Roualeyn Gordon Cumming

Hunting Adventures in South Africa

FIVE YEARS'
HUNTING ADVENTURES

IN

SOUTH AFRICA

BEING

*AN ACCOUNT OF SPORT WITH THE LION, ELEPHANT
BUFFALO, RHINOCEROS, CAMELOPARD, OSTRICH
HIPPOPOTAMUS, WILDEBEST, KOODOO
HYAENA, &c., &c.*

BY

ROUALEYN GORDON CUMMING, Esq.

OF ALTYRE

COMPLETE POPULAR EDITION

LONDON: SIMPKIN, MARSHALL. & CO
GLASGOW: THOMAS D. MORISON

INTRODUCTION.

As the reader who purposes to follow me through the five adventurous years I spent in the untrodden wilds of Southern Africa might like to know something of my previous career, I shall briefly state that the early portion of my life was spent in the County of Moray, where a love of natural history and of sport early engendered itself, and became stronger and more deeply rooted with my years. Salmon fishing and roe-stalking were my favourite amusements; and, during these early wanderings by wood and stream, the strong love of sport and admiration of Nature in her wildest and most attractive forms became with me an all-absorbing feeling, and my greatest possible enjoyment was to pass whole days and many a summer night in solitude, where, undisturbed, I might contemplate the silent grandeur of the forest and the ever-varying beauty of the scenes around. Long before I proceeded to Eton I took pride in the goodly array of hunting trophies which hung around my room.

In 1839 I sailed for India, to join my regiment, the 4th Madras Light Cavalry. Touching at the Cape of Good Hope, I had an opportunity of hunting several of the smaller antelopes, and obtained a foretaste of the splendid sport I was in after years so abundantly to enjoy. In India I procured a great number of specimens of natural history, and laid the foundation of a collection which has since swelled to gigantic proportions.* Finding that the climate did not agree with me, I retired from the service and returned home, where, resuming my old hunting habits, I was enabled, through the kindness of a wide circle of friends, to follow my favourite pursuit of deer-stalking so successfully that I speedily found myself in possession of a fine collection of select heads from most of the Scottish deer-forests. Growing weary, however, of hunting in a country where the game was strictly preserved, and where the continual presence of keepers and foresters took away half the charm of the chase, and longing once more for the freedom of nature, and the life of the wild hunter—so far preferable to that of the mere sportsman—I resolved to visit the rolling prairies and rocky mountains of the Far West, where my nature would find congenial sport with the bison, the wapiti, and the elk. With this view I obtained a commission in the Royal Veteran Newfoundland Companies. But I speedily discovered that the prospect of getting from the barrack-square would be small, and that I should have little chance of playing the Nimrod whilst attached

---

* Which may now be seen in my South African Museum at the Chinese Gallery in London.

to this corps. I accordingly effected an exchange into the Cape Riflemen, and in 1843 found myself once more in the country upon whose frontiers dwelt those vast herds of game which had so often fired my imagination, and made me long to revisit it.

Immediately upon landing I marched with my division of the army of occupation, under the command of Colonel Somerset, into the country of the Amaponda Caffres, where we lay for some time under canvas, and where our principal amusements were quail-shooting and throwing the assegai. Being disappointed in my expectations, and there being at that time no prospect of fighting, I made up my mind to sell out of the army, and to penetrate into the interior farther than the foot of civilized man had yet trodden—to vast regions which would afford abundant food for the gratification of the passion of my youth,—the collecting of hunting trophies and objects of interest in science and natural history. And in this I ultimately succeeded to my heart's desire.

With regard to my African adventures the following pages must speak for themselves. Let me here state, however, that I was the first to penetrate into the interior of the Bamangwato country, and that my axe and spade pioneered the way, which others have since followed. I should have pushed still farther but that the great losses I experienced in cattle and horses prevented me from so doing.

During the many years I spent in the wilderness, my waggon was my only home. Even this I often deserted; and alone, or attended only by savages, proceeded on distant hunting expeditions, leaving my few followers encamped around my baggage. Days and nights, on these occasions, have I passed in my solitary hunting-hole, near some drinking-place, watching the majestic carriage of the lion, the sagacious actions of the elephant, and the curious instincts of the countless varieties of game that have passed within a few yards of me, quite unaware of the proximity of man. Whatever on those occasions I witnessed worthy of attention, I noted in my journal whilst the impression was yet fresh in my memory—from this journal the following work is almost literally transcribed. Written under such circumstances, the reader will not look for the graces of style. The hand, wearied all day with grasping the rifle, is not the best suited for wielding the pen. If I have in simple language given pleasure to the sportsman, or added one page to the natural history of Southern Africa, or to our knowledge of its tribes, I shall think myself amply repaid for my many wanderings and watchings in a wild and savage land.

Altyre, June, 1850.

CONTENTS.

	PAGE
CHAPTER I.,	13

Preparations for a Hunting Expedition—Cape Traders—Travelling—Trader at a Farm—Danger of a Trader's Life—Articles for Barter—Dissuasions from the Enterprise—My Outfit—Hunting Rheebok—Wild Flowers.

CHAPTER II., ... 22

Mysteries of Inspanning—Cape Waggon and its Furniture—Departure from Grahamstown—My head Servant leaves me—Impassable state of the Roads—My Waggon in a fix—Change of Route—Singular Instinct of the Honeybird.

CHAPTER III., ... 32

Fearful Descent of De Bruin's Poort—District lately deserted by Elephants—Noble Forest-trees—The Great Fish River—Cunning Boers—Burning effects of the Sun—The Dutch Nöe's Green Tea Ointment—Skill of the Hottentots in "Tapping the Admiral"—Beautifully Wooded Country—The Village of Cradock—South African Climate—Countless Herds of Springbok—Mynheer Pocheter—The way to make a Friend on the Theba Flats—Hendrick Strydom—Hunting for Springbok—Extraordinary Migrations of these Antelopes.

CHAPTER IV., ... 44

A Bustard shot—Flight of Locusts—Quagga Shooting in the Dark—Curious Mistake—Ostriches—A Sportsman napping—Leave Strydom's Residence in quest of Wildebeests—Wildebeest Shooting—Meeting with a Brother Officer—Proceed to Colesberg—Additions to Equipments.

CHAPTER V., ... 52

Departure from Colesberg—Jaging Springbok—Vast Herds of Game—Swarms of Flies—Oology—A Nomad Boer's Encampment—Anecdote of the Gemsbok—Cobus rides down a splendid old Bull Gemsbok—A Night in the Desert—Paterson arrives—Bushmen—Their extraordinary Raids across the Desert.

CHAPTER VI., ... 61

Hard Chase of an Oryx—A Brindled Gnoo reduces himself to a "dead lock," and is taken—Paterson slays a Gemsbok and a Bull Wildebeest—He leaves for Colesberg—Ostrich-eggs—Novel method of carrying them—Anecdotes of the Ostrich—Affray with a Porcupine—He proves a rough Rider for my Horse—Narrow Escape from the Thrust of a dying Oryx—The grateful Water-root—Troops of Springboks cover the face of the land—Their Migrations—The finest shot at my leisure—Beer Vley.

CONTENTS.

CHAPTER VII., ... 69

Leave Beer Vley—A Bushboy captured and enlisted as a Follower—Famous Sport with Wildebeest and Quaggas from a Hunting-hole—Water fails, and we march to the Great Orange River—Beautiful Appearance of the River—Stink Vonteyn, a famous sporting quarter—An Ostrich's Nest—Bold Mountain Ranges—The Griqua Tribe, their Manners and Customs—An ancient Mimosa Forest—Residence of a Bushman—Successful Chase of a noble Bull Oryx.

CHAPTER VIII., ... 79

We leave Stink Vonteyn and reach the Vaal River—Wait-a-bit Thorns—Chase and kill a Buck Koodoo, and bivouac on the ground—Cobus and Jacob abscond—Roan Antelope—We recross the Vaal River—Griqua Encampment—Stink Vonteyn again—A Flight of Locusts—A Saltpan—Salubrious Climate—Boers attempt to carry off Ruyter—A Cameeldorn Forest—A Brindled Gnoo bayed by Wild Dogs—Habits of the latter.

CHAPTER IX., ... 89

The Riet River—Nomad Boer Encampments—Surly Reception at a Boer's Farm—Lions slain by the Boers—Cowardice of the Boers in Lion-hunting—Rumours of War between the Boers and Griquas—The Mirage of the Plains—Habits of the Blesbok—a knowing old Hog—A Snake under my Pillow—A Troop of Wild Dogs come upon me at night in my Shooting-hole—The Roar of Lions—Curious Facts concerning them.

CHAPTER X., ... 102

Boer Encampment—A Night in a Storm—A Fancy Costume—Fearful Encounter with a Lioness—"Colesberg" dreadfully mangled—Cowardice of Hottentots—We march back to Colesberg—Danger of being plundered by the Rebel Boers—Arrival at Colesberg—The Troops march against the Boers—The Battle of Schwart Coppice—Start for the distant Land of Elephants—The Hottentots make free with my Brandy, and mutiny—Leopards—Kuruman—Mr. Moffat, the good Missionary—Roasted Locusts.

CHAPTER XI., ... 113

Motito—The Bechuana Tribes—The mysterious great inland Lake—Blesbok and Wildebeest abundant—Park-like Country—We arrive at the beautiful Vale of Bakatla—Dr. Livingstone the Missionary—Native Fashions at Church—Determine to push on to Bamangwato—The Natives follow me for Venison—Great Variety of Game—A dangerous Fight with a herd of Buffaloes, two of which are slain—A Colony of Baboons—A Rhinoceros chases me round a Bush—Habits of the Beast—A noble Eland killed—An impromptu Steak—Slay a Rhinoceros, and lose my way in the Forest.

CHAPTER XII., ... 126

My Hottentots object to advance farther into the Interior—A Boar Hunt—We march through a charming Country—The Mountain Pass of Sesetabie—A Lion and Lioness inspect my Cattle, and the Lion pays for peeping—Hungry Hyænas sup upon the Cattle Furniture—The Camelopard—Description of its Habits—Booby,

CONTENTS.

a Bechuana Kraal—Gun Medicine—Disastrous Finale to an Incantation—Native Conspiracy to prevent my farther Progress.

CHAPTER XIII., ... 138

The Guides try to mislead me—The Cattle and Horses dying from Thirst—Search for Water—Melancholy Anticipations—Directed to a Pool by the flight of Birds—Chase and kill a Giraffe—Wandering Bechuanas point out my right Course—Miserable Condition of the Natives—Game Pitfalls—Mimosa Grove smashed by Elephants—A Rhinoceros charges me—Abundance of large Game—Lost in the Forest.

CHAPTER XIV., ... 146

The Bamangwato Mountains—The Elephants' Fountain—A troop of colossal Giraffes—Elephants drinking by Night—Habits of the African Elephant—Elephant Hunt—A Bull shot after a dangerous Encounter—Cutting out the Tusks—Extraordinary Rocks—Mountain-retreat of Sicomy, King of Bamangwato—His Cunning—Barter Muskets for Ivory—His Majesty's curious Gun-practice—Trading for Native Weapons.

CHAPTER XV., ... 161

Take leave of Sicomy—Digging for Water—The Elephants' Fountain again—A wounded Roan Antelope bays in the Water, and kills my Dogs right and left—Sicomy's Camp again—We march through a beautiful Valley—Curious Instinct of the Rhinoceros-bird—A mighty Bull Elephant shot after a hard Conflict—Mutchuisho's Attentions more charitable than pleasant—Cutting up an Elephant—A strange Scene—Baking the Flesh—Primitive Tobacco-pipes—Biltongue Festoons.

CHAPTER XVI., ... 175

Elephant spooring with the Natives—The Mystic Dice—Hunt in a Wait-a-bit Thorn Cover—Romantic Gorge in the Mountains—Sabié—Ancient Elephant Path—Ludicrous Native Signal—A noble Bull Elephant slain—Isaac, my Interpreter, dismissed—A Lioness bagged at one shot—Drunkenness and Disorder in Camp—My manner of taking the Field after the larger Game—Sicomy's Followers desert me.

CHAPTER XVII., ... 184

We march from Sabié—Track along a River-bed—The dry Grass on Fire for miles—Glorious Elephant-shooting—Cowardice of my After-rider—Strange circumstance at the Death of a Bull Elephant—A Sable Antelope—Tête-à-tête with a disabled Elephant—The Klipspringer Antelope—A pack of Wild Dogs capture and kill a Koodoo—The coming of Summer—Vast numbers of Birds visiting the Fountains—My trusty two-grooved Rifle bursts—My Snuffers, Spoons, and Candlesticks melted for Bullets—Elephants taking a Douche Bath—Two of them slain—Yet more Elephants—My Horse Colesberg dies of the African Distemper—Virulence of the Scourge.

CHAPTER XVIII., ... 194

Turn my Waggons towards the Colony—A Troop of Elephants in Indian File—Splendid Sport amongst them—Two of them break their Tusks in falling—The Rainy Season commences—Erection of a Bothy—The gigantic Nwana-tree—Sicomy's Mountain Kraal—Four of his Subjects become my Servants—Corriebely—The Natives astonished by my finding a Mine of Lead—Elephant-shooting—Leave the land of Elephants—Boötlonamy—Terrific Thunderstorm.

CHAPTER XIX., ... 203

All my Colonial Servants desert me—Pursue them in vain—Both Waggons get disabled—Melancholy Anticipations—Cut a Path through the Forest—A Sandy Desert—Cattle dying for want of Water—Troubles surmounted—Pallahs and Koodoos—A Lion and Leopard visit the Camp at Midnight—Another horse dies of Distemper—We reach Booby—One of the Axletrees breaks—The Bakatlas assist me—The Baggage-waggon upset in a River—The Distemper kills more Horses—Lions roaring—Arrive at Dr. Livingstone's—March upon Chouaney—The Ngotwani—A Herd of Buffaloes among the Reeds.

CHAPTER XX., ... 213

Arrive at Sichely's Kraal—Description of that Chief—His Wives—The Rain-makers—My Gun Medicine—Bakatla—A Kraal struck by Lightning—Reach Mr. Moffat's Station at Kuruman—Daring Robberies of the Bushmen—Campbellsdorp—Discover my runaway Hottentots—We cross the Vaal—The Inmates of a Farm terrified by my wild Appearance—Colesberg and Grahams-town—English Hounds in Africa.

CHAPTER XXI., ... 220

Set out again for the Far Interior—Fort Beaufort—Purchase fresh Steeds and Oxen—My old servant Corollus rejoins me—Elephant Fountain once more—Hunt Elephants—Corriebely—Obliged to act very decidedly with Sicomy—Horses and Oxen taken in Pits—Two Dogs killed by a Leopard—A file of Bakalahari Women carrying water to the Desert—A sleeping Rhinoceros shot—Hunting in the neighbourhood of Lotlokane and Letlochee—The Natives kill an Elephant—A grim Lion slain—Rheumatic Fever attacks me—Leave Bamangwato Country—The Game disturbed by Natives—Soobie—Watch nightly for Game from a place of Ambush—Vanquish a noble Lioness.

CHAPTER XXII., ... 232

A Lion shot from my Watching-hole at Midnight—Six Lions drink close beside me—A Lioness slain—A Rhinoceros bites the dust—Moselakose Fountain—My Shooting-hole surrounded with Game—Pallahs, Sassaybys, Zebras, etc.—A Rhoode-Rheebok shot—Extraordinary Circumstance—My fiftieth Elephant bagged—Interesting Fountains on the Hills—Leave my Waggons for the Hills—Struggle with a Boa Constrictor—Lions too numerous to be agreeable—Five Rhinoceroses shot as they came to drink—A Venomous Snake.

CHAPTER XXIII., ... 242

Sichely's Kraal again—The Ngotwani—Chase and kill a waterbuck—A portion of the Cattle recovered—A Leopard bayed by my Dogs and slain—Buffalo-shooting beside the Ngotwani—A Lion feeds on the Carcase—My Horse knocked down by the King of Brutes—Meet a grim Lion face to face at midnight!—He sheers off—These Animals unpleasantly bold—An amusing Chase with a Buffalo—Interesting Stalk in rocky ground—Leave my hunting-ground and encamp on Vaal River—Great Herds—In taking the Drift a Waggon sticks fast in the middle of the River—Great fear of losing all my Property—Rescue of the Waggon—Colesberg—A Farmer's Waggon capsized in the Fish River—Visit Strydom's farm and find it desolate—Arrival at Grahamstown.

CHAPTER XXIV., ... 251

Start on another Elephant-shooting Expedition—The Hart River—Numerous pack of Wild Dogs—Mahura, Chief of the Batlapis—Rumours of Wars—The Meritsane—Lotlokane—Encounter with two Lions on the Molopo—Chouaney—A tremendous Fight with a Buffalo—The River Limpopo—Huge Crocodiles—A splendid Hippopotamus falls to my Rifle—Immense Herds of Buffaloes crossing the River—The Serolomootlooque Antelope unknown to Naturalists—A herd of Hippopotami—Fine Sport beside the River.

CHAPTER XXV., ... 250

We cross the Limpopo—Rash Encounter with a Hippopotamus—Remarkable dome-like Rock—Two Serolomootlooques shot—Hollow Trees containing Honey—Gigantic Ant-hills—Hunting across the Limpopo—Another Boa Constrictor—A Visit from Seleka—A Sea-cow shot, which sinks—Resurrection of the Beast—Splendid Hippopotamus-shooting.

CHAPTER XXVI., ... 267

Seleka's Town among the Rocks—Elephant-hunting with Seleka and his Men—Trading with Seleka—A Lion and Lioness with their Cubs—An immense Herd of Hippopotami—Nine of them killed—Trap for inflicting poisoned Wounds on Sea-cows—We cross the Limpopo, and a Waggon sticks in the River—We trek down the Stream—Two of my best Horses killed and eaten by Lions—The Chief of the Bamalette visits me—Audacity of the Lions—A Horse killed in a Pitfall—A Chief flogged for catching and consuming a Horse.

CHAPTER XXVII., ... 274

We trek down the Limpopo—Abundance of Sea-cows—The Lotsane River—An immense Herd of Elephants—Combat with a first-rate old Bull—Rheumatic Fever attacks me, which determines our course homewards—Elephants smashing Forest-trees—A Lion carries off one of my men from the Fireside—The Beast occupied consuming him all night—The man-eating Lion slain—Three Hippopotami shot—One of the Dogs eaten by a Crocodile—The fatal "Tsetse" fly—The Fountain of Seboono—An old Bull-Elephant held in check without Gun or Dogs.

CHAPTER XXVIII., ... 285

Paapaa Fountain—Watch by Moonlight from a Shooting-hole—Remarkable Sport with Elephants—Four bagged and eight mortally wounded in one night—Elephant-hunting with Horse and Dogs by Moonlight—A Troop of Lions—The Vultures with the shadowy Wings—Another Dog snapped up by a Crocodile—The Skeleton of an Elephant shot by me discovered—The Tusks being gone, strong measures are adopted for their recovery.

CONTENTS.

CHAPTER XXIX., ... 295
We march up the Limpopo—The Guapa Mountains—Immense variety of Game—Stalk and shoot two Sable Antelopes—Several Hounds lost—Romantic Ravine in the Guapa Mountains—My Forest Home—Buck Koodoos—Stalking Sable Antelopes—Two of my Horses die from Tsetse—Continue our March—Countless Herds of Game.

CHAPTER XXX., ... 304
Leave the Potaquaine Country—Absurd Ceremony—My Cattle fail me—Send to the Missionary Station for Aid—Encamp near the Limpopo—Indescribable Fish—A young Secretary—Nearly all my Oxen die—Assistance arrives from Mr. Livingstone—We reach the Residence of Sichely—A Hunter's Monument—We continue our March through a beautiful Country—An Adventure with two savage Lionesses—A violent Tempest—Mahura—Bakalahari driving Game towards their Pitfalls—We cross the Orange River and reach Colesberg.

CHAPTER XXXI., ... 313
Start on my fifth and last Expedition into the Interior—Mr. Orpen accompanies me—Hurried March—Extraordinary Herd of Blesboks—The Hart River—Cattle attacked with Hoof Sickness—Three Lionesses fearfully mangle my pack of Dogs—Lion-hunts—Hyænas devour my Camp-stools—Meritsane—Six Buffaloes shot—Another Lion-hunt—Glorious Chase with Elands—Sichely's Kraal—We cross the Limpopo—A Lion attacks my Kraal and kills an Ox—A Field of Battle—Seboono—My hundredth Elephant!—We march down the Limpopo and hunt Hippopotami Attacked by Rheumatic Fever—Mr. Orpen nearly killed by a Leopard.

CHAPTER XXXII., ... 328
Mr. Orphen and myself in a helpless condition—We leave the low-lying Limpopo for the Mountains—Trading with Seleka—Ceremony to impart the power of successful Shooting—March to the Ngotwani and retrace our steps to the Limpopo—Enormous Herds of Buffaloes—An exciting Lion-hunt—Three of my Dogs killed—The noble Beast takes the water, followed by a Dog and a Crocodile—A bold Mountain-range—Abundance of Game—A brilliant Lion-hunt—Two killed out of a troop of four—Rhinoceros-hunting—Leave the Mariqua River—Sublime Scenery—Another Lion-Hunt—A Buffalo rips up my After-rider's Horse—Camelopard-Chase—Sudden encounter with two huge Lions—Arrival at Sichely's Kraal.

CHAPTER XXXIII., ... 340
The Pass of God—Hunt Sable and Roan Antelope—Sesetabie—My Cattle-losses in five Expeditions—My Cattle desperate for want of Water—Trading with Mahura—Inspanning young Oxen—We cross the Vaal River—The Country densely covered with Game—An Ostrich's Nest—Bloem Vonteyn—Multitudes of Antelope Skeletons cover the Plains—The Great Orange River—We are detained by the Flood—Twenty-three Men drowned in attempting to cross—We have to take the Waggons to pieces—Arrival at Colesberg—Determine to revisit Old England and transport my collection of Trophies thither.

THE LINE OF MARCH

CHAP. I.

FIVE YEARS'
HUNTING AND SPORTING
ADVENTURES IN SOUTH AFRICA.

CHAPTER I.

Preparations for a Hunting Expedition—Cape Traders—Travelling—Trader at a Farm—Dangers of a Trader's Life—Articles for Barter—Dissuasions from the Enterprise—My Outfit—Hunting Rheebok—Wild Flowers.

HAVING resolved to make a hunting expedition into the interior of Southern Africa, my first object was to seek out some experienced person, able to give me the necessary information as to what purchases I should require to make in the way of waggons and oxen, and as to my outfit in general, and I accordingly pitched upon an individual of the name of Murphy, a trader in the interior, who, I had reason to believe, was better acquainted than any other person in Grahamstown with the frontiers of the colony, and the adjoining territories of the Griqua and Bechuana tribes, situated beyond the Great Orange River. With this person I had already had the pleasure of becoming acquainted during the short time I was quartered in Grahamstown in the month of July, having been introduced to him by another trader, a man from my own land of Moray, famous among the Dutch Boers about and beyond the frontiers. This man's name was Andrew Thompson, of Forres, one of three brothers, all of whom followed the same adventurous line of life, and were as steady, hard-working, and determined young men as might be met with throughout the colony.

As, in the course of the following pages, I may have occasion to allude to these traders, and others of a similar avocation, it will perhaps be as well to give the reader a sketch of the manner in which their occupation is conducted. Each trader is supposed to be the proprietor of one or two ox-waggons. These they "load up," from the large stores of the merchants in Grahamstown and Port Elizabeth, with every species of merchandise which the far-dwelling isolated Dutch Boers are likely to require. So supplied, they set out on their long journey, which usually occupies from six to eight months; at the end of which they return to the colony, enriched with immense droves of sleek oxen and fat wethers, selected from the numerous herds and flocks of the pastoral dwellers in the interior. The waggons of a trader generally contain every requisite for a farmer's establishment; groceries, hardware, bales of cloth and canvas, haberdashery, saddlery, crockery—in short, everything, from an awl for the Boer to mend his "feldtschoens" or country shoes, to a roll of cherry-coloured or sky-blue riband to tie up the bonny brown locks of his fair daughters, whose beauty, like that of Skye terriers, I fear, in many cases, consists in their ugliness. They, however, sadly lack the "dégagée" appearance of the Skye terrier, as their general air and gait might be more aptly likened to a yard of pump-water.

As the trader advances up the country and effects exchanges, he leaves the cattle or sheep which he has bartered, in charge of their former master, picking them up on his return southward. When all his goods are disposed of, he generally winds up his barter by exchanging the waggon or waggons which bore them for cash or oxen, or both, and then, purchasing a horse, he returns in light marching order to the colony.

The price which a trader gives for a waggon is usually from 40*l.* to 60*l.*, and in war times often a thousand rix dollars, or 75*l.* The number of oxen which he usually obtains for it at the close of his journey is from forty to fifty, and these he is supposed to select himself. The value of the waggon is partly dependent on the character of the tent. Tents are of two kinds; the one being coarsely yet strongly constructed of green boughs fitting into iron staples along the sides of the waggon, and lashed together with strips of green hide so as to form a succession of arches overhead. These are kept in their position by means of long straight wands laid all along the outside of the arches, the whole framework being very strongly secured by the aforementioned strips of green hide. On the top of this are placed coarse Kaffir mats made of reeds, which act as a Scotchman (to use a seafaring phrase), to keep the waggon-sail, which is of stout canvas, from chafing. The other variety of tent is of a less homely build, and is termed by the colonists a cap-tent waggon. It requires the hand of a skilful waggon-builder, and is much more elaborately finished, the wood which supports and composes the tent being all neatly sawed and planed, and fastened together with iron rivets.

This description of waggon is preferred by the aristocracy among the Boers, as presenting a more distingué appearance, when they drive their fraus and children on a round of visits, which they are constantly doing; or when flocking to the "Nachmal," or communion, which happens three or four times in the year. The former, or common wand tent, however, possesses a great advantage over the cap-tent, inasmuch as, in the first place, it is cheaper by 10*l.*, and secondly, if broken in a capsize, which in Cape travelling is an affair of common occurrence, it is easily repaired on the spot; whereas the cap-tent waggon, if once upset, is irretrievably ruined.

When a trader arrives on a Boer's farm, he halts and walks up to the door to inquire where he is to "outspan," or unyoke the oxen, and also in what direction the oxen are to be driven to graze. At the door he is met by the baas, or master, generally pipe in mouth, who, cordially greeting him with one hand, raises his hat from his head with the other. The Boers lay great stress on this piece of etiquette, which has to be gone through with a whole string of juvenile Boers following in the rear, each encased in a very roomy pair of inexpressibles, and crowned with an immense broad rimmed tile, nearly half the size of its wearer. Permission to outspan being obtained, and a few complimentary speeches interchanged, the trader inquires of the Boer if he has any fat oxen to handle or barter, to which the Boer either at once replies in the negative, or more commonly says,

"I do not know. What have you got on your waggon?" The trader answers,

"I have got a little of everything, and all of the very best quality, and you shall have anything you require as low as a trader can possibly sell it. I shall presently unload a little for your inspection." The Boer politely says,

"No, no, mynheer, you must not offload; it would grieve me that mynheer should exert himself so much:" to which the trader replies,

"It is no trouble; we are accustomed to do it, and it is our business."

The trader then instructs his knecht, or head servant, to make a parade of the goods, and he then accompanies the Boer into the house, where dinner will shortly make its appearance, to which the Boer invariably, in the most hospitable manner, makes every white stranger welcome. Here, if the trader is wide awake to his own interest, he will pay marked attention to the Noë or frau, as no bargain or transaction of any nature can be ratified with a Dutchman without *her* full concurrence and approval. The Dutch are particularly cleanly in their establishments and cooking, and moreover possess a very fair notion of the culinary art, their tables in general being graced with several very excellent and substantial dishes. When dinner is over, all hands resort to the waggon and overhaul the merchandise, where it is ten to one but the Noë will find about fifty different articles which she will prevail upon her husband to believe indispensible in the private economy of his establishment. Thus when "handling" once begins, it often goes on briskly, and from a Boer who at the outset declared himself independent of the trader's supplies, as many as two or three, or even half a dozen, fat oxen may be obtained.

As the trader knows well from past experience that the Boer will be sure to endeavour to abate his prices, he makes a point of asking a little more than he intends to take, so as to be able to give in to the Boer's importunities, who, with a sly wink at his wife, congratulates himself on his shrewdness, and flatters himself that he has run a hard bargain.

When the trader has collected all his cattle, he drives them by steady marches, of from twenty to thirty miles in the twenty-four hours, which are performed chiefly during the night, to Grahamstown or Beaufort, where he disposes of them to butchers. At the former place they are purchased for the use of the town, and by the Government contractors for the supply of the troops. At Beaufort, which is on the high road to Cape Town, they are purchased for the supply of the Cape Town market. The payments for the cattle are seldom, if ever, made in hard cash, the poor trader having to content himself with approved bills, drawn at six and nine months, which in too many cases are never honoured, the defaulter being found either bankrupt, or to have bolted for England or California.

The life of a trader is hard and harrassing, and he is often liable to very heavy losses by deaths from severe drought, distempers, and other causes; also from the chances of war, oxen straying and being found no more, overstocked markets, and non-payments as above, besides the danger to which he is exposed from the attacks of wild beasts. During the time that he is engaged in driving his oxen, his rest is necessarily broken and disturbed, and, being compelled to watch his cattle every hour of the night, in all weathers, he is obliged always to have his clothes on, and to sleep when he can, after the manner of sea-captains in bad weather, who hang their nose on to a ratlin, and so take a nap. As an instance of the injury from chances of war, I may here allude to the severe losses sustained by my friend Mr. Peter Thompson, who, during the war which ravaged the colony in the years 1846 and 1847, was returning to Grahamstown with a large herd of some hundred fine oxen, the well-earned proceeds of a laborious and toilsome expedition, when he was attacked in De Bruin's Poort, a rugged and densely-wooded ravine, within one march of Grahamstown, by a band of the marauding Amaponda Kaffirs, armed with guns and assagais, who swept off the whole of his drove, he himself barely escaping with his life.

In years when the prices of cattle are low, these traders occasionally vary their line of march, and, forsaking the Boers for a season, they load up a suitable cargo, and direct their course for the Bechuana tribes, from whom they obtain ivory, karosses (skin cloaks), and ostrich-feathers, along with various curiosities, for which they obtain a ready sale in the Grahamstown market, where good ivory averages from 4s. to 4s. 6d. per pound. Karosses vary in price from £1 to £3 each, according to their size, kind, and quality. Ostrich-feathers used to fetch from £5 to £6 per pound, but, partly owing to the feathers being less worn by the votaries of fashion in London, and partly to the late disturbances throughout Europe, the prices have greatly fallen.* The articles required for trading with the Bechuana tribes consist of beads of all sizes and colours, brass and copper wire, knives and hatchets, clothing for both sexes, ammunition, guns, young cows, and she-goats. The two latter the trader obtains in barter from the Boers, Griqua and Koranna tribes, more immediately adjacent to the colony.

Some writers have erroneously stated that snuff and tobacco are a good circulating medium among the tribes in Southern Africa, but in the course of my experience I can scarcely remember having ever obtained the smallest article in barter for either, not even a drink of milk. The natives have certainly no objection to receive these articles when given gratuitously, but are far too wide awake to place any great value upon them. During my career in Southern Africa I have had much experience in trading with the Bechuana tribes, and, as I shall have occasion to refer to my trading exploits in the course of my narrative, I have entered into the above particulars that the reader may, at the outset, form an idea of the manner in which these things are conducted.

---

* From seventy-five to ninety good sized ostrich-feathers weigh a pound.

On making inquiries I had the pleasure to find that, contrary to my expectation, both Andrew Thompson and Murphy were still in Grahamstown, where I had left them about three months before, when I marched thence into Caffraria with my regiment; and the latter, whom I found to be a confirmed tippler, was able, in his few lucid moments, to give me much valuable information relative to the preparations which I required to make in the way of purchasing oxen and waggons, engaging servants, etc., etc.; also various wrinkles as to the conducting of my establishment, the hours of marching, and the line of country which I had chalked out for my first expedition. Poor Murphy! he was as kind-hearted a creature as ever breathed.

From the 1st till the 22nd of October I was actively employed in making the necessary purchases and arrangements for my coming expedition, and in forwarding my affairs, in which Murphy, during his sober intervals, most willingly assisted me. As the reader will observe, my establishment at my first outset was on a much more limited scale than upon subsequent expeditions. This was partly owing to the uncertainty which I felt as to the success of my sporting undertakings, and the length of time which I might feel inclined to devote to this line of life. I was much in the dark as to what sport I might expect to realize, and what difficulties I should have to encounter in the trip I was about to make; the truth being that I could not find a single individual, either among the natives or the military, who could in the smallest degree enlighten me on the subject.

The general impression amongst my military friends was, that any game which remained in the interior must have, ere then, retreated to such remote parts, far away in the territories of savage tribes, as to be utterly beyond the reach of any sportsman, however enterprising; and when they saw me bustling about making my purchases, they used to say to me, "It is all nonsense your laying out your money in this way. Why don't you rather go home at once to your own country? We shall see you returning in a month or two, like those fellows who went on a shooting trip last year, with a *coup-de-soleil* and an attack of dysentery, utterly disgusted with the country, and selling off all these things on which you are now expending so much capital."

The shooting party here alluded to consisted of one officer of the 7th Dragoons, two of the 27th, and others who, having obtained a few week's leave, and burning to distinguish themselves in a campaign against the feræ of Southern Africa, had hired a waggon, and penetrated as far as the Thebus mountain, where for a few days they enjoyed some good sport among the black wildebeest and springboks which abound on the plains surrounding that mountain; till, having broken the stocks of their rifles in falls from their horses while impetuously "jaging" the game, they returned to head-quarters, one suffering from *coup-de-soleil*, and the rest from dysentery brought on by drinking bad water, they having been unfortunate in the vley beside which they had fixed their encampment. My gallant friend, Lieutenant H——, of the 91st, was one of the most urgent in endeavouring to dissuade me from my steadfast purpose of trekking up the country, and recommended me rather to return with him to England, whither he was about to proceed. He and I had sent in our resignation of Her Majesty's service at the same time, and fortunately for us, by some mistake, our papers were mislaid at Cape Town, and not forwarded in the usual course, whereby we gained several months' pay. H——, who, like many others of the military, entertained a profound disgust for the colony and everything connected with it, at first could hardly believe that I was in earnest when I spoke of going up the country; and when convinced that such was my determination, he said, with a strong lisp which was habitual to him, "Good G—, Cummin! you are thurely mad to remain longer in thith country after you have obtained leave to return to dear old England. I athure you, I had rather be a thoe-black in England than live in thith beathtly country."

Notwithstanding these friendly dissuasions on the part of my acquaintance, I continued to prosecute my affairs so unremittingly that on the 22nd I considered my manifold arrangements complete, and, being much harassed and annoyed by the unavoidable delays to which I had been subjected, I was full of impatience to make a start. These delays were in a great measure occasioned by the weather, heavy and constant rains having fallen during the previous fourteen days, accompanied with a cold wind off the Southern Ocean. This, of necessity, materially interfered with and delayed me in my arrangements, and had also the effect of rendering the country perfectly unfit for locomotion, in many places cutting up the roads with rugged impassable watercourses, and in low-lying districts converting them into deep, impracticable quagmires.

It will here be necessary to give a detailed account of my outfit, to put the reader at once in possession of the extent and nature of my establishment and camp equipage. My first object was, of course, to secure a travelling waggon, and I had the good fortune to obtain an excellent new cap-tent one, complete with all its gear ready for inspanning, from Mr. Ogilvie of Grahamstown, for the sum of £60; which, as it eventually proved to be a right good one, was decidedly a bargain. I very soon, however, found out, as I extensively collected specimens of natural history, that one waggon was insufficient; and not long after, in the town of Colesberg, on the frontiers of the colony, I purchased a second, also a cap-tent waggon, with its necessary accompaniment, a span of oxen; and at a later period, as the reader will subsequently learn, I found it necessary to purchase a third, and became the proprietor of considerably more than a hundred draught oxen.

From an English farmer in the vicinity of Grahamstown, I obtained a span of twelve excellent, well-trained, black, züür-veldt oxen, which I judged suited for my work, they having been in the habit, with their late master, of bringing in very heavy loads of wood to the Grahamstown market. Their price was £3 each; and as it is not unusual to see an ox, in the best of spans, knock up on long marshes, by Murphy's advice I purchased two spare oxen of Mr. Thomson.

My stud of horses as yet consisted of but two, which had been my chargers in the regiment. These were "Sinon," a stallion which I had bought of Major Goodman of the 27th, and "The Cow," an excellent dark-brown gelding which I had obtained from Colonel Somerset of

"Ours." I did not think it wise to lay out more money in horse-flesh in Grahamstown, as I should shortly have to pass through the Hantam, where most of the Boers breed horses extensively, which are famed for their spirit and hardiness throughout the colony. I engaged four servants,—namely, an Englishman called Long, as head-servant, a thorough cockney, who, as I afterwards learnt, had formerly been a cab-driver in London, and whom I took into my service at Murphy's recommendation, Long being supposed to possess a certain degree of experience, having penetrated as far as the banks of the Orange River on a trading excursion on his own account; but his heart, as the event proved, inclined more to worship at the shrine of Venus than at that of Diana. A certain little dark-eyed damsel, who acted as laundress to the military, and who was employed all day in driving her mangle, seemed entirely to engross his thoughts—Long frequently observing that "there was that sweet little creature obliged to drive a mangle who ought rather to be sitting practising at her 'pihanne.'"

My other three servants were natives. A waggon-driver named Kleinboy, a stout active Hottentot, with the high cheek-bones and woolly head of his race, and who was quite *au fait* at his department. Like many others of his countrymen, he was subject to fits of sulks, and much preferred reclining for hours under my waggons, or in the shade of a bush practising on his violin, to looking after his master's work. My leader's name was Carollus: he was the third whom I had engaged in that capacity, the other two having absconded. He was a stout powerful fellow, descended from the Mozambique races. He entered my service under cover of night, having absconded from Kingsley of "Ours" —that gentleman, according to his assertion, being in the habit of administering a little wholesome correction with the jambok, which on further acquaintance with him I had reason to believe he richly merited. My third native servant was Cobus, a Hottentot of light weight, the son of a veteran in my regiment. He 'listed in the capacity of after-rider, and proved to be first-rate in his calling, being the best horseman I met with in South Africa. He also, like Kleinboy, was liable to fits of sulkiness, through which I eventually lost him, for on one occasion finding it necessary to inflict on him a summary chastisement, he deserted from my service in consequence.

The baggage, provisions, and general stores which I carried with me were as follows:—Two sacks, containing 300 lbs. of coffee, four quarter-chests of tea, 300 lbs. of sugar, 300 lbs. of rice, 180 lbs. of meal, 100 lbs. of flour, 5 lbs. of pepper, 100 lbs. of salt, an anker of vinegar, several large jars of pickles, half a dozen hams and cheeses, 2 cases of gin, 1 anker of brandy, 1 half-aum of Cape brandy, iron baking-pots with long legs, stewing and frying pans, saucepans and gridirons, tin water-buckets of various sizes, 2 large "fagie" or water-casks, an accompaniment which no Cape waggon is ever without, 2 large flasks of tar to be subsequently mixed with hard fat for greasing the wheels when required, 6 dozen pocket knives, 24 boxes of snuff, 50 lbs. of tobacco, 300 lbs. of white, coral, red, and bright blue beads of various sizes; 3 dozen tinder-boxes, 1 cwt. of brass and copper wire, which the Bechuana tribes, especially those dwelling to the east, readily barter and convert into ornaments for their legs and arms; 2 dozen sickles, 2 spades, 2 shovels, 1 pickaxe, 5 superior American axes, 2 augers, 1 stock and 36 bits, hatchets, planes, drawing-knives, several coarse chisels for waggon-work, a vice, blacksmith and carpenter's hammers, and a variety of other tools appertaining to both these professions. A gross of awls, a gross of sail-needles, 50 hanks of sail-twine, 2 bolts of sail-canvas, several rolls of stout woollen cloths, 2 dozen gown-pieces, 6 dozen Malay handkerchiefs; thread, needles, and buttons; ready-made jackets and trowsers for my people, several dozen coarse shirts, Scotch bonnets, and cockernonnys (as for shoes, colonial servants are supposed to make them for themselves); a few medicines, arsenical soap, English and coarse Boer's soap. Also, 1 large bell-tent, 1 mattress and bedding, 1 camp table and chair, and my canteen, which most fortunately I had resolved to retain when disposing of my other military equipments: I found it a most serviceable and convenient appendage during my five years' wanderings in Southern Africa. My saddlery consisted of 2 English hunting saddles, 2 common saddles for servants, and 1 pack-saddle to convey venison to camp. My ordnance was as follows:—3 double-barrelled rifles by Purdey, William Moore, and Dickson of Edinburgh—the latter a two-grooved, the most perfect and useful rifle I ever had the pleasure of using; 1 heavy single-barelled German rifle, carrying 12 to the lb. This last was an old companion, which had been presented to me, when a boy, by my dear and much-lamented friend, and brother-sportsman, the late James Duff of Innes House. With this rifle, about ten years before, I had brought down my first stag on the Paps of Jura, and subsequently bowled over many a princely master-stag and graceful roebuck in his summer-coat, throughout the glens and forests of my native land. The Purdey was also a tried friend, both it and the heavy German having been with me in several campaigns on the plains and in the jungles of Hindostan. I had also 3 stout double-barrelled guns for rough work when hard riding and quick-loading is required. Several lead-ladles of various sizes, a whole host of bullet-moulds, loading-rods, shot-belts, powder-flasks, and shooting-belts; 3 cwt. of lead, 50 lbs. of pewter for hardening the balls to be used in destroying the larger game; 10,000 prepared leaden bullets, bags of shot of all sizes, 100 lbs. of fine sporting gunpowder, 300 lbs. of coarse gunpowder, about 50,000 best percussion caps, 2000 gun-flints, greased patches and cloth to be converted into the same. I carried also several spare yokes, yoke-skeys, whipsticks, rheims, and straps, 2 sets of spare linchpins, all of which last articles belong to the waggon. With the above, and £200 in cash which I carried with me, I considered myself prepared to undertake a journey of at least twelve months amongst Boers or Bechuanas, independent of either.

While I was laying in these stores, I once or twice amused myself by riding in quest of rheebok in the rugged and precipitous high grounds lying immediately to the south of Grahamstown. On one of these occasions I was accompanied by my cousin, Colonel Campbell of the 91st (one of the bravest and most distinguished officers in the late Kafir war, and withal about the best rifle-shot and keenest sportsman then in the colony), a brother of Captain Campbell of Skipness, the author of the

"Old Forest-Ranger," a work highly approved amongst Indian Nimrods. The rheebok is a species of antelope generally found in all mountain districts throughout Southern Africa, from Table Mountain to the latitude of Kuruman or New Litakoo. Of the rheebok there are two varieties: the rhooye-rheebok, or red rheebuck; and the vaal rheebok, or grey rheebuck. The range of the vaal-rheebok, to the northward, ceases in the latitude of the Long Mountains lying to the south of Kuruman; the other variety is met with as far north as the mountains in the territory of Sichely, chief of the Baquaines, about fifty miles to the north of the Kurrichane range. Both of these antelopes frequent high and rocky mountains. The manner of hunting them is alike; and, when properly pursued, I think more nearly resembles Scotch Highland deerstalking than the pursuit of any other antelope.

Throughout the grassy mountains which the hunter must traverse in following this antelope, his eye is often gladdened by romantic dells and sparkling rivulets, whose exhilarating freshness strongly and pleasingly contrasts with the barren, rocky mountain heights and shoulders immediately contiguous. The green banks and little hollows along the margins of these streamlets are adorned with innumerable species of brilliant plants and flowering shrubs in wild profusion. Amongst these, to my eye, the most dazzling in their beauty were perhaps those lovely heaths for which the Cape is so justly renowned. These exquisite plants, singly, or in groups, here adorn the wilderness, with a freedom and luxuriance which, could the English gardener or amateur florist behold, he might well feel disheartened, so infinitely does Nature in this favoured clime surpass in wild exuberance the nurselings of his artificial care. I remember being particularly struck with two pre-eminently brilliant varieties, the one bearing a rose-coloured, the other a blood-red bell; and though I regret to say that I am but a poor botanist, even in the heat of the chase I paused, spell-bound, to contemplate with admiration their fascinating beauty.

Others, with their downy stems and waxen flowers of every gaudy hue, green, lilac, and various shades of pink, red, and crimson; some of them with brown lips to the bell, flourished in the richer hollows of their native glen, or bloomed with equal loveliness along the arid cliffs and fissures of the overhanging rocks. Almost equalling the heaths in beauty, and surpassing them in the additional attraction of their scented leaves, a whole host of geraniums fill the balmy breeze with their delicious perfume. These are too well known to admit of any novelty in description, but I may mention, *en passant*, that they attain a far larger growth in their native soil than I have been in the habit of seeing in our greenhouses. Small groups of the lofty, fair, conscious-looking iris, rear their graceful heads along the edges of the streams. Their fairy forms reflected in the waters, "they seem to stand like guardian Naiads of the strand."

Another tribe of plants, which particularly delighted me from old associations, though not so striking as many of its neighbours for perfume and brilliancy, was composed of several varieties of the light, airy fern, or bracken, which, whether gracefully overshadowing the mossy stones, eternally moistened by the bubbling spray of the stream, which they kissed as it danced along, or veiling the grey lichen-clad masses of rock in the hollows higher up, strongly reminded me of those so conspicuously adorning the wild glens in the mountains of my native land. Besides these, a thousand other gay flowers deck the hills and plains wherever the eye can fall. Endless varieties of the ixea, the hæmanthus, the amaryllis, the marigold, and a number of everlasting flowers, are scattered around with a lavish hand; also the splendid protea, whose sweets never fail to attract swarms of the insect tribes, on which several bright kinds of fly-catchers, their plumage glancing in the noonday sun, are constantly preying. Farther down these watercourses, in the dense, shady ravines, the jungle is ornamented with long tangled festoons of different creepers, among which the wild jessamine ranks foremost, hanging in fragrant garlands amid the shaggy lichens, and bunches of bright orange-coloured missletoe, for which the forest of Africa, in the vicinity of her sea-coasts, are so remarkable.

While touching on the floral beauties of the hills more immediately adjoining the sea-coast, I may remark that here are the great nurseries for heaths and geraniums. As the traveller advances up the country these gradually disappear, and, together with the animal kingdom, the vegetable world assumes entirely new features; the colonial forest-trees and bushes, herbs, and plants, being succeeded by a vast and endless world of loveliness; unseen, unknown, untrodden, save by those varied multitudes of stupendous, curious, and beautiful quadrupeds, whose forefathers have roamed its mighty solitudes from primæval ages, and with whom I afterwards became so intimately acquainted.

CHAPTER II.

Mysteries of Inspanning—Cape Waggon and its Furniture—Departure from Grahamstown—My head Servant leaves me—Impassable state of the Roads —My Waggon in a Fix—Change of Route—Singular Instinct of the Honeybird.

ON the 23rd of October, 1843, having completed my final arrangements, and collected and settled all outlying debts, the weather, which had been wet and stormy for many days past, assuming a more settled appearance, I resolved to "inspan" and "trek," which the reader will bear in mind mean to yoke and march. I accordingly communicated my intentions to my followers, and despatched my leader Carollus to the neighbouring mountains, where my cattle were supposed to be pasturing, to bring them up. He expended the greater part of the day in searching for them in vain about their wonted feeding-ground: at length, late in the afternoon, he chanced to meet a comrade, who informed him that the oxen he was seeking were safely lodged in the "skit-kraal," or pound, Colonel Somerset, of "Ours," having detected them in the act of luxuriating in a field of green forage. This pleasing intelligence demanded my immediate attendance at the skit-kraal, where, by a disembursement of nine shillings, I obtained their release.

Having secured my oxen, my next business was to find my servants, who were all missing. Long, as I expected, was found gallantly assisting the dark-eyed heroine of the mangle, and Kleinboy and Cobus were discovered in a state of brutal intoxication, stretched on the green-sward in front of one of the canteens, along with sundry other waggon-drivers and Hottentot Venuses, all in the same glorious condition, having expended on liquor the pay which they had extracted from me in advance on the plea of providing themselves with necessaries. Drunk as they were, Carollus, who was sober, managed to allure them to the waggons, and, Long assisting, the inspanning commenced. As no man who has not visited the Cape can form any idea of the manner in which this daily operation is performed, it will here be necessary to explain it, and to say a few more words concerning the structure of a waggon.

The Cape waggon is a large and powerful, yet loosely-constructed vehicle, running on four wheels. Its extreme length is about 18 feet, its breadth varying from $3\frac{1}{2}$ to 4 feet; the depth of the sides is about 2 feet 6 inches in front, but higher towards the back of the waggon. All along the sides two rows of iron staples are riveted, in which are fastened the boughs forming the tent, which arches over the waggon to a height of 5 feet, with an awning of Caffre mat, and a strong canvas sail over all, with "fore-clap" and "after-clap," which is the colonial name for two broad canvas curtains, that form part and parcel of the sail, and hang in front and rear of the waggon, reaching to within a few inches of the ground. In the front is placed a large chest occupying the extreme breadth of the waggon, on which the driver and two passengers of ordinary dimensions can sit abreast. This is called the fore-chest, and is secured from sliding forwards by two buffalo rheims, or strips of dressed hide, placed across the front of it, and secured to the sides. A A similar chest is fastened in like manner to the rear of the waggon, which is called the after-chest. Along the sides of the waggon, and outside it, are two longer and narrower chests called side-chests. These are supported by two horizontal bars of hard wood riveted to the bottom of the waggon. The side-chests are very convenient for holding tools, and all manner of odds and ends too numerous to mention. The fore and after chests are likewise extremely useful for containing clothing, ammunition, and a thousand small articles in daily use.

Along the sides of the tent are suspended rows of square-cut canvas bags, called side-pockets, in which the traveller keeps his hair-brushes and combs, razors, knives, tooth-brushes, soap, towels, or anything else which he may wish to have at hand. I used to devote one to contain my luncheon, which often consisted of a slice of elephant's trunk.

The traveller sleeps upon a sort of cot, termed a "cardell." This cardell is a light, strong, oblong frame, about eight feet in length, and occupying the breadth of the waggon. It is bored all round with small holes, through which strips of hide are interlaced, forming a sort of network on which the mattress rests. This cot is slung across the waggon, and is attached with thongs to the bows of the tent, its elevation being regulated by the cargo, which is carefully stowed away beneath it in the body of the waggon. Suspended underneath the hind part of the vehicle is a strong wooden framework called the trap, on which the pots and gridirons are lashed during a march. The waggon is steered by a pole, called the dissel-boom, to the end of which is fastened the trektow, a stout rope formed of raw buffalo-hide. It is pulled by a span, or team, consisting of twelve oxen, which draw the waggon by yokes fastened along the trektow at regular intervals by means of strips of raw hide. Passing through each end of the yoke, at distances of 18 inches from one another, are two parallel bars of tough wood about 18 inches in length; these are called yoke-skeys. In inspanning, the yoke is placed on the back of the neck of the ox, with one of these skeys on either side, and towards the ends are notches in which is fixed the strap, made of twisted hide; this, passing under the neck of the animal, secures him in the yoke.

Besides these straps, each pair of oxen is strongly coupled by the buffalo rheims, which are used in catching and placing them in their proper order, preparatory to inspanning them: a rheim is a long strip of prepared hide with a noose at the end; it is made either of ox or buffalo hide, and is about eight feet long. A waggon is also provided with a tar-bucket, two powerful iron chains which are called the rheim-chains, and a large iron drag called the rheim-schoen: also the invariable whip and jambok; the former consisting of a bamboo pole upwards of 20 feet in length, with a thong of about 25 feet, to the end of which is sewn with "rheimpys," or strips of dressed steinbok skin, the "after-slock," and to this again is fastened the "fore-slock," corresponding with the little whipcord lash of the English coachman. The "fore-slock," about which the waggon-drivers are very particular, is about a yard in length, and is formed of a strip of the supple skin of some particular variety of antelope prepared in a peculiar manner. The skins of only a few species of antelopes are possessed of sufficient toughness for this purpose. Those most highly prized amongst the colonists are the skins of the hartebeest, koodoo, blesbok, and bushbuck; when none of these are to be obtained they use the skin of a he-goat, which is very inferior. The colonial waggon-driver wields this immense whip with great dexterity and grace. As he cracks it he produces a report nearly equal to that of a gun, and by this means he signals to his leader, who is perhaps herding the oxen at the distance of a mile, to bring them up when it is time to inspan.

The "jambok" is another instrument of persuasion, indispensable in the outfit of every Cape waggon. It is made of the thick tough hide either of the white rhinoceros or hippopotamus. Its length is from six to 7 feet; its thickness at the handle is about an inch and a half, and it tapers gradually to the point. These jamboks are exceedingly tough and pliant, and are capable of inflicting most tremendous chastisement upon the thick hides of sulky and refractory oxen. Those manufactured from the skin of the hippopotamus are very much superior to those of the rhinoceros, being naturally of a much tougher quality. If properly prepared, one of these will last for many years. A smaller description of jambok is manufactured for the benefit of horses, and may be seen in the hands of every horseman in the colony.

When the leader brings up the oxen to the waggon to be inspanned, the waggon-driver if possible sends another Hottentot to his assistance, especially if any of the oxen in the span happen to be young or refrac-

tory. These, armed with a huge jambok in one hand, and a handful of stones in the other, one on either flank, with shouts, yells, and imprecations, urge forward the unwilling team towards the yokes, where the driver is standing with the twelve long buffalo rheims hanging on his left arm, pouring forth a volley of soothing terms, such as—
"Ah! now, Scotland! Wo ha, Blauberg! you skellum, keer dar Carollus for Blauberg, ye stand somar da, ich wichna wha yo hadachta ist." (Turn there for Blauberg; you stand there in an absent state, I do not know where your ideas are.) "Holland, you ould Myfooty!" ("Myfooty" is a common Hottentot term, which I would defy even themselves to construe. The Dutch word "somar," mentioned above, is also a word to which I think I could challenge the most learned schoolmaster in the colony to attach any definite meaning. It is used both by Boers and Hottentots in almost every sentence; it is an answer to every question; and its meanings are endless.) "Slangfeldt, you neuxel!" (Snakefield, you humbug!) "Wo ha, now, Creishmann!" (Crooked man.) "Orlam, you verdomde Kind, vacht un bidgte, ich soll you krae." (Civilized! you d—d child; wait a bit, I'll serve you out.) "Vitfoot, you duivel! slahm dar für Vitfoot, slahm ihm dat he barst!" (Whitefoot, you devil! flog there Whitefoot, flog him till he bursts.) "Englandt, you ould ghroote-pench! Ah now! Wo ha! Ye dat so lowe ist in die shwor plach, und dharum so vees at inspanning! Vacht un bidgte, ich soll a plach for you aitsuch. Ye lob da for nett so as ye will, mar ich soll you arter bring, whar ich kann you mach like baikam." (England, you old big-paunch! Ah no! Wo ha! You who are so lazy in the heavy place, and nevertheless so vicious at inspanning. Wait a little. I shall seek out a place for you! You tramp there in front, exactly as you please; but I will yoke you farther back, where I can reach you with facility.)

This last is said in allusion to "England's" having lately been in the habit of being yoked in the front of the team, and if it is very long the driver cannot reach the leading oxen with his whip without descending from the box, and, therefore, when a fore-ox becomes lazy, he is yoked farther back in the team, that he may have the full benefit of the persuasive "fore-slock."

While the driver's tongue is pouring forth this flow of Hottentot eloquence with amazing volubility, his hands and feet are employed with equal activity; the former in throwing the open noose of the rheim, lasso-like, over the horns of each ox, and drawing it tight round them as he catches him; the latter in kicking the eyes and noses of those oxen which the jamboks and shouts of the leaders behind have driven too far in upon him. At this moment "Blauberg," who is an old offender, and who acquired in early youth the practice which he has never relinquished of bolting from the team at the moment of inspanning, being this day unusually lively, not having had any severe work for some weeks, suddenly springs round, notwithstanding Kleinboy, well aware of his propensities, has got his particular rheim firmly twisted round his hand; and having once got his tail where his head ought to have been, and thus deprived Kleinboy of all purchase over him, he bounds madly forward, heedless of a large sharp stone with which one of the leaders salutes him in the eye. By his forward career, Carollus is instantly dashed to the ground; and Kleinboy, who has pertinaciously grasped the rheim in the vain hope of retrieving the matter, is dragged several yards along the ground, and eventually relinquishes the rheim, at the same time losing a good deal of the outer bark of his unfortunate hand. Away goes Blauberg in his headlong course, tearing frantically over hill and dale, his rheim flying from his horns like a streamer in the wind. His course lies right across the middle of the Cape-Corps barracks, where about forty or fifty riflemen who are lounging about, parade being over, rush to intercept his course, preceded by a pack of mongrel curs of every shape and size, but in vain. Blauberg, heedless of a shower of sticks and stones hurled at his devoted head, charges through the midst of them, nor is he recovered for the space of about two hours.

The rest of the team, seeing their driver sprawling on the ground, as a matter of course follow Blauberg's example: instantly wheeling to the right and left about, away they scamper, each selecting a course for himself, some with and others without the appendage of the streamers. The Hottentots, well aware that it will be useless to follow Blauberg in the usual way, as he would probably lead them a chase of four or five miles, now adopt the most approved method usually practised in such cases. They accordingly drive out a small troop of tamer oxen, with which they proceed in quest of the truant. This troop they cunningly induce Mr. Blauberg to join, and eventually return with him to the waggon—the driver, with pouting lips and the sweat running down his brow, pouring forth a torrent of threatened vengeance against the offending Blauberg. The inspanning is then once more commenced as before, and Blauberg, being this time cautiously placed in a central position, well wedged up by the other oxen, whereby he is prevented from turning about, is lassoed with the strongest rheim, and firmly secured to the steady old ox who has purposely been driven up beside him. The twelve oxen are soon all securely yoked in their proper places; the leader has made up his "fore-tow," which is a long spare rheim attached round the horns of each of the fore or front oxen, by which he leads the team, and inspanning is reported to be accomplished.

I omitted to mention that the two fore-oxen, and the two after-oxen, which are yoked one on either side of the "dissel-boom," or pole, are always supposed to be the steadiest, most intelligent, and tractable in the team. The two fore-oxen in particular, to be right good ones, require a combination of excellences, as it is indispensable for the safety of the waggon that they thoroughly understand their duty. They are expected, unguided by reins, to hold the rare-trodden roads which occur throughout the remoter parts of the colony either by day or night; and so well trained are these sagacious animals that it is not uncommon to meet with a pair of fore-oxen which will, of their own accord, hold the "spoor" or track of a single waggon which has perhaps crossed a plain six months previously.

In dangerous ground, however—where the narrow road winds through stones and rocks, or along the brink of a precipice; or where the road is much intersected by water-courses, and bordered by the eternal hillocks raised by the white ants, which are of the consistence of a brick, being formed during damp weather, of clay, which the sun afterwards hardens; or where the "aard-varcke," or ant-bear, with his powerful claws has undermined the road with enormous holes—the fore-oxen, however trustworthy, should never be left to their own devices, but the leader should precede them, leading by the tow. This safe and highly necessary precaution is however rarely practised by the ruffianly Hottentots if the "baas" or master is not present, these worthies preferring to sit still and smoke their pipes or play their violins during the march, to performing their duty, thus frequently exposing their master's property to imminent peril. It is thus that more than half the capsizes, broken axletrees, broken dissel-booms, and smashed cap-tents, daily occur throughout the colony. All being now in readiness, and some pots and spades, which the Hottentots as a matter of course had omitted to stow away in their proper places, being securely lashed on the trap and to the sides of the waggon, the illustrious Kleinboy brandishes his huge whip, and cracking it with a report which loudly reverberates throughout the walls and houses of the Cape-Corps barracks, shouts out, with stentorian lungs—

"Trek, trek, you duivels! Rhure y'lla dar vor, you skellums! Ane spoor trap, you neuxels! Tabelberg, you ould kring! Trek, you löwe paar marys. Schneeberg, you löwe Satan! Blauberg, you duivel's kind!"—(Draw, draw, you devils! Move yourselves forward, there, you skellums! Tramp all in the same track, you humbugs! Table Mountain, you old ring! Draw, you lazy troop of mares! Snow Mountain, you lazy Satan! Blue Mountain, you child of the devil!

At the same moment he catches the refractory Blauberg the most terrific wipe round the ribs with his fore-slock, accompanied by a sharp report like the discharge of a pistol, upon which a cloud of blue hair is seen to fly from the ox, and a long red streak, down which the blood copiously flows, denotes the power of the weapon the driver so mercilessly wields over the backs of his horny team. At last the huge and heavily-laden waggon is in motion, and rolls lightly along after the powerful oxen, which on level ground seem scarcely to feel the yokes which lie across their necks.

Requiring to pick up several large parcels at the stores of some of the merchants in the town, we trekked down the main street of Grahamstown; and in passing the shops of the butchers and bakers, laid in a large supply of bread and fresh meat for immediate use. Before we had proceeded far, some sharp-sighted Hottentots came running after us, calling out that a fountain of tiger's milk had started in the stern of the waggon; and on halting we discovered that several loose cases of gin which I had purchased for immediate use, and which had not been properly stowed, had sprung a leak. The Hottentots seemed to regret amazingly the loss of so much good liquor, and endeavoured with their hands to catch it as it fell.

Owing to the various delays which had occurred during the day, I did not get more than half a mile clear of Grahamstown when the sun went down; and there being then no moon, I deemed it expedient to halt for the night. We accordingly outspanned; and the Hottentots, having secured the oxen to the yokes, and picketed my two horses on the wheels, requested my permission to return to the town to take another farewell of their wives and sweethearts. This I did not deem altogether prudent; but, knowing well that if I withheld my consent they would go without it, I considered it best to comply with a good grace; and, granting a general leave of absence, took on myself the charge of the castle which was destined to be my home during the next five years.

The Hottentots, strange to say, according to their promise, returned to the waggon during the night, and next morning, at earliest dawn of day, I roused them, and we inspanned. When this was accomplished, my head servant Long not appearing, we marched without him; but we had only proceeded about three miles when he managed to overtake us, the road being hilly and very soft, owing to the recent rains. On coming up and recovering his breath, he expressed himself very much disgusted at my starting without him, when I took the liberty of explaining that I expected my servants to wait for me, and not that I should tarry for them. Our progress was considerably impeded by the bad state of the roads, and at ten A.M. we halted for breakfast beside a pool of rain-water, having performed a march of about nine miles. Here, having outspanned our oxen, we set about preparing our gipsy breakfast: one collected sticks for the fires, another filled the kettles at the adjoining "vley," while Long and I were busied in spreading the table and dusting the beefsteaks with salt and pepper.

Having permitted the oxen to graze for a few hours, we again inspanned, holding the high road for Somerset; and about sundown we halted for the night on the farm of a Mr. Fichett, a great sheep-farmer, who received me hospitably, and invited me to dine with him. Here I met Captain Codrington, who had lately sold out of the 7th Dragoons. Our march this day lay through a succession of low, undulating hills, richly clothed with a variety of grasses, herbs, and flowers, with here and there large patches of dwarfish evergreens. I had directed my Hottentots to kraal the oxen that night, with the intention of making an early start on the following morning, but the herd managed to lose them in the thick underwood. They were, however, recovered at an early hour on the following morning, and, having breakfasted, I was about to proceed, when Long, with a face worthy of his name, came up to me with a whole tissue of dire complaints about his personal inconveniences, the most galling of which appeared to be his having to sleep on the ground in the tent. On my friend's advancing these objections, I saw very plainly that he was not the man for my work, as the life before us was by no means likely to be one of luxury; so having made over to him his impedimenta, and paid him him his month's wages, I wished him a safe return to Grahamstown.

It was a lovely day, with a bright blue sky overhead, covered with light, fleecy clouds, and the trees and shrubs, freshened by the recent rains, emitted an aromatic perfume. Having proceeded some miles, we commenced ascending the Zuurberg range, where we were met by two waggons from Somerset, laden with oranges for the Grahamstown market, of which I purchased several dozen, and found them excellent. The drivers of these waggons informed me that the road in advance was almost impassable, owing to the recent heavy rains. Although their oxen were better than mine, and their waggons lighter by some thousand pounds, they had had great difficulty in coming on, and they recommended me to retrace my steps, and, crossing the country, try the other road by De Bruin's Poort. Notwithstanding their remonstrances, I resolved to push on and give it a trial.

About midday I outspanned for two hours, to let the cattle graze; after which, having proceeded a few miles, we found the road so cut up that we were obliged to abandon it, and trek along the rugged hill-side, holding a course parallel to it. Marching in front, and sinking up to my ankles in mud at every step, I endeavoured to select the hardest ground, on which the waggon might follow. The ground now every moment became worse and worse; the panting oxen, straining every nerve to keep it in motion, and halting every hundred yards to take breath. At length the wheels suddenly sank deep into the soil, and became immoveably fixed, upon which we made loose our shovels and pickaxe, and worked hard for half an hour, clearing away the soil in front of and around the wheels; which, being accomplished, we rigged out a fore-tow and extra yoke to inspan my two spare oxen, and then set our whole fourteen to draw, but they could not move the waggon an inch.

We then lightened it of a part of the cargo, and, after half an hour's further labour, we had relieved the waggon of upwards of three thousand pounds; but still the oxen, notwithstanding the most unmerciful application of both whip and jambok, failed to move it. The thought then struck me of pulling it out backwards; we accordingly cast loose the trektow, and, having hooked on the long span or team to the after-part of the waggon, we succeeded in extricating it from its deep bed. We next proceeded with much care and trouble to stow away the baggage which we had removed, and the oxen being again placed in their position we resumed our journey; but, before we had gone three hundred yards, the waggon again became engulfed, sinking into the earth to such a depth that I half expected it would disappear altogether. The nave of the wheel was actually six or eight inches below the surface. This put us at our wits' ends, and I began to think that, if this was to be our rate of travelling, my hair would be grey ere I reached the land of elephants.

A few minutes after this had occurred, another waggon meeting us from Somerset hove in sight, but shortly stuck fast within a quarter of a mile of us. Its owner, an Englishman, an Albany transport-rider or carrier, of the name of Leonard, now came up and requested me to lend him my oxen to assist him in his difficulties, which I did, he promising in return to help me out of mine; but it was not until unloaded of the entire cargo that they succeeded in extricating it; after which, with considerable trouble, they came up to us. We now hooked to my waggon both spans, amounting to twenty-six strong oxen, the drivers standing one on either side, with their whips ready at the given signal to descend upon the devoted oxen. I myself, with one of the Hottentots, armed with the jamboks, stood by the after-oxen, upon whom, in a dilemma of this sort, much depends. Every man and beast being at their post, the usual cry of "Trek, trek!" resounded on all sides, accompanied by a torrent of unearthly yells and abusive epithets; at the same time the whips were plied with energetic dexterity, and came down with startling reports on the backs of the oxen throughout all parts of the team.

The twenty-six oxen, thus urged, at the same moment concentrated their energies, laying a mighty strain on the gear. Something *must* yield, and accordingly my powerful buffalo trektow snapped asunder within a few feet of the dissel-boom. The trektow being strongly knotted together, a second attempt was made, when it again snapped in a fresh place. We then unhooked the long drag-chains from beneath the waggon, wherewith having fortified the trektow, we made a third trial. The cunning oxen, having now twice exerted themselves in vain, and being well aware that the waggon was fast, according to their usual custom, could not be induced to make any further effort, notwithstanding the waggon-drivers had inflicted upon them about an hour's terrific flogging, till the sides of half of them were running down with gore. In cases of this sort the oxen, instead of taking properly to their work, spring about in the yoke, and turn their tails round where their heads should be, invariably snapping the straps and yoke-skeas, and frequently splitting the yokes.

In the present instance my gear did not escape, for, after battling with the oxen till the sun went down, and smashing the half of my rheims, straps, and skeas, and splitting one of my yokes, we were obliged to drop it for the night. We cast loose the oxen, and, driving them up the hill-side, granted them their liberty until morning; and leaving our broken gear, pickaxes, spades, and other utensils scattered about the ground in grand confusion, tired and worn out we kindled a fire, and set about cooking our dinner. Leonard and his servants declared that they had not tasted anything but a little biscuit and coffee during the last three days, the Dutchmen along their road being very unfriendly and inhospitable to the English transport-riders.

Next morning we awoke refreshed by sound slumbers, and having despatched all the Hottentots, excepting one man, in quest of the oxen, Leonard and I were actively employed for two hours in digging out and off-loading the waggon, after which Leonard and the Hottentot set about preparing the breakfast, whilst I proceeded to darn my worsted stockings, having had the good fortune to obtain some hanks of worsted from the wife of a Scotch serjeant in Grahamstown, after vainly seeking that article in the shops of all the haberdashers in the town. While we were thus employed, Captain Codrington and Mr. Fichett rode up to us, and seemed very much amused at our situation. Having drunk a cup of coffee with me, Fichett and Codrington returned home, previously engaging me to dine with them, as I had resolved to retrace my steps and try another line of country.

About eleven A.M. the Hottentots returned with our oxen, when, with the united efforts of the teams, we succeeded in extricating my now lightened waggon. The two oxen I purchased from Thompson, though well-favoured, proving indolent in a heavy pull, I exchanged them with Leonard for the liberty to pick any two out of his span, giving him a sovereign to boot. His team consisted of twelve tough little red Zoolah oxen, from the district of Natal, which, like the Albany cattle, are termed "Zuur-feldt." This colonial phrase is applied to all oxen bred and reared near the sea-coast, in districts where the majority of the grass is sour. Those from about the frontiers of the colony, or anywhere beyond the Orange River, are termed "Sweet-feldt" oxen. The Zuur-feldt cattle possess a superiority over the Sweet-feldt as trek-oxen, inasmuch as they thrive on any pasture, whereas the latter die if detained more than a few days in Zuur-feldt districts.

Leonard's account of the road before me was so bad, his waggon having been upset four times on the preceding day, that I resolved to put about, and adopt the route through De Bruin's Poort, which had been recommended to me by the drivers of the Somerset orange-waggons. By this route I should avoid Somerset, and pass through the village of Cradock. My plans at this time were, in the first instance, to proceed direct to the Thebus Flats, where black wildebeest and springbok were reported to abound; and thence to march upon Colesberg, a village on the frontiers, where I expected to meet my cousin Colonel Campbell, of the 91st, by whose advice, in a great measure, I intended to be guided in my future movements.

We now reloaded my waggon, made all fast, and, having put everything in order, Leonard and I journeyed together to Fichett's farm, where I once more took up my quarters for the night. While actively busied with my oxen, I saw to-day for the first time the honey-bird. This extraordinary little bird, which is about the size of a chaffinch, and of a light-gray colour, will invariably lead a person following it to a wild-bees' nest. Chattering and twittering in a state of great excitement, it perches on a branch beside the traveller, endeavouring by various wiles to attract his attention; and having succeeded in doing so, it flies lightly forward in a wavy course in the direction of the bees' nest, alighting every now and then, and looking back to ascertain if the traveller is following it, all the time keeeping up an incessant twitter.

When at length it arrives at the hollow tree, or deserted white ant's hill, which contains the honey, it for a moment hovers over the nest, pointing to it with its bill, and then takes up its position on a neighbouring branch, anxiously awaiting its share of the spoil. When the honey is taken, which is accomplished by first stupifying the bees by burning grass at the entrance of their domicile, the honey-bird will often lead to a second and even to a third nest. The person thus following it ought to whistle. The savages in the interior, whilst in pursuit, have several charmed sentences which they use on the occasion. The wild-bee of Southern Africa exactly corresponds with the domestic garden-bee of England. They are very generally diffused throughout every part of Africa—bees'-wax forming a considerable part of the cargoes of ships trading to the Gold and Ivory Coasts, and the deadly district of Sierra Leone, on the western shores of Africa.

Interesting as the honey-bird is, and though sweet be the stores to which it leads, I have often had cause to wish it far enough, as, when following the warm "spoor" or track of elephants, I have often seen the savages, at moments of the utmost importance, resign the spoor of the beasts to attend to the summons of the bird. Sometimes, however, they are "sold," it being a well-known fact, both among the Hottentots and tribes of the interior, that they often lead the unwary pursuer to danger, sometimes guiding him to the midday retreat of a grizzly lion, or bringing him suddenly upon the den of the crouching panther. I remember on one occasion, about three years later, when weary with warring against the mighty elephants and hippopotami which roam the vast forests and sport in the floods of the fair Limpopo, having mounted a pair of unwonted shot-barrels, I sought recreation in the humbler pursuit of quail-shooting. While thus employed, my attention was suddenly invited by a garrulous honey-bird, which pertinaciously adhered to me for a considerable time, heedless of the reports made by my gun.

Having bagged as many quails and partridges as I cared about shooting, I whistled lustily to the honey-bird, and gave him chase; after following him to a distance of upwards of a mile, through the open glades adjoining the Limpopo, he led me to an unusually vast crocodile, who was lying with his entire body concealed, nothing but his horrid head being visible above the surface of the water, his eyes anxiously watching the movements of eight or ten large bull-buffaloes, which, in seeking to quench their thirst in the waters of the river, were crackling through the dry reeds as they cautiously waded in the deep mud that a recent flood had deposited along the edge. Fortunately for the buffaloes, the depth of the mud prevented their reaching the stream, and thus the scaly monster of the river was disappointed of his prey.

CHAPTER III.

Fearful Descent of De Bruin's Poort—District lately deserted by Elephants—Noble Forest-trees—The Great Fish River—Cunning Boers—Burning effects of the Sun—The Dutch Nöe's Green Tea Ointment—Skill of the Hottentots in "Tapping the Admiral"—Beautifully Wooded Country—The Village of Cradock—South African Climate—Countless Herds of Springbok—Mynheer Pocheter—The way to make a Friend on the Thebus Flats—Hendrick Strydom—Hunting for Springbok—Extraordinary Migrations of these Antelopes.

My trektow having been destroyed during the recent struggles, I was glad to purchase a new one from a man named Mackenzie in Fichett's employ, which he supplied me, together with a strong thornwood yoke, for £1. On leaving the farm we proceeded in an easterly course, and struck into a track which in a few hours led us into the high road leading from Grahamstown to Cradock. Having followed this road for several miles, we commenced descending through the De Bruin's Poort, where the road winds, in a deep, narrow, and rugged ravine, through dense evergreen underwood, in its descent to the lower ground adjacent to the banks of the Great Fish River. This poort, or mountain pass, the terror of waggon-drivers, being at all times perilous to waggons, was in the present instance unusually dangerous and impassable, the recent heavy rains having entirely washed away the loose soil with which the colonists had been in the habit of embanking the permanent shelves and ridges of adamantine rock over which the waggons must necessarily pass, while they had at the same time undermined an immense number of large masses of rocks and stones which had hitherto occupied positions on the banks above, and which now lay scattered along the rocky way, presenting an apparently insurmountable barrier to our further progress.

As we were the first who had travelled this road since the late inundations, it had not undergone the slightest repair, which, to have done properly, would have required the labour of a week. Having halted the waggon, and descended into the ravine for an inspection, accompanied by Kleinboy, I at once pronounced it, in its present state, to be impassable. Kleinboy, however, well aware that he would not be called upon to pay for damages, seemed to entertain a different opinion, evidently preferring to run all risks to encountering the Herculean labours of rolling all these boulders to one side.

Accordingly, having made up our minds to take the pass, we re-ascended to the waggon, and, having rheimed or secured the two hind wheels by means of the drag-chains, Kleinboy took his position on the box, and the waggon commenced its perilous descent, I following, in the firm expectation every moment of beholding its destruction. Jolting furiously along, it crashed and jumped from rock to rock; at one moment the starboard hind wheel resting on a projecting ledge of rock several feet in height, and the front wheel on the same side buried in a deep hollow, and next moment the larboard wheels suddenly elevated by a corresponding mass of rock on the opposite side, placing the waggon in such a position that it seemed as though another inch must inevitably decide its fate. I held my breath, doubting the possibility of its regaining the horizontal position. Righting, again, however, with fearful violence it was launched, tottering from side to side, down the steep stony descent, and eventually, much to my astonishment, the pass was won, and we entered upon the more practicable road beneath.

I could not help fancying how an English-built vehicle would have fared in a similar situation, and how a Brighton coachman would have opened his eyes could he have seen my Cape waggon in the act of descending this fine specimen of a colonial waggon-road, which I might aptly compare to the rugged mountain-bed of some Highland river. Having continued our journey till within an hour of sundown, we encamped for the night. The country through which we had passed was densely covered with one vast jungle of dwarfish evergreen shrubs and bushes, amongst which the speck-boom was predominant. This species of tree, which is one of the most abundant throughout the forests and jungles of Albany and Caffraria, is utterly unserviceable to man, as its pithy branches, even when dead, are unavailable for fuel. It is, however, interesting, as constituting a favourite food of the elephants which, about twenty-five years ago, frequented the whole of this country in large herds. The footpaths formed through successive ages by the feet of these mighty animals are still discernible on the sides and in the necks of some of the forest-clad hills; and the skulls and larger bones of many are at this moment bleaching in some of the forest-kloofs or ravines adjacent to the sea in Lower Albany.

From time immemorial these interesting and stupendous quadrupeds had maintained their ground throughout these their paternal domains, although they were constantly hunted, and numbers of them were slain, by the neighbouring active and athletic warriors of the Amaponda tribes, on account of their flesh—the ivory so much prized among civilised nations being by them esteemed of no value, the only purpose to which they adapt it being the manufacture of rings and ornaments for their fingers and arms. These gallant fellows, armed only with their assegais or light javelins of their own manufacture, were in the constant habit of attacking the gigantic animals, and overpowering them with the accumulated showers of their weapons. At length, however, when the white lords of the creation pitched their camps on the shores of Southern Africa, a more determined and general warfare was waged against the elephants on account of their ivory, with the more destructive engines of ball and powder.

In a few years, those who managed to escape from the hands of their oppressors, after wandering from forest to forest, and from one mountain-range to another, and finding that sanctuary there was none, turned their faces to the north-east, and trekked or migrated from their ancestral jungles to lands unknown. A small remnant, however, remained; and these, along with a few buffaloes, koodoos, and one solitary black rhinoceros, still found shelter in the vast jungles of the Zuurberg and Addo bush as late as the commencement of 1849.

When the colonists first settled in Albany they were in the habit of carrying on a very lucrative traffic with the chiefs of the neighbouring Amaponda tribes, from whom they obtained large quantities of ivory in barter for beans, brass wire, and other articles of little value.

Throughout the jungles of Albany and Caffraria, but more particularly in the deep kloofs and valleys, many varieties of noble forest-trees are found of considerable size and great beauty, several of which are much prized by the colonists on account of their excellence for waggon-work and house-building; of these I may enumerate the yellow-wood tree, the wild cedar, the stink-wood tree, and the black and the white iron-wood tree. The two latter are remarkable for toughness and durability, and are much used in the axletrees of waggons. The primitive system of wooden axletrees has of late years been superseded in some districts by patent iron ones; many, however, still use and prefer the old wooden axletrees, because waggons having those made of iron, in steep descents, run too freely after the team, to the injury of the two after-oxen; and, further, because a wooden axle, if broken, may be replaced in any remote part of the country; whereas a damaged iron axletree cannot be mended even by the skilful smiths throughout the towns and villages of the colony. The iron axles are especially apt to be broken in cold frosty mornings during the winter, when a waggon, immediately after being set in motion, has to pass through rough ground before the friction of the wheel has imparted to it a certain degree of heat.

On the following day a march of four hours brought us to the bank of the Great Fish River, having crossed an extensively open glade covered with several varieties of low shrubs and grasses and rough heather. Here for the first time I saw and shot the black koran, an excellent game bird, allied to the bustards, so abundant throughout South Africa. Its weight corresponds with that of our old cock grouse; its legs and neck are long like those of the ostrich; its breast and back are grey, and its wings black and white. They are everywhere to be met with where the country is at all level and open : when disturbed they take wing and fly over the plain in circles, much after the manner of the green plover or peewit, uttering a harsh grating cry. The best method of getting within range is to use a horse, and ride round them in a circle, gradually contracting it. To this open glade, whose name I have forgotton, the Nimrods about Grahamstown often resort, and indulge in the exciting sport of wild boar and porcupine hunting. This "chasse" is conducted on bright moonlight nights, with a gathering of rough strong dogs, the hunters being armed with a bayonet or spear, with which they despatch the quarry when brought to bay.

I found the Great Fish River, as I had anticipated, still flooded and impassable to waggons. It was, however, ebbing rapidly, and apparently would be fordable on the morrow. During the previous heavy rains, which were said not to have been equalled for twenty-seven years, it had risen to an immense height, and everywhere overflowed its banks. That part of the bank which formed the descent and ascent of the former waggon-road was, as a matter of course, entirely swept away, a steep wall on either side of the river remaining in its stead, flanked by a bank of deep and slimy mud. An immense deal of manual labour would consequently be necessary to form a road, by cutting down these walls, and clearing a channel through the mud, before a waggon could take the drift.

Accordingly, the work being considerable, I thought the sooner we set about it the better; so having cooked and partaken of a hot tiffin, we cast loose the pickaxes, spades, and shovels, stripped to our shirts, and, half wading, half swimming, succeeded in crossing the river, where, having laboured hard till sundown, and constructed a famous piece of road, we considered our task on that side as completed. Early on the following morning we resumed our labours on our side of the river, and about ten A.M. our path was finished. A party of Boers now hove in sight with three waggons, which they outspanned on the opposite bank, and drove their oxen into the neighbouring hills to graze. Presently observing us preparing to inspan, they beckoned to me to hold a conference with them across the stream, the object of which was to dissuade me from taking the drift until their oxen should return, under pretence of assisting us, but, in reality, fearing that we would stick fast, and that they should be *forced* to assist us, since, in the event of our waggon sticking before their oxen came up, they would be unable to pass us until we were extricated. I saw the move with half an eye, and instantly ordered my men to inspan with all possible despatch; when we got safely through the river and up the opposite bank, which was much more than I had anticipated.

It was a fearful pull for the poor oxen; the waggon stuck fast three times, and was within a hair's breadth of being upset. The water just came up to the bottom boards, but fortunately did not wet any part of the cargo. The Boers seemed much surprised at the success of our venture, as they always entertain the idea that an Englishman's oxen must be inferior to theirs, but this idea is grossly erroneous, the reverse being invariably the case. A Boer will hardly ever flog his oxen when they require it, which, though it may shock the ear of my fair reader, my regard to truth compels me to state is indispensable, oxen being of a strange, stubborn disposition, perfectly different from horses. This, at a future period, I had cause to ascertain practically, when, forsaken by my followers on the borders of the Kalihari desert, I was necessitated daily to inspan and drive my own oxen, which I did, with the assistance of a small Bushman, for a distance of about a thousand miles.

It is a common thing to see a Boer's oxen stick fast on a very moderate ascent, with not above 1000 lbs. or 2000 lbs. weight in the waggon, where an Albany transport-rider would pass him with a load of 6000 lbs. behind his bullocks; and it is by no means uncommon to see these Albany men discharging a load of even 8000 lbs. weight at the stores of the Grahamstown merchants, which they have transported with a team of fourteen oxen through the hilly country betwixt that town and Algoa Bay. After crossing the river, the road continued good for about three miles, but after that we found it washed away in many places. Once we stuck fast, and were obliged to dig the waggon out, and broke our trektow three times in extricating it. In other places we were obliged to leave the usual road, and cut a new way through the thorny trees with our axes, the road being cut up with watercourses six and eight feet deep. At midday we outspanned for two hours, to rest the oxen, on the farm of a Mr. Corrie. Here we met a "smouse," or trader, coming down the country with a drove of about a hundred and fifty very large well-conditioned oxen. He offered me a span at £3 a head; they were worth £12 each in England. I felt the sun rather oppressive.

About two P.M. we inspanned, and, having ascended a long and very steep hill, we entered upon a new line of country, of wide undulating open plains of rank waving grass, dotted over with the mud-built habitations of white ants. We held on for three hours after sundown, and halted for the night at an uninhabited dilapidated mansion, in which we lighted a fire and cooked our dinner. Having secured our oxen on the yokes, instead of permitting them to graze during the night, we were enabled to march next morning some time before the break of day; and as the rising sun gradually unveiled the landscape, I had the pleasure of beholding for the first time several small herds of springboks scattered over the plain. This exquisitely graceful and truly interesting antelope is very generally diffused throughout Southern Africa, and is more numerous there than any other variety; it is very nearly allied to the ariel gazelle of Northern Africa, and in its nature and habits reminded me of the saisin of India.

A few herds of springboks are still to be met with on the plains in the district of Somerset, on which I had now entered; but as this is one of the nearest districts to the abodes of men where this species remains, it is of course much hunted, and is annually becoming scarcer. The gentlemen farmers of the surrounding districts keep a good breed of greyhounds, with which they have excellent sport in pursuing these antelopes. On beholding the springboks I instantly directed my two horses to be saddled, and, desiring the Hottentots to proceed to a farm in advance and there outspan, I rode forth with Cobus, taking my two-grooved rifle to endeavour to obtain a shot. I found them extremely wild, and after expending a considerable deal of ammunition, firing at distances of from six to eight hundred yards, I rejoined my waggons, which I found drawn up on a Dutchman's farm, and left the antelopes scathless.

Owing to the exposure to the sun while working at the Fish River drift on the preceding days, and also to having discarded coat, waistcoat, and neckcloth since leaving Grahamstown, my arms, neck and shoulders were much swollen and severely burnt and blistered, causing me much pain, and at night preventing me from sleeping. The kind-hearted noë, or lady of the farm, commiserating my condition, and wishing to alleviate my pain, informed me that she had an excellent recipe for sunburn, which she had often successfully administered to her husband and sons. One of the chief ingredients of the promised balsam was green tea, which was to be reduced to powder, of which she directed me to send her a little by one of my servants. I do not know what the other components might have been, but I well know that, on applying the ointment to the raw and swollen parts, it stung me as though it had been a mixture of salt and vinegar, giving me intense pain, and causing me to hop and dance about like one demented, and wish the Boer noë and her ointment in the realms of Pluto, to the infinite delight and merriment of my sympathising Hottentots.

A peculiar expression in the eyes of these gentlemen and their general demeanour, inclined me to think that their potations had consisted of some more generous beverage than water during the morning's march; and on examining one of my liquor-cases, I found that I was minus a bottle and a half of gin since yesterday.

This is a common failing among this monkey-faced race, nineteen in every twenty Hottentots being drunkards, and they have, moreover, not the slightest scruple of conscience as to who is the lawful proprietor of liquor, so long as they can get access to it. No locks nor bolts avail; and thus on the Bay-road, the high road between Algoa Bay and Grahamstown, a constant system of tapping the admiral is maintained.

In this pursuit these worthies, from long practice, have arrived at considerable skill, and it is usually accomplished in the following manner :—If the liquor is in a cask, having removed one of the hoops, a gimlet is inserted, when, a bucket or two of spirit having been drawn off, the aperture is filled with a plug, and, the hoop being replaced, no outward mark is visible. The liquor thus stolen, if missed, and inquiries issued, is very plausibly set down to the score of leakage. A great deal of gin arrives in Grahamstown in square case-bottles, packed in slight red wooden cases. To these the Hottentots devote marked attention, owing to the greater facility of getting at them. Having carefully removed the lid and drained several of the bottles, either by drinking them or pouring their contents into the water-casks belonging to the waggons, they either replace the liquor with water and repack the case again as they found it, or else they break the bottles which they have drained and replace them in the case, at the same time taking out a quantity of the chaff in which they had been packed. This is done to delude the merchant into the idea that the loss of liquor occurred owing to breakage from original bad packing. The risk and damage entailed on the proprietors of waggons and owners of merchandise from the drivers indulging in such a system, on the precarious roads of the colony, may be imagined.

After breakfast we continued our march, when I was again tempted to saddle up and give chace to a troop of springboks, one of which I shot: we continued our march until sundown, when we halted beside a pool of rain-water. Here we found some young Boers and Hottentots, belonging to a neighbouring farm, actively employed in digging out a nest of wild bees; several of them had their eyes nearly closed from the stings which they had received. The spoils of the "bike," however, repaid their pains by twenty pounds of honey. On approaching the nest a large cluster of bees chose my sunburnt arm as a place of rendezvous, from which I could not remove them until I had obtained a bunch of burning grass.

Our march on the following day lay through a mountainous country abounding with rich pasture, covered in many places with picturesque thorny-mimosa trees, detached and in groups, imparting to the country the appearance of an English park. In the forenoon we halted for a couple of hours in a broad well-wooded hollow, where I found abundance of bustard, guinea fowl, black koran, partridge, and quail. At sundown we encamped at a place called Daka-Boer's Neck, on high ground, where the road crosses a bold precipitous mountain-range. The mountain road along which we trekked the following morning, was extremely steep and rugged : on my right, high above me, I observed a herd of upwards of a hundred horses, consisting chiefly of brood mares and their foals, pasturing on the hill-side. Three more marches brought us to the village of Cradock, which we reached at dawn of day on Saturday morning the 2nd of October, having twice again had occasion to cross the Great Fish River.

The country through which we passed was bold, mountainous, and barren, excepting along the banks of the river, which were adorned with groves of mimosa, willow, and whitethorn, clad with a profusion of rich yellow blossoms yielding a powerful and fragrant perfume. It was now the spring of the year, and, this season having been peculiarly favoured with rains, a vernal freshness robed these sometimes arid regions, and I consider that I first saw them under very favourable circumstances. On the northern bank, at one of the drifts where we crossed the Fish River, I observed the dry dung in an old sheep-kraal burning. It was smouldering away after the manner of Scotch peat ; and on my return from the interior about eighteen months after, on my way to Grahamstown, the dunghill was still burning, and had been burning all the time, and nevertheless only two-thirds were consumed. The immense time which these dunghills require to burn is very singular. It is quite a common occurrence for one of them to burn for three or four years; and I have been informed by several respectable farmers of Lower Albany, on whose veracity I could rely, that in that district one of these "middens," as they are termed in Scotland, burnt for seven years before it was consumed. The heaviest and most protracted rains seem to affect them but little, rarely if ever extinguishing them.

Cradock is a pretty little village situated on the eastern bank of the Great Fish River, by wich it is supplied with water and the gardens irrigated. It is inhabited by Dutch and English, and a goodly sprinkling of Hottentots, Mozambiques, and Fingoes. The principal street is wide and adorned with shady trees on every side, among which I observed lots of peach-trees covered with green fruit. The houses are large and well built, generally of brick, some in the old Dutch and some in the English style. Each house has got a considerable garden attached to it : these are tastefully laid out and contain all the vegetables most used in the English kitchen. Apples, pears, oranges, quinces, nectarines, and grapes abound. The vision is bounded on every side by barren, arid, rocky hills and mountains. I marched right through the town and outspanned about a quarter of a mile beyond it, and after breakfast I re-entered the village on foot to purchase necessaries for myself and servants. Numbers of Dutch Boers with their wives and families were assembling to hold their Nachmahl or sacrament.

About eleven A.M. we inspanned, and continued our journey about five miles, crossing the Great Fish River twice, when I halted for some hours upon its bank on account of my oxen, the grass in the vicinity of the town having been very bare. This was the fifth and last time that we crossed the Great Fish River. Here about a dozen waggons passed us on their way to Cradock, containing Dutch Boers with their fraus and families. Several of these were horse-waggons, drawn by eight and ten horses in each waggon, harnessed two abreast, and drawing by straps across their breasts instead of collars. These straps are generally manufactured of the skin of the lion when it is to be obtained, that being reckoned by the Boers to be tougher and more enduring than any other. These long teams are well managed and dexterously driven by the Boers, one man holding the reins and another the whip. In the afternoon I again inspanned, and continued my march till sundown. The road since I left Cradock had improved, and was now fine and level, leading through a wide, open, undulating strath along the north-eastern bank of the Fish River. The surrounding country presented in every direction endless chains of barren stony mountains; the bold range of the Rhinaster Bergs standing forth in grand relief to the westward; not a tree to be seen, except a few thorny mimosas in some of the more favoured hollows of the hills and along the banks of the river; the country covered with grass and heaths, dwarfish shrubs, and small thorny bushes.

The sun during the day was powerful, but a cool breeze prevailed from the south. Ever since I left Grahamstown the weather had been very pleasant, and seldom oppressively hot, saving in the low-lying hollows where the breezes are not felt. South Africa, though its climate is dry and sultry, is nevertheless very salubrious, being surrounded on three sides by the sea, off which a healthy breeze prevails throughout the greater part of the year. At certain seasons, however, northerly breezes prevail: these are termed by the colonists "hot winds." On these occasions the wind feels as though it were blowing off a furnace in a glass-foundry, being heated in its passage over the burning sands of the Great Kalihari desert.

In Cradock I engaged another Hottentot, named Jacob, in the capacity of after-rider. Having followed the course of the Fish River for a distance of about nine miles, our road inclined to the right in a more northerly direction, and we here bade the stream a final adieu. Two more marches through a succession of wide, undulating, sterile plains, bounded on all sides by bleak and barren mountains, brought us to the borders of the immense flats surrounding the Thebus Mountain.

Having followed along the eastern bank an insignificant little stream dignified by the appellation of the Brak River, I arrived at the farm of Mynheer Besta, a pleasant hospitable Boer, and a field-cornet of the district, which means a sort of resident magistrate. Here we halted to breakfast, and Besta, who is a keen sportsman, entertained me with various anecdotes and adventures which had occurred to him during the earlier days of his sporting career in Albany, where he had once resided. He informed me that the black wildebeest and springbok were extremely numerous on the plains immediately beyond his farm, which made me resolve to saddle up and go in quest of them as soon as I had breakfasted. The flesh of these animals forms one of the chief articles of food among the Boers and their servants who inhabit the districts in which they are abundant; and the skulls and horns of hundreds of black wildebeest and springbok were to be seen piled in heaps and scattered about the outhouses of the farm. Adjoining the house was a well-watered garden with very green trees and corn in it, which formed a most pleasing contrast with the surrounding barren country.

Having directed my men to proceed to the next farm along the banks of the Brak River, I rode forth with Cobus and held a northerly course across the flats. I soon perceived herds of springbok in every direction, which, on my following at a hard gallop, continued to join one another until the whole plain seemed alive with them. Upon our crossing a sort of ridge on the plain I beheld the whole country as far as my eye could reach actually white with springboks, with here and there a herd of black gnoos or wildebeest, prancing and capering in every direction, whirling and lashing their white tails as they started off in long files on our approach. Having pursued them for many hours, and fired about a dozen shots at these and the springboks at distances of from four to six hundred yards, and only wounded one, which I lost, I turned my horse's head for camp.

The evening set in dark and lowering, with rattling thunder and vivid flashes of lightning on the surrounding hills. I accordingly rode hard for my waggon, which I just reached in time to escape a deluge of rain which lasted all night. The Brak River came down a red foaming torrent, but fell very rapidly in the morning. This river is called Brak from the flavour of its waters, which, excepting in the rainy seasons, are barely palatable. My day's sport, although unsuccessful, was most exciting. I did not feel much mortified at my want of success, for I was well aware that recklessly jaging after the game in the manner in which I had been doing, although highly exhilarating, was not the way to fill the bag. Delight at beholding so much noble game in countless herds on their native plains was uppermost in my mind, and I felt that at last I had reached the borders of those glorious hunting-lands the accounts of which had been my chief inducements to visit this remote and desolate corner of the globe; and I rejoiced that I had not allowed the advice of my acquaintances to influence my movements.

As I rode along in the intense and maddening excitement of the chase, I felt a glad feeling of unrestrained freedom, which was common to me during my career in Africa, and which I had seldom so fully experienced; and notwithstanding the many thorns which surrounded my roses during the many days and nights of toil and hardship which I afterwards encountered, I shall ever refer to those times as by far the brightest and happiest of my life. On the following morning I rode through the Brak River to visit Mynheer Pocheter, with the intention of buying some horses from him, but he had none to dispose of. I met the old fellow coming in from the "feldt," with his long single-barrelled roer and enormous flint-lock, with the usual bullock's horn powder-flask dangling at his side. He had gone out with his Hottentot before the dawn of day, and taken up a position in a little neck in an uneven part of the plain, through which the springboks were in the habit of passing before sunrise.

In places of this description the Boers build little watching-places with flat stones, from which they generally obtain a shot every morning and evening, and at such distances as to insure success. To use their own words, "they secure a buck from these places, skot for skot," meaning a buck for every shot. On this occasion, however, our friend had been unfortunate, returning without venison, although I had heard the loud booming of his "roer" a short time previously. The report made by these unwieldy guns of the Boers, charged with a large handful of coarse gunpowder, is to be heard at an amazing distance through the calm atmosphere of these high table-lands; and during my stay on the flats adjoining Thebus Mountain, scarcely an hour elapsed at morning, noon, or eve, but the distant booming of some Dutchman's gun saluted the ear.

Mynheer Pocheter asked me in to take some breakfast with him, which I did, Cobus acting as interpreter, mine host not understanding a word of English, and I not having at that time acquired the Dutch language, with which I not long afterwards became thoroughly conversant. After breakfast I took leave of Mynheer Pocheter, and having directed the waggon to strike out of the direct road to Colesberg, and hold across country to the abode of a Boer named Hendrick Strydom, where the game was represented to me as being extremely plentiful, I again rode forth, accompanied by Cobus, to wage war with the springboks. We pricked over the plain, holding an easterly course, and found, as yesterday, the springboks in thousands, with here and there a herd of black wildebeest. Finding that by jaging on the open plain I could not get within four or five hundred yards of them, I left my horses and after-rider, and set off on foot to a low range of rocky hills, where I performed two difficult stalks upon a springbok and a wildebeest, both of which I wounded severely, but lost. When stalking in upon the springbok I took off my shoes, and had very great difficulty in finding them again. I experienced great distress from thirst. The sun was very powerful, and, notwithstanding the heavy rains of the preceding evening, a drop of water was nowhere to be found.

In the afternoon I came to a pool of mud; the little water it contained was almost boiling; I was, however, most thankful to find it, and tears of delight came into my eyes on discovering it. How trifling was this to the trials from thirst which I have often since undergone! Shortly after this I fell in with my servant, who, astonished at my long absence, had come in search of me with the horses. I was right glad to fall in with him, and, having got into the saddle, I rode hard across the plain for my waggon. On my way thither I took up a position behind a ridge, and directed Cobus to "jag" a herd of springbok towards me, which he did most successfully sending upwards of a hundred of them right in my teeth. I however was still unfortunate, firing both barrels into the herd without doing any apparent injury.

On reaching my waggon, which I found outspanned at the desolate abode of Mynheer Hendrick Strydom, I took a mighty draught of gin and water, and then walked, followed by my interpreter carrying a bottle of Hollands and glasses, to the door of Strydom, to cultivate the acquaintance of himself and frau, and wearing the garb of old Gaul, in which I generally hunted during my first expedition, to the intense surprise of the primitive Boers. Shaking Strydom most cordially by the hand, I told him that I was a "Berg Scott," or mountain Scotchman, and that it was the custom in my country, when friends met, to pledge one another in a bumper of spirits; at the same time, suiting the action to the word, I filled him a brimming bumper. This was my invariable practice on first meeting a Boer. I found it a never-failing method of gaining his good-will, and he always replied that the Scotch were the best people in the world.

It is a strange thing that Boers are rather partial to Scotchmen, although they detest the sight of an Englishman. They have an idea that the Scotch, like themselves, were a nation conquered by the English, and that, consequently, we trek in the same yoke as themselves; and further, a number of their ministers are Scotchmen. Hendrick Strydom was a tall, sunburnt, wild-looking creature, with light, sandy hair, and a long, shaggy red beard. He was a keen hunter, and himself and household subsisted, in a great measure, by the proceeds of his long single-barrelled "roer." His frau was rather a nice little woman, with a fresh colour, and fine dark eyes and eyebrows; and displayed her good taste by taking a fancy to me, but perhaps the tea and coffee which she found I bestowed with a liberal hand might account for her partiality.

These were Boers of the poorer order, and possessed but little of this world's goods. Their abode was in keeping with their means. It was a small mud cottage, with a roof which afforded scanty protection from the heavy periodical rains. The fire burnt on the hearthstone, and a hole in the roof served at once for a window and chimney. The rafters and bare mud walls were adorned with a profusion of skins of wild animals, and endless festoons of "biltongue" or sun-dried flesh of game. Green fields or gardens there were none whatever; the wild Karroo plain stretched away from the house on all sides; and during the night the springboks and wildebeests pastured before the door.

The servants consisted of one old Bushman and his wife, and the whole of their worldly possessions were an old waggon, a span of oxen, a few milk cows, and a small herd of goats and sheep. Strydom's revenue seemed principally to be obtained by manufacturing ashes, with which he was in the habit of loading up his waggon and trekking many days' journey into other districts, where he sold them to richer Boers.

The manner of obtaining this ash is first to dig up the bushes and collect them on the plains. There they are left until sufficiently dry to burn, when, a calm day being selected, they are set on fire, and the ashes are collected and stowed away in large sacks made of the raw skins of wildebeests and zebras, when they are fit for immediate use. These ashes are in great demand amongst all the Boers, as being an indispensable ingredient in the manufacture of soap. Every Boer in South Africa makes his own soap. There is a low, succulent, green bush from which the ashes are obtained, which is only found in certain districts, and in these desolate plains it was very abundant.

Strydom, having sympathised with me on my continued run of ill-luck, remarked that it was quite a common thing when "jaging" on the principle which I had followed. He said that he was aware that in hunting on that system an immense amount of ammunition was expended with little profit, and that he, being a poor man, very rarely indulged in it; but that if I would accompany him after I had taken my coffee, there being still about two hours of daylight, he would show me his method, and he thought it very probable that we should get a buck that evening. Accordingly, having partaken of coffee, Strydom and I stalked forth together across the wild and desolate-looking plain, followed by two Hottentots, large herds of graceful springboks pasturing on every side. He placed me behind a small green bush, about eighteen inches in height, upon a wide open flat, instructing me to lie flat on my breast; and having proceeded some hundred yards, and taken up a similar position, he sent the Hottentots round a herd of springboks which were feeding on the plain, to endeavour to move them gently towards us. It was a very beautiful thing altogether, and succeeded well. The whole herd came on slowly, right towards where I lay, until within a hundred yards, when I selected a fine fat buck, which I rolled over with a ball in the shoulder. This was the first fair shot that I had obtained at a springbok on these plains. I have always been reckoned by those who know my shooting to be a very fair rifle-shot, whether standing or running, but I do not profess to make sure work much beyond one hundred and ten paces, or thereabouts.

Two days before this, I brought down a koran flying, with single ball. Our chances for this evening being now over, and night setting in, I returned to the farm with Strydom in high spirits.

The springbok is so termed by the colonists on account of its peculiar habit of springing or taking extraordinary bounds, rising to an incredible height in the air when pursued. The extraordinary manner in which springboks are capable of springing is best seen when they are chased by a dog. On these occasions away start the herd, with a succession of strange perpendicular bounds, rising with curved loins high into the air, and at the same time elevating the snowy folds of long white hair on their haunches and along their back, which imparts to them a peculiar fairy-like appearance, different from any other animal. They bound to the height of ten or twelve feet, with the elasticity of an India-rubber ball, clearing at each spring from twelve to fifteen feet of ground without apparently the slightest exertion. In performing the spring, they appear for an instant as if suspended in the air, when down come all four feet again together, and, striking the plain, away they soar again as if about to take flight. The herd only adopt this motion for a few hundred yards, when they subside into a light elastic trot, arching their graceful necks and lowering their noses to the ground, as if in sportive mood. Presently pulling up, they face about, and reconnoitre the object of their alarm. In crossing any path or waggon-road on which men have lately trod, the springbok invariably clears it by a single surprising bound; and when a herd of perhaps many thousands have to cross a track of the sort, it is extremely beautiful to see how each antelope performs this feat, so suspicious are they of the ground on which their enemy, man, has trodden. They bound in a similar manner when passing to leeward of a lion, or any other animal of which they entertain an instinctive dread.

The accumulated masses of living creatures which the springboks exhibit on the greater migrations is utterly astounding, and any traveller witnessing it as I have, and giving a true description of what he has seen, can hardly expect to be believed, so marvellous is the scene.

They have been well and truly compared to the wasting swarms of locusts, so familiar to the traveller in this land of wonders. Like them they consume every green thing in their course, laying waste vast districts in a few hours, and ruining in a single night the fruits of the farmer's toil. The course adopted by the antelopes is generally such as to bring them back to their own country by a route different from that by which they set out. Thus their line of march sometimes forms something like a vast oval, or an extensive square, of which the diameter may be some hundred miles, and the time occupied in this migration may vary from six months to a year.

CHAPTER IV.

A Bustard shot—Flight of Locusts—Quagga Shooting in the Dark—Curious Mistake—Ostriches—A Sportsman napping—Leave Strydom's Residence in quest of Wildebeests—Wildebeest Shooting—Meeting with a Brother Officer—Proceed to Colesberg—Additions to Equipments.

AT an early hour on the morning of the 6th, while I was yet in bed, Hendrick Strydom and his frau were standing over my fire, alongside of my waggon, with a welcome supply of sweet milk, and hurrying on the indolent Hottentots to prepare my breakfast, and rouse their slothful master—the earliest dawn being, as he affirmed, the best time to go after the springboks. On hearing their voices I rose, and having breakfasted, we shouldered our "roers," walked about a mile across the plain, and took up positions behind two very low bushes, about three hundred yards apart, and instructed our Hottentots to endeavour to drive the springboks towards us. We had two beats, but were unlucky both times, each of us wounding and losing a springbok.

In the evening we went out again to hunt on the same principle, on a very wide flat to the west of his house, where we lay down behind very low bushes, in the middle of the bucks. We lay there on our breasts for two hours, with herds of springboks moving all round us, our Hottentots manœuvring in the distance. One small troop came within shot of me, when I sent my bullet spinning through a graceful doe, which bounded forward a hundred yards, and, staggering for a moment, fell over and expired. A little after this, I suddenly perceived a large paow or bustard walking on the plain before me. These birds are very wary and difficult to approach. I therefore resolved to have a shot at him, and lay like a piece of rock until he came within range, when I sent a bullet through him. He managed, however, to fly about a quarter of a mile, when he alighted; and on going up to the place half an hour after, I found him lying dead, with his head stuck into a bush of heath.

Strydom had two family shots, and brought down with each a well-conditioned buck. In high good humour with our success, we now proceeded to gralloch or disembowel the quarry; after which, each of us shouldering a buck, we returned home in heavy marching order. On the following day I had the pleasure of beholding the first flight of locusts that I had seen since my arrival in the colony. We were standing in the middle of a plain of unlimited length, and about five miles across, when I observed them advancing. On they came like a snow-storm, flying slow and steady, about a hundred yards from the ground. I stood looking at them until the air was darkened with their masses, while the plain on which we stood became densely covered with them. Far as my eye could reach—east, west, north, and south—they stretched in one unbroken cloud; and more than an hour elapsed before their devastating legions had swept by. I was particularly struck with this most wonderful and truly interesting sight; and I remember at the time my feeling was one of self-gratulation at having visited a country where I could witness such a scene. On this day and on the morrow Strydom and I continued to wage successful war against the springboks. We crossed the small stream called the Thebus River, and hunted on the plains to the east. On one occasion Hendrick brought down two fat bucks at one shot, which he assured me was not an uncommon event with him.

On the morning of the 9th, Strydom and I having resolved over night to go in quest of a troop of ostriches which his Hottentot reported frequenting the plains immediately adjacent to the Thebus Mountain, we started our Hottentots two hours before the dawn of day; and after an early breakfast we saddled up, and rode direct for the Thebus Mountain. This remarkable mountain, which I shall ever remember as the leading feature on the plains where I first really commenced my African hunting, is of peculiar shape, resembling a cone depressed at the apex, and surmounted by a round tower. It is also remarkable as being considerably higher than the surrounding mountains, with which the plains are bounded and intersected. As we rode along a balmy freshness prevaded the morning air. We passed through herds of thousands of springboks, with small herds of wildebeest scattered amongst them. I fired two or three very long shots without success. Strydom, however, was more fortunate. He fired into a herd of about a hundred bucks at three hundred yards, and hit one fine old buck right in the middle of the forehead, the ball passing clean through his skull. We hid him in a hole in the ground, and covered him with bushes, and then rode on to our Hottentots, whom we found waiting beside a small fountain in a pass formed by a wide gap in a low range of hills situated between two extensive plains which were thickly covered with game. I took up my position in a bush of rushes in the middle of the pass, and remained there for upwards of eight hours, during which our boys were supposed to be endeavouring to drive the game towards us.

The Boer took up the best pass about a quarter of a mile to my right. Before we had been an hour at our passes, the boys drove up four beautiful ostriches, which came and stood within fifty yards of Strydom, but, alas! he was asleep. About this time I was busy trying to remember and practise a childish amusement which once delighted me as much as rifle-shooting—namely, making a cap of rushes—when, on suddenly lifting up my eyes, I saw standing within eighty yards of me about a dozen beautiful springboks, which were coming up to the pass behind me. I snatched up my rifle, and, lying flat on my breast, I sent a bullet through the best buck in the troop, smashing his shoulder. He ran about fifty yards, and fell dead. I unfortunately left him lying exposed in the pass, the consequence of which was that three other troops of springboks, which were coming up as he had come, were turned to the right-about by his carcase.

It was amusing to see the birds and beasts of prey assembling to dispute the carcase with me. First came the common black and white carrion-crow, then the vultures; the jackals knew the cry of the vultures, and they too came sneaking from their hiding-places in the rocks and holes of the ant-bear in the plains, to share in the feast, whilst I was obliged to remain a quiet spectator, not daring to move, as the game was now in herds on every side of me, and I expected to see ostriches every moment. Presently a herd of wildebeest came thundering down upon me, and passed within shot. I put a bullet into one of these, too far behind the shoulder, which, as is always the case with deer and antelopes, did not seem to affect him in the slightest degree. In the afternoon we altered our positions, and sent the boys to drive the plain beside which I had been sitting all day. The quantity of bucks which were now before our eyes beat all computation. The plain extended, without a break, until the eye could not discern any object smaller than a castle. Throughout the whole of this extent were herds of thousands and tens of thousands of springboks, interspersed with troops of wildebeest. The boys sent us one herd of about three hundred springboks, into which Strydom let fly at about three hundred yards, and turned them and all the rest.

It was now late in the day, so we made for home, taking up the buck which Strydom had shot in the morning. As we cantered along the flats, Strydom, tempted by a herd of springboks, which were drawn up together in a compact body, jumped off his horse, and, giving his ivory sight an elevation of several feet, let drive at them, the distance being about five hundred yards. As the troop bounded away, we could distinguish a light-coloured object lying in the short heath, which he pronounced to be a springbok, and on going up we found one fine old doe lying dead, shot through the spine. This day, and every day since I arrived at these flats, I was astonished at the number of skeletons and well-bleached skulls with which the plains were covered. Thousands of skulls of springbok and wildebeest were strewed around wherever the hunter turned his eye.

The sun was extremely powerful all day, but, being intent on the sport, I did not feel it, until I found my legs burnt; my dress as usual was the kilt, with a grey stalking cap. On reaching home the following day a large party of natives, belonging to the chief Moshesh, arrived on the farm. These poor men were travelling in quest of employment. Numbers of natives annually visit the colony, and work for the Boers, making stone enclosures for their cattle, and large dams or embankments across little streams in the mouths of valley, for the purpose of collecting water in the rainy season, for the supply of their flocks and herds during the protracted droughts of summer. They are paid for their labour with young cows or she-goats. The recent rains having washed away the embankment of a dam situated in a distant range of hills, on the borders of the farm, Strydom engaged these men to repair it. The vicinity of the dam being a favourite haunt for quaggas, and it being necessary that Strydom should go there on the morrow, we resolved to hunt in the neighbouring district, in which were situated some high and rugged hills.

Accordingly next day we sallied forth, and I ascended to one of their highest pinnacles, where I managed to shoot a rhode-raebok. Joining Strydom shortly afterwards, we hunted over another range of the same hills, where we fell in with three quaggas and other game. Night was now fast setting in, so we descended from the hills, and made for home. Cantering along, we observed what we took to be a herd of quaggas and a bull wildebeest standing in front of us, upon which we jumped off our horses, and, bending our bodies, approached them to fire.

It was now quite dark, and it was hard to tell what sort of game we were going to fire at. Strydom, however, whispered to me that they were quaggas, and they certainly appeared to be such. His gun snapped three times at the wildebeest, upon which they all set off at a gallop. Strydom, who was riding my stallion, let go his bridle when he ran in to fire, taking advantage of which the horse set off at a gallop after them. I then mounted "The Cow," and after riding hard for about a mile I came up to them. They were now standing still, and the stallion was in the middle of them. I could make him out by his saddle; so, jumping off my horse in a state of intense excitement, I ran forward and fired both barrels of my two-groved rifle into the quaggas, and heard the bullets tell loudly. They then started off, but the stallion was soon once more fighting in the middle of them. I was astonished and delighted to remark how my horse was able to take up their attention, so that they appeared heedless of the reports of my rifle.

In haste I commenced loading, but to my dismay I found that I had left my loading-rod with Hendrick. Mounting "The Cow," I rode nearer to the quaggas, and was delighted to find that they allowed my horse to come within easy shot. It was now very dark, but I set off in the hope to fall in with Hendrick on the wide plain, and galloped along shouting with all my might, but in vain. I then rode across the plain for the hill to try to find some bush large enough to make a ramrod. In this, by the greatest chance, I succeeded, and, being provided with a knife, I cut a good ramrod, loaded my rifle, and rode off to seek the quaggas once more. I soon fell in with them, and, coming within shot, fired at them right and left, and heard both bullets tell, upon which they galloped across the plain with the stallion still after them. One of them, however, was very hard hit, and soon dropped astern. The stallion remained to keep him company.

About this time the moon shone forth faintly. I galloped on after the troop, and, presently coming up with them, rode on one side, and dismounting, and dropping on my knee, I sent a bullet through the shoulder of the last quagga; he staggered forward, fell to the ground with a heavy crash, and expired. The rest of the troop charged wildly around him, snorting and prancing like the wild horses in Mazeppa, and then set off at full speed across the plain. I did not wait to bleed the quagga, but, mounting my horse, I galloped on after the troop, but could not, however, overtake them. I now returned and endeavoured to find the quagga which I had last shot, but owing to the darkness, and to my having no mark to guide me on the plain, I failed to find him. I then set off to try for the quagga which had dropped astern with the stallion; having searched some time in vain, I dismounted and laid my head on the ground, when I made out two dark objects which turned out to be what I sought. On my approaching, the quagga tried to make off, when I sent a ball through his shoulder, which laid him low. On going up to him in the full expectation of inspecting for the first time one of these animals, what was my disappointment and vexation to find a fine brown gelding, with two white stars on his forehead! The truth now flashed upon me; Strydom and I had both been mistaken; instead of quaggas, the waggon-team of a neighbouring Dutchman had afforded me my evening's shooting!

I caught my stallion and rode home, intending to pay for the horses which I had killed and wounded; but on telling my story to Strydom, with which he seemed extremely amused, he told me not to say a word about it, as the owners of the horses were very avaricious, and would make me pay treble their value, and that if I kept quiet it would be supposed they had been killed either by lions or wild Bushmen. Strydom and I continued hunting springboks till the 17th, during which time we enjoyed a constant run of good luck, and so fascinating was the sport that I felt as though I never could tire of it.

It was, indeed, a country where a person who loved rifle-shooting ought to have been content. Every morning, on opening my eyes, the first thing which I saw, without raising my head from the pillow, was herds of hundreds of springboks grazing before me on the plains. On the 17th an old friend of Strydom's, a Boer from Magalisberg, outspanned on the farm. He had been to Grahamstown with a load of ivory, and was returning home with supplies of tea, coffee, clothing, etc., sufficient for two year's consumption. He was accompanied by his wife and two tall gawky-looking daughters, and half a dozen noisy geese which were secured in a cage on the trap of the waggon. This Boer informed me that I could get all the rarer animals, which I wished to shoot, in his vicinity, namely, sable antelope, roan antelope, eland, waterbuck, koodoo, pallah, elephant, black and white rhinoceros, hippopotamus, giraffe, buffalo, lion, etc. He told me he had shot elephants there with tusks weighing 100 lbs. each, and upwards of seven feet in length. He advised me not to visit that country before the end of April, as my horses would assuredly die of a never-failing distemper which prevails in the interior, within a certain latitude, during the summer months.

Being anxious now to devote my attention more particularly to black wildebeests, of which I had not yet secured a specimen, I resolved to take leave of my friend Hendrick Strydom, and proceed to the plains beyond the Thebus Mountain, where he informed me they abounded. Accordingly, about 9 P.M., having inspanned by moonlight, I took leave of my friend, having presented him with a coffee-mill and some crockery, to which his frau had taken a fancy, and also with a supply of coarse gunpowder, which is to a Boer a most acceptable gift. We held for the Thebus Mountain, steering across the the open plains and following no track, with springboks and wildebeests whistling and bellowing on every side of us. About midnight we halted by a fountain near the pass where a few days before I had lain in ambush for eight hours, and, as it was probable that the oxen would wander during the night, we secured them on the yokes. Two of my oxen and both my horses were reported missing when we left the farm, and I had left Cobas to seek for them.

In the afternoon of the next day my two servants joined me, bringing with them the lost oxen, but having failed to find the steeds. At night I took up a position in an old shooting-hole beside the vley, to watch for wildebeests. Several jackals, wildebeests, quaggas, and hyænas came to drink during the night, but, not being able to see the sight of my rifle, I did not fire. Here I remained until the bright star of morning had risen far above the horizon, and day was just beginning to dawn when, gently raising my head and looking round, I saw, on one side of me, four wildebeests, and on the other side ten. They were coming to drink; slowly and suspiciously they approached the water, and, having convinced themselves that all was right, they trotted boldly up and commenced drinking. Selecting the finest bull, I fired, and sent a bullet through his shoulder, when, splashing through the water, he bounded madly forward, and, having run about a hundred yards, rolled over in the dewy grass. I did not show myself, other game being in sight, but lay still in the hole. In about an hour an old springbok fed up to within three hundred yards of me, and continued browsing there for a considerable time. As no more wildebeests seemed to be approaching, and as I was very hungry, I put up my sight and took a cool, calculating aim at him, and sent the ball through the middle of his shoulder. I then left my hole, and, having inspected the wildebeest bull, which was a noble specimen, I walked up to my waggon and sent the boys to cut up the venison and preserve the head carefully.

On the following morning I woke as day dawned, and held for my hole beside the vley, but had not gone two hundred yards round the hillock when I saw an old springbok feeding, which I stalked, and broke his fore-leg. He went off towards the waggon, when the boys slipped "Gauger" (one of my greyhounds), who at once ran into him and pulled him down. Having lain about an hour at the vley, two old wildebeests approached up wind, and, suspecting the ground, described a wide semicircle, like our red-deer, I wounded one of them, but he did not drop. I however managed to send a ball through the shoulder of the other, when he ran several hundred yards, whisking his long white tail as if all right, and suddenly rolled over in full career. His skin had a delicious smell of the grass and wild herbs on which these animals lie and feed. On proceeding to my waggon, I found all my men asleep. Having gralloched the wildebeest, we bore him bodily to the waggon on the "lechteruit," which is a bar of hard wood used in greasing the waggon-wheels, when I immediately set about curing the head, it being a very fine one.

On the following morning Cobus returned, having found my two horses. While taking my breakfast I observed a gentleman approaching on horseback; this was Mr. Paterson, an officer of the 91st, a detachment of which was then quartered at Colesberg. Lieutenant Borrow, a brother officer of mine, had intrusted me with the care of a rifle which he was sending to Mr. Paterson, and, as I had been a long time on the road, he had now come to look after it. He was a keen sportsman, and I had much pleasure in meeting so agreeable a person in the wilderness. Having joined me in my rough breakfast with a true hunter's appetite, we rode forth together to look for a wildebeest I had wounded in the morning, expecting to find him dead. On reaching the ground we found five small herds of wildebeests charging about the plain, and for a long time could not discover the wounded one; at length I perceived an old bull with his head drooping, which I at once pronounced to be my friend. On observing him we dismounted and watched him for a short time. The others inclined to make of, but seemed unwilling to leave him. Being now convinced that this was the wildebeest we sought, we determined to give him chase, and try to ride into him; but, just as we had come to this resolution, he fell violently to the ground, raising a cloud of dust. On riding up to him we found him dead.

Paterson and I then made for the vley, and had not proceeded two hundred yards when, on looking back, I saw about thirty large vultures standing on the wildebeest, which in a very short space of time they would have devoured. On the morrow Paterson left me and rode back for Colesberg, having first extracted a promise that I would follow him within three days. I accordingly hunted until that time had expired, when I reluctantly inspanned and marched upon Colesberg. Three long marches brought us to the farm of a Boer named Penar, who had been recommended to me as having a good stamp of horses, and as being reasonable in his prices. I was however disappointed with his stud, and, finding him exorbitant in his prices, no business was transacted. The country continued much the same; wide Karroo plains, bounded by abrupt rocky mountains. One more long march brought us within five miles of Colesberg, where I halted for the night.

On the 27th, having taken an early breakfast, we trekked into Colesberg, where, having chosen a position for my camp, I outspanned and took up my quarters with Paterson. The village of Colesberg is so called from a conspicuous, lofty table-mountain in its immediate vicinity, which takes its name from a former governor of the colony. The town is situated in a confined hollow, surrounded on all sides by low rocky hills. The formation of these rocks is igneous, and the way in which they are distributed is very remarkable. Large and shapeless masses are heaped together and piled one above another, as if by the hand of some mighty giant of the olden times. The town is well supplied with water from a strong fountain which bursts from the base of one of these rocky hillocks above the level of the town, and by which the small gardens adjoining the houses are irrigated. Abundance of water is the only advantage that the situation can boast of.

In the town are several large stores, from which the Boers of the surrounding districts can obtain every necessary article in their domestic economy. Numbers of these farmers attend the market weekly with their waggons, bringing in the produce of their farms and gardens; and, on sacramental occasions, which happen four times every year, the town is inundated with Boers, who bring in their families in horse-waggons. Owing to the unsettled state of the country, troops were then stationed at Colesberg. The garrison consisted of about two hundred men of the 91st, under command of my cousin Colonel Campbell, and one company of the Cape mounted Rifles, commanded by Captain Donovan. Colesberg was in those days a pleasant quarter, as there was not much pipeclay, and very good shooting could be obtained within a few hours of cantonment.

In the forenoon we had some some rifle practice at a large granite stone above the town, which the privates of the 91st were wont to pepper on ball-practice days. On this occasion I saw some very good shooting by Campbell, Yarborough, Bailey, and Paterson, all officers of the 91st, and about the four best shots on the frontier. These four

Nimrods had a short time previously boldly challenged any four Dutchmen of the Graaf Reinet or Colesberg districts to shoot against them. The challenge was accepted by four Dutchmen, who of course got "jolly well licked."

After spending a few days very pleasantly with the garrison, I resolved to hunt on and about the frontiers until the end of March, at which time the horse distemper begins to subside, when I proposed starting on an elephant-hunting expedition into the more remote districts of the far interior. In Colesberg I purchased, by the kind recommendation of Captain Donovan, a second waggon of the cap-tent kind, which turned out to be an unusually good one. Its price was £50. I also purchased an excellent span of black and white oxen from a Dutch blacksmith in the town. From Donovan I bought a dark-brown horse, which I named Colesberg. His price was 300 dollars, and he was well worth double that sum, for a better steed I never crossed. I purchased from a Boer in the town another horse, well known to the garrison by the sobriquet of the "Immense Brute." He was once the property of Captain Christie of the 91st; when on one occasion having wandered, an advertisement appeared in one of the frontier papers relative to an "immense brute" in the shape of a tall bay horse, the property of Captain Christie, etc., etc., and ever since he had been distinguished by this elegant appellation. I exchanged my brown stallion with Colonel Campbell for au active grey, which I considered better adapted to my work. Glass was at this time at a premium in Colesberg, every window in the town having been smashed by a recent hailstorm. I loaded up my new waggon with barley, oats, and forage for my horses, they having very hard work before them—hunting the oryx, upon which I was more immediately bent, being more trying to horses than any other sport in South Africa.

My intention was to revisit Colesberg in four or five months, and refit, preparatory to starting for the far interior. I left the skulls and specimens of natural history which I had already collected in the charge of my friend Mr. Dickson, a merchant in Colesberg. During my stay in Colesberg my men were in a constant state of beastly intoxication, and gave me much trouble, and my oxen and horses were constantly reported in the "skit-kraal" or pound. I engaged one more Hottentot, named John Stofolus, as driver to the new waggon. He was an active stout little man, and very neat-handed at stuffing the heads of game, preserving specimens, or any other little job which I might give him to do. He was, however, extremely fond of fighting with his comrades, and was ever boasting of his own prowess; but when his courage was put to the proof in assisting me to hunt the more dangerous animals, he was found woefully deficient.

CHAPTER V.

Departure from Colesberg—Jaging Sprinkbok—Vast Herds of Game—Swarms of Flies—Oology—A Nomad Boer's Encampment—Anecdote of the Gemsbok—Cobus rides down a splendid old Bull Gemsbok—A Night in the Desert—Paterson arrives—Bushmen—Their extraordinary Raids across the Desert.

THE VULTURES AGAIN.

On the evening of the 2nd of December with considerable difficulty I collected my drunken servants, my oxen and horses, and taking leave of my kind entertainers, I trekked out of Colesberg, steering west for the vast Karroo plains, where the gemsbok were said to be still abundant. It was agreed that Campbell should follow me on the second day to hunt springbok and black wildebeest, in a district through which I was to travel; and Paterson had applied for a fortnight's leave, with the intention of joining me in the gemsbok country, and enjoying along with me, for a few days, the exciting sport of "jagging" that antelope. I did not proceed very far that evening, my men being intoxicated, and having several times very nearly capsized the waggons. I halted shortly after sundown, when, all the work with the oxen and horses falling upon me, and no fuel being at hand, I was obliged to content myself by dining on a handful of raw meal and a glass of gin and water. On the following day we performed two long marches, crossing the Sea-Cow River, and halted as it grew dark on a Boer's farm where the plains were covered with springbok. Here Campbell had instructed me to await his arrival, and next morning he was seen approaching the waggons, mounted on the "Immense Brute," and leading two others.

Having breakfasted, we started on horseback to "jag" springbok and wildebeest, ordering the waggons to proceed to a vley about four miles to the west. We galloped about the plains, loading and firing for about six hours. The game was very wild. I wounded three springboks and one wildebeest, but lost them all. Campbell shot two springboks. The first was entirely eaten by the vultures (notwithstanding the bushes with which we had covered him), and skinned as neatly as if done by the hand of man. The second had its leg broken by the ball, and was making off, when a jackal suddenly appeared on the bare plain, and, giving him chase, after a good course ran into him.

This is a very remarkable occurrence and not unfrequent. Often when a springbok is thus wounded, one or more jackals suddenly appear and assist the hunter in capturing his quarry. In the more distant hunting lands of the interior it sometimes happens that the lion assists the sportsman in a similar manner with the larger animals; and though this may appear like a traveller's story, it is nevertheless true, and instances of the kind happened both to myself and to Mr. Oswell of the H.E.I.C.S., a dashing sportsman, and one of the best hunters I ever met, who performed two hunting expeditions into the interior. Mr. Oswell and a companion were one day galloping along the shady banks of the Limpopo, in full pursuit of a wounded buffalo, when they were suddenly joined by three lions, who seemed determined to dispute the chase with them. The buffalo held stoutly on, followed by the three lions, Oswell and his companion bringing up the rear. Very soon the lions sprang upon the mighty bull and dragged him to the ground, when the most terrific scuffle ensued. Mr. Oswell and friend then approached and opened their fire upon the royal family, and, as each ball struck the lions, they seemed to consider it was a poke from the horns of the buffalo, and redoubled their attentions to him. At length the sportsman succeeded in bowling over two of the lions, upon which the third, finding the ground too hot for him, made off.

Next morning, having bathed and breakfasted, Campbell and I parted: he for Colesberg and I for the Karroo. I trekked on all day, and, having performed a march of twenty-five miles, halted at sundown on the farm of old Wessel, whom I found very drunk. My road lay through vast plains, intersected with ridges of stony hills. On these plains I found the game in herds exceeding anything I had yet seen—springbok in troops of at least ten thousand; also large bodies of quaggas, wildebeest, blesbok, and several ostriches. I had hoped to have purchased some horses from Wessel, but he was too drunk to transact any business, informing me that he was a Boer, and could not endure the sight of Englishmen, at the same time shoving me out of the house, much to the horror of his wife and daughters, who seemed rather nice people.

Two more days of hard marching, under a burning sun, brought me to the farm of Mynheer Stinkum, which I reached late on the evening of the 7th. He informed me that about fifteen miles to the west of his farm I should fall in with a Boer of the wandering tribe who would direct me to a remote vley in the Karroo, a good many miles beyond his encampment, to which he advised me at once to proceed and hunt in its vicinity. He represented that district as not having been recently disturbed by hunters, and doubted not but I should find gemsbok and other varieties of game abundant.

It being now summer, flies prevailed in fearful swarms in the abodes of the Boers, attracted thither by the smell of meat and milk. On entering Stinkum's house, I found the walls of his large sitting-room actually black with these disgusting insects. They are a cruel plague to the settlers in Southern Africa, and it often requires considerable ingenuity to eat one's dinner or drink a cup of coffee without consuming a number of them. When food is served up, two or three Hottentots or Bush-girls are always in attendance with fans made of ostrich-feathers, which they keep continually waving over the food till the repast is finished.

This morning I purchased a handsome chestnut pony from a Boer named Duprey, a field-cornet, from whom I obtained an egg of the bustard of the largest species for my collection, oology being a subject in which for many years of my life I had taken great interest, having in my possession one of the finest collections in Great Britain, amassed with much toil and danger. I have descended most of the loftiest precipices in the central Highlands of Scotland, and along the sea-shore, with a rope round my waist, in quest of the eggs of the various eagles and falcons which have their eyries in those almost inaccessible situations. Amongst Stinkum's stud was a handsome brown gelding, to which I took a great fancy; and after consulting for some time with his wife, he made up his mind to part with him. The lowest price was to be £18. After a good deal of bargaining, however, I persuaded him to part with him for £12 in cash, 15 lbs. of coffee, and 20 lbs. of gunpowder. I christened this horse "Sunday," in honour of the day on which I obtained him. This bargain being concluded, I inspanned, and trekked to the wandering Boer, whom I reached about an hour after sundown.

This man's name was Gous; he lived in a small canvas tent pitched between his two waggons, round which his vast flocks of sheep assembled every evening, his cattle and horses running day and night in a neighbouring range of grassy hills: his wife was one of the best-looking women I met among the Boers; she informed me that she was of French extraction. On the following morning I breakfasted with Gous in his tent: he had lots of flesh, milk, and wild honey, which last article was reported abundant that season. He offered to sell to me a brown horse of good appearance; his price was too high, but at a subsequent period we came to terms, and I bought him. After breakfast I inspanned, and having proceeded a few miles across a glowing plain, on which I counted fourteen tall ostriches stalking amid large herds of other game, I reached a periodical stream, where I outspanned, the sun being intensely powerful. Here I found another Boer, named Sweirs, encamped with his flocks and herds, having been obliged to leave his farms, situated far in the depths of the Karroo, from want of water. Sweirs was an elderly man, but had been a keen sportsman, and entertained me with many interesting anecdotes relative to the habits of the game and of his hunting adventures in his early days. He informed me that he remembered lions extremely abundant in those districts, and that a few were still to be met with. He related to me instances where he had seen the gemsbok beat off the lion, and he had also come upon the carcases of both rotting on the plain, the body of the lion being transfixed by the long sharp horns of the powerful gemsbok so that he could not extract them, and thus both had perished together: he also mentioned that, notwithstanding the agility of the springbok, he had often known the lion dash to the ground two, three, and four in quick succession in a troop.

Four of my oxen being footsore and unable to proceed, I left them in charge of old Sweirs, and in the cool of the evening I inspanned, and, having proceeded about five miles through an extremely wild and desolate-looking country, on clearing a neck in a range of low rocky hills I came full in view of the vley or pool of water beside which I had been directed to encamp. The breadth of this vley was about three hundred yards. One side of it was grassy and patronized by several flocks of Egyptian wild geese, a species of barnacle, wild ducks, egrets, and cranes. The other side was bare, and here the game drank, and the margin of the water was trampled by the feet of wild animals like an English horsepond. There being no trees beside which to form our camp, we drew up our waggons among some low bushes, about four hundred yards from the vley. When the sun went down I selected the three horses which were to carry myself and two after-riders in the chase of the unicorn on the following morning, and directed my boys to give them a liberal supply of forage to eat during the night.

The oryx, or gemsbok, to which I was now about to direct my attention more particularly, is about the most beautiful and remarkable of all the antelope tribe. It is the animal which is supposed to have given rise to the fable of the unicorn, from its long straight horns, when seen, *en profile*, so exactly covering one another as to give it the appearance of having but one. It possesses the erect mane, long sweeping black tail, and general appearance of the horse, with the head and hoofs of an antelope. It is robust in its form, squarely and compactly built, and very noble in its bearing. Its height is about that of an ass, and in colour it slightly resembles that animal. The beautiful black bands which eccentrically adorn its head, giving it the appearance of wearing a stall-collar, together with the manner in which the rump and thighs are painted, impart to it a character peculiar to itself. The adult male measures 3 feet 10 inches in height at the shoulder.

The gemsbok was destined by nature to adorn the parched karroos and arid deserts of South Africa, for which description of country it is admirably adapted. It thrives and attains high condition in barren regions, where it might be imagined that a locust would not find subsistence, and, burning as is the climate, it is perfectly independent of water, which, from my own observation, and the repeated reports both of the Boers and aborigines, I am convinced it never by any chance tastes. Its flesh is deservedly esteemed, and ranks next to the eland. At certain seasons of the year they carry a great quantity of fat, at which time they can more easily be ridden into. Owing to the even nature of the ground which the oryx frequents, its shy and suspicious disposition, and the extreme distances from water to which it must be followed, it is never stalked or driven to an ambush like other antelopes, but is hunted on horseback, and ridden down by a long, severe, tale-on-end chase. Of several animals in South Africa which are hunted in this manner, and may be ridden into by a horse, the oryx is by far the swiftest and most enduring. They are widely diffused throughout the centre and western parts of Southern Africa.

On the 10th of December, everything having been made ready overnight, I took coffee, saddled up, and started an hour before day-dawn, accompanied by Cobus and Jacob as after-riders leading a spare horse with my packsaddle. We held a south-westerly course, and at length reached the base of a little hillock slightly elevated above the surrounding scenery. Here I dismounted, and having ascended to the summit examined the country all around minutely with my spyglass, but could not see anything like the oryx. I was in the act of putting up my glass again, when to my intense delight I perceived, feeding within four hundred yards, in a hollow between two hillocks, a glorious herd of about five-and-twenty of the long-wished-for gemsbok, with a fine old bull feeding at a little distance by himself, their long sharp horns glancing in the morning sun like the cheese-toasters of a troop of dragoons.

I scarcely allowed myself a moment to feast my eyes on the thrilling sight before me, when I returned to my boys and with them concerted a plan to circumvent them. At this time I was very much in the dark as to the speed of the gemsbok, having been led by a friend to believe that a person even of my weight, if tolerably mounted, could invariably, after a long chase, ride right into them. This, however, is not the case. My friend was deceived in the opinion which he had formed. The fact of the matter was, that he had been hunting a long way to windward of a party who were hunting on the same plains with him, and several of the gemsboks which he had killed had previously been severely chased by the other party. In the whole course of my adventures with gemsbok I only remember four occasions, when mounted on the pick of my stud (which I nearly sacrificed in the attempt), that alone and unassisted I succeeded in riding the oryx to a stand-still. The plan which I adopted, and which is generally used by the Boers, was to mount my light Hottentots or Bushmen on horses of great endurance, and thus, as it were, convert them into greyhounds, with which I coursed the gemsbok as we do stags in Scotland with our rough deer-hounds. A "tail-on-end" chase is sometimes saved, in parts where the hunter, from a previous knowledge of the country, knows the course which the gemsbok will take; when, having first discovered the herd, the after-rider is directed to remain quiet until the hunter shall have proceeded by a wide semicircular course some miles to windward of the herd, which being accomplished, the Hottentot gives the troop a tremendous burst towards his master, who, by riding hard for their line, generally manages to get within easy shot as the panting herd strains past him.

We agreed that Jacob and I should endeavour to ride by a circuitous course a long way to windward of the herd, and that Cobus should then gave chase and drive them towards us. The wind was westerly, but the district to which this herd seemed to belong unfortunately lay to the northward. Jacob and I rode steadily on, occasionally looking behind us, and, presently taking up a commanding position, strained our eyes in the direction of the gemsboks in the full expectation of seeing them flying towards us. After waiting a considerable time and nothing appearing, I felt convinced that we were wrong, and in this conjecture I judged well. A slight inequality in the plain had concealed from our view the retreating herd, which had started in a northerly course. Cobus had long since dashed into the herd, and was at that moment flying across the plains after them, I knew not in what direction. After galloping athwart the boundless plains in a state bordering on distraction, I gave it up, and accompanied by Jacob returned to the waggons in anything but a placid frame of mind.

About two hours after, Cobus reached the waggon, having ridden the old bull to a stand-still. The old fellow had lain down repeatedly towards the end of the chase, and at length could proceed no farther, and Cobus, after waiting some time and seeing no signs of his master, had reluctantly left him. In the height of the day the sun was intensely powerful; I felt much disgusted at my want of luck in my first attempt, and, burning with anxiety for another trial, I resolved to take the field again in the afternoon, more especially as we had not a pound of flesh in camp. Between three and four P.M. I again sallied forth with the same after-riders leading a spare horse. We cantered across plains to the north-east, and soon fell in with ostriches and quaggas, and after riding a few miles through rather bushy ground, a large herd of hartebeest cantered across our path, and these were presently joined by two or three herds of quaggas and wildebeests, which kept retreating as we advanced, their course being marked by clouds of red dust: at length I perceived a herd of ash-coloured bucks stealing right away ahead of the other game; I at once knew them to be gemsbok, and gave chase at a hard canter.

I gradually gained upon them, and after riding hard for about two miles I ordered Cobus to go ahead and endeavour to close with them. At this moment we had reached the border of a slight depression on the plain, down which the herd led, affording me a perfect view of the exciting scene. The gemsbok now increased their pace, but Cobus's horse, which was a good one with a very light weight, gained upon them at every stride, and before they had reached the opposite side of the plain he was in the middle of the foaming herd, and had turned out a beautiful cow with a pair of uncommonly fine long horns. In one minute he dexterously turned her in my direction, and heading her, I obtained a fine chance, and rolled her over with two bullets in her shoulder. My thirst was intense, and, the gemsbok having a fine breast of milk, I milked her into my mouth, and obtained a drink of the sweetest beverage I ever tasted.

While I was thus engaged Cobus was shifting his saddle from the "Immense Brute" to the grey, which being accomplished I ordered him to renew the chase, and try to ride down the old bull for me. We fastened the "Immense Brute" to a bush beside the dead gemsbok, and then, mounting the horse which Jacob had been riding, I followed on as best I might. On gaining the first ridge I perceived the troop of oryx about two miles ahead of me ascending another ridge at the extremity of the plain, and Cobus riding hard for them about a mile astern, but rapidly gaining on them. Oryx and boy soon disappeared over the distant ridge, the boy still far behind.

The country here changed from grass and bushes to extreme sterility; the whole ground was undermined with the holes of colonies of meercat or mouse-hunts. This burrowed ground, which is common throughout these parts, was extremely distressing to our horses, the soil giving way at every step, and my steed soon began to flag. On gaining the distant ridge a wide plain lay before me. I looked in every direction, straining my eyes to catch a glimpse of Cobus and the oryx, but they were nowhere to be seen: at length, after riding about two miles farther in the direction which he seemed to hold when I had last seen him, I detected his white shirt on a ridge a long way to my right, and on coming up to him I found that he had ridden the old bull to a stand-still: the old fellow was actually lying panting beside a green bush. I thought him one of the most lovely animals I had ever beheld, and I could have gazed for hours at him, but I was now many miles from my waggons without a chance of water and dying of thirst, so I speedily finished the poor oryx, and having carefully cut off the head I commenced skinning him.

It was now late—too late to take home the cow oryx that night; the bull was much too far from my camp to think of saving any part of the flesh. I therefore sent off Cobus to the waggons to fetch water and bread, desiring him to meet me at the spot where the cow gemsbok was lying, where I resolved to sleep, to protect her from hyænas and jackals; but before Jacob and I had accomplished the skinning, and secured the skin and the head upon the horse, night had set in. My thirst was now fearful, and becoming more and more raging. I would have given anything I possessed for a bottle of water. In the hope of meeting Cobus, Jacob and I rode slowly forward, and endeavoured to find out the place; but darkness coming on, and there being no feature in the desert to guide me, I lost my way entirely, and after wandering for several hours in the dark, and firing blank shots at intervals, we lay down in the open plain to sleep till morning, having tied our horses to a thorny bush beside where we lay. I felt very cold all night, but my thirst continued raging. My clothes consisted of a shirt and a pair of knee-breeches. My bed was the bull's hide laid over a thorny bush, which imparted to my tough mattress the elasticity of a feather bed. Having slept about two hours, I awoke and found that our horses had absconded, after which I slept little. Day dawned and I rose, and on looking about neither Jacob nor I had the most remote idea of the ground we were on, nor of the position of our camp.

Within a few hundred yards of us was a small hill, which we ascended and looked about, but could not in the least recognise the ground. I however ascertained the points of the compass and the position of my camp by placing my left hand towards the rising sun. I was then returning to the spot where I had slept, when suddenly I perceived, standing within three hundred yards of me, the horse which I had fastened beside the cow oryx on the preceding evening, and on going up I found both all right. I immediately saddled the horse, and rode hard for camp, ordering Jacob to commence skinning the cow, and promising to send him water and bread as soon as I reached the waggons.

On my way thither I met Cobus on horseback, bearing bread and a bottle of water, wandering he knew not whither, having entirely lost his reckoning. My thirst had by this time departed, so I did not touch the water, but allowed him to take it on to Jacob. He informed me that John Stofolus was coming on with the baggage-waggon to take up the venison; and before riding far I fell in with him, having, with a Hottentot's usual good sense, come away without water in the casks. Having shown him how to steer, I rode on to the camp, which I was right glad to reach, and felt much refreshed with a good bowl of tea. I was actively employed during the rest of the day in preserving the two oryx-heads for my collection. In the evening a horseman on a jaded steed was seen approaching the waggons, accompanied by an after-rider leading a spare horse. This was my friend Paterson, who had succeeded in obtaining a fortnight's leave of absence, and with whom that evening, over a gemsbok stew, I "fought my battles o'er again." Our respective studs being considerably done up, and in need of rest, the following day was devoted to "dulce otium," washing our rifles, and writing up the log.

On the 14th we went out on foot after a troop of ostriches, one of which we wounded, and came home much exhausted. The very ground was as hot as the side of a stove. The following day we were visited by a party of Boers from the neighbouring encampments, who had come to see how we were getting on. Finding our brandy good, they made themselves very agreeable, and sat for many hours conversing with us. The leading subject of conversation was gemsbok and lion shooting, and the slaying and capturing of whole tribes of marauding Bushmen in bygone days. They informed us that when they first occupied these districts the game was far more abundant, and eland and koodoos were plentiful. Their herds of cattle were constantly attacked and plundered by the vindictive wild Bushmen. Unlike the Caffre tribes, who lift cattle for the purpose of preserving them and breeding from them, the sole object of the Bushmen is to drive them to their secluded habitations in the desert, where they massacre them indiscriminately, and continue feasting and gorging themselves until the flesh becomes putrid. When a Kaffir has lifted cattle, and finds himself so hotly pursued by the owners that he cannot escape with his booty, he betakes himself to flight, and leaves the cattle unscathed; but the spiteful Bushmen have a most provoking and cruel system of horribly mutilating the poor cattle, when they find that they are likely to fall into the hands of their rightful owners, by discharging their poisoned arrows at them, hamstringing them, and cutting lumps of flesh off their living carcases. This naturally so incenses the owners, that they never show the Bushmen any quarter, but shoot them down right and left, sparing only the children, whom they tame and convert into servants. The people who suffer from these depredations are Boers, Griquas, and Bechuanas, all of whom are possessed of large herds of cattle, and the massacres of the Bushmen, arising from these raids are endless.

The Boers informed us that in a country to the south-west of our actual possession, a tribe of these natives for many years were in the habit of practising raids with impunity upon the herds of the farmers in the Raw-feldt, assisted by a vast and impracticable desert which intervened between their country and the more fertile pastoral districts. They seemed to prefer extremely dry seasons for these incursions, their object in this being that their pursuers, who of course followed on horseback while they were always on foot, should not obtain water for the horses. Their own wants in this respect they provided for in the following curious manner. They had regular stages at long intervals in a direct line across the desert, where, assisted by their wives, they concealed water in ostrich-eggs, which they brought from amazing distances, and these spots, being marked by some slight inequality in the ground, they could discover either by day or night from their perfect knowledge of the country. They were thus enabled fearlessly to drive off a herd of cattle, whose sufferings from thirst gave them little concern, and to travel day and night, while their mounted pursuers, requiring light to hold the spoor, could necessarily only follow by day, and were soon obliged to give up the pursuit on account of their horses being withuot water.

CHAPTER VI.

Hard Chase of an Oryx—A Brindled Gnoo reduces himself to a "dead lock," and is taken—Paterson slays a Gemsbok and a Bull Wildebeest—He leaves for Colesberg—Ostrich-eggs—Novel method of carrying them—Anecdotes of the Ostrich—Affray with a Porcupine—He proves a rough Rider for my Horse—Narrow Escape from the Thrust of a dying Oryx—The grateful Water-root—Troops of Springboks cover the face of the land—Their Migrations—The finest shot at my leisure—Beer Vley.

AT an early hour on the morning of the 16th Paterson and I again took the field, accompanied by our three after-riders, and, having ridden several miles in a northerly direction, we started an oryx, to which Paterson and his after-rider gave immediate chase. I then rode in an easterly direction, and shortly fell in with a fine old cow oryx, which we instantly charged. She stole away at a killing pace, her black tail streaming in the wind, and her long, sharp horns laid well back over her shoulders. Aware of her danger, and anxious to gain the desert, she put forth her utmost speed and strained across the bushy plain. She led us a tearing chase of upwards of five miles in a northerly course, Cobus sticking well into her, and I falling far behind. After a sharp burst of about three miles, Cobus and the grey disappeared over a ridge about half a mile ahead of me. I here mounted a fresh horse, which had been led by Jacob, and followed. On gaining the ridge, I perceived the grey disappearing over another ridge, a fearfully long way ahead. When I reached this point I commanded an extremely extensive prospect, but no living object was visible on the desolate plain.

Whilst deliberating in which direction to ride, I suddenly heard a pistol-shot, some distance to my left, which I knew to be Cobus's signal that the oryx was at bay. Having ridden half a mile, I discovered Cobus dismounted in a hollow, and no oryx in view. He had succeeded in riding the quarry to a stand, and, I not immediately appearing, he very injudiciously had at once lost sight of the buck and left it. Having upbraided Cobus in no measured terms for his stupidity, I sought to retrieve the fortunes of the day by riding in the direction in which he had left the oryx. The ground here was uneven and interspersed with low hillocks. We extended our front and rode on up wind, and, having crossed two or three ridges, I discovered a troop of bucks a long way ahead. Having made for these, they turned out to be hartebeests.

At this moment I perceived three magnificent oryx a short distance to my left. On observing us, they cantered along the ridge towards a fourth oryx, which I at once perceived to be "embossed with foam and dark with soil," and knew to be the antelope sought for. Once more we charged her. Our horses had now considerably recovered their wind, but the poor oryx was much distressed; and after a chase of half a mile I jumped off my horse and sent a bullet through her ribs, which brought her to a stand, when I finished her with the other barrel. She proved a fine old cow with very handsome horns; the spot on which she fell being so sterile that we could not even obtain the smallest bushes with which to conceal her from the vultures, we covered her with my after-rider's saddlecloth, which consisted of a large blanket: the head, on which I placed great value, we cut off and bore along with us.

On my way home I came across Paterson's after-rider, "jagging" a troop of seven gemsbok, but fearfully to leeward, his illustrious master being nowhere in sight. An hour after I reached the camp Paterson came in, in a towering rage, having been unlucky in both his chases. I now despatched one of my waggons to bring home my oryx. It returned about twelve o'clock that night, carrying the skin of my gemsbok and also a magnificent old blue wildebeest (the brindled gnoo), which the Hottentots had obtained in an extraordinary manner. He was found with one of his fore legs caught over his horn, so that he could not run, and they hamstrung him and cut his throat. He had probably managed to get himself into this awkward attitude while fighting with some of his fellows. The vultures had consumed all the flesh of the gemsbok, and likewise torn my blanket with which I had covered her.

On the following day, all our steeds being very much done up, Paterson and I visited the neighbouring Boers to endeavour to buy and hire some horses. I bought one clipper of Mynheer Gous for £25, and called him "Grouse," and Paterson succeeded in hiring one, and with these, on the following day, we continued our campaign against the gemsboks. Paterson's after-rider not being well up to his work, I lent him Cobus, and on this occasion his perseverance was rewarded by a noble gemsbok which he rode down and slew, and also a fine bull blue wildebeest, which last animal is rather rare in these parts. We had one more day together, after which, much to my regret, Paterson was obliged to take leave of me, and start for Colesberg, his leave of absence having expired. One of his horses being footsore, I purchased him, in the hope of his soon recovering, which after a few days' rest he did: I call him "Paterson," after his old master. My stud now consisted of eight horses, but three of them were missing, and I despatched Jacob in quest of them, who returned on the third day bringing them with him, having followed the spoor upwards of fifty miles.

In the evening two of the Hottentots walked in to camp, bending under a burden of ostrich-eggs, having discovered a nest containing five-and-thirty. Their manner of carrying them amused me. Having divested themselves of their leather "crackers," which in colonial phrase means trousers, they had secured the ankles with rheimpys, and, having thus converted them into bags, they had crammed them with as many ostrich-eggs as they would contain. They left about half of the number behind concealed in the sand, for which they returned on the following morning. While encamped at this vley we fell in with several nests of ostriches, and here I first ascertained a singular propensity peculiar to these birds. If a person discovers the nest, and does not at once remove the eggs, on returning he will most probably find them all smashed. This the old birds almost invariably do, even when the intruder has not handled the eggs or so much as ridden within five yards of them.

The nest is merely a hollow scooped in the sandy soil, generally amongst heath or other low bushes; its diameter is about seven feet; it is believed that two hens often lay in one nest. The hatching of the eggs is not left, as is generally believed, to the heat of the sun, but, on the contrary, the cock relieves the hen in the incubation. These eggs form a considerable item in the Bushman's cuisine, and the shells are converted into water-flasks, cups, and dishes. I have often seen Bush-girls and Bakalahari women, who belong to the wandering Bechuana tribes of the Kalahari desert, come down to the fountains from their remote habitations, sometimes situated at an amazing distance, each carrying on her back a kaross or a network containing from twelve to fifteen ostrich-egg shells, which had been emptied by a small aperture at one end: these they fill with water and cork up the hole with grass.

A favourite method adopted by the wild Bushman for approaching the ostrich and other varieties of game is to clothe himself in the skin of one of these birds, in which, taking care of the wind, he stalks about the plain, cunningly imitating the gait and motions of the ostrich until within range, when, with a well-directed poisoned arrow from his tiny bow, he can generally seal the fate of any of the ordinary varieties of game. These insignificant-looking arrows are about two feet six inches in length; they consist of a slender reed, with a sharp bone head, thoroughly poisoned with a composition, of which the principal ingredients are obtained sometimes from a succulent herb, having thick leaves, yielding a poisonous milky juice, and sometimes from the jaws of snakes. The bow barely exceeds three feet in length; its string is of twisted sinews. When a Bushman finds an ostrich's nest he ensconces himself in it and there awaits the return of the old birds, by which means he generally secures the pair. It is by means of these little arrows that the majority of the fine plumes are obtained which grace the heads of the fair throughout the civilized world.

It was now the height of summer, and every day the heat of the sun was terrific, but there was generally a breeze of wind, and the nights were cool. Our vley was daily decreasing, and I saw that, unless we were visited by rains, it would soon be no more. On the morning of the 22nd I had rather an absurd adventure with a porcupine, which cost me my packsaddle, the only thing of the sort I had in camp. Long before daybreak I saddled up and rode north with my two after-riders and a spare horse with the packsaddle. As day dawned I came upon a handsome old porcupine, taking his morning airing. At first sight he reminded me of a badger. Unwilling to discharge my rifle, as it was probable that we were in the vicinity of oryx, I resolved to attempt his destruction with the thick end of my jambok, the porcupine, like the seal, being easily killed with a blow on the nose. I jumped off my horse, and after a short race, in which I frequently turned him, when he invariably doubled back between my legs, giving me the full benefit of his bristling quills. I succeeded in killing him with the jambok, but not till I had received several wounds in my hands. My boys the while sat grinning in their saddles, enjoying the activity of their "baas."

Having covered him with bushes, we rode on, and shortly came upon an immense, compact herd of several thousand "trekking" springboks, which were exceedingly tame, and in the middle of them stood two oryx. These we managed for the first time to drive in a southerly direction, being that in which the camp lay; and after a sharp and rather circular burst, I headed the finer, and bowled her over. She proved to be a young cow, about three years old. Having disemboweled her, and prepared her for the packsaddle with a *couteau-de-chasse*, by splitting the brisket, passing the knife along the gristly bones on one side of it, and breaking the back by a dexterous touch of the knife, where certain ribs well known to the hunter join the vertebræ, whereby the animal can more easily be balanced on the packsaddle, we succeeded with great difficulty in placing her on "Sunday," and rode slowly for the place where we had left the porcupine.

We placed him on the oryx, and secured him with a rheim, but we had not proceeded far when some of the quills pricked the steed, upon which he commenced bucking and prancing in the most frantic manner, which of course made matters ten times worse, causing the porcupine to beat the devil's tattoo on his back. The gemsbok's head, also, which, being a poor one, I had not cut off, unfortunately got adrift, and kept dangling about his haunches, the sharp horns striking his belly at every spring. He broke loose from Jacob, who led him, and set off across the country at a terrific pace, eventually smashing the packsaddle, but still failing to disengage himself from the gemsbok, whose hind and fore feet, being fastened together, slipped round under his belly, impeding his motions, and in this condition he was eventually secured, being considerably lacerated about the haunches by the horns of the oryx.

Next day Cobus and I fell in with the finest bull oryx I had yet met, which, after a severe chase, we rode into and slew. For some evenings previous a large bright comet had appeared in the south-west, having a tearing, fiery tale, which strange meteor, to the best of my recollection, shone brightly in the clear firmament for five or six weeks. We lived well, but lonelily. My camp abounded with every delicacy—tongues, brains, marrow-bones, kidneys, rich soup, with the most delicious venison in the world, etc., etc., and a constant supply of ostrich-eggs. The 25th was cool and cloudy, being the first day that the sky had been overcast since I had left the Thebus Flats.

In the afternoon I resolved to ride far into the oryx country, sleep under a bush, and hunt them on the following morning. I accordingly left my waggons about three P.M., with my two after-riders and a spare horse, and rode about fifteen miles in a northerly course, when we secured our horses to a bush, to leeward of which we slept. On my way thither I dismounted on an arid plain to breathe our steeds and dig up some bulbs of the water-root for immediate consumption, my thirst being very severe. While cantering along we passed several troops of hartebeests and ostriches, and late in the day I observed a small troop of oryx. With regard to water-root just referred to, it has doubtless saved many from dying of thirst, is met with throughout the most parched plains of the Karroo. It is a large oval bulb, varying from six to ten inches in diameter, and is of an extremely juicy consistence, with rather an insipid flavour. It is protected by a thin brown skin, which is easily removed with the back of a knife. It has small insignificant narrow leaves, with little black dotes on them, which are not easily detected by an inexperienced eye. The ground round it is generally so baked with the sun, that it has to be dug out with a knife. The top of the bulb is discovered about eight or nine inches from the surface of the ground, and the earth all round it must then be carefully removed. A knowledge of this plant is invaluable to him whose avocations lead him into these desolate regions. Throughout the whole extent of the great Kalahari desert, and the vast tracts of country adjoining thereto, an immense variety of bulbs and roots of this juicy description succeed one another monthly, there being hardly a season in the year at which the poor Bakalahari, provided with a sharp-pointed stick hardened in the fire, cannot obtain a meal, being intimately acquainted with each and all the herbs and roots which a bountiful hand has provided for his sustenance. There are also several succulent plants, having thick juicy leaves, which in like manner answer the purpose of food and drink.

Above all, a species of bitter water-melon is thickly scattered over the entire surface of the known parts of the great Kalahari desert. These often supply the place of food and water to the wild inhabitants of those remote regions, and it is stated by the Bakalahari that these melons improve in flavour as they penetrate farther to the west. Most of these roots are much eaten by the gemsboks, which are led by instinct to root them out. The elephants also, apprised by their acute sense of smell of their position, feed upon them, and whole tracks may be seen ploughed up by the tusks of these sagacious animals in quest of them.

On the 26th I raised my head from my saddle about one o'clock A.M., imagining the day was dawning, and, having roused my after-riders, we proceeded to saddle our horses; but I soon perceived that the bright moon, across which a bank of clouds was at that moment passing, had deceived me, and accordingly we off-saddled, and in a few minutes I was once more asleep. Towards morning a smart shower of rain suddenly falling on my face broke in abruptly on my slumbers, when we once more arose, and, when day dawned, we saddled up, and held a northerly course. We found the fresh tracks of hyænas not more than fifteen yards from our horses. Within a hundred yards of our bush we at once discovered the spoor of an old bull-gemsbok which had fed past us during the night; and we had proceeded but a short distance when we discovered a herd of seven noble oryx within a quarter of a mile of us, pasturing in a low hollow; upon which I directed Cobus to ride round and "jag" them up to me, whilst I took up a position in front.

The oryx presently charged past me; but Cobus had started after an old bull which I did not see, and which he rode to a stand. To these seven oryx I accordingly gave chase, and before the first mile I was riding within a hundred yards of them. Here we were joined by another fine herd of twenty-two oryx, nearly all full-grown, and carrying superb horns. On we swept at a thrilling pace, and, after riding upwards of another mile, I pulled up to have a shot; but "Grouse," which I rode, being very restless, the herd got a long way ahead before I could fire. I however wounded one fine old cow, which I ascertained some hours afterwards. Having fired, I resumed the chase, and, observing that the finest bull of the first herd seemed distressed, I endeavoured to cut him off from the herd, which I succeeded in doing, and, in the excitement of the moment, I determined to follow him as long as my horse could go. Away and away we wildly flew—the oryx leading me a cruel long chase due north, tail-on-end, from my waggons, over a very heavy country entirely undermined by the endless burrows of the mouse-hunts. My poor steed became at length completely knocked up, while the oryx seemed to gain fresh speed, and increase the distance between us. I felt that my horse could not do it.

One chance alone remained : there was still a shot in my left barrel. I pulled up, and, vaulting from my panting steed, with trembling hand and beating heart I cocked my rifle and let fly at the round stern of the retreating antelope. The ball passed within a few inches of his ear and raised the dust about fifty yards in advance of him; and I had the mortification of having to content myself with watching his lessening form as he retreated across the boundless waste. Faint and weary, and intensely mortified at the issue of my long-continued chase, my lips cracking, and my tongue and throat parched with raging thirst, I threw my bridle on my arm and led my weary steed homewards, and I inwardly wished that, instead of my being a man of fourteen stone weight, nature had formed me of the most Liliputian dimensions. I was now a fearful long way from my camp; hills that in the morning were blue before me were now equally blue far far behind me; "Grouse" could scarcely walk along with me, nor did he ever recover that morning's work.

Upon my return I observed Jacob making for me, leading a fresh horse, of which I stood not a little in need; he stated that he had seen an oryx standing at a distance on the plain, which bore the appearance of being wounded. We then made for this oryx, and on my overhauling her with my spyglass I saw plainly that she was badly hit. On my cantering up to her she ran but a short distance, when she gave in, and, facing about, stood at bay. I foolishly approached her without firing, and very nearly paid dearly for my folly, for, lowering her sharp horns, she made a desperate rush towards me, and would inevitably have run me through had not her strength at this moment failed her, when she staggered forward and fell to the ground.

On the following day the waters of my vley sank into the earth and disappeared; the water for some days past had become very "brack," making myself and my people very unwell.

On the 28th I had the satisfaction of beholding, for the first time, what I had often heard the Boers allude to—viz. a "trek-bokken," or grand migration of springboks. This was, I think, the most extraordinary and striking scene, as connected with beasts of the chase, that I have ever beheld.

For about two hours before the day dawned I had been lying awake in my waggon, listening to the grunting of the bucks within two hundred yards of me, imagining that some large herd of springboks was feeding beside my camp; but on my rising when it was clear, and looking about me, I beheld the ground to the northward of my camp actually covered with a dense living mass of springboks, marching slowly and steadily along, extending from an opening in a long range of hills on the west, through which they continued pouring, like the flood of some great river, to a ridge about a mile to the north-east, over which they disappeared. The breadth of the ground they covered might have been somewhere about half a mile. I stood upon the fore chest of my waggon for nearly two hours, lost in wonder at the novel and wonderful scene which was passing before me, and had some difficulty in convincing myself that it was reality which I beheld, and not the wild and exaggerated picture of a hunter's dream.

During this time their vast legions continued streaming through the neck in the hills in one unbroken compact phalanx. At length I saddled up, and rode into the middle of them with my rifle and after-riders, and fired into the ranks until fourteen had fallen, when I cried "Enough." We then retraced our steps to secure from the ever-voracious vultures the venison which lay strewed along my gory track. Having collected the springboks at different bushes, and concealed them with brushwood, we returned to camp, where I partook of coffee while my men were inspanning.

A person anxious to kill many springboks might have bagged thirty or forty that morning. I never, in all my subsequent career, fell in with so dense a herd of these antelopes, nor found them allow me to ride so near them. Having inspanned, we proceeded with the waggons to take up the fallen game, which being accomplished, we held for the small periodical stream beside which the wandering Boers were encamped, that point being in my line of march for Beer Vley. Vast and surprising as was the herd of springboks which I had that morning witnessed, it was infinitely surpassed by what I beheld on the march from my vley to old Sweirs's camp; for, on our clearing the low range of hills through which the springboks had been pouring, I beheld the boundless plains, and even the hill sides which stretched away on every side of me, thickly covered, not with "herds," but with "one vast herd" of springboks; far as the eye could strain the landscape was alive with them, until they softened down into a dim red mass of living creatures.

To endeavour to form any idea of the amount of antelopes which I that day beheld were vain; but I have, nevertheless, no hesitation in stating that some hundreds of thousands of springboks were that morning within the compass of my vision. On reaching the encampment of the Boers I outspanned, and set about cutting up and salting my venison; the Boers had likewise been out with their "roers," and shot as many as they could carry home. Old Sweirs acknowledged that it was a very fair "trek-bokken," but observed that it was not many when compared with what he had seen.

"You this morning," he remarked, "behold only one flat covered with springboks, but I give you my word that I have ridden a long day's journey over a succession of flats covered with them, as far as I could see, as thick as sheep standing in a fold." I spent the following two days with the Boers. Each morning and evening we rode out and hunted the springboks, killing as many as we could bring home. The vast armies of the springboks, however, did not tarry long in that neighbourhood; having quickly consumed every green herb, they passed away to give other districts a benefit, thus leaving the Boers no alternative but to strike their tents, and remove with their flocks and herds to lands where they might find pasture.

On the morning of the 31st I left this periodical stream, whose name was "Rhinoceros Pool," and held on for Beer Vley, which I reached in about eight hours. Our march was a very hot one, across a desolate barren country destitute of water. The country, though barren, was not, however, without game: I saw several herds of springboks, of from 500 to 2000 in each; also several troops of gigantic-looking ostriches, and abundance of bustard and Namaqua partridges. I shot two springboks, and broke the foreleg of a third. Beer Vley, at the southern end of which I had now encamped, is a very extensive, low-lying, level plain; its length might be somewhat about twenty miles, and its breadth averaging from one to two miles. Through the entire length of this grassy vley runs, in the rainy season, a deep stream of water, which meanders in a very serpentine course along the centre of the plain, and, overflowing its banks, irrigates and enriches the surrounding pasture. At that season, however, this channel was perfectly dry, and the plain was covered with rich green grass. The country surrounding Beer Vley is extremely desolate and sterile, consisting of low rocky hills and undulating sandy plains, barely covered with dwarfish scrubby shrubs and small karroo bushes.

On the morrow I removed my encampment about eight or nine miles farther down the vley, being obliged, from the broken and uneven nature of the ground, to march in a semicircular course, holding along the outside of the vley. I drew up my waggons on the plain close to the bank of a dry channel, with a fine large pool of running water in my vicinity. This was the finest place that can be described to shoot springboks, and also to select extraordinary specimens on account of their horns, which I was anxious to do. The country, on every side, was covered with immense herds of these antelopes, and they all seemed to have an inclination to come and feed close along the side of the watercourse beside which we lay. This channel being about ten feet deep, and extending throughout the entire length of the plain, I had only to study the wind, and could walk up within easy shot of any herd, and select what buck I pleased.

Here I remained for several days enjoying brilliant sport, and daily securing fine specimens of oryx, springboks, and other game. Here, also, I shot my first ostrich, a fine old cock. It was a very long shot; I gave my rifle several feet of elevation, yet nevertheless the ball struck him on the leg, breaking it below the knee, when he fell and was unable to rise. The power possessed by an ostrich in his leg can hardly be imagined. The thigh is very muscular, and resembles that of a horse more than of a bird. In the act of dying, he lashed out and caught me a severe blow on my leg, which laid me prostrate.

CHAPTER VII.

Leave Beer Vley—A Bushboy captured and enlisted as a Follower—Famous Sport with Wildebeest and Quaggas from a Hunting-hole—Water fails, and we march to the Great Orange River—Beautiful Appearance of the River—Stink Vonteyn, a famous sporting quarter—An Ostrich's Nest—Bold Mountain Ranges—The Griqua Tribe, their Manners and Customs—An ancient Mimosa Forest—Residence of a Bushman—Successful Chase of a noble Bull Oryx.

ON the 9th I considered I had sufficiently long enjoyed the sweets of Beer Vley; and accordingly, the waggons being properly packed, I inspanned in the afternoon, and trekked to the south. On the following morning we inspanned at the dawn of day, and retraced our steps to the Rhinoceros Pool. The heat continued most oppressive, the wind still northerly. We were infested with myriads of common flies, which proved a constant annoyance, filling tent and waggons to such a degree that it was impossible to sit in them. I rode out in the morning of the 11th, accompanied by an after-rider, and shot two springboks, which we bore to camp secured on our horses behind our saddles by passing the buckles of the girths on each side through the fore and hind legs of the antelopes, having first performed an incision between the bone and the sinews with the *couteau-de-chasse*, according to colonial usage.

The Boers had informed me of a small fountain one march in advance, where they recommended me to hunt for a short time, and this place I intended to be my next encampment. On the morrow we inspanned at earliest dawn, and trekked about ten miles in a north-easterly course across a barren extensive plain, steering parallel with the country frequented by the oryx. We drew up our waggons at a place where some Boers had been encamped during the winter months. Here we found a well with nothing but mud in it. I set to work with the spade and cleaned it out, and presently had good water for myself and people. I despatched one of my Hottentots on horseback to seek for water in advance for the horses and oxen. He shortly returned, and reported another deserted Boer encampment about a mile ahead, at which there was a stronger fountain, but considerably choked with mud.

Having breakfasted, I removed my waggons thither, and encamped. This fountain will be ever memorable in the annals of my African campaign, since on the following day I was there joined by a unique and interesting specimen of a Bushman, who has ever since faithfully followed my fortunes through every peril and hardship by sea and land; and is at the moment that I write brandishing in the Highlands of Scotland an imitation of a Cape waggon-whip which he has constructed, and calling out with stentorian lungs the names of the oxen composing the team which he, at a subsequent period, drove when he alone stood by me, all my followers having forsaken me in the far interior.

In the afternoon I saddled up, and started with my two after-riders and a spare horse, with the intention of sleeping in the oryx country, and hunting next day. We rode north through sandy plains and hollows on which large herds of gnoos and springboks were grazing. Just as the sun descended we started a fine old bull oryx. We discovered him in a bushy hollow; after a sharp burst Cobus managed to turn him, when, by heading him, I got within range, and finished him with a couple of shots. It was now dark; having off-saddled our horses, we knee-haltered them, and allowed them to graze for an hour; after which, having secured them to a neighbouring bush, we lay down to sleep on the hard ground. My pillow was the neck of the old bull; the jackal sang his coronach.

On the 13th I shot a fine old steinbok, and on nearing my encampment I discovered two different vleys, containing water. Upon reaching my camp I found a funny little fellow in the shape of the Bushboy before alluded to, awaiting my arrival. My Hottentots had detected his black woolly head protruding from the reeds adjoining the fountain, and had captured him. I presented him with a suit of new clothes and a glass of spirits, and we immediately became and have ever since continued the best of friends. He informed me that, when a child, he was taken by a party of Dutch Boers at a massacre of his countrymen, and from these he had subsequently absconded on account of their cruel treatment of him. The Boers had named him "Ruyter," probably after a certain Dutch admiral, which name he still bears.

In the afternoon I rode to one of the vleys, accompanied by two of my men, bearing pickaxes and spades and my bedding. We dug a shooting hole on the usual principle, about three feet deep and eight in diameter, on the lee side of the largest vley. In this hole I used to take my station every night—the jackals and hyænas growling around me— and await the coming of the dawn to get a sight of the game that came to drink. In this manner I enjoyed excellent sport among the wildebeests and quaggas until the 17th, when, through want of water for my oxen, I was compelled to march for the great Orange River, which was the nearest water, being distant upwards of thirty miles. We inspanned in the afternoon, and, having performed a march of twelve miles, holding a north-easterly course, I outspanned for a couple of hours to allow my oxen to graze; after which I again inspanned, and trekked about twelve miles farther by moonlight, when we halted till the day dawned, making fast the horses and oxen. The country here assumed a less sterile appearance than that which I had occupied during the last five weeks, being ornamented with a few ancient trees, bearing a leaf resembling that of the willow, and called by the Dutch "olean-wood;" there were also a few dwarfish thorny trees of a species of mimosa.

On the 18th we inspanned at the dawn of day, and after a march of about four hours through a wild and uninhabited country we suddenly found ourselves on the bank of the magnificent Orange River. This queen of African rivers forms a leading feature in the geography of Southern Africa. Its length, I believe, is somewhere about a thousand miles. It rises in the east, in the Vitbergen mountain-range, a little to the northward of the latitude of Port Natal, and, flowing westward, it is joined by the fair Vaal river about fifty miles below the spot where I had now arrived; thence it continues its course westward, and falls into the South Atlantic about five hundred miles to the north of the Cape of Good Hope. We made the river at a place called Davinar's Drift or ford, beside which was a comfortable Dutch farm. The owner was a young

Boer from the Cape district, and had obtained his present enviable position by marrying a fat old widow. Their chief riches consisted of sheep and goats, of which they possessed enormous flocks, which were in very fine condition, the country being suitable for pasturing these animals. Large herds of trekking springboks were feeding in sight of the homestead. I had passed several herds on my morning's march, and had shot three, which were in good order.

The Boers, contrary to my expectation, reported the river fordable, though I had been informed that it was very large. Before venturing to cross we were occupied for upwards of an hour in raising the goods liable to be damaged by water, by means of a platform consisting of green willow boughs, with which we filled the bottom of the waggons, and then replaced the cargo. The descent on our side was extremely steep, and we found it necessary to rheim, viz., to secure, by means of the drag-chains, both hind wheels of each waggon. The drift was extremely rough, and jolted the waggons about sadly. We, however, got safely through, and, having proceeded about half a mile up the opposite bank, we encamped.

No person who has not contemplated a magnificent river under similar circumstances can form an idea of the pleasure I felt in reaching this oasis of the desert. For many weeks past our lot had been cast in the arid plains of the parched karroo, where there had often been barely sufficient water for our cattle to drink, with cloudless skies and an intense burning sun over our heads, and no tree nor bush of any description whose friendly shade might shelter us from the power of its rays. Here, "o' the sudden," a majestic river rolled before our delighted eyes, whose fertile banks were adorned with groves clad in everlasting verdure. At the spot where we crossed, the river reminded me of the appearance exhibited by certain parts of the river Spey in summer during a spate. The breadth of the Orange River, however, is in general about three hundred yards. The whole of the banks are ornamented with a rich fringe of weeping willows, whose branches dip into the stream, and also of many other trees and bushes whose blossoms and pleasing foliage yielded the most delicious balmy perfume.

Numerous flocks of the feathered tribe by their beautiful plumage and melodious notes increased the charm of this lovely scene. The entomologist could likewise have found abundance of interesting objects in his department, the ground and trees swarming with curious, if not gaudy, insects. My first move after halting was to enjoy a delightful bath; after which, having donned my best apparel, I recrossed the river on horseback to visit the happy couple whose farm I have previously described.

I found them civil and communicative, and obtained from them a supply of vegetables, which to me were most acceptable, having tasted nothing of that sort for many weeks. They informed me that about fifteen miles in a northerly direction there was a saltpan, in the vicinity of which I might find koodoos and sassaybys, in addition to the varieties of game which I had already hunted. I walked through their garden, which, besides vegetables in great variety, contained several kinds of fruit-trees, such as peaches, apricots, etc.; these throve well, their branches being laden with abundance of fruit. On the forenoon of the 19th, having twice enjoyed the luxury of bathing, I saddled up, and rode north to an extensive range of rocky hills to seek for koodoos. Crossing an extensive plain which intervened, I came upon an ostrich's nest, containing two eggs; the cock was sitting on the nest, and, imagining that we would pass without observing him, he allowed us to ride within sixty yards before he started. I found the hills for which I rode of so stony and rocky a character that it was impossible to ride through them. They, however, bore a goodly coating of rank grass of various kinds, and the hollows contained a few dwarfish bushes. Leaving my steed in charge of my after-rider, I traversed, with my rifle, several of these rocky ranges, but failed to find any traces of koodoos. It was the sort of country exactly suited for the raebok, to which I have already alluded, and of these antelopes I discovered three small herds.

On ascending to the summit of the highest hill in my vicinity, I commanded a grand panoramic view of the surrounding scenery. An endless succession of bold mountains, of considerable height, extended as far as I could see in a northerly and easterly direction. Some of them were tabular, but others of conical and pyramidal shapes towered above their fellows; their abrupt forms standing forth in grand relief above the surrounding country. Throughout all these mountain-ranges plains of considerable extent, more or less undulating, intervened.

At one P.M. on the following day I inspanned and trekked north to the saltpan, which we reached in the dark. The general character of the country became richer after crossing the Orange River. The plains were adorned with a more luxuriant coating of grass and in greater profusion; and the small karroo bushes were replaced by others of fairer growth, and of a different variety. Most of these yielded a strong aromatic perfume, but more particularly when the ground had been refreshed by a shower of rain; on which occasions the African wilderness diffuses a perfume so exquisite and balmy, that no person that has not experienced its delights can form an idea of it. Our march lay through an extensive undulating country. We passed several troops of hartebeests and springboks, and saw for the first time one sassayby, a large antelope allied to the hartebeest, and of a purple colour. Mountain ranges bound the view on every side, and I could discover by means of my spyglass that strips of forests of mimosa stretched along their bases. The saltpan to which we had come was of an oval shape, and about a quarter of a mile in diameter.

It was a low basin, whose sides sloped gently down, but the middle was a dead level of fine sand. Upon this sand, throughout the greater part of the pan, lay a thick layer of good coarse salt, varying from one to four inches in depth. Heavy rains fill the pan or basin with water, and, the dry season succeeding, the water disappears, and large deposits of salt are found. These pans or salt-licks are met with in several parts of South Africa. Those which mainly supply the colony with good salt are situated between Utenage and Algoa Bay; they are of considerable extent, and yield a surprising quantity. Ostriches and almost every variety of antelope frequent these pans for the purpose of licking the brack or salt ground, to which they are very partial. The pan which we had reached was formerly visited by Boers and Griquas for the purpose of obtaining salt, but had of late years been abandoned for others yielding it of a better quality. The country around was consequently undisturbed; and, being utterly uninhabited, was lonely and as still as the grave.

On the morning of the 21st I left my waggons encamped beside the salt-pan, and, having proceeded about half-a-mile in a northerly direction along a seldom trodden waggon-track, I discovered a fountain of excellent water, but very strongly impregnated with saltpetre. This fountain I afterwards learnt is termed by the Boers "Cruit Vonteyn," or Powder Fountain, its waters resembling the washings of a gun-barrel; but the Griquas more elegantly call it "Stink Vonteyn." At breakfast-time I was joined by a party of ruffianly Griquas, who were proceeding with a dilapidated-looking waggon, which had no sail, to hunt hartebeests and blue wildebeests, in the vicinity of a small fountain to the north-east where game was reported abundant.

They were accompanied by several wild-looking, naked Bushmen attendants, whom they had captured when young, and domesticated. These drove their shooting-horses loose behind the waggon, grazing as they went along. I also observed a couple of milch-cows with calves among their loose oxen, a healthy luxury without which that race of people seldom proceed on a journey. The country occupied by the Griquas extends from Rhama, a village on the Orange River, about thirty miles to the east of my present position, to Griquastadt their capital, a village situated about a hundred miles to the northward of the junction of the Vaal with the Orange River. They are governed by a chief, whose name is Waterboer. These men are of Hottentot origin, and in general possess the distinguishing features of that race, such as broad, flat noses, high cheek bones, small, elephant eyes, thick lips, woolly hair, and other Hottentot peculiarities, which, in the present enlightened state of society, it were superfluous to enumerate.

They are, however, so mixed up with crosses of other tribes that every ramification of breed between Boers, Bechuanas, Mozambiques, Corannas, Namaqua Hottentots, Bushmen, etc., may be found located within their territory. All of these intermarry. Some of them have long black hair, while the craniums of others, such as the Bushmen, are adorned with detached tufts of sickly-looking crisp wool, and the issue of such unions exhibit locks singularly varied.

Another tribe of men in every way similar to these Griquas inhabit an extensive and fertile country immediately to the east of their territory. These men term themselves Bastards. Their chief's name is Adam Kok. The name of their capital is Philipolis, a small village about thirty miles to the north of Colesberg. Their country is bounded on the south by the Great Orange River, and is about the most desirable district in Southern Africa for farming purposes, there being abundance of fountains throughout its whole extent capable of being led out to irrigate the land, without which no gardens can be formed, nor wheat grown in that country. Rich pasture is abundant. Cattle and sheep thrive and breed remarkably well; goats, also, an animal valuable to the South African settler, but for which only certain districts are suitable, are here very prolific.

The goat in many districts is subject to a disease called by the Boers "brunt sickta," or burnt sickness, owing to the animals afflicted with it exhibiting the appearance of having been burnt. It is incurable; and if the animals infected are not speedily killed, or put out of the way, the contagion rapidly spreads, and it is not uncommon for a farmer to lose his entire flock with it. This sad distemper also extends itself to the *feræ naturæ*. I have shot hartebeests, black wildebeests, blesbucks, and springbucks with their bodies covered with this disease. I have known seasons when the three latter animals were so generally affected by it, that the vast plains throughout which they are found were covered with hundreds of skulls and skeletons of those that had died therefrom.

One of the chief recommendations of the Bastard's country is its admirable suitableness for breeding horses. Large herds of these may be seen throughout their country pasturing high on the mountain sides, or scattered in troops over its grassy plains. The deadly distemper so prevalent along the frontiers of the colony is here of comparatively rare occurrence. In the far interior, however, it is so virulent during five or six months of the year, that it is often impossible to save a single horse, and through its ravages I was annually in the habit of losing the greater part of my stud.

The chiefs of the Griquas and Bastards are in close alliance with the English government, which protects them from the attacks of the rebel Dutch Boers. These, well aware of the excellent qualities of the Bastard's country, are possessed with a strong desire to appropriate it. The language spoken by both these tribes is Dutch. They have in general embraced the Christian religion, and several worthy missionaries have, for several years past, devoted their lives to the improvement of their temporal and eternal condition. The dress worn by the men consists of home-made leathern jacket, waiscoat, and trousers, feldtschoens, or home-made shoes, a Malay handkerchief tied round the head, and on Sundays and other great occasions a shirt and a neckcloth. The females wear a close-fitting corset reaching to the small of the waist, below which they sport a petticoat like the women of other countries. These petticoats are sometimes made of stuffs of British manufacture, and at other times of soft leather prepared by themselves. Their head-dress consists of two handkerchiefs, one of black silk, the other of a striped red and green colour, usually termed Malay handkerchiefs. They are very fond of beads of every size and colour, which they hang in large necklaces round their necks. They have one description of bead peculiar to themselves and to the tribes extending along the banks of the Great Orange River to its junction with the sea. This bead is formed of the root of a bush found near the mouth of the Orange River, and possesses a sweet and peculiar perfume. Every Griqua girl wears at least one of these; and no traveller who has once learnt to prize this perfume can inhale it again without its inadvertently recalling to his memory the fine dark eyes and fair forms of the semi-civilized nymphs frequenting the northern bank of the Orange stream.

Their houses somewhat resemble a bee-hive or ant-hill, consisting of boughs of trees stuck into the ground in a circular form, and lashed down across one another overhead so as to form a framework, on which they spread large mats formed of reeds. These mats are also used instead of waggon-sails, and are very effectual in resisting both sun and rain. The diameter of these dome-shaped huts varies from ten to fifteen feet. On changing their quarters, which they are occasionally compelled to do on account of pasture, it will easily be understood that they have little difficulty in removing their house along with them.

A strong pack-ox can travel with the whole concern placed on his back; and on occasions of their migration I have seen a pack-ox carrying not only its master's house on its back, but also a complete set of dairy utensils, all manufactured of wood, a couple of skin bags containing thick milk, various cooking utensils, and, surmounting all, the guidwife, with one or two of her children. They are all possessed of flocks and herds of goats, sheep, and cattle. A description of the houses and manner of living of these people may serve to convey an idea of all the tribes that border on the Vaal and Orange Rivers to the sea. They are, without exception, of an indolent disposition, and averse from hard work of any description. Much of their time is spent in hunting, and large parties annually leave their homes and proceed with their waggons, oxen, and horses on hunting expeditions into the far interior, absenting themselves for a period of from three to four months.

They are a people remarkable for their disregard for truth, a weakness which I regret to state I found very prevalent in Southern Africa. They are also great beggars, generally commencing by soliciting for "trexels," a trexel being a pound of tea or coffee. Knowing the gallantry of our nation, they affirm this to be a present for a wife or daughter, whom they represent as being poorly. If this is granted they continue their importunities, successively fancying your hat, neckcloth, or coat; and I have known them on several occasions coolly request me to exchange my continuations for their leathern inexpressibles, which they had probably worn for a couple of summers.

When this party of Griquas came up to me, being anxious to see as much as possible of the natives of those parts which I traversed, I invited them to halt and drink coffee with me, an invitation which a Griqua was never yet known to decline. They informed me that, in the mountain ranges to the north-east, koodoo were to be met with, and they invited me to accompany them on their *chasse.* When breakfast was finished they sent their waggon in advance, with instructions to wait for their arrival at the fountain, where they intended to pitch their camp; and, having saddled up, we all set forward and rode east to hunt koodoos and hartebeests, or any other game we might fall in with. After riding three or four miles, on approaching the base of the hills we entered an ancient forest of mimosas, every tree being a study for an artist. There was also a considerable undercover of various sweet-smelling shrubs and bushes.

Here steinbok and duyker were abundant. This venerable forest extended all around the bases of various ranges of rocky hills which stretched in different directions through these plains. Close in, at the foot of one of the hills, we discovered a Bushman residence, consisting of three small huts, each about four feet high, and about eight in diameter. They were formed of boughs of trees, thatched over with rank grass drawn up by the roots. The natives, as usual, had fled on our approach, and no living creature was to be seen. I entered each of the huts, and found lots of well "braid" (or dressed) skins of all the wild beasts of these parts. All their dishes were made either of ostrich-eggs or of the shells of land tortoises, and these were ranged round the floor on one side of the hut. Most of the ostrich-eggshells contained water.

We crossed the hills by a stony neck; and having proceeded some distance through several well-wooded glades and hollows in the table-land of the hills, we suddenly looked forth upon a noble prospect. A wide grassy plain, covered with picturesque mimosas and detached clumps of evergreen bushes, stretched away from the bases of the hills on which we stood. Beyond, the landscape was shut in by the bold and abrupt forms of rugged mountain ranges, which were coloured with a softened blue tint. Having descended into this fine picturesque plain, we held north, riding parallel with the hilly chain. Presently, my comrades adopting a course which did not strike me as the most likely to fall in with game, I chose a line of march for myself, and, following along under the mountain chain, I soon lost sight of them, and saw them no more that day. On this occasion I had taken the field without any after-rider.

Having ridden about a mile farther, I started a doe koodoo, the first I had seen, and shortly after I started another, with a young one, which I determined to secure, there being no flesh in our camp. Having pursued it a short distance, I came suddenly upon a troop of koodoos, consisting of three bucks and several does. Two of the bucks were old fellows, and carried magnificent, wide-set, long, spiral horns. To these I instantly directed my attention, when they at once made, as koodoos invariably do, for the adjacent rocky hills. Their pace was a succession of long bounds over the thorny bushes, which sadly distressed my poor steed. I nevertheless gained on them, and would have assuredly secured one, had they not reached a stony barrier of sharp, hard rocks, over which they disappeared, and where my horse could not follow. I was much struck with the noble appearance of these two buck koodoos, and felt very chagrined in having been unfortunate with them. Having lost the koodoos, I turned my face to the south, and rode along the skirts of the forest, in hope of falling in with my comrades.

I had ridden about a mile, when I suddenly perceived a gallant herd of nine old oryxes cantering towards me, all of them carrying horns of immense length and beauty, surpassing anything I had hitherto seen. They were preceded by four beautifully striped zebras, the first I had met with, and followed by two brilliant red hartebeests. In half a minute I was flying along within sixty yards of the troop of oryxes, carefully studying the horns of each, and at a loss to decide which was the finest, they were all so very handsome. As I swept along I deplored my folly in having taken the field without my after-riders; I nevertheless entertained hopes of success, as these antelopes had evidently been followed by the Griquas from whom I parted. They led me a long and severe chase along the skirts of the hills, the wind fortunately blowing right across them.

After riding hard for several miles I felt my horse very much distressed, and was on the point of giving up the pursuit, when I observed one old bull make a momentary halt under a mimosa, evidently very much blown. This gave me fresh hope; I resolved to follow him as long as my horse could go, and once more I gave chase with renewed speed. I was soon riding opposite to him, within sixty yards, with the hill on the other side, and by a desperate effort I managed to cut him off from his comrades, and turn his head down the wind. His fate was now sealed, and I at once felt that he was mine. From this moment his pace decreased, and, after another half mile of sharp galloping down hill, in which I gained upon him at every stride, I was riding within fifteen yards of his handsome, round stern. His tongue was now hanging from his mouth, and long streaks of foam streamed back on his sides. Suddenly, on rounding a thorny bush, he pulled up in his career, and, facing about, stood at bay. I sprang breathless and worn out from my panting steed, and with a shaking hand sent a bullet through his shoulder, when he fell and breathed his last.

This noble oryx carried the finest horns I had met with, and I had, moreover, the satisfaction of knowing that he was the finest in the herd. Having off-saddled and knee-haltered my horse, I commenced cutting off the head of the oryx, which I accomplished with some trouble, the skin at the neck being an inch in thickness. I then broke thorny branches from a neighbouring mimosa, which I heaped over the carcase, to protect it from the vultures. This being accomplished, I returned to camp, carrying the head on the pommel of the saddle before me, and my rifle over my shoulder. On occasions like this I have often felt that I should have been the better for a third hand for the management of my steed. At an early hour on the following morning I left my waggons, accompanied by two after-riders, to look for koodoos, and secure the skin of the oryx of the preceding day. Contrary to my expectations, the hyænas had not discovered him. The flesh, however, owing to the heat of the weather was unserviceable. I rode with my boys deployed into line along the likely part of the old mimosa forest, hoping to fall in with koodoos. Here I shot two fine old steinboks, with very good horns, and these I carefully preserved for my collection. By firing I lost a chance of koodoos, as I presently discovered fresh spoor of a troop of these antelopes, which my shots had disturbed.

Returning towards my waggons, I rode through a gorge in the mountains where I had started a pack of about thirty wild dogs in the morning. Observing a number of vultures sitting on the rocks about the place from which the dogs had started, I at once knew that they had killed some animal; and on riding up I discovered the skeleton of an old doe koodoo, which they had run into and consumed. They had not cracked the marrow-bones, which the hyænas would have done if left there till after sunset. These, therefore, my Hottentots hastily took possession of, the marrow of the thigh-bones of the koodoo being by them esteemed a great delicacy. Springing from their horses, they triumphantly seized the skeleton; and, each selecting for himself a couple of stones, they sat down on the ground, cracked the marrow-bones, and greedily devoured their raw contents.

On reaching the waggons we found an extremely ancient and shrivelled-looking Bushman, who chattered just like a monkey. He signed to me that I had visited his hut on the preceding day, but that he feared the Griquas who accompanied me. He also intimated that he feared the Boers; but he knew from the appearance of my waggons that they belonged to an Englishman. He also signified to me that, when the moon should rise, blue wildebeests would come and drink at "Stink Vonteyn." This fact I had already ascertained from personal observation, having seen their spoor by the water. In the evening, having taken several cups of strong coffee to keep me awake, I walked to the fountain with four of my followers, bearing spades and pickaxe, and my bedding to watch for wild animals. Having constructed a shoot-hole, my men retired, and I took up my position for the night, which was mild and lovely, with good moonlight. After watching several hours I fell asleep.

About midnight my light sleep was disturbed by the tramp of approaching wild animals. I peeped from my hole, and saw a herd of about twenty shaggy blue wildebeests, or brindled gnoos, cautiously advancing to the water. They were preceded by a patriarchial old bull, the finest in the herd. I fired at him, and heard the ball tell upon his shoulder, upon which he and the whole troop galloped off in a northerly direction, enveloped in a cloud of red dust. Being thirsty, I then walked up to the eye of the fountain, and having imbibed a draught of its sulphurous waters, in a very few minutes I was once more asleep.

On the 23rd I stood up in my hole at dawn of day, and, having donned my old grey kilt and Badenoch brogues, I took up the spoor of the herd of brindled gnoos. After I had proceeded a short distance I perceived the head of the old bull looking at me over a small rise on the bushy plain. The head disappeared, and I heard a loud noise of tramping, as of an animal endeavouring to gallop upon three legs. On gaining this rise I again saw the handsome head, with its strangely-hooked, fair-set horns, gazing at me from the long grass some hundred yards in advance. He had lain down. I held as though I intended to go past him; but before I neared him he sprang to his feet, and endeavoured to make off from me. Poor old bull! I at once perceived that it was all over with him. He was very faint from loss of blood, and one fore leg was broken in the shoulder. He made a tottering run of about a hundred yards, and again lay down, never more to rise. I walked up to within eighty yards of him, and sent a bullet through his heart. Receiving the ball, he rolled over on his side, and expired without a groan.

I then made for my waggons, and despatched men with a span or team of oxen to slip the wildebeest to camp. He afforded us a welcome supply of excellent flesh, as he was in fine condition. I breakfasted on an ostrich-egg, Kleinboy having found a nest the preceding day. He had unfortunately taken only eight of the eggs out of the nest, foolishly leaving the other twelve, which on his return, he found smashed by the old birds, according to their usual custom.

CHAPTER VIII.

We leave Stink Vonteyn and reach the Vaal River—Wait-a-bit Thorns—Chase and kill a Buck Koodoo, and bivouac on the ground—Cobus and Jacob abscond—Roan Antelope—We recross the Vaal River—Griqua Encampment—Stink Vonteyn again—A Flight of Locusts—A Saltpan—Salubrious Climate—Boers attempt to carry off Ruyter—A Cameeldorn Forest—A Brindled Gnoo bayed by Wild Dogs—Habits of the latter.

On the evening of the 24th we inspanned, and, leaving "Stink Vonteyn," marched upon the Vaal River, distant about twenty-five miles. Our road lay through soft sand, rendering the work very severe for the oxen. About two A.M. on the following morning we reached the fair Vaal River by fine moonlight. Having sent mounted men through the stream to ascertain its depth, and finding a passage practicable, I resolved at once to cross it—a rule generally adopted by all experienced in the country, among whom a general maxim prevails never to defer the passage of a river if at all fordable when they reach it. Endless are the stories related by South African travellers, who, by failing to adopt this plan have been compelled to remain for weeks, and even months, on the banks of its various rivers. The current here being very powerful, I mounted the leaders of my teams, and in a few minutes my long double line of oxen was stoutly stemming the rapid stream, which reached half way up their sides. We got both the waggons across in safety. The water had just reached the bottom of my cargoes, but did not damage anything.

The bank on the farther side was extremely steep and stony, and required every ox to exert himself to the utmost. The river here is very beautiful; broad and rapid streams are succeeded by long, deep, and tranquil pools, termed by the natives "zekoe ychots," signifying sea-cow or hippopotamus holes; these vast and wondrous amphibious animals having, not many years since, been plentiful along the entire length of the Vaal River. The hippopotamus, however, like the elephant, is of a very shy and secluded disposition, and rapidly disappears before the approach of civilization. I drew up my waggons on a commanding open position on the northern bank of the stream. The margin of the Vaal, like the Orange River, is richly clad with dense groves of various evergreen trees, among which drooping willows predominate, whose long waving fringes dip gracefully into the limpid waters as they glide along in their seaward course. All along the banks of both these rivers huge trunks of trees are strewn, having been borne thither by the mighty floods to which they are annually subject. A short distance above my position was a beautiful island, adorned with trees of the richest verdure.

About three P.M. I rode north-east to look for roan antelopes, which, next to the eland, are the largest in the world; and being incapable of great speed, may at times be ridden into with a good horse. I was accompanied by Cobus and Jacob. We found the country covered with bushes, of which the majority were of a most impracticable description, reminding me of a kill-devil, an implement used in angling, they being covered with thorns on the fish-hook principle. This variety of mimosa is waggishly termed by the Boers "vyacht um bige," or wait-a-bit thorns, as they continually solicit the passing traveller not to be in a hurry; if he disregards which request, the probability is that he leaves a part of his shirt or trousers in their possession. Here and there were hills covered with sharp adamantine rocks, throughout which, however, there was abundance of excellent grass and fine green bushes. In short, it was just the country to suit the taste of the rock-loving koodoos. Having proceeded some miles, we discovered fresh spoor of a troop of them at the foot of one of the ranges of rocky hills. We then crossed the ridge, still finding spoor, and the country becoming more and more likely.

Suddenly, on raising our eyes, we saw standing on the hill side, within three hundred yards of us, five buck koodoos, four of which were tearing old fellows carrying extremely fine horns; and majestic as they were, the elevated position which they occupied imparted to them a still more striking appearance. We galloped towards them, on which they bounded higher up the rocky hill, and stood for a few seconds looking at us.

I had seen many sights thrilling to a sportsman, but few to surpass what I then beheld. I think an old buck koodoo, when seen standing broadside on, is decidedly one of the grandest-looking antelopes in the world. They now broke into two lots, the two finest bucks holding to the left, and to these we gave chase. They led us over the most terrific ground for horses that can be imagined. It consisted of a mass of large sharp adamantine pieces of rock; even the rock-frequenting koodoos themselves made bad weather of it. Cobus, on this occasion, rode in a manner which astonished me. He was mounted on "The Cow," which steed, having in its youth led an unrestrained life, as most Cape horses do, in the rugged mountains of the Hantam, bounded along the hill side in a style worthy of a klipspringer. A flat of considerable extent, covered with tall bushes, intervened between us and a long range of high table-land to the northward, along the base of which, for an extent of many miles, stretched a dense forest of wait-a-bit thorns and mimosas.

This forest was the head-quarters of the koodoos, and for it they now held, breaking away across the above-mentioned flat. That forest, however, the finest koodoo was destined never to reach. As soon as we got clear of the rocky ground our horses gained upon them at every stride; and Cobus, who was invariably far before me in every chase, was soon alongside of the finest. Here, in the dense bushes, we lost sight of his comrade. Cobus very soon prevailed on the koodoo to alter his tack, and strike off at a tangent from his former course; when, by taking a short cut like a greyhound running cunning, I got within range, and with a single ball I rolled him over in the dust. I felt more pleasure in obtaining this fine specimen of a buck koodoo than anything I had yet shot in Africa. He was a first-rate old buck, and carried a pair of ponderous, long, wide-set spiral horns.

Owing to the nature of the ground which they frequent, it is a very difficult matter to ride them down, and they are more usually obtained by stalking or stealing stealthily upon them. When, however, the hunter discovers a heavy old buck koodoo on level ground, there is no great difficulty to ride into him, his speed and endurance being very inferior to that of the oryx. I could have stood contemplating him for hours, but darkness was fast setting in; so, having off-saddled and knee-haltered our horses, we carefully removed the head and commenced skinning him. The skin of the koodoo, though thin, is extremely tough, and is much prized by the colonists for "foreslocks," or lashes for ox-waggon whips. The koodoo-skin was my mattress, my saddle was my pillow; and supperless I lay down to rest, without any covering save an old shirt and a pair of leather crackers. The excitement of the thrilling sport which I had enjoyed prevented my sleeping until a late hour; and when at length I closed my eyes, I dreamt that we were surrounded by a troop of lions, and, awaking with a loud cry, startled my men and horses.

On the 26th we arose at earliest dawn, and having packed the trophies of the koodoo, and a part of his flesh, upon my spare horse, I despatched Jacob with him to camp, while Cobus and I held north-east to seek for roan antelope. I sought that day and the two following for these antelopes, but saw no traces of them.

On the morning of the 30th I inspanned, and trekked some miles farther up the northern bank of the Vaal, and encamped opposite where the Riet or Reed River joins it. The stream here is extremely beautiful, being about a hundred and fifty yards in breadth, with sloping banks richly adorned with shady evergreen groves, and fringed with lofty reeds—a never-failing prognosticator of a sleepless night, a virulent species of mosquito being always abundant where reeds are met with. Several large bustards were stalking on a small bushy flat, as we drew up the waggons. I went after these, and made a fine off-hand shot at an old cock at a hundred and fifty yards. Here I lost Cobus and Jacob, my two Hottentot after-riders. Returning from the bustards to my waggons, where I expected to find my breakfast waiting me, I discovered these two worthies, whose duty it was to be preparing it, quietly reclining under the shade of a mimosa, and enjoying the soothing influence of their short clay pipes.

Being now beyond the pale of magisterial law, I deemed that a little wholesome correction might prove beneficial, which I accordingly administered. This so disgusted these high-minded youths, that after breakfast they embraced the opportunity of my bathing to abscond from my service. I imagined that they had sneaked into the bushes, and would soon return. I, however, saw no more of them until several months after, when I met them at Colesberg, which place they had reached, assisted by the Bastards, through whose country they had passed. Cobus, though a first-rate after-rider, was a great scamp and mischief-maker; and I learned from my remaining people that it was by his persuasion Jacob had left me.

In the forenoon, the sun being extremely powerful, I built for myself a bower under an old willow beside the river. In this bower I made my bed, and might have had a sound sleep by way of a change, had not the mosquitos and midges assaulted me throughout the whole night, so that I hardly closed my eyes. The 31st was a charming cool day, the sky beautifully overcast. Having enjoyed a good swim in the waters of the

Vaal, I breakfasted, after which I saddled up, and rode north to seek for roan antelope. I was accompanied by Carollus, the native of Mozambique, who was much too heavy to act as after-rider, and by the little Bushboy named Ruyter, who had joined me on the plains of the karoo. This Bushboy, although he had learnt to ride among the Boers, had an indifferent seat on horseback, and would never push his horse to overtake any antelope if the ground were at all rough.

Having explored the country to a considerable distance, in the course of which we fell in with four sassaybys and a troop of hartebeests, I resolved to make for home, as the darkening sky and distant thunder to the southward threatened a heavy storm. I had not long, however, determined on returning, when the wind, which had been out of the north, suddenly veered round, and blew hard from the south. In less than half an hour the rain descended in torrents, the wind blew extremely cold, and the rain beat right in my face; the peals of thunder were most appalling, the most fearful I think I had ever heard, the forked lightning dancing above and around me with such vividness as to pain my eyes: I thought every moment would be my last. I shifted my saddle from "Sunday" to "The Cow," and we pricked along at a smart pace.

We were entering a thicket of thorny bushes, when a very large grey-looking antelope stood up under one of them. I could not see his head, but I at once knew that it was the long-sought-for roan antelope, or bastard gemsbok. Carollus quickly handed me my little Moore rifle, secure from the pelting storm in one of Mr. Hugh Snowie's patent waterproof covers. The noble buck now bounded forth, a superb old male, carrying a pair of grand scymitar-shaped horns. He stood nearly five feet high at the shoulder. "The Cow" knew well what he had to do, and set off after him with right good will over a most impracticable country. It was a succession of masses of adamantine rock and stone, and dense bushes with thorns on the boat-hook principle. In a few minutes my legs below the knee were a mass of blood, and my shirt, my only covering, was flying in streamers from my waist. The old buck at first got a little ahead, but presently, the ground improving, I gained upon him, and after a sharp burst of about two miles we commenced ascending a slight acclivity, when he suddenly faced about and stood at bay, eyeing me with glowing eyes and a look of defiance.

This was to me a joyful moment. The buck I had for many years heard of and longed to meet now stood at bay within forty yards of me. I dismounted, and, drawing my rifle from its holster, sent a bullet through his shoulder, upon which he cantered a short distance and lay down beside a bush. On my approach he endeavoured to charge, but his strength failed him. I then gave him a second shot in the neck, just where I always cut off the head. On receiving it he rolled over, and, stretching his limbs, closed his eyes upon the storm, which all this time raged with increasing severity.

I felt extremely cold. I had lost my shirt in the chase, and all that was left me was my shoes and leather knee-breeches. I nevertheless took some time to inspect the beautiful and rare antelope which I had been fortunate enough to capture. He proved to be a first-rate specimen: his horns were extremely rough and finely knotted. I now proceeded to cut off his head and "gralloched" him, all of which I accomplished before my followers came up. They stumbled on me by chance, having lost sight of me in the denseness of the storm. Having shifted my saddle from "The Cow" to "Colesberg," I ordered them to follow, and I rode hard for camp, which was distant many miles. At sunset the storm ceased, and my boys arrived with the head. The following day was the 1st of February. In the morning I despatched two men to bring home the skin of the roan antelope and a supply of the venison, which was in high condition. Strange to say, they found the buck all safe, having escaped the attacks both of hyænas and vultures.

My meal-bag was reported almost empty; and this being a dangerous country for the horse-sickness, a distemper which rages during February, March, and April, I resolved to recross the Vaal River and bend my course for the land of blesboks, a large and beautiful violet-coloured antelope, which is found, together with black wildebeests and springboks, in countless thousands on the vast green plains of short sour grass situated about a hundred and fifty miles to the eastward of my then position. My purpose was to amuse myself hunting in these parts until the beginning of April, when the most dangerous period of the horse-sickness would be past; and after that to revisit Colesberg, where I intended to store the specimens of natural history which I had already accumulated, and, having refitted and laid in a store of supplies, to start for the remote districts of the far interior in quest of elephant, rhinoceros, giraffe, buffalo, eland, and other varieties of large and interesting game to be found in those secluded regions.

Before removing from my present encampment I had another hard day among the sharp rocks and wait-a-bit thorns to the northward of the Vaal, when I fell in with a troop of about twelve young ostriches, which were not much larger than guinea-fowls. I was amused to see the mother endeavour to lead us away exactly like a wild duck, spreading out and drooping her wings, and throwing herself down on the ground before us as if wounded, while the cock bird cunningly led the brood away in an opposite direction.

On the afternoon of the 3rd of February we inspanned, and retraced our steps to the drift, which we reached in the dark: I however crossed the river and encamped on the opposite bank. On the following day I marched to a small kraal of Griquas, in hope of obtaining some corn. Our march was a heavy one, through a sandy country adorned in parts with very ancient-looking, picturesque trees of the "cameel-dorn" species. From the site of these kraals I obtained a distant view of both the Vaal and Orange River. I found these Griquas very importunate, flocking round my waggons and begging for tea, coffee, tobacco, gunpowder, etc. Some of these ruffians formed a plot to make me give up the Bushboy who had entered my service, but, on my threatening them with the vengeance of the Government if they interfered with any men in my service, they relinquished the idea. On the morrow it was ascertained that the oxen, having missed the fountain, had wandered very far in search of water: they were recovered more than half way back to the Vaal River. I purchased eight "emirs" or measures of wheat from one of the Griquas, and also a couple of goats for slaughter. In the afternoon we inspanned, and trekked to "Stink Vonteyn," already mentioned. On the march I shot a large hawk, a species of buzzard, with ball, and also a steinbok, at a hundred and sixty yards.

On the following morning the Namaqua partridges, which every morning and evening visit the vleys and fountains in large coveys for the purpose of drinking, mustered in great force at "Stink Vonteyn." Of these birds I have met with three varieties. They are abundant wherever extensive open sandy districts occur, as far as I have penetrated into Southern Africa. By watching the flight of these birds in the mornings and evenings I have discovered the fountains in the desert, when unassisted and forsaken by the natives. As they fly they repeatedly utter a soft melodious cry, resembling the words "pretty, pretty dear." They are excellent eating, and a person so disposed, by mounting a pair of shot-barrels, might, any morning or evening, secure a large bag of them.

In the forenoon I observed the base of an extensive range of hills to the northward concealed for miles, as if by thick clouds or mist, which steadily advanced towards us, holding a southerly course. This was a flight of countless myriads of locusts, in my opinion one of the most remarkable phenomena that a traveller can behold. They resembled very much a fall of snow, when it gently descends in large light flakes. The sound caused by their wings reminded me of the rustling of the summer breeze among the trees of the forest. In the afternoon I hunted in a mountain range to the westward of the saltpan named by the Boers and Bastards "Sautpan's berg;" and in the evening I visited the old Bushman's hut, whom I found at home with a litter of very small Bush-children: these he signified to me were his grand-children. I lay down to sleep beneath an aged mimosa in their vicinity, and about midnight the wind set in from off the Southern Ocean, and, having no covering but my shirt, I felt it piercingly cold. Sleep was out of the question, and I was right glad when I heard the sparrow's chirp announcing the dawn of day.

Notwithstanding these nocturnal exposures, my health since leaving my regiment had been perfect—not a twitch of rheumatism, a complaint from which I suffered while in India, although I had ceased to wear flannel, which I had previously done for years : I can therefore confidently recommend the country to those that suffer from that most grievous affliction. Colds, coughs, and sore throats are of rare occurrence ; and scientific persons, in whose opinions I can place the utmost reliance, have informed me that the frontier districts of the colony, and still more the remoter districts to the northward, are the finest in the world for persons labouring under any pulmonary complaint. At times I felt very lonely when I returned to camp for want of some old companion to welcome me and discuss with me in the evenings, over my gipsy fire, the adventures and incidents of the day: in general, however, when the sport was good I enjoyed excellent spirits.

On reaching my waggons I breakfasted, after which we inspanned and trekked east along a very rarely trodden old waggon-track, making for a small fountain situated on the borders of a large pan, which lay in a broad hollow in the centre of an extensive open tract of undulating country. Here the entire country was of a soft sandy character, and utterly uninhabited; the plains were covered with long rough heath and other low scrubby bushes, intermingled with much sweet grass. Ranges of hills of goodly height and considerable extent intersected the plains, and bounded the view at various distances on every side. Ancient forests of picturesque and venerable mimosas, interspersed with high grey-leaved bushes, detached and in groups, stretched along the bases of these mountain-ranges, their breadth extending about a mile into the surrounding extensive campaign country. We reached the small fountain in the dark, our road leading through the saltpan, where we halted for an hour, for the purpose of collecting salt, with which we had little difficulty in filling two large sacks.

On the march, as we crossed a vast plain, a flight of locusts passed over our heads during upwards of half an hour, flying so thick as to darken the sun; they reached in dense clouds as far as we could see, and maintained an elevation of from six to three or four hundred feet above the level of the plain. Woe to the vegetation of the country on which they alight! In the afternoon two mounted Boers were observed leading a spare horse, and following on our track. While they were yet afar off, Ruyter, the little Bushboy, recognised them as old acquaintances, and pronounced one of them to be the brother of the master from whom he had absconded. I at once guessed the object of their visit, and was right in my conjecture. By some clue they had ascertained that the boy was in my possession, and were now following me in the hope of recovering him.

Accordingly, when they rode up and requested me to halt the waggons for a conference, I received them very gruffly, and replied, that, the water being distant, I had no time for conferences until I should arrive there. Having repeated their request, and finding that I paid them no regard, they took up a position in the rear, and followed my waggons to the halting-place. Here they began to pester me with a long yarn concerning their claims to the Bushboy, when I stopped their pratings by ordering them to drop the subject, promising them a hearing in the morning; and having directed my people to place refreshments before the Boers, I wished them good night, and retired.

On the following morning they renewed their importunities, stating many things which I knew to be false; upon which I informed them that the nation to which I belonged was averse to slavery, and that I could not think of acceding to their demand. They then saddled up, and departed as wise as they had come, telling me that the matter should not rest there. The little Bushman seemed highly amused with the whole proceeding; and as the Boers mounted their steeds and rode away, leading the spare horse, he shrieked with delight, exclaiming in Low Dutch—

"Yah, yilla forfluxta Boera, yilla had de chadachta me te chra, mar ik heb noo a ghroote baas, dat sall yilla neuk;" signifying "Yes, you worthless Boers, you thought to get hold of me; but I have now a great master, who will serve you out." The Boers having departed, and my oxen and horses having effaced all original traces around the fountain, I described a circle a little distance from it to ascertain if it was much frequented. This is the manner in which spoor should at all times be sought for. I found a tolerable abundance of the spoor of various wild animals, and I therefore resolved to remain here some days for the purpose of hunting. I removed my waggons to an adjacent hollow, where I drew them up entirely concealed from view, and then constructed a shooting-hole beside the fountain, where for several mornings, at early dawn, I shot hartebeests as they came to drink.

On the morning of the 12th I rode north-east with attendants, and after proceeding several miles through an open country, we entered a beautiful forest of cameeldorn trees, and rode along beneath a range of steep rocky hills. The country gave me the idea of extreme antiquity, where the hand of man had wrought no change since the Creation. In a finely-wooded broad valley or opening among the hills we fell in with a magnificent herd of about sixty blue wildebeests. As they cantered across the grassy sward, tossing their fierce-looking, ponderous heads, their shaggy manes and long, black, bushy tails streaming in the breeze, they presented an appearance at once striking and imposing; and to a stranger they conveyed rather the idea of buffaloes than anything belonging to the antelope tribe, to which, indeed, wildebeests, both black and white, are but remotely allied, notwithstanding the classification of naturalists. Returning to camp with the trophies of a hartebeest, of which antelope I discovered several fine troops, I started a strand wolfe, or fuscous hyæna, which I rode into and slew.

About midnight on the 16th, weary with tossing on my restless couch, I arose, and taking my two-grooved rifle, a pillow, and a blanket, I held for my shooting-hole beside the fountain. The remainder of the night was very cool, with a southerly breeze. At dawn I looked from my hole, and seeing no game approaching, I rolled my blanket tight around me and tried to sleep. In this manner I had lain for about half an hour, when I was suddenly startled by a large heavy animal galloping past within six feet of me. I at once knew that it must be either some beast which had been coming to drink and had got my wind, or one hunted, which, according to the custom of deer and the larger antelopes, had rushed for refuge to the water in its distress. In the latter conjecture I was right; for, on cautiously peeping through the stones which surrounded my hole, I had the pleasure to behold a fine bull brindled gnoo dash into the waters of the fountain within forty yards of me, and stand at bay, followed by four tearing, fierce-looking wild dogs. All the four had their heads and shoulders covered with blood, and looked savage in the extreme. They seemed quite confident of success, and came leisurely up to the bull, passing within a few yards of me, their eyes glistening with ferocious glee.

My anxiety to possess this fine old bull, and also a specimen of the wild dog, prevented my waiting to see more of the fun. I deliberated for a few seconds whether I would shoot the bull first or one of the hounds, and ended by shooting the gnoo and the largest hound right and left. The bull, on receiving the ball, bounded out of the fountain; but suddenly wheeling about, he re-entered it, and, staggering violently for a moment, subsided in its waters. The hound got the bullet through his heart, and, springing forward from his comrades, instantly measured his length upon the gravel. I then quickly reloaded my rifle, lying on my side—a proceeding which, I may inform those who have not yet tried it, is rather difficult to accomplish. Whilst I was thus occupied the three remaining hounds reluctantly withdrew, and described a semicircle to leeward of me for the purpose of obtaining my wind and more correctly ascertaining the cause of their discomfiture. Having loaded, I re-opened my fire, and wounded another, when they all made off.

I could not help feeling very reluctant to fire at the jolly hounds. The whole affair reminded me so very forcibly of many gallant courses I had enjoyed in the Scottish deer forests with my own noble deerhounds, that I could not divest myself of the idea that those now before me deserved a better recompense for the masterly manner in which they were pursuing their desperate game. One hound in particular bore a strong expression of dear old Factor in his face, a trusty stag-hound bred by myself, whose deeds, though not renowned in verse like Ossian's Oscar and Luath, were perhaps little inferior either in speed or prowess to those famed in ancient song.

The wild dogs, or "wilde honden," as they are termed by the Dutch Boers, are still abundant in the precincts of the Cape colony, and are met with in great numbers throughout the interior. These animals invariably hunt together in large organized packs, varying in number from ten to sixty, and by their extraordinary powers of endurance, and mode of mutual assistance, they are enabled to run into the swiftest, or overcome the largest and most powerful antelope. I have never heard of their attacking the buffalo, and I believe that the animal pursued in the present instance is the largest to which they give battle. Their pace is a long never-tiring gallop, and in the chase they relieve one another, the leading hounds falling to the rear when fatigued, when others, who have been husbanding their strength, come up and relieve them. Having succeeded in bringing their quarry to bay, they all surround him, and he is immediately dragged to the ground, and in a few minutes torn to pieces and consumed.

They are of a bold and daring disposition, and do not entertain much fear of man, evincing less concern on his approach than any other carnivorous animal with which I am acquainted. On disturbing a pack, they trot leisurely along before the intruder, repeatedly halting and looking back at him. The females bring forth their young in large holes, in desolate open plains. These burrows are connected with one another underground. When a troop of wild dogs frequenting these holes observe a man approaching, they do not, as might be supposed, take shelter in the holes, but, rather trusting to their speed, they rush forth, even though the intruder should be close upon them, and retreat across the plain, the young ones, unless very weak, accompanying them. The devastation occasioned by them among the flocks of the pastoral Dutch Boers is inconceivable. It constantly happens that when the careless shepherds leave their charge, in quest of honey or other amusement, a pack of these marauders comes across the defenceless flock. A sanguinary massacre in such cases invariably ensues, and incredible numbers of sheep are killed and wounded. The voracious pack, not contented with killing as many as they can eat, follow resolutely on, tearing and mangling all that come within their reach.

Their voice consists of three different kinds of cry, each being used on special occasions. One of these cries is a sharp angry bark, usually uttered when they suddenly behold an object which they cannot make out. Another resembles a number of monkeys chattering together, or men conversing while their teeth are chattering violently from cold. This cry is emitted at night when large numbers of them are together, and they are excited by any particular occurrence, such as being barked at by domestic dogs. The third cry, and the one most commonly uttered by them, is a sort of rallying note to bring the various members of the pack together when they have been scattered in following several individuals of a troop of antelopes. It is a peculiarly soft melodious cry, yet, nevertheless, it may be distinguished at a great distance. It very much resembles the second note uttered by the cuckoo which visits our islands during the summer months, and, when heard in a calm morning echoing through the distant woodlands, it has a very pleasing effect. They treat all domestic dogs, however large and fierce, with the utmost scorn, waiting to receive their attack, and then, clanishly assisting one another, they generally rend them in pieces. The domestic dogs most cordially reciprocate their animosity, and abhor their very voices, at what distance soever heard, even more than that of the lion, starting to their feet, and angrily barking for hours. This interesting though destructive animal seems to form the connecting link between the wolf and the hyæna.

But to return to the bull. Having summoned my men, and with considerable difficulty dragged the ponderous carcase of the old bull out of the water, we found that he had been cruelly lacerated by the hounds. It appeared to me that they had endeavoured to hamstring him. His hind legs, haunches, and belly were dreadfully torn; he had lost half his tail, and was otherwise mutilated. Poor old bull! I could not help commiserating his fate. It is melancholy to reflect that, in accordance with the laws of nature, such scenes of pain must ever be occurring; one species, whether inhabiting earth, air, or ocean, being produced to become the prey of another. At night I watched the water, with fairish moonlight, and shot a large spotted hyæna.

I continued here hunting hartebeests until the 21st, when I inspanned at an early hour and trekked due east till sundown, when I halted near a small fountain of fine water, having performed a march of about twenty-five miles. Our road lay through a wild uninhabited country, producing sweet grass in abundance, but destitute of water. On the morning of the 22nd, having breakfasted, I rode south-west, with after-riders, and found the game abundant, but wild and shy, having been recently hunted by Boers.

CHAPTER IX.

The Riet River—Nomad Boer Encampments—Surly Reception at a Boer's Farm—Lions slain by the Boers—Cowardice of the Boers in Lion-hunting—Rumours of War between the Boers and Griquas—The Mirage of the Plains—Habits of the Blesbok—a knowing old Hog—A Snake under my Pillow—A Troop of Wild Dogs come upon me at night in my Shooting-hole—The Roar of Lions—Curious Facts concerning them.

WE inspanned before the dawn of day on the 23rd of February, and after steering east and by north for a distance of about twelve miles we found ourselves on the southern bank of the Riet river, where we outspanned. Along the banks, both above and below me, several families of the nomad Boers were encamped with their tents and waggons. Their overgrown flocks and herds were grazing on the plains and grassy hill-sides around. Five of these Boers presently came up to my waggons, and drank coffee with me. They seemed much amused with the details of my sporting adventures, which I was now able to give them in broken Dutch, in which language, from lately hearing no other spoken, I was daily becoming more proficient. On learning that I had not as yet enjoyed any blesbok shooting, they said they were certain I should be delighted with the sport.

The borders of the country inhabited by the blesboks they stated to be about four days distant in a north-easterly direction, and that on reaching it I should fall in with those antelopes in countless herds, along with black wildebeest, springbok, and other game. The Boers supplied me liberally with milk. In the height of the day we all bathed in the Riet river, and in the afternoon I continued my journey eastward. The breadth of the Riet river here is about thirty yards. It rises about one hundred miles to the eastward, and, flowing westerly, joins the Vaal river opposite Campbell's dorp.

On the third day after making the Riet river we crossed below a very picturesque waterfall, and resumed our march along its northern bank. The day was cool and pleasant, the sky overcast; the hot days of summer were now past, and the weather was most enjoyable. Continuing my march in the afternoon, I left the Riet river on my right, and held on through an open sandy country richly covered with abundance of sweet grass, and intersected by mountain ranges of very considerable extent. At sunset I encamped beside a Boer's farm, who received me hospitably, and asked me to dine with him.

During dinner, according to the custom of the Boers, he pestered me with a thousand questions, such as, What was my nation? Where was I from? Where was I bound for? Why I travelled about alone in such a manner. Where was my farm? Were my father and mother living? How many brothers and sisters I had? Was I married? And had I never been married in the whole course of my life? On my replying in the negative to this last question, the Boer seemed petrified with astonishment, and the family gazed at one another in utter amazement.

On the farm was a fine specimen of the African wild boar, which was perfectly tame, and took vegetables from the hands of the children. On the following day I performed two long marches, and again halted on the farm of a Boer, whose name was Potcheter. I found this man particularly bitter against the Government. On my going up to him to inquire where I should outspan, he was very surly, and would scarcely deign to speak to me. Of this, however, I took no notice, but took the liberty of informing him that when I had outspanned I should come up to the house and make the acquaintance of Mrs. Potcheter. As I wheeled about and walked away from him, I overheard him remark to three other gruff-looking Boers who stood beside him that I was "a verdomd Englishman."

Notwithstanding this cold reception, on returning to the house I soon managed to get into their good graces, and took dinner with them. During dinner the conversation turned on politics, when a keen discussion arose concerning the present administration of the Government. This being at all times a disagreeable subject, I thought it time to change the conversation to sporting subjects, in which the Boers always take intense interest. I accordingly mentioned to one of the young ladies who sat next to me that I had in my waggon a large work containing engravings of all the most interesting animals in the world; on which she instantly expressed a strong desire to see it. I then produced my "Museum of Animated Nature," which never failed to enchant the Boers, and to put an end to all political discussions; shooting and wild animals engrossing the conversation during the rest of the evening.

These Boers informed me that I should see herds of blesboks on the following day. They also stated that lions frequented the bushy mountain ranges which look down upon the plains frequented by the blesboks, and they mentioned that a considerable party of Boers had mustered that day upon a farm a few miles in advance, to hunt a troop of lions which had killed some horses on the preceding day. From the conversation which I overheard among themselves, I learnt that a war was brewing between the emigrant Boers on the northern bank of the Orange River and the Bastard and Griqua tribes. The rumour of this war threw my followers, who also heard the news from the servants of the Boers, into a state of great alarm. I resolved, however, that my movements should not be influenced by these reports.

At an early hour on the following morning a young Boer rode up to the farm, and informed us that the party who had been lion-hunting on the preceding day had bagged two fine lions, a male and female. As the farm lay directly in my line of march, I mounted Colesberg, and, directing my followers to follow with the waggons, I rode hard for the farm, to inspect the noble game. On my way thither I met a horse-waggon, drawn by eight horses, containing some of the party who had mustered for the battue. Arriving on the farm, I found the lion and lioness laid out on the grass in front of the house, and the Boer's Hottentots busy skinning them. Both lions were riddled with balls, and their heads were shot all to pieces.

This is generally the way in which the Boers serve their lions after they have killed them, fearing to approach, though dead, until they have expended a further supply of ammunition. A Hottentot is then ordered to approach and throw a stone at him; the Boers then ask if he is dead, and on the Hottentot replying, "Like so, baas," he is ordered to pull him by the tail before the hunters will venture to approach. My little Bushman informed me that he had often been out lion-hunting during his captivity with the Boers. On one of these occasions a Boer, who had dismounted from his horse to fire, was dashed to the ground by the lion before he could regain his saddle. The brute, however, did not injure him, but merely stood over him, lashing his tail, and growling at the rest of the party, who had galloped to a distance in the utmost consternation, and, instead of approaching within easy shot of the lion, to the rescue of their comrade, opened their fire upon him from a great distance, the consequence of which sportsmanlike proceeding was, that they missed the lion, and shot their comrade dead on the spot. The lion presently retreated, and, none daring to follow him, he escaped.

The Boer on whose farm I had arrived was a tall, powerful, manly-looking fellow. He informed me that he was a Dane. He was in great distress about two favourite dogs which the lions had killed during the attack on the preceding day. Three more were badly wounded, and their recovery seemed doubtful. He confirmed the reports of an impending war between the Boers and Griquas, which I had previously heard, and he asked me if I was not afraid, in times of war, to remain hunting, with only a few followers, in the wilderness. Being anxious to commence my operations against the blesboks, I resumed my march shortly after mid-day. On taking leave, the Dane presented me with some meal and a couple of loaves of bread, a luxury to which I had been an utter stranger for many months, and which, together with vegetables, I may further add I hardly ever tasted during the five hunting expeditions which I performed in Southern Africa. Another short march in a north-easterly direction brought me to the western borders of the boundless regions inhabited by the blesboks. I drew up my waggons beside a vley of rain-water, in open country, the plains before me being adorned with herds of black wildebeest, springbok, and blesbok.

I had now reached the borders of a country differing entirely from any I had hitherto seen. The sweet grass, which had heretofore been so abundant, became very scarce, being succeeded by short, crisp, sour pasturage, which my cattle and horses refused to eat. A supply of forage for these, however, could generally be obtained by driving them to the stony killocks and rocky mountain ranges which at various distances from one another intersected the campaign country. The plains were firm and hard, and admirably suited for riding; they were pastured short and bare by the endless herds of game which from time immemorial had held possession of these extensive domains. Although intersected occasionally by mountain ranges, these plains often extend to amazing distances, without any landmark to break the monotony of their boundless and ocean-like expanse. At other times the eye is relieved by one or more abrupt pyramidal or cone-shaped hills, which serve as a landmark to the hunter, whereby to regain his encampment after the excitement of the chase.

When the sun is powerful, which it is during the greater part of the year, an enduring mirage dances on the plain wherever the hunter turns his bewildered eyes. This mirage restricts the range of vision to a very moderate distance, and is very prejudicial to correct rifle-shooting. The effect produced by this optical illusion is remarkable: hills and herds of game often appear as if suspended in mid-air. Dry and sun-baked vleys, or pans covered with a crystallized efflorescence, constantly delude the thirsty traveller with the prospect of water; and more than once I have ridden towards a couple of springboks, magnified a hundred-fold, which I had mistaken for the white tilts of my waggons.

This vast tract of bare, sour pasturage, which is peculiarly the inheritance of the black wildebeest, the springbok, and the blesbok, but more particularly of the latter, occupies a central position, as it were, in Southern Africa. On the west of my present encampment, as far as the shores of the South Atlantic Ocean, no blesboks are to be found. Neither do they extend to the northward of the latitude of the river Molopo, in 25° 30', of which I shall at a future period make mention, although their herds frequent the plains along its southern bank. To the south a few small herds are still to be found within the colony, but their head-quarters is to the northward of the Orange River; whence they extend in an easterly direction throughout all the vast plains situated to the west of the Witbergen range.

The blesbok, in his manners and habits, very much resembles the springbok, which, however, it greatly exceeds in size, being as large as an English fallow-deer. It is one of the true antelopes, and all its movements and paces partake of the grace and elegance peculiar to that species. Its colour is similar to that of the sassayby, its skin being beautifully painted with every shade of purple, violet, and brown. Its belly is of the purest white, and a broad white band, or "blaze," adorns the entire length of its face. Blesboks differ from springboks in the determined and invariable manner in which they scour the plains, right in the wind's eye, and also in the manner in which they carry their noses close along the ground. Throughout the greater part of the year they are very wary and difficult of approach, but more especially when the does have young ones. At that season, when one herd is disturbed, and takes away up the wind, every other herd in view follows them; and the alarm extending for miles and miles down the wind, to endless herds beyond the vision of the hunter, a continued stream of blesboks may often be seen scouring up wind for upwards of an hour, and covering the landscape as far as the eye can see.

The springboks, which in equal numbers frequent the same ground, do not in general adopt the same decided course as the blesboks, but take away in every direction across the plains, sometimes with flying bounds, beautifully exhibiting the long, snowy-white hair with which their backs are adorned, and at others walking slowly and carelessly out of the hunter's way, scarcely deigning to look at him, with an air of perfect independence, as if aware of their own matchless speed.

The black wildebeests, which also thickly cover the entire length and breadth of the blesbok country, in herds averaging from twenty to fifty, have no regular course, like the blesboks. Unless driven by a large field of hunters, they do not leave their ground, although disturbed. Wheeling about in endless circles, and performing the most extraordinary variety of intricate evolutions, the shaggy herds of these eccentric and fierce-looking animals are for ever capering and gambolling round the hunter on every side. While he is riding hard to obtain a family shot of a herd in front of him, other herds are charging down wind on his right and left, and, having described a number of circular movements, they take up positions upon the very ground across which the hunter rode only a few minutes before.

Singly, and in small troops of four or five individuals, the old bull wildebeests may be seen stationed at intervals throughout the plains, standing motionless during a whole forenoon, coolly watching with a philosophic eye the movements of the other game, eternally uttering a loud snorting noise, and also a short, sharp cry which is peculiar to them. When the hunter approaches these old bulls, they commence whisking their long white tails in a most eccentric manner; then springing suddenly into the air, they begin prancing and capering, and pursue each other in circles at their utmost speed. Suddenly they all pull up together, to overhaul the intruder, when two of the bulls will often commence fighting in the most violent manner, dropping on their knees at every shock; then quickly wheeling about, they kick up their heels, whirl their tails with a fantastic flourish, and scour across the plain enveloped in a cloud of dust.

Throughout the greater part of the plains frequented by blesboks, numbers of the sun-baked hills or mounds of clay formed by the white ants occur. The average height of the ant-hills, in these districts, is from two to three feet. They are generally distant from one another from one to three hundred yards, being more or less thickly placed in different parts. These ant-hills are of the greatest service to the hunter, enabling him with facility to conceal himself on the otherwise open plain. By means of them I was enabled to hide, and select out of the herds the bucks and bulls carrying the finest heads for my collection.

On the 28th, having breakfasted, I rode forth with two after-riders, to try for blesboks, and took up positions on the plain, lying flat on my breast behind ant-hills, while my after-riders, one of whom led my horse, endeavoured to move them towards me. We found the blesboks abundant, but extremely wary. I wounded several, but did not bag one. I however shot two springboks, which were fat, and whose flesh we stood much in need of. I had several chances of wildebeests, but I had resolved not to fire at them.

The following day was the 1st of March. After an early breakfast I again took the field, with my after-riders and a spare horse. There was thunder and lightning on all sides, and I expected the day would set in wet: it all passed over, however, with a few showers, and the weather was delightfully cool. I lay behind ant-hills, while my men, extending to the right and left, endeavoured to drive the game towards me. Late in the day I bagged a fine old blesbok; it was a family shot, running at two hundred yards. I also shot a springbok, and mortally wounded another; both were very long shots.

The blesbok is one of the finest antelopes in the world, and is allowed to be the swiftest buck in Africa. He nevertheless attains very high condition, and at this period was exceedingly fat. I was surprised and deli_hted with the exquisite manner in which his beautiful colours are blended together. Nothing can exceed the beauty of this animal. Like most other African antelopes, his skin emitted a most delicious and powerful perfume of flowers and sweet-smelling herbs. A secretion issues from between his hoofs which has likewise a pleasing perfume.

The 3rd was a charmingly cool day. At an early hour in the morning I was visited by a party of Boers, some of whom I had previously met. They were proceeding to hunt wildebeest and blesbok, and were mounted on mares, each of which was followed by a foal. They requested me to join them in their "jag," but I excused myself, preferring to hunt alone. Having partaken largely of my coffee, the Boers mounted their mares and departed, holding a south-easterly course. As soon as they were out of sight I saddled up and rode north, with two after-riders, to try for blesboks. I found the country extremely pleasant to ride on. It resembled a well kept lawn. Troops of graceful springbok and blesbok were to be seen cantering right and left, and large herds of black wildebeests in every direction, now charging and capering, and now reconnoitring. I took up positions on the plain behind the ant-hills. In the forenoon I wounded one blesbok, and late in the day I made a fine double shot, knocking over two old blesboks right and left, at a hundred and a hundred and fifty yards. I also shot one springbok.

While "gralloching" a buck, one of the Boers rode up to me to say that his brother had wounded a wildebeest, which stood at bay on the plain; and his ammunition being expended, he would feel obliged by my coming to his assistance. I accordingly accompanied the Boer to where his brother stood sentry over the wounded bull, when I lent him my rifle, with which he finished his bull with a bullet in the forehead.

On the following day I hunted to the north-east of my camp, and made a fine shot at a blesbok, knocking him over at a hundred and fifty yards. Returning to camp in a low-lying grassy vley, I started a herd of "vlacke varcke," or wild hogs. The herd consisted of seven half-grown young ones and three old ones, one of which carried a pair of enormous tusks, projecting eight or nine inches beyond his lip. Being well mounted and the ground favourable, I at once gave chase and was soon at their heels. My horse was "The Grey." I selected the old boar for my prey, and immediately separated him from his comrades. After two miles of sharp galloping, we commenced ascending a considerable acclivity, when I managed to close with him, and succeeded in turning his head towards my camp. He now reduced his pace to a trot, and regarded me with a most malicious eye, his mouth a mass of foam. He was entirely in my power, as I had only to spring from my horse and bowl him over. I felt certain of him, but resolved not to shoot as long as his course lay in the direction of the waggons.

At length, surprised at the resolute manner in which he held for my camp, I headed him; when, to my astonishment, he did not in the slightest swerve from his course, but trotted along behind my horse like a dog following me. This at once roused my suspicions, and I felt certain that the cunning old fellow was making for some retreat, so I resolved to dismount and finish him. Just, however, as I had come to this resolution, I suddenly found myself in a labyrinth of enormous holes, the burrows of the ant-bear. In front of one of these the wild boar pulled up, and, charging stern foremost into it, disappeared from my disappointed eyes, and I saw him no more. I rode home for my men; and, returning, we collected grass and bushes and eadeavoured to smoke him out, but without success.

On the 7th we inspanned at dawn of day, and trekked east about ten miles, encamping beside a small isolated farmhouse, which had been lately vacated by some Boer owing to the impending war with the Griquas. Here we found plenty of old cow-dung for fuel—an article which, throughout the whole of the blesbok country, is very scarce, there often being great difficulty in obtaining sufficient fuel to boil the kettle for coffee. Beside the farmhouse were two strong springs of excellent water, in which cresses flourished. Game was abundant on all sides; wildebeests and springboks pasturing within a few hundred yards of the door as we drove up. Below the fountains was a small garden, in which I found a welcome supply of onions and other vegetables.

On the 12th I bagged two bull wildebeests and two springboks to the northward of my camp. In the evening I took my pillow and "komberse," or skin blanket, to the margin of a neighbouring vley, where I had observed doe blesboks drink. Of these I had not yet secured a single specimen, which I was very anxious to do, as they likewise carry fine horns, which, though not so thick as those of the males, are more gracefully formed. Shortly after I had lain down, two porcupines came grunting up to me, and stood within six feet of where I lay. About midnight an old wildebeest came and stood within ten yards of me, but I was too lazy to fire at him. All night I heard some creature moving in the cracked earth beneath my pillow; but, believing it to be a mouse, I did not feel much concerned about the matter. I could not, however, divest myself of a painful feeling that it might be a snake, and wrapped my blanket tight round my body. Awaking at an early hour the following morning, I forgot to look for the tenant who had spent the night beneath my pillow. No blesbok appearing, I stalked an old sprinkbok through the rushes and shot him. Having concealed him, I held for camp, and despatched two men to bring home the venison and my bedding.

While taking my breakfast I observed my men returning, one of them carrying a very large and deadly serpent. I at once felt certain it was he that I had heard the previous night beneath my pillow; and on asking them where they had killed it, they replied "In your bed." On approaching the bedding, they had discovered the horrid reptile sunning itself on the edge of my blanket, until on perceiving them it glided in beneath it. It was a large specimen of the black variety of the puff adder, one of the most poisonous serpents of Africa, death ensuing within an hour after its bite.

On the 15th I had a very good day's sport. As the day dawned I peeped from my hole, and saw troops of blesboks feeding on every side of me, but none came within range. I shot one springbok; and having concealed him in the rushes, I walked to camp. After breakfast, I took the field with Kleinboy and Bushman, and rode north to try for blesboks. While lying behind an ant-hill on the bare plain, a herd of about thirty wildebeests came thundering down upon me, and the leading bull nearly jumped over me. Into one of these I fired; he got the ball too far back, however, and made off, but was found by one of my men the following day. Presently Kleinboy rode up, and stated that while he was driving the blesboks he had observed an old stag hartebeest standing in the shade of some tall green bushes in the adjacent range of hills. I resolved to stalk him in the most approved Highland fashion; so, having made an accurate survey of the ground with my spyglass, I rode within a quarter of a mile of him, and then proceeded to creep in upon him on my hands and knees.

In this manner I got within sixty yards of him, where I lay flat on my breast for several minutes until he should give me his broadside. Presently he walked forth from the cover of the bush beneath which he had been standing, when I sent a ball in at his right shoulder, which rested on the skin in his left haunch. Wheeling about, he bounded over an adjacent ridge and was out of sight in a moment. On gaining this ridge I was just in time to see the noble hartebeest stagger for a moment, and then subside into the long grass in a hollow below me. He was a princely old stag, carrying splendid horns and a beautiful coat of new hair. I thought I could never sufficiently admire him. Having removed the head and skin, we made for the camp, and on my way thither I was tempted to try a long shot at one of two old blesboks that kept capering to leeward of us. Sitting down on the grass, and resting both my elbows on my knees (a manner of firing much practised by the Boers), I let fly at a blesbok, and made one of the finest shots I had ever seen, sending the ball through the middle of his shoulder at upwards of two hundred and fifty yards. On receiving it he cantered forward a short distance and fell dead.

The rifle I used in those days was a double-barrelled two-grooved one, by Dixon of Edinburgh, with which I managed to make such superior shooting to that which I could perform with the old style of rifle, that I considered the latter as a mere "popgun" in comparison with the other. In the evening I took up my position in my shooting-hole to the northward of camp. About an hour after the moon rose, a troop of wildebeests came and stood within thirty yards of me. I fired, and a very large bull with one horn fell to the shot. If I had allowed this bull to lie there, my chance of further sport was over for that night and the following morning. I therefore took the old fellow by his horn, and, exerting my utmost strength and taking time, I managed to drag him as he fell, and still living, to a hollow beside the water, in which I concealed him. In half an hour another troop of wildebeests came and stood snuffing on the spot where he had fallen. I fired, and a fine old bull received the ball in the shoulder, and bounding forward one hundred yards rolled over in the dust. In about an hour a third troop of wildebeests came and stood within thirty yards of me. At one of these I let fly, and heard the ball crack loudly on his shoulder.

On the 16th I hunted on the plains to the north-east, killing one springbok, and at night I watched the distant vley to the northward of my camp, and got a fright which I shall remember to my dying day. Soon after the moon rose, a troop of wildebeests came within range; at one of these I fired, and he dropped to the shot, the ball passing through the spine. A little after this I discharged my other barrel at a large spotted hyæna, and then I returned my rifle to its holster without loading either barrel, and presently I was asleep.

I had not slept long when my light dreams were influenced by strange sounds. I dreamt that lions were rushing about in quest of me, and, the sounds increasing, I awoke with a sudden start, uttering a loud shriek. I could not for several seconds remember in what part of the world I was, or anything connected with my present position. I heard the rushing of light feet as of a pack of wolves close on every side of me, accompanied by the most unearthly sounds. On raising my head, to my utter horror I saw on every side nothing but savage wild dogs, chattering and growling. On my right and on my left, and within a few paces of me, stood two lines of these ferocious-looking animals cocking their ears and stretching their necks to have a look at me; while two large troops, in which there were at least forty of them, kept dashing backwards and forwards across my wind within a few yards of me, chattering and growling with the most extraordinary volubility. Another troop of wild dogs were fighting over the wildebeest I had shot, which they had begun to devour.

On beholding them I expected no other fate than to be instantly torn to pieces and consumed. I felt my blood curdling along my cheeks and my hair bristling on my head. However, I had presence of mind to consider that the human voice and a determined bearing might overawe them, and accordingly, springing to my feet, I stepped on to the little ledge surrounding the hole, where, drawing myself up to my full height, I waved my large blanket with both hands, at the same time addressing my savage assembly in a loud and solemn manner. This had the desired effect: the wild dogs removed to a more respectful distance, barking at me something like collies. Upon this I snatched up my rifle and commenced loading, and before this was accomplished the entire pack had passed away and did not return.

These had not been gone many minutes when twelve or fifteen large hyænas were hard at work on the wildebeest. I fired two shots at them at different times during the night, but none fell to my shots. Heedless of me they continued their banquet, and long before morning nothing was left of the wildebeest save a few of the larger bones. On the two following mornings I was annoyed by a cunning old bull wildebeest, which, having discovered my retreat, kept sentry over me, and successively drove away every troop of his fellows that approached my vley to drink. He kept feeding just out of rifle-range, and not only warned his comrades of their danger by fixing his eye on my place of concealment and snorting loudly, but when this failed he drove the other wildebeests from me in the most determined manner, like a collie dog driving sheep. Before leaving my hole, however, on the second morning, I had my revenge. A troop of cows, heedless of his warnings, approached the vley. In his anxiety for their safety he neglected his own; and coming for the first time within long rifle-range, I put up my after-sights and let drive at his ribs. The ball took effect, and, kicking up his heels and flourishing his long white tail, the old bull bounded forth, and disappearing over a ridge I saw him no more.

The night of the 19th was to me rather a memorable one, as being the first on which I had the satisfaction of hearing the deep-toned thunder of the lion's roar. Although there was no one near, to inform me by what beast the haughty and impressive sounds which echoed through the wilderness were produced, I had little difficulty in divining. There was no mistake about it; and on hearing it I at once knew, as well as if accustomed to the sound from my infancy, that the appalling roar which was uttered within half a mile of me was no other than that of the mighty and terrible king of beasts. Although the dignified and truly monarchical appearance of the lion has long rendered him famous amongst his fellow quadrupeds, and his appearance and habits have often been described by abler pens than mine, nevertheless I consider that a few remarks, resulting from my own personal experience, formed by a tolerably long acquaintance with him both by day and by night, may not prove uninteresting to the reader.

There is something so noble and imposing in the presence of the lion, when seen walking with dignified self-possession, free and undaunted, on his native soil, that no description can convey an adequate idea of his striking appearance. The lion is exquisitely formed by nature for the predatory habits which he is destined to pursue. Combining in comparatively small compass the qualities of power and agility, he is enabled, by means of the tremendous machinery with which nature has gifted him, easily to overcome and destroy almost every beast of the forest, however superior to him in weight and stature.

Though considerably under four feet in height, he has little difficulty in dashing to the ground and overcoming the lofty and apparently powerful giraffe, whose head towers above the trees of the forest, and whose skin is nearly an inch in thickness. The lion is the constant attendant of the vast herds of buffaloes which frequent the interminable forests of the interior; and a full-grown one, so long as his teeth are unbroken, generally proves a match for an old bull buffalo, which in size and strength greatly surpasses the most powerful breed of English cattle: the lion also preys on all the larger varieties of the antelopes, and on both varieties of the gnoo. The zebra, which is met with in large herds throughout the interior, is also a favourite object of his pursuit.

Lions do not refuse, as has been asserted, to feast upon the venison that they have not killed themselves. I have repeatedly discovered lions of all ages which had taken possession of, and were feasting upon, the carcases of various game quadrupeds which had fallen before my rifle. The lion is very generally diffused throughout the secluded parts of Southern Africa. He is, however, nowhere met with in great abundance, it being very rare to find more than three, or even two, families of lions frequenting the same district and drinking at the same fountain. When a greater number were met with, I remarked that it was owing to long-protracted droughts, which, by drying nearly all the fountains, had compelled the game of various districts to crowd the remaining springs, and the lions, according to their custom, followed in the wake. It is a common thing to come upon a full-grown lion and lioness associating with three or four large young ones nearly full-grown; at other times, full-grown males will be found associating and hunting together in a happy state of friendship: two, three, and four full-grown male lions may thus be discovered consorting together.

The male lion is adorned with a long, rank, shaggy mane, which in some instances almost sweeps the ground. The colour of these manes varies, some being very dark, and others of a golden yellow. This appearance has given rise to a prevailing opinion among the Boers that there are two distinct varieties of lions, which they distinguish by the respective names of "Schwart fore life" and "Chiel fore life:" this idea, however, is erroneous. The colour of the lion's mane is generally influenced by his age. He attains his mane in the third year of his existence. I have remarked that at first it is of a yellowish colour; in the prime of life it is blackest, and when he has numbered many years, but still is in the full enjoyment of his power, it assumes a yellowish-grey, pepper-and-salt sort of colour. These old fellows are cunning and dangerous, and most to be dreaded. The females are utterly destitute of a mane, being covered with a short, thick, glossy coat of tawny hair. The manes and coats of lions frequenting open-lying districts utterly destitute of trees, such as the borders of the great Kalahari desert, are more rank and handsome than those inhabiting forest districts.

One of the most striking things connected with the lion is his voice, which is extremely grand and peculiarly striking. It consists at times of a low, deep moaning, repeated five or six times, ending in faintly audible sighs; at other times he startles the forest with loud, deep-toned, solemn roars, repeated five or six times in quick succession, each increasing in loudness to the third or fourth, when his voice dies away in five or six low, muffled sounds, very much resembling distant thunder. At times, and not unfrequently, a troop may be heard roaring in concert, one assuming the lead, and two, three, or four more regularly taking up their parts, like persons singing a catch.

Like our Scottish stags at the rutting season, they roar loudest in cold, frosty nights; but on no occasions are their voices to be heard in such perfection, or so intensely powerful, as when two or three strange troops of lions approach a fountain to drink at the same time. When this occurs, every member of each troop sounds a bold roar of defiance at the opposite parties; and when one roars, all roar together, and each seems to vie with his comrades in the intensity and power of his voice. The power and grandeur of these nocturnal forest concerts is inconceivably striking and pleasing to the hunter's ear. The effect, I may remark, is greatly enhanced when the hearer happens to be situated in the depths of the forest, at the dead hour of midnight, unaccompanied by any attendant, and ensconced within twenty yards of the fountain which the surrounding troops of lions are approaching. Such has been my situation many scores of times; and though I am allowed to have a tolerably good taste for music, I consider the catches with which I was then regaled as the sweetest and most natural I ever heard.

As a general rule, lions roar during the night; their sighing moans commencing as the shades of evening envelop the forest, and continuing at intervals throughout the night. In distant and secluded regions, however, I have constantly heard them roaring loudly as late as nine and ten o'clock on a bright sunny morning. In hazy and rainy weather they are to be heard at every hour in the day, but their roar is subdued. It often happens that when two strange male lions meet at a fountain a terrific combat ensues, which not unfrequently ends in the death of one of them. The habits of the lion are strictly nocturnal; during the day he lies concealed beneath the shade of some low bushy tree or wide-spreading bush, either in the level forest or on the mountain side. He is also partial to lofty reeds or fields of long rank yellow grass, such as occur in low-lying vleys. From these haunts he sallies forth when the sun goes down, and commences his nightly prowl. When he is successful in his beat, and has secured his prey, he does not roar much that night, only uttering occasionally a few low moans : that is, provided no intruders approach him, otherwise the case would be very different.

Lions are ever most active, daring, and presuming in dark and stormy nights; and consequently on such occasions the traveller ought more particularly to be on his guard. I remarked a fact connected with the lions' hour of drinking peculiar to themselves : they seemed unwilling to visit the fountains with good moonlight. Thus, when the moon rose early, the lions deferred their hour of watering until late in the morning; and when the moon rose late, they drank at a very early hour in the night. By this acute system many a grisly lion saved his bacon, and is now luxuriating in the forests of South Africa, which had otherwise fallen by the barrels of my "Westley Richards." Owing to the tawny colour of the coat with which nature has robed him he is perfectly invisible in the dark; and although I have often heard them loudly lapping the water under my very nose, not twenty yards from me, I could not possibly make out so much as the outline of their forms.

When a thirsty lion comes to water, he stretches out his massive arms, lies down on his breast to drink, and makes a loud lapping noise in drinking, not to be mistaken. He continues lapping up the water for a long while, and four or five times during the proceeding he pauses for half a minute as if to take breath. One thing conspicuous about them is their eyes, which, in a dark night, glow like two balls of fire. The female is more fierce and active than the male, as a general rule. Lionesses which have never had young are much more dangerous than those which have. At no time is the lion so much to be dreaded as when his partner has got small young ones. At that season he knows no fear, and, in the coolest and most intrepid manner, he will face a thousand men. A remarkable instance of this kind came under my own observation which confirmed the reports I had before heard from the natives.

One day, when out elephant-hunting in the territory of the "Baseleka," accompanied by two hundred and fifty men, I was astonished suddenly to behold a majestic lion slowly and steadily advancing toward us with a dignified step and undaunted bearing, the most noble and imposing that can be conceived. Lashing his tail from side to side, and growling haughtily, his terribly expressive eye resolutely fixed upon us, and displaying a show of ivory well calculated to inspire terror amongst the timid "Bechuanas," he approached. A headlong flight of the two hundred and fifty men was the immediate result; and, in the confusion of the moment, four couples of my dogs, which they had been leading, were allowed to escape in their couples. These instantly faced the lion, who, finding that by his bold bearing he had succeeded in putting his enemies to flight, now became solicitous for the safety of his little family, with which the lioness was retreating in the back-ground. Facing about, he followed after them with a haughty and independent step, growling fiercely at the dogs which trotted along on either side of him. Three troops of elephants having been discovered a few minutes previous to this, upon which I was marching for the attack, I, with the most heartfelt reluctance, reserved my fire. On running down the hill side, to endeavour to recall my dogs, I observed, for the first time, the retreating lioness with four cubs. About twenty minutes afterwards two noble elephants repaid my forbearance.

Among Indian Nimrods a certain class of royal tigers is dignified with the appellation of "man-eaters." These are tigers, which, having once tasted human flesh, show a predilection for the same, and such characters are very naturally famed and dreaded among the natives. Elderly gentlemen of similar tastes and habits are occasionally met with among the lions in the interior of South Africa, and the danger of such neighbours may be easily imagined. I account for lions first acquiring this taste in the following manner: the Bechuana tribes of the far interior do not bury their dead, but unceremoniously carry them forth, and leave them lying exposed in the forest or on the plain, a prey to the lion and hyæna, or the jackal and vulture; and I can readily imagine that a lion, having thus once tasted human flesh, would have little hesitation, when opportunity presented itself, of springing upon and carrying off the unwary traveller or "Bechuana" inhabiting his country. Be this as it may, man-eaters occur; and on my fourth hunting expedition a horrible tragedy was acted one dark night in my little lonely camp by one of these formidable characters, which deprived me, in the far wilderness, of my most valuable servant.

In winding up these few observations on the lion, which I trust will not have been tiresome to the reader, I may remark that lion-hunting, under any circumstances, is decidedly a dangerous pursuit. It may, nevertheless, be followed, to a certain extent, with comparative safety by those who have, naturally, a turn for that sort of thing. A recklessness of death, perfect coolness and self-possession, an acquaintance with the disposition and manners of lions, and a tolerable knowledge of the use of the rifle, are indispensable to him who would shine in the overpoweringly exciting pastime of hunting this justly-celebrated king of beasts.

CHAPTER X.

Boer Encampment—A Night in a Storm—A Fancy Costume—Fearful Encounter with a Lioness—"Colesberg" dreadfully mangled—Cowardice of Hottentots—We march back to Colesberg—Danger of being plundered by the Rebel Boers—Arrival at Colesberg—The Troops march against the Boers—The Battle of Schwart Coppice—Start for the distant Land of Elephants—The Hottentots make free with my Brandy, and mutiny—Leopards—Kuruman—Mr. Moffat, the good Missionary—Roasted Locusts.

ON the 22nd of March I rode south to a distant farm, for the double purpose of obtaining some corn or meal, and of hearing the news of the impending war between the Boers and Griquas. On reaching the farm I found that a large party of Boers were here encamped together: they had mustered for mutual protection. Their tents and waggons were drawn up on every side of the farm-house, forming a very lively appearance. The Boers informed me that all their countrymen, and also the Griquas, were thus packed together in "lagers," or encampments, and that hostilities were about to commence. They remonstrated with me on what they were pleased to term my madness, in living alone in an isolated position in such sharp times, and invited me to place myself for protection under their banner. I endeavoured to persuade them to get up a party to hunt the lion; but this they declined to do, remarking that "a lion (like Johnnie Gordon's bagpipes) was not to be played with." Returning to my camp I bowled over a springbok at one hundred and fifty yards.

On the 23rd, having breakfasted, I rode north, with after-riders, to try for blesboks. It was a cool day, with a strong easterly breeze, and we found the game extremely wild. As we proceeded, vast herds kept streaming on up the wind, darkening the plain before us, in countless thousands. About two miles north of the bushy mountain where I had heard the lion roar, far in the vast level plain, were some bushy mimosa trees. Within a few hundred yards of these we discovered an old bull wildebeest, newly killed by a lion and half eaten. His large and striking foot-prints were deeply embedded in the sand, and so fresh that they seemed to have been imprinted only a few minutes before. Moreover, there was not a single vulture near the carcase. We therefore felt convinced that the lion must be lying somewhere near us, having hidden himself on our approach. We searched for some time in the adjacent hollows, where the grass was very rank, but in vain. The game now became more and more wild, taking away into another district in long strings, like our island red-deer when hard driven; I accordingly gave it up, and turned my horse's head for camp. On my way thither I bagged one blesbok and two bull wildebeests: one of these got the bullet through his heart, but nevertheless stood at bay for some time after.

On reaching camp I suddenly resolved to take men and horses with me, and spend the night in the vicinity of the lion, and search early for him on the following morning. Accordingly, while dinner was preparing, I occupied myself in cleaning and loading my three double-barrelled rifles; after which, having dined, I rode with Kleinboy and John Stofolus to my hole by the vley, where my bedding lay day and night. This spot was within a few miles of where we expected to fall in with the lion in the morning. We secured the three horses to one another, as there was no tree or bush within miles of us; but these I could dispense with, for I knew very well by the looks of the Hottentots that they would not sleep much, but would keep a vigilant eye over our destinies. I spent a most miserable night. The wind, which had been blowing so fresh in the height of the day, had subsided to a calm when the sun went down, and was now succeeded by an almost death-like stillness, which I too well knew was the harbinger of a coming tempest.

We had not lain down an hour when the sky to leeward became black as pitch. Presently the most vivid flashes of lightning followed one another in quick succession, accompanied by terrific peals of thunder. The wind, which, during the day, had been out of the north-east, now, as is usual on such occasions, veered right round and came whistling up from the south-west, where the tempest was brewing; and in a few minutes more it was upon us in all its fury, the rain descending in torrents on our devoted heads, while vivid flashes of lightning momentarily illumined, with the brilliancy of day, the darkness that reigned around. In a very few minutes the whole plain was a sheet of water, and every atom of my clothes and bedding was thoroughly saturated. My three rifles had excellent holsters, and with the help of two sheep-skins, which I used instead of saddle-cloths, I kept them quite dry. In two hours the tempest had passed away, but light rain fell till morning, until which time I lay on the wet ground, soaked to the skin. About midnight we heard the lion roar a mile or so to the northward; and a little before the day dawned I again heard him in the direction of the carcase which we had found on the preceding day. Soon after this I gave the word to march. We then arose and saddled our horses. I found my trousers lying in a pool of water, so I converted a blanket into a long kilt by strapping it round my waist with my shooting-belt. The costume of my followers was equally unique.

We held for the north end of the lion's mountain at a sharp pace, which we gained before it was clear enough to see surrounding objects. As the light broke in upon us we reduced our pace, and rode slowly up the middle of the vast level plain towards the carcase of the wildebeest, with large herds of wildebeests, springbok, blesbok, and quaggas on every side of us, which were this day as tame as they had been wild on the previous one. This is generally the case after a storm. The morn was cloudy; misty vapours hung on the shoulders of the neighbouring mountains, and the air was loaded with balmy perfume, emitted by the grateful plants and herbs. As we approached the carcase, I observed several jackals steal away, and some half-drowned-looking vultures were sitting round it. But there was no appearance of the lion. I spent the next half-hour in riding across the plain looking for his spoor; but I sought in vain. Being cold and hungry, I turned my horse's head for camp, and rode slowly along through the middle of the game, which would scarcely move out of rifle-range on either side of me.

Suddenly I observed a number of vultures seated on the plain about a quarter of a mile ahead of us, and close beside them stood a huge lioness, consuming a blesbok which she had killed. She was assisted in her repast by about a dozen jackals, which were feasting along with her in the most friendly and confidential manner. Directing my followers' attention to the spot, I remarked, "I see the lion;" to which they replied, "Whar? whar? Yah! Almagtig! dat is he;" and instantly reining in their steeds and wheeling about, they pressed their heels to their horses' sides, and were preparing to betake themselves to flight. I asked them what they were going to do?

To which they answered, "We have not yet placed caps on our rifles." This was true; but while this short conversation was passing the lioness had observed us. Raising her full, round face, she overhauled us for a few seconds and then set off at a smart canter towards a range of mountains some miles to the northward; the whole troop of jackals also started off in another direction; there was, therefore, no time to think of caps. The first move was to bring her to bay, and not a second was to be lost. Spurring my good and lively steed, and shouting to my men to follow, I flew across the plain, and, being fortunately mounted on Colesberg, the flower of my stud, I gained upon her at every stride. This was to me a joyful moment, and I at once made up my mind that she or I must die.

The lioness having had a long start of me, we went over a considerable extent of ground before I came up with her. She was a large full-grown beast, and the bare and level nature of the plain added to her imposing appearance. Finding that I gained upon her, she reduced her pace from a canter to a trot, carrying her tail stuck out behind her, and slewed a little to one side. I shouted loudly to her to halt, as I wished to speak with her, upon which she suddenly pulled up, and sat on her haunches like a dog, with her back towards me, not even deigning to look round. She then appeared to say to herself, "Does this fellow know who he is after?" Having thus sat for half a minute, as if involved in thought, she sprang to her feet, and, facing about, stood looking at me for a few seconds, moving her tail slowly from side to side, showing her teeth, and growling fiercely. She next made a short run forwards, making a loud, rumbling noise like thunder. This she did to intimidate me; but, finding that I did not flinch an inch nor seem to heed her hostile demonstrations, she quietly stretched out her massive arms, and lay down on the grass. My Hottentots now coming up, we all three dismounted, and, drawing our rifles from their holsters, we looked to see if the powder was up in the nipples, and put on our caps.

While this was doing the lioness sat up, and showed evident symptoms of uneasiness. She looked first at us, and then behind her, as if to see if the coast were clear; after which she made a short run towards us, uttering her deep-drawn murderous growls. Having secured the three horses to one another by their rheims, we led them on as if we intended to pass her, in the hope of obtaining a broadside. But this she carefully avoided to expose, presenting only her full front. I had given Stofolus my Moore rifle, with orders to shoot her if she should spring upon me, but on no account to fire before me. Kleinboy was to stand ready to hand me my Purdey rifle, in case the two-grooved Dixon should not prove sufficient. My men as yet had been steady, but they were in a precious stew, their faces having assumed a ghastly paleness, and I had a painful feeling that I could place no reliance on them.

Now, then, for it, neck or nothing! She is within sixty yards of us, and she keeps advancing. We turned the horses' tails to her. I knelt on one side, and, taking a steady aim at her breast, let fly. The ball cracked loudly on her tawny hide, and crippled her in the shoulder, upon which she charged with an appalling roar, and in the twinkling of an eye she was in the midst of us. At this moment Stofolus's rifle exploded in his hand, and Kleinboy, whom I had ordered to stand ready by me, danced about like a duck in a gale of wind. The lioness sprang upon Colesberg, and fearfully lacerated his ribs and haunches with her horrid teeth and claws; the worst wound was on his haunch, which exhibited a sickening, yawning gash, more than twelve inches long, almost laying bare the very bone. I was very cool and steady, and did not feel in the least degree nervous, having fortunately great confidence in my own shooting; but I must confess, when the whole affair was over I felt that it was a very awful situation and attended with extreme peril, as I had no friend with me on whom I could rely.

When the lioness sprang on Colesberg, I stood out from the horses, ready with my second barrel for the first chance she should give me of a clear shot. This she quickly did; for, seemingly satisfied with the revenge she had now taken, she quitted Colesberg, and, slewing her tail to one side, trotted sulkily past within a few paces of me. Taking one step to the left, I pitched my rifle to my shoulder, and in another second the lioness was stretched on the plain a lifeless corpse. In the struggles of death she half turned on her back, and stretched her neck and fore arms convulsively, when she fell back to her former position; her mighty arms hung powerless by her side, her lower jaw fell, blood streamed from her mouth, and she expired. At the moment I fired my second shot, Stofolus, who hardly knew whether he was alive or dead, allowed the three horses to escape. These galloped frantically across the plain; on which he and Kleinboy instantly started after them, leaving me standing alone and unarmed within a few paces of the lioness, which they, from their anxiety to be out of the way, evidently considered quite capable of doing further mischief.

Such is ever the case with these worthies, and with nearly all the natives of South Africa. No reliance can be placed on them. They will to a certainty forsake their master in the most dastardly manner in the hour of peril, and leave him in the lurch. A stranger, however, hearing these fellows recounting their own gallant adventures, when sitting in the evening along with their comrades round a blazing fire, or under the influence of their adored "Cape smoke" or native brandy, might fancy them to be the bravest of the brave. Having skinned the lioness and cut off her head, we placed her trophies upon Beauty, and held for camp. Before we had proceeded a hundred yards from the carcase, upwards of sixty vultures, whom the lioness had often fed, were feasting on her remains.

We led poor Colesberg slowly home, where having washed his wounds, and carefully stitched them together, I ordered the cold water cure to be adopted. Under this treatment his wounds rapidly healed, and he eventually recovered. The sky remained overcast throughout the day. When the shades of evening set in, terror seemed to have taken possession of the minds of my followers, and they swore that the mate of the lioness, on finding her bones, would follow on our spoor and revenge her death. Under this impression they refused to remain about the waggons or in the tent after the sun went down; and having cut down the rafters and cupboards of the Boer's house for fuel, they kindled a large fire in the kitchen, where they took up their quarters for the night.

I continued hunting here until the 29th, when I deemed it high time to return to Colesberg, for the purpose of packing and storing my curiosities, increasing my establishment, and refitting generally, preparatory to starting for the distant land of elephants in the far forests of the interior. The distemper or horse sickness, which rages in those parts during the summer months, might be expected shortly to be past, there was therefore not much time to lose. The morning was spent in stowing the waggons, greasing the wheels, securing the pots, gridirons, spades, etc., and overhauling the yokes, rheims, straps, and other gear, preparatory to inspanning, and in the afternoon we inspanned, and, turning our faces to the south, marched upon Colesberg.

On the march I killed two springboks; and having proceeded ten miles we halted for the night. It rained heavily till morning. My oxen were in fine condition, and having done very little work of late, they were very fresh and obstreperous. On the following day we crossed the Riet river. The country was very heavy, owing to the recent rains, and some of my gear, which was rotten, broke repeatedly, causing much delay. At sundown we halted at a lager, or encampment of Boers. Here about a dozen families were congregated together for mutual protection. These men were all rebels and our enemies, being, at that very moment, at war with our allies, the Griquas and Bastards, whom we shortly afterwards assisted against the Boers. I deemed it rather a rash step thus coolly to march through the enemy's country, bearding as it were the lion in his den. There was, however, no help for it; so I resolved to take the bull by the horns, and put on a bold face. The least that I might have expected was to have my waggons most thoroughly ransacked and plundered, if not taken from me altogether. This they would certainly have done if they had thought that I was an Englishman; but by saying I was a berg Scot, or mountain Scotsman, backed by the garb of Old Gaul, which I always wore, I convinced them that I was a Scotsman. Many of the clergyman among the Boers being Scots, they entertain a predilection for my countrymen.

These Boers happened to be short of coffee, a beverage of which they are extremely fond. I had fortunately a large supply in my waggons; and as I was on my way to Colesberg, I had no objection to dispose of it. Accordingly, by presenting the ladies of the leading families with a few half-pounds of coffee, and selling them the remainder of my stock at a moderate price, I managed to secure the good graces of the whole,

and they were pleased to express their opinion that I was a "ghooe carle," or good fellow. On hearing that a few days previous I had bagged a savage lioness, and on beholding her trophies, they seemed quite astonished, remarking to one another—
"Mi scapsels! vat zoorten mens is de?" signifying, "My stars and garters! what sort of man is this?"

In the course of the evening and during the night several armed parties of Boers halted at this lager to refresh, and then passed on to join the head-quarters of their army, which was encamped about forty miles to the southward, at a place called "Schwart Coppice." Each of these Boers was provided with one or more packhorses bearing his commissariat and ammunition, and many of them had Hottentot and Bushman after-riders. Their sole weapon consisted of their roer or long gun; each wore a leathern shooting-belt round his waist, and a large bullock's horn containing powder dangled by his side.

On the 31st I continued my march, and on the evening of the 2nd of April I reached Philipolis, a missionary station, and the chief town of the Bastards' country. My road had led between the encampments of the contending parties. Troops of mounted Boers had been scouring the country in every direction, plundering all they could lay their hands on, and sweeping off the cattle and horses of the Bastards. Halting at an encampment of Bastards on the preceding day, I was much amused by their taking me for a missionary. My costume was not very clerical, consisting of a dirty shirt and an old Gordon tartan kilt. From a Bastard in the vicinity of Philipolis I obtained two large rough dogs, in exchange for three pounds of coffee and a little tea. The names of these dogs were "Bles" and "Flam." Bles was of an extremely fierce and savage disposition. On the evening of the 3rd we encamped on the northern bank of the mighty Orange River, at a place called "Boata's Drift," which is nearly opposite Colesberg. Our march had been through a succession of mountains, covered with excellent pasture to their summits. It had rained heavily throughout the day.

After inspecting the drift or ford on the following morning, we calculated that the river was too high for the waggons to cross; and by sending a man over on horseback, according to the most approved custom, we ascertained that a passage for the waggons was impracticable. I accordingly instructed my men to proceed to Norval's Punt, situated a long march higher up the river, there to cross and join me in Colesberg on the evening of the following day; and having breakfasted, I saddled "The Immense Brute," and, taking the ford high up, I managed to cross the river in safety, the current having twice taken my horse off his legs. In two hours I entered the village of Colesberg, where I found the officers of the 91st and all my other friends in great force.

My waggons did not make their appearance in Colesberg until the afternoon of the third day. I took up my quarters with my old friend Mr. Paterson, who also kindly accommodated the half of my stud in his stables, and the other half I picketed in the stables of my old regiment the Cape Mounted Rifles. My oxen I permitted to run day and night in the neighbouring mountains. On the 7th we offloaded the waggons, and made a grand parade of my heads and hunting trophies in front of

Paterson's house, which was situated in the centre of the village: this attracted crowds of persons throughout the day. In the afternoon of the 8th, Mr. Rawstorne, the resident magistrate, received despatches from Adam Kok, chief of the Bastards, stating that the Boers had commenced active hostilities, and craving assistance from government. Accordingly, in the evening an order was issued that all the available force in the garrison should march upon the Orange River next day. This I considered an intense bore, as I should thereby lose the society of all my friends. On the following morning all was bustle and preparation throughout the village, the military preparing for the march, and the merchants loading up their waggons with commissariat for the supply of the troops, while many a dark-eyed nymph wiped the hot tear from her expressive eye, and heaved a deep-drawn sigh as she reflected on the absence of her lover and the casualties of war.

At half-past twelve the men mustered on the parade-ground, and marched out of the village for Alleman's Drift. Paterson politely requested me to occupy his quarters as long as I remained in Colesberg, and not to spare his cellar, which contained most excellent wine. On the following day, while actively employed in forwarding my affairs, a friend informed me that all my oxen were safely lodged in the skit-kraal, or pound, from which I released them, after a deal of trouble and annoyance, by a small pecuniary disbursement. In the evening the village was agitated by a report that a skirmish had taken place between the Boers and the Bastards, in which several had fallen on both sides, and that it was the intention of the Boers to pillage Colesberg. On the 15th, in company with Messrs. Gibbon and Draper, two merchants of Colesberg, I rode out to visit my friends of the 91st, who were encamped at Alleman's Drift, on the south side of the river. At this spot the Orange River and the surrounding scenery are very beautiful, reminding me of Highland scenery. At one bold sweep of the river the waters are hemmed in by stupendous granite-rocks, which cause a deep and sweeping rapid. Below are long deep pools, enclosed by banks adorned with drooping willows and everlasting verdure.

I found my friends the military employed, according to the most approved system in the army, luxuriating in brandy and cheroots. The privates, availing themselves of the proximity of the river, were enjoying the recreations of angling and dragging the river with nets. They captured lots of mullet and barbel, averaging from one to four pounds in weight.

A party of artillery and a detachment of the 7th Dragoon Guards were reported *en route* from Fort Beaufort, to assist the 91st in their operations against the Boers. Skirmishes were daily occurring between the belligerents on the opposite side, and expresses from Adam Kok were continually arriving in camp, soliciting assistance. The manner in which these skirmishes were conducted was very amusing, and illustrative of the high courage of the contending parties. Every day, having breakfasted, the Boers and Bastards were in the habit of meeting and peppering away at one another till the afternoon, when each party returned to its respective encampment. The distance at which they stood from one another might be somewhere above a couple of miles, and they fired at one another peeping over ranges of coppice or low rocky hills, while large herds of springboks and wildebeests kept quietly pasturing on the goreless field of battle between them.

Some of these neutrals, I was informed, occasionally fell before the hissing balls of the redoubted warriors. Before dismissing the subject of the rebellion of '45, I may state that soon after this, the 91st and Cape Corps men being reinforced with a party of artillery and a detachment of the 7th Dragoon Guards, they crossed the Orange River, and advanced upon the Boers' position by forced marches, when the Boers were charged by the dragoons, and put to flight, and their waggons and commissariat fell into our hands. On this occasion the Boers had two pieces of ordnance, of which they were supposed to have obtained possession some years previously at Port Natal. Over one of these presided a Frenchman of low stature; and while little Monsieur was actively employed in ramming down one of their home-made ball, which were constructed of lead, a Cape Corps man ran up, and sent a bullet through the centre of his skull. Thus ended the memorable battle of Schwart Coppice ; and since that time the valorous Bastards have been loud in their own praises, declaring that "they are the boys to put the Boers up to the time o' day."

On the forenoon of the 16th I rode through the river to visit a gentleman of the name of Bain, who was then living on one of Mr. Fossey's farms. Mr. Bain had made several trips into the interior, and gave me much valuable information and dazzling accounts of the sport I might expect. He recommended my trekking down the Orange River to a drift near Rhama, and thence proceeding by Campbellsdorp to Kuruman, a missionary station, distant from Colesberg about two hundred and fifty miles, where I should obtain a Bechuana interpreter, and all necessary information from the resident missionary. On the following day, having taken leave of my kind friends and brother sportsmen, I rode into Colesberg. Here I had the pleasure of meeting two Nimrods, Messrs. Murray and Oswell, proceeding, like myself, on a hunting expedition into the far interior—the former a keen salmon fisher from the banks of Tay ; the latter a civilian in the Honourable East India Company's service. During my stay in Colesberg I was actively employed storing my collection and refitting. All my specimens were carefully sewn up in canvas, and nailed down in cases ; and perishable articles, such as skins and stuffed heads, were heremetically sealed, being carefully soldered up in tin cases by old Mr. Privet, the tinsmith, one of the leading members of the community of Colesberg.

I covered my waggons with new sails, and had the wheels and ironwork carefully overhauled by the blacksmith. I purchased from various parties several excellent horses and trek-oxen, and increased my kennel of dogs to twelve stout, rough, serviceable-looking curs. From Mr. Williams of the commissariat I purchased a large elephant-gun, carrying four to the pound. I engaged two additional Hottentots, named Johannus and Kleinfeldt, and replenished my supplies in every department ; and on the 22nd, everything being ready, I resolved, if possible, to get under way that afternoon. With inconceivable trouble I managed to collect all my runaway men, dogs, oxen, and horses together ; and, after much bustle and angry altercation with my inebriated and swarthy crew, my caravan was in motion, and started on its distant journey.

We were followed by the female acquaintances of our Hottentots, screaming, yelling, and cursing at their men, at the same time catching up handfuls of red dust, which they tossed into the air with true Hottentot action. Having no hair fortunately to rend, they contented themselves with scratching their woolly pates and rending their petticoats, which they soon reduced to tatters. Among other articles with which I loaded up while in Colesberg was a number of common muskets, which had been represented to me as being the most available to barter for ivory with the tribes of the far interior. These I afterwards turned to good account, and regretted that I did not possess ten times as many of them. As it was not improbable that, in the event of my encamping too near to Colesberg that evening, my followers would avail themselves of the opportunity to levant under cover of night, and return to the embraces of their wives and sweethearts, I made up my mind, having once succeeded in setting them in motion, to give them a good spell of it; and accordingly, there being good moonlight, I did not permit them to outspan until after midnight.

I held a westerly course, steering for the Saltpan's Drift, about four days' journey down the Orange River, where I intended crossing. By adopting this course I avoided the hostile Boers, who were scouring the country across the river immediately opposite to Colesberg.

On the fourth day I reached Saltpan's Drift, which I crossed with considerable difficulty, the waggons repeatedly sticking fast in the deep sand. The opposite bank was extremely steep, and required an hour's cutting with our pickaxes and shovels. We passed the farms of several Boers, from whom I purchased three excellent dogs, named "Wolf," "Prince," and "Bonteberg." On one of these farms were half-a-dozen ostriches, which the Boer endeavoured to persuade me to purchase. Continuing our march, on the 28th we passed through the Griqua kraal named Rhama. In the morning, on proceeding to rouse my men, I discovered Kleinboy very coolly smoking his pipe over my loose, dilapidated powder-casks; upon which I seized the culprit, and handled him rather roughly. This so disgusted my friend that he dashed his pipe on the ground with true Hottentot action, and swore he would go no farther with me. The appearance, however, of a fine fat sheep, which I purchased a few minutes after from a Griqua, induced Mr. Kleinboy to alter his mind on the subject, and he sulkily returned to his duty.

On the 4th of May we made the fair Vaal River, which we crossed at my old drift. Here a party of Korannas rode up to the waggons, mounted on pack-oxen. The bridles consisted of thongs attached to sticks passed through a hole in the animals' noses, and the saddle was a sheepskin secured with a thong across the back. In the evening we trekked half way to Campbellsdorp. On the march my dogs killed two fine porcupines, by tearing off their heads, the only vulnerable part, but getting at the same time their own noses and shoulders full of the quills. On the following day we passed through Campbellsdorp, where I was kindly welcomed by Mr. Bartlett, the resident missionary, from whom I received a liberal present of bread and vegetables.

On the third day after leaving Campbellsdorp we reached Daniel's Kuil, a krall of Griquas under Waterboer. The country through which we passed was level and uninteresting, no hill nor landmark relieving the ocean-like expanse and sameness of the scene in any direction. In parts the country was covered as far as I could see with a species of bush, averaging about nine feet in height, having a grey leaf and bunches of small grey blossoms, yielding a very sweet and powerful aromatic perfume. In the evening we continued our march to Kramer's Fonteyn, a very powerful fountain, whose waters issue hot from the earth, as if they were mixed with boiling water. Leaving Kramer's Fonteyn on the 9th, we held for Koning, a very distant water on the road to Kuruman. Towards midnight my men commenced driving furiously, and I ascertained that they were under the influence of liquor, which I imagined they had obtained from the Griquas. On ordering them to halt and outspan, Mr. Kleinboy only drove the harder, so I found it necessary to send him flying off the box.

A short time after I had been asleep I was wakened by a commotion amongst my cattle, and found that my men had commenced inspanning the oxen, stating that they intended to proceed no farther, but to return with the waggons to the colony. Finding remonstrance vain, I had recourse to my double-barrelled rifle, upon which my followers for the moment relinquished their intention of inspanning, and, retiring to the shelter of a neighbouring bush, they shortly fell asleep. I kept sentry over the waggons during the remainder of the night, with my rifle in my hand and a hatchet by my side. At dawn of day on the following morning I roused my ruffians, and ordered them to inspan, which orders they mechanically obeyed, swearing, however, that this was the last time they would inspan my oxen.

Having proceeded about ten miles, we arrived at Koning: this was a vley of fine spring-water, about six hundred yards in length, densely covered with lofty reeds from twelve to fifteen feet high. This place is said never to be without lions. Here was spoor of zebras and hartebeests. In the afternoon I observed that my men were again in liquor. I had at first imagined that the Griquas had supplied them with brandy, but upon examining my liquor-case I discovered that one had been broken into and two bottles of brandy stolen. This was a second night of anxiety and trouble. I kept watch over my goods and cattle, with my rifle in my hand, till morning. The night was piercingly cold, and in the morning the ground was white with hoar-frost, and a thick coating of ice covered the pools of water. At midday on the 11th we left Koning, and continued our march to Kuruman, halting at sundown without water.

On our left our view was bounded by the Kamhanni Mountains, an extensive rocky chain. In every other direction a vast endless plain extended as far as the eye could strain. The plains were covered with rank yellow grass, interspersed with clumps of grey-leaved bushes. Shortly before outspanning we started three leopards that were consuming a duiker. Throughout all this country game was very scarce.

Since crossing the Vaal, with the exception of feathered game, I had shot only one springbok and one steinbok.

On the following day we reached Kuruman, or New Litakoo, a lovely green spot in the wilderness, strongly contrasting with the sterile and inhospitable regions by which it is surrounded. I was here kindly welcomed and hospitably entertained by Mr. Moffat and Mr. Hamilton, both missionaries of the London Society, and also by Mr. Hume, an old trader, long resident at Kuruman. The gardens at Kuruman are extensive and extremely fertile. Besides corn and vegetables they contained a great variety of fruits, amongst which were vines, peach-trees, nectarines, apple, orange, and lemon trees, all of which in their seasons bear a profusion of the most delicious fruit. These gardens are irrigated with the most liberal supply of water from a powerful fountain which gushes forth, at once forming a little river, from a subterraneous cave, which has several low narrow mouths, but within is lofty and extensive. This cave is stated by the natives to extend to a very great distance under ground.

The natives about Kuruman and the surrounding districts generally embrace the Christian religion. Mr. Moffat kindly showed me through his printing establishment, church, and school-rooms, which were lofty and well built, and altogether on a scale which would not have disgraced one of the towns of the more enlightened colony. It was Mr. Moffat who reduced the Bechuana language to writing and printing; since which he has printed thousands of Sichuana Testaments, as also tracts and hymns, which were now eagerly purchased by the converted natives. Mr. Moffat is a person admirably calculated to excel in his important calling. Together with a noble and athletic frame, he possesses a face on which forbearance and Christian charity are very plainly written, and his mental and bodily attainments are great. Minister, gardener, blacksmith, gunsmith, mason, carpenter, glazier—every hour of the day finds this worthy pastor engaged in some useful employment—setting, by his own exemplary piety and industrious habits, a good example to others to go and do likewise.

Mr. Moffat informed me that a missionary named Dr. Livingstone, who was married to his eldest daughter, had lately established a missionary station among the Bakatlas at Mabotsa, in the vale of Bakatla, about fourteen days' journey to the north-east. Thither he recommended me at once to proceed, as few of the larger varieties of game could now be expected to be found to the southward of Bakatla. He represented to me that my falling in with elephants, even throughout the vast forests in the country immediately beyond Bakatla, was very uncertain, and recommended me, if I was determined to have good elephant-shooting, to endeavour to push on to the remote and endless forests beyond the mountains of Bamangwato, in the territory of Sicomy, the great and paramount chief of the extensive country of the Bamangwato. There would also be a probability of obtaining ivory in barter from Sicomy, he being reported to possess large quantities of that valuable commodity. By Mr. Moffat's assistance I engaged a Bechuana in the capacity of interpreter in the Dutch and Sichuana languages. From Mr. Hume

I purchased a supply of wheat, and on the following day I set all my people to work on a mill of Mr. Moffat's to reduce this wheat to flour.

On the 15th I took leave of my friends at Kuruman, and continued my journey in a north-easterly course through a heavy sandy country of boundless level plains, stretching away on every side, covered with rank yellow grass, which, waving in the breeze, imparted the idea of endless fields of ripe corn. At sundown we crossed the Matluarin river, an insignificant stream, and encamped on its northern bank. On the march we saw a few blue wildebeests and ostriches. At dawn of day on the following morning we pursued our journey through the same description of country, varied however with detached clumps of thorny mimosas. On the march we crossed a swarm of locusts, resting for the night on the grass and bushes. They lay so thick that the waggons could have been filled with them in a very short time, covering the large bushes just as a swarm of young bees covers the branch on which it pitches. Locusts afford fattening and wholesome food to man, birds, and all sorts of beasts; cows and horses, lions, jackals, hyænas, antelopes, elephants, etc., devour them. We met a party of Batlapis carrying heavy burdens of them on their backs. Our hungry dogs made a fine feast on them. The cold frosty night had rendered them unable to take wing until the sun should restore their powers. As it was difficult to obtain sufficient food for my dogs, I and Isaac took a large blanket, which we spread under a bush, whose branches were bent to the ground with the mass of locusts which covered it; and having shaken the branches, in an instant I had more locusts than I could carry on my back: these we roasted for ourselves and dogs.

Soon after the sun was up, on looking behind me, I beheld the locusts stretching to the west in vast clouds, resembling smoke; but the wind, soon after veering round, brought them back to us, and they flew over our heads, for some time actually darkening the sun. In the evening I continued my march by moonlight, and halted within a few miles of Motito, an extensive kraal of the Batlapis, a tribe of Bechuanas. The nights were piercing cold, the grass being every morning covered with white frost.

CHAPTER XI.

Motito—The Bechuana Tribes—The mysterious great inland Lake—Blesbok and Wildebeest abundant—Park-like Country—We arrive at the beautiful Vale of Bakatla—Dr. Livingstone the Missionary—Native Fashions at Church—Determine to push on to Bamangwato—The Natives follow me for Venison—Great Variety of Game—A dangerous Fight with a herd of Buffaloes, two of which are slain—A Colony of Baboons—A Rhinoceros chases me round a Bush—Habits of the Beast—A noble Eland killed—An impromptu Steak—Slay a Rhinoceros, and lose my way in the Forest.

At an early hour on the 17th I outspanned at Motito, where I was kindly received by Monsieur Loga and Mr. Edwards, the former a French missionary stationed at Motito, and the latter an English missionary from Mabotza. Another French missionary, named Monsieur Lemue, belonging to the station, was absent. The women at Motito wear heavier ornaments of beads than any with whom I am acquainted. As I have now reached the southern borders of that vast tract of Southern Africa inhabited by the numerous tribes of the Bechuanas, it will be necessary, before proceeding further, to give a sketch of their manners and customs.

They are a lively and intelligent race of people, and remarkable for their good humour : they are well formed, if not starved in infancy. They possess pleasing features and very fine eyes and teeth; their hair is short and woolly; the colour of their complexion is of a light copper. The various tribes live in kraals, or villages, of various sizes, along with their respective chiefs. Their wigwams are built in a circular form, and thatched with long grass; the floor and wall, inside and out, are plastered with a compound of clay and cow-dung. The entrances are about three feet high and two feet broad. Each wigwam is surrounded with a hedge of wickerwork, while one grand hedge of wait-a-bit thorns surrounds the entire kraal, protecting the inmates from lions and other animals.

The dress of the men consists of a kaross, or skin cloak, which hangs gracefully from their shoulders; and another garment, termed tsecha, which encircles their loins, and is likewise made of skin. On their feet they wear a simple sandal formed of the skin of the buffalo or camelopard. On their legs and arms they carry ornaments of brass and copper of different patterns, which are manufactured by themselves. The men also wear a few ornaments of beads round their necks and on their arms. Around their necks, besides beads, they carry a variety of other appendages, the majority of which are believed to possess a powerful charm to preserve them from evil. One of these is a small hollow bone, through which they blow when in peril; another is a set of dice formed of ivory, which they rattle in their hands and cast on the ground to ascertain if they are to be lucky in any enterprise in which they may be about to engage; also a host of bits of root and bark which are medicinal. From their necks also depend gourd snuff-boxes made of an extremely diminutive species of pumpkin, trained to grow in a bottle-like shape.

They never move without their arms, which consist of a shield, a bundle of assagais, a battle-axe, and a knobkerry. The shields are formed of the hide of the buffalo or camelopard; their shape among some tribes is oval, among others round. The assagai is a sort of light spear or javelin, having a wooden shaft about six feet in length attached to it. Some of these are formed solely for throwing, and a skilful warrior will send one through a man's body at one hundred yards. Another variety of assagai is formed solely for stabbing. The blades of these are stouter, and the shafts shorter and thicker, than the other variety. They are found mostly among the tribes very far in the interior. Their battle-axes are elegantly formed, consisting of a triangular-shaped blade, fastened in a handle formed of the horn of the rhinoceros. The men employ their time in war and hunting, and in dressing the skins of wild animals. The dress of the women consists of a kaross depending from the shoulders, and a short kilt formed of the skin of the pallah, or some other antelope. Around their necks, arms, waists, and ankles they wear large and cumbrous coils of beads of a variety of colours, tastefully arranged in different patterns.

The women chiefly employ their time in cultivating their fields and gardens, in which they rear corn, pumpkins, and water-melons; and likewise in harvesting their crops and grinding their corn. Both men and women go bareheaded: they anoint their heads with "sibelo," a shining composition, being a mixture of fat and a grey sparkling ore, having the appearance of mica. Some of the tribes besmear their bodies with a mixture of fat and red clay, imparting to them the appearance of Red Indians. Most of the tribes possess cattle; these are attended to and milked solely by the men, a woman being never allowed to set foot within the cattle-kraal. Polygamy is allowed, and any man may keep as many wives as he pleases: the wife, however, has in the first instance to be purchased.

Among tribes possessed of cattle the price of a wife is ten head of cattle; but among the poorer tribes a wife may be obtained for a few spades with which they cultivate their fields. These spades, which are manufactured by themselves, are fastened in the end of a long shaft, and are used as our labourers use the hoe. Rows of women may be seen digging together in the fields singing songs, to which they keep time with their spades.

The name of the chief at Motito was Motchuara, a subordinate of the great chief Mahura. He was very anxious that I should remain a day with him, for the purpose of trading in ostrich-feathers and karosses; but being anxious to push forward, I resumed my march in the afternoon, and trekked on till near midnight, when I encamped in an extensive forest of grey and ancient-looking cameeldorn trees. These were the finest I had yet seen in Africa, each tree assuming a wide-spreading and picturesque appearance. They were detached and in groups, like oaks in an English deer-park. Many of them were inhabited by whole colonies of the social grosbeak, a bird with whose wonderful habitations the branches were loaded. These remarkable birds, which are about the size and appearance of the British greenfinch, construct their nests and live socially together under one common roof, the whole fabric being formed of dry grass, and exhibiting at a short distance the appearance of a haycock stuck up in the tree. The entrances to the nests are from beneath. They are built side by side, and when seen from below resemble a honeycomb.

At dawn of day on the following morning we continued our march through the venerable cameel-dorn forest. The road was extremely heavy, consisting of soft loose sand. Having proceeded about six miles, emerging from the forest, we entered once more on a wide-spreading open country, covered in some parts with bushes, and in others only with grass. Another hour brought us to Little Chooi, a large saltpan, where we obtained water for ourselves and cattle from a deep pit made by men. In sight were a few zebras, ostriches, and springboks.

In the forenoon a number of cattle, belonging to Mahura, came to drink at the pit. Some of these carried enormous wide-spreading horns. Mahura and his tribe possess immense herds of cattle, the majority of which they "lifted" or obtained in war from other Bechuana tribes.

Some years before this, Mahura, assisted by another tribe, had attacked Sobiqua, king of the Bawangketse, a tribe inhabiting the borders of the great Kalahari desert, whom they routed, and succeeded in driving off the majority of their vast herds. Upon this, Sobiqua and his tribe fled with the remainder of the cattle across a portion of the desert to the westward, and for some years located themselves on the borders of a vast inland lake. This mysterious lake the natives in the vale of Bakatla state to be situated due west from their position; while the natives of Bamangwato, situated two hundred and fifty miles to the northward, always pointed out to me the north-west as its position. They represented to me that the natives on its banks were possessed of canoes; that its waters were salt; and that every day the waters retired to feed, and again returned, by which I understood that this lake, whatever it may be, is affected by some tide.

At three P.M. we inspanned, and held on till midnight with fine moonlight, crossing a desert and sandy country. In the vicinity of Chooi we passed an extensive range of old pitfalls, formed by the natives for entrapping game. They were dug in the form of a crescent, and occupied an extent of nearly a quarter of a mile. On the march I observed some enormous trunks of trees that had been destroyed by fire in bygone years. On the following day we reached Loharon, an uninteresting and desolate spot, where we encamped for the day beside a pool of rainwater. Here I observed a few hartebeests, sassaybys, and zebras. On the 20th, having breakfasted, we inspanned, and continued our march till sunset. We passed through a very level country, covered with detached bushes. The dulness of the scene, however, was enlivened by a wondrous flight of locusts, the largest I had ever beheld. The prospect was obscured by them as far as we could see, resembling the smoke arising from a thousand giant bonfires; while those above our heads darkened our path with a double flight—the one next the ground flying north, while the upper clouds of them held a southerly course. The dogs, as usual, made a hearty meal on them.

We continued our march by moonlight, halting at midnight in a vast open plain beside a small pool of rain-water. After breakfast I rode forth in quest of springboks, of which I bagged a couple. I fell in with blue and black wildebeests, zebras, ostriches, and blesboks. The plains here were bare and open, resembling the country frequented by the blesboks to the southward of the Vaal, with which country I subsequently ascertained it to be connected, in a due southerly course, by an endless succession of similar bare plains, throughout the entire extent of which the blesbok and black wildebeest are abundant. While galloping after a herd of zebras, "The Immense Brute" put his foot into a hole, and came down with great violence on his head, pitching me over his bows. I saved my rifle at the risk of sacrificing my collar-bone; and would have escaped without further injury than the loss of a portion of the bark of my cheek, had not my horse described a somersault, coming down with the broad of his back on the calf of my right leg, and bruising it so severely as to incapacitate me from walking for several days.

About midday we resumed our march, and in the evening we reached Great Chooi, a very large saltpan at present full of water. Here I found, for the first time, the bones and skull of a rhinoceros long killed. My interpreter informed me that the rhinoceros had long left that country; to his surprise, however, we discovered fresh spoor by the fountain. Continuing our march, on the 22nd we entered on a new description of country: boundless open plains being succeeded by endless forests of dwarfish trees and bushes, the ground slightly undulating, and covered with a variety of rich grasses and aromatic herbs. The old and seldom-trodden waggon-track which we followed seemed a favourite footpath for a troop of lions, their large and heavy spoor being deeply imprinted in our path. At sundown we encamped on the Siklagole River, a periodical stream, in the gravelly bed of which fine spring-water could be obtained by digging. As we were in great want of flesh, my hungry pack being nearly starving, I resolved to rest my oxen on the following day, and hunt for eland, the spoor of several of which we discovered beside our encampment.

On the morning of the 23rd I rode east with after-riders and a pack-horse. The country through which we passed resembled a vast interminable park, being adorned with a continued succession of picturesque dwarfish forest-trees single and in groups. Such, with the exception of a few grassy open plains, is the character of the country from Siklagolé, as far as the mountains of Bakatla. We failed to fall in with elands, but I succeeded in bringing down two zebras and a hartebeest, which, along with sassaybys, oryx, and ostriches, now became daily more abundant. On the 31st we reached the Kurrichane mountain range. Having crossed these, we proceeded up a valley about three miles, when we reached a gorge in the mountains which connected this fine valley with the great strath or vale of Bakatla. Through this gorge ran a stream of the purest crystal water. Our road lay along the margin of this stream, across large masses of stone and ledges of rock, which threatened every moment the destruction of our waggons.

Following the stream for half a mile, we arrived at Mabotza, the kraal of Mosielely, king of the Bakatlas, a tribe of Bechuanas. Here I was kindly received by Dr. Livingstone, the resident missionary. The vale of Bakatla, which I had now reached, is one of the most beautiful spots in Africa. It is a broad and level strath extending from east to west, and bounded by picturesque rocky mountains, beautifully wooded to their summits. In parts the strath is adorned with groves and patches of beautiful forest-trees of endless variety; in others it is open, carpeted with a goodly coating of luxuriant grass. A large portion of the valley, opposite to the town, is cultivated by the Bakatla women, and a succession of extensive corn-fields stretched away to the northward of the kraal. These had lately been denuded of their crops, but a goodly show of pumpkins and water-melons still remained on the fields. The following day was Sunday, and I attended Divine service in a temporary place of worship that had been erected by the missionaries. It was amusing to remark, in the costume of the Bakatlas on this occasion, the progress of the march of civilization. All those who had managed to get hold of some European article of dress had donned it, some appearing in trousers without shirts, and others in shirts without trousers.

The 2nd of June was the coldest day I had experienced in Africa, a cutting cold wind blowing off the Southern Ocean. On the morning of the 2nd I was waited upon by Mosielely, attended by a number of his nobility and others of the tribe, who flocked around my waggons importunately requesting snuff. The appearance of the chief was mild, but not dignified. One of his generals, with whom he seemed to be on very intimate terms, was a jolly-looking old warrior with a wall eye, and a face strongly marked with the small-pox. This man's name was "Siemi." He had killed about twenty men in battle with his own hand, and bore a mark of honour for every man. This mark was a line tattooed on his ribs. Mosielely presented me with a bag of sour milk, and requested that I would tarry with him for a few days for the purpose of trading.

I informed him that I was now anxious to push on to the country of the elephants, but would trade with him on my return. This intimation seemed very much to disappoint the king, who was anxious to exchange karosses for guns and ammunition. But I had resolved to part with my muskets solely for ivory, which article Mosielely on this particular occasion did not possess. The Bakatlas work a great deal in iron, manufacturing various articles, with which they supply the neighbouring tribes. They obtain their iron from ore, which they procure by excavating in the surrounding mountains. This ore is smelted in crucibles, a great deal of the metal being wasted, and only the best and purest being preserved. They use a sort of double bellows, consisting of two bags of skin, by which the air is forced through the long tapering tubes of the two horns of the oryx. The person using the bellows squats between the two bags, which he raises and depresses alternately, working one with each hand. Their hammer and anvil consists of two stones. They nevertheless contrive to turn very neat workmanship out of their hands, such as spears, battle-axes, assagais, knives, sewing-needles, etc. The men of this tribe also manufacture large wooden bowls, which they cut out of the solid piece, the tool they use for this purpose being a small implement shaped like an adze.

Dr. Livingstone informed me that large game was abundant on all sides to the northward of Bakatla. He stated that herds of elephants occasionally visited the territories of the adjoining chiefs, sometimes frequenting a district for half a summer; but that, at present he was not aware of any elephants in the forests adjacent to Bakatla. He represented the distant and unexplored forests beyond Bamangwato, the territory of Sicomy, as being allowed by the natives to be the country where elephants were at all times abundant. There was also a prospect of obtaining their ivory in barter for my muskets. I accordingly resolved, in the first instance, to direct my attention mainly to elephants, and not to tarry in any district, however favourable, for the purpose of hunting other varieties of game.

Dr. Livingstone stated that I should experience considerable difficulty in reaching Bamangwato, since there was no path nor track of any description to guide me thither. My only chance of getting there seemed to depend on being able to obtain Bechuana guides from Caachy, a subordinate chief of a branch of the "Baquaina" tribe, then resident at a place called "Booby," situated about eighty miles to the north-west of Bakatla. Without these guides it would be almost impossible to proceed, as the waters were few and very far between. The probability, however, was that these guides would be refused, since it is the invariable policy of African chiefs to prevent all travellers from penetrating beyond themselves.

Bamandwato is distant upwards of two hundred miles to the northward of Bakatla, from which it is separated by rugged and apparently impassable mountain ranges, extensive sandy deserts, which are destitute of water, and vast and trackless forests. Isaac, my interpreter, already began to lose heart, and raised a thousand objections to my proceeding to so distant a country. He recommended my rather hunting in the territory of "Sichely," the paramount chief of the Baquaines, situated about fifty miles to the north of Bakatla, where he assured me we should find elephants. Perceiving that his remonstrances did not avail, and that I was inexorable, he proposed resigning his commission, and was with difficulty prevailed on by Dr. Livingstone to agree to accompany me farther.

On the 3rd I took leave of my kind friend Dr. Livingstone, and started for Bamangwato. I was accompanied by a large party of the Bakatla men and two Baquaines. They followed me in the hope of obtaining flesh, a report having spread through the tribe that I was a successful hunter. The Bechuanas are extremely fond of flesh, which they consider the only food befitting men. Corn and milk they reckon the food of women. Having no flesh at home, and being seldom able to kill large game for themselves, they entertain great respect for those who kill plenty of venison for them, and they will travel to very great distances for the purpose of obtaining it. We proceeded in a westerly course, and held up the lovely valley of Bakatla, through open glades and patches of ancient forests.

I had ridden only a short distance across the valley when I fell in with a troop of blue wildebeests, one of which I wounded and immediately lost in rocky ground. I then rode on, and crossed a ridge of stony hills covered with thick jungle, after which I entered upon another grassy and well-wooded valley. Presently I observed seven majestic buck koodoos standing on the mountain side high above me. In trying to stalk these I disturbed a troop of graceful pallahs and a herd of zebras, which clattered along the mountain, and spoiled my stalk with the koodoos. I now observed a large herd of buffaloes reclining under a clump of mimosa-trees a little farther up the valley. Descending from my position, I secured my horse to a tree, and proceeded to stalk in on the buffaloes. While I was doing this, a herd of zebras, which I had not observed, got my wind and came cantering through the cover within a few yards of me. When I reached the spot where I had seen the buffaloes they were gone; having followed up the spoor, however, for a short distance, I overtook them; when I shot the patriarch of the herd, which, as usual, brought up the rear.

Early on the 4th we inspanned and continued our march for Booby, a large party of savages still following the waggons. Before proceeding far I was tempted by the beautiful appearance of the country to saddle horses to hunt in the mountains westward of my course. I directed the waggons to proceed a few miles under guidance of the natives, and there await my arrival. I was accompanied by Isaac, who was mounted on the Old Grey, and carried my clumsy Dutch rifle of six to the pound. Two Bechuanas followed us, leading four of my dogs. Having crossed a well-wooded strath, we reached a little crystal river, whose margin was trampled down with the spoor of a great variety of heavy game, but especially of buffalo and rhinoceros. We took up the spoor of a troop of buffaloes, which we followed along a path made by the heavy beasts of the forest through a neck in the hills; and emerging from the thicket, we beheld, on the other side of a valley which had opened upon us, a herd of about ten huge bull buffaloes. These I attempted to stalk, but was defeated by a large herd of zebras, which, getting our wind, charged past and startled the buffaloes. I ordered the Bechuanas to release the dogs; and spurring Colesberg, which I rode for the first time since the affair with the lioness, I gave chase. The buffaloes crossed the valley in front of me, and made for the succession of dense thickets in the hills to the northward.

As they crossed the valley, by riding hard I obtained a broadside shot at the last bull, and fired both barrels into him. He, however, continued his course, but I presently separated him, along with two other bulls, from the troop. My rifle being a two-grooved, which is hard to load, I was unable to do so on horseback, and followed with it empty, in the hope of bringing them to bay. In passing through a grove of thorny trees I lost sight of the wounded buffalo; he had turned short and doubled back, a common practice with them when wounded. After following the other two at a hard gallop for about two miles, I was riding within five yards of their huge broad sterns. They exhaled a strong bovine smell, which came hot in my face. I expected every minute that they would come to bay, and give me time to load; but this they did not seem disposed to do. At length, finding I had the speed of them, I increased my pace; and going ahead, I placed myself right before the finest bull, thus expecting to force him to stand at bay; upon which he instantly charged me with a low roar, very similar to the voice of a lion. Colesberg neatly avoided the charge, and the bull resumed his northward course.

We now entered on rocky ground, and the forest became more dense as we proceeded. The buffaloes were evidently making for some strong retreat. I, however, managed with much difficulty to hold them in view, following as best I could through thorny thickets. Isaac rode some hundred yards behind, and kept shouting to me to drop the pursuit, or I should be killed. At last the buffaloes suddenly pulled up, and stood at bay in a thicket within twenty yards of me. Springing from my horse, I hastily loaded my two-grooved rifle, which I had scarcely completed when Isaac rode up and inquired what had become of the buffaloes, little dreaming that they were standing within twenty yards of him. I answered by pointing my rifle across his horse's nose, and letting fly sharp right and left at the two buffaloes.

A headlong charge accompanied by a muffled roar was the result. In an instant I was round a clump of tangled thorn-trees; but Isaac, by the violence of his efforts to get his horse in motion, lost his balance, his saddle, and big Dutch rifle, all came to the ground together, with a heavy crash, right in the path of the infuriated buffaloes. Two of the dogs, which had fortunately that moment joined us, met them in their charge, and, by diverting their attention, probably saved Isaac from instant destruction. The buffaloes now took up another position in an adjoining thicket. They were both badly wounded, blotches and pools of blood marking the ground where they had stood. The dogs rendered me assistance by taking up their attention, and in a few minutes these two noble bulls breathed their last beneath the shade of a mimosa grove. Each of them in dying repeatedly uttered a very striking, low, deep moan. This I subsequently ascertained the buffalo invariably utters when in the act of expiring.

On going up to them I was astonished to behold their size and powerful appearance. Their horns reminded me of the rugged trunk of an oak-tree. Each horn was upwards of a foot in breadth at the base, and together they effectually protected the skull with a massive and impenetrable shield. The horns, descending, and spreading out horizontally, completely overshadowed the animal's eyes, imparting to him a look the most ferocious and sinister that can be imagined. On my way to the waggons I shot a stag sassayby, and while I was engaged in removing his head a troop of about thirty doe pallahs cantered past me, followed by one princely old buck. Snatching up my rifle, I made a fine shot, and rolled him over in the grass.

Early in the afternoon I despatched men with a packhorse to bring the finer of the two buffalo-heads. It was so ponderous that two powerful men could with difficulty raise it from the ground. The Bechuanas who had accompanied me, on hearing of my success, snatched up their shields and assagais, and hastened to secure the flesh, nor did I see any more of them, with the exception of the two Baquaines, who remained with me, being engaged in a plot with my interpreter to prevent my penetrating to Bamangwato. Isaac did not soon forget his adventure with the buffaloes; and at night over the fire he informed my men that I was mad, and that any man who followed me was going headlong to his own destruction. At an early hour on the 5th I continued my march through a glorious country of hill and dale, throughout which water was abundant.

Beautifully wooded hills and mountains stretched away on every side; some of the mountains were particularly grand and majestic, their summits being surrounded by steep precipices and abrupt parapets of rock, the abodes of whole colonies of black-faced baboons, which, astonished to behold such novel intruders upon their domains, leisurely descended the craggy mountain sides for a nearer inspection of our caravan. Seating themselves together upon a broad ledge, they seemed to hold a council as to the propriety of permitting us to proceed farther through their territories. Having advanced about nine miles, I drew up my waggons on the bank of a rivulet, where the spoor of large game was extremely abundant. In the bed of the stream I discovered the scaly skin of a manis, which had been newly eaten by some bird of prey. This extraordinary animal, which in its habits partakes of the nature of the hedgehog, is about three feet in length, and is covered all over with an impenetrable coat of mail, consisting of large rough scales about the size and shape of the husk of an artichoke; these overlap one another in an extraordinary and very beautiful manner. Its tail is broad, and likewise covered with scales; on being disturbed it rolls itself into a ball: the manis is met with throughout the interior of South Africa, but it is rare, and very seldom seen.

Of the rhinoceros there are four varieties in South Africa, distinguished by the Bechuanas by the names of the borèlé or black rhinoceros, the keitloa or two-horned black rhinoceros, the muchocho or common white rhinoceros, and the kobaoba or long-horned white rhinoceros. Both varieties of the black rhinoceros are extremely fierce and dangerous, and rush headlong and unprovoked at any object which attracts their attention. They never attain much fat, and their flesh is tough, and not much esteemed by the Bechuanas. Their food consists almost entirely of the thorny branches of the wait-a-bit thorns. Their horns are much shorter than those of the other varieties, seldom exceeding eighteen inches in length. They are finely polished with constant rubbing against the trees. The skull is remarkably formed, its most striking feature being the tremendous thick ossification in which it ends above the nostrils. It is on this mass that the horn is supported. The horns are not connected with the skull, being attached merely by the skin, and they may thus be separated from the head by means of a sharp knife. They are hard and perfectly solid throughout, and are a fine material for various articles, such as drinking cups, mallets for rifles, handles for turner's tools, etc., etc. The horn is capable of a very high polish. The eyes of the rhinoceros are small and sparkling, and do not readily observe the hunter, provided he keep to leeward of them. The skin is extremely thick, and only to be penetrated by bullets hardened with solder.

During the day the rhinoceros will be found lying asleep or standing indolently in some retired part of the forest, or under the base of the mountains, sheltered from the power of the sun by some friendly grove of umbrella-topped mimosas. In the evening they commence their nightly ramble, and wander over a great extent of country. They usually visit the fountains between the hours of nine and twelve o'clock at night, and it is on these occasions that they may be most successfully hunted, and with the least danger. The black rhinoceros is subject to paroxysms of unprovoked fury, often ploughing up the ground for several yards with its horn, and assaulting large bushes in the most violent manner. On these bushes they work for hours with their horns, at the same time snorting and blowing loudly, nor do they leave them in general until they have broken them into pieces. The rhinoceros is supposed by many, and by myself among the rest, to be the animal alluded to by Job, chap. xxxix. verses 10 and 11, where it is written, "Canst thou bind the unicorn with his band in the furrow? or will he harrow the valleys after thee? Wilt thou trust him because his strength is great? or wilt thou leave thy labour to him?" evidently alluding to an animal possessed of great strength and of untameable disposition, for both of which the rhinoceros is remarkable.

All the four varieties delight to roll and wallow in mud, with which their rugged hides are generally encrusted. Both varieties of the black rhinoceros are much smaller and more active than the white, and are so swift that a horse with a rider on his back can rarely overtake them. The two varieties of the white rhinoceros are so similar in habits, that the description of one will serve for both; the principal difference consisting in the length and set of the anterior horn; that of the muchocho averaging from two to three feet in length, and pointing backwards; while the horn of the kobaoba often exceeds four feet in length, and inclines forward from the nose at an angle of 45°. The posterior horn of either species seldom exceeds six or seven inches in length. The kobaoba is the rarer of the two, and it is found very far in the interior, chiefly to the eastward of the Limpopo. Its horns are very valuable for loading rods, supplying a substance at once suitable for a sporting implement and excellent for the purpose. Both these varieties of rhinoceros attain an enormous size, being the animals next in magnitude to the elephant. They feed solely on grass, carry much fat, and their flesh is excellent, being preferable to beef. They are of a much milder and more inoffensive disposition than the black rhinoceros, rarely charging their pursuer. Their speed is very inferior to that of the other varieties, and a person well mounted can overtake and shoot them. The head of these is a foot longer than that of the borèlé. They generally carry their heads low, whereas the borèlé, when disturbed, carries his very high, which imparts to him a saucy and independent air. Unlike the elephants, they never associate in herds, but are met with singly or in pairs. In districts where they are abundant, from three to six may be found in company, and I once saw upwards of a dozen congregated together on some young grass, but such an occurrence is rare.

It was on the 4th of June that I beheld for the first time the rhinoceros. Having taken some coffee, I rode out unattended, with my rifle, and before proceeding far I fell in with a huge white rhinoceros, with a large calf, standing in a thorny grove. Getting my wind, she set off at top speed through thick thorny bushes, the calf, as is invariably the case, taking the lead, and the mother guiding its course by placing her horn, generally about three feet in length, against its ribs. My horse shied very much at first, alarmed at the strange appearance of "Chukuroo," but by a sharp application of spur and jambok I prevailed upon him to follow, and presently, the ground improving, I got alongside, and, firing at a gallop, sent a bullet through her shoulder. She continued her pace with blood streaming from the wound, and very soon reached an impracticable thorny jungle, where I could not follow, and instantly lost her. In half an hour I fell in with a second rhinoceros, being an old bull of the white variety. Dismounting, I crept within twenty yards, and saluted him with both barrels in the shoulder, upon which he made off, uttering a loud blowing noise, and upsetting everything that obstructed his progress.

Shortly after this I found myself on the banks of the stream beside which my waggons were outspanned. Following along its margin, I presently beheld a bull of the borèlé, or black rhinoceros, standing within a hundred yards of me. Dismounting from my horse I secured him to a tree, and then stalked within twenty yards of the huge beast under cover of a large strong bush. Borèlé, hearing me advance, came on to see what it was, and suddenly protruded his horny nose within twenty yards of me. Knowing well that a front shot would not prove deadly, I sprang to my feet and ran behind the bush. Upon this the villain charged, blowing loudly, and chased me round the bush. Had his activity been equal to his ugliness, my wanderings would have terminated here, but by my superior agility I had the advantage in the turn. After standing a short time eyeing me through the bush, he got a whiff of my wind, which at once alarmed him. Uttering a blowing noise, and erecting his insignificant yet saucy-looking tail, he wheeled about, leaving me master of the field, when I sent a bullet through his ribs to teach him manners.

Finding that rhinoceroses were abundant in the vicinity, I resolved to halt a day for the purpose of hunting, and after an early breakfast on the 6th I rode south-east with the two Baquaines. They led me along the bases of the mountains, through woody dells and open glades, and we eventually reached a grand forest grey with age. Here we found abundance of spoor of a variety of game, and started several herds of the more common varieties. At length I observed an old bull eland standing under a tree. He was the first that I had seen, and was a noble specimen, standing about six feet high at the shoulder. Observing us, he made off at a gallop, springing over the trunks of decayed trees which lay across his path; but very soon he reduced his pace to a trot. Spurring my horse, another moment saw me riding hard behind him. Twice in the thickets I lost sight of him, and he very nearly escaped me; but at length, the ground improving, I came up with him, and rode within a few yards behind him.

Long streaks of foam now streamed from his mouth, and a profuse perspiration had changed his sleek grey coat to an ashy blue. Tears trickled from his large dark eye, and it was plain that the eland's hours were numbered. Pitching my rifle to my shoulder, I let fly at the gallop, and mortally wounded him behind; then spurring my horse, I shot past him on his right side, and discharged my other barrel behind his shoulder, when the eland staggered for a moment and subsided in the dust. The two Baquaines soon made their appearance, and seemed delighted at my success. Having kindled a fire, they cut out steaks, which they roasted on the embers: I also cooked a steak for myself, spitting it upon a forked branch, the other end of which I sharpened with my knife and stuck into the ground.

This magnificent animal is by far the largest of all the antelope tribe, exceeding a large ox in size. It also attains an extraordinary condition, being often burthened with a very large amount of fat. Its flesh is most excellent, and is justly esteemed above all others. It has a peculiar sweetness, and is tender and fit for use the moment the animal is killed. Like the gemsbok, the eland is independent of water, and frequents the borders of the great Kalahari desert in herds varying from ten to a hundred. It is also generally diffused throughout all the wooded districts of the interior where I have hunted. Like other varieties of deer and antelope, the old males may often be found consorting together apart from the females, and a troop of these, when in full condition, may be likened to a herd of stall-fed oxen. The eland has less speed than any other variety of antelope; and, by judicious riding, they may be driven to camp from a great distance. In this manner I have often ridden the best bull out of the herd, and brought him within gunshot of my waggons, where I could more conveniently cut up and preserve the flesh, without the trouble of sending men and pack-oxen to fetch it. I have repeatedly seen an eland drop down dead at the end of a severe chase, owing to his plethoric habit. The skin of the eland I had just shot emitted, like most other antelopes, the most delicious perfume of trees and grass.

Having eaten my steak, I rode to my waggons, where I partook of coffee, and having mounted a fresh horse I again set forth, accompanied by Carollus leading a packhorse, to bring home the head of the eland and a supply of the flesh: I took all my dogs along with me to share in the banquet. We had not proceeded far when the dogs went ahead on some scent. Spurring my horse, I followed through the thorny bushes as best I might, and emerging on an open glade, I beheld two huge white rhinoceroses trotting along before me. The dogs attacked them with fury, and a scene of intense excitement ensued. The Old Grey, on observing them, pricked up his ears and seemed only half inclined to follow, but a sharp application of the spur reminded him of his duty, and I was presently riding within ten yards of the stern of the largest, and sent a bullet through her back.

The Old Grey shied considerably and became very unmanageable, and on one occasion, in consequence, the rhinoceros, finding herself hemmed in by a bend in a watercourse, turned round to charge: I had a very narrow escape. Presently, galloping up on one side, I gave her a bad wound in the shoulder, soon after which she came to bay in the dry bed of a river. Dismounting from my horse, I commenced loading, but before this was accomplished she was off once more. I followed her, putting on my caps as I rode, and coming up alongside I made a fine shot from the saddle, firing at the gallop. The ball entered somewhere near her heart. On receiving this shot she reeled about, while torrents of blood streamed from her mouth and wounds, and presently she rolled over and expired, uttering a shrill screaming sound as she died, which rhinoceroses invariably do while in the agonies of death.

The chase had led me close in along the northern base of a lofty detached mountain, the highest in all that country. This mountain is called by the Bechuanas the Mountain of the Eagles. The eland which I had shot in the morning lay somewhere to the southward of this mountain, but far in the level forest. Having rounded the mountain, I began to recognise the ground, and presently I had the satisfaction to behold a few vultures soaring over the forest in advance, and, on proceeding a short distance farther, large groups of these birds were seated on the grey and weather-beaten branches of the loftiest old trees of the forest. This was a certain sign that the eland was not far distant; and on raising my voice and loudly calling on the name of Carollus, I was instantly answered by that individual, who, heedless of his master's fate, was actively employed in cooking for himself a choice steak from the dainty rump of the eland. That night I slept beneath the blue and starry canopy of heaven. My sleep was light and sweet, and no rude dreams or hankering cares disturbed the equanimity of my repose.

CHAPTER XII.

My Hottentots object to advance farther into the Interior—A Boar Hunt—We march through a charming Country—The Mountain Pass of Sesetabie—A Lion and Lioness inspect my Cattle, and the Lion pays for peeping—Hungry Hyænas sup upon the Cattle Furniture—The Camelopard—Description of its Habits—Booby, a Bechuana Kraal—Gun Medicine—Disastrous Finale to an Incantation—Native Conspiracy to prevent my farther Progress.

At an early hour on the 7th we arose, and, having loaded the pack-horse with a burden of flesh and fat, I despatched one of the Baquaines with him to camp. Carollus and I then rode for the rhinoceros to secure the horn. On nearing the carcase, a noble bull-buffalo stood within thirty yards of me, but I had omitted to put on my caps. Lions had consumed a large part of the rhinoceros, and had sneaked off on hearing us approach, leaving, as is usual, matted locks from their shaggy grey manes sticking on the broken points of the projecting ribs. My dogs on scenting them ran barking angrily in the direction which the lions had held, springing up into the air with their hair bristling along their backs. With considerable difficulty we separated the horn of the muchocho from the skin by means of a long sharp knife. It was nearly three feet in length, and measured almost a foot in diameter at the base. This being accomplished, we returned to camp.

Here I found that Isaac had not been idle in forwarding his own views. I at once saw that my followers had something unusual on their minds; blackness and dismay were plainly written on every countenance. I had scarcely seated myself beside the fire, when Isaac approached me with a slow funereal step, and horror depicted in his face, and asked me if I had heard the news. I replied, What news? He went on to state that on the preceding evening two men of the Bamangwato tribe had passed my waggons on their way to Bakatla, to warn that tribe of the on coming of the cruel and warlike Matabili (whose powerful chief, Moselekatse, has been so ably described in the pages of my fellow-sportsman, Captain Harris). These they represented as having a few days previously attacked and plundered various Bechuana tribes to the northward, and that they were now advancing by rapid marches to devastate the country and murder the inhabitants of these parts.

This I at once knew to be a fabrication to prevent my penetrating farther, and I laughed at Isaac and told him he had dreamed it; to which he replied, "Yes, you will not listen to my advice when you are warned of danger, but both you and your men will one day acknowledge the truth of my forebodings." I had considerable difficulty in calming the minds of my followers, and prevailing on them to proceed farther with me.

In the afternoon we continued our journey to the northward, through a country of increasing loveliness. Beautifully wooded hills and valleys, captivating to the sportsman's eye, stretched away on every side, with rivulets of crystal waters in the valleys, and the spoor of large game very abundant. On the march my dogs dashed up the wind, and in two minutes the peaceful forest was disturbed by their united voices, angrily barking around some animal which they had brought to bay. Snatching up my rifle, I rushed to the scene of conflict, and found them actively baying a fierce and grisly boar, whose foaming jaws were adorned with a pair of tusks so enormous as to resemble horns, each of them being upwards of a foot in length. It was some time before I could obtain a clear shot, owing to the eagerness of my dogs, but at length an opening occurred, when I dropped the grim boar with a bullet in the heart. Night had scarcely set in when lions commenced to roar in concert on every side of us, and continued their deep and awful music until the sun rose next day.

On the 8th we performed a short march before breakfast, halting beside a stream of delicious water. In the afternoon we resumed our march, and halted at sundown beside the broad and sandy bed of a periodical river, through which ran a crystal stream, where we started a troop of eight or ten bull-buffaloes, one of which my dogs immediately brought to bay, when I finished him with two balls behind the shoulder.

On the 9th we continued our march through a lovely and romantic country, steering for Sesetabie, an extremely bold and picturesque pass, in the lofty mountains in which the "Kouloubeng" or "river of wild boars," a tributary to the Ngotwani, takes its rise. As the waggons proceeded I walked in advance with my rifle, and presently brought down a sassayby. While following a herd of pallahs, the waggons got ahead of me; and on overtaking them, I found them drawn up beside a sweet little rocky river, at a short distance from the mountain pass, which from its appearance we expected would prove a barrier to our farther progress.

Kleinboy and Isaac had started in pursuit of a large herd of upwards of one hundred buffaloes, which had thundered up the river-side on the approach of the waggons; presently we heard them fire, and on their return to the waggons they stated that they had mortally wounded an enormous bull. They had certainly wounded a buffalo, but, as I afterwards ascertained, the ball had struck him on the hind leg, within a few inches of the ground.

Having breakfasted, I went out on foot with Isaac, and, directing him to follow up the spoor of his wounded buffalo, I proceeded to ascend a lofty mountain-range to the westward of the pass. Here I fell in with large colonies of baboons and a few klipspringers. I also saw for the first time green parrots and grey squirrels. A number of interesting birds, possessing melodious voices, and plumage more or less gaudy, adorned the groves and forests since I had crossed the range of the Kurrichane mountains; but throughout my career in the forests of the interior my attention was necessarily so taken up with the pursuit of larger, and to me more interesting objects of the chase, that I could rarely bestow upon the feathered creation more than a short and passing glance of admiration. Having ascended to the summit of the highest mountain of the chain, I obtained a glorious view of the surrounding country.

It was truly a fair and boundless prospect; beautifully wooded plains and mountains stretched away on every side to an amazing distance, until the vision was lost among the faint blue outlines of the distant mountain-ranges. Throughout all this country, and vast tracts beyond, I had the satisfaction to reflect that a never-ending succession of herds of every species of noble game which the hunter need desire pastured there in undisturbed security; and as I gazed I felt that it was all my own, and that I at length possessed the undisputed sway over a forest, in comparison with which the tame and herded narrow bounds of the wealthiest European sportsman sink into utter insignificance.

Returning to my waggons, I ascertained from Isaac, who had arrived there a few minutes previously, that he had failed to find his wounded buffalo. The truth was that he had not been in quest of it, fearing to follow up the spoor; a wounded buffalo being deemed by the Bechuanas as dangerous as a lion. Having inspanned, we proceeded to take the bold mountain-pass of Sesetabie, and wound along the margin of the stream, which danced and sparkled down its abrupt and rocky channel, forming a pleasing succession of babbling streams and foaming waterfalls. As we advanced farther up the gorge the path became extremely contracted, there being barely sufficient room to admit of the waggons passing between the steep and rocky brink of the stream, and the rugged base of the lofty, inaccessible mountain which towered on our left. On the opposite side the mountain forming the eastern bulwark of the pass rose precipitately from the water's edge, presenting an impassable barrier. It was a wild and lonely glen, hitherto untrodden, save by the wild denizens of the forests, which from time immemorial had roamed these solitudes.

Large stones and masses of granite rock obstructed our progress, and several hours were occupied in rolling these to one side before we could venture to bring on the waggons. The rocky way was imprinted with the spoor of the large herd of buffaloes which my followers had that morning disturbed, and while my men were engaged with the granite boulders, having detected blood upon the stones, I proceeded to take up the spoor of the wounded buffalo, taking several couple of my dogs along with me. Having followed it a short distance up the pass, I reached a point where two streams met from opposite directions, and here the buffalo had held along the reed-clad margin of the western branch of the stream, which wound along the depths of a lonely and densely wooded valley, embosomed amid rocky mountains. At this spot my dogs, not being led, snuffed up the wind, and instantly disappeared over the ridge above me. Having proceeded on the spoor some distance, still finding blood, which enabled me to distinguish it from the spoor of others of the herd which had accompanied him, I suddenly heard trampling in the grove on the rocky hill-side above me; and on looking up I beheld four splendid old bull buffaloes, walking leisurely along; I made a running stalk after these, and was presently within twenty yards of them, when, upon my whistling shrilly, the buffaloes halted, and looked about at me.

Selecting the finest head, I fired at the centre of his forehead, and in another instant the buffalo was rolling down the mountain side a lifeless mass. I then returned to the spoor I had been following, and was shortly joined by my dogs, which had heard the report of my rifle. I had not proceeded far when I started the wounded bull out of a bed of reeds; he limped along the margin of the stream on three legs, one of his hind legs being shot off above the spurs. My dogs at once brought him to bay, and I finished him with a shot behind the shoulder. The sun was some time under before I reached the waggons, which we drew up on a narrow open glade above the junction of the two streams. All night long lions and hyænas prowled around, and the dogs maintained an incessant barking. At dawn of day on the following morning I despatched a part of my men with a packhorse and all the dogs for a supply of flesh, and the finer head of the two fallen buffaloes; they found them, as I had anticipated, half consumed by lions and hyænas.

It was a cold, windy morning, and I lay in my waggon longer than usual. My other Hottentots thought proper to leave their charge, and go in quest of honey under the guidance of the garrulous honey-bird. I had lain about twenty minutes in my waggon after they had all started, and was occupied in reading a book, when suddenly I heard the oxen come trotting along in front of the waggons, as if sharply driven. On raising my head from my pillow I perceived a lioness following within twenty yards of them, and next moment her mate, a venerable-looking lion, with a shaggy mane which swept the ground, appeared in the yellow grass in front of the oxen, waiting for her to put them to flight. The plot had evidently been preconcerted between them, this being the usual manner in which the lion attacks the buffaloes. Fortunately the oxen would not run for them, and the lions seemed surprised at the confidence of their game. On springing to my feet and shouting to them, they joined one another, and stood together beneath a shady tree within a hundred and twenty yards of the waggons. My horses were pasturing at a short distance from the lions, feeding towards me, and on these they seemed now to meditate an attack, their intention being divided between the horses and myself.

In such a position of affairs I considered it high time to give these bold intruders a hint whose cattle they were so carefully herding. Snatching up my two-grooved rifle, which at all times hung loaded in my waggon, I at once ran forward under cover of a convenient bushy tree which intervened, and on gaining this bush I was within seventy yards of the lions. Here a forked branch afforded an admirable rest. I placed my rifle in the fork, and, taking the old lion low, I let fly, hitting him in the shoulder; the two then wheeled about, and, bounding forward with angry growls, disappeared among the trees.

From the cool state I was in when I fired, and the steady aim which the forked branch had afforded me, I felt convinced that the lion, if not dead, must be mortally wounded, but I prudently resolved not to proceed in quest of him alone. Presently some of my men, who had gone to the carcase of a buffalo I had slain the previous day, returned bringing the dogs; and, having informed them of what had happened, I proceeded to take up the spoor of the wounded lion. On reaching the spot where the lions had stood, my dogs at once commenced barking angrily and looking sharply round in every direction their hair bristling on their backs. I at once discovered blood, which increased as I proceeded from small red drops to large frothy blotches; and before advancing two hundred yards, on approaching a dense green bush, my dogs, which led the way, sprang suddenly to one side, barking with great vehemence. By this I knew that the lion was dead, and, on cautiously rounding the bush, taking care at the same time to give it a wide berth, I had the satisfaction to behold a princely lion stretched lifeless on the ground.

He was in the prime of life, having fine sharp teeth; and it being now the dead of winter he carried the most luxuriant coat of hair, the rankness of his flowing mane exceeding in beauty anything I had hitherto seen. I considered myself extremely fortunate in having secured so noble a specimen of the lion with so little danger, and I at once set men to work to unrobe him, which they were not long in accomplishing.

About midday we inspanned, and trekked on till sundown through a country the most wild and primitive that can be conceived. We proceeded under the guidance of two Bechuanas, who had joined us on the preceding day, and were proceeding to Booby. The two Baquaines who had accompanied me from Bakatla had forsaken my standard after I had shot the bull eland; so liberal a supply of flesh being far too powerful a temptation to admit of their proceeding beyond it. On gaining the neck of the mountain-pass our march for a few miles wound through beautifully-wooded grassy hills, after which we descended into a rugged and densely wooded valley, intersected with deep watercourses which threatened momentarily the destruction of my axletrees. So dense was the jungle that we were obliged repeatedly to halt the waggons, and cut out a pathway with our axes before they could advance. Emerging from this valley, we entered upon a more level country, still, however, densely covered with forest-trees and bushes in endless variety. Here water was very abundant. We crossed several streams and marches whose margins were a mass of the spoor of wild animals; that of rhinoceros, buffalo, and camelopard being most abundant. At one stream the fresh spoor of a troop of lions was deeply imprinted in the wet sand.

Although I am now acquainted with the native names of a number of the trees of the African forests, yet of their scientific names I am utterly ignorant. The shoulders and upper ridges of the mountains throughout all that country are profusely adorned with the graceful sandal-wood tree, famed on account of the delicious perfume of its timber. The leaf of this tree emits at every season of the year a powerful and fragrant perfume, which is increased by bruising the leaves in the hand. Its leaf is small, of a light silvery grey colour, which is strongly contrasted by the dark and dense evergreen foliage of the moopooroo-tree, which also adorns the upper ridges of the mountain ranges. This beautiful tree is interesting, as producing the most delicious and serviceable fruit that I have met with throughout those distant parts; the poorer natives subsisting upon it for several months, during which it continues in season. The moopooroo is of the size and shape of a very large olive. It is at first green, but, gradually ripening, like the Indian mango, it

THE GIRAFFE AND ITS HABITS. 131

becomes beautifully striped with yellow, and when perfectly ripe its colour is the deepest orange. The fruit is sweet and mealy, similar to the date, and contains a small brown seed. It covers the branches, and when ripe the golden fruit beautifully contrasts with the dark green leaves of the tree which bears it.

Besides the moopooroo, a great variety of fruits are met with throughout these mountains and forests, all of which are known to, and gathered by, the natives. I must, however, forego a description of them, as it would swell these pages to undue bounds. Throughout the densely-wooded dells and hollows of the mountains the rosewood-tree occurs, of considerable size and in great abundance.

Throughout the night we were beset by a daring troop of hyænas, which, notwithstanding the vigilance of my dogs, consumed a part of my buffalo trektow and also a number of straps from off the yokes. The dogs kept up a loud and incessant barking until the day dawned, when I shot one of the hyænas, and the rest made off.

On the 11th we were in the yoke soon after daybreak. It was a bitterly cold morning, ice a quarter of an inch in thickness covering the pools of water. We were now clear of the extensive mountain-ranges through which our road had wound since leaving Bakatla, and were approaching towards the south-eastern limits of the great Kalahari desert, on whose borders Booby is situated. We continued our march, steering north-west; in which direction the distant blue hills (pointed out to me as the position of Booby) shot abruptly above the unvaried sameness of the intervening forest scenery. To the west, one eternal ocean-like expanse of grey forest stretched away in a level and unbroken plain, terminated only by the far horizon. Having performed a march of three hours, we crossed a small stream, where I outspanned to breakfast.

This day was to me rather a memorable one, as the first on which I saw and slew the lofty graceful-looking giraffe or camelopard, with which, during many years of my life, I had longed to form an acquaintance. These gigantic and exquisitely beautiful animals, which are admirably formed by nature to adorn the fair forests that clothe the boundless plains of the interior, are widely distributed throughout the interior of Southern Africa, but are nowhere to be met with in great numbers. In countries unmolested by the intrusive foot of man, the giraffe is found generally in herds varying from twelve to sixteen; but I have not unfrequently met with herds containing thirty individuals, and on one occasion I counted forty together; this, however, was owing to chance, and about sixteen may be reckoned as the average number of a herd. These herds are composed of giraffes of various sizes, from the young giraffe of nine or ten feet in height, to the dark chesnut-coloured old bull of the herd, whose exalted head towers above his companions, generally attaining to a height of upwards of eighteen feet. The females are of lower stature and more delicately formed than the males, their height averaging from sixteen to seventeen feet. Some writers have discovered ugliness and a want of grace in the giraffe, but I consider that he is one of the most strikingly beautiful animals in the creation; and when a herd of them is seen scattered through a grove of the picturesque parasol-topped acacias which adorn their native plains, and on whose uppermost shoots they are enabled to browse by the colossal height with which nature has so admirably endowed them, he must indeed be slow of conception who fails to discover both grace and dignity in all their movements.

There can be no doubt that every animal is seen to the greatest advantage in the haunts which nature destined him to adorn, and amongst the various living creatures which beautify this fair creation, I have often traced a remarkable resemblance between the animal and the general appearance of the locality in which it is found. This I first remarked at an early period of my life, when entomology occupied a part of my attention. No person following this interesting pursuit can fail to observe the extraordinary likeness which insects bear to the various abodes in which they are met with. Thus, among the long green grass we find a variety of long green insects, whose legs and antennæ so resemble the shoots emanating from the stalks of the grass that it requires a practised eye to distinguish them. Throughout sandy districts varieties of insects are met with of a colour similar to the sand which they inhabit. Among the green leaves of the various trees of the forest innumerable leaf-coloured insects are to be found; while, closely adhering to the rough grey bark of these forest-trees, we observe beautifully coloured grey-looking moths of various patterns, yet altogether so resembling the bark as to be invisible to the passing observer.

In like manner among quadrupeds I have traced a corresponding analogy, for, even in the case of the stupendous elephant, the ashy colour of his hide so corresponds with the general appearance of the grey thorny jungles which he frequents throughout the day, that a person unaccustomed to hunting elephants, standing on a commanding situation, might look down upon a herd and fail to detect their presence. And further, in the case of the giraffe, which is invariably met with among venerable forests, where innumerable blasted and weather-beaten trunks and stems occur, I have repeatedly been in doubt as to the presence of a troop of them, until I had recourse to my spyglass; and on referring the case to my savage attendants, I have known even their optics to fail, at one time mistaking these dilapidated trunks for camelopards, and again confounding real camelopards with these aged veterans of the forest.

Although we had now been travelling many days through the country of the giraffe, and had marched through forests in which their spoor was abundant, our eyes had not yet been gifted with a sight of "Tootla" himself; it was therefore with indescribable pleasure that, on the evening of the 11th, I beheld a troop of these interesting animals.

Our breakfast being finished, I resumed my journey through an endless grey forest of cameel-dorn and other trees, the country slightly undulating, and grass abundant. A little before the sun went down my driver remarked to me, "I was just going to say, Sir, that that old tree was a camelopard."

On looking where he pointed, I saw that the old tree was indeed a camelopard, and, on casting my eyes a little to the right, I beheld a troop of them standing looking at us, their heads actually towering above the trees of the forest. It was imprudent to commence a chase at such a late hour, especially in a country of so level a character, where the chances were against my being able to regain my waggons that night. I, however, resolved to chance everything; and directing my men to catch and saddle Colesberg, I proceeded in haste to buckle on my shooting-belt and spurs, and in two minutes I was in the saddle. The giraffes stood looking at the waggons until I was within sixty yards of them, when galloping round a thick bushy tree, under cover of which I had ridden, I suddenly beheld a sight the most astounding that a sportsman's eye can encounter. Before me stood a troop of ten colossal giraffes, the majority of which were from seventeen to eighteen feet high. On beholding me they at once made off, twisting their long tails over their backs, making a loud switching noise with them, and cantered along at an easy pace, which, however, obliged Colesberg to put his best foot foremost to keep up with them.

The sensations which I felt on this occasion were different from anything that I had before experienced during a long sporting career. My senses were so absorbed by the wondrous and beautiful sight before me that I rode along like one entranced, and felt inclined to disbelieve that I was hunting living things of this world. The ground was firm and favourable for riding. At every stride I gained upon the giraffes, and after a short burst at a swingeing gallop I was in the middle of them, and turned the finest cow out of the herd. On finding herself driven from her comrades and hotly pursued, she increased her pace, and cantered along with tremendous strides, clearing an amazing extent of ground at every bound; while her neck and breast, coming in contact with the dead old branches of the trees, were continually strewing them in my path.

In a few minutes I was riding within five yards of her stern, and, firing at the gallop, I sent a bullet into her back. Increasing my pace, I next rode alongside, and, placing the muzzle of my rifle within a few feet of her, I fired my second shot behind the shoulder; the ball, however seemed to have little effect. I then placed myself directly in front, when she came to a walk. Dismounting, I hastily loaded both barrels, putting in double charges of powder. Before this was accomplished she was off at a canter. In a short time I brought her to a stand in the dry bed of a watercourse, where I fired at fifteen yards, aiming where I thought the heart lay, upon which she again made off. Having loaded, I followed, and had very nearly lost her; she had turned abruptly to the left, and was far out of sight among the trees. Once more I brought her to a stand, and dismounted from my horse. There we stood together alone in the wild wood. I gazed in wonder at her extreme beauty, while her soft dark eye, with its silky fringe, looked down imploringly at me, and I really felt a pang of sorrow in this moment of triumph for the blood I was shedding. Pointing my rifle towards the skies, I sent a bullet through her neck. On receiving it she reared high on her hind legs and fell backwards with a heavy crash, making the earth shake around her. A thick stream of dark blood spouted far from the wound, her colossal limbs quivered for a moment, and she expired.

I had little time to contemplate the prize I had won. Night was fast setting in, and it was very questionable if I should succeed in regaining my waggons; so, having cut off the tail of the giraffe, which was adorned with a bushy tuft of flowing black hair, I took "one last fond look," and rode hard for the spoor of the waggons, which I succeeded in reaching just as it was dark.

No pen nor words can convey to a sportsman what it is to ride in the midst of a troop of gigantic giraffes: it must be experienced to be understood. They emitted a powerful perfume, which in the chase came hot in my face, reminding me of the smell of a hive of heather honey in September. The greater part of this chase led through bushes of the wait-a-bit thorn of the most virulent description, which covered my legs and arms with blood long before I had killed the giraffe. I rode as usual in the kilt, with my arms bare to my shoulder. It was Chapelpark of Badenoch's old grey kilt, but in this chase it received a deathblow which it never afterwards recovered.

On the 12th we performed two long marches through thickly wooded plains, the spoor of camelopard being extremely abundant. On the 13th we cast loose the cattle at dawn of day. Breakfast being finished, we inspanned, and having proceeded about eight miles through the forest, steering for a range of rocky mountains, we reached a gorge in the same. Here we crossed a small river; and having followed its banks about three miles, we reached Booby, a residence of Bechuanas, being a branch of the tribe of the Baquaines, and governed by a subordinate chief, who was then absent on a visit. I was, however, welcomed by his nephew, named Caachy, a man of pleasing exterior and prepossessing manners, who shortly afterwards became, and now is, chief of that tribe.

As the manner in which Caachy succeeded to the chieftainship was peculiar, I may here relate the circumstances attending it. Throughout all the Bechuana tribes an absurd belief prevails in witchcraft and supernatural agencies of every kind. They also believe that for every transaction there is a medicine which will enable the possessor to succeed in his object. Thus they think those among themselves who work in iron, do so under the power of medicine. Their rain-makers by the power of their medicines can propitiate the friendly clouds during the protracted droughts of summer. They have medicines to protect them from the lightning's stroke, from the deadly bite of the viper, and from the fatal spring of the lion. They further believe that there is a medicine for guns, the possession of which will cause the gun to shoot well; and likewise one for the gunpowder, which will give it strength.

During my visit to Booby I obtained from the natives some interesting specimens of native arms and other curiosities, for which they required gunpowder, their chief having in his possession one or two muskets. When the chief and his men proceeded to use my powder, they missed all they fired at; the Bechuana mode of firing being to withdraw the face from the gun, from a natural impulse of fear, before drawing the trigger, and to look back over the left shoulder instead of at the animal they expect to kill. The cause of their missing they at once ascribed to the powder, which they affirmed required medicine. Accordingly, the chief and all the long-headed men in Booby assembled in the forum; and having placed the unworthy gunpowder upon a large kaross, they all sat round it, and commenced a variety of ceremonies and incantations with a view of imparting to it that power which they considered it had lost. At length some wiseacre among the soothsayers informed the king that the presence of fire was indispensable on the occasion. Fire was accordingly introduced along with the other medicines, and a censer of hot embers was passed frequently over the powder. Suddenly, however, an unlucky spark sprang from the censer into the heap of powder, which of course instantly exploded, and, the quantity being very considerable, the Booby men and their chief were blown heels over head on every side—several of the party, and among others the chief, being so severely burnt, that they shortly died. So much for Bechuana medicines.

The kraal of Booby is encompassed on three sides by rocky hills, which to their summits are densely clad with sandal-wood trees. The sides of these mountains in parts are extremely precipitous, and are the abodes of baboons and klipspringers. On the march, as we approached Booby, I took my rifle and ascended to the base of one of these precipices, where I shot two immense baboons. One of them was sitting on the shelf of a rock very high above me; and on receiving the shot he fell about a hundred feet without a break. The valleys between the mountains are extensively cultivated by the women, as also a large level piece of ground to the north-eastward of the kraal. The costume of this tribe was the same I have already described as worn by the Bechuanas; but I remarked that they used the atrocious mixture of red clay and grease more freely than their neighbours. The Booby men flocked around my waggons, evidently much gratified with so novel a sight, and continued with me until nightfall. Shortly after I reached Booby a party of Baquaines arrived from Sichely. They had been sent to endeavour to dissuade me from visiting Bamangwato, and to inform me that Sichely had ivory and karosses, with which to purchase all my guns; and that, above all, he wished me to promise to reserve my big Dutch rifle for him. I informed these men that I was determined to visit Sicomy, but that I would keep the Dutch rifle for their chief, as he requested it.

Having informed Caachy that I intended to march next day, he expressed surprise, and said I made his heart sore. That evening there was a meeting of all the wise men in Booby to consult how I could best be prevented from journeying on to Bamangwato. On the morning of the 14th I felt far from well, probably having drunk too much of Caachy's beer on the preceding evening. Before I was inclined to turn out, the regent with all his great men were standing thick around my waggons. I pretended to be asleep; so they kindled fires, around which they squatted. Presently I arose, and gave the regent his breakfast. I told him that I wished him to send men along with me to Bamangwato. He replied that there was war in that country, and that he was afraid of Moselekatse. I then said, that, though he would not give me men, I possessed medicine which would enable me to discover the way without his assistance; and I informed him that, if he persisted in withholding guides, I should inform Sicomy, the great and paramount chief of Bamangwato, that they endeavoured to prevent the white men from visiting his domains. Upon this Caachy changed his story, and said that four men should accompany me to Bamangwato, and return with me. His plan however was, that these men should guide me in a wrong direction; and pretending that the waters had failed, they were eventually to lead me to Sichely, who resided to the eastward of Booby.

This being arranged, I gave Caachy some presents, and requested him to take charge of my buffalo and other heads until my return, which he promised to do, and ordered men to bear them directly to his kraal. About midday we inspanned and left Booby, accompanied by nearly the whole tribe, every man carrying two or three assagais and a battle-axe. They followed us in the hope that I would shoot large game for them. The guides at first held north-east; but presently drawing off that course, and steering due east, I halted, and said that was not the road to Bamangwato. They replied, they held that course on account of water. I then directed them to place an assagai on the ground with its head pointing to Bamangwato. Thereupon the savages laid down one of their assagais, and, having pretended for some minutes to be discussing among themselves the exact position of Bamangwato, they ended by pointing it due east, declaring that Bamangwato lay in that direction.

I told them that I had a needle in my pocket which I had rubbed with medicine, by which I could tell if their spear pointed to Sicomy's country. Knowing that Bamangwato lay a little to the east of north, I said that by turning the needle three times round my left wrist it would point a little to the left-hand side of the country I required. On hearthis the savages looked at one another with surprise, and pressed round me to see if my needle possessed the power I represented. Slipping my fingers into my shooting-belt, I then pulled out my pocket compass, and, passing it three times round my left wrist with the utmost gravity, I whistled shrilly; and on opening the compass I placed it on the ground before them. Snatching one of their assagais, I placed it beside the compass a little to the east of north, and told them that it was there Bamangwato lay. They were struck with astonishment, and at once considered me as working by supernatural agency.

Having done this, I inquired of the guides if they would lead me to waters in that direction. They all shouted that that was the desert, and that no man had ever found water there. Having said this, they all turned right about, and, retreating for about two hundred yards, they squatted on the ground. Isaac and I then approached them; but they sat in silence, and looked on the ground. I asked them why they all sat thus. They answered that they would proceed no farther with me. I replied that I was happy to hear it, and that I could find the way better without them. I returned to my waggons, and ordered my men to turn about and retrace their steps to the nearest water. The savages then requested me to halt and speak with them. I told them to go home to their captain, as their presence troubled me; and having proceeded a few hundred yards, I encamped beside a pool of water.

It was plain to me that Isaac, my interpreter, was in league with the Baquaines in their designs against me; but as I did not intend to part with him, because his presence gave confidence to my people, I deemed it best to pretend that I believed him to be sincere. My flesh being exhausted, I resolved to halt for a day for the purpose of hunting before proceeding farther; and having obtained a good supply, to steer through the forest by compass a little to the east of north, and to search for water with my horses in advance of the waggons. I felt poorly in health, and was much troubled in mind. My situation was by no means an enviable one. I was far in the interior of Africa, alone and friendless, surrounded by a tribe of men who would do anything to prevent my attaining my object; but fear restrained them from using violence. What I most dreaded was their stealing my oxen or horses, which they could easily accomplish, as I was encamped in a thick forest; my men also were faint-hearted and anxious to return towards home.

That night I slept little, from vexation and anxiety. The whole tribe of the Booby men lay encamped beside us. They lay on the ground around a number of fires, with a hedge of thorny bushes placed in a semicircle to windward of each party. After breakfast I rode east to hunt, accompanied by Kleinboy leading a packhorse; about thirty of the Bechuanas followed us in the hope of flesh. Having proceeded about two miles, I perceived a large herd of blue wildebeests and zebras. I signed to the Bechuanas to lie down, and then rode slowly forward as if to pass to leeward of the herd. Having probably never before seen a horseman, they allowed me to approach within a hundred yards, when I sprang from my horse, and with my first barrel dropped a fat blue wildebeest. The Bechuanas then rushed forward, but I beckoned to them to lie down. Having loaded I galloped in pursuit of the troop, and after riding a short distance hard in their dusty wake, through a thinly-wooded part of the forest, I pulled up and was on my feet just as the leading cow wheeled about. I fired right and left, and shot two fat old cows. Both ran a short distance and fell. The Bechuanas now came up with Kleinboy, greatly delighted at my success. I presented them with the bull and one of the cows for their chief, and having placed the remaining cow upon my packhorse, we returned to camp.

Here I found Caachy with all his retinue: they had come out to endeavour by cunning speaking to lead me astray. Having saluted Caachy, I said that I had yesterday promised to kill some game for him, and that I had now fulfilled my word, upon which he thanked me. I then remarked that his men did not lead me as Dr. Livingstone had told me to ride; to which he replied that the road was circuitous, and that they led me so on account of water. At length he had almost persuaded me to follow his guides, but I said I would rest till to-morrow, having determined that, as I had no friend whom I might consult, I would revolve the subject in my mind that night, and determine finally in the morning. Caachy then drank coffee with me and departed.

In the evening I inquired of the guides concerning the waters and the distances betwixt them. They replied that the first water was a moderate day's journey, but after that I must ride more than two days without water: they also persevered in pointing to the east as my course. I now plainly saw that their intention was to lead me far astray, and finally to bring me to Sichely, their own paramount chief. I therefore resolved to adhere to my first resolution of steering my own course by the compass, but I kept this intention secret, fearing that they might steal some of my oxen.

CHAPTER XIII.

The Guides try to mislead me—The Cattle and Horses dying from Thirst—Search for Water—Melancholy Anticipations—Directed to a Pool by the flight of Birds—Chase and kill a Giraffe—Wandering Bechuanas point out my right Course—Miserable Condition of the Natives—Game Pitfalls—Mimosa Grove smashed by Elephants—A Rhinoceros charges me—Abundance of large Game—Lost in the Forest.

On the morning of the 16th a large party of Caachy's men were still encamped beside us, and were under the impression that they had succeeded in prevailing upon me to follow them. Having filled all my water-casks, I ordered my men to inspan, the Bechuanas cracking their jokes and fancying that I should ride east as they led; but to their astonishment, having inspanned, I told them that they had better all return to their captains, as I would shoot no more game for them, and I then ordered my men to ride for a conspicuous tree in the distance, bearing N.N.E. The Bechuanas sat still for some time to see how I would steer, and presently they shouldered their assagais and followed in our wake. This was a bold step on my part: the country looked very unlikely for water, and the Bechuanas swore that there was none for seven day's journey in that direction.

Our march lay through a boundless forest, with no hill nor landmark to give an idea where to search for water. Fortune, however, followed me here as usual: if I had lived all my life in the country, I could not have taken a more direct course for the spot I wished to reach. After we had proceeded some miles, a rising ground arose in our path, from the summit of which I fancied that a view might be obtained of the country in advance. This view only served to damp my hopes, the prospect exhibiting one slightly undulating, ocean-like expanse of forest and dense thorny jungles.

We halted for a few minutes to breathe the oxen, when the Bechuanas all came up, and sat down on the ground beside us. I asked them why they had not gone home as I had told them. They replied that they followed me because they were afraid that I should lose myself and my oxen. We held on, steering by compass N.N.E. All the Bechuanas now forsook me except the four ill-favoured men whom Caachy had pointed out to me as my guides. These four, contrary to my expectations, followed in our wake at some distance. I walked a hundred yards in advance of the waggons with my compass in my hand, having ordered the men to follow my footsteps. After travelling for several hours the country became more open, and presently we entered upon a wide tract that had been recently burned by the Bakalahari, or wild inhabitants of the desert. Here the trees and bushes stood scorched and burnt, and there was not a blade of grass to cheer the eye—blackness and ashes stretched away on every side wherever I turned my anxious glance. I felt my heart sink within me as I beheld in dim perspective my famished and thirsty oxen returning some days hence over this hopeless desert, all my endeavours to find water having failed, and all my bright hopes of elephant-hunting dashed and crowned with bitter disappointment: it was indeed a cheerless prospect. I had no friend to comfort or advise me, and I could hear my men behind me grumbling, and swearing that they would return home; the guides, who had now come up, asking them why they followed me to destruction.

At length we reached the farther side of this dreary waste of ashes, but now an equally cheerless prospect was before me. We entered a vast forest, grey with extreme age, and so thick that we could not see forty yards in advance. We were obliged occasionally to halt the waggons and cut down trees and branches to admit of their passing; and to make matters still worse, the country had become extremely heavy, the waggons sinking deep in soft sand. My men began to show a mutinous spirit by expressing their opinions aloud in my presence. I remonstrated with them, and told them that, if I did not bring them to water next day before the sun was under, they might turn the oxen on their spoor. We continued our march through this dense forest until nightfall, when I halted for the night beside a widespreading tree: here I cast my oxen loose for an hour, and then secured them on the yokes by moonlight.

I felt very sad and unhappy in my mind, for I considered that the chances were against me, and I shuddered at the idea of returning to the colony, after coming so very far, without shooting or even seeing what my heart most ardently desired, viz. a wild bull elephant free in his native jungle. I took some wine, and, coming to the fire which the men had kindled for the night beneath a magnificent old cameel-dorn tree, I affected great cheerfulness and contentment, and, laughing at the four Bechuanas, I told them that I was not a child that they should lead me astray, but that I was an old warrior and a cunning hunter, and could find my way in strange lands. I laughed, but it was the laugh of despair, for I expected that next evening they would be laughing at me, on seeing me compelled to retrace my steps. One of the greatest difficulties that presented itself was, that, if I rode in advance to search for water, it would be almost impossible to find my way back to the waggons through that vast and trackless forest. I went to bed but tried in vain to sleep.

Care and anxiety kept me awake until a little before morning, when I fell asleep for a short time and dreamt that I had ridden in advance and found water. Day dawned, and I awoke in sorrow. My hopes were like a flickering flame; care sat upon my brow. I cast loose my horses and oxen, and prepared some breakfast; I then directed my men to catch "The Cow" and "Colesberg," and give them some corn. I asked the guides if they could lead me to water in a northerly direction, when they replied that no man ever found water in the desert. I did not talk more with them, but ordered my men to remain quiet during the day and listen for shots, lest I should lose my way in returning; and having given them ammunition to reply, I saddled up and held N.N.E. through thick forest, accompanied by Kleinboy. The ground was heavy, being soft sand, and the grass grew at intervals in detached bunches. We rode on without a break or a change, and found no spoor of wild animals to give me hope. I saw one duiker, but these antelopes are met with in the desert, and are independent of water.

At last we reached a more open part of the forest, and emerging from the thicket I perceived a troop of six giraffes standing looking at us about two hundred yards to my right; but this was no time to give them chase, which I felt very much inclined to do. I allowed them to depart in peace, and continued my search for water. In this open glade I found two or three vleys that had once contained a little water, but they were now hard and dry. Re-entering the dense forest, we held one point more to the east, and rode on as before. For miles we continued our search, until my hopes sank to a very low ebb; and Kleinboy swore that we should never regain the waggons. At length I perceived a sassayby walking before me: this antelope drinks every day ;—"fresh vigour with the hope returned." I once more pressed forward and cantered along, heedless of the distance which already intervened betwixt me and my camp and the remonstrances of my attendant, who at last reigned up his jaded steed, and said that he would not follow me farther to my own destruction. I then pointed to the top of a distant grey tree that stretched its bare and weather-beaten branches above the heads of its surrounding comrades, and said, that, if we saw nothing to give us hope when we reached that tree, I would abandon the search, and hunt during that season in Sichely's mountains to the east of Booby.

But fate had ordained that I should penetrate farther into the interior of Africa; and before I reached the old grey tree I observed a small flight of Namaqua partridges flying across my path in a westerly direction. It was impossible to tell, until I should see a second flock of these, flying at a different angle, whether the first flock had come from, or were going to, water. For this I accordingly watched, nor watched long in vain. A considerable distance ahead of me I detected a second flight of these birds likewise flying westerly; and it was evident, from their inclination, that they held for the same point as the first had done. Shortly afterwards the first flight returned, flying high above our heads, uttering their soft melodious cry of "pretty dear, pretty dear." I then rode in the direction from which the birds had come, and before proceeding far we discovered a slight hollow running north and south. This I determined to follow, and presently I discovered fresh spoor of a rhinoceros: this was a certain sign that water was somewhere not very distant.

Once more my dying hopes revived. I looked north at the glorious sky, which on this day was quite different from anything I had beheld for months. It was like one of those glorious days when the bright blue sky in my own dark land is seen through ten thousand joyous fleecy clouds, and all nature seems to strive in its sunny hour to make poor unhappy man forget his cares and sorrows. I took it as a favourable omen, and, stirring my good and lively steed, I cantered along the glade. The hollow took a turn, on rounding which I perceived that I was in an elevated part of the forest; and I, for the first time, obtained a distant view of the surrounding scenery. Far as the eye could strain

TREACHERY OF THE GUIDES. 141

it was all forest without a break; but there was now an undulating country before me, instead of the hopeless level through which I had come. I felt certain of success. We soon discovered vleys that had recently contained water; and at last a large pool of excellent water, enough to supply my cattle for several days. This was to me a joyous moment; it was a grand step towards attaining my object, and, as my difficulties had seemed to increased, my wish and determination to overcome them had become stronger. I knew that, whether I reached Bamangwato or not, if I could now only manage to travel north about eight days' journey I should fall in with elephants.

I was extremely fortunate in regaining my waggons, which I did without a turn in my course. On reaching them I at first pretended not to have discovered water; and I said to the guides, "There is nothing but dense wood in this country; can you not show me water? my oxen will die." They replied that they knew the country from infancy, and that if I wanted water I must travel till sunset, steering south of east. I then surprised them by saying, "Now I see that you wish to lead me astray; for I have seen abundance of water, and I will find my way to Bamangwato, though you do all in your power to prevent me." Having inspanned, we held for the water, which I succeeded in reaching at a late hour. I still felt very anxious and full of care; but this first bold and successful step seemed to have made a strong impression on the guides, who still followed in our wake. It appeared to me that the orders they had received from their chief were, to endeavour to lead me astray, and bring me to Sichely; but that, in the event of my finding the way myself, they were to accompany me to Sicomy to ensure his friendship and to convince him of their chief's sincerity.

On the morning of the 18th, shortly after the day dawned, I was lying awake thinking whether I should hunt or explore the country in advance, my men having as usual wasted their food and already consumed the bull wildebeest which I had shot for them two days previously, when suddenly I heard the voices of men a little distance down the glade. Fortune seemed determined to favour me. The guides, who sat by our fire, had not heard the voices; if they had been aware of men being near us they would have run to meet them, and warned them to lead me astray. Springing from my bed, I hastily donned my attire, and, proceeding in the direction of the voices, I discovered a party of ten Bechuanas squatted round a fire which they had just kindled. These men belonged to Booby; they had been hunting jackals at a place called Boötlonamy, which is halfway from Booby to Bamangwato, and they were now returning home with their spoils. They at once pointed out to me the correct line of march for Bamangwato, and advised me of a fine vley in the forest one march in advance.

Having breakfasted, I inspanned, and after trekking for about six hours through dense forest we reached the vley. On the march it was necessary to have constant recourse to our axes to clear a path for the waggons. I was much delighted with the little loch to which we then came: it covered about an acre, in shape a circle, and its margin was imprinted with the fresh spoor of a variety of wild animals, such as giraffe, rhinoceros, buffalo, sassayby, pallah, zebra, lion, etc. We encamped beneath two wide-spreading shady trees, and I at once saddled up, and rode forth with Kleinboy to hunt, our flesh being at an end. I had ridden about half a mile in a north-easterly course, through shady groves of mokala-trees, when suddenly I observed a stately giraffe walk slowly across my path, and crop the leaves from the upper branches of a mokala-tree about a hundred yards in advance This was a fine lookout: with hasty hand I shifted my saddle from "Sunday" to the Old Grey, and ordering Kleinboy to set the packsaddle on "Sunday," and listen for shots, I rode slowly towards the giraffe.

As I advanced I perceived another giraffe standing looking at me a little to my left, which gave the alarm by starting off, when I stirred my steed, and on rounding an intervening clump of trees I came full in sight of a troop of eight giraffes, cantering before me. In another minute I was in the middle of them; and selecting a fine fat cow, I rode hard at her, and fired my first shot at the gallop. She got it through her ribs, and the blood flowed freely. Again and again I broke her from the troop, and again she joined them. At length I fired my second shot at her stern; after which, by heading her, I brought her to a stand, when I sprang from the fidgety, snorting Old Grey, and, hastily loading both barrels, I fired right and left for her heart. Her colossal frame shook convulsively for a few seconds, when, tottering forward, she subsided in the dust with tremendous violence.

Four signal-shots brought Kleinboy and the packhorse, and also Isaac with the four guides. The chase was all in thick forest, and had led me to within a few hundred yards of the waggons. The hungry guides seemed enchanted at the prospect of such a banquet. They at once kindled a fire, and slept that night beside the carcase. I returned to the waggons with my horses laden with flesh. My mind was now once more at rest. I went to my bed and slept soundly. During the night lions roared around us.

On the 19th I rose at dawn of day, and took a stroll through the forest. Here I found some old dung of elephants; and observing several full-grown trees torn up by the roots, and others that had been shivered by the gigantic strength of those animals. The guides, finding that they prevailed nothing, at length volunteered to lead me to Bamangwato by a northerly course, and promised that I should not lack for water. We inspanned, and held on till sundown, proceeding in a north-easterly course, when we halted in dense forest without water. Our march lay through an interesting country well adapted for hunting the eland and giraffe. The forest was in many places thin and open, with here and there gigantic old trees of picturesque appearance standing detached, some half-dead, and others falling to pieces from age. The soil was soft yet firm, and admirably suited for riding. The spoor of eland and giraffe was abundant.

On the 20th we inspanned at dawn of day, and having proceeded about five miles we reached a miserable little kraal or village of Bakalahari. Here was a vley of water, beside which we outspanned. Starvation was written in the faces of these inhabitants of the forest. In their vicinity were a few small gardens, containing water-melons and a little corn. Occasionally they have the luck to capture some large animal in a pitfall, when for a season they live in plenty. But as they do not possess salt, the flesh soon spoils, when they are compelled once more to roam the forest in quest of fruits and roots, on which, along with locusts, they in a great measure subsist. In districts where game is abundant, they often construct their pits on a large scale, and erect hedges in the form of a crescent, extending to nearly a mile on either side of the pit. By this means the game may easily be driven into the pitfalls, which are carefully covered over with thin sticks and dry grass; and thus whole herds of zebras and wildebeests are massacred at once, which capture is followed by the most disgusting banquets, the poor starving savages gorging and surfeiting in a manner worthy only of the vulture or hyæna. They possess no cattle, and, if they did, the nearest chief would immediately rob them. All that part of the country abounded with the pitfalls made by these and others of the Bakalahari. Many of these had been dug expressly for the giraffe, and were generally three feet wide, and ten long; their depth was from nine to ten feet. They were placed in the path of the Camelopard, and in the vicinity of several of these we detected the bones of giraffes, indicating the success that had attended their formation.

At midday we resumed our march, halting at sunset without water. The first of this march lay through dense forest, where we were obliged to cut a pathway with our axes. Here the spoor of eland was abundant. In the evening we passed through an open tract very thinly wooded, where I saw abundance of springbok and blue wildebeest. At midnight the dogs giving chase to some animal, I sprang out of bed; and following them in my shirt, I found them standing over a jackal. The guides skinned him, and, having baked him in the ashes, they consumed him.

On the 22nd, ordering my men to move on to the fountain of Boötlonamy, I rode forth with Ruyter, and held east through a grove of lofty and widespreading mimosas, most of which were more or less damaged by the gigantic strength of a troop of elephants, which had passed there about twelve months before. Having proceeded about two miles with large herds of game on every side, I observed a crusty-looking old bull borèlé, or black rhinoceros, cocking his ears one hundred yards in advance. He had not observed us; and soon after he walked slowly towards us, and stood broadside to, eating some wait-a-bit thorns within fifty yards of me. I fired from my saddle, and sent a bullet in behind his shoulder, upon which he rushed forward about one hundred yards in tremendous consternation, blowing like a grampus, and then stood looking about him. Presently he made off. I followed, but found it hard to come up with him. When I overtook him I saw the blood running freely from his wound.

The chase led through a large herd of blue wildebeests, zebras, and springboks, which gazed at us in utter amazement. At length I fired my second barrel, but my horse was fidgety, and I missed. I continued riding alongside of him, expecting in my ignorance that at length he would come to bay, which rhinoceroses never do; when suddenly he fell flat on his broadside on the ground, but, recovering his feet, resumed his course as if nothing had happened. Becoming at last annoyed at the length of the chase, as I wished to keep my horses fresh for the elephants, and being indifferent whether I got the rhinoceros or not, as I observed that his horn was completely worn down with age and the violence of his disposition, I determined to bring matters to a crisis; so, spurring my horse, I dashed ahead, and rode right in his path.

Upon this the hideous monster instantly charged me in the most resolute manner, blowing loudly through his nostrils; and although I quickly wheeled about to my left, he followed me at such a furious pace for several hundred yards, with his horrid horny snout within a few yards of my horse's tail, that my little bushman, who was looking on in great alarm, thought his master's destruction inevitable. It was certainly a very near thing; my horse was extremely afraid, and exerted his utmost energies on the occasion. The rhinoceros, however, wheeled about and continued his former course; and I, being perfectly satisfied with the interview which I had already enjoyed with him, had no desire to cultivate his acquaintance any further, and accordingly made for camp. We left the fountain of Boötlonamy the same day, and marched about six miles through an old grey forest of mimosas, when we halted for the night. Large flocks of guinea-fowls roosted in the trees around our encampment, several of which I shot for my supper.

On the 23rd we inspanned by moonlight, and continued our march through a thinly-wooded level country. It was a lovely morning; the sun rose in great splendour, and the sky was beautifully overcast with clouds. Having proceeded about ten miles, the country became thickly covered with detached forest-trees and groves of wait-a-bit thorns. The guides now informed us that the water, which is called by the Bechuanus "Lepeby," was only a short distance in advance; upon which I saddled steeds, and rode ahead with the Bushman, intending to hunt for an hour before breakfast. Presently we reached an open glade in the forest, where I observed a herd of zebras in advance; and on my left stood a troop of springboks, with two leopards watching them from behind a bush. I rode on, and soon fell in with a troop of hartebeests, and, a little after, with a large herd of blue wildebeests and pallahs. I followed these for some distance, when they were reinforced by two other herds of pallahs and wildebeests. Three black rhinoceroses now trotted across my path. Presently I sprang from my horse, and fired right and left at a princely bull blue wildebeest. He got both balls, but did not fall; and I immediately lost sight of him in the dense ranks of his shaggy companions.

The game increased as we proceeded, until the whole forest seemed alive with a variety of beautifully coloured animals. On this occasion I was very unfortunate; I might have killed any quantity of game if venison had been my object; but I was trying to get a few very superior heads of some of the master bucks of the pallahs. Of these I wounded four select old bucks, but in the dust and confusion caused by the innumerable quantity of the game I managed to lose them all.

We had now ridden many miles from the waggons; and feeling faint from want of food, I dropped the chase in disgust, and, without looking at my compass, ordered the Bushman to go ahead. My attention had been so engrossed with the excitement of the pursuit, that I had not the remotest idea of the course I had taken, and the whole country exhibited such an aspect of sameness, that there was no landmark nor eminence of any description by which to steer. Having ridden many miles through the forest, I at length asked the Bushman, in whom on such occasions I generally placed great confidence, if he was sure he was riding in the right direction, and, as he appeared quite confident, I allowed him to proceed.

At length he said that we had gone a little too far to the left, and led me away several miles to the right, which was westerly; whereas the waggons eventually proved to be a long way to the east. I felt convinced that we were wrong, and, reining up, a discussion arose between us, the Bushman still maintaining that we must ride west, whilst I was certain that our course should be east. I now adopted my own opinion, and, having ridden many miles in an easterly direction, we were at one time close upon the waggons, when the thick-headed Bushman declared that if I persevered we should never see the waggons again, and I with equal stupidity, yielded to his advice, and a south-westerly course was once more adopted. Having ridden for many miles, I again reined up, and again told the Bushman we were wrong; upon which he for the first time acknowledged that he knew nothing at all about the matter, but stated it to be his impression that we ought to ride farther to the west. My head was so confused that I lost all recollection of how we had ridden; and while I was deliberating what I should do, I observed a volume of smoke a long way to the north, which I at once imagined had been kindled by my followers to guide their lost master ·to the waggons.

With revived spirits, I stirred my jaded steed and made for the smoke; but, alas! this only served to lead me farther astray. After riding many miles in that direction, I discovered that the fire was at an amazing distance, and could not have been kindled by my men; it was the wild Bakalahari of the desert burning the old dry grass. I was now like a seaman in a hurricane—at my wit's end—I knew not how to ride nor what to do. The sun, which had just risen when I left the waggons, was about to set. There was no landmark whatever by which to steer; I might wander for days, and not discover water.

To find the waggons was comparatively a trifle. I thought little of them; it was the thought of water that harrowed my mind. Already the pangs of thirst began to seize me. I had ridden all day, under the hot sun, and had neither eaten nor drunk since early the preceding evening. I felt faint and weary; and my heart sank as horrible visions of a lingering death by maddening thirst arose before me. Dismounting from my horse, I sat down to think what I should do. I knew exactly by my compass the course we had been steering since we left Booby. I accordingly resolved to ride south-west for many miles, the course of the waggons having been north-east, and then to send Ruyter across the country a little to the north of west, while I should hold a corresponding course in an easterly direction. By this means one of us could not fail to find the spoor, and I arranged that at nightfall we should meet at some conspicuous tree. Having thus resolved, I mounted my horse, which was half dead with thirst and fatigue, and, having ridden south-west for several miles, I and Ruyter separated at a conspicuous tree, and rode in opposite directions. Before riding far I recognised the country as being the spot where I had seen the leopards in the morning. I at once followed Ruyter, and fired several signal shots, which he fortunately heard, and soon joined me. We then rode due east, and eventually, to my inexpressible gratification, we discovered the spoor of the waggons, which we reached after following it for about four miles in a north-easterly direction.

Our poor horses were completely exhausted, and could barely walk to camp. I found my waggons drawn up beside the strong fountain of Lepeby, which, issuing from beneath a stratum of white tufous rock, formed an extensive deep pool of pure water, adorned on one side with lofty green reeds. This fountain was situated at the northern extremity of a level bare vley, surrounded by dense covers of the wait-a-bit thorns. Such a peculiar sameness characterized the country, that a person wandering only a few hundred yards from the fountain would have considerable difficulty in regaining it. It was night when I reached the waggons, and two or three cups of coffee soon restored me to my wonted vigour.

On the following morning, from earliest dawn until we trekked, which we did about ten A.M., large herds of game kept pouring in to drink from every side, completely covering the open space, and imparting to it the appearance of a cattle-fair; blue wildebeests, zebras, sassaybys, pallahs, springboks, etc., capered fearlessly up to the water, troop after troop, within two hundred yards of us. In former years a tribe of Bechuanas had frequented this fountain, and I beheld the skeletons of many rhinoceroses and of one elephant bleaching in the sun; but the powerful and cruel Matabili had attacked the tribe, and driven them to seek a home elsewhere. I shot a pallah and a wildebeest, which we secured behind the waggons. About ten A.M. we inspanned, and within a mile of Lepeby we passed through another similar open vley, containing a strong fountain of delicious water. We continued our march till sundown through an undulating open country, thinly covered with detached trees and thorny bushes, and encamped in a sandy desert without water.

CHAPTER XIV.

The Bamangwato Mountains—The Elephants' Fountain—A troop of colossal Giraffes—Elephants drinking by Night—Habits of the African Elephant—Elephant Hunt—A Bull shot after a dangerous Encounter—Cutting out the Tusks—Extraordinary Rocks—Mountain-retreat of Sicomy, King of Bamangwato—His Cunning—Barter Muskets for Ivory—His Majesty's curious Gun-practice—Trading for Native Weapons.

On the 25th, at dawn of day, we inspanned, and trekked about five hours in a north-easterly course, through a boundless open country sparingly adorned with dwarfish old trees. In the distance the long-sought mountains of Bamangwato at length loomed blue before me. We halted beside a glorious fountain, which at once made me forget all the

Colesberg declines being mounted.

CHAP. XIV.

cares and difficulties I had encountered in reaching it. The name of this fountain was Massouey, but I at once christened it "the Elephant's own Fountain." This was a very remarkable spot on the southern borders of endless elephant forests, at which I had at length arrived. The fountain was deep and strong, situated in a hollow at the eastern extremity of an extensive vley, and its margin was surrounded by a level stratum of solid old red sandstone. Here and there lay a thick layer of soil upon the rock, and this was packed flat with the fresh spoor of elephants. Around the water's edge the very rock was worn down by the gigantic feet which for ages had trodden there.

The soil of the surrounding country was white and yellow sand, but grass, trees, and bushes were abundant. From the borders of the fountain a hundred well-trodden elephant footpaths led away in every direction, like the radii of a circle. The breadth of these paths was about three feet; those leading to the northward and east were the most frequented, the country in those directions being well wooded. We drew up the waggons on a hillock on the eastern side of the water. This position commanded a good view of any game that might approach to drink. I had just cooked my breakfast, and commenced to feed, when I heard my men exclaim, "Almagtig keek de ghroote clòmp cameel;" and, raising my eyes from my sassaby stew, I beheld a truly beautiful and very unusual scene. From the margin of the fountain there extended an open level vley, without a tree or bush, that stretched away about a mile to the northward, where it was bounded by extensive groves of wide-spreading mimosas.

Up the middle of this valey stalked a troop of ten colossal giraffes, flanked by two large herds of blue wildebeests and zebras, with an advanced guard of pallahs. They were all coming to the fountain to drink, and would be within rifle-shot of the waggons before I could finish my breakfast. I however continued to swallow my food with the utmost expedition, having directed my men to catch and saddle Colesberg. In a few minutes the giraffes were slowly advancing within two hundred yards, stretching their graceful necks, and gazing in wonder at the unwonted waggons. Grasping my rifle, I now mounted Colesberg, and rode slowly towards them. They continued gezing at the waggons until I was within one hundred yards of them, when, whisking their long tails over their rumps, they made off at an easy canter. As I pressed upon them they increased their pace; but Colesberg had much the speed of them, and before we had proceeded half a mile I was riding by the shoulder of the dark-chestnut old bull, whose head towered high above the rest.

Letting fly at the gallop, I wounded him behind the shoulder; soon after which I broke him from the herd, and presently, going ahead of him, he came to a stand. I then gave him a second bullet, somewhere near the first. These two shots had taken effect, and he was now in my power, but I would not lay him low so far from camp, so, having waited until he had regained his breath, I drove him half-way back towards the waggons. Here he became obstreperous; so, loading one barrel, and pointing my rifle towards the clouds, I shot him in the throat, when, rearing high, he fell backwards and expired. This was a magnificent specimen of the giraffe, measuring upwards of eighteen feet in height. I stood for nearly half an hour engrossed in the contemplation of his extreme beauty and gigantic proportions; and, if there had been no elephants, I could have exclaimed, like Duke Alexander of Gordon when he killed the famous old stag with seventeen tine, "Now I can die happy." But I longed for an encounter with the noble elephants, and I thought little more of the giraffe than if I had killed a gemsbok or an eland.

In the afternoon I removed my waggons to a correct distance from the fountain, and drew them up among some bushes about four hundred yards to leeward of the water. In the evening I was employed in manufacturing hardened bullets for the elephants, using a composition of one of pewter to four of lead; and I had just completed my work when we heard a troop of elephants splashing and trumpeting in the water. This was to me a joyful sound; I slept little that night.

On the 26th I arose at earliest dawn, and having fed four of my horses I proceeded with Isaac to the fountain to examine the spoor of the elephants which had drunk there during the night. A number of the paths contained fresh spoor of elephants of all sizes, which had gone from the fountain in different directions. We reckoned that at least thirty of these gigantic quadrupeds had visited the water during the night.

We hastily returned to camp, where, having breakfasted, I saddled up, and proceeded to take up the spoor of the largest bull elephant, accompanied by after-riders and three of the guides to assist in spooring. I was also accompanied by my dogs. Having selected the spoor of a mighty bull, the Bechuanas went ahead, and I followed them. It was extremely interesting and exciting work. The foot-print of this elephant was about two feet in diameter, and was beautifully visible in the soft sand. The spoor at first led us for about three miles in an easterly direction, along one of the sandy footpaths, without a check. We then entered a very thick forest, and the elephant had gone a little out of the path to smash some trees, and to plough up the earth with his tusks. He soon, however, again took the path, and held along it for several miles.

We were on rather elevated ground, with a fine view of a part of the Bamangwato chain of mountains before us. Here the trees were large and handsome, but not strong enough to resist the inconceivable strength of the mighty monarchs of these forests. Almost every tree had half its branches broken short by them, and at every hundred yards I came upon entire trees, and these the largest in the forest, uprooted clean out of the ground, or broken short across their stems. I observed several large trees placed in an inverted position, having their roots uppermost in the air. Our friend had here halted, and fed for a long time upon a large wide-spreading tree which he had broken short across within a few feet of the ground. After following the spoor some distance farther through the dense mazes of the forest, we got into ground so thickly trodden by elephants that we were baffled in our endeavours to trace the spoor any farther; and after wasting several hours in attempting by

CHAP. XIV.—1 Cameleopard hunting at Massouey.

MY FIRST ELEPHANT.

casts to take up the proper spoor, we gave it up, and with a sorrowful heart I turned my horse's head towards camp.

Having reached the waggons, while drinking my coffee I reviewed the whole day's work, and felt much regret at my want of luck in my first day's elephant hunting, and I resolved that night to watch the water, and try what could be done with elephants by night-shooting. I accordingly ordered the usual watching-hole to be constructed; and having placed my bedding in it, repaired thither shortly after sundown. I had lain about two hours in the hole, when I heard a low rumbling noise like distant thunder, caused (as the Bechuanas affirmed) by the bowels of the elephants which were approaching the fountain. I lay on my back, with my mouth open, attentively listening, and could hear them ploughing up the earth with their tusks. Presently they walked up to the water, and commenced drinking within fifty yards of me. They approached with so quiet a step, that I fancied it was the footsteps of jackals which I heard; and I was not aware of their presence until I heard the water, which they had drawn up in their trunks and were pouring into their mouths, dropping into the fountain. I then peeped from my sconce with a beating heart, and beheld two enormous bull elephants, which looked like two great castles, standing before me. I could not see very distinctly, for there was only starlight. Having lain on my breast some time taking my aim, I let fly at one of the elephants, using the Dutch rifle carrying six to the pound. The ball told loudly on his shoulder, and uttering a loud cry he stumbled through the fountain, when both made off in different directions.

All night large herds of zebras and blue wildebeests capered around me, coming sometimes within a few yards. Several parties of rhinoceroses also made their appearance. I felt a little apprehensive that lions might visit the fountain, and every time that hyænas or jackals lapped the water I looked forth, but no lions appeared. At length I fell into a sound sleep, nor did I again raise my head until the bright star of morn had shot far above the eastern horizon.

Before proceeding further with my narrative, it may here be interesting to make a few remarks on the African elephant and his habits. The elephant is widely diffused through the vast forests, and is met with in herds of various numbers. The male is very much larger than the female, consequently much more difficult to kill. He is provided with two enormous tusks. These are long, tapering, and beautifully arched; their length averages from six to eight feet, and they weigh from sixty to a hundred pounds each. In the vicinity of the equator the elephants attain to a greater size than to the southward; and I am in the possession of a pair of tusks of the African bull elephant, the larger of which measures ten feet nine inches in length, and weighs one hundred and seventy-three pounds. The females, unlike Asiatic elephants in this respect, are likewise provided with tusks. The price which the largest ivory fetches in the English market is from £28 to £32 per hundred and twelve pounds.

Old bull elephants are found singly or in pairs, or consorting together in small herds, varying from six to twenty individuals. The younger bulls remain for many years in the company of their mothers, and these are met together in large herds of from twenty to a hundred individuals. The food of the elephant consists of the branches, leaves, and roots of trees, and also of a variety of bulbs, of the situation of which he is advised by his exquisite sense of smell. To obtain these he turns up the ground with his tusks, and whole acres may be seen thus ploughed up. Elephants consume an immense quantity of food, and pass the greater part of the day and night in feeding. Like the whale in the ocean, the elephant on land is acquainted with, and roams over, wide and extensive tracts. He is extremely particular in always frequenting the freshest and most verdant districts of the forest; and when one district is parched and barren, he will forsake it for years and wander to great distances in quest of better pasture.

The elephant entertains an extraordinary horror of man, and a child can put a hundred of them to flight by passing at a quarter of a mile to windward; and when thus disturbed, they go a long way before they halt. It is surprising how soon these sagacious animals are aware of the presence of a hunter in their domains. When one troop has been attacked, all the other elephants frequenting the district are aware of the fact within two or three days, when they all forsake it, and migrate to distant parts, leaving the hunter no alternative but to inspan his waggons, and remove to fresh ground. This constitutes one of the greatest difficulties which a skilful elephant-hunter encounters. Even in the most remote parts, which may be reckoned the head-quarters of the elephant, it is only occasionally, and with inconceivable toil and hardships, that the eye of the hunter is cheered by the sight of one. Owing to habits peculiar to himself, the elephant is more inaccessible, and much more rarely seen, than any other game quadruped, excepting certain rare antelopes. They choose for their resort the most lonely and secluded depths of the forest, generally at a very great distance from the rivers and fountains at which they drink. In dry and warm weather they visit these waters nightly; but in cool and cloudy weather they drink only once every third or fourth day.

About sundown the elephant leaves his distant midday haunt, and commences his march towards the fountain, which is probably from twelve to twenty miles distant. This he generally reaches between the hours of nine and midnight; when, having slaked his thirst and cooled his body by spouting large volumes of water over his back with his trunk, he resumes the path to his forest solitudes. Having reached a secluded spot, I have remarked that full-grown bulls lie down on their broadsides, about the hour of midnight, and sleep for a few hours. The spot which they usually select is an anthill, and they lie around it with their backs resting against it; these hills, formed by the white ants, are from thirty to forty feet in diameter at their base. The mark of the under tusk is always deeply imprinted in the ground, proving that they lie upon their sides. I never remarked that females had thus lain down, and it is only in the more secluded districts that the bulls adopt this practice; for I observed that, in districts where the elephants were liable to frequent disturbance, they took repose standing on their legs beneath some shady tree.

Having slept, they then proceed to feed extensively. Spreading out from one another, and proceeding in a zigzag course, they smash and destroy all the finest trees in the forest which happen to lie in their course. The number of goodly trees which a herd of bull elephants will thus destroy is utterly incredible. They are extremely capricious, and on coming to a group of five or six trees they break down not unfrequently the whole of them, when, having perhaps only tasted one or two small branches, they pass on and continue their wanton work of destruction. I have repeatedly ridden through forests where the trees thus broken lay so thick across one another that it was almost impossible to ride through the district; and it is in situations such as these that attacking the elephant is attended with most danger. During the night they will feed in open plains and thinly wooded districts; but as day dawns, they retire to the densest covers within reach, which nine times in ten are composed of the impracticable wait-a-bit thorns; and here they remain drawn up in a compact herd during the heat of the day. In remote districts, however, and in cool weather, I have known herds to continue pasturing throughout the whole day.

The appearance of the wild elephant is inconceivably majestic and imposing. His gigantic height and colossal bulk, so greatly surpassing all other quadrupeds, combined with his sagacious disposition and peculiar habits, impart to him an interest in the eyes of the hunter which no other animal can call forth. The pace of the elephant when undisturbed is a bold, free, sweeping step; and from the peculiar spongy formation of his foot, his tread is extremely light and inaudible, and all his movements are attended with a peculiar gentleness and grace. This, however, only applies to the elephant when roaming undisturbed in his jungle; for when roused by the hunter, he proves the most dangerous enemy, and far more difficult to conquer than any other beast of chace.

On the 27th, as day dawned, I left my shooting-hole, and proceeded to inspect the spoor of my wounded elephant. After following it for some distance I came to an abrupt hillock, and, fancying that from the summit a good view might be obtained of the surrounding country, I left my followers to seek the spoor, while I ascended. I did not raise my eyes from the ground until I had reached the highest pinnacle of rock. I then looked east, and to my inexpressible gratification I beheld a troop of nine or ten elephants quietly browsing within a quarter of a mile of me. I allowed myself only one glance at them, and then rushed down to warn my followers to be silent. A council-of-war was hastily held, the result of which was my ordering Isaac to ride hard to camp, with instructions to return as quickly as possible, accompanied by Kleinboy, and to bring me my dogs, the large Dutch rifle, and a fresh horse. I once more ascended the hillock to feast my eyes upon the enchanting sight before me; and, drawing out my spyglass, I narrowly watched the motions of the elephants. The herd consisted entirely of females, several of which were followed by small calves.

Presently, on reconnoitring the surrounding country, I discovered a second herd, consisting of five bull elephants, which were quietly feeding about a mile to the northward. The cows were feeding towards a rocky ridge that stretched away from the base of the hillock on which I stood. Burning with impatience to commence the attack, I resolved to try the stalking-system with these, and to hunt the troop of bulls with dogs and horses. Having thus decided, I directed the guides to watch the elephants from the summit of the hillock, and with a beating heart I approached them. The ground and wind favouring me, I soon gained the rocky ridge towards which they were feeding. They were now within one hundred yards, and I resolved to enjoy the pleasure of watching their movements for a little before I fired. They continued to feed slowly towards me, breaking the branches from the trees with their trunks, and eating the leaves and tender shoots. I soon selected the finest in the herd, and kept my eye on her in particular. At length two of the troop had walked slowly past at about sixty yards, and the one which I had selected was feeding with two others on a thorny tree before me.

My hand was now as steady as the rock on which it rested, so, taking a deliberate aim, I let fly at her head a little behind the eye. She got it hard and sharp, just where I aimed, but it did not seem to effect her much. Uttering a loud cry, she wheeled about, when I gave her the second ball, close behind the shoulder. All the elephants uttered a strange rumbling noise, and made off in a line to the northward at a brisk ambling pace, their huge fanlike ears flapping in the ratio of their speed. I did not wait to load, but ran back to the hillock to obtain a view.

On gaining its summit the guides pointed out the elephants; they were standing in a grove of shady trees, but the wounded one was some distance behind with another elephant, doubtless its particular friend, who was endeavouring to assist it. These elephants had probably never before heard the report of a gun; and, having neither seen nor smelt me, they were unaware of the presence of man, and did not seem inclined to go any farther. Presently my men hove in sight, bringing the dogs; and when these came up I waited some time before commencing the attack, that the dogs and horses might recover their wind. We then rode slowly towards the elephants, and had advanced within two hundred yards of them when, the ground being open, they observed us, and made off in an easterly direction; but the wounded one immediately dropped astern, and next moment she was surrounded by the dogs, which, barking angrily, seemed to engross her attention.

Having placed myself between her and the retreating troop, I dismounted to fire within forty yards of her, in open ground. Colesberg was extremely afraid of the elephants, and gave me much trouble, jerking my arm when I tried to fire. At length I let fly; but, on endeavouring to regain my saddle, Colesberg declined to allow me to mount; and when I tried to lead him, and run for it, he only backed towards the wounded elephant. At this moment I heard another elephant close behind; and on looking about I beheld the "friend," with uplifted trunk, charging down upon me at top speed, shrilly trumpeting and following an old black pointer named Schwart, that was perfectly deaf, and trotted along before the enraged elephant quite unaware of what was behind him. I felt certain that she would have either me or my horse. I however determined not to relinquish my steed, but to hold on by the bridle.

My men, who of course kept at a safe distance, stood aghast with their mouths open, and for a few seconds my position was certainly not an enviable one. Fortunately, however, the dogs took off the attention of the elephants; and just as they were upon me I managed to spring into the saddle, where I was safe. As I turned my back to mount, the elephants were so very near that I really expected to feel one of their trunks lay hold of me. I rode up to Kleinboy for my double-barrelled two-grooved rifle: he and Isaac were pale and almost speechless with fright. Returning to the charge, I was soon once more alongside, and, firing from the saddle, I sent another brace of bullets into the wounded elephant. Colesberg was extremely unsteady, and destroyed the correctness of my aim.

The friend now seemed resolved to do some mischief, and charged me furiously, pursuing me to a distance of several hundred yards. I therefore deemed it proper to give her a gentle hint to act less officiously, and accordingly, having loaded, I approached within thirty yards, and gave it her sharp, right and left, behind the shoulder, upon which she at once made off with drooping trunk, evidently with a mortal wound. I never recur to this my first day's elephant-shooting without regretting my folly in contenting myself with securing only one elephant. The first was now dying, and could not leave the ground, and the second was also mortally wounded, and I had only to follow and finish her; but I foolishly allowed her to escape, while I amused myself with the first, which kept walking backwards, and standing by every tree she passed. Two more shots finished her: on receiving them she tossed her trunk up and down two or three times, and, falling on her broadside against a thorny tree, which yielded like grass before her enormous weight, she uttered a deep hoarse cry and expired. This was a very handsome old cow elephant, and was decidedly the best in the troop. She was in excellent condition, and carried a pair of long and perfect tusks.

I was in high spirits at my success, and felt so perfectly satisfied with having killed one, that, although it was still early in the day, and my horses were fresh, I allowed the troop of five bulls to remain unmolested, foolishly trusting to fall in with them next day. How little did I then know of the habits of elephants, or the rules to be adopted in hunting them, or deem it probable I should never see them more!

Having knee-haltered our horses, we set to work with our knives and assagais to prepare the skull for the hatchet, in order to cut out the tusks, nearly half the length of which, I may mention, is embedded in bone sockets in the fore part of the skull. To cut out the tusks of a cow elephant requires barely one-fifth of the labour requisite to cut out those of a bull; and when the sun went down we had managed by our combined efforts to cut out one of the tusks of my first elephant, with which we triumphantly returned to camp, having left the guides in charge of the carcase, where they volunteered to take up their quarters for the night. On reaching my waggons I found Johannus and Carollus in a happy state of indifference to all passing events; they were both very drunk, having broken into my wine-cask and spirit-case.

On the 28th I arose at an early hour, and, burning with anxiety to look forth once more from the summit of the hillock which the day before brought me such luck, I made a hasty breakfast, and rode thither with after-riders and my dogs. But, alas! I had allowed the golden opportunity to slip. This day I sought in vain; and although I often again ascended to the summit of my favourite hillock on that and on the succeeding year, my eyes were destined never again to hail from it a troop of elephants.

Early on the following morning I proceeded to inspect the sandy foot-paths leading from the fountain, and at once discovered the spoor of two mighty bull elephants that had drunk there during the night. These I followed, but did not succeed in coming up with the objects of my search.

We were now within two days' march of the kraal of the great chief Sicomy, king of the extensive territory of Bamangwato. This chief was reported to be in the possession of large quantities of ivory; and as I had brought a number of muskets and other articles for barter, I was anxious to push on, and first get over my trading before resuming elephant-hunting; more especially since it was not improbable that, having once led the way, other adventurers might follow in my track, and perhaps spoil my market. Taking this into consideration, I deemed it proper on the morning of the 30th to march upon the kraal of Sicomy; and accordingly, about 10 A.M. we inspanned, and held for the Bamangwato mountains, whose summits we could see peering above the intervening forest in an easterly direction. On our march we passed near to the carcase of the elephant which I had slain three days before. The number of vultures which were here congregated was truly wonderful. My guides had baked a part of the trunk and two of the feet of the elephant, and these they now brought to the waggons.

It was ever to me a source of great pleasure to reflect that, while enriching myself in following my favourite pursuit of elephant-hunting, I was feeding and making happy the starving families of hundreds of the Bechuana and Bakalahari tribes, who invariably followed in my waggons, and assisted me in my hunting, in numbers varying from fifty to two hundred at a time. These men were often accompanied by their wives and families, and when an elephant, hippopotamus, or other large animal was slain, all hands repaired to the spot, when every inch of the animal was reduced to biltongue, viz., cut into long narrow strips, and hung in festoons upon poles, and dried in the sun: even the entrails were not left for the vultures and hyænas, and the very bones were chopped to pieces with their hatchets to obtain the marrow, with which they enriched their soup.

On the following morning, which was the 1st of July, we inspanned at dawn of day, and late in the afternoon we reached Lesausau, having performed an extremely arduous and fatiguing march. Our route during the greater part of the day lay through dense jungle and thorny thickets, where it was necessary to clear a way with our axes before the waggons could pass. The ground also was in many places extremely rocky, and threatened the destruction of my wheels and axletrees, causing us much labour, it being indispensable to remove the masses of rock to one side. As we neared Lesausau, we entered upon a broad level strath, adorned throughout its length and breadth with a variety of picturesque acacia and other trees, which stood at intervals as if they had been planted by the hand of man. On either side, the mountains rose abruptly from the plain, and they now assumed a very bold and striking appearance, their sides and summits consisting of huge masses of rock piled one above another, some of which seemed so balanced upon their exalted and narrow pedestals,

> "As if an infant's touch could urge
> Their headlong passage down the verge."

A light and feathery fringe of dwarfish trees and varieties of gigantic cacti adorned the sides and upper ridges of these rugged mountains, and as we proceeded, I observed finely wooded wild ravines, stretching away into the bosom of the mountains.

Here we were joined by three of Sicomy's men, who informed us that they were in daily apprehension of an attack from the Matabili, who they heard were marching against them. In consequence of this, Sicomy and all his tribe had forsaken their kraals, and were now living in wild caves and other secluded retreats in the sides and on the summits of these rocky mountains. They led us round the base of a bold projecting rock, and then up a wild and well-wooded rocky ravine, bearing no traces of men. On raising our eyes, however, we perceived the summits of the rocks covered with women and children, and very soon detached parties of Sicomy's warriors came pouring in from different directions, to gaze upon the white man, I being the first that many of them had seen. These men were all armed and ready for action, each bearing an oval shield of ox, buffalo, or camelopard's hide, a battle-axe, and three or four assagais. They wore karosses of jackal's and leopard's skins, which depended gracefully from their shoulders: and many of them sported a round tuft of black ostrich-feathers on their heads, while others had adorned their woolly hair with one or two wavy plumes of white ones. Both men and women wore abundance of the usual ornaments of beads and brass and copper wire.

We were presently met by a messenger from Sicomy, saying that the king was happy we had arrived, and that he would shortly come to see me. We proceeded up the bold and narrow ravine of Lesausau, as far as it was practicable, the water being situated at its upper extremity. Soon after we had encamped Sicomy drew nigh, accompanied by a large retinue of his principal men and warriors. He appeared to me to be about thirty years of age, and was of middle stature. His distinguishing feature is a wall-eye, which imparts to his countenance a roguish look that does not belie the cunning and deceitful character of the man. As he came up to the waggons I met and shook hands with him, and invited him to partake of coffee with me. I could see that he was enchanted at my arrival. He talked at a very rapid pace, and assumed an abrupt and rather dictatorial manner, occasionally turning round and cracking jokes with his councillors and nobility. He was very anxious to ascertain from Isaac the contents of the waggons, and he said that he would buy everything I had brought, and that he would give me a large bull elephant's tusk for each of my muskets.

This was a fishing remark to hear what I should say; so I replied that the muskets cost many teeth in my own country, and that I had not stolen them. I had resolved to maintain a firm and independent manner in my dealings with him, treating him at the same time with the utmost affability. I told him that other men feared to come so far to trade with him, but that his friend Dr. Livingstone had directed me to come, and had sent him a present by me. I then gave him Dr. Livingstone's present, with a similar one from myself, consisting of beads, snuff, and ammunition. It amused me to observe the timid and cringing demeanour of the men of Booby when seated in the presence of the king. Approaching him with the utmost humility, they saluted him by stretching out their hands and clapping the palms together, saying at the same time:

"Rumèla, cosi," signifying, Hail, king! which his majesty was graciously pleased to acknowledge by squinting at them with his cockeye, and saying "Eh," which is the invariable Bechuana acknowledgement of a salutation. Often, however, when I saluted the natives, they acknowledged my salutation by saying "Eh! keitumēla, cosi a Machoa;" signifying, "Eh! thank you, king of the white men." Having saluted the king, the Booby men at once proceeded to expatiate upon the difficulty they had had in prevailing upon the great white man to visit his dominions, and the meritorious manner in which they had conducted me thither; for which the king expressed his gratitude, and ordered "boyalwa," or native beer, to be placed before them. Sicomy remained long at the waggons, engaged in deep and constant conversation with my interpreter and several of his elder councillors, and at a late hour he departed, promising to visit us early on the following day. Fearing that any of his people might come and trade with me during his absence, the king instructed his uncle Mutchuisho, with a retinue, to remain beside the waggons during the night.

At an early hour on the following morning the king made his appearance, attended by a number of his warriors, all carrying their battle-gear. I was still in bed, and seeing the king peeping into my waggon I pretended to be asleep. Presently I observed a savage coming up the glen bearing on his shoulders a bull-elephant's tooth, which he laid under the waggon. Coffee was now announced, so I arose, and the king breakfasted with me. I had resolved to say as little as possible about the trading, and to appear very indifferent, a system indispensable in trading with the natives, which at all times progresses slowly, but much more so if the trader allows them to imagine that he is very anxious to obtain possession of their goods.

In trading with the Bechuanas the most difficult point is agreeing about the price of any article in the first instance; and often when trad-

has once commenced, and the natives are satisfied with the price, exchanges are effected rapidly. It is generally necessary for the trader to ask a little more than he expects to get, that he may appear to yield to their importunity, otherwise they would not deal with him. They never conclude a bargain in a hurry, and always deem it necessary to ask the advice of nearly every one present before they can make up their minds; and if it should happen that any one individual present disapprove of the bargain, the exchange is for the time at an end.

I have more than once been prevented from effecting a sale, which I had all but concluded, by some old wife, who happened to be passing at the moment, exclaiming that I was too high in my prices, although she was perfectly ignorant of our transaction.

While Sicomy was taking his coffee, he told me that he had despatched men to bring elephants' teeth, which he said were at a distance, and that he would purchase everything as quickly as possible, that I might be enabled to leave the country before the Matabili should come. This rumour about the Matabili I at the time suspected to be a fabrication, but I subsequently ascertained that it was a fact.

In the forenoon I occupied myself in writing the journal in my waggon, and I could see that the king was annoyed at my indifference about the trading. At length he asked me to come out of the waggon, saying that he had got a present for me, and he brought forward the elephant's tusk which lay beneath the waggon. Having thanked him, I expressed myself satisfied with his present; and in return I immediately presented him with what he reckoned an equivalent in beads. He asked me the price of my muskets, and I answered four large bull's teeth for each. He then retired to an adjacent grove of shady trees, where he sat consulting with his men for hours. Two men at length appeared, coming from opposite directions, each bearing a bull's tooth. When these arrived, Sicomy ordered them to be placed before me, and, calling Isaac, he inflicted on me a long harangue, talking all manner of nonsense, and endeavouring to obtain a musket for these two teeth. At length a third tusk was brought, but it was a small one.

It was now late in the afternoon, so I told the king that I was going to take a walk in the mountains to obtain a view of his country. He said that he was going to buy one of the muskets immediately, and requested that I would not leave the waggons. After sitting talking with his men till it was near sunset, he once more offered me two tusks for a gun. I replied that I had already spoken. He then said he was going home, and that he did not know if he would come again to trade with me. If the king had indeed resolved not to trade with me, no request on my part would have altered the case. So I replied that I had never asked him to purchase anything, and was perfectly indifferent whether he did or not; that there were other chiefs who were anxious to purchase my goods; and that my reason for visiting his territory was to enjoy the sport of elephant-hunting. Having thus spoken, I wished him good evening, and shouldering my rifle, I stalked up the rocky ravine and shot two baboons.

At an early hour on the following morning Sicomy was at the waggons; and having breakfasted, he commenced as on the previous day to endeavour to purchase a gun with two tusks. At length I said that he should have one for three tusks, provided they were large. After a protracted discussion, the third tusk was produced, when I handed him a musket. He next bothered for a bullet-mould, which I also gave him into the bargain. Having obtained the mould, he insisted on having a lead-ladle. This I said I could not give him with one gun; but promised if he dealt liberally with me he should have one. He continued his importunity about the ladle till late in the afternoon, when he began to talk about buying a second gun. Three tusks were brought, and we had nearly concluded a bargain, when some of his councillors told him that he ought to have received powder and bullets along with the first gun. He commenced to pester me on this subject; but I stoutly resisted, and told him the bargain was concluded. He, however, continued to harp on this string till a late hour, when I told him, as I had done the preceding day, that I must now take a walk; and I remarked that, if he thought he had given too much for my gun, he had better return it, and take away his tusks. Having consulted a short time with his wise men, he returned the gun, and resumed possession of his tusks. I then shouldered my rifle, and held for the wells, to give the dogs water.

These wells were situated at a great distance from my camp, and yielded a very moderate supply of water. Here I met with large parties of the Bamangwato women drawing water, which they bore in earthen vessels balanced on their heads to their elevated retreats in the mountains. The pits where my oxen drank were very distant from the camp, and were reported not to yield a sufficient supply of water, the consequence of which was that my horses and oxen had already greatly fallen off in condition. In this state of things I resolved that my stay at Bamangwato should not exceed another day, and I determined if possible to come to terms with Sicomy on the following morning. On returning to the waggons, Carollus came up to me and reported half the oxen missing. This threw me into a state of great alarm. I at once suspected treachery, and I well knew that if Sicomy had taken them they would not easily be recovered. I instantly despatched two mounted men in different directions, with instructions to ride hard and seek the spoor, and these returned at a late hour, having found them.

On reviewing my trading I could not help feeling annoyed at the dilatory mode in which it progressed. I had now spent two entire days endeavouring to trade, yet no exchanges had been effected. For this, however, there was no help. I could not have acted otherwise, and on the following day I reaped the benefit of my unyielding resolution.

Although I voted the trading an intense bore, it was nevertheless well worth a little time and inconvenience, on account of the enormous profit I should realise. The price I paid for the muskets was £16 for each case containing twenty muskets; and the value of the ivory I required for each musket was upwards of £30, being about 3000 per cent., which I am informed is reckoned among mercantile men to be a very fair profit. Sicomy was in those days in the possession of very large quantities of splendid ivory, and still considerable quantities pass annually through his hands. Since I first visited Bamangwato, and taught the natives the use of fire-arms, they have learnt to kill the elephant themselves; but previous to my arrival they were utterly incapable of subduing a full-grown elephant, even by the united exertions of the whole tribe. All the ivory which Sicomy then possessed, and the majority of that which still passes through his hands, is obtained from elephants slain with assagais by an active and daring race of Bushmen inhabiting very remote regions to the northward and north-west of Bamangwato.

The manner in which Sicomy obtained this ivory was by sending a party of his warriors to the Bushmen, who first obtained the tusks in barter for a few beads, and then compelled some of the poor Bakalahari, or wild natives of the desert, over whom Sicomy conceives that he has a perfect right to tyrannize, to bear them on their shoulders across extensive deserts of burning sand to his head-quarters at Bamangwato. So great was the fatigue endured by the poor Bakalahari on these occasions, that many of them died of exhaustion before reaching Bamangwato. At an early hour on the 4th, Sicomy not appearing, I proceeded to visit him at his mountain residence, accompanied by Isaac and a party of his own men. We wound along the base of the mountains for a distance of half a mile, and then commenced ascending the almost perpendicular and rugged mountain side, consisting of immense masses of rock heaped together in dire confusion. Having gained the summit, which was of a tabular character, we advanced a short distance through a succession of heaps of disjointed masses of rock, and presently we reached the chief's temporary retreat; which consisted of a small circular hut, composed of a framework of boughs of trees, interlined with twigs and covered with grass. A number of similar huts were erected around the royal dwelling, on areas which his men had cleared among the rocks. This, however, was the abode of only a very small part of his tribe, which was extensively scattered over different parts of the mountain range, and occupied sundry distant cattle outposts.

I found Sicomy seated before his wigwam, in earnest conversation with his councillors. He seemed pleased to see me, and thanked me for my visit. I shook hands with him, and informed him that, owing to the scarcity of water at Lesausau, I could not prolong my visit to him; and that I had come to take my leave, and had brought him a few presents, which I then laid before him. He thanked me, and said that I was very good, and that he was happy that I had visited his country; but that one thing made his heart sore, viz. that we had not been able to trade. I replied that that was his fault, and not mine, having offered him my goods on equally liberal terms as I did to others. I then expressed myself anxious to depart. Hereupon Sicomy requested me to remain with him another day, promising to bring me abundance of tusks, and to purchase all my muskets. To this I replied that I was still willing to deal with him, if he would only deal fairly; but I gave him to understand that this was positively the last day I could remain with him.

We then all started for the waggons, where this day the barter went on as briskly as it had been dilatory on the two preceding ones. The king continued drinking coffee and taking snuff at a tremendous rate, and large bowls of his boyalwa kept continually arriving, and were freely circulated throughout the day. Sicomy gave me three bull's tusks for each of the first two muskets, I giving him some powder and lead to boot; after which the price fell to two tusks for each musket. With this rate of exchange the whole assembly seemed perfectly satisfied, and the trading went on without a murmur. Athletic savages were constantly coming and going throughout the day in three different directions, bearing on their shoulders the precious spoils of the elephants of the Kalahari; and when the sun went down all my muskets were disposed of, and I found myself in the possession of a very valuable lot of ivory.

I also effected several exchanges of beads and ammunition for the tusks of cow elephants. I had resolved to purchase fine specimens of the native costume and arms, etc., but ivory being the most important article, it was best to defer all minor transactions until our trade in it was concluded. The king seemed highly delighted with his purchases, and insisted on discharging each of the muskets as he bought it. It was amusing to see the manner in which he performed this operation. Throwing back his kaross, and applying the stock to his naked shoulder, he shut his good eye, and kept the wall-eye open, to the intense amusement of the Hottentots, who were his instructors on the occasion. Each report caused the utmost excitement and merriment among the warriors, who pressed forward and requested that they also might be permitted to try their skill with these novel implements of war.

The king had in his possession a most wonderful knobkerry, which I was determined to obtain. It was made of the horn of the kobaoba, a very rare species of the rhinoceros, and its chief interest consisted in its extraordinary length, which greatly exceeded anything I had ever seen of the kind before, or have since met with. Handing Sicomy my snuff-box, I pointed to the kerry, and asked him where the kobaoba had been killed. He replied that that kerry had been sent him by a chief who resided at an amazing distance on the borders of the Lake of Boats. I then asked him to present it to me, that I might have something to keep in remembrance of him; but he replied that it belonged to his wife, and he could not part with it. Presently, however, while sipping his coffee, he said that if I chose I might purchase it. I asked him what he required for it, and he answered, the cup which he then held full of gunpowder. Accordingly, when his majesty had drained the cup, I handed him the powder, and became possessor of the kobaoba kerry, which is now in my possession, and on which I place a very great value. It was now night, and king said that he would sleep by the waggons, as it was too late to go home.

A number of his men prepared for the bivouac, some collecting logs for the nocturnal watch-fire, which the Bechuanas invariably keep up, while others were occupied in forming circular hedges of thorny branches around the fires, within which they carefully levelled the ground with

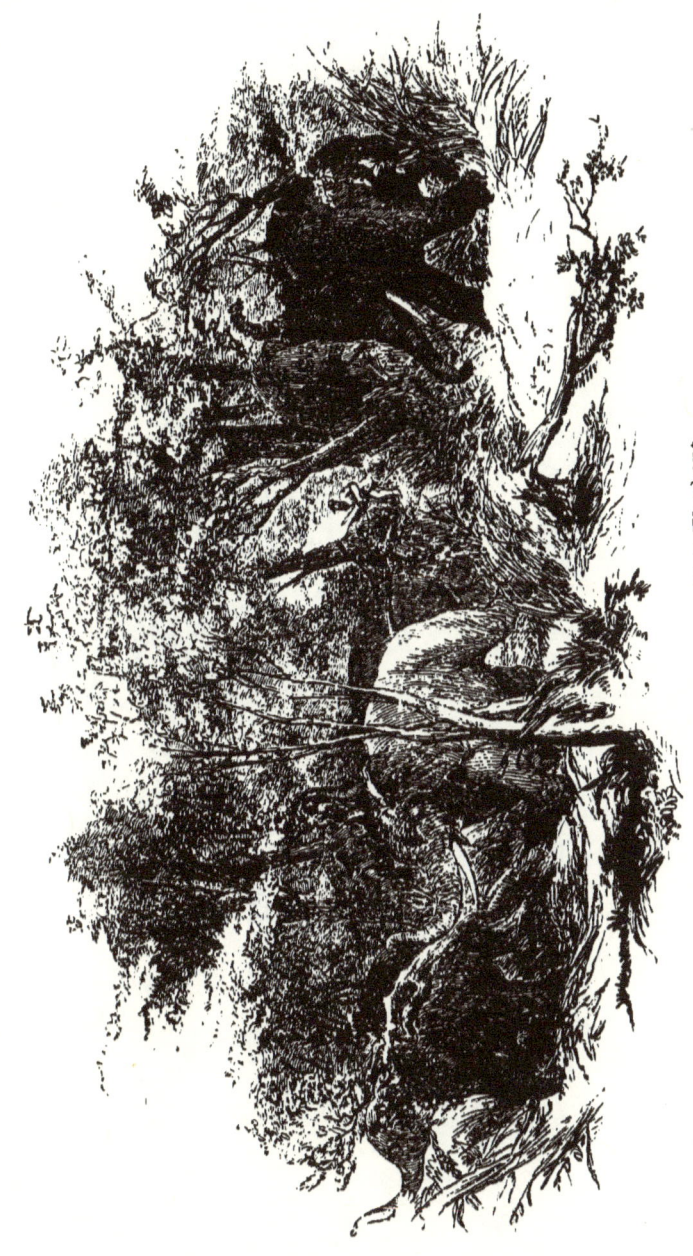

Riding out the best Bull Elephant

CHAP. XV.

pointed sticks, preparatory to spreading out their couches, which consist of long dried grass, and extend in a circular form around the fire. On these couches the Bechuanas sleep, with the soles of their feet to the fire, with no other covering than a light kaross. They lie huddled together like silver spoons on a tray, and the number of individuals around each fire is usually about a dozen. Before retiring to rest I informed Sicomy that I should march on the morrow as soon as my oxen had drunk, and I expressed my wish to trade with his people for karosses and armour at an early hour. Sicomy promised that these articles should be forthcoming, and at once informed his people of my wish.

At an early hour on the morning of the 5th I commenced to trade with Sicomy's men for karosses and Bechuana arms, of each of which I obtained some very fine specimens. With these, as with the ivory, there was considerable discussion before the prices could be agreed on in the first instance, after which exchanges were effected rapidly. I had, however, to pay them long prices for their "chakas" or battle-axes, on which all the Bechuana tribes place a very great value.

I had intended to penetrate beyond Bamangwato, with a wish to explore the country, and for the purpose of hunting elephants; but owing to gross misrepresentations made to me by Isaac relative to Sicomy's wishes on the subject, and partly owing to the threatened attack from the Matabili, I resolved for the present not to extend my peregrinations beyond Bamangwato, but to occupy my time for the remainder of that season in hunting throughout the fine country between Bamangwato and Sichely's mountains. As Isaac's character, however, gradually unfolded itself to me, and as I became more intimate and conversant with the natives, I discovered that he had interpreted Sicomy's wishes to me in utterly false colours; and I afterwards ascertained from the natives, whose language I very soon began to understand, that Sicomy and his people were not only willing, but anxious, that I should remain and hunt elephants in their territory. In consequence of this, as the reader will shortly learn, being informed by Sicomy's men that the invasion by the Matabili was no longer apprehended, I returned to Bamangwato, and penetrated into the extensive forests to the northward and eastward of that mountain range, where for several months I continued hunting elephants, accompanied by large parties of Sicomy's men.

CHAPTER XV.

Take leave of Sicomy—Digging for Water—The Elephants' Fountain again—A wounded Roan Antelope bays in the Water, and kills my Dogs right and left—Sicomy's Camp again—We march through a beautiful Valley—Curious Instinct of the Rhinoceros-bird—A mighty Bull Elephant shot after a hard Conflict—Mutchuisho's Attentions more charitable than pleasant—Cutting up an Elephant—A strange Scene—Baking the Flesh—Primitive Tobacco-pipes—Biltongue Festoons.

ABOUT eleven o'clock A.M. on the 5th of July, everything being ready, I took leave of Sicomy and retraced my steps for Corriebely. It caused me much pain and anxiety to observe that my cattle were extremely hollow-looking and spiritless from want of water; not one of them having obtained a sufficiency of that essential of life since they had last drunk at Corriebely, and several appearing so distressed that I entertained considerable fears of their being able to reach that fountain. I was accompanied by a small party of Sicomy's men, who followed me in the hope of obtaining flesh.

Having proceeded about a mile, I missed my greyhound "Flam," which had been doubtless stolen by Sicomy's orders, he being notorious for his predilection for that variety of dog. I therefore at once despatched a messenger to the king, to say that I required him to find my dog; and shortly after this men overtook me, bearing a kaross, which they said the king had sent to purchase one of my dogs. I replied that they had already taken the dog, but that I would not have the kaross. They then departed, and I continued my march. After trekking about six miles we reached a deep gravel-hole beside a mass of red granite rock, at the bottom of which there was about a bucketful of spring water; and here was the fresh spoor of a huge bull elephant, which had scooped out large portions of the gravel with his trunk on the preceding evening, but on turning about he had entirely undone what he had accomplished by trampling it down again into the well with his huge feet.

On inspecting the spot I fancied that by digging we might obtain a little water for the unfortunate cattle, which at this moment was an object of the utmost importance, the fountain of Corriebely being still very distant. I accordingly set to work hard with all my followers, assisted by the Bechuanas; and having removed an immense quantity of the gravel, I had the satisfaction to discover a small spring of excellent water, which issued from beneath the granite rock and ran as fast as we could catch it in our pails. I then placed my large flesh-pot near the pit, and, ordering the men to bring up the cattle in small detachments, we baled out the water as fast as they could drink it, the buckets being handed along by a line of men extending up the gravel bank to the cattle: and thus in a short time every one of them obtained a sufficiency. This opportune supply of water was to me invaluable, my poor dogs having also been much distressed and requiring water no less than the cattle.

With renewed spirits we continued our journey, and at sundown we halted about half-way to Corriebely. On the march two of the oxen evinced distress, and we were obliged to outspan them and allow them to follow slowly with the loose cattle. About ten o'clock on the following morning I reached Corriebely, and was most thankful to have succeeded in bringing all my wretched cattle alive to a fountain where they could drink their fill. While breakfasting, three of Sicomy's men approached, leading my greyhound Flam; they said that they were sent by Sicomy, who, on hearing that she was missing, had at once issued orders for her recovery.

In the afternoon we inspanned, and marched to the scene of the fall of my first elephant, where we halted for the night. On reaching

Massouey I commenced examining the elephants' footpaths on the side on which were my strongest hopes. I had almost made the circuit of the fountain, and hope had died within me, when, lo ! broad and long, and fresh as fresh could be, the enormous spoor of two mighty bull elephants which had drunk there during the night. This was glorious! I had great faith in the spooring powers of the Bamangwato men, and I felt certain that at length the day had arrived on which I was to kill my first bull elephant. The Bechuanas at once took up the spoor, and went ahead in a masterly manner; and with buoyant spirits I followed in their steps. The spoor led about due west, a direction in which I had not yet been. Having followed it for many miles through this desert country, we reached a district where the bushes, to whose berries Kuopkop was so partial, grew in great abundance; and here the elephants had commenced to feed upon their roots, ploughing up the sand extensively with their tusks. We now entered upon ground much frequented by elephants, their traces, of various dates, extending on all sides, crossing and recrossing one another in every direction : and by this means we eventually lost the spoor.

After a fruitless search of several hours, and many vain endeavours to retrieve the day by trying back on the spoor and making wide casts to the right and left, I was completely beaten, and compelled to drop it, the Bechuanas sitting down and sulkily refusing to proceed farther. We now bent our steps homeward. We had not ridden many miles when we observed a herd of fifteen camelopards browsing quietly in an open glade of the forest. After a very severe chase, in the course of which they stretched out into a magnificent widely-extended front, keeping their line with a regularity worthy of a troop of dragoons, I succeeded in separating a fine bull, upwards of eighteen feet in height, from the rest of the herd, and brought him to the ground within a short distance of the camp. The Bechuanas expressed themselves delighted at my success. They kindled a fire and slept beside the carcase, which they very soon reduced to biltongue and marrow-bones.

On the morning of the 8th I walked to the fountain, and examined all the elephants' footpaths, but there was no fresh spoor. Having breakfasted, I rode for a conical hill, distant from the waggons about five miles in a northerly direction, from whose summit I fancied that elephants might be seen. It was a charming cool day, with a fine bracing wind, the sky beautifully overcast with clouds. I rode along, holding the elephants' footpaths. The marks of their strength were visible in every grove, and all the large trees in the vicinity of the muddy vleys, which at this season were dry, were plastered with sunbaked mud to a height of twelve feet from the ground. On reaching the base of the conical hill I secured my horse to a tree, and ascended to its summit, from which I carefully examined the distant forest landscape with my spyglass, but sought in vain for elephants.

In the evening I took my heavy single-barrelled rifle, and sauntered towards the fountain. A large herd of blue wildebeests were slowly advancing up the vley to drink. I accordingly took up a position behind a low bush near which they must pass, and lay flat on the ground, waiting their approach. Presently I raised my head to see how they were coming on, when I perceived a pair of the rare and beautiful roan antelope or bastard gemsbok warily approaching the fountain. These came up, and were passing within a hundred and twenty yards of me, when, selecting the buck, I let fly, and missed. The whole herd of wildebeests now wheeled to the right-about, and thundered down the vley, enveloped in a cloud of dust; but the two roan antelopes, which had probably never before heard the report of a gun, stood looking about them, while I hastily loaded, lying flat on my side. This being accomplished, I again let fly, and the old buck dropped to the shot; the ball had entered his shoulder, and he lay kicking and roaring until I had almost reloaded, when he regained his feet and made off after his comrade.

At this moment "Argyll" and "Bonteberg," two right good dogs, came up, having heard the shots, and, perceiving the bastard gemsboks, they gave chase. To my surprise the wounded buck, instead of turning to bay, now set off at a rapid pace. He had not gone far, however, when he turned, and stood at bay for about a minute. Two or three more of the dogs heard their comrades barking, and came up to the buck, which then broke bay and made off through the bushes, and in another moment all was still. It was now almost dark, and I followed in the direction which the buck had held, when suddenly I heard a rushing noise, and in another instant the wounded buck met me face to face, closely pursued by five of the dogs. He was making for the water, where he would have bayed, but I unluckily turned him. Owing to light rain which was falling at the moment, I had unfortunately slipped my rifle into a water-proof holster, which prevented my firing, and the buck held close past the waggons, where more dogs joined in the chase.

On reaching camp I inquired of the men if they had seen the buck, and they answered Yes, but that he was not wounded. This I fancied must be the case, and that the dogs had followed the fresh buck; and as two of them made their appearance, I thought that the affair was at an end. In the mean time, however, Kleinboy had seen the chase, and, hastily bridling a horse, had followed. He now rode breathless to the waggons, and reported that the buck was at bay beyond a low ridge within half a mile of camp, and that he was killing the dogs right and left. Seizing my rifle, I mounted a horse and followed after Kleinboy in the dark. Presently I heard the music of my pack, and on coming up I found the bastard gemsbok lying beside a bush, with the dogs barking round him. Three dogs that had followed me from camp, on seeing the buck lying, rushed in upon him, when he struck furiously right and left, and killed one dead on the spot, severely wounding another behind the shoulder; these were Vitfoot and Argyll, two of my best dogs. Again he struck right and left, and knocked over Wolf and Flam with amazing violence, severely injuring their stomachs. He had killed Bles, my stoutest and fiercest dog, before I came up, the horn having entered his heart.

It was a long time before I could fire, for the night was dark, and the buck lay on the ground, with the surviving dogs still pressing close around him. At length he stood up, when I shot him dead with a single shot. He proved to be the wounded buck, having received my first shot in the shoulder. This was a first-rate specimen of the roan antelope, and carried a pair of superb scimitar-shaped horns, which were long and fairly set, and beautifully knotted. Before leaving Massouey two more noble giraffes fell before my rifle, also several fat elands and other varieties of game.

After remaining in the neighbourhood of the fountain for several days, and finding that it was entirely deserted by the elephants, I determined to retrace my steps, and seek for them beyond Bamangwato, and on the 18th we again came to the camp of Sicomy upon the Rocky Mountains. I found the king in a kraal which I had not hitherto visited. He was seated beneath a low shady tree, with a few friends and some of his wives. A number of splendid koodoos' skulls and horns lay rotting about the kraal, among which were several pairs exceeding any I had yet beheld. Casting my eyes to the south-east, I obtained a very distant view of the country in that direction. From the base of the mountain on which I stood stretched a dead level park through a bold opening in the mountains. This park was regularly ornamented with groves and forest-trees, and extended without the slightest break or change as far as I could see. The scene exactly resembled the ocean when viewed from the summit of some bold mountain standing near its shore. Having partaken of the king's beer, I descended to my waggons, when we continued our march along the aforesaid valley. I was accompanied by Sicomy's brother; and on looking behind me as we proceeded, I beheld long strings of the natives following in our wake, and small detached parties kept pouring down from the rocks and glens on every side, until my suite exceeded two hundred men.

We held a northerly course, and on the second day we reached Letlochee, a strong perpetual fountain, situated in an abrupt and rocky ravine. This ravine lay in a range of low rocky hills, which were bounded on the north and west by a wide and gently sloping basin or hollow, diversified with extensive groves and open glades. This hollow extended to a breadth of from six to eight miles, and was much frequented by elands and giraffes, and beyond it stretched the boundless extent of the sandy Kalahari desert. Here I daily enjoyed excellent sport with these two varieties of game; but though elephants occasionally visited the water, and we followed on their tracks to an amazing distance, we always failed to obtain a view of them.

On the forenoon of the 23rd a native came and informed me that he had discovered a white rhinoceros lying asleep in thick cover to the south. I accordingly accompanied him to the spot and commenced stalking in upon the vast muchocho. He was lying asleep beneath a shady tree, and his appearance reminded me of an enormous hog, which in shape he slightly resembles. He kept constantly flapping his ears, which they invariably do when sleeping. Before I could reach the proper distance to fire, several "rhinoceros-birds," by which he was attended, warned him of his impending danger by sticking their bills into his ear, and uttering their harsh, grating cry. Thus aroused, he suddenly sprang to his feet and crashed away through the jungle at a rapid trot, and I saw no more of him.

These rhinoceros-birds are constant attendants upon the hippopotamus and the four varieties of rhinoceros, their object being to feed upon the ticks and other parasitic insects that swarm upon these animals. They are of a greyish colour, and are nearly as large as a common thrush; their voice is very similar to that of the mistletoe-thrush. Many a time have these ever-watchful birds disappointed me in my stalk, and tempted me to invoke an anathema upon their devoted heads. They are the best friends the rhinoceros has, and rarely fail to awaken him even in his soundest nap. "Chukuroo" perfectly understands their warning, and, springing to his feet, he generally first looks about him in every direction, after which he invariably makes off.

I have often hunted a rhinoceros on horseback, which led me a chase of many miles and required a number of shots before he fell, during which chase several of these birds remained by the rhinoceros to the last. They reminded me of mariners on the deck of some bark sailing on the ocean, for they perched along his back and sides; and as each of my bullets told on the shoulder of the rhinoceros, they ascended about six feet into the air, uttering their harsh cry of alarm, and then resumed their position. It sometimes happened that the lower branches of trees, under which the rhinoceros passed, swept them from their living deck, but they always recovered their former station; they also adhere to the rhinoceros during the night. I have often shot these animals at midnight when drinking at the fountains, and the birds, imagining they were asleep, remained with them till morning, and on my approaching, before taking flight, they exerted themselves to their utmost to awaken Chukuroo from his deep sleep.

In the evening one of the parties sent out to seek for the spoor of elephants returned to camp, stating that a small tribe of Bakalahari, who resided in a range of mountains to the east, reported these beasts to frequent the forests in the vicinity of their abode, and Mutchuisho, Sicomy's uncle, who attended me whilst hunting his country, accordingly requested me to hold myself in readiness to accompany him in quest of the elephants at an early hour next day. It was customary with me to console myself, when hope had almost died under a long-continued run of bad luck, by saying to myself that "Patience will have her perfect work," thus making up my mind that a man who is a good stalker and a fair rifle-shot must eventually obtain by perseverance whatever game be seeks to kill. But in the present instance things looked so bad that I had begun to think it not improbable that I might be compelled to leave the Bamangwato country without again even seeing what my heart so ardently desired, viz. an old bull elephant free in his native forests; and day and night I mourned my folly in losing the opportunity which I had neglected on the 27th day of June.

But patience *will* have her perfect work, and the day had at last arrived which was to repay my steady perseverance with complete success. At an early hour on the 24th, upon the strength of the report brought to us on the preceding evening, I took the field with Isaac and Kleinboy as after-riders, accompanied by Mutchuisho and a hundred and fifty of his tribe. We held a north-easterly course, and, having proceeded about five miles through the forest, we reached a fountain, where I observed the spoor of a herd of cow elephants, two days old. Here we made a short halt, and snuff was briskly circulated, while the leading men debated on the course we were to follow, and it was agreed that we should hold for the Bakalahari kraal. Having continued our course for several miles, we rounded the northern extremity of a range of rocky monntains which rose abruptly in the forest and stretched away to the south of east in a long-continued chain. Here we were met by men whom Mutchuisho had despatched before daybreak, who said that the Bakalahari women had that morning seen elephants. This was joyous news. My hopes were high, and I at once felt certain that the hour of triumph was at hand. But disappointment was still in store for me. We all sat down on the grass, while men were despatched to bring the Bakalahari, and when these came we ascertained that it was only spoor and not elephants they had seen. We held on for an inspection of it; and here I was further to be disappointed, the spoor proving to be two days old.

The country now before me was a vast level forest extending to the north and east for about twenty miles without a break. At that distance, however, the landscape was shut in by blue mountain ranges of considerable height, and two bold conical mountains standing close together rose conspicuous above the rest. These mountains the Bamangwato men informed me were their ancient habitation, and that of their forefathers, but the cruel Matabili had driven them from thence to the rocky mountains which they now occupy. We continued our course in an easterly direction, and twice crossed the gravelly bed of a periodical river, in which were several small springs of excellent water. These springs had been exposed by elephants, which had cleared away the gravel with their trunks. Around these springs the spoor of rhinoceros was abundant. After proceeding several miles through a dry and barren tract, where wait-a-bit thorns prevailed, we entered upon more interesting ground.

The forest was adorned with very picturesque old trees of various sorts and sizes, which stood singly and in shady groups, while the main body of the forest consisted of a variety of trees of other sorts, averaging the height of a giraffe. The elephants had left abundant traces of their presence, but all the marks were old. Fresh spoor of giraffe was imprinted on the ground on every side, and we presently saw a large herd of these, standing scattered through the forest to our left. They were glorious fellows, but I was now in pursuit of nobler game: the natives were leading me to some distant fountain, where they expected we should discover spoor.

On we sped through the depths of the forest, our view being confined to about fifty yards on every side. Presently emerging upon a small open glade, I observed a herd of brindled gnoos and two or three troops of pallahs; and soon after a second herd of about fifteen camelopards stood browsing before us, and, getting our wind, dashed away to our left. We had proceeded about two miles farther, and it was now within two hours of sunset, when, lo! a thorny tree, newly smashed by an elephant. Some of the natives attentively examined the leaves of the broken branches to ascertain exactly when he had been there; while some for the same purpose overhauled the spoor. It was the spoor of a first-rate bull; he had fed there that morning at the dawn of day. The ground was hard and bad for spooring, but the natives evinced great skill; and following it for a short distance, we came to ground where a troop of bull elephants had pastured not many hours before. Here the thorny trees on every side were demolished by them, and huge branches and entire trees were rent and uprooted, and lay scattered across our path, having been carried several yards in the trunks of the elephants before they stood to eat the leaves: the ground also was here and there ploughed up by their tusks in quest of roots; and in these places the enormous fresh spoor—that thrilling sight to a hunter's eye—was beautifully visible.

All this was extremely interesting and gratifying; but I had been so often disappointed, and it was now so very near sunset, that I entertained but faint hopes of finding them that evening. Mutchuisho was very anxious that I should see the elephants; he had divested himself of his kaross, and, carrying one of the muskets which Sicomy had bought from me, he led the spooring party, consisting of about fifteen cunning old hands. The great body of the men he had ordered to sit down and remain quiet until the attack commenced. Having followed the spoor for a short distance, old Mutchuisho became extremely excited, and told me that we were close to the elephants. A few minutes after several of the spoorers affirmed that they had heard the elephants break a tree in advance; they differed, however, about the direction, some saying it was in front, and others that it was away to our left. Two or three men quickly ascended the tallest trees that stood near us, but they could not see the elephants. Mutchuisho then extended men to the right and left, while we continued on the spoor.

In a few minutes one of those who had gone off to our left came running breathless to say that he had seen the mighty game. I halted for a minute, and instructed Isaac, who carried the big Dutch rifle, to act independently of me, while Kleinboy was to assist me in the chase; but, as usual, when the row began, my followers thought only of number one. I bared my arms to the shoulder, and, having imbibed a draught of aqua pura from the calabash of one of the spoorers, I grasped my trusty two-grooved rifle, and told my guide to go ahead. We proceeded silently as might be for a few hundred yards, following the guide; when he suddenly pointed, exclaiming, "Klow!" and before us stood a herd of mighty bull elephant, packed together beneath a shady grove about a hundred and fifty yards in advance. I rode slowly towards them; and as soon as they observed me they made a loud rumbling noise, and, tossing their trunks, wheeled right about and made off in one direction, crashing through the forest and leaving a cloud of dust behind them. I was accompanied by a detachment of my dogs, who assisted me in the pursuit.

The distance I had come, and the difficulties I had undergone, to behold these elephants, rose fresh before me. I determined that on this occasion at least I would do my duty, and, dashing my spurs into "Sunday's" ribs, I was very soon much too close in their rear for safety. The elephants now made an inclination to my left, whereby I obtained a good view of the ivory. The herd consisted of six bulls; four of them were full-grown, first-rate elephants; the other two were fine fellows, but had not yet arrived at perfect stature. Of the four old fellows, two had much finer tusks than the rest, and for a few seconds I was undecided which of these two I would follow; when, suddenly, the one which I fancied had the stoutest tusks broke from his comrades, and I at once felt convinced that he was the patriarch of the herd, and followed him accordingly. Cantering alongside, I was about to fire, when he instantly turned, and, uttering a trumpet so strong and shrill that the earth seemed to vibrate beneath my feet, he charged furiously after me for several hundred yards in a direct line not altering his course in the slightest degree for the trees of the forest, which he snapped and overthrew like reeds in his headlong career.

When he pulled up in his charge, I likewise halted; and as he slowly turned to retreat I let fly at his shoulder, "Sunday" capering and prancing and giving me much trouble. On receiving the ball the elephant shrugged his shoulder, and made off at a free majestic walk. This shot brought several of the dogs to my assistance which had been following the other elephants, and on their coming up and barking another headlong charge was the result, accompanied by the never-failing trumpet as before. In his charge he passed close to me, when I saluted him with a second bullet in the shoulder, of which he did not take the slightest notice. I now determined not to fire again until I could make a steady shot; but although the elephant turned repeatedly, "Sunday" invariably disappointed me, capering so that it was impossible to fire.

At length exasperated, I became reckless of the danger, and, springing from the saddle, I approached the elephant under cover of a tree, and gave him a bullet in the side of the head, when, trumpeting so shrilly that the forest trembled, he charged among the dogs, from whom he seemed to fancy that the blow had come; after which he took up a position in a grove of thorns, with his head towards me. I walked up very near, and as he was in the act of charging, I (being in those days under wrong impressions as to the impracticability of bringing down an elephant with a shot in the forehead) stood coolly in his path until he was within fifteen paces of me, and let drive at the hollow of his forehead, in the vain expectation that by so doing I should end his career. The shot only served to increase his fury—an effect which, I have remarked, shots in the head invariably produce; and continuing his charge with incredible quickness and impetuosity, he all but terminated my elephant-hunting for ever.

A large party of the Bechuanas who had come up yelled out simultaneously, imagining I was killed, for the elephant was at one moment almost on the top of me: I however escaped by my activity, and by dodging round the bushy trees. As the elephant was charging, an enormous thorn ran deep into the sole of my foot, the old Badenoch brogues, which I that day sported, being worn through; and this caused me severe pain, laming me throughout the rest of the conflict.

The elephant held on through the forest at a sweeping pace; but he was hardly out of sight when I was loaded and in the saddle, and soon once more alongside. About this time I heard Isaac blazing away at another bull; but when the elephant charged, his cowardly heart failed him, and he very soon made his appearance at a safe distance in my rear. My elephant kept crashing along at a steady pace, with blood streaming from his wounds; the dogs, which were knocked up with fatigue and thirst, no longer barked around him, but had dropped astern. It was long before I again fired, for I was afraid to dismount, and "Sunday" was extremely troublesome. At length I fired sharp right and left from the saddle: he got both balls behind the shoulder and made a long charge after me, rumbling and trumpeting as before. The whole body of the Bamangwato men had now come up, and were following a short distance behind me. Among these was Mollyeon, who volunteered to help; and being a very swift and active fellow, he rendered me important service by holding my fidgety horse's head while I fired and loaded. I then fired six broadsides from the saddle, the elephant charging almost every time, and pursuing us back to the main body in our rear, who fled in all directions as he approached.

The sun had now sunk behind the tops of the trees: it would very soon be dark, and the elephant did not seem much distressed, notwithstanding all he had received. I recollected that my time was short, therefore at once resolved to fire no more from the saddle, but to go close up to him and fire on foot. Riding up to him I dismounted, and, approaching very near, I gave it him right and left in the side of the head, upon which he made a long and determined charge after me; but I was now very reckless of his charges, for I saw that he could not overtake me, and in a twinkling I was loaded, and, again approaching, I fired sharp right and left behind his shoulder. Again he charged with a terrific trumpet, which sent "Sunday" flying through the forest.

This was his last charge. The wounds which he had received began to tell on his constitution, and he now stood at bay beside a thorny tree, with the dogs barking around him. These, refreshed by the evening breeze, and perceiving that it was nearly over with the elephant, had once more come to my assistance. Having loaded, I drew near and fired right and left at his forehead. On receiving these shots, instead of charging he tossed his trunk up and down, and by various sounds and motions, most gratifying to the hungry natives, evinced that his demise was near. Again I loaded, and fired my last shot behind his shoulder: on receiving it, he turned round the bushy tree beside which he stood, and I ran round to give him the other barrel, but the mighty old monarch of the forest needed no more; before I could clear the bushy tree he fell heavily on his side, and his spirit had fled. My feelings at this moment can only be understood by a few brother Nimrods, who have had the good fortune to enjoy a similar encounter. I never felt so gratified on any former occasion as I did then.

By this time all the natives had come up; they were in the highest spirits, and flocked around the elephant laughing and talking at a rapid pace. I climbed on to him, and sat enthroned upon his side, which was as high as my eyes when standing on the ground. In a few minutes night set in, when the natives, having illuminated the jungle with a score of fires, and formed a semicircle of bushes to windward, lay down to rest without partaking of a morsel of food. Mutchuisho would not allow a man to put an assagai into the elephant until the morrow, and placed two relays of sentries to keep watch on either side of him. My dinner consisted of a piece of flesh from the temple of the elephant, which I broiled on the hot embers. In the conflict I had lost my shirt, which was reduced to streamers by the wait-a-bit thorns, and all the clothing that remained was a pair of buckskin knee-breeches.

The night was very cold, it being now the dead of the African winter. Having collected dry grass, I spread it beside my fire, and lay down for the night with no other covering than an old sheepskin, which I had used for a saddle-cloth. Shortly after I had dropped asleep, Mutchuisho, commiserating my bare condition, spread an old jackal kaross over me. This kaross, as all Bechuana garments are, was thickly tenanted by small transparent insects, usually denominated lice. These virulent creatures, probably finding my skin more tender than that of the owner of the kaross, seemed resolved to enjoy a banquet while they could; and presently I awoke with my whole body so poisoned and inflamed that I felt as if attacked with a severe fever. All further rest that night was at an end. I returned the kaross to Mutchuisho, with grateful acknowledgments for his polite intentions; and piling dry wood on the fire, which emitted a light as bright as day, I aroused the slumbering Kleinboy to assist me in turning my buckskins outside in, when an animating "chasse" commenced, which terminated in the capture of about fourscore of my white-currant coloured visitors. I then lit another fire opposite to the first, and spent the remainder of the night squatted between the two, thus imbibing caloric before and behind.

As the sun rose on the morning of the 25th, Mutchuisho gave the word to cut up the elephant, when a scene of blood, noise, and turmoil ensued, which baffles all description. Every native there, divested of his kaross and armed with an assagai, rushed to the onslaught; and in less than two hours every inch of the elephant was gone, and carried by the different parties to their respective temporary locations, which they had chosen beneath each convenient tree that grew around.

The manner in which the elephant is cut up is as follows:—The rough outer skin is first removed, in large sheets, from the side which lies uppermost. Several coats of an under skin are then met with. This skin is of a tough and pliant nature, and is used by the natives for making water-bags, in which they convey supplies of water from the nearest vley or fountain (which is often ten milles distant) to the elephant. They remove this inner skin with caution, taking care not to cut it with the assagai; and it is formed into water-bags by gathering the corners and edges, and transfixing the whole on a pointed wand. The flesh is then removed in enormous sheets from the ribs, when the hatchets come into play, with which they chop through, and remove individually, each colossal rib. The bowels are thus laid bare; and in the removal of these the leading men take a lively interest and active part, for it is throughout and around the bowels that the fat of the elephant is mainly found.

There are few things which a Bechuana prizes so highly as fat of any description; they will go an amazing distance for a small portion of it. They use it principally in cooking their sun-dried biltongue, and they also eat it with their corn. The fat of the elephant lies in extensive layers and sheets in his inside, and the quantity which is obtained from a full-grown bull, in high condition, is very great. Before it can be obtained, the greater part of the bowels must be removed. To accomplish this, several men eventually enter the immense cavity of his inside, where they continue mining away with their assagais, and handing the fat to their comrades outside until all is bare. While this is transpiring with the sides and bowels, other parties are equally active in removing the skin and flesh from the remaining parts of the carcase. The natives have a horrid practice on these occasions of besmearing their bodies, from the crown of the head to the sole of the foot, with the black and clotted gore; and in this anointing they assist one another, each man taking up the fill of both his hands, and spreading it over the back and shoulders of his friend.

Throughout the entire proceeding an incessant and deafening clamour of many voices and confused sounds is maintained, and violent jostling and wrestling are practised by every man, elbowing the breasts and countenances of his fellows, all slippery with gore, as he endeavours to force his way to the venison through the dense intervening ranks, while the sharp and ready assagai gleams in every hand. The angry voices and gory appearances of these naked savages, combined with their excited aud frantic gestures and glistening arms, presented an effect so wild and striking, that when I first beheld the scene I contemplated it in the momentary expectation of beholding one half of the gathering turn their weapons against the other.

The trunk and feet are considered a delicacy, and a detachment are employed on these. The four feet are amputated at the fetlock joint, and the trunk, which at the base is about two feet in thickness, is cut into convenient lengths. Trunk and feet are then baked, preparatory to their removal to head-quarters. The manner in which this is done is as follows:—A party, provided with sharp-pointed sticks, dig a hole in the ground for each foot and a portion of the trunk. These holes are about two feet deep, and a yard in width; the excavated earth is embanked around the margin of the hole. This work being completed, they next collect an immense quantity of dry branches and trunks of trees, of which there is always a profusion scattered around, having been broken by the elephants in former years. These they pile above

ELEPHANT COOKING.

the holes to the height of eight or nine feet, and then set fire to the heap. When these strong fires have burnt down, and the whole of the wood is reduced to ashes, the holes and the surrounding earth are heated in a high degree.

Ten or twelve men then stand round the pit, and rake out the ashes with a pole about sixteen feet in length, having a hook at the end. They relieve one another in quick succession, each man running in and raking the ashes for a few seconds, and then pitching the pole to his comrade and retreating, since the heat is so intense that it is scarcely to be endured. When all the ashes are thus raked out beyond the surrounding bank of earth, each elephant's foot and portion of the trunk is lifted by two athletic men, standing side by side, who place it on their shoulders; and approaching the pit together, they heave it into it. The long pole is now again resumed, and with it they shove in the heated bank of earth upon the foot, shoving and raking until it is completely buried in the earth. The hot embers, of which there is always a great supply, are then raked into a heap above the foot, and another bonfire is kindled over each, which is allowed to burn down and die a natural death; by which time the enormous foot or trunk will be found to be equally baked throughout its inmost parts. When the foot is supposed to be ready, it is taken out of the ground with pointed sticks, and is first well beaten, and then scraped with an assagai, whereby adhering particles of sand are got rid of. The outside is then pared off, and it is transfixed with a sharp stake for facility of carriage.

The feet thus cooked are excellent, as is also the trunk, which very much resembles buffalo's tongue. The reason why such large fires are requisite is owing to the mass of the flesh that must be baked. In raking the sand on the foot, the natives are careful not to rake the red-hot embers in with it, which would burn and destroy the meat; whereas the sand or earth protects it, imparting an even and steady heat. When the natives have cut up the elephant, and removed the large masses of flesh, etc., to their respective temporary kraals around, they sit down for a little to rest and draw their breath, and for a short time smoking and snuffing are indulged in.

The Bechuana pipe is of a very primitive description, differing from any I had ever seen. When they wish to smoke they moisten a spot of earth, not being particular whence they obtain the water. Into this earth they insert a green twig, bent into a semicircle, whose bend is below the said earth, and both ends protruding. They then knead the moist earth down with their knuckles on the twig, which they work backwards and forwards until a hole is established, when the twig is withdrawn, and one end of the aperture is enlarged with the fingers, so as to form a bowl to contain the tobacco. The pipe is thus finished and ready for immediate use, when tobacco and fire are introduced, and the smoker drops on his knees, and resting on the palms of his hands, he brings his lips in contact with the mud at the small end of the hole, and thus inhales the grateful fumes. Large volumes of smoke are emitted through the nostrils, while a copious flow of tears from the eyes of the smoker evinces the pleasure he enjoys. One of these pipes will serve a large party, who replenish the bowl and relieve one another in succession.

The natives, having drawn their breath, once more devote their attention to the flesh, which they next reduce to biltongue, cutting every morsel into thin strips from six to twenty feet in length. These strips are of the breadth and thickness of a man's two fingers. When all is reduced to biltongue they sally forth with their tomahawks, and cut down a number of poles of two sorts, for uprights and cross-poles. The uprights are eight feet long, and forked at one end. They place them upright in the ground around their respective trees, laying the cross-poles resting on the forks, and these are adorned with endless garlands of the raw meat, which is permitted to hang in the sun for two or three days, when it will have lost much of its weight, and be stiff and easy to be carried. They then remove the biltongue from the poles, and, folding it together, they form it into bundles, which are strongly lashed and secured with long strips of the tough inner bark of thorny mimosas. Their work in the forest is now completed, and, each man placing one bundle on his head, and slinging several others across his shoulders, returns to his wife and family at head-quatters.

The appearance which the flesh of a single elephant exhibits when reduced to strips and suspended from the poles is truly surprising, the forest far around displaying a succession of ruby festoons, and reminding one of a vineyard laden with its clustering fruits. When the skull of my elephant was ready for the axe, Mutchuisho caused a party to hew out for me the tusks—a work of great labour and needing considerable skill. In the present instance the work was clumsily executed, the natives hacking and injuring the ivory in removing the bone with their little tomahawks. In consequence of this I invariably afterwards performed the task myself, using superior American hatchets, which I had provided expressly for the purpose. When the tusks had been extracted, I saddled up, and started for the camp, accompanied by my after-riders and a party of the natives bearing the ivory, with a supply of baked foot and trunk and a portion of the flesh. The natives had appropriated all the rest, and when I left them they were quarelling over the remnant of the skull, whose marrowy bones were in high demand. They fought for every chip as it flew from the axe, and chewed it raw. On our way to camp we passed through the kraal of the Bakalahari, situated in the mountain range. In the valleys they had formed considerable gardens, in which corn and water-melons were extensively grown. I was right glad to reach my comfortable camp and get a bowl of coffee.

On the evening of the 26th men kept pouring into camp heavily laden with the flesh of the elephant, a large part of which was for Sicomy: they halted with me for the night, and resumed their march in the morning.

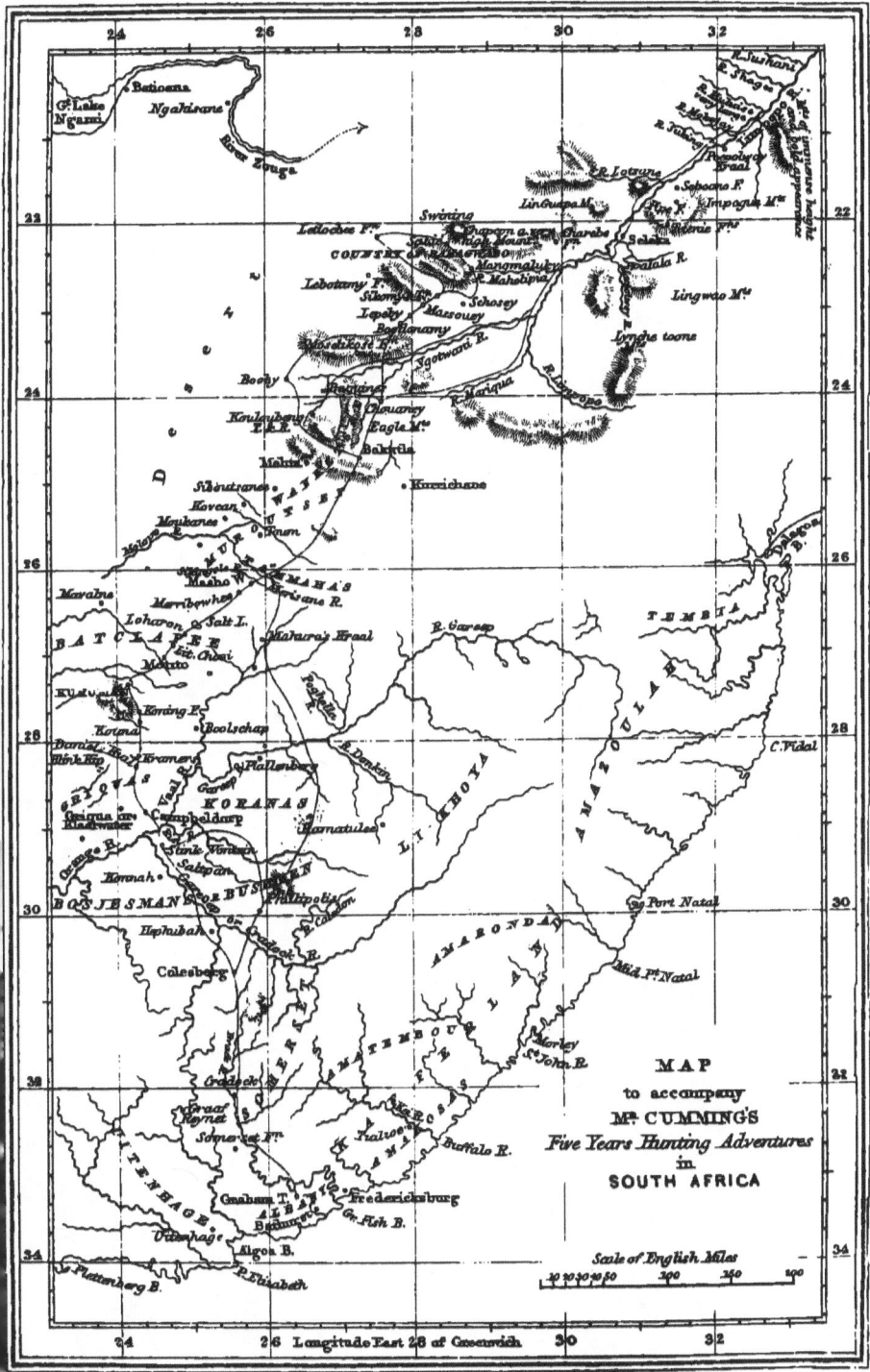

CHAP. XVI.

CHAPTER XVI.

Elephant spooring with the Natives—The Mystic Dice—Hunt in a Wait-a-bit Thorn Cover—Romantic Gorge in the Mountains—Sabié—Ancient Elephant Path—Ludicrous Native Signal—A noble Bull Elephant slain—Isaac, my Interpreter, dismissed—A Lioness bagged at one shot—Drunkenness and Disorder in Camp—My manner of taking the Field after the larger Game—Sicomy's Followers desert me.

ON the 27th of July I resolved to move my waggons further to the east, and informed the waggon-drivers of my intentions: they however raised many objections, and all but gave me a direct refusal. As I was not aware of the position of the waters, and knowing well that Isaac would not assist me in discovering them, I deemed it prudent first to make an excursion to the east on horseback. I accordingly stowed some ammunition and a washing-rod in my old game-bag (to the inside of which, by the by, adhered a goodly coating of the scales of grilse and salmon, along with sundry speckled and blood-stained feathers of the grouse and partridge), and having made bread and ground coffee sufficient for three days' consumption, I ordered two of my men to be ready to accompany me next morning. My interpreter's countenance never lacked a scowl; and, instead of forwarding my interests, he actively employed his energies in sowing dissension betwixt me and the natives, and disseminating mutiny among the Hottentots. I discovered that all along he had deceived me, and carefully concealed the direction where most elephants abounded, and I began to think that, in justice to myself, it was high time that he should be ignominiously dismissed the service.

On the 28th, as I was breakfasting, natives arrived and reported fresh spoor within a mile of camp. I therefore resolved to defer for the present the trip to the eastward on which I had determined; but it so happened that the spoor which was reported led me in that direction, and was the means of introducing me to a succession of fine hunting-districts, throughout which elephant and rhinoceros were abundant. Everything being ready, I proceeded to take up the spoor; accompanied by after-riders and about a hundred of the Bamangwato men, fresh parties having joined me: it was the spoor of a small troop of cow elephants. Mutchuisho and the spooring party took it up in a masterly manner, and went along at a rapid pace all day, with scarcely a check, until we found the elephants. The spoor led us first through a gorge in the mountains, which I mentioned as having rounded on the 24th; after which we followed it in an easterly course, skirting the base of the mountain chain. The country increased in beauty as we advanced; and, having followed the spoor some hours, it led us into a new variety of country, and, as I fancied, into a new climate. Here large trees were abundant, and the grass and leaves were much greener than in the country we had left behind. We crossed the gravelly beds of two periodical rivers. In one of these I observed the recent spoor of a herd of bull elephants deeply imprinted in the sand. This day the wind, which had for weeks been cold and blighting, blowing off the icebergs of the Southern Ocean, shifted to north-east, and breathed warm and balmy upon us.

As we advanced the work of elephants became more and more apparent on the trees and in the earth, and late in the afternoon, we reached ground where a large herd of cows had fed that morning. Here we had a short check, when Mutchuisho rated the trackers for their negligence; and, having despatched parties to try back upon the spoor, and extended others to make casts on our right and left, he leisurely ensconced himself beneath a shady tree, and proceeded, along with several of his cronies, to enjoy the luxury of taking snuff, which important ceremony having been duly performed, they began with the utmost gravity to smooth a portion of the ground before them, preparatory to casting the mystic dice which most of the Bechuanas carry strung around their necks. These dice, which are of sundry indescribable shapes, are formed of ivory, and the Bechuanas invariably appeal to them before entering upon any project of importance to ascertain the probability of its ultimate success. Having unstrung the dice, which are four in number, they rattle them between their hand, and drop them on the ground, when the long-headed old men carefully study the directions of the points, and decide the merits of the case accordingly.

In the present instance the dice spoke favourably, auguring the speedy capture of an elephant; and one of the trackers at this moment coming up, and stating that his comrades had regained the spoor, we sprang to our feet, and again held on. We had proceeded about half a mile when we suddenly beheld a herd of about twelve old cow elephants, some of which were accompanied by little calves, feeding high on the side of the rocky mountains, about five hundred yards to our right. The intervening ground was a dense and almost impenetrable mass of wait-a-bit thorny bushes, averaging twenty feet in height, every inch of which was to be dreaded as the hooks upon a "kill-devil." On perceiving the elephants we halted, and Mutchuischo despatched two men to windward, in the hope of driving them from the impracticable ground they occupied into the level forest where we stood. The elephants, however, were much too wide awake to leave their stronghold of wait-a-bit bushes. On getting the wind of the men they tossed their trunks, and, wheeling about, they held along the mountain side at a rapid pace until they reached an impenetrable jungle of thorns, from which all our efforts proved unavailing to dislodge them.

This jungle densely covered the sides and bottom of a wide semicircular basin or hollow in the mountains; it was throughout so dense, that a man on foot could scarcely penetrate it. When the elephants started I rode hard after them, followed by my after-riders, and, not understanding the intentions of the elephants, we followed on through the mazes of the jungle in an elephant path, until we reached the centre of the thicket, when we suddenly found ourselves upon them. The dogs then ran in barking, when a general trumpeting took place, and a charging and crashing in all directions, and, owing to the extremely dangerous nature of the ground, I was glad to beat a precipitate retreat.

Once more all was quiet; my dogs were jaded with the sun, and would not fight. Fancying that the elephants had gone ahead, and fearing to lose them, I again pushed on, holding the footpath as before; when crash came a second charge of elephants at our very elbows, accompanied by a trumpeting which caused our ears to tingle. They charged upon us from opposite directions, and we were actually in the very middle of them. They were extremely fierce, and, but for the dogs, not a man of us had escaped to tell the tale. Fortunately, the dogs, which they seemed to think designed the capture of their calves, engrossed their whole attention; whereas, by reason of the colour of the horses on which we rode, they took us for gregarious creatures like themselves; and actually grazing our animals' haunches with their legs, they left us scatheless and pursued the dogs. I seldom remember a more startling or dangerous position; it was a decided case of "De'il tak the hin'most." Spurs and jamboks were energetically plied; there was no time to select a path. Placing my head below my horse's neck and trusting to Providence, I charged through the thickest of the thorns, and presently found myself out of the way of the elephants. I know nothing which so effectually teaches a hunter the art of riding through "Vacht um bigé," or "wait-a-bit" jungle, in an artistical manner, as hearing the trumpet of an enraged elephant, which is following about a spear's length in his wake. After a few such lessons he will have learnt to bring his breast in contact with the side of his horse's neck, his head being well under it, whereby his prominent feature will be secured, and, agitating his persuaders, he will drive through the most impracticable "wait-a-bits," with apparently the facility with which an Eton boy takes a header into the Thames at the Lion's Leap.

With very great difficulty we got clear of the cover, and gained the level forest on the lower side. By this time the natives had lined the side of the mountain above the cover, and were shouting and yelling in the hope of driving out the elephants; but not a man would venture in. Presently some of them came round to me, and I proposed to go in on foot, but they would not hear of it, saying that the elephants were extremely fierce, and would kill me to a certainty. I then proposed that all the natives should enter the jungle in a line, and try to drive them out, but they said that no power could force the elephants from their stronghold until night set in.

The elephants now shifted their ground a little, forcing their way through the jungle to the higher side of the basin. Leaving the horses in charge of a native, I went round to the line of men above. Here I commanded a fine view of the exasperated elephants, being high above them, and distant about two hundred and fifty yards, and I observed that they displayed considerable cunning in their movements. Placing my rifle on a forked branch, and giving it the proper elevation, I let drive at the nearest cow, and wounded her severely. The shot reverberated through the dale, and the dogs once more ran into the midst of them, when a general charge and trumpeting ensued, which was truly terrific. They rushed after the dogs, following them up to a great distance, crashing through and upsetting the high bushy wait-a-bits and other trees like grass. They then turned and formed in two separate detachments, standing thick together; but two wicked old cows that had calves stood far out from the others, with their heads turned to us, ready to charge whatever might approach.

I saw that it was extremely dangerous to attack them, but the sun was now fast sinking behind a shoulder of the mountains, so I resolved to defy all chances and enter the cover. I first, however, fired two shots at the elephants that formed the advanced piquets; both cows got it in the ribs, and, finding themselves wounded, retreated to the main body, where they stood smashing the trees with rage, and, catching up volumes of the red dust with their trunks, threw it in clouds above their backs. Mutchuisho and I now descended into the jungle, and crept stealthily along, listening for the breathing of the elephants. They had moved to the lower side, and were standing thick together within one hundred yards of the outside. On ascertaining their position, we emerged from the cover, and followed along the outside until we were opposite them. I then stalked in within twenty yards, and fired at the side of the head of the elephant that stood next to me; and before the smoke had cleared my back was to them, and I was running for the outside of the cover at my utmost speed. The elephants held their ground; so, having loaded, I again drew near and fired sharp right and left into another, and turning my back I ran for it once more. Re-entering the cover a third time, I was listening which way they had gone, when, casting my eyes to the left, a noble elephant lay dead before me. The ball had penetrated to her brain, and she had dropped dead upon the spot.

A little after this an old cow came charging after the dogs, and took up a position in the jungle close beside us. We heard her preparing for a second charge, when the natives beat a precipitate retreat, but I very rashly waited to receive her, and just as she cleared the cover I let fly at her forehead. Regardless of my shot, she came down upon me at a tremendous pace, shrilly trumpeting. It was rather a near thing, for I was burdened with my rifle and rhinoceros-horn loading-rod, and my shooting-belt containing about forty rounds of ammunition. I escaped her by my speed, and the instant she halted I faced about, and gave her the other barrel behind the shoulder.

Night now set in, and I saw no more of the elephants. A number of them were wounded and must have died; I, however, felt satisfied with the one I had secured. The natives made me more cautious than I should otherwise have been, and, had we found them at an earlier hour, I should probably have killed one half the troop. Weary and hungry, we formed our kraals and kindled fires; after which, having partaken of the elephant, I lay down to sleep beside my fire.

On the 29th I sent Carollus to the waggons with instruction to bring all the horses and the Bushman, with bread, coffee, and ammunition. In the forenoon I ascended the neighbouring mountain-range, to obtain a view of the surrounding country. On clearing the first ridge I looked down upon a bold and romantic gorge, which here intersected the mountain chain, connecting the forests on either side. Far below me through the bottom of the ravine twined the gravelly bed of a periodical river, which in the rainy season flows in an easterly direction. Though in all other parts this gravelly channel was now dry, yet just at this spot, deep in the bosom of the mountains, its bed was covered with delicious spring water to a depth of several inches; and here the elephants had excavated sundry holes, about two feet deep, for the purpose of drinking. I descended to the water by an elephant-path, and stood long contemplating the interesting spot. The bed of the river was deeply imprinted with the spoor of elephants, buffaloes, and rhinoceros, of various dates. The gorge was wide and open by the water, and its abrupt and rocky sides were adorned with a profusion of trees and shrubs. A little farther down the gorge was more confined, the river winding through huge perpendicular walls of rock, that raised their giant forms on both sides to a height of several hundred feet.

From the basis of these stupendous ramparts to the margin of the river on either side was a sloping bank, along which grew an avenue of picturesque acacias of enormous bulk and lofty stature; beneath these were well-beaten paths of elephants, and the sides of the trees were well polished to the usual distance from the ground. Leaving the river, I ascended to the summits of loftier hills beyond, where I commanded a glorious prospect of the endless grey forests which stretched away as far as I could see over slightly undulating country, the faint blue outline of extensive mountain ranges bounding the landscape to the east. Descending from my lofty station, I discovered four bull-buffaloes feeding in the valley far beneath me; I left them undisturbed, and bent my steps towards the carcase of the elephant.

In the evening Carollus arrived, bringing the horses and ammunition, and accompanied by a numerous body of the natives. At an early hour on the 30th I started with Mutchuisho and a numerous retinue to search for elephants in an easterly direction; and we crossed the gravelly bed of the river Mahalapia, about a mile below the gorge I had visited on the preceding day. In after years I renewed my acquaintance with the Mahalapia, on the banks of the fair Limpopo, into which it empties itself several days' journey to the east.

This was one of the loveliest spots I had seen in Southern Africa: a bold bend of the river was adorned with groves of remarkably lofty and picturesque acacias. Three trees in particular, of the same description, graced the spot, which in size and beauty surpassed any I had hitherto met with, carrying their thickness to an immense height from the ground, when they divided into goodly branches, which stretched away in beauty to the skies.

Here, in the bed of the river, we took up the spoor of a huge bull elephant; and having followed it a short distance through the verdant forest, we started the old fellow, but no man saw him. The great body of the natives never would be quiet, and ever pressed upon the spooring party, notwithstanding my remonstrances. One native heard him, but said he thought it was a rhinoceros. In half a minute, however, we discovered our mistake, and there ensued a general rush upon the spoor, at a pace which must shortly have overtaken him, for he had not started in great alarm. Whistling to my dogs, they took up the scent and went ahead; but as I galloped after them, expecting every instant to behold the elephant, whose spoor I now saw beneath my horse's feet, an unlucky troop of camelopards dashed across our path, and away went all the dogs, leaving me in the lurch just as I was upon the elephant. The trackers, however, soon came up, and we again held briskly on; but had not proceeded far when we entered upon ground so covered with fresh footmarks that the trackers in their haste overran the spoor we followed, and a long check was the result. Here, to add to my annoyance, another large herd of camelopards came cantering up the wind, and dashed away before us, to spread further alarm.

Old Mutchuisho now came up in a state of intense excitement, his watery eyes fixed upon the ground, and his tongue going like perpetual motion. He blew up the trackers right and left, who seemed to quail before his menacing aspect, and redoubled their energies in the doubtful pursuit. Presently one of these, loudly smacking his "nether end," intimated that he had hit off the proper spoor. This peculiar signal, I remarked, was used by the Bechuanas to warn one another on various occasions. In spooring game it was invariably practised; and when a line of men were threading the mazes of the forest, each warned the man behind him of any rough sticks, stones, or thorns which lay across the path, by the same elegant and friendly gesture.

We resumed the spoor at a rapid pace, with a widely extended front, and presently on my left I heard the joyous signal of the presence, "Klow;" and, cantering in that direction, I came full in sight of an enormous bull elephant, marching along at a free majestic pace, and in another minute I was riding by his side. The horse which I bestrode on this occasion was "The Cow," one of my best and steadiest shooting-horses; and the forest being tolerably suited for the sport, I was not long in finishing the elephant. I fired thirteen bullets at his head and shoulder; on receiving the last two shots sharp right and left behind the shoulder, he made a rapid charge, and disappeared among the trees. Cautiously following, I discovered him lying in an upright position, with his two fore-legs stretched out before him. Fancying he was still alive, I fired both barrels at his ear; but though the balls rang loudly on his venerable head, the noble elephant heeded not their force; his ancient spirit had departed.

This was a very large old elephant; but his tusks were much destroyed, being worn down, and having been broken (probably in rocky ground) in former years. Mutchuisho appeared in the highest glee, and despatched messengers through the gorge in the mountains, the name of which is Sabié, to advise Sicomy of the death of the elephant. The chase had led me to within rifle range of the three veteran acacias I admired in the morning. I made my bower and a couch of grass beneath a shady wait-a-bit thorn-tree, and encircled my fire with a hedge of the same description.

I resolved to bring on my waggons to the pass of Sabié, where there was sufficient water for all my cattle, my intention being to continue hunting through the forests to the eastward, returning to Bamangwato by a different route. I, however, foresaw that I must give Isaac his dismissal before proposing such a measure; and accordingly I rode to camp on the 1st day of August, and informed Mr. Isaac that his valuable services could for the future be dispensed with, requesting at the same time that he would make himself scarce as quickly as possible. I then explained to my Hottentots my future course; and having directed them to inspan and follow me to Sabié, under guidance of the natives, I mounted the Old Grey, and started to return to my bower on the bank of the Mahalapia. The country between Letlochee and Sabié was almost impracticable for waggons, the forest in many parts being extremely dense, and sundry difficult nullahs intervening. I therefore did not expect them to reach their destination till the afternoon of the following day. My men, however, did not appear until the evening of the third day. They did not seem at all to fancy the idea of following me farther through the wilderness; but finding they could make no better of it, they submitted to their fate; and no sooner had I turned my back than Mr. Kleinboy proposed that they should drown their sorrows in the bowl. This brilliant idea was unanimously seconded by all the rest. Axes and hatchets were immediately resorted to, the liquor was obtained, and before I had been gone an hour all hands were mortal drunk.

At an early hour on the following day I started with about sixty natives to look for elephants. We filled our water kalabashes at an elephant's hole in the bed of the Mahalapia, and held east through the forest; and presently we discovered the fresh spoor of two bull elephants. As we were threading the spoor, the dogs dashed up wind on some scent, and the forest was awakened with their music. I imagined they had found the elephants, and pressed through the thicket at my utmost speed. As I approached I heard a hoarse noise like the voice of an elephant; but my eye sought in vain for his lofty back towering above the wait-a-bits. I then fancied it must be a buffalo; but on rounding the thick bush, behind which my dogs were barking, I came full in sight of an angry lioness, which stood lashing her tail, and growling fiercely at the dogs.

Observing the lioness, I shouted to the natives, who were pressing forward, that it was "Tao," when a headlong retreat was the immediate result, a number of the party taking refuge in the trees. I dismounted, and, advancing to within twenty yards of the lioness, I waited till she turned her head, when I fired at the back of her neck, and stretched her lifeless on the ground. The bullet had passed along the spine, and, penetrating the skull, rested in her brain. On shouting to the natives, for a long time none of them would venture to approach, and, when at length they did, their astonishment knew no bounds at beholding their formidable enemy so easily disposed of. Having resumed the spoor of the elephants, we soon ascertained that the hubbub with the lioness had started them; and after following the spoor some distance through dense jungle, and over very rocky ground, along the mountain side, the trackers declared themselves to be fairly beaten and we gave it up.

At an early hour on the 3rd I again held east with a large retinue to seek for elephants. We took up spoor at the fountains where I discovered borèlè on the preceding day. This spoor led us in a south-easterly course, first through verdant forest, and then over an extremely rugged ridge that stretched into the forest from the mountain chain. Beyond this ridge was an extensive and almost impracticable jungle of wait-a-bit thorns, and in this jungle we now heard the rumbling sound of elephants. As we advanced I perceived from the nature of the ground that success was very doubtful, and in a few minutes the dogs, winding the elephants, ran in upon them and gave tongue; a crashing and trumpeting ensued, and all the natives shouted out "Machoa" (signifying white man). With the utmost difficulty I pressed through the jungle, and obtained a view of one of the elephants, around which my dogs were barking angrily; but perceiving that it was a small cow, and knowing well that if I shot her the natives would not take up the spoor again for at least a couple of days, I reserved my fire; and the dogs being jaded by the sun, and returning to my call, we left the elephants to their own devices.

A few minutes afterwards we discovered the fresh spoor of two enormous bull elephants, which had pastured towards the hills. Having followed it a short distance, we came upon some dung, the outside of which the sun had not yet dried; from which we might presume that the elephants were at that moment in the same valley with ourselves. Two young men were despatched in haste to ascend the beetling crags of the adjacent mountain, from which they could obtain a bird's-eye view of the length and breadth of that and the surrounding valleys. The main body of the natives squatted on the ground, and I sat down to eat some bread and elephant, and take a drink of water. I had scarcely time to finish my luncheon when the two young men returned breathless with excitement to report that they had discovered the two bull elephants browsing in a grove of thorny trees on the mountain side within a quarter of a mile of us. I approached under cover of a bushy tree, on clearing which I beheld two of the finest elephants in Africa standing broadside on within fifty yards. The finer of these had one of his tusks broken short off by the lip; I therefore chose his comrade which carrried a pair of very long and perfect tusks. I had hard work with this elephant, and the sun was under before I laid him low.

On the 4th I rode for my bower on the Mahalapia, in the hope of finding my waggons waiting for me; but I had misgivings about my men, who ought to have appeared on the evening of the 2nd. On reaching my bower where the former elephant had died, I found the fires still smoking, but every man had disappeared: Carollus, whom I had ordered to await me, had vanished with the rest. I now fancied that I must have missed the natives who had passed me on their way to the elephant of the previous day, and that Carollus had joined the waggons wherever they might be.

I was right in my conjecture, and presently, on firing a signal shot, I received an answer from the waggons, which were drawn up in the romantic gorge of Sabié, as near as might be to the water. Drunkenness and disorder had prevailed during my absence, as I had feared; my

EQUIPMENT FOR THE FOREST.

chests were broken open, the fine captents of both my waggons were most seriously damaged, oxen had been lost, and horses ridden off their legs in search of them. It appeared that Mr. Kleinboy had been the chief delinquent. Under the influence of the liquor, and anxious to distinguish himself, he had resolved to try his hand in hunting the giraffe. Accordingly he saddled Colesberg, my favourite steed, and borrowed one of my 80 guinea rifles, armed with which he had sped through the forest he knew not whither; and eventually becoming bewildered, he had lost himself entirely. In this condition he was fortunately discovered by a party of Bakalahari, who conducted him safely to my camp.

I had at length got into the way of making myself tolerably comfortable in the field, and from this date I seldom went in quest of elephants without the following impedimenta, viz., a large blanket, which I folded and secured before my saddle, as a dragoon does his cloak; and two leather sacks, containing a flannel shirt, warm trousers, and a woollen nightcap, spare ammunition, washing-rod, coffee, bread, sugar, pepper and salt, dried meat, a wooden bowl, and a teaspoon. These sacks were carried on the shoulders of the natives, for which service I remunerated them with beads. They also carried my coffee-kettle, two calabashes of water, two American axes, and two sickles, which I used every evening to cut grass for my bed, and likewise for my horses to eat throughout the night. My after-rider carried extra ammunition and a spare rifle; and my own personal appointments consisted of a wide-awake hat, secured under my chin by "rheimpys," or strips of dressed skin, a coarse linenby shirt, sometimes a kilt, and sometimes a pair of buckskin knee-breeches, and a pair of "veldtschoens," or home-made shoes. I entirely discarded coat, waistcoat, and neckcloth, and I always hunted with my arms bare. My heels were armed with a pair of powerful persuaders, and from my left wrist depended by a double rheimpy an equally persuasive sea-cow jambok.

Around my waist I wore two leathern belts or girdles. The smaller of these discharged the duty of suspenders, and from it on my left side depended a plaited rheimpy, eight inches in length, forming a loop in which dangled my powerful loading rod, formed of a solid piece of horn of the rhinoceros. The larger girdle was my shooting-belt: this was a broad leather belt, on which were fastened four separate compartments made of otter-skin, with flaps to button over of the same material. The first of these held my percussion-caps, the second a large powder-flask, the third and fourth, which had divisions in them, contained balls and patches, two sharp clasp-knives, a compass, flint and steel. In this belt I also carried a loading mallet, formed from the horn of the rhinoceros; this and the powder-flask were each secured to the belt by long rheimpys, to prevent my losing them. Last, but not least, in my right hand I usually carried my double-barrelled two-grooved rifle, which was my favourite weapon. This, however, I subsequently made up my mind, is not the proper tool for a mounted man, especially when quick loading is necessary.

I remember having a discussion with the commanding officer of a regiment of heavy dragoons on this subject, and he and I agreed that nothing can surpass a double-barrelled smooth bore for practical utility. When a two-grooved rifle has been once or twice discharged, the bullet requires considerable power to drive it home; and to a mounted man this is extremely inconvenient. I consider that no regiment in the service was more effectually armed than my own old corps, the Cape Mounted Rifles, who were furnished with short double-barrelled smooth-bored pieces, carrying a ball of twelve to the pound, and having stout percussion-locks. Give me a weapon of this description to war against the larger game of Africa. To accelerate loading, the hunter ought to have his balls stitched up in their patches, and well greased before taking the field. This was my invariable custom: I found it a great convenience, and after a little practice I could load and fire in the saddle, although riding in rough ground at a swingeing gallop.

On the evening of the 12th a herald from Sicomy stood up in the centre of my camp, and loudly proclaimed that it was the king's orders that on the following day every man should return to head-quarters; and accordingly next day all hands shouldered their impedients and forsook me. I could not rightly divine the cause of this mysterious command; but I attributed it to some plotting scheme of Isaac's, who I understand was living with Sicomy. I saw very plainly that Mutchuisho was against the move. In consideration of his services, I begged his acceptance of several considerable presents, and I also sent some presents to the king. On parting, Mutchuisho promised shortly to return, and he informed me that he had instructed a party of Bakalahari to assist me in my hunting during his absence.

CHAPTER XVII.

We march from Sabié—Track along a River-bed—The dry Grass on Fire for miles—Glorious Elephant-shooting—Cowardice of my After-rider—Strange circumstance at the Death of a Bull Elephant—A Sable Antelope—Tête-à-tête with a disabled Elephant—The Klipspringer Antelope—A pack of Wild Dogs capture and kill a Koodoo—The coming of Summer—Vast numbers of Birds visiting the Fountains—My trusty two-grooved Rifle bursts—My Snuffers, Spoons, and Candlesticks melted for Bullets—Elephants taking a Douche Bath—Two of them slain—Yet more Elephants—My Horse Colesberg dies of the African Distemper—Virulence of the Scourge.

I REMAINED at Sabié, hunting elephant and rhinoceros with various success, till the morning of the 22nd of August, when I inspanned, and marched for Mangmaluky, which we reached at sundown, when I drew up my waggons in an open grassy glade on a rather elevated position, commanding a fine view of the bold outline of the surrounding mountains. On the march I shot a white rhinoceros in the act of charging down a rocky face, with all the dogs in full pursuit of him. The ball disabled him in the shoulder, when, pitching upon his head, he described the most tremendous somersault, coming down among the stones and bushes with the overwhelming violence of an avalanche.

Headlong Charge of a Wounded Elephant.

CHAP. XVII.

FIGHT WITH AN ELEPHANT.

On the 27th I cast loose my horses at earliest dawn of day, and then lay half asleep for two hours, when I arose to consume coffee and rhinoceros. Having breakfasted, I started with a party of the natives to search for elephants in a southerly direction. We held along the gravelly bed of a periodical river, in which were abundance of holes excavated by the elephants in quest of water. Here the spoor of rhinoceros was extremely plentiful, and in every hole where they had drunk the print of the horn was visible. We soon found the spoor of an old bull elephant, which led us into a dense forest, where the ground was particularly unfavourable for spooring; we, however, threaded it out for a considerable distance, when it joined the spoor of other bulls. The natives now requested me to halt, while men went off in different directions to reconnoitre.

In the mean time a tremendous conflagration was roaring and crackling close to windward of us. It was caused by the Bakalahari burning the old dry grass to enable the young to spring up with greater facility, whereby they retained the game in their dominions. The fire stretched away for many miles on either side of us, darkening the forest far to leeward with a dense impenetrable canopy of smoke. Here we remained for about half an hour, when one of the men returned, reporting that he had discovered elephants. This I could scarcely credit, for I fancied that the extensive fire which raged so fearfully must have driven, not only elephants, but every living creature out of the district. The native, however, pointed to his eye, repeating the word "Klow," and signed to me to follow him. My guide led me about a mile through dense forest, when we reached a little well-wooded hill, to whose summit we ascended, whence a view might have been obtained of the surrounding country, had not volumes of smoke obscured the scenery far and wide, as though issuing from the funnels of a thousand steamboats. Here, to my astonishment, my guide halted, and pointed to the thicket close beneath me, when I instantly perceived the colossal backs of a herd of bull elephants. There they stood quietly browsing on the lee side of the hill, while the fire in its might was raging to windward within two hundred yards of them.

I directed Johannus to choose an elephant, and promised to reward him should he prove successful. Galloping furiously down the hill, I started the elephants with an unearthly yell, and instantly selected the finest in the herd. Placing myself alongside, I fired both barrels behind his shoulder, when he instantly turned upon me, and in his impetuous career charged head foremost against a large bushy tree which he sent flying before him high in the air with tremendous force, coming down at the same moment violently on his knees. He then met the raging fire, when, altering his course, he wheeled to the right-about. As I galloped after him I perceived another noble elephant meeting us in an opposite direction, and presently the gallant Johannus hove in sight, following his quarry at a respectful distance. Both elephants held on together, so I shouted to Johannus, "I will give your elephant a shot in the shoulder, and you must try to finish him." Spurring my horse, I rode close alongside, and gave the fresh elephant two balls immediately behind the shoulder, when he parted from mine, Johannus following; but before many minutes had elapsed that mighty Nimrod reappeared, having fired one shot and lost his prey.

In the mean time I was loading and firing as fast as could be, sometimes at the head, and sometimes behind the shoulder, until my elephant's fore-quarters were a mass of gore, notwithstanding which he continued to hold stoutly on, leaving the grass and branches of the forest scarlet in his wake.

On one occasion he endeavoured to escape by charging desperately amid the thickest of the flames; but this did not avail, and I was soon once more alongside. I blazed away at this elephant, until I began to think that he was proof against my weapons. Having fired thirty-five rounds with my two-grooved rifle, I opened fire upon him with the Dutch six-pounder; and when forty bullets had perforated his hide, he began for the first time to evince signs of a dilapidated constitution. He took up a position in a grove; and as the dogs kept barking round him, he backed stern foremost among the trees, which yielded before his gigantic strength. Poor old fellow! he had long braved my deadly shafts, but I plainly saw that it was now all over with him; so I resolved to expend no further ammunition, but hold him in view until he died. Throughout the chase this elephant repeatedly cooled his person with large quantities of water, which he ejected from his trunk over his back and sides; and just as the pangs of death came over him, he stood trembling violently beside a thorny tree, and kept pouring water into his bloody mouth until he died, when he pitched heavily forward, with the whole weight of his fore-quarters resting on the points of his tusks.

A most singular occurrence now took place. He lay in this posture for several seconds, but the amazing pressure of the carcase was more than the head was able to support. He had fallen with his head so short under him that the tusks received little assistance from his legs. Something must give way. The strain on the mighty tusks was fair; they did not, therefore, yield; but the portion of his head in which the tusk was imbedded, extending a long way above the eye, yielded and burst with a muffled crash. The tusk was thus free, and turned right round in his head, so that a man could draw it out, and the carcase fell over and rested on its side. This was a very first-rate elephant, and the tusks he carried were long and perfect.

On the 28th I saddled up, and rode for the waggons, steering my course by the lofty pyramidal mountain, in whose vicinity they were drawn up. The remainder of the day was spent in constructing a loading-rod of rhinoceros-horn, and writing up the log. At an early hour on the 29th I started a party of the natives, bearing my impedimenta, to await me at the carcase of the last elephant; and in the forenoon I held thither, accompanied by Johannus. Cantering along through the forest, I came suddenly in full view of one of the loveliest animals which graces this fair creation. This was an old buck of the sable antelope, the rarest and most beautiful animal in Africa. It is large and powerful, partaking considerably of the nature of the ibex. Its back and sides are of glossy black, beautifully contrasting with the belly, which is white as driven snow. The horns are upwards of three feet in length, and bend strongly back with a bold sweep, reaching nearly to the haunches.

This animal was first discovered by Captain Harris, of the Bombay Engineers, in 1837. As I subsequently devoted a great deal of time in the pursuit of this antelope, I shall not here make any remarks concerning him. The one which was now before me was the first I had seen, and I shall never forget the sensations I experienced on beholding a sight so thrilling to the sportsman's eye. He stood with a small troop of pallahs right in our path, and had unfortunately detected us before we saw him. Shouting to my pack, I galloped after him; but the day was close and warm, and the dogs had lost their spirit with the sun. My horse being an indifferent one, I soon lost ground, and the beautiful sable antelope, gaining a rocky ridge, was very soon beyond my reach, and vanished for ever from my view. I then rode on for the carcase of the elephant, where I took up my quarters for the night, but I sought in vain to close my eyelids: the image of the sable antelope was still before me, and I slept little throughout the night.

On the 31st I held south-east in quest of elephants, with a large party of the natives. Our course lay through an open part of the forest, where I beheld a troop of springboks and two ostriches, the first I had seen for a long time. We held for Towannie, a strong fountain in the gravelly bed of a periodical river: here two herds of cow elephants had drunk on the preceding evening, but I declined to follow these; and presently, at a muddy fountain a little in advance, we took up the spoor of an enormous bull, which had wallowed in the mud and then plastered the sides of several of the adjacent veteran-looking trees. We followed the spoor through level forest in an easterly direction, when the leading party overran the spoor, and casts were made for its recovery. Presently I detected an excited native beckoning violently a little to my left, and, cantering up to him, he said that he had seen the elephant. He led me through the forest a few hundred yards, when, clearing a wait-a-bit, I came full in view of the tallest and largest bull elephant I had ever seen. He stood broadside to me, at upwards of one hundred yards, and his attention at the moment was occupied with the dogs, which, having winded him, were rushing past in search of his exact position, while the old fellow seemed to gaze at their unwonted appearance with surprise.

Halting my horse, I fired at his shoulder, and secured him with a single shot. The ball caught him high upon the shoulder-blade, rendering him instantly dead lame; and before the echo of the bullet could reach my ear, I plainly saw that the elephant was mine. The dogs now came up and barked around him, but, finding himself incapacitated, the old fellow seemed determined to take it easy, and, limping slowly to a neighbouring tree, he remained stationary, eyeing his pursuers with a resigned and philosophic air.

I resolved to devote a short time to the contemplation of this noble elephant before I should lay him low; accordingly, having off-saddled the horses beneath a shady tree which was to be my quarters for the night and ensuing day, I quickly kindled a fire and put on the kettle, and in a very few minutes my coffee was prepared. There I sat in my forest home, coolly sipping my coffee, with one of the finest elephants in Africa awaiting my pleasure beside a neighbouring tree.

It was, indeed, a striking scene; and as I gazed upon the stupendous veteran of the forest, I thought of the red deer which I loved to follow in my native land, and felt that, though the Fates had driven me to follow a more daring and arduous avocation in a distant land, it was a good exchange which I had made, for I was now a chief over boundless forests, which yielded unspeakably more noble and exciting sport.

Having admired the elephant for a considerable time, I resolved to make experiments for vulnerable points, and, approaching very near, I fired several bullets at different parts of his enormous skull. These did not seem to affect him in the slightest; he only acknowledged the shots by a "salaam-like" movement of his trunk, with the point of which he gently touched the wound with a striking and peculiar action. Surprised and shocked to find that I was only tormenting and prolonging the sufferings of the noble beast, which bore his trials with such dignified composure, I resolved to finish the proceeding with all possible despatch; accordingly I opened fire upon him from the left side, aiming behind the shoulder; but even there it was long before my bullets seemed to take effect. I first fired six shots with the two-grooved, which must have eventually proved mortal, but as yet he evinced no visible distress; after which I fired three shots at the same part with the Dutch six-pounder. Large tears now trickled from his eyes, which he slowly shut and opened; his colossal frame quivered convulsively, and, falling on his side, he expired. The tusks of this elephant were beautifully arched, and were the heaviest I had yet met with, averaging 90 lbs. weight apiece.

In case any fair reader may misinterpret my motive for killing this elephant in the manner which I describe, I will remark that my object was *not* to uselessly torture the animal, but to put an end to its life and pain in the quickest manner possible. I had often lamented having to inflict so many wounds on the noble animals before they fell.

To any sportsman, or person understanding such matters, this explanation is not required.

On the 1st of September—so full of interest to the British Nimrod— we saddled our steeds and steered our course for Mangmaluky. Cantering along the base of a mountain range, I started two klipspringers, which went bounding up the mountain side with the elasticity of an India-rubber ball, selecting for their path the most prominent points of the large fragments of rock of which the mountain-side was chiefly composed. I shot one of these, being the first of the species I had killed, though in subsequent years, while hunting the sable antelope, I secured a number of fine specimens. This darling little antelope frequents precipitous rocky hills and mountains, and bounds along over the broken masses of rock with the most extraordinary ease and agility: it may often be seen perched, like a chamois, on the sharp pinnacle of some rock or stone, with its four feet drawn up close together. Its hoofs are different from those of other antelopes, being suited solely for rocky ground, and are so formed that the weight of the animal rests upon their tips. On looking down a precipice I have often seen two or three of this interesting antelope lying together on a large flat mass of rock, and sheltered from the power of the noonday sun by the friendly shade of some sandal-wood or other mountain tree. They are about half the size of the Scottish roebuck, whose winter coat the texture of their hair very much resembles, but it is stiffer and of a yellower colour.

On the afternoon of the 2nd, as I was sitting in my waggon writing up my journal, a koodoo charged past me, closely followed by a pack of hungry wild dogs, which maintained their position although all my kennel joined them in the chase, and, holding on, the wild dogs killed the koodoo just as it reached the water where my oxen drank. On the 3rd I took the field with Johannus and a small party of Bakalahari, and held a northerly direction. After following the spoor of four bull elephants for many miles in a semicircular course, we came up with them in extremely dangerous and unfavourable ground, when I was fortunate enough to secure the finest, after a severe and dangerous conflict, during which, on three separate occasions, I narowly escaped destruction. The horse I rode was "Colesberg," which, as usual, capered and balked me when I tried to fire from his back; when I dismounted, he seemed to take a pleasure in jerking my arm as I was taking aim; and on the elephant charging he declined permitting me to regain the saddle.

This elephant was a first-rate bull, with large and perfect tusks: he fell within three hundred yards of the fountains, where I found a black rhinoceros which I wounded on the 31st of August. The sun was powerful throughout the day; the months of winter were gone by, and summer was rapidly advancing. The trees were budding and putting forth leaves, which loaded the passing breeze with a sweet and balmy fragrance. In low-lying districts the young grass had already commenced to shoot forth its tender blades, and all nature seemed to pant for the grateful rains to robe herself in her mantle of summer verdure.

In the evening I laved in the fountain my sunburnt eyes, which were sore and irritated from the constant strain necessarily concomitant on spooring; after which I sat for a long time silently contemplating the tranquil scene. As the sun went down, the number of the feathered tribe that visited the fountains was truly surprising: turtle-doves, and extremely small long-tailed pigeons, were most abundant. These kept collecting from every side, uttering their gentle notes, till the trees and bushes around the glade were thickly covered with them. I also observed four distinct varieties of partridge; and guinea-fowls attended in flocks of from twenty to sixty. On the 4th, having few followers, I was occupied from early dawn until the sun was under in cleaning the skull and hewing out the tusks of my bull elephant; and on the following day I returned to camp with a party of Bakalahari bearing them upon their shoulders. On the 6th I took the field with about forty natives and held through the forest in a south-easterly direction. Falling in with two white rhinoceroses, one of which carried an unusually long horn, I was induced to give her chase; and by hard riding I soon overtook and finished her with four shots behind the shoulder.

In the afternoon I was engaged for three or four hours combating with a vicious elephant, which I finished with thirty-five bullets in the shoulder, in an impracticable jungle of wait-a-bit thorns. The conflict was greatly prolonged by the "Immense Brute," which capered continually, and constantly destroyed the correctness of my aim. While I was fighting with this elephant, my dogs were combating with a younger bull, which they hunted backwards and forwards in the same thicket with myself. This elephant took up a position beside the one which had fallen, and the dogs continued barking around him. My rifle being now extremely dirty, I experienced considerable difficulty in ramming home the balls, notwithstanding the power of my rhinoceros-horn loading-rod. This being accomplished, I ran cautiously within twenty yards of this second elephant, and, resting my rifle on a branch, I aimed for his heart and pressed the trigger.

Alas! it was for the last time. The barrel burst with a terrific explosion, sending the locks and half the stock flying right and left, and very nearly sending me to "the land of the leal." I, however, received no futher damage than a slight burn on my left arm, and the loss for many days of the use of my left ear, a fragment of the barrel having whizzed close past it. At first I was so stunned that I knew not if I were wounded or not, and on recovering from the shock my person underwent a strict scrutiny. Before I discovered these elephants I was faint from thirst, and quite done up with the power of the sun, owing to which I considered that I did not attack the elephant so bravely as I might otherwise have done.

The loss of my trusty two-grooved rifle, in such a remote corner of the world, was irreparable, and cut me to the heart. It was my mainstay; and as I thought of the many services it had performed for me in the hour of need, I mourned over it as David mourned for Absalom. On the evening of the 7th I returned to Mangmaluky under a burning sun, which continued oppressive throughout the day. Having lost my two-grooved rifle, I resolved to try what could be done with the double-barrelled Moore and Purdey rifles, carrying sixteen to the pound, and I accordingly set about casting hardened bullets to suit them. For this purpose I had brought in with me a quantity of solder, but I now had the mortification to discover that all that I had possessed of this important article had mysteriously vanished by some underhand transaction betwixt my followers and Sicomy. I was thus reduced to the extremity of melting the contents of my old military canteen to harden the bullets; and upon overhauling it, I ascertained that the tray of the snuffers, the spoons, candlesticks, teapots, and two drinking-cups, were admirably suited for this purpose, and I accordingly sentenced them to undergo the fiery ordeal of the ladle.

In the evening I had much pleasure to behold my old friend Mutchuisho walk into my camp, followed by a numerous party of the natives. He seemed glad to see me, and we at once arranged to make an expedition to the eastward on the following day. Accordingly, on the morning of the 9th I took the field with Johannus and Mutchuisho and about eighty men, and proceeded in a south-easterly direction. We continued our course till the sun went down without finding fresh spoor, when we halted for the night to leeward of a fountain, where we hoped that elephants would come to drink. The heat throughout the day had been most oppressive, the dense level forest rendering it still more insupportable.

On the morrow we cast loose the horses to graze long before the dawn of day. No elephants had visited the fountain, so after an early breakfast we saddled up, and again held on in an easterly direction through boundless forests, till I found myself in a country which I had not hitherto visited. Passing along beneath a rocky hillock we started a detachment of hideous hyænas, which sought shelter from the sun beneath the shadow of the rocks. We passed several large herds of lovely camelopards, and I also obtained two very deadly chances of rhinoceros, both fine old bulls ; but knowing well from past experience that my policy was to keep my followers hungry, I refrained from firing a single shot.

In the afternoon we reached a small vley, where five first-rate bull elephants had drunk on the preceding evening. Here my followers all sat down and rested for a quarter of an hour, a wild duck swimming fearlessly beside us. We then took up the spoor, but, as it was late in the day, I had not the slightest expectation of success, and was so done up with the power of the sun that I felt it irksome to sit in the saddle. The spoor led east, right away from camp, but the elephants seemed to have proceeded slowly, having extended widely from one another, and rent and uprooted an amazing number of goodly trees. Presently the spoor took a turn to our left, when I grieved to remark that we were following it down the wind ; thus we eventually started the elephants, which were feeding in the forest at no great distance, but, owing to a check among the trackers, we were not aware of this until the elephants had gained a considerable start.

On finding that they were gone, Johannus and I went off on the spoor at a rapid pace, but I had not the slightest expectation of overtaking them ; for it was so late that, even if I had already commenced the attack, the chances were that before I could finish one the night would have set in. It is much easier to hold the spoor of a herd of elephants that have been alarmed than to follow those which have been undisturbed, since the former adopt a decided course and follow one another in a direct line. Thus we were enabled to hold the spoor at a gallop without a check until our horses began to evince distress ; and, despairing of success, I was just going to pull up, when I heard Johannus exclaim,

"Sir, sir, dar stand illa," and, looking before me, I beheld five enormous old bull elephants walking slowly along.

They seemed heated by the pace at which they had retreated, and were now refreshing themselves with large volumes of water, which nature enables them to discharge from their capacious stomachs, and shower back upon their bodies with their extraordinary trunks. I overtook these elephants in open ground, which enabled me at once to make a fine selection. I had never before obtained so satisfactory a view of a herd of bulls: they really looked wondrous vast. It is a heart-stirring sight to behold one bull elephant; but when five gigantic old fellows are walking slowly along before you, and you feel that you can ride up and vanquish whichever one you fancy, it is so overpoweringly exciting that it almost takes a man's breath away; but it was now too late in the day to part with my breath for a single moment.

Johannus whispered to me to wait a little, to allow the horses to recover their wind; but Wolf dashing in upon them, I was obliged to follow to obtain an accurate selection of the tusks. Spurring my horse, in another moment I was in the middle of them, closely followed by Johannus; and in a twinkling the finest bull had received the contents of the Moore and Purdey behind the shoulder. I was now joined by Wolf, who rendered me important service by considerably engrossing the attention of the elephant, running barking before him as he charged. I was in a precious hurry, as the sun was setting, and I kept loading and firing at duelling distance. On receiving the twenty-fourth shot he stood trembling violently for several seconds, and then fell heavily forward on his tusks, after which he rolled over and rested on his side. I reckoned this to be a fortunate conclusion after the hard and toilsome day I had spent under the power of a scorching sun. Mutchuisho and the natives soon made their appearance, all in wondrous good humour at our success.

The nearest water to this elephant was in a vley situated several miles to the eastward; and when the natives had constructed a number of water-bags of the under skin of the elephant, a watering party was despatched with these and a number of calabashes which they always carried along with them. This party rejoined us at the hour of midnight, and reported that while they were filling their water-bags at one side of the vley a troop of bull elephants were drinking at the other. Accordingly, on the morrow I went in quest of these, accompanied by Mutchuisho and a small party, and on the second day I came up with them and bagged an old bull whose tusks were the stoutest I had ever seen.

After a most weary and toilsome spoor of two days I cast loose the steeds at earliest dawn of the 3rd, and soon after we heard the hoarse cry of an elephant within half a mile of us. I permitted my horses to graze while the dew was on the grass, after which I sent them along with the dogs to water with a party of Bakalahari at a fountain reported three miles distant, and in the mean time I regaled myself with coffee and rhinoceros.

It is extraordinary how soon the mind accustoms itself to everything, good or bad. There I sat taking my breakfast, with a troop of princely elephants feeding within a few minutes' ride of me, with as much indifference as if I were going woodcock-shooting. I certainly did not feel half so anxious about the matter as I usually did when taking my breakfast on a fine May morning, with a southerly wind, before starting to fish my native river. This indifference was probably owing to the reduced state of my system from improper diet and constant toil.

When the Bakalahari returned with the dogs and horses, they reported fresh spoor of bull elephants by the fountain; and at the same moment another party, whom Mutchuisho had despatched in the direction of the cry, returned to say that it was a herd of bulls which we had heard that morning. This was very pleasing intelligence, for I had fancied that the elephants must be a troop of cows, whose traces we had observed on the preceding evening. Everything being ready we made for the elephants, and, as we approached them, an old bull rhinoceros was detected standing within forty yards, which, as if aware that I dared not fire on him, kept trotting along the path before me. We discovered the elephants quietly browsing on very unfavourable ground, the greater part of the forest consisting of the ever-recurring wait-a-bits. The troop was composed of three old bulls, two of which carried stumpy and broken tusks.

On the evening of the 20th, after bowling over another elephant with a splendid pair of tusks, I returned to camp, where, to my utter horror, I found my favourite Colesberg dangerously ill. Guessing that it was the distemper, I had him up instantly and bled him freely, but to no purpose. Finding him worse on the morrow, I bled him again, but before midday he died in great pain, and shortly after life had departed a copious discharge of white foam issued from his nostrils, by which I knew that his illness was the African distemper.

This bitter scourge of the African sportsman prevails throughout every district of the interior during the greater part of the year. At no season is the hunter's stud exempt from its ravages; it is most prevalent however during the summer months, generally commencing with the early rains. There are various opinions among the horse-breeders of the colony regarding its prevention and cure; but notwithstanding all that has been done and said, the subject still remains wrapped in utter mystery. The distemper rarely visits districts adjacent to the sea, and is also unusual in mountain districts. In proportion as the traveller advances from the sea, so will he find the sickness prevalent. In all years it is not alike, and every fifth or seventh year it ravages the farms on the frontier districts, where a farmer often loses from fifty to a hundred horses in a single season. Bleeding is generally believed to act as a preventive. When a horse is attacked with it he almost invariably comes up to his master's waggon, or the door of his dwelling-place, as if soliciting assistance in his deep distress, and when led away to a distance, unless he be secured, the poor animal will continue to return to his master's dwelling. This was the case with my much-lamented Colesberg, of the free and fiery indomitable spirit.

I had also the mortification to observe that the "Immense Brute" was affected, evincing symptoms similar to those of Colesberg, on which I had him caught and bled him freely. About the hour of midday we got under way, when I trekked till sundown in a south-westerly course, steering for the mountains of Bamangwato. I formed my encampment beside a little fountain, whose name I never ascertained.

CHAPTER XVIII.

Turn my Waggons towards the Colony—A Troop of Elephants in Indian File—Splendid Sport amongst them—Two of them break their Tusks in falling—The Rainy Season commences—Erection of a Bothy—The gigantic Nwana-tree—Sicomy's Mountain Kraal—Four of his Subjects become my Servants—Corriebely—The Natives astonished by my finding a Mine of Lead—Elephant-shooting—Leave the land of Elephants—Boötlonamy—Terrific Thunderstorm.

HAVING so far succeeded in the object of my expedition, and both my waggons being now heavily laden with the tusks of elephants and a large collection of the spoils of the chase, with a number of other interesting curiosities, I at length resolved once more to turn my face towards the distant dwellings of my countrymen. On the 23rd of September, however, although harassed in my mind, and fearing to lose all my horses if I did not speedily forsake the country, I yielded to my inclination, and the persuasions of Mutchuisho, once more to take the field, and follow the spoor of two bull elephants, reported to have visited a distant fountain. Before starting I gave Johannus my phlegme, and a hasty lesson in the art of bleeding, with instructions to bleed copiously any of my stud evincing the slightest symptoms of distemper. We held an easterly course, and at sundown on the second day I bagged a white rhinoceros and a fine old bull elephant, beside whose carcase I bivouacked as usual. On the forenoon of the 25th I saddled up and held for camp, accompanied by only one attendant.

It was a glorious day, with a cloudy sky, and the wind blew fresh off the Southern Ocean. Having ridden some miles in a northerly direction, we crossed the broad and gravelly bed of a periodical river, in which were abundance of holes excavated by the elephants, containing delicious water. Having passed the river, we entered an extensive grove of picturesque cameel-dorn trees, clad in young foliage of the most delicious green. On gaining a gentle eminence about a mile beyond this grove, I looked forth upon an extensive hollow, where I beheld for the first time for many days a fine old cock ostrich, which quickly observed us and dashed away to our left. I had ceased to devote my attention to the ostrich, and was straining my eyes in opposite direction, when Kleinboy called out to me,

"Dar loup de old carle;" and turning my eyes to the retreating ostrich, I beheld two first-rate old bull elephants, charging along at their utmost speed within a hundred yards of it. They seemed at first to be in great alarm, but, quickly discovering what it was that had caused their confusion, they at once reduced their pace to a slow and stately walk. This was a fine look-out, the country appeared to be favourable for an attack, and I was followed by Wolf and Bonteberg, both tried and serviceable dogs with elephants. Owing to the pace at which I had been riding, both dogs and horses were out of breath, so I resolved not to attack the elephants immediately, but to follow slowly, holding them in view.

The elephants were proceeding right up the wind, and the distance betwixt us was about five hundred yards. I advanced quietly towards them, and had proceeded about half way, when, casting my eyes to my right, I beheld a whole herd of tearing bull elephants standing thick together on a wooded eminence within three hundred yards of me. These elephants were almost to leeward. Now the correct thing to do was to slay the best in each troop, which I accomplished in the following manner :—I gave the large herd my wind, upon which they instantly tossed their trunks aloft, "a moment snuffed the tainted gale," and, wheeling about, charged right down wind, crashing through the jungle in dire alarm. My object now was to endeavour to select the finest bull, and hunt him to a distance from the other troop before I should commence to play upon his hide. Stirring my steed, I galloped forward. Right in my path stood two rhinoceroses of the white variety, and to these the dogs instantly gave chase. I followed in the wake of the retreating elephants, tracing their course by the red dust which they raised and left in clouds behind them.

Presently emerging into an open glade, I came in full sight of the mighty game; it was a truly glorious sight; there were nine or ten of them, which were, with one exception, full-grown, first-rate bulls, and all of them carried very long, heavy, and perfect tusks. Their first panic being over, they had reduced their pace to a free, majestic walk, and they followed one leader in a long line, exhibiting an appearance so grand and striking that any description, however brilliant, must fail to convey to the mind of the reader an adequate idea of the reality. Increasing my pace, I shot alongside, at the same time riding well out from the elephants, the better to obtain an inspection of their tusks. It was a difficult matter to decide which of them I should select, for every elephant seemed better than his neighbour; but, on account of the extraordinary size and beauty of his tusks, I eventually pitched upon a patriarchal bull, which, as is usual with the heaviest, brought up the rear.

I presently separated him from his comrades, and endeavoured to drive him in a northerly direction. There is a peculiar art in driving an elephant in the particular course which you may fancy, and, simple as it may seem, it nevertheless requires the hunter to have a tolerable idea of what he is about. It is widely different from driving in an eland, which also requires judicious riding: if you approach too near your elephant or shout to him, a furious charge will certainly ensue, whilst, on the other hand, if you give him too wide a berth, the chances are that you will lose him in the jungle, which, notwithstanding his size, is a very simple matter, and, if once lost sight of, it is more than an even bet that the hunter will never again obtain a glimpse of him. The ground being favourable, Kleinboy called to me to commence firing, remarking very prudently that he was probably making for some jungle of wait-a-bit thorns, where we might eventually lose him. I continued, however, to reserve my fire until I had hunted him to what I considered to be a safe distance from the two old fellows which we had first discovered.

At length closing with him, I dared him to charge, which he instantly did in fine style, and as he pulled up in his career I yelled to him a note of bold defiance, and, cantering alongside, I again defied him to the combat. It was thus the fight began, and, the ground being still favourable, I opened a sharp fire upon him, and in about a quarter of an hour twelve of my bullets were lodged in his forequarters. He now evinced strong symptoms of approaching dissolution, and stood catching up the dust with the point of his trunk and throwing it in clouds above and around him. At such a moment it is extremely dangerous to approach an elephant on foot, for I have remarked that, although nearly dead, he can muster strength to make a charge with great impetuosity. Being anxious to finish him, I dismounted from my steed, and, availing myself of the cover of a gigantic nwana-tree, whose diameter was not less than ten feet, I ran up within twenty yards, and gave it him sharp right and left behind the shoulder.

These two shots wound up the proceeding; on receiving them, he backed stern foremost into the cover, and then walked slowly away. I had loaded my rifle, and was putting on the caps, when I heard him fall over heavily; but, alas! the sound was accompanied by a sharp crack, which, I too well knew, denoted the destruction of one of his lovely tusks; and, on running forward, I found him lying dead, with the tusk, which lay under, snapped through the middle.

I did not tarry long for an inspection of the elephant, but, mounting my horse, I at once set off to follow on the spoor of the two old fellows which the ostrich had alarmed. Fortunately I fell in with a party of natives, who were on their way to the waggons with the impedimenta, and, assisted by these, I had sanguine hopes of shortly overtaking the noble quarry. We had not gone far when two wild boars, with enormous tusks, stood within thirty yards of me, but this was no time to fire, and a little after a pair of white rhinoceroses stood directly in our path. Casting my eyes to the right, I beheld within a quarter of a mile of me a herd of eight or ten cow elephants, with calves, peacefully browsing on a sparely wooded knoll. The spoor we followed led due south, and the wind was as fair as it could blow. We passed between two twin-looking abrupt pyramidal hills, composed of huge disjointed blocks of granite, which lay piled above each other in grand confusion. To the summit of one of these I ascended with a native, but the forest in advance was so impenetrable that we could see nothing of the game we sought. Descending from the hillock we resumed the spoor, and were enabled to follow at a rapid pace; the native who led the spooring party being the best tracker in Bamangwato. I had presently very great satisfaction to perceive that the elephants had not been alarmed, their course being strewed with branches which they had chewed as they slowly fed along.

The trackers now became extremely excited, and strained their eyes on every side in the momentary expectation of beholding the elephants. At length we emerged into an open glade, and, clearing a grove of thorny mimosas, we came full in sight of one of them. Cautiously advancing, and looking to my right, I next discovered his comrade, standing in a thicket of low wait-a-bits, within a hundred and fifty yards of me; they were both first-rate old bulls, with enormous tusks of great length. I dismounted, and warily approached the second elephant for a closer inspection of his tusks. As I drew near he slightly turned his head, and I then perceived that his farther one was damaged towards the point, while at the same instant his comrade, raising his head clear of the bush on which he browsed, displayed to my delighted eyes a pair of the most beautiful and perfect tusks I had ever seen.

Regaining my horse, I advanced towards this elephant, and when within forty yards of him he walked slowly on before me in an open space, his huge ears gently flapping, and entirely concealing me from his view. Inclining to the left, I slightly increased my pace, and walked past him within sixty yards, upon which he observed me for the first time; but probably mistaking "Sunday" for a hartebeest, he continued his course with his eye upon me, but showed no symptoms of alarm. The natives had requested me to endeavour, if possible, to hunt him towards the water, which lay in a northerly direction, and this I resolved to do. Having advanced a little, I gave him my wind, when he was instantly alarmed and backed into the bushes, holding his head high and right to me.

Thus he stood motionless as a statue, under the impression probably that owing to his Lilliputian dimensions I had failed to observe him, and fancying that I would pass on without detecting him. I rode slowly on, and described a semicircle to obtain a shot at his shoulder, and, halting my horse, I fired from the saddle; he got it in the shoulder-blade, and, as slowly and silently I continued my course, he still stood gazing at me in utter astonishment. Bill and Flam were now slipped by the natives, and in another moment they were barking around him. I shouted loudly to encourage the dogs and perplex the elephant, who seemed puzzled to know what to think of us, and, shrilly trumpeting, charged headlong after the dogs. Retreating, he backed into the thicket, then charged once more, and made clean away, holding the course I wanted.

When I tried to fire, "Sunday" was very fidgety, and destroyed the correctness of my aim. Approaching the elephant, I presently dismounted, and, running in, gave him two fine shots behind the shoulder; then the dogs, which were both indifferent ones, ran barking at him. The consequence was a terrific charge, the dogs at once making for their master, and bringing the elephant right upon me. I had no time to gain my saddle, but ran for my life. The dogs, fortunately, took after "Sunday," who, alarmed by the trumpeting, dashed frantically away. Though in the midst of a most dangerous affray, I could not help laughing to remark horse, dogs, and elephant all charging along in a direct line.

The dogs, having missed their master, held away for Kleinboy, who had long disappeared I knew not whither. "Sunday" stood still, and commenced to graze, while the elephant, slowly passing within a few yards of him, assumed a position under a tree beside him. Kleinboy presently making his appearance, I called to him to ride in and bring me my steed, but he refused and asked me if I wished him to go headlong to destruction. "Sunday" having fed slowly away from the elephant, I went up and he allowed me to recapture him. I now plainly saw that the elephant was dying, but I continued firing, to hasten his demise. Towards the end he took up a position in a dense thorny thicket, where for a long time he remained.

Approaching within twelve paces, I fired my last two shots, aiming at his left side, close behind the shoulder. On receiving these he backed slowly through the thicket, and, clearing it, walked gently forward about twenty yards, when he suddenly came down with tremendous violence right on his broadside. To my intense mortification, the heavy fall was accompanied by a loud sharp crack, and on going up I found one of his matchless tusks broken off short by the lip. This was a glorious day's sport: I had bagged in one afternoon probably the two finest bull elephants in Bamangwato, and, had it not been for the destruction of their noble trophies, which were the two finest pair of tusks I had obtained that season, my triumph on the occasion would have been great and unalloyed.

I was now languid and faint from excessive thirst, and the nearest water was still very remote. Being joined by the natives, we quickly proceeded to divest the side of the elephant of a large sheet of the outer skin, when of the under one we constructed a pair of water-bags, with which two of the natives set out, leading along with them the dogs and horses; nor did they rejoin us till after midnight, having lost their reckoning by the way. Their comrades who were with me, conjecturing the cause of the delay, requested me to fire signal-shots at intervals throughout the night, which was the means of their eventually reaching their destination. At an early hour on the following day, leaving Kleinboy with the natives to look after the ivory, I set out with two men, to show them where the other elephant lay, and thence to continue my way to camp.

The weather had hitherto been favourable for the toilsome pursuit of elephant-hunting, little rain having fallen since I first entered the country. At length, however, the rainy season was at hand, and we were constantly visited by the most appalling thunderstorms, accompanied by overwhelming torrents of rain, which filled the hitherto dry nullahs and gravelly water-courses with running streams, and converted the parched forest and arid plains into blossoming verdure and grassy meads. While hunting I was often overtaken by the rains, and on these occasions I still managed to keep myself tolerably comfortable, by compelling the natives to erect for me a bothy, or temporary hut. This duty they often proved reluctant to perform; but I invariably managed to gain my point, by explaining to them that, if my guns and powder were exposed to the rain, they would die, and then I could kill no more elephants for them.

When attended by a large party the erection of a good substantial bothy was a simple and easy proceeding, and was accomplished in the following manner:—One party, armed with tomahawks, went in quest of long forked poles, which they cut in lengths of ten feet; a second party gathered green brushwood; and the third collected a large quantity of long dry grass, which they tore out of the ground by the roots. The poles were set up in a circular position, the forked ends meeting and resting against one another overhead, then the brushwood was tightly interlaced between the poles, leaving a small low aperture for the door, and the fabric was effectually thatched with the long grass, the conical summit being usually crowned either with the enormous ear or a portion of the hide of an elephant. Such was the bothy which the natives were wont to build for me when overtaken by storms, or when the sky looked threatening, during the remainder of that and all the subsequent seasons that I hunted among the Bechuana tribes.

But it often happened, when I had lain down for the night with no other roof above me than the vaulted canopy of heaven, that my placid slumbers were rudely disturbed by rain falling like a water-spout on my face. Such events as these were extremely disagreeable, more especially when it came down so heavily as to preclude the possibility of maintaining our usual watch-fires. In weather like this the prowling tyrant of the forest is ever most active in search of his prey, and our ears were occasionally greeted with the deep-toned voices of troops of lions, as attracted by the smell of our beef, they prowled around our encampments.

I continued hunting to the eastward of Bamangwato until the 3rd of October, during which time I added four other noble elephants, besides rhinoceroses and other animals, to my already satisfactory list of game. It is about this latitude that the traveller will first meet with the gigantic and castle-like nwana, which is decidedly the most striking and wonderful tree among the thousands which adorn the South African forests. It is chiefly remarkable on account of its extraordinary size, actually resembling a castle or tower more than a forest-tree. Throughout the country of Bamangwato the average circumference of these trees was from thirty to forty feet; but on subsequently extending my researches in a north-easterly direction, throughout the more fertile forests which clothe the boundless tracts through which the fair Limpopo winds, I daily met with specimens of this extraordinary tree averaging from sixty to hundred feet in circumference, and maintaining this thickness to a height from twenty to thirty feet, when they diverge into numerous goodly branches, whose general character is abrupt and horizontal, and which seem to terminate with a peculiar suddenness. The wood of this tree is soft and utterly unserviceable; the shape of the leaf is similar to that of the sycamore-tree, but its texture partakes more of the fig-leaf; its fruit is a nut, which in size and shape resembles the egg of the swan.

A remarkable fact, in connection with these trees, is the manner in which they are disposed throughout the forest. They are found standing singly, or in rows, invariably at considerable distances from one another, as if planted by the hand of man; and from their wondrous size and unusual height (for they always tower high above their surrounding compeers), they convey the idea of being strangers or interlopers on the ground they occupy.

The rains having fallen, the country was already adorned with a goodly coating of verdant grass, and my oxen, having done little else than feed and rest themselves for several months, were now full of spirit and in fine condition, and rattled along before my heavily laden waggons, over rugged hills and through the trackless mazes of the forest, at a rapid and willing pace, and on the evening of the 4th of October I once more formed my encampment at Lesausau, in the Bamangwato Mountains, in the neighbourhood of Sicomy's kraal.

Here I was quickly welcomed by Sicomy, who visited me in company with a numerous body of his tribe. He expressed himself much gratified at seeing me return in safety from the dangerous pursuit in which I had been employed, remarking that he was anxious about me in my absence, for, if any casualty had befallen me, my king, he said, would be certain to seek restitution at his hands. His Majesty was pleased to compliment me on my extraordinary success and skill in hunting, and observed that the medicine of the white man must indeed be strong.

In the course of the evening he amused me with the quaintness of his questions, asking me if my father and mother were alive, how many brothers and sisters I had, if the flocks and herds of my king were extremely abundant, and if his subjects were more numerous than his own. On informing him that our chief was a woman, he seemed much tickled by the disclosure; and when I said that her subjects were as numerous as the locusts, he looked round on his warriors with an evident grin of disbelief, and then inquired of me if all my countrymen could vanquish the elephants as easily as I did. This was a puzzler: so I replied that I could not say; but I knew that the hearts of all my nation were very strong, like the heart of the lion when his cubs are small. The whole assembly was greatly moved by this bright remark, and a general murmur of surprise and admiration extended through the dusky ranks as each man repeated to his neighbour the surpassing courage of my lion-hearted countrymen. Old Mutchuisho understood my gibberish better than any of the rest, and acted in the capacity of interpreter between me and the king.

Our conversation was maintained partly by means of signs, my attainments in the Sichuana language being as yet but limited. Mutchuisho now intimated to me that two friends of Sicomy's, with their two attendants, wished to accompany me to the colony in the capacity of cattle-herds, who promised at the same time to make themselves generally useful in the way of collecting firewood and carrying venison home to the waggons. To this proposal I fortunately agreed, and the four aspirants came forward, and were duly introduced to me. The names of these four Bechuanas were Mollyee, Mollyeon, Kapain, and Kuruman: the two former belonged to the aristocracy, and were old friends of mine, having often assisted me in the field. These men agreed to serve me faithfully as far as the sea and back again to the country of their chief, in consideration of which I promised on my part to reward them with a cow and musket each.

Mollyee and Mollyeon were brothers; they were tall, active-looking savages, with large, bright, sparkling eyes and a pleasing cast of features. Kapain was a short, thickset, noisy individual, remarkable for his ugliness, and was the funniest fellow in all Bamangwato. Kuruman was a good-natured boy of about sixteen years of age; his face was prepossessing, resembling that of a girl more than the sex to which he professed to belong. I entertained Sicomy with stewed meat and coffee, and he and his retinue remained that night in my encampment. Before retiring to rest he intimated to me, through Mutchuisho, that he wished to trade with me on the ensuing day, which I said I should be happy to do until the hour of midday, when I would positively inspan and leave Lesausau.

Accordingly, at an early hour on the morrow sundry fine tusks and some good specimens of native arms and costume made their appearance, which I obtained in barter for beads, ammunition, and other articles. On inquiring of the king what had become of Isaac, he said that he had long since returned to Kuruman in company with a son of "old Seretse," a Bechuana of distinction residing in the vicinity of Kuruman. This individual, whose name, being translated, signifies "*mud*," is remarkable for his bitterness against the advancement of the Christian religion and for the number of his progeny. Bidding adieu to Sicomy at midday on the 5th, I continued my march for Corriebely, which I reached about noon on the following day. I was accompanied, as usual, by a number of the natives, in the hope of obtaining a supply of flesh, elephants being reported to have revisited Massouey. Heavy rains had fallen throughout this district, and the country now presented an entirely new appearance, rank young grass having everywhere sprung up, and the plains and forests displaying a profusion of the richest verdure. It was here that I had concealed a large quantity of lead, in a hole beneath the ashes of my fire, before recrossing the mountains of Bamangwato.

Proceeding to the spot, I had the satisfaction to observe that the ground appeared to have been undisturbed; and, returning to the waggons, I commenced to unlash from the side of one of these a shovel. The natives, who always watched my movements with great attention, at once observed me, and a large party followed me to my former fireplace. Here, to their surprise, I began to excavate; and on beholding the lead they seemed utterly astounded, and I could read very plainly in their faces that, had they known it was there, they would have saved my oxen the trouble of transporting it across the sandy deserts betwixt me and Bakatla. On reaching Massouey, and examining the fountain, I sought in vain for the tracks of elephants; the natives, nevertheless, declared that one or two herds of these were still to be met with in the district, which I inclined to credit; and this report turned out to be correct, for the succeeding day I followed and succeeded in bagging a whole herd of eight bull and cow elephants, after a most exciting chase. The natives were overjoyed at my success, and, while talking over the circumstance to each other, I observed that they frequently drew their hands across their mouth, a gesture commonly made use of by them when a "clean sweep" (as in the present instance) had been made, either in the chase or in their combats with each other.

I continued hunting at Massouey till the 12th, when, bidding a long farewell to the land of elephants, I inspanned, and marched upon Lepeby, which I reached at an early hour on the following day, having travelled several hours during the night, availing myself of the bright moonlight. When last I visited this fine fountain the game drank at it in numerous herds, but now not an animal of any kind came near it, with the exception of a few rhinoceroses. This I always found to be the case at the fountains during the summer months, when the game are very independent of water, owing to the more abundant moisture contained in the young grass. In the forenoon I went birdnesting among the reeds and rushes which grew around the fountain. Hundreds of birds resembling the redpole were busy building their grassy nests, which they ingeniously suspended between the tops of the reeds. In the rushes I found two nests of the water-hen, containing eggs, which, along with the nests, exactly corresponded with these in Scotland. Two beautifully-painted wild geese, an egret, or white heron, and about twenty teal, ornamented the fountain, and were so tame that they permitted me to approach within a few yards of them.

At an early hour on the 16th I trekked for Boötlonamy, which I reached at sundown on the same evening, and drew up the waggons under an impenetrable grove of picturesque mimosas, which were then gaily decked with a profusion of highly scented yellow blossoms, brightly contrasting with their summer vestment of delicious green. Here I continued hunting for several days, and enjoyed excellent sport, daily securing several fine specimens of the different varieties of game frequenting the district. On one occasion while hunting I started a secretary from off her nest, which was built on the top of a very dense green tree, with thorns on the fish-hook principle. With much difficulty I cut my way to the large thorny branch on which the nest was built, and, to proceed farther being impossible, from the denseness of the thorns, I cut through this branch with my knife, and by dragging it down I got hold of the eggs, which were the size and shape of a turkey's, and the colour of a buzzard's egg.

On the forenoon of the 19th we were visited by a most terrific storm. The thunder was the most appalling I had ever heard, resembling the simultaneons discharge of a thousand pieces of artillery: it burst close over my head with a report so sudden and tremendous, that I involuntarily trembled, and the sweat ran down my brow. At other times the thunder rumbled on every side, and rolled away with a long-protracted sound, which had not died before fresh explosions burst above and around me. The lightning was so vivid that it pained my eyes; it seemed so near, that I fancied every moment it must strike the waggons, which would certainly have proved extremely inconvenient, as I had 300 lbs. of gunpowder stowed in one of them beneath my bed.

About sundown the storm had passed away, having exquisitely purified the atmosphere, while the grateful earth and fragrant forest emitted a perfume of overpowering sweetness. I then sauntered out with my rifle towards where the oxen were grazing, and, falling in with a herd of brindled gnoos, I shot a couple of shaggy old fellows, firing right and left. The storm set in again about ten P.M. with thunder and lightning, which continued throughout the greater part of the night.

CHAPTER XIX.

All my Colonial Servants desert me—Pursue them in vain—Both Waggons get disabled—Melancholy Anticipations—Cut a Path through the Forest—A Sandy Desert—Cattle dying for want of Water—Troubles surmounted—Pallahs and Koodoos—A Lion and Leopard visit the Camp at Midnight—Another horse dies of Distemper—We reach Booby—One of the Axletrees breaks—The Bakatlas assist me—The Baggage-waggon upset in a River—The Distemper kills more Horses—Lions roaring—Arrive at Dr. Livingstone's—March upon Chouaney—The Ngotwani—A Herd of Buffaloes among the Reeds.

I HAD now arrived at a period of considerable importance in my lonely expedition, an event here occurring which caused me a world of trouble and anxiety, yet which was nevertheless finally beneficial in its results, as it taught me what difficulties a man may surmount when he is pressed by adversity, and it was also the means of my becoming an accomplished waggon-driver. I allude to my being abandoned by all my colonial servants, with the exception of Ruyter, the little Bushman. I attributed this unmanly and dastardly proceeding mainly to their despair of succeeding in bringing the waggons safely across the sandy deserts intervening betwixt me and the distant missionary station of Bakatla, on account of the broken state of one of the axletrees of my travelling waggon, Kleinboy in one of his drunken fits having driven it against a tree with such violence that one of the wooden arms of the fore axletree was cracked right across, so that little now held the wheel excepting the linchpin and the iron skein. I remarked on the 22nd that there was something unusual on the minds of my colonial followers, for none of them could look me in the face; and in the evening I spoke harshly to them concerning some ground coffee which I had missed from my canteen.

On the 23rd of October I was lying asleep in my waggon, a little before the day dawned, when Ruyter awoke me, to report that my four Hottentots had decamped during the night. He said that each of them had taken with him a large bundle of biltongue or sun-dried meat, and that they had tried hard to prevail on him to accompany them. This was a rather startling announcement, for I had barely enough of hands to perform the work when they were with me, and the four savages from Bamangwato were, like myself, quite unaccustomed to the laborious and intricate art of waggon leading and driving, and the inspanning and outspanning of oxen. Imagining that the Hottentots would not persevere in so rash and unwarranted a measure, and that they would assuredly change their minds and retrace their steps to their master when they reflected on the step they had taken, I did not endeavour to overtake them, but employed the morning in stowing the waggons, lashing down pots, spades, axes, etc., in their proper places, and overhauling the gear preparatory to marching.

Having breakfasted, I and the little bushman, assisted by the savages, lassoed, sorted, and yoked twenty-four oxen, placing twelve before each waggon, when we cracked our whips and started for Boötlonamy. Mollyee and Mollyeon led the teams, and Kapain and Kuruman followed behind the waggons, driving the horses and loose oxen. In former days I had acquired considerable experience in driving tandem and four-in-hand; but I had now undertaken a pursuit of a widely different character. I soon, however, became quite *au fait* in the mysteries connected with the driving of oxen, and learnt to inspan and drive my own waggons with nearly the same expedition as before the desertion of the Hottentots.

The vley of Boötlonamy being firm and hard, we rattled along it at our wonted pace; but in the evening, as we cleared the vley, and entered on the sandy tracts beyond, the oxen, having discovered that their new drivers could not wield the whips with the rapidity and execution of the old, declined to move along the heavy sand beyond the pace they fancied, often halting of their own accord. Eventually, in ascending a sandy ridge, the Bushman's waggon stuck fast in the deep sand, and in trying to drag it out the oxen broke the "disselboom," or pole. Finding that the labours we had undertaken were greater than I had calculated upon, I resolved to ride on the morrow in pursuit of the runaways; and accordingly at daybreak on the following day, leaving the waggons and their valuable contents at the mercy of the savages, I started with the Bushman and a spare horse to endeavour to overtake them.

There was no water where the waggons stood, so I instructed Mollyeon to proceed with the cattle in quest of that essential requisite. I held along my old waggon-track, where we traced the footsteps of the Hottentots; and having ridden some miles, we reached the spot where they had slept, and where the ashes of the fire still were smouldering. I followed up their spoor till mid-day, when I accidentally took up the spoor of a party of Bakalahari, which we followed in a westerly direction, imagining that the Hottentots were with them. This spoor we eventually lost in stony ground, and then we rode back to where we had lost the right spoor, which after some search we found, and once more held on.

Our steeds were now fatigued, for we had ridden sharp, and they were faint with thirst, as we were also; but we sought in vain for water in the vleys which had contained it when we last passed through the country. A little before the sun went down we reached three small pools of water left by the recent rains, and here the Hottentots had drunk and were at that moment hiding in a bush within a hundred yards of me, as I discovered on the ensuing day. I however failed to observe them; and fancying that they had held on to a larger vley, where I had encamped on my way to Bamangwato, we proceeded for that place, but, night setting in, we at length lost our way in the intricacies of the forest.

Faint, hungry, and thirsty, we now desisted from our fruitless search, and on looking for my matches I found to my intense mortification that I had lost them; and being on this occasion minus my shooting-belt and rifle, we spent the night without a fire, thereby incurring great danger of losing the horses and ourselves by lions. Scarcely had we off-saddled when two huge rhinoceroses came up and stood within twenty yards of us, and would not for a long time be persuaded to depart. Some time after I observed a dark-looking object prowling around us, and evidently anxious to cultivate the acquaintance either of ourselves or the horses. It was a hyæna. Rising from my comfortless couch, I pelted him with stones, when he took the hint and made off. The horses were completely done up, and when knee-haltered would not feed. One of them on being off-saddled lay stretched upon the ground, and after a while, on endeavouring to walk, repeatedly rolled over on his side.

On the 25th I cast loose the horses as soon as it was clear, and ascended to the summit of a pyramidal little hill beside which we had slept, to ascertain from thence whither I had wandered; but the view from this hill did not help to elucidate matters, endless forests stretching away on every side without a mark to assist my memory. I now resolved to seek no longer for my ruffianly Hottentots, but to retrace my spoor to the water I had discovered on the preceding evening, and halt there for a day until the horses should sufficiently recover their strength to carry us back to the waggons. By adhering to the horses' tracks, I reached the water at an early hour, and here I discovered the fresh tracks of the Hottentots on the top of our horses' spoor of the preceding evening.

I had, however, resolved not to ride another yard after them; I accordingly off-saddled, and remained there for the remainder of the day. In the vicinity of the water we discovered the spot where the Hottentots had slept during the night. Although possessed of flint and steel, they had not kindled a fire, having nevertheless collected fuel for that purpose previous to our arrival on the preceding evening. This, as I afterwards learnt from themselves, was to prevent our discovering their position, in case we had returned that evening. I spent most of the day in endeavouring to make fire, which I failed to accomplish for want of tinder. This was extremely annoying, for I had brought along with me both tea and coffee, as also a kettle, and a haunch of springbok.

On the morning of the 26th we cast loose our horses, and proceeded to consume raw meat and water. While thus breakfasting, a pair of superb roan antelopes approached the water, advancing within easy range before they noticed us. We saddled up and rode for the waggons, which we reached in the afternoon, having off-saddled for an hour by the way. I found the waggons as I had left them, and also the savages, who had fortunately discovered a small vley of rain-water about two miles to the southward of their position, where they had daily refreshed themselves and the cattle.

My situation was by no means an enviable one, and my mind was burdened with anxiety. One of the waggons was fast in deep sand, with the dissel-boom broken, and the fore-axle of the other was cracked, so that at any moment it was likely to give way; and if this should happen on the line of march while crossing the desert and far from water, I should have had no alternative but to abandon the waggon to its fate. Moreover, owing to the indolent disposition of the Hottentots, everything connected with the gear was broken and out of order, while the hatchets appeared to have been used in chopping gun-flints, and all their handles were in similar condition.

I arose at dawn on the morning of the 27th, and, having cast loose the horses and oxen, I rummaged out my tools, and in two hours I got out the broken dissel-boom, and put in a new one, which I formed from the stem of a tough mimosa. This being accomplished, I yoked twelve oxen to the waggon which was sticking in the sand, but tried in vain to make them drag it out, for the cunning animals knew that it was fast, and would not exert themselves to attempt to extricate it. After inconceivable trouble and repeatedly shifting the positions of the various oxen in the span, I at length made a fortunate arrangement of the oxen. The brutes for once pulled all together, and once more the waggon was in motion. I then inspanned the other team, and we reached the water without further trouble. As we neared the water I detected a giraffe browsing within a quarter of a mile; this was well, for we required flesh.

Commanding silence, I hastily outspanned, and, having saddled the Old Grey, I rode with Ruyter to where we last had seen the "Tootla." Having proceeded a short distance through the forest, I again discovered him within a hundred yards of me. He proved to be a young bull, and led me a severe chase over very heavy ground. Towards the end I thought he was going to beat me, and I was about to pull up, when suddenly he lowered his tail, by which I knew that his race was run. Urging my horse, I was soon alongside of him, and with three shots I ended his career. Having obtained for the present both flesh and water, my next lookout was to consider how I was to cross the sandy desert which lay betwixt me and the kraal of Booby. It was very evident that I could not return by the route I had previously held, having already ascertained that that country to ox-waggons was now impassable, all the waters being dry.

On explaining this to my Bamangwato followers, Mollyeon stated that he had once traversed that country in a dry season many years before, and that he and his comrades had obtained water in some deep pits, which had been excavated by Bakalahari in a rocky part of the desert, considerably to the eastward of my former route. He said we should require the greater part of two days to reach this water, our route thither lying across a soft sandy soil, varied in many places by almost impenetrable forest; he moreover seemed a little doubtful as to whether we should be able to discover the place, and, when we did, whether the pits might not prove dry. This was certainly a bright lookout, more especially as the next water (which he represented as a perpetual fountain) was two days beyond the uncertain pits.

On the 28th I was occupied about the waggons all the day, putting sundry things to rights. I had thoughts of trekking on the following day, and could not divest myself of the most dismal forebodings, for I felt certain that the heavier waggon would again stick fast, or that the cracked axletree would come in contact with some tree, and leave me in the desert a hopeless wreck, remote from water or any assistance. I had certainly good reason to be uneasy. On the 29th I waited till the sun was up, that the cattle might drink plentifully, when I immediately inspanned, and commenced my anxious journey. For the first ten or twelve miles we proceeded along a hollow, where the soil was in general tolerably firm; but on leaving this hollow we entered upon a most impracticable country, the waggons sinking about four inches in the soft sand. Though I held on I had not the slightest hope of getting through it, for every hundred yards required the utmost exertion both of ourselves and oxen; yet I had the best of two days more of it to expect before I could reach the promised water. To increase our difficulties our progress was presently opposed by an interminable forest, where the trees stood so close together as often to bar the possibility of the waggons passing betwixt them.

On these occasions it became imperative upon me to turn pioneer, and in the course of the day I felled with the axe not less than fifty trees. In this manner I held on till the sun went down, when I halted in dense forest and cast loose the oxen for an hour; after which, with infinite trouble, I lassoed the two teams and made them fast on the trektow, in their proper places, ready to inspan at dawn of day. I had also nine horses to catch and make fast, and none to assist me but the little Bushman; for the savages were so lazy, awkward, and disobliging, that one Hottentot would have assisted me more than the whole pack of them.

On the 30th I inspanned before it was light, and again held on, as on the preceding day, through heavy sand and interminable forest, where it was necessary to keep the axes in constant operation. In the afternoon we reached the promised watering-place, but on springing from the waggon, and running anxiously forward for an inspection of the pits, I had the mortification to find that all they contained was a little mud, in which sundry heterogeneous insects were sprawling. The Bechuanas, however, signified to me that, by clearing out the pits and digging a little, water would make its appearance. Accordingly, having outspanned the jaded oxen, I unlashed the spades, which were vigorously plied, when the water began very reluctantly to trickle in from every side.

We thus cleared out the three most likely pits, and in two hours I obtained a very moderate supply of water for each of the oxen, which I gave them individually out of my large flesh-pot. My poor horses did not get a drop; and we now proceeded to inspan, and resume our march beneath a burning sun of unusual intensity. The sand became, if possible, worse than ever, and the waggons repeatedly stuck fast. We held through a jungle of the most virulent wait-a-bit thorns, which reduced my waggon-sails to ribbons; and when the sun went down I halted for the night, and cast loose my wretched oxen for an hour.

On the 31st my vans were again in motion before daylight; and about four P.M., to my infinite delight and great relief, I got clear of the desert, and reached a strong perennial fountain situated in a finely-wooded valley on the northern borders of the mountain country, extending to the southward, with little intermission, as far as the chain of the Kurrichane range. Towards the end of the march it was necessary to descend into a rugged valley, and cross a very awkward watercourse, in which the baggage-waggon was within a hair-breadth of being capsized. Ascending from this valley, we crossed a precipitous ridge, where large disjointed masses of rock threatened the momentary destruction of the waggons.

As I was yoking one of the oxen, which had broken his yokeskey and got out of his place, I received from a vicious ox in front a severe kick on the cap of the knee, which gave me intense pain and laid me prostrate on the ground. I however managed to drive the waggon to its destination, where, after lying for a few minutes, the pain increased so much that I lay panting on my bed. Just as I had outspanned, and before my knee had stiffened, a herd of zebras approached the fountain to drink. This was a godsend at such a moment, our flesh being at an end and the dogs starving. In torture as I was, I managed to make a limping stalk towards them, when I obtained a fine double-shot and brought down a brace of fine old mares.

The following day was the 1st of November; my knee was much better, and in the afternoon I went out with Ruyter and shot two koodoos and a pallah. I shot one of the koodoos from the saddle as he bounded past me at a hundred yards. At night, as I lay down, I heard a lion roar in the vicinity of camp, and presently I was asleep. In a few hours I was awoke by an unusual disturbance in the camp, and, raising my head, I saw the Bechuanas standing close together round the fire with their faces outwards, while they shrieked and talked with unusual volubility. I guessed at once that a lion caused the rumpus; and I was right. The dogs were barking loud and angrily, and kept rushing back occasionally to the fire, as if pursued by some animal. The night was pitch dark, so that nothing could be seen; but Mollyeon told me that a lion and a leopard were prowling around us, endeavouring to obtain the venison of the zebras, which hung in festoons in the trees beside us; and next moment I heard the voices of both, for the lion roared and the leopard shrieked wildly as they sprang after the dogs.

At length their boldness increased; the lion chased the dogs with angry growls within twenty yards of where we stood, and the leopard actually sprang into the centre of my larder beside the fire, and was making off with a large fragment of ribs, when the dogs went gallantly at him. He turned upon them, and so terribly lacerated two that they soon after died from their wounds. We now snatched up large flaming brands from the fire, and, meeting the lion as he advanced, we sent them flying in his face, when I fancy he made off. I feared to use my rifle lest I should shoot the dogs. The horses and oxen, although much alarmed, did not endeavour to break loose, being still very much fatigued from the hardships they had undergone.

On the morning of the 2nd I shot a koodoo, which antelope seemed here to be tolerably abundant; and about midday, as I sat writing beneath the waggon, I observed a troop of zebras approaching the fountain, followed by a string of koodoos, three of which carried unusually fine horns. While I sat looking at them through my spyglass, I directed Ruyter to bring up the horses, when we saddled the "Grey" and the "Chestnut Pony," and rode slowly towards them, till they started, when we gave them chase. They took right up the face of a stony ridge, and as they disappeared over its summit the Bushman was riding within a spear's length of the finest buck.

Before, however, I could gain the ridge, the "Old Grey" refused to proceed farther, when, dismounting, I resumed the chase on foot, but failed to fall in with my after-rider, who eventually brought the koodoo to a stand. Retracing my steps, I directed my attention to my poor "Old Grey," which was evidently attacked with the African distemper. With considerable difficulty I brought him to the camp, where I instantly bled him, but to no purpose, and in another hour the "gallant grey" lay down and "stretched his stiff limbs to rise no more." At night the lion feasted on the body, and when he was full the leopard and hyænas finished it.

On the morning of the 3rd I left this fountain and held for Booby, which I reached at midday on the 5th. On my way thither we one evening fell in with a large herd of elands, out of which I captured a first-rate bull. I was kindly welcomed by Caachy, now the chief of Booby, the former chief having been blown up in my absence as already mentioned. Caachy informed me that my runaway Hottentots had reached his kraal, and were very much exhausted by their march. He had assisted them with corn, and passed them on to Bakatla. They informed this chief that I had dismissed them from my service, having engaged other servants at Bamangwato.

I remained at Booby till midday on the 7th, and obtained several very fine karosses and other native curiosities in barter from the tribe. The king supplied me liberally with boyalwa, or native beer, which I thought most excellent, but found that it possessed a soporific tendency, inducing me on one occasion to lie down and sleep for half the day while the king and his nobility were waiting to trade with me. A large body of the natives accompanied me from Booby, some of them leading pack-oxen which were sent by Caachy to convey the venison of sundry rhinoceroses which I engaged to shoot for him. These men led me towards Bakatla by a different route from that which I had formerly adopted.

Early on the 13th, while taking coffee, I was met by a party from Bakatla who had been kindly depatched by Dr. Livingstone, the resident missionary, on hearing of my abandonment by my colonial servants. The party consisted of a Bechuana, named Mabal, belonging to Kuruman (who assisted Dr. Livingstone in teaching the children of the Bakatlas), and three of the Bakatla tribe. These men reached me just at the proper moment; for, having inspanned, before we had proceeded three hundred yards the damaged axletree broke short across, and the wheel rolling away the waggon came down on its side. This was a catastrophe I had for some time anticipated, and I was only thankful that it had been deferred so long. We outspanned, and, having unloaded the waggon, we put a support under it, and took out the forestell, and I then set about making a false axletree of tough thorn-wood. The vertical sun was extremely powerful, and both my ankles gave me severe and never-ceasing pain from wounds inflicted by the cruel wait-a-bits and inflammation induced by the unvarying animal diet on which I had so long subsisted. In the afternoon of the following day I got the false axletree fixed in its proper position, and having loaded up the waggon we were once more ready for a start.

On the 15th we inspanned, and, having passed through the bold mountain gorge of Sesetabie, we encamped on the margin of a periodical river whose precipitous banks and broad channel of deep soft sand caused me considerable apprehensions of difficulties for the morrow.

On the 16th I unlashed my spades and pickaxe, and worked hard for several hours cutting down the precipitous banks of the river and constructing a road for the waggons to pass; after which we inspanned and took the stream. I drove my waggon safely through; but, alas! not so with the baggage-waggon. Twice it stuck fast in the treacherous sand while crossing the river's bed, but the sturdy oxen pulled it out, and had dragged it more than half-way up the almost perpendicular bank, when the native who led the long team, unmindful that a waggon was behind them, suddenly turned the leading oxen short towards the river's bank, thus rendering it impossible for the driver to steer his after-oxen. The waggon was dragged off the fine road which I had made for it, and after quivering for a moment as if loth to meet its fate, it fell heavily over and rolled down the bank with a most terrific crash, smashing the fine capped tent, and sending the ivory and all my highly-valued trophies flying into the bed of the river in a mass of the most dire confusion.

This was enough to vex any man, but I had now become so seasoned to adversity that I only laughed at the capsize as though the accident had happened to a foe; and having unyoked the oxen, we commenced carrying the heavy ivory and other articles up the bank to the level ground beyond; after which we righted the waggon, and a team of oxen dragged it up the bank. I then set to work to repair the tent with green boughs, and before sunset we had again replaced the greater part of the cargo. As the sun went down "The Cow" died from the distemper which had carried off my other two horses. The night set in with thunder, lightning, and rain; jackals and hyænas prowled around us, and soon found the remains of my lamented charger, on which they feasted till the dawn of day.

The 17th ushered in a lovely morning, and the sky was beautifully overcast with clouds. When I got things dry I finished stowing the waggon, and we then trekked, holding on till the evening, when the axle-tree which I had made burst, and the linchpin giving way the wheel rolled off, leaving me once more a wreck. While securing my few remaining horses, I remarked that a handsome little bay horse, named "Hutton," evinced symptoms of the distemper, but I did not bleed him, as it seemed to be of no avail. Heavy rain continued falling throughout the night, and next morning the ground where we had outspanned was a mass of deep mud.

At an early hour all hands were busy in again unloading the broken waggon, and before night I had finished another axletree and fixed it in its place. The day throughout was dark and gloomy—heavy clouds hung low on the mountain of the eagles, reminding me of the mist I was wont to see in the distant country of the Gael, and our ears were repeatedly saluted with the subdued voices of a troop of lions which were moaning in concert around its base. In the evening the horse called "Hutton" died, and scarcely had night set in when his doleful coronach was wildly re-echoed by the shrill voices of a score of jackals, which the lions hearing soon came to their assistance, and presently we heard them feasting on his remains.

On the morning of the 19th we resumed our march, and at a late hour on the evening of the 20th we reached the missionary station at Bakatla, where I was kindly received by Dr. Livingstone and his amiable lady. They had been anxious concerning my fate, and entertained great apprehensions for my safety. Mrs. Livingstone had seen my Hottentots as they passed through Bakatla, where they remained only one day; and that lady represented them as bearing the appearance of men who had been guilty of crime. She had endeavoured, but without success, to prevail upon them to rejoin their master and return to their duty. Dr. Livingstone at the time was absent on a visit to Sichely, superintending the erection of a dwelling-house and place of public worship at that chief's kraal, named "Chouaney," whither he intended shortly to remove, there being another missionary, named Mr. Edwards, already stationed at Bakatla, who was then absent on a visit to the colony. Dr. Livingstone informed me that at present there was war between the Baquaines, of whom Sichely is chief, and the Bakatlas, and that the latter were in daily expectation of an attack.

The 23rd was Sunday, when Dr. Livingstone showed me, on comparing notes, that I had lost a day during my sojourn in the far interior. I attended Divine service, and had considerable difficulty to maintain my gravity as sundry members of the congregation entered the church clad in the most unique apparel. Some of these wore extraordinary old hats ornamented with fragments of women's clothes and ostrich-feathers. These fine hats they were very reluctant to take off, and one man sat with his beaver on immediately before the minister until the doorkeeper went up to him and ordered him to remove it. At dinner we had a variety of excellent vegetables, the garden producing almost every sort in great perfection; the potatoes in particular were very fine. To-day another of my stud, named Yarborough (so called in honour of a gallant major of the 91st from whom I purchased him), died of the distemper, and was immediately consumed by the starving curs of the Bakatlas. Being anxious to visit Sichely and his tribe, Dr. Livingstone and I resolved to leave Bakatla and march upon Chouaney with one of my waggons on the ensuing day; the Doctor's object being to establish peace between the two tribes, and mine to enrich myself with ivory and karosses and other objects of interest.

On the morning of the 24th I off-loaded the baggage waggon, and stowed its contents in Dr. Livingstone's premises, after which the Doctor and I started for Chouaney, which bore a little to the east of north. Our road lay through the most perfect country. On clearing the romantic valley of Bakatla we descended into another beautiful valley, through which meandered the crystal waters of the Ngotwani, an interesting stream, which, flowing in a north-easterly direction, falls into the Limpopo about sixty miles below its junction with the Mariqua. The Ngotwani contains several varieties of fish, which are of good flavour, and afford the angler steady average sport both with bait and fly. After following some distance along the finely-wooded banks of the Ngotwani, and having twice crossed its stream, we entered upon an extensive open tract of country adorned with a carpet of the most luxuriant herbage.

This interesting plain was beautifully wooded towards the mountain ranges which bound it on every side, and the Ngotwani twined in a serpentine course along the middle of it, forming in one part an extensive vley or marsh about four miles long and a quarter of a mile in breadth. This vley was now beautified with a dense crop of waving green reeds, averaging about fourteen feet in height, and forming a favourite resort of buffaloes and their invariable attendants the lions. Dr. Livingstone told me that a party of Baquaines were to leave Chouaney on the ensuing day to visit this vley, for the purpose of cutting a supply of the long rank reeds with which to thatch his new church and dwelling-house; and he said that he should wish me, if opportunity presented itself, to shoot some large game on which these men might feed.

We were marching quietly along and were nearly opposite the centre of the reeds, when, on emerging from a grove of thorny mokala trees, casting our eyes to the right, we suddenly beheld a numerous herd of buffaloes grazing on the open plain betwixt us and the vley. Their dark imposing squadrons extended over a great space of ground, and we reckoned that there might have been between six and eight hundred of them. I immediately saddled "Sunday," and rode towards them. As I drew near they stood gazing at me for a minute, and then, panic-stricken, the whole herd started off together, making for the nearest wood.

Pressing my horse, I was soon ahead of them, and by shouting I turned them right about, when they thundered along in a compressed mass, and held for the reeds. Their amazing numbers greatly impeded their progress, and I had no difficulty in keeping alongside of them. I kept on their right flank to enable me more conveniently to fire, and on one occasion, on my riding very near the foremost of the herd, a large division of those behind me suddenly extended to the right and increased their pace, and, on looking over my shoulder, I found myself almost surrounded by their helmeted squadrons. As I galloped along I endeavoured to select the finest head, but among so many it was no easy matter to make a choice, and as soon as I selected one he disappeared among the ranks of his companions. At length, riding at the gallop, I let fly right and left into the herd, and next moment they had gained the margin of the lofty reeds.

Here the whole herd suddenly halted and faced about with the regularity and precision of a regiment of cavalry, when, having overhauled me for half a minute, they charged headlong into the soft muddy vley, and in another moment they were hidden from my view. I marked the reeds bowing before them far on my right and left as they splashed and struggled through the marshy vley, and presently they gained the other side, when, emerging from the reeds, they held across the open plain, steering for their strongholds in the woods beyond. As the clouds of dust behind me cleared away, I looked back and beheld a fine old cow stagger for a moment and then fall dead, and near her stood a wounded calf, whose mother had remained beside it, being loth to leave her offspring.

I now returned to Dr. Livingstone, when we brought up the waggon for the fallen buffaloes, and halted for the night. Just as we had outspanned, a blue wildebeest, having observed the oxen, and taking them for buffaloes, fearlessly approached the waggon, when, advancing under cover of one of the oxen, I bowled him over with my rifle. Early on the following morning the reed-cutters from Chouaney hove in sight, and were not a little gratified to find so bountiful a supply of their favourite "niama," or flesh, awaiting their arrival. The afternoon was cold and rainy, and at a late hour we outspanned at Chouaney, where we were immediately welcomed by a messenger from Sichely, who expressed himself highly gratified at our arrival and promised to come and breakfast with me next morning.

CHAPTER XX.

Arrive at Sichely's Kraal—Description of that Chief—His Wives—The Rainmakers—My Gun Medicine—Bakatla—A Kraal struck by Lightning—Reach Mr. Moffat's Station at Kuruman—Daring Robberies of the Bushmen—Campbellsdorp—Discover my runaway Hottentots—We cross the Vaal—The Inmates of a Farm terrified by my wild Appearance—Colesberg and Grahamstown—English Hounds in Africa.

At an early hour on the 26th of November Sichely presented himself with a large retinue. The appearance of this chief was prepossessing, and his manner was civil and engaging; his stature was about five feet ten inches, and in his person he inclined to corpulency. His dress consisted of a handsome leopard-skin kaross, and on his arms and legs, which were stout and well turned, he wore a profusion of brass and copper ornaments manufactured by tribes residing a long way to the eastward. In the forenoon I accompanied Sichely to his kraal situated in the centre of the town, and alongside of it stood respectively the kraals of his wives, which were five in number. These kraals were neatly built, and were of a circular form, the walls and floors being smoothly plastered with a composition of clay and cow-dung, and secured from the weather by a firm and well-constructed thatch of long dry grass. Each kraal was surrounded by an area enclosed with a strong impenetrable fence six feet in height. The town was built on a gentle slope on the northern side of a broad extensive strath, throughout the whole extent of which lay wide fields and gardens enclosed with hedges of the wait-a-bits.

A short time previous to my arrival, a rumour having reached Sichely that he was likely to be attacked by the emigrant Boers, he suddenly resolved to secure his city with a wall of stones, which he at once commenced erecting. It was now completed, entirely surrounding the town, with loopholes at intervals all along through which to play upon the advancing enemy with the muskets which he had resolved to purchase from hunters and traders like myself.

I was duly introduced to the five queens, each of whose wigwams I visited in succession. These ladies were of goodly stature and comely in their appearance; they all possessed a choice assortment of very fine karosses of various descriptions, and their persons were adorned with a profusion of ornaments of beads and brass and copper wire. Sichely professed and was believed by his tribe to be a skilful rainmaker, viz. one having the power of creating rain when required for the fields and gardens.

The rainmaker's art is a regular profession among the Bechuanas, and the individuals who practise it are much esteemed and highly venerated among their fellow-men. They are supposed to work by supernatural agency; and acting probably on the general principle that a prophet is not without honour save in his own country, they invariably practise their arts amongst tribes remote from their own particular districts. Their birth and original place of residence are always involved in mystery, and they pretend to have been suddenly created in some lonely cave, or on the summit of a mountain, from which they came in a state of manhood without undergoing the usual ordeal of birth. Some of these rainmakers attain to much higher reputation than their fellow necromancers: an illustrious character of this description is much sought after, and is often sent for from an amazing distance by a chief on whose dominions the periodical thunderstorms (which are often very partial) have failed to descend.

The modes in which they propitiate the clouds are various. The one most commonly practised is, by collecting a few leaves of each individual variety of tree in the forest, which they allow to simmer in large pots over a slow fire, and, while a sheep is killed by pricking it in the heart with a "lemue" or long sewing-needle, the rainmaker is employed in performing a variety of absurd incantations. The steam arising from the simmering leaves is supposed to reach and propitiate the clouds, and the remainder of the day is spent in dances which are joined in by all the tribe and kept up till midnight, being accompanied with songs having a long-continued chorus in which all join, and the burden of which is the power and praises of the rainmaker. It often, however, happens that the relentless clouds decline attending to the solicitations of the rainmaker, and the fields of young corn become parched and withered.

Other schemes are then resorted to. A number of the young men sally forth, and, forming an extensive circle, they enclose the rocky face of some mountain-side in which the rock-loving klipspringer is likely to be met with, when, by gradually contracting their circle like our Highlanders of old, they generally manage to catch alive sundry klipspringers, whose voices are supposed to attract rain. The unfortunate little antelopes thus captured are paraded round the kraal, while the rainmaker, by pinching and tormenting them, induces them to scream. But as it often happens that these and his other machinations prove unavailing, the rainmaker is at times obliged eventually to make a moonlight flitting and cut and run for it, when the services of another of the fraternity are courted.

When the rainmakers fail to fulfil their promises they always ascribe their want of success to the presence of some mysterious agency which has destroyed the effect of their otherwise infallible nostrums. One of these anti-rainmaking articles is ivory, which is believed to have great influence in driving away rain, in consequence of which, in the summer season, they produce it only as the sun goes down, at which time it is brought for the trader's inspection carefully wrapped up in a kaross. I remember on one occasion incurring the censure of a whole tribe, who firmly believed me to have frightened the rain from their dominions by exposing a quantity of ivory at noonday; and on another occasion the chief of a certain tribe commanded a missionary with whom I am acquainted to remove all the rafters from the roof of his house, these having been pointed out by the rainmaker as obstructing the success of his incantations.

The Griquas, taking advantage of the superstitions of the Bechuanas, often practise on their credulity, and, a short time before I visited Sichely, a party of Griquas who were hunting in his territory had obtained from him several valuable karosses in barter for a little sulphur, which they represented as a most effectual medicine for guns, having assured Sichely that by rubbing a small quantity on their hands before proceeding to the field they would assuredly obtain the animal they hunted.

It happened in the course of my converse with the chief that the subject turned on ball practice, when, probably relying on the power of his medicine, the king challenged me to shoot against him for a considerable wager, stipulating at the same time that his three brothers were to be permitted to assist him in the competition. The king staked a couple of valuable karosses against a large measure filled with my gunpowder, and we then at once proceeded to the waggon, where the match was to come off, followed by a number of the tribe. Whilst Sichely was loading his gun, I repaired to the fore-chest of the waggon, where, observing that I was watched by several of the natives, I proceeded to rub my hands with sulphur, which was instantly reported to the chief, who directly joined me, and, clapping me on the back, entreated me to give him a little of my medicine for his gun, which I of course told him he must purchase. Our target being set up, we commenced firing; it was a small piece of wood six inches long by four in breadth, and was placed on the stump of a tree at the distance of one hundred paces. Sichely fired the first shot, and very naturally missed it, upon which I let fly and split it through the middle. It was then set up again, when

Sichely and his brothers continued firing, without one touching it, till night setting in put an end to their proceedings. This of course was solely attributed by all present to the power of the medicine I had used.

When Dr. Livingstone was informed of the circumstance he was very much shocked, declaring that in future the natives would fail to believe him when he denounced supernatural agency, having now seen it practised by his own countryman. I obtained several very fine karosses, as also ivory, ostrich-feathers, and sundry interesting curiosities, in barter from Sichely and his tribe; and at noon on the 27th we took leave of Sichely and started for Bakatla. In the evening of the following day I lost another horse of the distemper: it was the "Immense Brute;" and next morning the chesnut pony also died. About midnight an immense herd of buffaloes came feeding slowly towards us, and, imagining our oxen to belong to their own party, they continued to advance until we were actually surrounded by them. I then arose in my sleep, and, having remarked in Sichuana to the natives that the buffaloes were very good, I once more lay down, utterly unconscious of what I had done or spoken.

On the afternoon of the 29th we outspanned at Bakatla. A party of Baralongs were then on a visit to Mosielely on a trading excursion for skins for the manufacture of karosses. The head-quarters of these men was situated to the westward of Motito, on the borders of the great Kalahari desert. Night set in with a terrific thunderstorm, which prevailed for several hours: the lightning was most painful to the eyes, and deafening peals of thunder continually burst above and around us. From the proximity of the explosions we entertained considerable fears for the safety of the natives in the town, for the lightning appeared repeatedly to strike in that direction; and when the storm had subsided, a messenger from the king came down to the missionary's dwelling-house to report that the kraal occupied by the six strangers had been struck by the electric fluid, and that one of them was killed on the spot, and the other five were more or less affected by the shock. Dr. Livingstone informed me that this melancholy event would entail great alarm and uneasiness upon Mosielely, since all the tribes would blame him for the accident.

The following day was Sunday, and in the forenoon Dr. Livingstone and I visited Mosielely, and inspected the kraal that had been struck by lightning. We found the natives engaged in the most absurd idolatrous rites to cleanse the kraal and the survivors from the effects of the electricity. Unlike the Romans of old, these five individuals did not consider themselves honoured by the partiality which the lightning had evinced for them; huddled together, we found them lying speechless and terrified upon the ground, their hearts having died within them. On the 1st of December, with Dr. Livingstone's kind assistance, I commenced making a new axletree for the waggon, and by the evening of that day week we had completed a good, substantial axletree of seasoned hard wood, mounted with iron skeins, and secured it in its place.

The greatest difficulty we encountered in the accomplishment of our work was in welding the iron skeins and fixing them in their proper places. During my stay at Bakatla I traded extensively with the natives, and obtained from them a number of karosses and various curiosities and articles of interest. It was the heat of summer, and the sun at noon was extremely overpowering; the atmosphere, however, was occasionally refreshed by thunderstorms, accompanied with grateful showers of rain, which, of course, was attributed to the power of the rainmaker, and the vale rang nightly with loud and joyous songs, re-echoing his praises in a prolonged chorus. Before leaving Bakatla my horse "Sunday" died of the distemper, which reduced my stud from ten to two; and, before dismissing this subject, I may mention that I managed to save these two from the distemper, and succeeded in bringing them back to the colony, by preventing them from eating grass and by keeping them covered at night with blankets.

On the 11th I took leave of my kind host Dr. Livingstone, and, after a steady march of many days, on the 2nd of January I reached Kuruman, where I was entertained by Mr. Moffat with his usual kindness and hospitality. The following day was Sunday, when I attended Divine service in the large church morning and evening, and saw sixteen men and women who had embraced the Christian faith baptized by Mr. Moffat. It was now the fruit season, and the trees in the gardens of the missionaries were groaning under a burden of the most delicious peaches, figs, and apples. The vines bore goodly clusters of grapes, but these had not yet ripened. My runaway Hottentots had passed through Kuruman some time previous to my arrival, and it was reported that disease had overtaken them at the missionary station of Campbellsdorp, where they were now all four stretched upon a bed of sickness, and in a state of the most abject want and misery. Isaac had likewise made his appearance in due course, and he now came boldly forward to claim his wages, which I honestly paid him. I left in Mr. Moffat's kind keeping one of the waggons with its contents (which we stowed away in a room obligingly lent me by Mr. Moffat for the purpose), and also the whole of my oxen, with the exception of one span, with which, on the evening of the 7th, I set out for Koning, which I reached at an early hour on the following morning, having marched during the greater portion of the night.

Leaving Koning on the afternoon of the 8th, I resumed my march for Daniel's-kuil. Between Koning and Daniel's-kuil occur two interesting caves, long famous as affording a residence and protection to hordes of marauding Bushmen. The larger of these caves is situated on the west side of the waggon-track; it is of great size, and contains a perpetual fountain of delicious water, and its sides have been adorned by its Lilliputian inhabitants with correct likenesses of most of the game quadrupeds of Africa, as also unicorns, which of course they never saw, and must therefore have heard spoken of by other men. From this cave the Bushmen were wont to sally forth not very long since and lift fat cattle from the sleek herds of their more industrious neighbours the Griquas and Bechuanas.

Returning with these cattle, their custom was to drive them all into the cave, whence, being well supplied with water, they did not again proceed until the flesh was either rotten or consumed. It was in vain that the exasperated owners of the cattle followed on their traces to the Bushman-cave, for here they well knew it was madness to follow farther, as inevitable death would be the result, by the poisoned arrows of their subtle foes within. At length the Bushmen became so frequent and daring in their attacks, that a number of the Bechuanas held "a great talk" on the subject (as they say in America), and ended by resolving to attack the Bushmen, and accomplish their destruction at whatever cost.

Accordingly, when the next robbery was committed, the Bechuanas marched upon the Bushman-cave, armed with large oval shields and battle-axes; and, entering the cave, they steadily advanced under cover of their shields, while the Bushmen's arrows rattled thick upon them like a storm of hail. The Bechuanas thus continued to advance until they came to close quarters, when they cut them down with their battle-axes. The other cave is situated to the eastward of the waggon-track; here, on a similar occasion, fire was made use of to smoke out the Bushmen, when those who escaped death by suffocation fell by the battle-axes and assagais of their foes without.

When driven to extremity the Bushmen are extremely plucky, and show fight to the last. In the year 1847, a Bechuana chief, named Assyabona, who is nearly related to Mahura, despatched a strong party of his tribe, armed with guns and assagais, to accomplish the destruction of a strong horde of wild Bushmen, whose robberies had become so daring and extensive that they were the terror of all who dwelt a hundred miles around them. On this occasion a great number of Bushmen were destroyed, having been overtaken in open ground. One determined fellow, having hastily collected several of the quivers of his dying comrades, which were full of poisoned arrows, ensconced himself within three large stones, from which position he for a long time defied the whole hostile array of Bechuanas, shooting two of them dead on the spot, and wounding a number of others. Though continuing gallantly to defend himself, he seemed aware that he could not possibly escape; and while peppering at the Bechuanas and upbraiding them with cowardice, he called out to them, that, if they had not killed his brother (who lay dead beside him, and who was a famous marksman among his fellows), it would have gone hard with them that day. He was eventually finished with a shot in the forehead by a son of Mahura, chief of the Batlapis, as he was in the act of discharging one of his diminutive yet deadly shafts.

On the 10th I marched from Daniel's-kuil, and early on the 12th I encamped at Campbellsdorp where I found Mr. Bartlett and Captain Cornelius Kok in great force. Here I at length overtook my runaway Hottentots. Sickness and starvation had done their work upon them, and they were so altered in their appearance that I scarcely knew them. They were now acting as servants to the Griquas who had nursed them in their illness, and they were working hard to earn their bread. On inquiring of them why they had forsaken me, they said that they had started in a rash and thoughtless moment, and that, although they almost immediately repented the step they had taken, fear and shame prevented them from returning to their duty.

Commiserating their condition, I presented them with the amount of their wages during the time they had remained with me, and, being now quite independent of their services, I allowed them to remain with the masters they had chosen. I here met an extremely plausible individual, a Dutchman, from the Bo-land or Cape district, who was *got up* in his rig at considerable expense. This fellow was swindling the Griquas right and left, purchasing from them all their best cattle at extravagant prices, and settling for them with paper notes, which *naturally* were forged. He represented himself as being one of a wealthy firm in Cape Town, and stated that two of his partners were then purchasing cattle among the Boers to the eastward, from whom they had already collected two thousand head; which cool assertion the Griquas were silly enough to believe, and he left their country for the Bo-land with a large drove of fat oxen. Eventually, however, he was brought to justice, and I afterwards heard of his being safely quartered in the jail of Beaufort.

At a late hour on the 13th I outspanned my waggons on the fragrant bank of the lovely Vaal river by clear moonlight, and on the morrow, the water being then fortunately low, I crossed the river with little difficulty, and on the 20th I took the drift of the Great Orange River, but with very faint hopes that my worn-out oxen would succeed in dragging me through its treacherous sands, more especially since two Boers who had crossed an hour previous had deemed it necessary to inspan sixteen tearing well-conditioned oxen into their light waggons. I was right in my conjecture, for with infinite flogging and shouting I got the waggon half-way through, when it stuck fast, and no efforts could prevail upon the oxen to move it a yard farther. A Griqua offered to lend me on hire a fresh span of able-bodied oxen, when, with the help of these and some of my best, I got safely through, and once more encamped within Her Majesty's dominions. While the waggon was sticking in the middle of the river a Boer took the drift from the opposite side with a light new waggon and twelve superb oxen, which bore him through in gallant style. Resuming my march for Colesberg, I trekked on till near midnight, when I lost my way in the dark. The country here was parched and arid, not a blade of grass for the weary oxen, but hopeless sterility stretched far around.

On the 21st I left the Bushman to bring on the waggon while I walked ahead under a most terrific sun to the farm where I had purchased Prince and Bonteberg, while *en route* to the far interior. My costume consisted of a dilapidated wide-awake hat, which had run the gauntlet with many a grove of wait-a-bits, a dusty-looking ragged shirt, and a pair of still more ragged-looking canvas trousers, which were, moreover, amputated, above the knee, while my face was adorned with a shaggy red beard, which *tout ensemble* imparted to me the appearance of one escaped from Bedlam. As I drew near the farm its inmates took fright at my wild appearance, and two of the Boers, timidly projecting their heads from the half-closed door, loudly shouted to me to lay down my gun. I however pretended not to understand, and advancing boldly I wished them good morning.

One of these was the owner of the farm, and the man from whom I had bought the dogs, yet nevertheless he failed to recognise me. He still appeared to be much alarmed, and evidently looked upon me as a dangerous character; but, commiserating the transparent texture of my continuations, he offered to lend me a pair of leather "crackers." Declining the proffered apparel, I entered the house without ceremony, and having come to an anchor I requested some milk. Here I was immediately recognised by the children as "de carle wha heb vor Bonteberg ha-quoch," viz., the man that bought Bonteberg.

On the 26th I marched at dawn of day, and in four hours I entered the village of Colesberg, where I found my old friends, the 91st, replaced by a detachment of the 45th. My first move was to visit the post-office, where I was very much disappointed to find no letters awaiting my arrival. Having off-loaded my waggon, I handed it over to Mr. Arnott, the resident blacksmith, to undergo repairs, of which it stood much in need. My Bechuana followers were extremely struck with the size and appearance of Colesberg, and the movements of the military elicited their unfeigned delight and approbation. On the 28th the village of Colesberg was enlightened with the presence of Mr. Kleinboy, who arrived with waggons from Kuruman. Having sought me out, he declared himself thoroughly penitent for all his former misdemeanours, and, expressing a wish again to join the service, I re-enlisted him.

On the 1st of February I left Colesberg, and reached Grahamstown on the forenoon of the 22nd, when I took up my residence with Captain Hogg of the 7th Dragoon Guards, in my old quarters at the barracks of the Cape Mounted Rifles. The officers of the 7th had brought out with them a pack of fox-hounds, which, while they lasted, afforded excellent sport, but unfortunately the climate of Southern Africa, especially near the coast, is so very unfavourable for well-bred English dogs, that, although no trouble nor expense was spared in the management of these hounds, and fresh drafts were constantly exported from England, and litters of pups carefully reared in the colony, the pack nevertheless had considerably diminished. These hounds were under the especial surveillance of Captain Hogg, who hunted them in a manner which evinced his consummate skill and judgment in the manly and ennobling pursuit of the chase.

CHAPTER XXI.

Set out again for the Far Interior—Fort Beaufort—Purchase fresh Steeds and Oxen—My old servant Corollus rejoins me—Elephant Fountain once more—Hunt Elephants—Corriebely—Obliged to act very decidedly with Sicomy—Horses and Oxen taken in Pits—Two Dogs killed by a Leopard—A file of Bakalahari Women carrying water to the Desert—A sleeping Rhinoceros shot—Hunting in the neighbourhood of Lotlokane and Letlochee—The Natives kill an

PREPARING FOR ANOTHER CAMPAIGN.

Elephant—A grim Lion slain—Rheumatic Fever attacks me—Leave Bamangwato Country—The Game disturbed by Natives—Soobie—Watch nightly for Game from a place of Ambush—Vanquish a noble Lioness.

I CONTINUED in Grahamstown until the 7th day of March, when I set out once more on my weary journey for the distant forests of the far interior. Before leaving the town I settled my accounts with the merchants from whom I had obtained supplies, and who evidently seemed to consider my returning to the colony as a very doubtful event. I engaged a discharged soldier of the 91st, named George Martin, in the capacity of head servant. This man hailed from Haddington, and bore an excellent character on leaving the regiment. He was accustomed to the charge of horses, in which he took a great interest.

My most important purchases in the sporting department consisted of a valuable double-barrelled rifle, with spare shot-barrels, by Westley Richards, which I obtained from Captain Hogg; and two right good steeds, one of which was a very superior coal-black gelding, which I purchased of Captain Walpole of the Engineers for £20, which was considerably below its value. I named this horse Black Jack; in paces and disposition he very much resembled my lamented Colesberg, and he was altogether one of the finest horses I ever mounted. His end was sudden and severe; for on a subsequent expedition, along with another of my favourite horses, he was torn to pieces and consumed by a troop of ruthless lions. The other horse which I purchased was a grey; and as it is probable that this horse may be introduced in future pages, under the designation of the "Old Grey," I trust the reader will not be confounded with the idea of the resurrection of the original "Old Grey."

On the morning of the 9th I reached Fort Beaufort, when I encamped at the mess-house of the 7th. I continued there until the morning of the 15th, when I resumed my march for the interior. In Fort Beaufort I purchased four right good horses from the officers of the garrison; one of these was a jet black steed, and was named by his late master Schwartland. This horse was one of the finest shooting-horses in Southern Africa, and understood his work so well that he seemed to follow the game with all the eagerness of a greyhound, and yet he would suddenly halt in full career when I wished to fire, if I merely placed my hand upon his neck. From his back I subsequently shot many elephants and other game, and his name will often appear in after pages. At the farm of Messrs. Nelson and Blane I purchased two more horses, which I called Brown Jock and Mazeppa, and also a span of oxen and some milch cows.

On the 2nd of April I entered the village of Colesberg, where I was actively employed in making final preparations for my distant campaign until the 9th. I engaged two Hottentot servants named Booi and Kleinfeldt, the latter individual being one of those who had forsaken my banner at Boötlonamy, and I purchased two more valuable steeds, which increased my stud to ten very superior young horses. I also purchased a number of rough long-legged serviceable dogs of a variety of breeds, which, with several other ragged-looking tykes, that I subsequently purchased from Boers along the line of march, increased my kennel to about twenty business-like dogs. At sunrise on the 9th we marched out of the village and held on until we reached the Orange River at Boata's Drift, where we outspanned beneath the shade of a grove of willows.

Having crossed the river on horseback, it proved too deep to take the waggons over, but I had the consolation to remark that the waters were on the ebb, and by the forenoon of the following day they had so far subsided that I was enabled to cross the great river without wetting my cargo. The ascension of the opposite side proved extremely severe, being an almost perpendicular bank of soft sand, and I was obliged to relieve the waggon of half its load before the oxen could drag it to the more practicable road beyond.

I was now all anxiety to reach my Fountain of Elephants, and pushed on with all speed for Massouey. On the 15th, just as I had reached the Bastard kraal of Rhama, I fell in with my old servant Carollus, who had absconded from me at Boötlonamy. He was in company with the waggons belonging to Mr. David Hume, the trader, on their return to the colony, but, meeting with his old companions Kleinfeldt and Kleinboy, he resolved to turn about and re-enter my service, which I was not sorry for, as I was short of hands for the distant expedition I was about to make. I also fell in with Captain Arkwright and Mr. Christie, who were proceeding up the country on a similar expedition to my own.

On the 16th of May I halted at Chouaney, at the residence of Dr. Livingstone, who told me that one or two troops of elephants had been frequenting the district. With one of these I fell in on the 20th, when I had an opportunity of testing the sportsmanlike qualities of my new servant Martin. The troop consisted of nine bull elephants, the finest of which I shot, but Martin, after selecting the poorest of the lot, ultimately lost him. We now pressed on as rapidly as possible for my favourite fountain Massouey, which we at length reached on the 29th.

I felt sincere pleasure in revisiting this very interesting spot. I found it well frequented by the elephants. Two troops of cows and three old bulls had drunk there on the preceding night. When the waggons came up to my old halting-place I took a hasty breakfast, and then started on the spoor of an enormous old bull. After following him north for about six miles we lost him in the spoor of a troop of cows; I accordingly followed the spoor of the cows, and soon came up with them. The troop consisted in all of about ten, but there were only three full-grown cows in the troop; each of these three, unluckily, went off in different directions. I rode within twenty yards of the best, and, halting, I put two balls close behind her shoulder, and, calling to Martin to finish her, I galloped after the second best. I soon got a view of her, and in three minutes I had turned her head towards camp, and presently I rolled her over with about six shots. Martin and the Bushman not appearing when two hours had elapsed, I rode to camp, where, to my astonishment, I found my servant, who had actually lost my elephant through the most inexcusable want of pluck. I was very much annoyed, and regretted having attacked the troop at all.

At dawn of day Mollyeon and I walked to the fountain to seek for elephants' spoor. A troop of cows, several small bulls, and two well-grown bulls, had drunk during the night, besides an unusual number of rhinoceroses, perhaps twenty. I made a hasty breakfast, and then took up the spoor of the two best bulls, with one after-rider. The spoor led nearly south-east. After following it for about six miles we found ourselves in an elevated part of the forest, which commanded a fine view of the mountains to the east, and here Mollyeon climbed to the summit of a sandal-wood tree to try if he could see the elephants. He could not see those we were spooring; but he saw three other bull elephants, about three parts grown, feeding slowly along, steering about north; after a short and dangerous conflict I slew the best with five bullets.

We then followed up the spoor of one of our first elephants, which had now taken a northerly course. After following it up very sharply for about five miles through very open country, we reached some dense wait-a-bit cover, where we discovered our friend hiding himself within twenty yards of us. He took away at once through the thickest of the cover, and on my approaching for a shot he made the most terrific charge after me, sending large thorny trees flying like grass before him. When he halted after his charge, I sent a ball through his ribs, and he then made clean away, and got into better country. Here I fought with him for about an hour, and gave him sixteen shots from the saddle. My horse was extremely troublesome, and invariably destroyed the correctness of my aim; the elephant was fierce and active, and made repeated charges with very destructive intentions; at length he turned and regained the dense thorny cover, in which I lost him.

On the morning of June 1st, before the sun rose, Mollyeon and I walked to the fountain to see if elephants had drunk. Ten bull elephants had been there, and had all gone off together, holding a south-easterly course; this was glorious. I started on the spoor with five natives, and Kleinfeldt as after-rider on Dreadnought. I took eight of my dogs, all led in strings, and rode Schwartland, my best shooting-horse. After following the spoor for about five miles, we found ourselves to leeward of the elephant I had shot on Saturday, and here the elephants had smelt the blood, and started off in great fear, going clean away through open country, steering one point west of south. They got into an old elephant footpath, and held steadily on for many miles, not halting to break one branch, or to plough the ground. The leading native said he did not expect to see them; and I was certainly of the same opinion. At length they got into a thickly wooded part of the country, and, although they were still holding clean away up wind, they had occasionally halted to feed. Here I started an oryx. We presently reached the border of a very wide open country, where the spoor took a turn to the east. We proceeded a few hundred yards farther, when we had the unexpected satisfaction to behold the mighty squadron drawn up in the open cover, in open order, two hundred yards ahead. Some of them stood motionless as statues, others moved slowly here and there, and browsed upon the trees.

The troop consisted of ten bull elephants: eight of them were about three parts grown; the other two were enormous old bull elephants, in magnificent condition. We halted and gave the dogs water, and I then rode slowly round the elephants to ascertain which was the best. After riding twice along their front, they all, as if by one accord, turned their faces to me, and advanced leisurely within forty yards, giving me an excellent opportunity of making my choice. At length they saw me, and, sounding the alarm, all made off together in great consternation. I galloped alongside of them to make my final choice, and selected the largest elephant. I had some difficulty in getting him clear of his comrades, some of which were extremely fierce, and were trumpeting along, with their tails and trunks aloft. At length I got him clear: all my dogs had gone off to the right and left after other elephants, and Dreadnought came galloping up to me, having thrown my after-rider, who did not succeed in recapturing him.

My elephant now, hearing the barking and trumpeting on every side, halted beside a bushy tree, with his head high, and right to me; but presently turning his broad-side, I gave it him sharp right and left after the shoulder; and the dogs, hearing the shots, came to my assistance. The conflict now became fast and furious; I had very pleasant work with this fine old elephant. My horse behaved very well, and his fury and attention were chiefly directed towards the dogs, who stuck well to him; but he was by far the toughest elephant to finish that I had ever engaged with. I gave him thirty-five balls, all about and behind his shoulder, and discharged at distances varying from fifteen to thirty-five yards, before he would halt and die. At length he reduced his pace to a very slow walk; blood flowed from his trunk and all his wounds, leaving the ground behind him a mass of gore; his frame shuddered violently, his mouth opened and shut, his lips quivered, his eyes were filled with tears; he halted beside a thorny tree, and having turned right about he rocked forwards and backwards for a few seconds, and, falling heavily over, his ancient spirit fled. The natives now came up, and, having promised to go on the spoor of my horse Dreadnought, I returned to Massouey, having off-saddled for an hour.

No elephants having drunk at the fount for some days, on the 5th I resolved to leave my favourite Massouey. I accordingly marched about one P.M. I passed Corriebely an hour before dark; there was water enough for the horses. Here I met Mutchuisho with a large party of Bechuanas, sent by Sicomy to endeavour to make me come and trade with him. I halted for an hour after sunset, and then inspanned and trekked on till the moon went down, when I halted near my old outspanning-place, having performed a very long and difficult march.

On the 6th, a very cold morning, we trekked at dawn of day, and in about three hours reached Lesausau, a bold and romantic gorge in the Bamangwato mountains, in the depth of which was a strong fountain. Sicomy soon made his appearance, and bothered all day; but he did not produce any ivory. At night I watched the fountain in the bold ravine, and shot two old black rhinoceroses, bull and cow, with my smooth bore carrying six to the pound. Both of these ran considerable distances, but were found by the natives. Along with the cow *borèlè* were two other old bulls, who fought together for three hours alongside of me.

On the 7th Sicomy made his appearance early, and towards evening bought powder and lead with seven elephants' teeth. Soon after this bargain was concluded he ordered men to take away the teeth, and he threw me back the powder; but on my kicking back the powder, and swearing I would shoot the first man who touched the ivory, he relinquished the idea.

On the succeeding day Sicomy prowled about the waggons all day, and bothered me so that I at last lost my temper, and swore at him. The natives held a consultation for a few minutes, which ended by their saying that they were all going to leave me. I said that I was happy to hear it. Then they decamped to a man; but in an hour four of my old acquaintances appeared, and said that the captain wished me to come and see him; but I replied that I was sick, and going to sleep. In another hour he made his appearance; and on asking him what I had done that he had called all his men away, he replied that they had gone away to have a sleep. Presently Arkwright and Christie rode up to my waggons: theirs were at hand. On the march they had lost one ox and two horses in pitfalls, and their "butler," while running to the assistance of the steeds, had been himself engulphed in another pitfall, which, fortunately, however, lacked the usual sharp-pointed stake for impaling the game, which the probabilities are that he would have converted into a "rump steak." At night Arkwright and I watched the water, but did not get a shot.

On the 9th Sicomy brought me ivory. He asked me to go to my hunting-ground, saying that he would trade with me there. He was very anxious to separate the two parties. As soon as possible, therefore, I inspanned, and trekked down the broad strath, steering south, although the natives asserted that I should find no water, and tried to guide me north. After trekking about eight miles, much to the annoyance of the Bamangwatos, I discovered the residence of the Bakaas, where I halted for the night, having sent a message to Schooey, the old chief, that I would trade with him next day.

The next day the old chief, with his wives and nobility, appeared at an early hour, and by midday I had purchased several tusks of elephants; also two very fine karosses of leopard-skin, etc. I then inspanned, and in two hours I got clear of the Bamangwato mountains, when I held about east, through thick forest, halting for the night beside a small fount, where the horses could not drink. On the march pallah were abundant and very tame.

On the morning of the 12th Sicomy came to my fireside, and said he was going to trade with me. A party of Bakalahari had arrived a little before, bearing twenty-nine elephants' teeth. After some trouble we set the trading agoing, and in about three hours I had purchased ten bull and ten cow elephants' teeth for ten muskets, and seven other cow elephants' teeth for powder, lead, and flints. I then bought two kobaoba knobkerries. At this moment natives came in, and reported elephants to have drunk within a mile during the night. This caused an immense bustle: in twenty minutes I was under way, with two after-riders and a party of good spoorers, followed by about a hundred and fifty starving natives. We took up the spoor a mile to the south, and followed it due east until the sun went down, when we halted for the night. While spooring we found the country in flames far and wide, but we crossed the fire, and took up the spoor beyond. We saw a troop of eight fat male elands, and a troop of eight giraffes.

Next day we followed the spoor for several miles in an easterly course, when it took a turn to the north-west, through most horrible wait-a-bit thorns. About midday we came up with the elephants. The troop consisted of one mighty old bull, and two bulls three-parts grown. I first shot the best of the two small bulls, and then the old bull. The natives and all my dogs had kept him in view, and one fellow had pricked him in the stern with an assagai. Upon the strength of this the Bechuanas came up and claimed him as theirs when he fell; but on my threatening to leave their country they relinquished the idea.

On the 16th and 17th I bagged two first-rate bull elephants in the level forests to the eastward of Mangmaluky.

On the 18th, after breakfast, I rode to Mangmaluky, to water my horses. One old bull elephant had been there, but the natives had too much flesh, and would not spoor. I rested all day, expecting my waggons, but they did not appear. At night a panther came within ten yards of my fire, and killed Cradock and disabled Wolf, my two best elephant-dogs.

On the 21st I held south, down a beautiful wide valley full of very green trees of various kinds. This was evidently a favourite haunt with the elephants: every tree bore their marks. At the southern end of this valley was one of the most interesting fountains I ever beheld; the water came gushing down through the wildest chasms, formed of one succession of huge masses of rock of all shapes and sizes, thrown loosely together in some places, and in others piled high one above another, as if by the hand of some giant. All the ground and rock about the fountain were covered with a layer of elephants' dung about a foot deep. We had proceeded about half-way up the valley when we heard elephants trumpeting ahead of us: it was a very fine troop of cows. There was one cow in the troop larger, I think, than any I had ever seen.

On this occasion I was extremely unfortunate. I began by sending two balls into the shoulder of the fine cow just as they were charging into a dense cover of wait-a-bits. The dogs took after two calves, which I was obliged to shoot; the natives, in attempting to assagai them, killed Bluma and wounded Alert in the loin. The elephants were hiding in the thorns, and no man knew or seemed to care where they were. At this moment we beheld another fine troop of cow elephants going along the wooded mountain-side opposite to us. I immediately made for them, and had the mortification to see them gain a neck in the mountain just above my head as I got within two hundred yards of them. I now returned to the thorny cover, where we found the cows concealed. The natives eventually drove them out on the wrong side of the cover without warning me, and, to my extreme vexation, this fine troop of cows got away without my killing one. I was extremely sorry to lose the large cow elephant: she carried a pair of most beautiful and perfect teeth. I slept near the fountain, where I picked up a piece of a tooth of a cow elephant.

On the 29th of June I reached a water called Lothokane, and hunted in the neighbourhood for several days, bagging some very fine elephants.

On the 13th of July I held west with Mollycon and about twenty natives on the spoor of bull elephants two days old. In the desert I came upon a troop of about twenty elands, the best of which I rode into and slew. In the evening we took up fresher spoor of three old bull elephants; but night setting in, we halted beneath a shady tree.

Early in the morning we resumed the spoor, which led us due west along the borders of the desert without a check until sundown. We had now spoored these elephants a very great distance, and the horses had not had water since the morning of the preceding day. I felt compassion for the thirsty steeds, and was on the point of turning, when lo! a string of Bakalahari women were seen half a mile before us, each bearing on her head an immense earthen vase and wooden bowl containing water. They had been to a great distance to draw water at a small fountain, and were now returning to their distant desert home. This was to us a perfect godsend. The horses and dogs got as much as they could drink, and all our vessels were replenished. The sun being now under, we halted for the night.

At sunrise we resumed the spoor, and after following it for about ten miles, and finding that these elephants had gone clean away into the desert beyond the reach of man, we gave it up, and made for the fountain where the women had drawn the water on the preceding day. On reaching the fountain we found that four bull elephants had drunk there during the night. It was a soft, sandy soil, and the spoor was beautifully visible. I had never seen larger spoor than that of two of these; they had fed slowly away from the fountain, and we followed on with high hopes of seeing them that day.

At length we got into a more densely wooded country, and presently observed the elephants standing in the forest about one hundred yards off. Having succeeded in securing the dogs, I shifted my saddle to Jock, and rode slowly forward to inspect the mighty game. Two of the elephants were but three parts grown; the other two were very large, but one of them was a great deal taller and stouter than the other. This immense elephant, which was, I think, decidedly the largest I had ever seen, had unfortunately both his tusks broken short off close to the lip; I therefore hunted his comrade, who carried a pair of very beautiful and perfect tusks. At the sixth shot he came to a stand and presently fell. I then dismounted and ran up to him, when he rose to his feet and stood some time, and then walked a few paces and fell again and died. On going up to him I found that he carried the finest teeth I had yet obtained; they must have weighed one hundred pounds each. He was an extremely old bull, and had been once much wounded with assagais, the blades of two of which were found in his back.

On the 17th I made for camp, and held through a fine open country lying north-west from Corriebely. In following some ostriches I came upon an extremely old and noted black rhinoceros lying fast asleep in some low wait-a-bits, the birds having tried in vain to waken him. I fired from the saddle: the first ball hit him, as he lay, in the shoulder; the second near his heart, as he gained his feet. In an instant the dogs were round him; he set off down hill at a steady canter, and led me a chase of a mile, when he came to a stand, his shoulder failing him. At this instant I beheld a troop of about twenty fine elands trotting before me on the open slope; I therefore quickly finished the black rhinoceros with two more balls, and then gave chase to the elands. I bagged the two best in the troop, a bull and cow, the latter about the fattest I have ever seen. I brought the bull within one hundred yards of the chukuroo.

At dawn next day I shot, from the spot I had slept on, a springbok, running, through the heart, at one hundred yards. After cutting off the horns of the black rhinoceros, I held on for Letlochee, and slept at Lebotane, a very strong and perpetual fountain.

On the 19th at sunrise I continued my march upon Letlochee, and presently detected an old buck koodoo, to which I gave chase. Just as I came up to him my horse fell and got away from me, whereby I lost the koodoo. My after-rider soon appeared and caught my steed, and once more we held on, and, presently gaining the ridge of the vast basin in which Letlochee lies, we started a second buck koodoo, to which I and the dogs gave chase, and, after a long and rocky chase, I shot him: he was an old buck with very wide-set horns. I then off-saddled for an hour, and once more held for camp. Presently I started a large troop of giraffes, to which I gave chase, and after a very hard and long run I rode into a princely old bull, which I drove within half a mile of camp, and then bowled over with a shot in the heart. Jock on this occasion was very much done up. On the 24th I left Letlochee, and marched upon Lotlokane.

In the forenoon of the next day I rode out to look for koodoos, without success. While riding through the forest I came upon the bloody spoor of an elephant; he had been evidently hunted by natives. The elephant was not far away, for, following the spoor a few hundred yards, I came upon about sixty natives who were hanging the flesh in garlands upon the thorny trees all around. This was an old bull elephant, and was quite lame, when the Bechuanas found him, from a ball-wound in the shoulder. On returning to camp, one of my Hottentots, who had been after some strayed oxen, stated that he had come upon a buffalo newly killed by a lion, and that the lion was lying in the bushes close by, watching his prey. Having taken some coffee, I saddled up three horses, and rode for the lion, with Booi and Kleinboy carrying my Moore and Westley Richards, and accompanied by all my dogs.

As we approached the carcase of the buffalo, which lay in a wait-a-bit thorn cover, the dogs all dashed away to my left, and in an instant

LION AND ANTELOPE SHOOTING.   229

they gave tongue, which was immediately followed by the deep and continued growling of the lion; he seemed to be advancing right to where we stood. I turned my head to ask Kleinboy for my shooting-horse, which he had ridden to the field of battle, but my trusty after-riders had fled on hearing the first growl of the advancing lion. I beheld Booi swept out of the saddle by the bough of a tree, and fall heavily to the ground with my pet rifle; while Kleinboy, with my other gun, was charging panic-stricken in another direction. After a short chase I came up with Kleinboy, who did not lack my blessing; and having changed horses and got my gun from him, I galloped to meet the grim lion.

Ye Gods! what a savage he looked. The whole of his mane was deeply tinged with the blood of the buffalo, and the rays of the declining sun added to it a lustre which imparted to the now exasperated lion a look of surpassing fierceness. He was making for the adjacent rocky mountains, and he marched along in front of the dogs with his tail stuck straight out, stepping along with an air of the most consummate pride and independence. There was not a moment to lose, so I galloped forward on one side, and then rode in slowly to get a near shot; as he came on I rode within thirty yards of him, and, halting my horse, I fired for his heart from the saddle. On receiving the ball he wheeled about, when I gave him the second a little below the first; he then walked or ran about ten yards forward and fell dead. This was a very large old lion; he had cleaned his buffalo very nicely, dragging up all the offal into a heap at a distance from the carcase, and he watched it all day to keep away the vultures, etc. The buffalo carried a very fine head.

On the 26th, feeling in very indifferent health, I remained at home, and stretched the lion's skin.

The next day after breakfast I rode up the wild glen above camp, intending to seek for bastard gemsbok on the other side of the mountains. I had ridden half-way up the glen, when, lo! the long-wished-for lovely sable antelope stood right in my path; a princely old buck: he stood about two hundred yards ahead looking at me. Having heard that dogs can easily catch this antelope, and having all my dogs at my heels, I sent them ahead, and fired a shot to encourage them; in half a minute they were at the heels of the potaquaine, and turned him down hill. He crossed the glen before me, and dashed up a very rough and rocky pass in the rocks to my right, the dogs following, but considerably thrown out. I listened to hear a bay, but listened in vain. To follow on horseback was impossible; I therefore galloped round to an opposite point, and listened with breathless anxiety, standing in my stirrups to catch one sharp note from my trusty dogs. Nor did I wait long: in a distant hollow in the rocks I could faintly here my dogs at bay.

My heart beat high; it must be the sable antelope, and the dogs would never leave him. Already I felt that he was mine, and with a joyous heart I urged Mazeppa over the most fearful masses of adamantine rock, and at last came into the hollow, where my dogs were keeping up a furious bay. Some thick bushes concealed the game from my view; I peeped over these, and, to my intense disappointment, instead of the sable antelope I beheld an old bull koodoo fighting gallantly for his life. I bowled him over with a shot in the heart; and rode to follow two other sable antelopes which I had seen on the face of a rocky hill while galloping round the rocks to seek for my dogs. I had ridden a few hundred yards, when, high above me on the shoulder of a rocky and well-wooded mountain on the opposite side of the ravine, I detected a fourth sable antelope, a fine old buck. I then rode into the deep ravine, and, having secured the steeds, I stripped to my shirt, and ascended the bold face to stalk him.

I held for a little to the leeward of where I had marked him; the Bushman followed with Boxer on a string. When I gained the summit I proceeded with extreme caution, and at length beheld him through the trees within a hundred yards of me; I crept about ten yards nearer, and then lay till he should move; this he presently did. He walked obligingly forward, and stood broadside in all his glory, with his magnificent scimitar-shaped horns sweeping back over his haunches. I fired. The ball broke his fore-leg in the shoulder, and he dropped on his face, but, recovering himself, he gained his legs, and limped slowly over the ridge. Boxer immediately appeared, and was beside me just as I peeped over the ridge, and beheld the wounded buck looking back within fifty yards of me. On seeing Boxer, he turned about, and, as he turned, I sent my second ball through his ribs. He then disappeared, and stumbled down the rocky mountain side, with Boxer at his heels. I followed as fast as could be, and found him half-way down the mountain, sitting on his haunches at bay, where I finished him with a shot in the heart. This was a magnificent sable antelope in the prime of life; he was very fat, and the flesh was excellent.

On the 28th I rode through the hills in quest of potaquaine, and went over a deal of rough ground on foot, and saw spoor, but no potaquaine. In the evening I took some bedding up the glen, and slept there.

I had lain in great pain all night, and in the morning of the 29th I found myself attacked with acute rheumatic fever. I had just strength to gain my waggons, when the disease came on in fall force, swelling up all the joints of my body, and giving me the most excruciating torture. I could not move hand nor foot nor turn on my bed. I had no medicine except salts; these I made use of, and bled myself, and in about eight days the intense pains left me, but left me so weak that I could not stand.

On the morning of the 4th of August I determined to leave the Bamangwato country and to return to Sichely by way of Massouey, which place I reached on the 15th. It was, however, infested by natives, and all the game gone. I accordingly trekked for Lepeby, which I reached the next day. Here too the natives had gathered, so I proceeded on to Soobie; where I found the skull of a very large lion, which the natives said had been killed by another lion.

At night I lay by the water with Kleinboy; abundance of game came and drank, but it was too dark to shoot with any certainty. About midnight a lion and a lioness came within ten yards of us before we noticed them. I was lying half asleep, but detected Kleinboy removing the big rifle from my side: he made a lucky shot, the ball passed through the lion's heart. He bounded forward about fifty yards, and, groaning fearfully, he died. Presently we heard the hyænas and jackals feasting on him, and before morn he was consumed. After some time the lioness re-approached the water to seek her mate, and drew nearer and nearer to us, roaring most fearfully; it was truly enough to make the stoutest heart quail. Kleinboy's quite failed him; and presently, hearing other lions approaching on the opposite side of the fount, I certainly felt that we were in danger, and accordingly agreed to light a fire, which was soon blazing cheerfully. I continued to watch the water from my deadly lair, both by day and night, till the 1st of September, enjoying extraordinary sport, and securing uncommonly fine specimens of the heads of all the varieties of game frequenting the district.

On the 1st of September, about twelve o'clock, Mollyee came and told me that my cattle-herd had come upon four wildebeests killed by a troop of lions. I immediately sent for the steeds and rode to the spot, with Martin and the Bushman as after-riders, and accompanied by all my dogs. On reaching the ground, the dogs immediately took up scent, and went beating up the wind. I rode after, hunting them on, and presently I missed Boxer and Alert. Wolf now beat up a scent to windward, on which he afterwards went off at full speed, and was soon heard at bay with a lion. Just as Wolf started I heard a dog bark to leeward, and, riding hard in that line, I found Lassie barking at a large bush, in which the lions had taken shelter, but were gone. I was followed by poor cripple Argyll, who went boldly in and took up the scent. I lost sight of Argyll in the bushes. I then turned my face, as Wolf had gone, and rode hard to seek him; at length he came up to me, quite exhausted with his exertions.

I rode back to seek Boxer, Alert, and Argyll. On coming to the place where Argyll had gone off, I found lions' spoor, and the spoor of the dogs on the top of. After holding this spoor for a few hundred yards I met my dogs, who, returning, led me to the game I sought—it was a noble lioness. As I approached I first beheld her great round face and black-tipped ears peeping over the low bushes. On riding up she obstinately kept her full front to me, although the dogs were barking close around her; at length she exposed a raking side shot, and the ball smashed her shoulder. She then charged among the dogs without doing any harm.

At my second shot Schwartland was unsteady and spoilt my aim; the ball, however, passed through the middle of her foot from side to side. I beckoned to Martin for my Moore, and, having got it, I rode up within a few yards of the lioness and gave her a shot, which crippled her in her other shoulder. She then fell powerless on the ground, and I fired my fourth shot for her heart: on receiving it she rolled over on her side and died. I cut off her head and the ten nails of her two fore feet and rode to camp, where I found that the rascally Hottentots, taking advantage of Martin's absence, had boned all my rich game-broth, replacing it with cold water. It blew a very stiff breeze of wind while I was hunting the lions, which entirely prevented me from hearing the dogs bark. The evening being very cold and windy, I did not watch the water. Lions roared around our camp all night.

CHAPTER XXII.

A Lion shot from my Watching-hole at Midnight—Six Lions drink close beside me—A Lioness slain—A Rhinoceros bites the dust—Moselakose Fountain—My Shooting-hole surrounded with Game—Pallahs, Sassaybys, Zebras, etc.—A Rhoode-Rheebok shot—Extraordinary Circumstance—My fiftieth Elephant bagged—Interesting Fountains on the Hills—Leave my Waggons for the Hills—Struggle with a Boa Constrictor—Lions too numerous to be agreeable—Five Rhinoceroses shot as they came-to drink—A Venomous Snake.

ON the afternoon of the 3rd of September I watched the fountain. Towards sunset one blue wildebeest, six zebras, and a large herd of pallahs, were all drinking before me. I lay enjoying contemplation for at least fifteen minutes, and, most of them having then slaked their thirst, I sent a ball through the heart of the best headed pallah. I then took a long shot at the blue wildebeest bull, and sent the other ball into his shoulder. I now came to the camp, and ordered the pallah to be placed in front of my hole beside the water, to attract the lions. Having taken my coffee, I returned to the water with Kleinboy and Mollyee. It was bright moonlight.

We had scarcely lain down when the terrible voice of a lion was heard a little to the east; the jackals were feasting over the remains of the white rhinoceros of yesterday, and only one or two occasionally came and snuffed at the pallah. Presently a herd of zebras, accompanied by elands, approached the water, but were too timid to come in and drink: a troop of wild dogs now came boldly up, and were walking off with the pallah, when I fired into them. They made off, but immediately returning, and again seizing my pallah, I fired again, and wounded one of them.

Soon after we had lain down a thundering clattering of hoofs was heard coming up the vley, and on came an immense herd of blue wildebeest. They were very thirsty, and the leading cow very soon came boldly up and drank before me. I sent a ball through her; she ran sixty yards up the slope behind me, and fell dead. Her comrades then thundered across the vley, and took up a position on the opposite rising ground. In two minutes the hyænas and jackals had attacked the carcase of this wildebeest. Soon after this a lion gave a most appalling roar on the bushy height close opposite to us, which was succeeded by a deathlike stillness which lasted for nearly a minute. I had then only one shot in my four barrels, and I hastily loaded the other barrel of my Westley Richards, and with breathless attention I kept the strictest watch in front, expecting every moment to see the mighty and terrible king of

CHAP. XXII.—1

Stopping a Poacher.

beasts approaching; but he was too cunning. He saw all the other game fight shy of the water, so he made a circuit to leeward to get the wind off the fountain. Soon after he roared I heard a number of jackals bothering him, as if telling him to come across the vley to the wildebeest: he growled from side to side, as if playing with them, and after this all was still.

I had listened with intense anxiety for about fifteen minutes longer, when I heard the hyænas and jackals give way on either side behind me from the carcase of the wildebeest, and, turning my head slowly round, I beheld a huge and majestic lion, with a black mane which nearly swept the ground, standing over the carcase. He seemed aware of my proximity, and lowering his head he at once laid hold of the wildebeest and dragged it some distance up the hill. He then halted to take breath, but did not expose a broadside, and in a quarter of a minute he again laid hold of the wildebeest and dragged it about twelve yards farther towards the cover, when he again raised his noble head and halted to take breath.

I had not an instant to lose; he stood with his right side exposed to me in a very slanting position; I stretched my left arm across the grass, and, taking him rather low, I fired: the ball took effect, and the lion sank to the shot. All was still as death for many seconds, when he uttered a deep growl, and slowly gaining his feet he limped toward the cover, roaring mournfully as he went. When he got into the thorny bushes he stumbled through them as he moved along, and in half a minute I heard him halt and growl fearfully, as if dying. I had now every reason to believe that he was either dead or would die immediately, and if I did not seek him till the morning I knew very well that the hyænas and jackals would destroy him. I accordingly went up to camp, and, having saddled two horses, I and Martin rode to seek him, taking all the dogs, led in strings by the natives.

On reaching the carcase of the wildebeest we slipped the dogs, and they went off after the hyænas and jackals: we listened in vain for the deep growl of the lion, but I was persuaded that he was dead, and rode forward to the spot where I had last heard him growl. Lassie, now coming up, commenced barking at a bush in front of me, and, riding round, I had the immense satisfaction to behold the most magnificent old black-maned lion stretched out before me.

The ball had entered his belly a little before the flank, and traversed the length and breadth of his body, crippling him in the opposite shoulder. No description could give a correct idea of the surpassing beauty of this most majestic animal, as he lay still warm before me. I lighted a fire and gazed with delight upon his lovely mane, his massive arms, his sharp yellow nails, his hard and terrible head, his immense and powerful teeth, his perfect beauty and symmetry throughout; and I felt that I had won the noblest prize that this wide world could yield to a sportsman. Having about fifteen natives with me, I sent for rheims and the lechteruit, and we bore the lion to camp.

On my way from the water to get the horses and dogs, I shot an extremely old bull black rhinoceros with a single ball: he dropped to the shot. His horns were quite worn down and amalgamated, resembling the stump of an old oak-tree.

On the afternoon of the 4th I deepened my hole and watched the water. As the sun went down two graceful springboks and a herd of pallah came and drank, when I shot the best pallah in the troop. At night I watched the water with Kleinboy: very soon a black cow rhinoceros came and drank, and got off for the present with two balls in her. A little afterwards two black rhinoceroses and two white ones came to the water-side. We both fired together at the finest of the two black rhinoceroses; she ran three hundred yards, and fell dead. Soon after this the other black rhinoceros came up again and stood at the water-side; I gave her one ball after the shoulder; she ran a hundred yards and fell dead. In half an hour a third old borèlé appeared, and, having inspected the two dead ones, he came up to the water-side. We fired together; he ran two hundred yards and fell dead. I felt satisfied with our success, and gave it up for the night.

By the following evening the natives had cleared away the greater part of two of the rhinoceroses which lay right in the way of the game approaching the water; I, however, enforced their leaving the third rhinoceros, which had fallen on the bare rising ground, almost opposite to my hiding-place, in the hope of attracting a lion, as I intended to watch the water at night. Soon after the twilight had died away, I went down to my hole with Kleinboy and two natives, who lay concealed in another hole, with Wolf and Boxer ready to slip in the event of wounding a lion.

On reaching the water I looked towards the carcase of the rhinoceros, and, to my astonishment, I beheld the ground alive with large creatures, as though a troop of zebras were approaching the fountain to drink. Kleinboy remarked to me that a troop of zebras were standing on the height. I answered, "Yes;" but I knew very well that zebras would not be capering around the carcase of a rhinoceros. I quickly arranged my blankets, pillow, and guns in the hole, and then lay down to feast my eyes on the interesting sight before me. It was bright moonlight, as clear as I need wish, and within one night of being full moon. There were six large lions, about twelve or fifteen hyænas, and from twenty to thirty jackals, feasting on and around the carcases of the three rhinoceroses. The lions feasted peacefully, but the hyænas and jackals fought over every mouthful, and chased one another round and round the carcases, growling, laughing, screeching, chattering, and howling without any intermission.

The hyænas did not seem afraid of the lions, although they gave way before them; for I observed that they followed them in the most disrespectful manner, and stood laughing, one or two on either side, when any lions came after their comrades to examine pieces of skin or bones which they were dragging. I had lain watching this banquet for about three hours, in the strong hope that, when the lions had feasted, they would come and drink. Two black and two white rhinoceroses had made their appearance, but, scared by the smell of the blood, they had made off.

Nocturnal adventure with Six Lions

CHAP. XXII.—2

At length the lions seemed satisfied. They all walked about with their heads up, and seemed to be thinking about the water; and in two minutes one of them turned his face towards me, and came on; he was immediately followed by a second lion, and in half a minute by the remaining four. It was a decided and general move, they were all coming to drink right bang in my face, within fifteen yards of me.

I charged the unfortunate, pale, and panting Kleinboy to convert himself into a stone, and knowing, from old spoor, exactly where they would driuk, I cocked my left barrel, and placed myself and gun in position. The six lions came steadily on along the stony ridge, until within sixty yards of me, when they halted for a minute to reconnoitre. One of them stretched out his massive arms on the rock and lay down; the others then came on, and he rose and brought up the rear. They walked, as I had anticipated, to the old drinking-place, and three of them had put down their heads and were lapping the water loudly, when Kleinboy thought it necessary to shove up his ugly head. I turned my head slowly to rebuke him, and again turning to the lions I found myself discovered.

An old lioness, who seemed to take the lead, had detected me, and, with her head high and her eyes fixed full upon me, she was coming slowly round the corner of the vley to cultivate further my acquaintance! This unfortunate proceeding put a stop at once to all further contemplation. I thought, in my haste, that it was perhaps most prudent to shoot this lioness, especially as none of the others had noticed me. I accordingly moved my arm and covered her: she saw me move and halted, exposing a full broadside. I fired; the ball entered one shoulder and passed out behind the other. She bounded forward with repeated growls, and was followed by her five comrades all enveloped in a cloud of dust; nor did they stop until they had reached the cover behind me, except one old gentleman, who halted and looked back for a few seconds when I fired, but the ball went high.

I listened anxiously for some sound to denote the approaching end of the lioness; nor listened in vain. I heard her growling and stationary, as if dying. In one minute her comrades crossed the vley a little below me, and made towards the rhinoceros. I then slipped Wolf and Boxer on her scent, and, following them into the cover, I found her lying dead within twenty yards of where the old lion had lain two nights before. This was a fine old lioness, with perfect teeth, and was certainly a noble prize; but I felt dissatisfied at not having rather shot a lion, which I had most certainly done if my Hottentot had not destroyed my contemplation.

On the 8th, as I and Kleinboy watched the under water about midnight, we heard a black rhinoceros blowing beside the upper water. We very rashly walked up within about eighteen yards of him, with no other shelter than a small bush. On perceiving us the borèlé at once turned his head to me and advanced slowly: Kleinboy, who was on my right and had a good chance, fortunately fired without orders, and the ball entered the shoulder with a fine direction. Borèlé then charged madly and furiously, through trees and bushes, right towards camp, making the most tremendous blowing noise, and halting in a stony open flat close to the waggons: he stood, and staggered about for a minute or two, and then fell. On coming up to him I found him a magnificent specimen, carrying three distinct horns.

After breakfast on the 10th, the oxen having drunk, we inspanned and marched to Bötolonamy, which we reached at sunset.

After a march of three days, during which the cattle and horses nearly died of thirst, we reached Moselakose, a retired fountain in a bold glen, or gorge, in the first mountain chain before us. As we approached this fine fountain, the poor, thirsty, loose cattle rushed ahead to the water, not a little gratified by the sight.

I found the spoor of game abundant at the water; accordingly I outspanned at a considerable distance from it, and at once set about making a hole from which to shoot the game as they came up to drink.

After breakfast on the 16th I rode to the water and again lay in my hole. There were large herds of game standing within a few hundred yards of me when I lay down, and soon after the horses had disappeared they came on from all sides and completely surrounded me. It was of no consequence that they got my wind, and frequent alarms were sounded—the thirsty game to windward would not heed the alarm, and, standing their ground fearlessly, they gave the others confidence. There were standing within shot of me at once about three hundred pallahs, about twelve sassaybys, and twenty zebras. I could only make out two very fair heads in all that vast herd of pallahs, and these were not to be compared with my best Soobie heads; I, therefore, amused myself by watching the game, and did not fire, having resolved to wait quietly, in the hope of some rarer game appearing, such as koodoo, sable antelope, or wild boar, etc. At length I observed three shy, strange-looking antelopes approach the water, with large bushy tails and furry-looking reddish-grey hair. They were three rhoode-rheeboks, a buck and two does. I had never before heard that either of the rheeboks frequented these parts; being anxious to certify that this antelope did so, I shot the buck through the heart.

The next day I again rode to the water and lay down, with large herds of pallahs, etc., in view: soon after the horses were gone they came in and surrounded me, the same as the day before. It was a fine show of game: there were about two hundred pallahs, about fifty blue wildebeests, thirty zebras, and thirty sassaybys—all at once drinking and standing within easy shot of me. After watching them for a short time I selected a fine old cow blue wildebeest, and fired, when this vast body of game thundered, panic-stricken, away on every side. As the dust cleared away the gnoo was to be seen standing alone, and in about ten minutes she staggered, fell, and died. Fifteen minutes afterwards two herds of pallahs approached from different directions.

I was overhauling them, when up came two tearing wild boars and stood broadside before me, with their long tails stuck right up. I took the best behind the shoulder; he ran off with his comrade up a very rocky hill above the fountain, leaving the stones red in his wake, and, feeling himself unable to proceed farther, he charged and staggered violently

Drawing a Snake.
CHAP. XXII.—3

about the stones, and, at last, gave in, having broken both his under-teeth; like any other pig, he also squealed violently when the struggles of death came over him.

A similar circumstance occurred as I watched the waters on the 20th. Having shot a sassayby, he immediately commenced choking from the blood, and his body began to swell in a most extraordinary manner; it continued swelling, with the animal still alive, until it literally resembled a fisherman's float, when the sassayby died of suffocation. It was not only his body that swelled in this extraordinary manner, but even his head and legs, down to his knees.

The 21st was a bitter cold morning, with a strong wind from the south-west. I rode to my hole at the fountain before the morning star appeared. Shortly, becoming impatient of lying still, I rose from my hole to examine what game had drunk during the night, and, to my astonishment, I at once discovered the spoor of a mighty bull elephant, which must have drunk there not many hours before. I went in haste to camp, and, having made all ready for a three-days' trip, I took up the spoor with two after-riders and six natives. It led us in an easterly course—first, through a neck in the mountains, and then skirting them for about five miles through thick cover and over hard adamantine rocks and sharp stones. The elephant had fed as he went along, and we soon came up with him standing in a thicket. When we first caught sight of him he was within twenty yards of us, a bushy tree nearly concealing him from our view. I first observed one of his tusks, and then I had to despatch Kleinboy to catch the cowardly natives, who were making off at top speed with my dogs on strings. The dogs fought well with him; it was very rocky ground, and I gave him one deadly shot before he was aware of our presence. I then hunted him into softer ground and slew him with the tenth shot.

This fellow made up my fiftieth elephant bagged in Africa; not to mention numbers lost.

On our way to camp, while following an old established elephant and rhinoceros footpath, I observed a grey mass beneath a bush, with something which looked like a shining black horn stuck out on one side; it was within about eighteen yards of our path. When I got alongside of it I saw that it was a princely old bull buffalo, with a very remarkably fine head. He had lain his head flat on the ground and was crouching, in the hope that we should ride past without observing him, just as an old stag or a roebuck does in Scotland. I gave the dogs the signal of the presence of game, when, as dogs invariably will do, they dashed off in the wrong direction. The buffalo sprang to his feet, and in one instant he was lost in the thicket.

From the quantity of buffalo's spoor on the north side of this mountain range, I made up my mind that there must be some strong water on that side of the hills, as only one or two buffaloes occasionally came to drink at the fountain where I was encamped; the natives all declared that there was none. I, however, on the 22nd, determined to ride thither to explore, and accordingly started with Kleinboy and the Bushman. We held first about west, and then crossed the mountains by a succession of very rocky valleys and ravines. When we had gained the highest part of the rock, which opened to us the forests to the north, a troop of seven doe koodoos and three rhooze-rheeboks started on the opposite side of the ravine. The dogs, observing the koodoos, gave immediate chase; and after a very fine and bold course they brought one to bay far in the valley below, which Kleinboy shot.

I had, in the mean time, ridden ahead, following an old established game footpath, and after proceeding two or three miles I had the satisfaction to discover a beautiful fountain in a deep rocky ravine on the north side of the mountains. Here was fresh spoor of black and white rhinoceros, buffalo, wildebeest, sassayby, koodoo, klipspringer, etc. A little after this I was met by my after-riders, who had likewise discovered a ravine containing water a little to the east. There they had started two bull buffaloes, three buck koodoos, and a troop of rheebok. I then rode to inspect this water, and took up the spoor of the buffaloes, in the hope of bringing them to bay with the dogs. I held up the hollow on their spoor, and presently observed one of them standing among some trees to my left. The dogs were snuffing about close under his nose; nevertheless they failed to observe him, but set off at top speed on some other scent; nor did they return for about ten minutes. The buffalo did not seem startled by the dogs, but walked slowly over the rocky ridge.

I was following briskly after him, when I observed his comrade lying right in our path; we squatted instantly, but he got our wind and was off. I followed, and got a shot across the ravine, wounding him behind the shoulder. When the dogs came up I tried to put them on this spoor, but they dashed up the ravine and started three other buffaloes, which they failed in bringing to bay, nor did I again see the dogs till I had been two hours in camp. I nearly killed myself by running after them, for I was on foot, the ground being too bad for the horses.

On reaching the steeds I rode hard for camp, as the day was far spent. Passing the mouth of another bold ravine, we crossed very well beaten paths, which led me to suspect that this ravine also contained a fountain. We had ridden about half-way to camp when a fine old bull eland came charging up to leeward, having got our wind. I sprang from the back of Mazeppa, and gave him both barrels as he passed me. We then gave him chase through very thick cover, and after a sharp burst of about a mile I shot him from the saddle: he carried a very fine head, and was, notwithstanding the lateness of the season, in very good condition.

On the 23rd, in the forenoon, I rode to explore the suspected ravine of the day before, and having crossed the mountain chain I came upon the fresh spoor of a very large troop of cow elephants leading towards the spot. I at once determined to follow it, and despatched the Bushman to camp for the dogs and Kleinboy's gun, etc. I rode slowly ahead on the spoor, imagining the elephants at a great distance, when, on gaining a ridge, I came full upon the troop drawn up within twenty-five yards of me. There were perhaps from twenty-five to thirty of them. The instant I came upon them they got my wind, and, rumbling, away they went in three divisions into the impenetrable cover.

The ground that I had now reached was one solid mass of sharp adamantine blocks of rock, so that a horse could with difficulty walk on it. I held along the ridge above the cover, and in half a minute I heard one division of the elephants crashing through the cover after me. They came on a little above me, and another troop held the same course a little before me, so that I had considerable difficulty in getting clear of them, and when I did so I held for the level ground beneath the dense cover. Here I fell in with one elephant with a calf: she had only one tooth. I gave her a shot behind the shoulder; and next minute, while trying to head her in the dense cover, she very nearly ran me down in her charge, and being without dogs I lost her immediately.

I then gave up the elephants in vexation with the ground, and rode to explore the ravine. My wounded elephant, however, happened to take the same course above me in the cover, and I once more fell in with her. She was going slowly along the hill-sides, keeping in the thickest cover, with a rocky ground, where my horse would be of no service to me. I might now have got her, but as she had only one tooth I was not anxious about her, so I held up the bold ravine.

Here, as I expected, I found a strong fountain in a solid rocky basin not more than ten feet wide: it was a very interesting spot, approachable by three different rugged passes, the sides of which were furrowed by broad footpaths established through ages. The large stones and masses of rock were either kicked to the side or packed into a level "like a pavement;" even the solid adamantine rock was worn hollow by the feet of the mighty game which most probably for a thousand years had passed over it. Here I found fresh spoor of most of the larger game, and, resolving to play havoc by light of the coming moon, I left the glen and rode for camp.

On the 25th, after breakfast, I started with bedding and provisions to hunt for a few days on the other side of the hills. We visited the first water and established a place of concealment with rocks and green boughs on the rock. While we were making this bothy a wild boar hove in view, but, observing us, he escaped. We then held on to the farther ravine, and on my way thither I nearly rode down a fine old bastard gemsbok, which got away among the rocks. I repaired an old hiding-hole at this water, building it up with fragments of rock. I then sent the steeds to a proper distance, put out my fire, and lay down to watch for the night.

First came a pallah, closely followed by a wild dog. The pallah escaped, the wild dog presently returned, and observing my retreating men he barked loudly; ten minutes after, about eight wild dogs came up the glen and drank. Night now set in, and the moonlight was very faint. Presently an occasional loud displacement of rock and stone announced the approach of large game: it was two old bull buffaloes; they came and drank, and went away without approaching within shot. Soon after fourteen buffaloes came; but before these had finished drinking they got an alarm and charged panic-stricken up the rugged mountain side. They had winded two lions, which came up to the fountain-head, and drank within eighteen yards of me, where they lay lapping loudly and occasionally halting for four or five minutes, but, from their light colour and the masses of rock that surrounded them, I could not see to fire. About ten minutes after they had drunk I fancied that they were still lingering, and on throwing a stone their step was heard retreating among the dry leaves and stones.

Soon after this six old bull buffaloes approached from a glen behind us: they walked very slowly, standing long to listen. When the leader came up within twenty yards of us, Kleinboy and I fired together; it ran thirty yards and in two minutes fell. His comrades, after considering the matter for five minutes, came on once more: we again took the leader, and he also dropped. His comrades, as before, retreated, but soon returning we wounded a third, which we did not get. The moon was now under and it was very dark; the buffaloes however were determined to try it on once more, and coming up a fourth and last time we shot another old bull. In about ten minutes lions were very busy on the carcase of the first buffalo, where they feasted till morning, taking another drink before they went away. Towards daybreak we wounded a white rhinoceros, and soon after two black rhinoceroses fought beside us, but I was too sleepy to rise.

On the 26th I rose at earliest dawn to inspect the heads of the three old buffaloes; they were all enormous old bulls, and one of them carried a most splendid head. The lions had cleaned out all his entrails: their spoor was immense. Having taken some buffalo breast and liver for breakfast, I despatched Ruyter to the waggons to call the natives to remove the carcases, whilst I and Kleinboy held through the hills to see what game might be in the next glen which contained water. On our way thither we started a fine old buck koodoo, which I shot, putting both barrels into him at one hundred yards. As I was examining the spoor of the game by the fountain I suddenly detected an enormous old rock-snake stealing in beneath a mass of rock beside me. He was truly an enormous snake, and, having never before dealt with this specimen of game, I did not exactly know how to set about capturing him. Being very anxious to preserve his skin entire, and not wishing to have recourse to my rifle, I cut a stout and tough stick about eight feet long, and having lightened myself of my shooting-belt I commenced the attack. Seizing him by the tail I tried to get him out of his place of refuge; but I hauled in vain, he only drew his large folds firmer together; I could not move him. At length I got a rheim round one of his folds about the middle of his body, and Kleinboy and I commenced hauling away in good earnest.

The snake, finding the ground to hot for him, relaxed his coils, and, suddenly bringing round his head to the front, he sprang out at us like an arrow, with his immense and hideous mouth opened to its largest dimensions, and before I could get out of his way he was clean out of his hole, and made a second spring, throwing himself forward about eight or ten feet and snapping his horrid fangs within a foot of my naked legs. I sprang out of his way, and getting a hold of the green bough I had cut I returned to the charge.

The snake now glided along at top speed : he knew the ground well, and was making for a mass of broken rocks where he would have been beyond my reach, but before he could gain this place of refuge I caught him two or three tremendous whacks on the head. He however held on, and gained a pool of muddy water, which he was rapidly crossing when I again belaboured him, and at length reduced his pace to a stand. We then hanged him by the neck to a bough of a tree, and in about fifteen minutes he seemed dead, but he again became very troublesome during the operation of skinning, twisting his body in all manner of ways. This serpent measured fourteen feet.

At night no game visited the water, being scared by the strong smell of the carrion. Lions however were so numerous that we deemed it safe to shift a position we had taken down the glen, for they trotted past within twenty yards of us, growling fearfully. We fired off the big gun to scare them for the moment while we shifted to our baggage at the fountain-head, where we instantly lighted a large fire. The lions, for a short time after this, kept quiet, when they again returned, and the fire being low they soon commenced upon the buffalo the natives had left within fifty yards of us, and before morning two of them came up and looked into our bothy, when Boxer giving a sharp bark, and I suddenly awaking and popping up my head, they bounded off.

In the evening of the 28th I shot an old bull koodoo. At night I watched the water near my camp with Kleinboy. After a long time had elapsed an enormous old bull muchocho or white rhinoceros came slowly on, and commenced drinking within fifteen yards of us, and next minute a large herd of zebras and blue wildebeest. It was long before the muchocho would turn his side ; when he did, we fired together, and away he went with zebras and wildebeests concealed in a cloud of dust. Next came an old bull borèlè; we fired together, and he made off, blowing loudly, after charging round and round, seeking some object on which to wreak his vengeance. Next came another borèlè; and he got two bullets into his person. The fourth that came was another old bull muchocho; he ran forty yards and fell. And fifth came a cow borèlè; she fell dead to the shots. Three other rhinoceroses came about me, but I was too drowsy to watch any longer, and fell asleep.

When day dawned I rose to see if the wounded chukuroos had gone far, and how like were their horns. We got the two old bull muchochos and a bull and a cow borèlè : both the muchochos and the bull borèlè carried very fine horns; the two former were very fat. I immediately set all the natives to work to clear away the flesh and bring a supply to camp. The heat in the middle of the day was very oppressive ; in the evening I lay by the fountain. Two troops of pallahs and a herd of sassaybys came up, when I shot the best stag sassayby in the troop : he got a raking shot at a hundred yards, and, after galloping after his comrades a couple of hundred yards at top speed, he fell violently over in the dust. Wishing to give my man Martin some diversion, I told him to come up to the water at sunset with Kleinboy and the two big guns to watch all night for rhinoceros. As we were making our beds ready we suddenly observed a superb old bull buffalo coming briskly on to drink: he was already in full sight of us; there was no time to get the horses out of the way, and there they stood saddled and bridled beside the water. In an instant we were out of sight in the hole.

On came the buffalo, but, detecting the saddlery, he eyed the steeds with great suspicion: one of these was fortunately "the pony," who entered a great dislike to buffaloes, having been once furiously charged by one; accordingly, when the pony beheld the buffalo he cocked his ears at him, and, turning right about face, he held away for his comrades: then the old buffalo came on; he was going to make a cast to leeward, but to this I objected, and, taking him a raking shot at eighty yards, I shot him in the heart; he ran forty-six yards and fell dead. But little game appeared during the night, scared by the blood of last night's carnage. About midnight I put a ball through a hyæna. A little before the moon was under a fine old borèlé stood within fifteen yards of us. Directing Martin and Kleinboy to present, and await my signal to fire, I covered Borèlé, but before I had given any signal Martin thought proper to fire with the borèlé standing almost tail on end to us; we of course lost him, and, after consigning Martin and the borèlé to the shades below, I lay down to rest in anything but a smooth temper.

These fountains afforded me excellent shooting for about a fortnight longer, during the whole of which time I watched nightly in my different hiding-holes, and bagged buffaloes, rhinoceros, koodoos, zebras, and other game. One night, while so engaged, a horrid snake which Kleinboy had tried to kill with his loading-rod flew up at my eye, and spat poison into it. Immediately I washed it well out at the fountain. I endured great pain all night, but next day the eye came all right.

CHAPTER XXIII.

Sichely's Kraal again—The Ngotwani—Chase and kill a waterbuck—A portion of the Cattle recovered—A Leopard bayed by my Dogs and slain—Buffalo-shooting beside the Ngotwani—A Lion feeds on the Carcase—My Horse knocked down by the King of Brutes—Meet a grim Lion face to face at midnight!—He sheers off—These Animals unpleasantly bold—An amusing Chase with a Buffalo—Interesting Stalk in rocky ground—Leave my hunting-ground and encamp on Vaal River—Great Herds—In taking the Drift a Waggon sticks fast in the middle of the River—Great fear of losing all my Property—Rescue of the Waggon—Colesberg—A Farmer's Waggon capsized in the Fish River—Visit Strydom's farm and find it desolate—Arrival at Grahamstown.

ON the 16th of October we inspanned, and trekked steadily on for Sichely under a most terrific sun, and halted at sundown without water: the country was covered with spoor of all the larger varieties of game including elephants.

On the 17th I inspanned, and trekked a couple of miles, when I found myself once more on the banks of the Ngotwani, which, except at its source, was this year generally dried up; we however found a spot in its gravelly bed where, by digging, we obtained sufficient water for all. The natives in charge of the loose cattle chose to remain behind all night, I having too well supplied them with flesh. Though my remaining stud of six horses and twelve trek-oxen were thus absent all night, I was not anxious about them, trusting to the usual good herding of the natives. When, however, they came up after breakfast, they were minus all the oxen, without being able to give any account of them, further than that they imagined that they were with us: I accordingly despatched two of my men on horseback to take up their spoor.

On the 18th I arose before it was clear, and rode up the banks of the river with my dogs to seek for water-buck, and presently arrived where another considerable river's bed joins the Ngotwani. Near this spot I came upon an old waterbuck, the first I had ever seen. He was standing among some young thorn-trees, within sixty yards, and had his eye full upon me. Before I could pull up my horse he was off at a rapid pace, and crossed the river's bed above me. I shouted to the dogs, and fired a shot to encourage them; they had a pretty fair start, and in half a minute the buck disappeared over a rocky ridge, with three or four of my best dogs within thirty yards of his stern. I knew that he would make for the nearest water; accordingly I kept my eye down the river, and listened with an attentive ear for the baying of the dogs.

Presently the noble buck appeared ascending a rocky pyramidal hill down the river side, with the agility of a chamois, and only one dog, Boxer, my best, at his heels. I then galloped down the river side at top speed to meet him, but was too late: I however fired a long shot to encourage Boxer. Next moment, in ascending the opposite bank of the Ngotwani, my horse fell and rolled down the bank very nearly on the top of me. One of the barrels of my favourite ball gun was thereby stove, by coming in violent contact with a piece of rock. Jock, on gaining his legs, declined being caught, and made off for camp, followed by my after-rider: Alert at this moment came up to me, having eight or ten inches of the skin of his breast and forearm ripped clean up by the waterbuck.

I now fancied that I had lost him, but a little after I heard Boxer's voice coming down the river side with the buck, having once more turned him. I ran up the bank of the Ngotwani at my best pace to meet them, and found the waterbuck at bay in a deep pool of water, surrounded by high banks of granite rock. He would not stand at bay, but swam through the deep water and broke bay on the opposite side. Boxer, however, held on and followed him up the river, and once more turned him to this pool. I met them coming down the watercourse, and sent a ball into the buck's throat, which made blood flow freely from his mouth. He held stoutly on, however, and plunged into the deep pool, there standing at bay under a granite rock. I then headed him, and from above put a bullet between his two shoulder-blades, which dropped him dead on the spot. He died as a waterbuck ought, in the deep water. My success with this noble and very beautiful antelope gave me most sincere pleasure.

I had now shot noble specimens of every sort of game in South Africa, excepting a few small bucks common in the colony, and the hippopotamus. Having contemplated the waterbuck for some time, I cut off his handsome head, which I bore to camp in triumph. The next day I succeeded in bringing down another fine waterbuck after a hot chase.

On the 19th Kleinboy returned without the lost oxen: the natives said that they had been found by Bakalahari, and were driven to Sichely. Next day the half of them were sent by the chief, with a message that no more had been found, but that spoor had been seen.

On the morning of the 22nd I rode into camp, after unsuccessfully following the spoor of a herd of elephants for two days in a westerly course. Having partaken of some refreshment, I saddled up two steeds and rode down the bank of the Ngotwani with the Bushman, to seek for any game I might find. After riding about a mile along the river's green bank I came suddenly upon an old male leopard, lying under the shade of a thorn grove, and panting from the great heat. Although I was within sixty yards of him he had not heard the horses' tread. I thought he was a lioness, and, dismounting, took a rest in my saddle on the old grey, and sent a bullet into him. He sprang to his feet and ran half way down the river's bank and stood to look about him, when I sent a second bullet into his person, and he disappeared over the bank. The ground being very dangerous, I did not disturb him by following then, but I at once sent Ruyter back to camp for the dogs.

Presently he returned with Wolf and Boxer, very much done up with the sun. I rode forward, and on looking over the bank the leopard started up and sneaked off alongside of the tall reeds and was instantly out of sight. I fired a random shot from the saddle to encourage the dogs, and shouted to them; they however stood looking stupidly round and would not take up his scent at all. I led them over his spoor again and again, but to no purpose; the dogs seemed quite stupid, and yet they were Wolf and Boxer, my two best.

At length I gave it up as a lost affair, and was riding down the river's bank when I heard Wolf give tongue behind me, and, galloping back, I found him at bay with the leopard, immediately beneath where I had fired at him: he was very severely wounded, and had slipped down into the river's bed and doubled back, whereby he had thrown out both the dogs and myself. As I approached he flew out upon Wolf and knocked him over, and then, running up the bed of the river, he took shelter in a thick bush: Wolf, however, followed him, and at this moment my other dogs came up, having heard the shot, and bayed him fiercely. He sprang out upon them and then crossed the river's bed, taking shelter beneath some large tangled roots on the opposite bank. As he crossed the river I put a third bullet into him, firing from the saddle, and as soon as he came to bay I gave him a fourth, which finished him. This leopard was a very fine old male: in the conflict the unfortunate Alert was wounded, as usual, getting his face torn open; he was still going on three legs, with all his breast laid bare by the first waterbuck.

In the evening I directed my Hottentots to watch a fine pool in the river, and do their best while I rode to a distant pool several miles up the Ngotwani, reported as very good for game, to lie all night and watch: my Totties, however, fearing "Tao,"* disobeyed me. As I rode along the river's bank I suddenly met a very old bull buffalo coming down the river on my side, with a troop of beautiful water does coming down on the opposite side. I sprang from my horse, and running down the bank towards him I sent a bullet through his correct part, and a second as he charged up the bank. He ran forty yards and stood looking about, and, detecting me, he turned towards me, looking very much as if he were going to charge. I thought I was in for it, and stood ready to spring down into the long reeds; his course was, however, run; he gazed but for a few seconds, and falling over he expired. This bull had many old wounds by lions. On reaching the water I was bound for, I found it very promising, and, having fastened my two horses to a tree beneath the river's bank, I prepared a place of concealment close by and lay down for the night.

The river's banks on each side were clad with groves of shady thorn-trees. After I had lain some time, squadrons of buffaloes were heard coming on, until the shady grove on the east bank of the water immediately above me was alive with them. After some time the leaders ventured down the river's bank to drink, and this was the signal for a general rush into the large pool of water: they came on like a regiment of cavalry at a gallop, making a mighty din and obscuring the air with a dense cloud of dust. At length I sent a ball into one of them, when the most tremendous rush followed up the bank, where they all stood still, listening attentively. I knew that the buffalo was severely wounded, but I did not hear him fall.

Some time after I fired at a second, as they stood on the bank above me; this buffalo was also hard hit, but did not then fall. A little after I fired at a third on the same spot; he ran forty yards, and falling groaned fearfully: this at once brought on a number of the others to butt their dying comrade, according to their benevolent custom. I then crept in towards them, and, firing my fourth shot, a second buffalo ran forward a few yards, and falling groaned as the last; her comrades, coming up, served her in the same manner. A second time I crept in, and, firing a fifth shot, a third buffalo ran forward and fell close to her dying comrades: in a few minutes all the other buffaloes made off, and the sound of teeth tearing at the flesh was heard immediately.

I fancied it was the hyænas, and fired a shot to scare them from the flesh. All was still: and, being anxious to inspect the heads of the buffaloes, I went boldly forward, taking the native who accompanied me along with me. We were within about five yards of the nearest buffalo, when I observed a yellow mass lying alongside of him, and at the same instant a lion gave a deep growl. I thought it was all over with me. The native shouted "Tao," and, springing away, instantly commenced blowing shrilly through a charmed piece of bone which he wore on his necklace. I retreated to the native; and we then knelt down. The lion continued his meal, tearing away at the buffalo, and growling at his

---

* Tao, the native name for lion.

wife and family, whom I found next day by the spoor had accompanied him. Knowing that he would not molest me if I left him alone, I proposed to the native to go to our hole and lie down, but he would not hear of it, and entreated me to fire at the lion. I fired three different shots where I thought I saw him, but without any effect; he would not so much as for a moment cease munching my buffalo. I then proceeded to lie down, and was soon asleep, the native keeping watch over our destinies. Some time after midnight other lions were heard coming on from other airts, and my old friend commenced roaring so loudly that the native thought it proper to awake me.

The first old lion now wanted to drink, and held right away for the two unfortunate steeds, roaring terribly. I felt rather alarmed for their safety; but, trusting that the lion had had flesh enough for one night, I lay still, and listened with an attentive ear. In a few minutes, to my utter horror, I heard him spring upon one of the steeds with an angry growl, and dash him to the earth; the steed gave a slight groan, and all was still. I listened to hear the sound of teeth, but all continued still. Soon after this "Tao" was once more to be heard munching the buffalo. In a few minutes he came forward, and stood on the bank close above us, and roared most terribly, walking up and down, as if meditating some mischief. I now thought it high time to make a fire, and, quickly collecting some dry reeds and little sticks, in half a minute we had a cheerful blaze. The lion, which had not yet got our wind, came forward at once, to find out what the deuce was up; but, not seeing to his entire satisfaction from the top of the bank, he was proceeding to descend by a game-path into the river-bed within a few yards of us. I happened at the very moment to go to this spot to fetch more wood, and, being entirely concealed from the lion's view by the intervening high reeds, we actually met face to face!

The first notice I got was his sudden spring to one side, accompanied by repeated angry growls, whilst I involuntarily made a convulsive spring backwards, at the same time giving a fearful shriek, such as I never before remembered uttering. I fancied just as he growled that he was coming upon me. We now heaped on more wood, and kept up a very strong fire until the day dawned, the lions feasting beside us all the time, notwithstanding the remonstrances of the little native, who, with a true Bechuana spirit, lamenting the loss of so much good flesh, kept continually shouting and pelting them with flaming brands.

The next morning, when it was clear, I arose and inspected the buffaloes. The three that had fallen were fine old cows, and two of them were partly consumed by the lions. The ground all around was packed flat with their spoor; one particular spoor was nearly as large as that of a borèlé. I then proceeded to inspect the steeds: the sand around them was also covered with the lion's spoor. He had sprung upon the Old Grey, but had done him no further injury than scratching his back through the skin: perhaps the lion had been scared by the rheims, or, on discovering his spare condition, had preferred the buffalo.

On the 24th we marched at dawn of day, and held up the Ngotwani, halting at the fine large pool of water where I had shot the three cow buffaloes two nights previously. I had left Ruyter and some natives to look after my flesh, and these reported lions to have surrounded them all night, coming boldly up within a few yards of them, and only retreating when burning brands were sent flying at their heads.

In the forenoon I shot a very beautifully coloured wild goose with my Moore, putting two bullets through him. In the afternoon I rode up the Ngotwani to explore, I found it generally well supplied with deep pools of water, and surrounded with fine green trees, chiefly thorn. I made a clever shot at two wild geese, waiting until their heads were in line, and then pinking them both with one bullet. At night I lay beside a favourite drinking-place with the game; in two hours large herds of buffaloes were trampling on the bank above me; at length the leaders came down and commenced drinking, which was instantly followed by a general rush of thirsty buffaloes. I got one good shot, but the dust which instantly followed obscured them for another chance. I, however, let drive into them when they halted to listen in the thicket above me. I heard one fall and die.

A little after this a noble lion presented himself on the bank above me, and was immediately saluted with a bullet in his ribs. The buffaloes capered about the banks, and at length they descended by a steep and unusual place to drink, crashing the reeds before them. There were three or four old lions roaring close about me all night, and feasting on my game. In the course of the night I fired three other long shots at the buffaloes, and towards morning, a very large lion and a lioness presenting themselves on the horizon of the bank, about twenty yards above me, I sent a ball into the lion; he bounded off, and presently we heard him growling as if dying; he lay a long time in one spot. I could hear the lioness bothering him to stand up, to which he objected, growling fearfully. I felt convinced that he was mine, and I had good hopes of the other lion. In the morning, when it was clear, I arose to see what game had died; I found two fine old cow buffaloes with very handsome heads, but, to my great regret, both the lions had made off. The day was extremely warm. I felt in need of rest, and slept most of the day by the water's margin, under cover of the long reeds.

The 26th was a cool cloudy morning, and looked like much rain. I was in the saddle before the sun rose, and rode down the river to seek waterbuck, accompanied by all my dogs. I had not ridden far when the dogs dashed up the wind, and started a large herd of cow buffaloes, to which I gave chase. They led me a long gallop right round camp, and ended by taking down wind up the Ngotwani, and sought shelter in the thorny thickets along its banks. Here, as a troop of them charged past me, I dismounted and shot one fine old cow; she brought up in a thicket, but took two more balls before she fell.

The dogs were now coursing up and down the river's bank after an old cow, with her two calves of this and last year. At length all three took into a deep pool some hundred yards long, and swam up and down and from side to side, followed by all the dogs. I wounded the old cow, but would not finish her then, and I next shot the two calves, one of which sank to the bottom, but soon after floated. I then came home to my camp for the natives to draw the flesh. Returning, we found the old cow still there, but standing in deep muddy water. She carried a very fine head, but, unfortunately, a bullet had splintered the point of one of the horns. While we were cutting up the *veal* the old cow came to the side, and got away. I came shortly afterwards, however, upon a very fine old cow buffalo, newly killed by a lion, and was astonished to find that it was my friend of the morning, with the splintered horn. The lion, ever prowling about, had detected her, and, after a sharp chase, had knocked her over. She bore the most fearful marks of his teeth on her throat, and all her back was marked by his terrible claws. I thought that there had been a long chase, as the buffalo was covered with foam from the lion's mouth.

Having inspected the buffalo I held on up the bank of the river for a couple of miles—banks densely wooded—and I then turned my face for home, having had a good bathe, and been saluted by a crocodile, who popped up his nose close beside me. I rode out a little distance from the river's bank, and presently came upon four waterbucks. The dogs at once gave chase, and broke a buck from the herd, which in one minute was standing at bay in the river, when I galloped up, and, dismounting, I shot him.

Soon after this, while skirting some rocky hills bordering on the river, I detected a very fine old waterbuck standing high up on the snmmit of one of these. I stalked him in true Highland fashion; and when within seventy yards I sent my right ball through his shoulder. The buck bounded over the ridge, and was out of sight in a moment. On gaining the ridge, with my gun at the ready, I came once more within range, when I sent a second bullet through his ribs. While following his bloody spoor I heard groans on the bank a little above me, and, going forward, I found a noble waterbuck lying dying, with the blood streaming from his mouth. When the life was gone I cut off his head, which was borne to camp before my after-rider.

The morning of the 27th was extremely hot, but I nevertheless resolved to pack up and march to Chouaney. Accordingly, after much trouble and management in stowing away all my lumber, we got under way about eleven A.M., and reached Sichely's a little after sundown. On the march one of my waggon's after-wheels rolled off, but very fortunately, the axletree escaped. I found Mr. Livingstone at his devotions, and he informed me that it was Sunday.

The next day was deliciously cloudy, with some slight showers of rain. In the evening Sichely came down to see me, bringing my four lost oxen which he had at length made up his mind to restore. Three of Sichely's men engaged to accompany me to the colony, their wages to be three guns and two cows.

I now proceeded slowly by way of Lotlokane, Motito, and Campbellsdorp, and encamped on the Vaal River on the 11th of November. Here I was obliged to wait for several days, owing to the great body of water coming down rendering a passage impossible.

On the 16th, however, the river having subsided, I inspanned my two waggons, and took the drift with the heaviest waggon, drawn by fourteen oxen. I led the team on horseback, and, several Griquas assisting us, we took the drift very high, and got a little more than half-way through when two of my oxen became entangled in the gear, and, being dragged along, my driver foolishly halted the waggon. The result of this foolish management was, that the oxen instantly turned right-about-face, and stood with their heads up water, the stream being too powerful for them to stand still otherwise. We spent a fruitless hour of very harassing work, trying to right the oxen, which was, however impossible, and at length we were obliged to cut away the trektow, and get the oxen ashore.

Here, after resting them for a little, we inspanned them in the trektow, and, taking them some distance above the isolated waggon, we swam them down, and tried to fix the trektow on the dissel-boom; but in this we failed, the stream carrying away the cattle before they made the waggon. We had then to go ashore and repeat the process. In the next attempt the oxen were brought too near the waggon, and, getting foul of it, we had great difficulty in extricating them. One ox remained there for half an hour before we got him clear, the strong current holding him against the waggon. We next got over the oxen and trektow of the other waggon, and made several attempts with these, but without success.

The day was now waning away, and both men and oxen were very much knocked up. It was most distressing work, and it was greatly aggravated by the cruel, sharp stones which composed the river's bed, and the virulent invisible doublegee-thorns with which the banks were strewed. I began to despair of getting the waggon out that day; and from the appearance of the weather toward the sources of the river for some time past, we had every reason to expect a flood at any moment. It was a dismal prospect, and my heart was ill at ease. Late in the day we made loose my strong new buffalo trektow, and bent it on to the dissel-boom, and then, bringing in the oxen, we managed to fasten the tow on to this one. I also placed several men on the wheels. This time we very nearly succeeded; the waggon started and proceeded several yards, when one of the tows gave way, and we were again left in the lurch. Once more we made the attempt, and again failed, the oxen becoming entangled with the gear. The sun was now under, and, all hands being most completely done up, we desisted for the night. My men came off to the waggon with three of my steeds, and I rummaged out some flesh, meal, and coffee, with some sleeping toggery and cooking utensils; we then left the desolate waggon, with great doubts of ever boarding it again.

I could not help thinking of Robinson Crusoe when he visited for the last time the wreck of his ship. I rested but little that night, and I had good reason to be anxious; for if the river should come down at all, it would be impossible to do anything with the waggon next day, and I could not expect anything but to see a tearing flood. If this had happened I should have been utterly ruined, for nearly all my worldly property was contained in the waggon. I sent a message to Mr.

Hughes, requesting him to assist me in my troubles with men and oxen next day, although it was the Sabbath.

I had the gratification to find at daydawn that the river had fallen a little during the night; and I had just finished my breakfast when four Griquas came up, bearing a long stout rope, which Mr. Hughes had forwarded for my use. These men informed me that he had sent men out in different directions to seek for three spans of his oxen to be brought to my assistance. We then set about getting the gear in order, and very soon two spans of the oxen appeared with another party of Griquas. We next made fast one end of the rope to the dissel-boom, and to the other end of this rope we fastened the large buffalo trektow, which reached slanting across the strong current to shallower water where the oxen could stand. We then brought in two span of oxen, and fastened the end of their tow on the buffalo, and put the oxen in motion. They laid a mighty strain on the long tow, and the waggon moved slightly, when a strong rheim, that with many turns fastened two of the trektows, gave way, and left me once more in trouble.

The river had at this moment increased about six inches, and was now stronger than on the preceding day; moreover it was still increasing. This put me at once in great consternation; my hopes, which a little before were very high, now sank, and I expected in a few hours perhaps to see my waggon overwhelmed and swept away. This, however, was not the case; the river did not increase much more, and in our second attempt we were successful. The trektows were on this occasion knotted together, the oxen all trekked fair and together, and the heavily-laden waggon, with its precious contents, was rescued from a watery grave. We hailed its rescue with continued cheers: the oxen held stoutly on, and dragged the waggon without a check right out to the shallow water on the border of the river. We then shortened the gear, and, having inspanned two after-bullocks, we pulled the waggon right out of the river's bed and outspanned on the top of the high bank.

The next move was to get the other waggons through. The Griquas at first made some demur, saying that it was Sunday; but I very soon got rid of that objection, by telling them that I would prepare some food and coffee for them, when they set to work with a good will, and in two hours more the other three waggons were brought safely through, and were high and dry.

On the 8th we entered the village of Colesberg. All the forenoon I was busy off-loading two of the waggons. We spread out the curiosities in the market-ground, making no end of a parade: it was truly a very remarkable sight, and struck all beholders with astonishment.

On the 13th I left Colesberg, and set out on my way to Grahamstown; passing on the 17th the Thebus flats. On the march I saddled up, and, leaving the waggons, I rode across country for Hendrick Strydom's farm, where I had commenced my sporting career in South Africa. As I rode across the flats I found springbok and black wildebeest still abundant. On reaching the residence of my former friend, I found the blackness of desolation pictured there. The house was falling to pieces, and the grass grew rank where the pot was wont to boil. In a melan-

CHAP. XXV.

A Waltz with a Hippopotamus.

choly mood I then turned my face for the farm where I had ordered my waggons to halt; and, as I rode along, I mused on the fleeting and transient nature of all human condition. On the 25th I reached Fort Beaufort, where I dined with some old acquaintances at the mess of the 7th.

On the 29th we marched to the Fish River at dawn of day. Here I found about sixty waggons waiting the fall of the river to get through. Some of us set to work to clear away a bank of mud on the opposite side, after which a good many waggons, lightly laden, crossed the river; but on attempting to bring through my large waggon, she stuck fast, but was at length extricated with the help of another span. We saved her just in time, for the river was increasing fast when we got her out, and in another half-hour was running a rapid torrent, at least ten feet deep. I found several very jolly farmers, English and Scotch,. lying on the opposite side; in particular, one Annesley, of whom I had heard a great deal. This man was a regular "brick," a thorough Scotsman from the borders. He came up to me at once, and asked me to come and have a glass of whisky with him: he was accompanied by his family; his eldest daughter was a very fine girl.

By the 1st of February the river had fallen most rapidly. After some work in clearing the mud on both sides, waggons began to cross, and a great rumpus was kept up during the remainder of the day. I got my second waggon through about eleven A.M. Soon after I had got through good old Annesley took the drift, and on approaching the opposite side his waggon had the most fearful capsize in deep water, seriously damaging a quantity of very valuable property. In an instant we were all at his assistance, and in a very short time we got out his wife and family and damaged cargo and righted his waggon for him. I brought him over dry clothes, and spent about three hours in assisting him in his difficulty. I then inspanned and trekked on to Boatasberg, where I halted about midnight, with good moonlight.

On the 2nd I marched into Grahamstown, where I sold my ivory well, the ivory and ostrich-feathers realising in the market somewhere about £1000.

CHAPTER XXIV.

Start on another Elephant-shooting Expedition—The Hart River—Numerous pack of Wild Dogs—Mahura, Chief of the Batlapis—Rumours of Wars—The Meritsane—Lotlokane—Encounter with two Lions on the Molopo—Chouaney—A tremendous Fight with a Buffalo—The River Limpopo—Huge Crocodiles—A splendid Hippopotamus falls to my Rifle—Immense Herds of Buffaloes crossing the River—The Serolomootlooque Antelope unknown to Naturalists—A herd of Hippopotami—Fine Sport beside the River.

I REMAINED in Grahamstown for some weeks, being undecided as to my future plans. At last, however, I decided upon making another elephant-shooting expedition. I accordingly started for the far interior on the 11th of March, and, having resolved to try a short cut through the territories of the chief Mahura, I crossed the Vaal river on the 5th of May, far to the eastward of my former track.

Early on the 7th we entered upon the broad strath through which the Hart River flows. Here we discovered a small fountain, where we halted for the night. We marched early on the 8th, holding up the strath parallel with the Hart River. Presently we came upon the largest pack of wild dogs I had ever seen: there were about forty of them. They went off very leisurely, and when my dogs chased them they turned about and showed fight. We were in motion most of the day; very large herds of cattle were to be seen pasturing on all sides.

On the 12th we marched before breakfast to within three miles of Mahura. Having taken breakfast, I rode ahead with Ruyter, and called on Mr. Ross, the resident missionary. We walked together to the town and visited Mahura and his brother; the expressions of neither of these men were at all in their favour. I told Mahura that I wanted an ox with very large horns, which he promised to provide. He asked me if we were still at war with the Tambookie tribes. He also mentioned that ten men of the Bastards had been shot by Mochesse's natives Mr. Ross informed me that Mahura was at present meditating war upon a tribe to the north-east, and also that Mochuarra, the chief at Motito, meditated an attack upon Sichely. In the evening-my waggons came up, when I directed them to draw up in a grove of cameel-dorn about a mile beyond the town.

The next day Mahura sent a party of men to inquire who had given me permission to outspan where I now stood, and ordering me to inspan and return to the town. These men were very insolent and overbearing in their manner. I accordingly at once assumed a very high tone, and said that, if Mahura was particular as to where I outspanned, he ought to have told me so on the preceding evening; that as to returning, I would on no account return; and that if the chief's heart was against me I would not wait to trade with him, but would at once proceed on my journey. I also told them that Mahura was not my chief, and that I cared not for his words. They then became still more insolent, and said that I should learn what Mahura could do before sunset, and they departed to report my words to their tyrannical chief.

Mahura was sitting in the missionary's house: accordingly I rode thither and arrived along with these men. On my words being reported, he was at first exceedingly wroth, and said that in consequence of what I had said he would not permit me to proceed through his country. I only smiled at threats; and he eventually cooled down, and took leave of us apparently in good humour. In the evening he returned and took tea with Mr Ross and myself, and then accompanied me to camp; he rode on horseback in a large white great-coat, accompanied by his brother and two other mounted attendants. I showed him all my rifles, with which he expressed himself much pleased; having drunk his coffee, he took a friendly leave, promising to visit me early next day.

True to his word, Mahura came and breakfasted with me, after which I obtained six karosses from him in barter for ammunition. I then presented him with a whipstick and two pound of powder, and walked down to the missionary's house, ordering my men to inspan. Mahura promised to come thither and take leave of me, but did not keep his word. About midday I marched, holding a spoor of three waggons some months old, said to lead me into my old course at Great Chooi.

On the 20th we reached the bank of the Meristane, two miles below my old spoor. On the march we saw for the first time spoor of the black rhinoceros, also pallah and koodoo on the mountain, and hartebeests on the open country,

On the 22nd we marched at early dawn, and, having proceeded about four miles, left the main road to Bakatla, and held across-country to our right for my old out-spanning place at Lotlokane; two hours more brought us thither. I did not find the vast herds of game congregated here as usual, water being everywhere abundant; the grass over the whole country was remarkable, being much higher than my oxen.

On the 23rd, when within two miles of the Molopo, the dogs took up the scent of lions. I then halted my waggons, and, having saddled up my two horses, I rode with Ruyter in quest of them, accompanied by ten of my dogs, who kept the scent for a short distance, and at last lost it altogether, and went off in the scent of some hartebeests. I now rode forward to the Molopo, which I made about one mile lower down than the drift. This darling little river is here completely concealed by lofty reeds and long grass which densely clothe its margin to a distance of at least a hundred yards. On each side reitbuck were very abundant. On making the river we started one of these. I rode up the river side, and immediately observed two old lions come slowly out from the adjoining cover and slant off toward the reeds. I galloped forward to endeavour to get between them and the reeds; in this I succeeded. The lions, imagining that we were some species of game, did not attempt to retreat, but stood looking in wonder until I was within fifty yards of them, and right between the last lion and the reeds. I was struck with wonder and admiration at the majestic and truly awful appearance which these two noble old lions presented.

They were both very large; the first, a "schwart fore-life," or black-maned lion,—the last, which was the finest and the oldest, a "chiell fore-life," or yellow-maned lion. The black-maned lion, after looking at me for half a minute, walked slowly forward and bounded into the reeds; the dark-brown lion would fain have done the same, but I was now right between him and his retreat. He seemed not at all to like my appearance, but he did not yet feel certain what I was, and, fancying that I had not observed him, he lay down in the long grass. Ruyter now came up with my rifle. Having loaded in the saddle, I waited a minute for all my dogs to come up, they having gone off after the reitbuck, and I then rode slowly forward towards the lion as if to pass within twenty-five yards of him. Not one of the dogs was yet aware of the lion, and they came on behind my horse.

This move on my part lost me the lion, for by so doing I laid open the ground of retreat between him and the reeds; and on coming within twenty or twenty-five yards of him, and whilst in the act of reining in my horse to fire, he took his eye off me, examined the ground between him and the reeds, and, seeing the coast clear, he suddenly bounded forward, and, before I could even dismount from my panic-stricken steed, was at the edge of the reeds, which he entered with a lofty spring, making the water fly as he pitched into it. Several of the dogs entered after him, but immediately retreated, barking over their shoulders in great fear. Thus I lost this most noble lion, which, with better management, I might easily have slain. I ought to have approached him on foot, leading my steed, and I ought not to have laid open the ground of retreat.

On the 27th we trekked to Chouaney, which we reached at sundown, and remained there to trade next day. I obtained from Sichely two natives to accompany me to the Limpopo, their pay being a musket each. I got also from the chief twelve elephants' teeth, several very fine karosses, native arms, and other curiosities.

About midday we marched, and slept near the Ngotwani, along whose banks my course lay for the Limpopo. The country through which the Ngotwani twines is soft and sandy, and in general covered with dense thorny jungle which greatly impeded our progress, having constantly to cut a passage before the waggons could advance. Several lions commenced roaring around us soon after the sun went down.

On the evening of the next day I had a glorious row with an old bull buffalo: he was the only large bull in a fine herd of cows. I found their spoor while walking ahead of the waggons, and, following it up, I came upon a part of the herd feeding quietly in a dense part of the forest. I fired my first shot at a cow, which I wounded. The other half of the herd then came up right in my face, within six yards of me. They would have trampled on me if I had not sung out in their faces and turned them. I selected the old bull and sent a bullet into his shoulder. The herd then crashed along through the jungle to my right, but he at once broke away from them and took to my left. On examining his spoor, I found it bloody. I then went to meet my waggons, which I heard coming on, and, ordering the men to outspan, I took all my dogs to the spoor. They ran it up in fine style, and in a few minutes the silence of the forest was disturbed by a tremendous bay. On running towards the sound I met the old fellow coming on towards the waggons, with all my dogs after him. I saluted him with a second ball in the shoulder; he held on and took up a position in the thicket within forty yards of the waggons, where I finished him. He carried a most splendid head.

On the 8th of June we made the long-wished-for fair Limpopo an hour before sunset. I was at once struck with this most interesting river: the trees along its banks were of prodigious size and very great beauty. At the very spot where I made the water, a huge crocodile lay upon the sand on the opposite side; on observing me he dashed into the stream.

The next day I rode ahead of the waggons with Ruyter, and hunted along the bank of the river. I immediately shot a waterbuck. This animal and pallah were very abundant. As I advanced I found large vleys along the river side, a favourite haunt of the waterbuck. After breakfast I again rode forth with fresh horses with my Bushman. We still found waterbuck and pallah very abundant. I presently gave chase to a herd of the former to try their speed; but as they led me into the midst of a labyrinth of marshy vleys, I gave it up.

At that instant the Bushman whispered "Sir, Sir;" and looking to my right, two princely old bull buffaloes stood in the jungle within forty yards of me. They got my wind, and started before I could get ready to fire. They held along the river-bank ahead of me, but not requiring them I did not give chase. After this I came upon a huge crocodile basking on the sand, which instantly dashed into the stream. I now got into a vast labyrinth of marshes of great extent. Several species of wild duck and a variety of water-fowl were extremely abundant and very tame, hundreds passing before my eye at once; guinea-fowl, three sorts of large partridge, and two kinds of quail being likewise numerous.

I presently wounded a noble old waterbuck as he dashed past me in marshy ground. In following him up I met an old buck pallah, which I killed on the spot with a shot in the middle of the breast. Following on after the wounded waterbuck, along the high bank of the river, which was, however, concealed from my view by the dense cover, I suddenly heard a loud splash, and, coming suddenly clear of the cover, I beheld the lovely waterbuck standing broadside on an island in the middle of the river. Before I could dismount to fire, he dashed into the water and swam to the opposite bank. I grasped my trusty little Moore and waited till he won the *terra firma*, when with one well-directed shot I dropped him on the spot. A very strange thing then occurred; the buck in his death-pangs slid down into the river, and continuing his struggles he swam half-way across the river back to the island, where he lay upon a sand-bank. I then divested myself of my leathers, spurs, and veldtschoens, and was wading in to fetch him, when the river carried him off, and, fearing the horrible crocodiles, I did not attempt to follow. It was now late, and I rode for my waggon-spoor, which I failed to find until I had returned to where we had that morning breakfasted. I had been following the turns of the river, and the waggons had taken a short cut across the country. I reached them in the dark by great good luck.

On the 10th I rode ahead of my waggons at day-dawn: thick mist was rolling along the Limpopo. Presently I saw two crocodiles in the stream below me. A little after I had the pleasure to find, for the first time, the spoor of sea-cows or hippopotami. I had never before seen it, but I knew it must be theirs; it was very similar to the spoor of borèlé, or black rhinoceros, but larger, and had four toes instead of three. Before returning to my waggons I tried to ride down a waterbuck which I turned off from the river, but in this I failed, though I managed to keep close to him in the chase, and eventually to knock him up along with my horse.

I again sallied forth with the Bushman and fresh steeds, and, directing the waggons to take the straight course, I followed the windings of the river. Presently, looking over the bank, I beheld three enormous crocodiles basking on the sand on the opposite side. I was astonished at their awful appearance and size, one of them appearing to me to be sixteen or eighteen feet in length, with a body as thick as that of an ox.

On observing us they plunged into the dead water by the side of the stream. The next minute, one of them popping up his terrible head in the middle of the stream, I made a beautiful shot, and sent a ball through the middle of his brains. The convulsions of death which followed were truly awful. At first he sank for an instant to the shot, but instantly striking the bottom with his tail he shot up above the water, when he struggled violently, sometimes on his back and then again on his belly, with at one time his head and fore feet above the water, and immediately after his tail and hind legs, the former lashing the water with a force truly astounding. Clouds of sand accompanied him in all his movements, the strong stream carrying him along with it, till at length the struggle of death was over, and he sank to rise no more.

Following the windings of the river I detected a small crocodile basking on the sand, when I gave him a shot and he instantly plunged into the river. A little farther on I wounded a third as he lay on a promontory of sand, and he likewise made the water. A little farther down the stream, yet another crocodile, a huge old sinner, lay basking on the sand. I determined to make a very correct shot in this case, and set about stalking him. Creeping up behind the trunk of a prostrate old tree, I took a rest and sent the ball into his nostril, when he plunged into the river, colouring the water with his blood.

We now got into a fine green turn of the river, where I saw a great many waterbucks. I shot one buck pallah, and immediately after I came suddenly upon a troop of five or six beautiful leopards. At the next bend of the river three huge crocodiles lay on the sand on the opposite side. Stalking within easy range, I shot one of them in the head: his comrades instantly dashed into the water, but he lay as if dead on the high sand. A second shot, however, through the ribs brought him back to life. On receiving it he kept running round and round, snapping his horrid jaws fearfully at his own wounded side. In the convulsions of death he made one run clean away from the water, but another unlucky turn brought his head toward the river, into which he eventually rolled.

Galloping along from this place to my waggons, I came suddenly upon a lion and lioness lying in the grass below a gigantic old mimosa. Dismounting from my horse, I took a couple of shots at the lion, missing him with my first, but wounding him with my second shot, when he rose with several angry short growls and bounded off. A few hundred yards farther on I found my waggons drawn up, and on reaching them my men informed me that they had just seen two huge hippopotami in the river beneath. Proceeding to the spot, we found them still swimming there. I shot one, putting three balls into his head, when he sank, but night setting in we lost him.

At dawn of day on the 12th a noise was heard for about twenty minutes up the river, like the sound of the sea, accompanied by the lowing of buffaloes. It was a herd crossing the river. I rode thither to look at them, and was retracing my steps to camp, when, within three hundred yards of my waggons, I beheld an old bull-buffalo standing contemplating my camp, with my followers looking at him in great consternation. They set the dogs after him, when he took away up the river. As the ground was extremely bad for riding, being full of deep holes, and all concealed with long grass, it was some time before I could get away after the dogs; and when I had ridden a short distance I met them all returning, their feet being completely done up with the long march from the colony.

I now turned my face once more for camp, when I heard one of my dogs at bay behind me. Galloping up to the spot, I found my dog "Lion" standing barking at an old waterbuck in an open flat. The buck, on observing me, made away for the river, and, joining a herd of does, they dashed into the stream, and were immediately upon the opposite bank. I was in a sequestered bend of the river, where the banks for several acres were densely clad with lofty reeds and grass which towered above my head as I sat on my horse's back. Beyond the reeds and grass were trees of all sizes, forming a dense shade; this is the general character of the banks of the Limpopo, as far as I have yet seen.

I was slowly returning to my camp, in anything but good humour at my want of success with the game I had just been after, when, behold, an antelope of the most exquisite beauty, and utterly unknown to sportsmen or naturalists, stood broadside in my path, looking me full in the face. It was a princely old buck of the serolomootlooque of the Bakalahari, or bushbuck of the Limpopo. He carried a very fine wide-set pair of horns. On beholding him I was struck with wonder and delight. My heart beat with excitement. I sprang from my saddle, but before I could fire a shot this gem of beauty bounded into the reeds, and was lost to my sight. At that moment I would have given half what I possessed in this world for a broadside at that lovely antelope, and I at once resolved not to proceed farther on my expedition until I had captured him, although it should cost me the labour of a month.

The antelope having entered the reeds, I gave my horse to my after-rider, and with my rifle on full cock and at the ready I proceeded to stalk with extreme caution throughout the length and breadth of the cover; but I stalked in vain; the antelope had vanished, and was nowhere to be found. I then returned to my steed, and rode slowly up the river's bank towards my camp. I had ridden to within a few hundred yards of the waggons, and was meditating how I should best circumvent the serolomootlooque, when once more this lovely antelope crossed my path; I had been unwittingly driving him before me along the bank of the river. He trotted like a roebuck into the thick cover, and then stood broadside among the thorn bushes.

I sprang from my saddle, and, guessing about his position, I fired and missed him; he then trotted along a rhinoceros's footpath, and gave me a second chance. Again I fired, and before my rifle was down from my shoulder the serolomootlooque lay prostrate in the dust. The ball had cut the skin open along his ribs, and, entering his body, had passed along his neck, and had lodged in his brains, where we found it on preparing the head for stuffing. I was not a little gratified at my good fortune in securing this novel and valuable trophy; he was one of the most perfect antelopes I had ever beheld, both in symmetry and colour. I had him immediately conveyed to camp, where I took his measurement, and wrote out a correct description of him for the benefit of naturalists. I christened him the "Antelopus Roualeynei," or "bushbuck of the Limpopo."

The next day I breakfasted before the sun rose, and then rode down the river's bank with Ruyter. I first shot an old buck pallah, and having ridden a few miles farther I came upon two fine old waterbucks fighting, when I stalked in within a hundred yards, and shot them both right and left. The heads were fair specimens, but, having many better, I reluctantly left them to perish in the feldt. Hereabouts I found fresh spoor of hippopotami of the preceding night. I followed this spoor to a considerable distance along the margin of the river, and at last I came upon the troop. They were lying in a shady, sequestered bend of the river, beneath some gigantic shady trees. In this place the water in heavy floods had thrown up large banks of sand, in which they had hollowed out their beds. The spot was surrounded with dense underwood and reeds, and was adjacent to a very deep and broad stream, into which their footpaths led in every direction.

I was first apprized of my proximity to them by a loud cry from one old bull, who took alarm at the sudden flight of a species of heron: his cry was not unlike that of an elephant. He stood in water which reached half way up his side, shaking his short ears in the sun; every half-minute he disappeared beneath the water, when, again parading half of his body, he uttered a loud snorting, blowing noise. On observing him, I dismounted, and every time he disappeared I ran in, until I stood behind the tall reeds within twenty yards of him. Here I might have dropped him with a single ball, but I unfortunately made up my mind not to molest them until next day, when I should have men to assist me to get them out. Presently he observed me, when he dived, and swam round a shady promontory into the deep stream, where he and his comrades kept up a continual loud blowing noise. I returned to camp, and, having ordered my men to inspan, I tried a drift on horseback, and crossed the Limpopo, but, the water coming over my saddle, I did not attempt to bring through my waggons. We accordingly held on our course on the north-western bank of the river, and outspanned about a mile above the place where I had found the hippopotami.

When the sun went down the sea-cows commenced a march up the river. They passed along opposite to my camp, making the most extraordinary sounds—plowing, snorting, and roaring, sometimes crashing through reeds, and sometimes swimming gently, and splashing and sporting through the water. There being a little moonlight, I went down with my man Carey, and sat some time on the river's bank contemplating these wonderful monsters of the river. It was a truly grand and very extraordinary scene; the opposite bank of the stream was clad with trees of gigantic size and great beauty, which added greatly to the interest of the picture.

On the 14th, after a very early breakfast, I proceeded with three after-riders, two double-barrelled rifles, and about a hundred rounds of ammunition, to the spot where I had yesterday found the hippopotami; but they had taken alarm, and were all gone. The spoor leading up the river, I rode along the banks, examining every pool until my steed was quite knocked up, but found not a single sea-cow. The spoor still led up the river; they had made short cuts at every bend, sometimes taking the direct line on my side, and sometimes on the other. Finding that I must sleep in the feldt if I followed on, I despatched Ruyter to camp for my blankets, coffee-kettle, biscuit, etc., and fresh steeds. I searched on foot, and penetrated every thicket and every dense jungle of reeds that overhung the river, until at last, faint with hunger and fatigue, I sought some game on which to make luncheon, and had good fortune to fall in with a young doe of the "Antelopus Roualeynei," which I shot, and in a few minutes she was roasting on a mighty fire.

Ruyter, at this moment coming up, brought a welcome supply of biscuit and coffee, and reported my horse "Flux," about my very best, to have died of horse-sickness. After luncheon I continued my search for hippopotami; and just as the sun went down I started an old fellow from beneath some tall reeds, which hung over a deep broad pool. On hearing me approach he dived with a loud splash, and immediately reappeared with a blowing noise a little farther up the river, and within twenty yards of the bank. Having looked about him, he again dived, and continued his course up the river, which could be traced from the wave above.

I ran in front of him, and when he came up the third time I was standing opposite to him, ready with my rifle at my shoulder. I sent the bullet into his brain, when he floundered for one moment at the surface, and then sank to the bottom. There he most probably only remained for half an hour, but in a few minutes night set in, and I had thus the extreme mortification to lose my hippopotamus, the second one which I had shot. We slept beneath a shady tree; at midnight a few drops of rain fell, and I feared a drenching; it, however, passed away. In the course of the day we saw several large crocodiles, three of which I shot. One of these lay upon an island; I shot him dead on the spot; he did not gain the water.

CHAPTER XXV.

We cross the Limpopo—Rash Encounter with a Hippopotamus—Remarkable dome-like Rock—Two Serolomootlooques shot—Hollow Trees containing Honey—Gigantic Ant-hills—Hunting across the Limpopo—Another Boa Constrictor—A Visit from Seleka—A Sea-cow shot, which sinks—Resurrection of the Beast—Splendid Hippopotamus-shooting.

ON the 17th of June, having found a good drift, I crossed the Limpopo with my waggons, and drew them up in a green and shady spot. I then rode a long way down the eastern bank in quest of hippopotami, and late in the evening I found one, which I did not molest, trusting to find him next day.

On the 18th a dense mist hung over the river all the morning.

Ordering the waggons to follow in an hour, I rode ahead to seek the sea-cow of the previous night, but after a long search I gave it up as a bad job, and, kindling a fire to warm myself, I awaited the waggons, which presently came up. Here I halted for two hours, and then once more rode ahead to seek hippopotami. The river became more promising for sea-cow. At every turn there occurred deep, still pools, with occasional sandy islands densely clad with lofty reeds, and with banks covered with reeds to a breadth of thirty yards. Above and beyond these reeds stood trees of immense age and gigantic size, beneath which grew a long and very rank description of grass, on which the sea-cow delights to pasture.

I soon found fresh spoor, and after holding on for several miles, just as the sun was going down, and as I entered a dense reed cover, I came upon the fresh lairs of four hippopotami. They had been lying sleeping on the margin of the river, and, on hearing me come crackling through the reeds, had plunged into the deep water. I at once ascertained that they were newly started, for the froth and bubbles were still on the spot where they had plunged in. Next moment I heard them blowing a little way down the river. I then headed them, and, with considerable difficulty, owing to the cover and the reeds, I at length came down-right above where they were standing. It was a broad part of the river, with a sandy bottom, and the water came half-way up their sides. There were four of them, three cows and an old bull; they stood in the middle of the river, and, though alarmed, did not appear aware of the extent of the impending danger.

I took the sea-cow next me, and with my first ball I gave her a mortal wound, knocking loose a great plate on the top of her skull. She at once commenced plunging round and round, and then occasionally remained still, sitting for a few minutes on the same spot. On hearing the report of my rifle two of the others took up stream, and the fourth dashed down the river; they trotted along, like oxen, at a smart pace as long as the water was shallow. I was now in a state of very great anxiety about my wounded sea-cow, for I feared that she would get down into deep water, and be lost like the last one; her struggles were still carrying her down stream, and the water was becoming deeper. To settle the matter I accordingly fired a second shot from bank, which, entering the roof of her skull, passed out through her eye; she then kept continually splashing round and round in a circle in the middle of the river. I had great fears of the crocodiles, and I did not know that the sea-cow might not attack me. My anxiety to secure her, however, overcame all hesitation; so, divesting myself of my leathers, and armed with a sharp knife, I dashed into the water, which at first took me up to my arm-pits, but in the middle was shallower.

As I approached Behemoth her eye looked very wicked. I halted for a moment, ready to dive under the water if she attacked me, but she was stunned, and did not know what she was doing; so, running in upon her, and seizing her short tail, I attempted to incline her course to land: It was extraordinary what enormous strength she still had in the water. I could not guide her in the slightest, and she continued to splash, and plunge, and blow, and make her circular course, carrying me along with her as if I was a fly on her tail. Finding her tail gave me but a poor hold, as the only means of securing my prey, I took out my knife, and cutting two deep parallel incisions through the skin on her rump, and lifting this skin from the flesh, so that I could get in my two hands, I made use of this as a handle; and after some desperate hard work, sometimes pushing and sometimes pulling, the sea-cow continuing her circular course all the time and I holding on at her rump like grim Death, eventually I succeeded in bringing this gigantic and most powerful animal to the bank. Here the Bushman quickly brought me a stout buffalo-rheim from my horse's neck, which I passed through the opening in the thick skin, and moored Behemoth to a tree. I then took my rifle and sent a ball through the centre of her head, and she was numbered with the dead.

At this moment my waggons came up within a few hundred yards of the spot, where I outspanned, and by moonlight we took down a span of select oxen and a pair of rheim chains, and succeeded in dragging the sea-cow high and dry. We were all astonished at her enormous size; she appeared to be about five feet broad across the belly. I could see much beauty in the animal, which Nature has admirably formed for the amphibious life it was destined to pursue.

We were occupied all the morning of the 19th cutting up and salting the select parts of the sea-cow; of the skull I took particular charge. She was extremely fat, more resembling a pig than a cow or a horse. In the evening I rode down the river, and shot a brace of waterbucks, after which I left the river-bank and rode to the summit of an adjacent hill, from which I obtained a fine view of the surrounding country. Many bold blue mountain ranges stood to the north and north-west; to the east and south-east were also mountain ranges; whilst to the south a very remarkable light-coloured rock, in the form of a dome, shot high above the level of the surrounding forest.

The next day at dawn I rode down the river-side to seek serolomootlooques, and ordered my waggons to follow in a couple of hours. After riding a few miles, I observed a serolomootlooque of surpassing beauty standing on the top of the opposite bank of the river; he stood with his breast to me, and from the broad belt of reeds on this side of the water it was impossible to get nearer than a hundred yards of him. Taking a deliberate aim, I fired off-hand, and heard the ball tell upon him. Here the river was deep, requiring swimming, and I had fears of the crocodiles. I sent the Bushman across, however, on horseback, who immediately discovered blood, and presently came upon the buck, and found his fore-arm smashed in the shoulder. I went over, and, starting the buck in the cover, put a bullet in his ribs. He then got into some thick reeds, when I took up a position on one side, and ordered Ruyter to beat up the cover. The buck broke near me, when I sent a third bullet right through and through his shoulder; and the tough old buck still scorning to fall, I quickly fired my other barrel, and most unluckily cut his lovely horn off at the base. The buck now charged headlong into a thick bush, and died. His head, before I destroyed it, was perhaps the finest along the banks of the Limpopo; the horns were of extraordinary length, and had a most perfect set and turn.

We now swam our steeds back to the saddlery, and presently overtook the waggons. I deposited my damaged trophy, and mounting fresh steeds, rode once more ahead. I was not ten minutes away from the waggons when I started another serolomootlooque, a first-rate old buck, very nearly as good as the last. Imagining our horses were some beasts of the forest, he turned to look at us, when I shot him in the heart. The waggons being close at hand, the buck was deposited in my larder, and I once more rode forth.

After proceeding many miles along the borders of the river, on emerging into an open space running parallel with the stream, I came upon large herds of pallahs, blue wildebeests, zebras, and to my utter astonishment, a herd of about ten bull elands. I was not aware that they were met with in these parts. I gave chase, and soon selected the best bull in the herd, a ponderous grey old fellow; he began at once to trot, though all the rest were still at a gallop. After a sharp ride of a few miles I turned this eland, and brought him back close on the river, when I shot him in the shoulder, holding out my rifle with one hand, like a pistol. I then rode back to seek my waggons, which I failed to find, they not having come on as I had ordered. I fancied that the natives had led them some short cut, and that the river might have a great bend; so, being faint and hungry, I rode back to the eland, where I had left my Bushman, kindled a fire, and roasted and ate flesh and liver of the eland. As night was on, I skinned his side which lay uppermost that I might have some covering, as I had neither coat nor waistcoat. When, however, the sun went down, signal shots disclosed to me the position of the waggons; they had come within half a mile of where the eland died.

On the 21st I rode some distance down the river with Ruyter in quest of sea-cow and serolomootlooques; we found fresh spoor of the former, and I shot one doe of the latter. Ruyter drove her up to me by beating the reeds; he also started a fine old buck, which did not break cover. As I rode along I saw six crocodiles and a great number of monkeys of two varieties; also several deadly serpents, one of them a cobra very similar to the Indian cobra. Bees were very abundant along the Limpopo, the gigantic old hollow trees affording them abundant homes. My natives brought me some fine honey while I was taking my breakfast; they found it in an old ant-hill. I was astonished to observed along the banks of the river enormous trees from three to four feet in diameter, cut down by Bakalahari, only for the sake of the honey which they contain. The Bakalahari fell them with immense trouble and perseverance with little tomahawks of their own formation.

The ant-hills along the Limpopo and throughout this part of Africa are truly wonderful; it is common to see them upwards of twenty feet high and one hundred feet in circumference. They are composed of clay, which hardens in the sun like a brick; they have generally one tall tapering spire in the middle of the fabric, the base of the spire being surrounded with similar projections of smaller height. The natives informed me that we were opposite to the tribe Seleka, whom they tried to persuade me to visit, but I resolved to stick to the Limpopo.

On the 22nd we came upon the Macoolwey, a large clear running river, joining the Limpopo from the south-east: here I bagged a princely waterbuck.

At dawn of the succeeding day I rode forth to try to cross the Limpopo and hunt for serolomootlooques, but I failed to find a drift. I then rode some distance along the bank of the Macoolwey seeking a passage; but I was still unsuccessful. I then retraced my steps to the Limpopo, determined to get through, cost what it might, as the banks looked very promising for serolomootlooques. I discovered a drift, but deep. I returned to camp for fresh horses, and rode forth with two after-riders, and a packhorse carrying bedding, as I had resolved to hunt for serolomootlooques over the river for a couple of days. We got safely through, and held up the stream. I sought every turn of the water on foot, the boys leading my horse, but failed to fall in with a buck serolomootlooque. I therefore retraced my steps down the river to a spot where buffaloes had drunk on the preceding evening, and there I spent the night.

In the morning I rode down to a likely cover for serolomootlooques opposite the drift. Here I started one old buck, but did not fire; he went off barking exactly like a roebuck, which they very much resemble in form, gait, voice, and habit. Following on after this buck, I started two does, one of which I shot. Here I left one of my after-riders with two of the steeds, whilst I and Ruyter rode down the bank of the Limpopo to explore. I found the river wearing quite a different appearance below its junction, being very much broader—nearly as large, indeed, as the Orange River. Crocodiles of enormous size were to be seen at every turn, and I shot four huge fellows. We then fell in with a large rock serpent, or "metsapallah," about eleven feet long, which I shot with a ball through the head, and brought to camp slung round my neck.

Having resolved over-night to rob a colony of bees of their precious stores, and to try for the old serolomootlooque at the drift, I started on the 25th at day-dawn, with two after-riders, one of them carrying a large tin pail for the expected honey. After crossing the river I stalked carefully through the cover where the serolomootlooque dwelt. I started him and another buck, but failed to obtain a shot. I then set my after-riders to beat up the cover, and they started them two or three times, but I was still unsuccessful. We now started for the bees' nest, which was in an old hollow tree. I kindled a large fire in front of the hole, and having smoked them with dry grass took out the honey, which was excellent. I got, however, about fifty stings on my hands and arms. In the afternoon I inspanned, and crossed the Macoolwey a few miles above its junction with the Limpopo. The natives again tried hard to lead me to Seleka, but I would not leave the Limpopo, and accordingly sheered off to its banks, which I reached by bright moonlight. Here we heard hippopotami snorting in the river, and lions roared near us all night long. Next day I had the luck to shoot two very fine old buck serolomootlooques.

On the 27th I rode down the river at dawn of day, and ordered my waggons to follow in two hours. Whilst riding along the river's bank, some distance beyond the limits of yesterday's ride, opposite to a broad sandbank densely covered with reeds, I heard a loud plunge, which was immediately followed by the welcome blowing sound of sea-cows. I instantly divested myself of my leather trousers, and went down into the reeds, where I came suddenly upon a crocodile of average size, lying in a shallow back stream; and on his attempting to gain the main river, I shot him with a bullet in the shoulder: he lay dead on the spot. This was the first crocodile which I had managed to lay my hands upon, although I had shot many. The sound of my rifle alarmed the sea-cows; some took up, and some down the river. I was unfortunate with them, shooting two and losing them both. As I was seeking the wounded hippopotami, my waggons came up. Soon after breakfast, the chief Seleka, with a number of his aristocracy, paid me a visit; and in the afternoon I rode down the river, ordering my waggons to follow, and found the fresh spoor of a mighty old bull elephant.

I rode forth at sunrise on the 28th, ordering my waggons to follow in two hours. Seleka had sent men down the river, before it was clear, to seek sea-cows; and they soon came running after me to say that they had found some. I accordingly followed them to the river, where, in a long, broad, and deep bend, were four hippopotami, two full-grown cows, a small cow, and a calf. At the tail of this pool was a strong and rapid stream, which thundered along in Highland fashion over large masses of dark rock.

On coming to the shady bank, I could at first only see one old cow and calf. When they dived I ran into the reeds, and as the cow came up I shot her in the head; she, however, got away down the river, and I lost her. The other three took away up the river, and became very shy, remaining under the water for five minutes at a time, and then only popping their heads up for a few seconds. I accordingly remained quiet behind the reeds, in hope of their dismissing their alarms. Presently the two smaller ones seemed to be no longer frightened, popping up their entire heads, and remaining above water for a minute at a time; but the third, which was by far the largest, and which I thought must be a bull, continued extremely shy, remaining under the water for ten minutes at a time, and then just showing her face for a second, making a blowing like a whale, and returning to the bottom. I stood there with rifle at my shoulder, and my eye on the sight, until I was quite tired. I thought I should never get a chance at her, and had just resolved to fire at one of the smaller ones, when she shoved up half her head and looked about her. I made a correct shot; the ball cracked loudly below her ear, and the huge body of the sea-cow came floundering to the top. I was enchanted; she could not escape. Though not dead she had lost her senses, and continued swimming round and round, sometimes beneath and sometimes at the surface of the water, creating a fearful commotion.

Hearing my waggons coming on, I sent a message to my followers to outspan, and to come and behold Behemoth floundering in her native element. When they came up I finished her with a shot in the neck, upon which she instantly sank to the bottom, and disappeared in the strong rapid torrent at the tail of the sea-cow hole. There she remained for a long time, and I thought that I had lost her, but the natives said that she would soon reappear. Being in want of refreshment, I left my people to watch for the resurrection of Behemoth, and I held to the waggon to feed. While taking my breakfast there was a loud hue-and-cry among the natives, that the koodoo had floated and was sailing down the river. It was so, and my Hottentots swam in and brought her to the bank. Her flesh proved most excellent. In the afternoon I rode down the river with Ruyter, and shot one very splendid old waterbuck with a princely head, which I kept.

The next day, after proceeding a few miles, I killed a very fine buck of the serolomootlooque. I again rode down the river's bank, with two after-riders, to seek hippopotami, the natives reporting that they were to be found in a pool in advance, where another river joined the Limpopo. After riding a short distance I found the banks unusually green and shady, and very much frequented by the sea-cow; and presently in a broad, deep, and long still bend of the river, I disturbed the game I sought.

They were lying in their sandy beds among the rank reeds at the river's margin, and on hearing me galloping over the gravelly shingle between the bank and the reeds, the deposit of some great flood, they plunged into their native stronghold in dire alarm, and commenced blowing, snorting, and uttering a sound very similar to that made by the musical instrument called a serpent. It was a fairish place for an attack, so, divesting myself of my leather trousers, I ordered my after-riders to remain utterly silent, and then crept cautiously forward, determined not to fire a shot until I had thoroughly overhauled the herd to see if it did not contain a bull, and at all events to secure, if possible, the very finest head amongst them.

The herd consisted of about fourteen hippopotami; ten of these were a little farther down the stream than the other four. Having carefully examined these ten, I made out two particular hippopotami decidedly larger than all the others. I then crept a little distance up the river behind the reeds, to obtain a view of the others. They were two enormous old cows with two large calves beside them. The old ones had exactly the same size of head as the two best cows below; I accordingly chose what I thought the best of these two, and, making a fine shot at the side of her head, I at once disabled her. She disappeared for a few seconds, and then came floundering to the surface, and continued swimming round and round, sometimes diving, and then reappearing with a loud splash and a blowing noise, always getting slowly down the river, until I re-attacked and finished her a quarter of a mile farther down, about an hour after.

The other sea-cows were now greatly alarmed, and only occasionally put up their heads, showing but a small part, remaining but a few seconds at a time. I, however, managed to select one of the three remaining ones, and, making a most perfect shot, I sent a bullet crashing into her brain. This caused instantaneous death, and she sank to the bottom. I then wounded two more sea-cows in the head, both of which I lost. The others were so alarmed and cunning that it was impossible to do anything with them.

The one I had first shot was now resting with half her body above water on a sandbank in the Limpopo, at the mouth of the other river Lepalala, which was broad, clear, and rapid. From this resting-place I started her with one shot in the shoulder and another in the side of the head; this last shot set her in motion once more, and she commenced struggling in the water in the most extraordinary manner, disappearing for a few seconds and then coming up like a great whale, setting the whole river in an uproar. Presently she took away down the stream, holding to the other side, but, again returning, I finished her with a shot in the middle of the forehead.

This proved a most magnificent specimen of the female of the wondrous hippopotamus, an animal with which I was extremely surprised and delighted. She far surpassed the brightest conceptions I had formed of her, being a larger, a more lively, and in every way a more interesting animal than certain writers had led me to expect. On securing this fine sea-cow I immediately cut off her head and placed it high and dry: this was a work of considerably difficulty for four men. We left her body in the water, being of course, unable to do anything with it there. It was well I secured the head when I did, for next morning the crocodiles had dragged her away.

I held up the river to see what the other sea-cows were doing, when to my particular satisfaction, I beheld the body of the other huge sea-cow which I had shot in the brain floating in the pool where I had shot her, and stationary within about twenty yards of the other side. I then held down the river to the tail of the pool, where the stream was broad and rapid and less likely to hold crocodiles, and here, although cold and worn out, I swam across to secure my game. The waggons now came up, and two of my Hottentots swam over to my assistance; but just as we were going in to secure the sea-cow, she became disengaged from the invisible fetters that had held her, and which turned out to be the branch of a gigantic old tree that some flood had lodged in the bottom of the pool. The sea-cow now floated down the middle of the river; when she neared the tail of the pool, we swam in and inclined her course to shore, and stranded her on a fine gravel bank.

This truly magnificent specimen was just about the same size as the first, and apparently older, but her teeth were not so thick. Ordering the natives at once to cut off her huge head, and having seen it deposited safely on the bank along with that of her comrade, I held for my waggons, having to cross the Lepalala to reach them. I was very cold and worn out, but most highly gratified at my good fortune in first killing, and then in securing, two out of the four best sea-cows in a herd of fourteen.

CHAPTER XXVI.

Seleka's Town among the Rocks—Elephant-hunting with Seleka and his Men—Trading with Seleka—A Lion and Lioness with their Cubs—An immense Herd of Hippopotami—Nine of them killed—Trap for inflicting poisoned Wounds on Sea-cows—We cross the Limpopo, and a Waggon sticks in the River—We trek down the Stream—Two of my best Horses killed and eaten by Lions—The Chief of the Bamalette visits me—Audacity of the Lions—A Horse killed in a Pitfall—A Chief flogged for catching and consuming a Horse.

On the 1st of July I inspanned at sunrise and marched to the town of the Baseleka, which I reached in about four hours, having crossed the Lepalala on the way. I outspanned on the bank of the river. Seleka's town is built on the top and sides of a steep and precipitous white quartz rock, which rises abruptly, and forms a very remarkable feature in the green forest scenery which surrounds it. In the evening Seleka brought down four fairish bull elephant's teeth, which I bought for four muskets.

On the morrow I took an early breakfast, and then held east with Seleka and about a hundred and fifty of his men to seek elephants, they having heard from the Bakalahari of the position of a troop of bulls. This day I might reckon as the beginning of my elephant-hunting this season. As the country appeared to me well adapted for the sport, and as I regretted not a little that my men and a good stud of horses should be idle at the waggons while they might be bringing me in fifty pounds once or twice a-week, I armed and mounted John Stofolus and Carey, both of whom vaunted much of their courage and skill. I instructed them, in the event of our finding, to select a good elephant, and, if not able to kill him, at least to hold him in view until I had finished mine, which I promised to do as quickly as possible, and then to come to their assistance.

We had not proceeded far from the white rock when we entered a forest frequented by elephants, and we very soon came upon the fresh spoor of a troop of about ten fine bulls. The spooring was conducted very properly, the old chief taking the greatest care of the wind, keeping his followers far back, and maintaining silence, extending picquets in advance, and to the right and left, and ordering them to ascend to the summits of the tallest trees to obtain a correct view of the surrounding forest. Presently the mighty game was detected. Old Schwartland was led alongside of me, and my dogs were all in the couples, eight in number. I quickly mounted, and, riding slowly forward, obtained a blink of one of the elephants.

I called to the natives to slip the dogs, and then dashed forward for a selection. I chose the last, and gave him a shot as he passed me, and then riding hard under his stern I yelled like a demon to clear him from his comrades and to bring the dogs to my assistance. The dogs came as I expected to my elephant, and I shot him from the saddle in a business-like style, loading and firing with great rapidity; he took from fifteen to twenty shots before he fell. All this time I listened in vain for shots from John or Carey. The former did not even consider himself safe in the same forest with the elephants, and had slunk away from Carey while in sight of a splendid bull; nor did we hear more of him that day. Carey did but little better, for he lost his elephant immediately, one charge being sufficient.

The natives were now fighting with an immense old bull: hearing them, I rode in their direction, and came upon Carey stationary in the forest. Here the dogs took up the scent of an elephant, and I followed them, but they eventually dropped it. I then tried to retrace my steps to the dead elephant, which I did by chance, having lost my way in the level boundless jungle and wandered far. I found a few natives, who reported their captain and most of his men to be still engaged with the elephant, and they said that Carey had joined them in the chase. I off-saddled for a little, but, hearing the cries of the natives in the distance, I saddled old Schwartland, and rode onward till I found the natives and Carey quite done up, and on the point of dropping the game. The elephant, although red with blood, and resembling a porcupine from the number of the assagais, was little the worse for all that he had received. I then attacked him, and, with eight or ten shots, ended his career.

Next morning, Bakalahari coming up and reporting to have heard elephants during the night, old Seleka and I went in quest of them. We were joined by the gallant and vaunting John Stofolus; who had slept at the waggons, and swore that he had lost his way in a long chase after an elephant. Both he and Carey expressing regret for their previous mismanagement, and vowing to prove themselves men this day, I allowed them to accompany me. We soon took up the spoor of one old bull, which led us into a forest thoroughly ploughed up and broken with bull elephants. Here this fine fellow joined a glorious squadron of from twenty to thirty mighty bulls. When we discovered their position I dashed forward, shouting to the dogs, and was instantly in the middle of them. Then followed a wondrous scene. The elephants, panic-stricken, charged forward, levelling the forest before them, trumpeting, with trunks and tails aloft, as the dogs mingled with them.

Looking back over my shoulder I beheld the elephants come crashing on behind and within a few yards of me. I then pressed forward, overtook about ten bulls that were inclining to the west, rode under their sterns, chose the best, and, yelling at the top of my voice, I separated him from his comrades, and brought my dogs to my assistance. In a few minutes he had many mortal wounds. Not hearing my trusty John and Carey fire, and the elephant's course being right towards camp, I ceased firing and drove him on before me. Presently these worthies came up to me, having been after a most splendid bull—the cock of the troop—which I in my haste, had ridden by. They had fired two or three shots, and then left him.

I now saw that all my hunting this season must depend on my own single hand, as my followers, instead of a help, were a very great hinderance and annoyance to me. If I had been alone that day I should most certainly have taken more time, and have selected the elephant they had lost, which the natives said carried extremely large and long teeth. Presently, my elephant declining to proceed farther, and, becoming extremely wicked, I recommenced firing, and at last he fell, having received twenty-nine balls, twenty-seven of these being in a very correct part. This was an enormous first-rate bull; but his teeth, though large, being not the best in the troop, I felt very much dissatisfied.

On the forenoon of the 5th I traded with Seleka for karosses of pallah's skin and tusks of elephants, and in the evening I walked up to inspect the town, and climbed to the summit of the quartz rock on which the citadel of Seleka is situated. Here I viewed the surrounding country; chains of mountains of moderate height shot above the level forest in every direction, but mostly to the east and south.

The next day, after breakfast, I saddled up steeds and took the field for elephants, accompanied by two after-riders. We were soon joined by the greater part of the Seleka tribe, and held about south, following the bank of the river Lepalala, which we eventually crossed. Having proceeded some distance through a tract but little frequented by elephants, men who had been sent to seek in a south-westerly direction came and reported that they had found. We then held at once for a steep and very rocky hill which rose abruptly in the forest, and on the west side of which the elephants had been seen. We had ascended about half-way up this hill, the natives following on in a long string and detached parties, when we discovered that we had nearly hemmed in a huge and most daring old lion, with his partner and a troop of very small cubs. I had passed him within about sixty yards, and was a little above him on the hill before I was aware of his presence. He gave us notice of his proximity by loud and continued growling, advancing boldly with open jaws towards the natives. These fled before him; and the lioness having now slunk away with her cubs, and some of our dogs having attacked him, he turned right about and followed slowly after his mate, growling fearfully.

We feared that all this noise might have started the elephants: when, however, we had gained a commanding point on the shoulder of the hill, we could see them standing in a thick low forest a short distance from the base of the hill; it was a troop of very middling cow elephants with a number of calves of all sizes: about half a mile to the north we could see another troop of cows. I wished to attack these, but the natives prevailed upon me to attack the nearest troop. Leaving the greater part of the natives to watch our movements from this elevated position, I descended the hill and held for the mighty game. I felt rather nervous on this ocassion. I was not in good health, and the forest here was not well adapted for the sport, the cover being thick, with a great deal of bad wait-a-bit thorns.

When we came upon the troop they were considerably scattered, and we first approached two very indifferent cows, which, hearing us, instantly retreated into the thick cover. I would not follow these, but at once slipped my dogs in the hope that they would find me better elephants. The dogs then ran forward in different directions, and immediately a loud trumpeting followed from three detachment of cows. Galloping forward, I obtained a view of them all. There was but one right good cow in the troop: she brought up the rear of a detachment which came crashing past on my right, making for the densest cover round the base of the hill. This cow carried two fine long white tusks, one of them with a very sharp point. On attacking her she at once separated from her comrades, and every one of my dogs took, as is usual, away after the calves; galloping up alongside and very near this cow, and firing from the saddle I bowled her over with a single ball behind the shoulder.

On the 11th we marched at dawn of day, holding north-east, and halted on the bank of the Limpopo. There the waggons remained, whilst I hunted the banks of the river, bagging two first-rate bull elephants and one hippopotamus. One of these elephants I shot across the Limpopo, under the mountains of Guapa; I fought him in dense wait-a-bit jungle from half-past eleven till the sun was under, when his tough old spirit fled, and the venerable monarch of the forest fell, pierced with fifty-seven balls. On the 17th we inspanned and trekked about five miles down the stream, when I halted beside a long deep hippopotamus hole, in which were two bulls and one cow, but it being late I did not trouble them.

The next day I rode down the river to seek sea-cows, accompanied by my two after-riders; taking, as usual, my double-barrelled rifles. We had proceeded about two miles when we came upon some most thoroughly beaten old-established hippopotamus paths, and presently, in a broad, long, deep, and shaded pool of the river, we heard the sea-cows bellowing. There I beheld one of the most wondrous and interesting sights that a sportsman can be blessed with. I at once knew that there must be an immense herd of them, for the voices came from different parts of the pool; so, creeping in through the bushes to obtain an inspection, a large sandy island appeared at the neck of the pool, on which stood several large shady trees.

The neck of the pool was very wide and shallow, with rocks and large stones; below it was deep and still. On a sandy promontory of this island stood about thirty cows and calves, whilst in the pool opposite, and a little below them, stood about twenty more sea-cows, with their heads and backs above water. About fifty yards farther down the river again, showing out their heads, were eight or ten immense fellows, which I think were all bulls; and about one hundred yards below these in the middle of the stream stood another herd of about eight or ten cows with calves, and two huge bulls. The sea-cows lay close together like pigs; a favourite position was to rest their heads on their comrades' sterns and sides. The herds were attended by an immense number of the invariable rhinoceros birds, which, on observing me, did their best to spread alarm throughout the hippotami. I was resolved to select if possible a first-rate old bull out of this vast herd, and I accordingly delayed firing for nearly two hours, continually running up and down behind the thick thorny cover, attentively studying the heads. At length I determined to go close in and select the best head out of the eight or ten bulls which lay below the cows. I accordingly left the cover and walked slowly forward in full view of the whole herd to the water's edge, where I lay down on my belly and studied the heads of these bulls. The cows, on seeing me, splashed into the water and kept up a continual snorting and blowing till night set in.

After selecting for a few minutes I fired my first shot at a splendid bull, and sent the ball in a little behind the eye. He was at once incapacitated, and kept plunging and swimming round and round, wearing away down the pool, until I finished him with two more shots. The whole pool was now in a state of intense commotion. The best cows and the bulls at once became very shy and cunning, showing only the flat roofs of their heads, and sometimes only their nostrils. The younger cows were not so shy, producing the whole head; and if I had wished to make a bag I might have shot an immense number. This however was not my object; and as there was likely to be a difficulty in securing what I did kill, I determined only to fire at the very best. When, therefore, the sun went down I had not fired a great many shots, but had bagged five first-rate hippopotami, four cows and one bull, and besides these there were three or four more very severely wounded which were spouting blood throughout the pool.

The next day I removed my waggons to the bank where I had waged successful war with the hippopotami. Here we halted beneath a shady tree with a very dark green leaf, and having drawn up the waggons we cast loose the trektows, and marching the two spans of oxen down to the edge of the river we dragged out one of the sea-cows high and dry. After breakfast I rode down the river with Carey to seek those I had wounded. Having ridden about three miles down the river, we heard sea-cows snorting; and on dismounting from my horse and creeping in through very dense thorny cover which here clothed the banks, I found a very fine herd of about thirty hippopotami basking in the sun: they lay upon a sand-bank in the middle of the river, in about three feet of water. After taking a long time to make a selection I opened my fire and discharged my four barrels: one sea-cow lay dead, and two others were stunned and took to the other side, but eventually recovered and were not numbered with the slain. I continued with them till sundown and fired a good many shots, but only bagged one other cow: they were very shy and cunning.

On the 20th I again rode down the river to the pool, and found a herd of sea-cows still there; so I remained with them till sundown, and bagged two very first-rate old sea-cows, which were forthcoming next day. This day I detected a most dangerous trap constructed by the Bakalahari for slaying sea-cows. It consisted of a sharp little assagai or spike most thoroughly poisoned, and stuck firmly into the end of a heavy block of thorn-wood about four feet long and five inches in diameter. This formidable affair was suspended over the centre of a sea-cow path at a height of about thirty feet from the ground by a bark cord which passed over a high branch of a tree and thence to a peg on the other side, where it was fastened. To the suspending cord were two triggers so constructed that, when the sea-cow struck against the cord which led across the path, the heavy block above was set at liberty, which instantly dropped with immense force with poisonous dart, inflicting a sure and mortal wound. The bones and old teeth of sea-cows which lay rotting along the bank of the river here evinced the success of this dangerous invention. I remained in the neighbourhood of the pool for several days, during which time I bagged no less than fifteen first-rate hippopotami, the greater portion of them being bulls.

At dawn of day on the 28th we inspanned and marched up the river to the drift. All hands worked hard in cutting down the bank on the opposite side, the Bakalahari assisting us; and in the afternoon we got the cap-tent waggon, which was very lightly laden, through the river, with twelve oxen. The baggage-waggon stuck fast in the mud, and remained there all night, with the fore-wheels half way up the bank, and the after-chest under the water; and although we put twenty oxen to it, we could not get it out.

The next day our first work was to reduce the bank on which the waggon stood, after which, with considerable difficulty, we got it out with twenty of my best oxen. The whole day we were busy drying the innumerable contents of the fore and after chests of each waggon, almost everything being thoroughly saturated, and I sustained considerable loss in fine powder, percussion-caps, biscuit, tea, coffee, sugar, and a number of other articles, some of which were damaged and some entirely destroyed.

I marched at dawn of day on the 30th. Seleka and his men and my hired Baquaines had done all in their power to prevent my proceeding farther; but as they could not conceal the waters from me, my course being to follow the Limpopo, I was perfectly independent of them. They remained by me until I crossed the Limpopo, and then they all turned home. I was now once more without natives, and held down the north-western bank of the river, but very soon Bakalahari joined us, and their numbers increased as we held on. I had the good luck this day to bag five more first-rate hippopotami.

The next day, after assisting my men to get out some of the sea-cows, I rode down the river with two after-riders to explore. Having ridden a few miles, I came upon a troop of twelve, the best of which I disabled and killed the next day. This was a most splendid old cow, and carried tusks far superior to any we had yet seen; in the afternoon I bagged six more.

From a continued run of good luck in all my hunting expeditions with my horses and oxen, in regard to lions and Bakalahari pitfalls, I had become foolishly careless of them, and I had got into a most dangerous custom of allowing the cattle to feed about the waggons long after the sun was under. I was always boasting of my good luck, and used to say that the lions knew that the cattle belonged to me, and feared to molest them. This night, however, a bitter lesson was in store for me. The sun as usual had been under an hour before I ordered my men to make fast my horses: the oxen had of their own accord come to the waggons and lain down; the horses, however, were not forthcoming. My hired natives, who were now anxious to prevent my proceeding farther from their country, were wilfully neglecting their charge, and, instead of looking after my cattle, they were exchanging the flesh and fat of my sea-cows for assagais, etc., with the Bakalahari.

The night was very dark, and the horses were sought for in vain. I remarked to Carey that it was some since we had heard the voice of a lion; but a few minutes after we heard the low moan of the king of beasts repeated several times at no great distance, and in the very direction in which my horses were supposed to be.

The next day the sun had been up two hours, and my horses could not yet be found. I entertained no apprehensions, however, from the lion, but rather suspected some plot between Seleka and my natives to drive my cattle back, and so force me to retrace my steps. I therefore ordered John Stofolus and Hendrick to take bridles and a supply of meat, and to follow up the spoor wherever it might lead; and being anxious to see which way it went, I took a rifle and followed in quest of it myself. Observing a number of vultures to the west, and hearing the voices of natives in that direction, I proceeded thither at top speed.

To my utter horror, I found my two most valuable and especially favourite veteran shooting-horses lying fearfully mangled and half consumed by a troop of ruthless lions. They were "Black Jock" and "Schwartland," the former a first-rate young horse, worth £24, the latter aged, but by far my most valuable steed, being perhaps the best shooting-horse in Southern Africa; he knew no fear, and would approach as near as I chose to elephant or lion, or any description of game. From his back I had shot nearly all my elephants last year; and so fond was I of this horse, that I never rode or even saddled him until we had found elephants, when I used him in the fight and then immediately off-saddled.

With a sickening heart I turned from this most painful scene, and, utterly dejected, I returned to camp. As there was much to do about the waggons, and as two of my men were absent seeking the lost horses, I did not immediately go in quest of the lions; this I however did in the afternoon, taking all my dogs, but I failed to find them. A large party of the natives from the south-west, the Bamalette, reached me late in the day; their object was flesh, and to endeavour to persuade me to come and trade with them. They had fallen in with three of my steeds, the others were found by my men near the drift where I had last crossed the river. I formed a very strong kraal for my cattle, and made all fast at sundown. Very soon after, the troop of lions came up to my camp on the spoor of the horses, fancying that they could repeat the tragedy of last night; they fought with my dogs in the most daring manner, off and on, until near dawn of day, driving them in to the fire-side. The cattle were very restive, and nearly broke away, but the kraal was good and saved them.

In the morning, ordering my waggons to follow, I rode down the river, followed by at least two hundred natives, to secure the hippopotami shot two days previous. Six of these were forthcoming, and we set about getting them to the side: they lay upon the rocks in the middle of the river. One of these proved to be an out-and-outer, a tearing old bull with tusks which far surpassed anything I had yet seen, and quite perfect; I was very much gratified with this fine trophy. There were also two of the cows which carried immense and perfect tusks. When the waggons came up, I found myself minus another steed: a fine young mare had fallen into a Bakalahari pitfall, and had been suffocated.

On the 5th I rode down the river and fell in with a large herd of about thirty hippopotami: they lay upon some rocks in the middle of a very long and broad pool. I wounded seven or eight of these in the head, and killed two, a bull and a cow, both of which we found next day. At night the lions prowled around our camp, and fought with the dogs until the morning: they came boldly in between the fires of the natives, who lay around my camp.

The next day I ordered my waggons to come on, and I rode ahead to the pool where I had last shot. When the waggons came up, I detected the head Bakalahari of the kraal beside which my mare had been killed; he was talking with my cattle herds, with whom he seemed to be on very intimate terms. This killing of my horse was either intentional or most culpably careless, as the pits were left covered, and the cattle driven to pasture in the middle of them; I accordingly deemed it proper that this man should be made an example of; so, calling to my English servant, Carey, to assist me, we each seized an arm of the guilty chief, and I then caused Hendrick to flog him, with a sea-cow jambok; after which I admonished him, and told him that if the holes were not opened in future I would make a more severe example as I proceeded. The consequence of this salutary admonition was that all the pitfalls along the river were thrown open in advance of my march, a thing which I had never before seen among the Bechuana tribes. In the afternoon I rode down the river a few pools, and found a very fine herd of about thirty hippopotami. I wounded three or four of these, and killed one.

CHAPTER XXVII.

We trek down the Limpopo—Abundance of Sea-cows—The Lotsane River—An immense Herd of Elephants—Combat with a first-rate old Bull—Rheumatic Fever attacks me, which determines our course homewards—Elephants smashing Forest-trees—A Lion carries off one of my men from the Fireside—The Beast occupied consuming him all night—The man-eating Lion slain—Three Hippopotami shot—One of the Dogs eaten by a Crocodile—The fatal "Tsetse" fly—The Fountain of Seboono—An old Bull-Elephant held in check without Gun or Dogs.

I RESOLVED now to cease for a time hunting sea-cows, and to trek ahead in good earnest. I accordingly took considerable trouble in stowing the waggons properly. We then trekked down the river until sundown. I rode ahead of the waggons to explore, and was struck with astonishment at the number of the hippopotami. They seemed to increase the farther I trekked down the river; every pool had its herd; they were extremely fearless, allowing me to approach within fifteen yards of them. In the morning I found myself minus my hired natives: these ruffians, fearing to receive a chastisement similar to that of the chief of the Bakalahari, which they felt they deserved, thought it best to get out of the way in time, and had cut the service. The chief

CHAP. XXVII.

The Fate of poor Hendrick.

Matsaca brought me ivory, which I obtained in barter for muskets and some ammunition.

On the 8th we trekked at dawn of day, and after proceeding a few miles came upon the Lotsane, one of those gravelly-bedded rivers, with only water in occasional spots, such as are met with in the Bamangwato country. Here was much spoor of elephant; and the natives pressing me to halt and hunt, I outspanned and got everything ready for a trip from the waggons.

The next morning I started with a party of natives to seek elephants. We held along the banks of the Lotsane for several miles, holding a north-westerly course; after which we left the river and held south-west; and, at last, followed down to the Limpopo, and so home to camp, without finding a single fresh spoor. Here I found my old friends from Bamangwato, Mollyeon and Kapain, with a party. I was glad to see these men, as I knew they would assist me in my hunting, and they could also converse with me.

On the 10th, at dawn of day, I rode down the river, and ordered my waggons to follow. I found sea-cows more and more abundant: every pool had its herd: the margin of the river on each side was trampled down by elephants, rhinoceroces, buffaloes, etc. Having ridden about six miles, I found the fresh spoor of a troop of bull elephants. I off-saddled, and in an hour the waggons came up, when I took up the spoor, accompanied by Carey, Hendrick, and Ruyter. After following the spoor for some miles, the natives lost it. A little distance ahead of us was a rocky hill, to the summit of which I ascended. This spot commanded a good view of the adjacent forest. I at once detected an immense herd of elephants. They were drinking in a wide open spot on a gravelly-bedded river which falls into the Limpopo, called by the natives Suking.

We then made a turn to leeward and came in upon this fine herd; it was the largest I had ever seen; there must have been upwards of one hundred elephants before my eye at once. The troop consisted chiefly of cows and calves; I however detected one fine well-grown bull, carrying very fair tusks. I rode slowly towards him, followed by my men, and the natives leading the dogs. We advanced unobserved until we were within twenty yards of some of the outside cows. Here I enjoyed a fine view of the herd; they stood drinking on a vast surface of granite rock, and, though no trees intervened between us and them, they took not the slightest notice of us.

At length I gave the bull a shot in the shoulder and then followed him up. He stumbled, and fell once upon the slippery rock, but, recovering his feet, went off at a pace which I could hardly equal on the dangerous ground. By good luck, most of my dogs came to my assistance, and I slew him in a few minutes with eight or ten shots. I had directed Hendrick and Carey to try to hold some of the cows for me until I was ready with the bull; accordingly, these doughty Nimrods followed and turned four cows for a short time, and then left them, without even firing a shot to advise me of their course; the consequence of which was, that I knocked up myself, my dogs, and horses, in chasing the retreating herd to a great distance, to no purpose.

On the following day I shot another bull elephant and a white rhinoceros; and on the afternoon of the 12th, returning to camp weary and worn, I came unexpectedly upon a bull elephant of unusual size, standing in the shade on the margin of the Limpopo. He took refuge in an extensive jungle of impracticable wait-a-bits, where it was impossible to do anything on horseback, and I was therefore obliged to hunt him on foot. I slew him with thirty bullets after an extremely severe and dangerous combat of about two hours. I afterwards felt much the worse for this severe exertion.

On the 14th I despatched Hendrick to bring on the waggons, which came up in the afternoon. Night set in warm, calm, and still, with a good moonlight. Elephants, sea-cows, and panthers kept up a continued music above and below us along the river until I fell asleep.

On the 15th I felt very ill, but in the forenoon I went down to the river, where I shot two sea-cows. In the evening, feeling worse, I bled myself, but strong fever was on me all night.

Next morning I marched, halting at sundown on the Mokojay, a gravelly-bedded periodical river, where elephants occasionally drank.

On the 18th at dawn of day I took leave of Mollyeon and Kapain of Bamangwato, as they would not follow me farther. We then inspanned, and held down the Limpopo. I regretted to observe that the spoor of elephants did not seem to increase in the same ratio as I had allowed myself to imagine. We were in an extremely remote and secluded corner of the world, quite uninhabited; yet the elephants, though frequenting it, were decidedly scarce. I felt extremely weak and nervous from the fever and the quantity of blood which I had lost, in so much that I started at my own shadow, and several times sprang to one side when the leaves rustled in the bushes. I walked along the bank of the river with my gun loaded with small shot, intending to shoot a partridge for my breakfast. Presently I came upon the fresh dung of bull elephants, and at the same moment my people at the waggons saw two old bull elephants within two hundred yards of them; and the wind being favourable, they walked unsuspiciously away.

A singular piece of good luck here occurred; on beholding the elephants my weakness (brought on by bleeding) and my nervousness of mind immediately left me.

Having caught and saddled steeds, I attacked these two noble elephants, and had the good fortune to secure them both, while my oxen were standing close by in their yokes, and my people were looking on. I was enabled to do this by the assistance of my dogs, who kept one of the elephants in play until his comrade was mortally wounded, when I galloped hard to their assistance, and secured him before the first had fallen to the ground.

On the 20th, early in the morning, I rode some distance down the river, with one after-rider, to explore. I found the country here not much frequented by elephants; I, however, found the fresh spoor of one troop, but I was much too weak to follow it. Following an elephant path in very rocky ground, I came suddenly within ten yards of an old bull buffalo, who instantly charged me most fiercely, and had not my horse been most particularly active I could not have escaped him : so headlong was his charge that he lost his footing in the rocky ground, and fell with amazing violence, getting up and retreating quite crippled with the fall. A little after this I had ascended to the summit of a tree to obtain a view of the surrounding forest, when two white rhinoceroses came trotting up, despite my shouting, and stood within fifteen yards of my already terrified steeds.

My fever still continuing on me, and the natives having deserted, I determined upon turning my face homewards. Accordingly, on the 21st, I ordered my men to inspan and retrace their spoor. A troop of lions had killed some game within a few hundred yards of us, and had been roaring very loudly all the morning : these gave us a parting salute as we were inspanning. Their voices sounded to me ominous, perhaps from the nervous state of my health. I thought they said, " Yes, you do well to retrace your rash steps ; you have just come far enough." I must acknowledge that I felt a little anxious as to the safety of proceeding farther on several accounts. First, the natives had spoken of Moselekatse, now resident not very far in advance, as one who would most unquestionably murder me, and seize all my property. They also told me that I should lose all my cattle by the fly called "Tsetse;" and I had also reason to believe the country in advance not very healthy for man.

My followers received my orders to turn homewards with sincere gratification : we trekked till sundown, halting on the march for a sick ox, which we eventually left behind a prey to the lions, and slept on the Mokojay, where the Bamangwato men had left me.

On the 29th we arrived at a small village of Bakalahari. These natives told me that elephants were abundant on the opposite side of the river. I accordingly resolved to halt here and hunt, and drew my waggons up on the river's bank, within thirty yards of the water and about one hundred yards from the native village. Having outspanned, we at once set about making for the cattle a kraal of the worst description of thorn-trees. Of this I had now become very particular, since my severe loss by lions on the first of this month ; and my cattle were, at night, secured by a strong kraal, which enclosed my two waggons, the horses being made fast to a trektow stretched between the hind-wheels of the waggons. I had yet, however, a fearful lesson to learn as to the nature and character of the lion, of which I had at one time entertained so little fear ; and on this night a horrible tragedy was to be acted in my little lonely camp of so very awful and appalling a nature as to make the blood curdle in our veins. I worked till near sundown at one side of the kraal with Hendrick, my first waggon-driver—I cutting down the trees with my axe, and he dragging them to the kraal. When the kraal for the cattle was finished, I turned my attention to making a pot of barley-broth, and lighted a fire between the waggons and the water, close on the river's bank, under a dense grove of shady trees, making no sort of kraal around our sitting-place for the evening.

The Hottentots, without any reason, made their fire about fifty yards from mine; they, accordingly to their usual custom, being satisfied with the shelter of a large dense bush. The evening passed away cheerfully. Soon after it was dark we heard elephants breaking the trees in the forest across the river; and once or twice I strode away into the darkness some distance from the fireside, to stand and listen to them. I little, at that moment, deemed of the imminent peril to which I was exposing my life, nor thought that a bloodthirsty man-eater lion was crouching near, and only watching his opportunity to spring in the midst of us, and consign one of our number to a most terrible death.

About three hours after the sun went down I called to my men to come and take their coffee and supper, which was ready for them at my fire; and after supper three of them returned before their comrades to their own fireside, and lay down; these were John Stofolus, Hendrick, and Ruyter. In a few minutes an ox came out by the gate of the kraal and walked round the back of it. Hendrick got up and drove him in again, and then went back to his fireside and lay down. Hendrick and Ruyter lay on one side of the fire under one blanket, and John Stofolus lay on the other. At this moment I was sitting taking some barley-broth; our fire was very small, and the night was pitch-dark and windy. Owing to our proximity to the native village the wood was very scarce, the Bakalahari having burnt it all in their fires.

Suddenly the appalling and murderous voice of an angry bloodthirsty lion burst upon my ear within a few yards of us, followed by the shrieking of the Hottentots. Again and again the murderous roar of attack was repeated. We heard John and Ruyter shriek "The lion! the lion"! still, for a few moments, we thought he was but chasing one of the dogs round the kraal; but, next instant, John Stofolus rushed into the midst of us almost speechless with fear and terror, his eyes bursting from their sockets, and shrieked out, "The lion! the lion! He has got Hendrick; he dragged him away from the fire beside me. I struck him with the burning brands upon his head, but he would not let go his hold. Hendrick is dead! Oh, God! Hendrick is dead! Let us take fire and seek him."

The rest of my people rushed about, shrieking and yelling as if they were mad. I was at once angry with them for their folly, and told them that if they did not stand still and keep quiet the lion would have another of us; and that very likely there was a troop of them. I ordered the dogs, which were nearly all fast, to be made loose, and the fire to be increased as far as could be. I then shouted Hendrick's name, but all was still. I told my men that Hendrick was dead, and that a regiment of soldiers could not now help him, and, hunting my dogs forward, I had everything brought within the cattle kraal, when we lighted our fire and closed the entrance as well as we could.

My terrified people sat round the fire with guns in their hands till the day broke, still fancying that every moment the lion would return and spring again into the midst of us. When the dogs were first let go, the stupid brutes, as dogs often prove when most required, instead of going at the lion, rushed fiercely on one another, and fought desperately for some minutes. After this they got his wind, and, going at him, disclosed to us his position: they kept up a continued barking until the day dawned, the lion occasionally springing after them and driving them in upon the kraal. The horrible monster lay all night within forty yards of us, consuming the wretched man whom he had chosen for his prey. He had dragged him into a little hollow at the back of the thick bush, beside which the fire was kindled, and there he remained till the day dawned, careless of our proximity.

It appeared that when the unfortunate Hendrick rose to drive in the ox, the lion had watched him to his fireside, and he had scarcely lain down when the brute sprang upon him and Ruyter (for both lay under one blanket), with his appalling murderous roar, and, roaring as he lay, grappled him with his fearful claws, and kept biting him on the breast and shoulder, all the while feeling for his neck; having got hold of which, he at once dragged him away backwards round the bush into the dense shade.

As the lion lay upon the unfortunate man he faintly cried "Help me, help me! Oh, God! men, help me!" After which the fearful beast got a hold of his neck, and then all was still, except that his comrades heard the bones of his neck cracking between the teeth of the lion. John Stofolus had lain with his back to the fire on the opposite side, and on hearing the lion he sprang up, and, seizing a large flaming brand, he had belaboured him on the head with the burning wood; but the brute did not take any notice of him. The Bushman had a narrow escape; he was not altogether scatheless, the lion having inflicted two gashes in his seat with his claws.

The next morning, just as the day began to dawn, we heard the lion dragging something up the river-side under cover of the bank. We drove the cattle out of the kraal, and then proceeded to inspect the scene of the night's awful tragedy. In the hollow, where the lion had lain consuming his prey, we found one leg of the unfortunate Hendrick, bitten off below the knee, the shoe still on his foot; the grass and bushes were all stained with his blood, and fragments of his pea-coat lay around. Poor Hendrick! I knew the fragments of that old coat, and had often marked them hanging in the dense covers where the elephant had charged after my unfortunate after-rider. Hendrick was by far the best man I had about my waggons, of a most cheerful disposition, a first-rate waggon-driver, fearless in the field, ever active, willing, and obliging: his loss to us all was very serious. I felt confounded and utterly sick in my heart; I could not remain at the waggons, so I resolved to go after elephants to divert my mind. I had that morning heard them breaking the trees on the opposite side of the river. I accordingly told the natives of the village of my intentions; and having ordered my people to devote the day to fortifying the kraal, I started with Piet and Ruyter as my after-riders. It was a very cool day. We crossed the river, and at once took up the fresh spoor of a troop of bull elephants.

These bulls unfortunately joined a troop of cows, and when we came on them the dogs attacked the cows, and the bulls were off in a moment, before we could even see them. One remarkably fine old cow charged the dogs. I hunted this cow, and finished her with two shots from the saddle. Being anxious to return to my people before night, I did not attempt to follow the troop. My followers were not a little gratified to see me returning, for terror had taken hold of their minds, and they expected that the lion would return, and, emboldened by the success of the preceding night, would prove still more daring in his attack. The lion would most certainly have returned, but fate had otherwise ordained. My health had been better in the last three days : my fever was leaving me, but I was, of course, still very weak. It would still be two hours before the sun would set, and, feeling refreshed by a little rest, and able for further work, I ordered the steeds to be saddled, and went in search of the lion.

I took John and Carey as after-riders, armed, and a party of the natives followed up the spoor and led the dogs. The lion had dragged the remains of poor Hendrick along a native footpath that led up the river-side. We found fragments of his coat all along the spoor, and at last the mangled coat itself. About six hundred yards from our camp a dry river's course joined the Limpopo. At this spot was much shade, cover, and heaps of dry reeds and trees deposited by the Limpopo in some great flood. The lion had left the footpath and entered this secluded spot. I at once felt convinced that we were upon him, and ordered the natives to make loose the dogs. These walked suspiciously forward on the spoor, and next minute began to spring about, barking angrily, with all their hair bristling on their backs : a crash upon the dry reeds immediately followed—it was the lion bounding away. Several of the dogs were extremely afraid of him, and kept rushing continually backwards and springing aloft to obtain a view. I now pressed forward and urged them on; old Argyll and Bles took up his spoor in gallant style and led on the other dogs. Then commenced a short but lively and glorious chase, whose conclusion was the only small satisfaction that I could obtain to answer for the horrors of the preceding evening. The lion held up the river's bank for a short distance and took away through some wait-a-bit thorn cover, the best he could find, but nevertheless open. Here, in two minutes, the dogs were up with him, and he turned and stood at bay. As I approached he stood, his horrid head right to me, with open jaws growling fiercely, his tail waving from side to side.

On beholding him my blood boiled with rage. I wished that I could take him alive and torture him, and, setting my teeth, I dashed my steed forward within thirty yards of him and shouted, " *Your* time is up, old fellow." I halted my horse, and, placing my rifle to my shoulder, I waited for a broadside. This, next moment, he exposed, when I sent a bullet through his shoulder and dropped him on the spot. He rose, however, again, when I finished him with a second in the breast. The Bakalahari now came up in wonder and delight. I ordered John to cut off his head and forepaws and bring them to the waggons, and mounting my horse I galloped home, having been absent about fifteen minutes. When the Bakalahari women heard that the man-eater was dead, they all commenced dancing about with joy, calling me *their father*.

On the 6th of September, there being no flesh in camp, I galloped up the river-side to slay a hippopotamus, and presently heard a troop of them chanting behind me: I had ridden past them and not observed them. With these I was unlucky: I wounded six or seven, but did not bag one; they became very shy and cunning after the first shot, only protruding their noses. At midday I returned to camp and drank tea, after which I galloped down the river to a favourite sea-cow pool about a mile below my waggons: I was accompanied by natives carrying my rifles. I found an immense herd of at least thirty hippopotami lying upon the rocks in the middle of the river. I shot the best bull and two fine old cows, and wounded a fourth. The bull and two cows soon floated, and all three rested together on a ledge of rocks in the middle of the river. I then sent for John and Adonis, and with the assistance of the Bakalahari we got them into shallow water, where we could work upon them.

I was occupied most of the next day in superintending the cutting up of the flesh of the sea-cows, and reducing the same to biltongue, which we hung in garlands upon ox-rheims stretched between the trees, surrounding them by a strong kraal of thorn-trees.

In the evening a large party of Seleka's Bechuanas arrrived at my camp. On the 8th one of my horses died of horse sickness; it was of course my favourite, being my best shooting-horse. On reaching camp after my last hunting excursion, "Lion," my very best dog, was reported consumed by a huge crocodile, whe frequented the spot where we drew water: for such little pleasing varieties the African hunter must make up his mind; they are mere occurrences of every day.

I saddled up at an early hour, and went in quest of elephants with Seleka's men. We crossed the Limpopo and then held east through the forest for the strong fountain called Seboono. I was unlucky here, however, as I also was next day, although we hunted by a splendid fountain in a more southerly direction. When under the mountains I met with the famous fly called "tsetse," whose bite is certain death to oxen and horses. This "hunter's scourge" is similar to a fly in Scotland called "kleg," but a little smaller; they are very quick and active, and storm a horse like a swarm of bees, alighting on him in hundreds and drinking his blood. The animal thus bitten pines away and dies at periods varying from a week to three months, according to the extent to which he has been bitten.

On the 10th the chief Pocoolway arrived with a large retinue: he was a short stout man, of a prepossessing expression, and both in appearance and manner much reminded me of a certain Scottish Earl.

After three or four days' unsuccessful hunting I resolved on the 14th, there being good moonlight, to try what might be done with the elephants by night-shooting at the fountains, and I determined to make Carey shoot with me, he using the big rifle of six to the pound, and I my single-barrelled two-grooved of eight to the pound. In the forenoon we were occupied making very hard bullets and sorting our ammunition, etc., etc., for a week's expedition, and at mid-day we started, followed by about sixty natives. We crossed the Limpopo, and held about east, right away through the forest, for the fountain which I had visited on the 8th. On our lines of march we found no fresh spoor: the day was extremely hot, and the shuffling Bechuanas chose to lag behind in the forest until they lost me entirely, with the exception of three or four who kept up with Piet my after-rider, carrying my gun, and leading "Filbert" and "Frochum," two of my best dogs. Not one of these men knew the country, and they had no Bakalahari men with them to act as guides.

When I reached the small fountain which lies west of the famous fountain for which I was steering, I told Piet to come on with the natives, and that I would ride ahead to the large fountain. I then galloped ahead, and made the fountain on its lee side. On slowly emerging from the thorny thicket through which I rode, I was astonished to behold two superb old bull elephants standing before me in the open space between the cover and the fountain. Both of them carried enormous tusks; one bull however was much taller and stouter than his comrade; I had very rarely seen his match, and his tusks at once took my eye as being perhaps the finest I had ever beheld. Here then was I standing without gun or dogs, and with a very jaded steed, beside, as I afterwards had good reason to believe, the very best elephant in all that district, and in perhaps many of the surrounding parts. I would have given anything at that moment for my gun and dogs.

I felt much perplexed what to do, but at length I resolved that it was best to hold the elephants in my view, and in the event of their being started to endeavour to hold the larger bull in play, and hunt him always back toward the fountain, until assistance should arrive. It was well that I came to so shrewd a resolution, for I had not stood sentry over them for many minutes, when, some straggling party having missed the fountain, and passing to windward, they suddenly tossed up their trunks, and, snuffing the tainted gale, they crashed past me down-wind at top speed.

Now came the tug of war. I had no child's play before me: alone and unassisted, and on a very jaded steed, I had resolved to endeavour what no two of my men had ever accomplished for me. I had not only to stick by the elephant wherever he chose to go, which was all I required of my people when endeavouring to assist me in my hunting, but I must also drive him back and keep him by the fountain, or else all my exertions would be fruitless.

I had very slight hope of success, but he was well worthy of a tough struggle, and I determined that he should have it. I thought what my feelings would be that night by my fireside if I let him escape, and on the other hand how highly I should prize his noble trophies if I succeeded. I at once dashed after him and separated him from his comrade. When he found that I had the speed of him he turned at once upon me and charged furiously back toward the fountain, after which he tried to conceal himself among the trees, and, having stood motionless for some time with his head towards me, he crashed away through the forest to the southward. I soon headed him again, yelling with all my might. Of course another charge followed: I eventually managed however to drive him back close to the fountain; still no assistance hove in sight. My after-rider, though he had been there before, had missed the fountain. It was he and the natives with him who had started the elephants: they had crossed the fountain to windward, and were wandering about with my gun and dogs some miles beyond me.

It were long to describe all the turns and twists I had with this princely old bull. I certainly did my duty, and stuck by him like a good old deer-hound by his stag. At length the elephant became extremely fierce, following up his charges with most determined intent to crush me and my steed, which, at first very much jaded, was now so completely done up that he could barely hold his own. I myself felt much exhausted, and my throat was becoming so sore and hoarse that my shouting was for the present nearing to a close. In this state of things I could not have held him much longer. Help was, however, at hand. Carey and Mutchuisho, with a large party of the natives, were at this moment carefully following up the spoor of my horse where I had first ridden ahead to the fountain, and were passing a considerable distance to leeward of where I was at bay, or rather, I should say, baying, when my hoarse voice fell on Carey's ear, and he instantly called silence among the natives and sat listening in his saddle. A second time my voice fell on his ear, and he at once held forward right for me, contrary to the opinion of the thick-headed natives, who swore that the voice came from behind.

Fortunately at this very moment the elephant made a furious charge after me, accompanied by a tremendous trumpet which at once sealed his fate. They all heard it, and "Cooley" and "Affriar," two right good dogs, were instantly released from the couples and flew to my assistance, followed by Carey and the natives. Right glad was I when I saw black Cooley come up to help me. I at once felt that the elephant was mine, being certain that further assistance was at hand, and, with revived spirits, I yelled with all my might. In two minutes up came Carey on horseback, but without a gun. I called out to him, "For God's sake, Carey, bring me a gun! here is the finest elephant in Africa; I have held him at bay and fought with him for nearly two hours." Carey rode back and brought me his single-barrelled smooth bore, carrying twelve to the pound, and gave me eight bullets out of his belt, expressing immense regret that my gun was not forthcoming. Carey had always an absurd idea that his gun could not kill an elephant: to-day, however, it was in other hands. "My good fellow," I said, "it is all right; the elephant is ours."

I then opened my fire on him from the saddle. I put my seventh bullet through his heart: on receiving it he made a short charge and stood trembling for a few seconds, when he fell forward on his breast and so lay; but as he evinced a desire to alter his position, which was a very good one for cutting out the teeth, I dismounted, and, going close up to him, I put two bullets into his ear, when he expired. The tusks of this elephant equalled my expectations; one of them, as usual, was more perfect than its fellow. I had never seen their match but önce.

On reviewing the whole afternoon's work, I considered myself extremely fortunate in capturing this noble prize, and I felt most gratified with the satisfactory termination of my exertions. Piet and his party heard my shots, and they presently came up to us; coffee and other good things were soon spread out on a sheep-skin, and a comfortable sofa being quickly constructed of soft grass, covered with a kaross, I lay down to rest, the happiest of the happy.

The 15th was an extremely hot day. Carey and I were occupied all the morning cutting out the tusks of the big bull elephant; we took particular care not to let the blood fall upon them. In the evening we made hiding-places beside the fountain from which to shoot elephants, and when the sun went down we returned thither and took up our positions for the night. Unfortunately the dead elephant lay directly to windward of the southern margin of the fountain, on which side were all the best elephant-footpaths. The consequence was that every elephant as he came up got the wind of the natives and turned right about. Late in the night a troop of eight or ten bull elephants walked slowly across the vley with their heads to the north. I rushed forward to get before them in the wind, and running down the edge of the thorn cover I got within thirty yards of the last bull, which was the best in the troop. Observing me move, he stood with his tusks up and his head directed towards me in a very suspicious manner for two minutes, when his fears died away, and he turned to me his left side. I then gave him a deadly shot which brought blood from his trunk, as I ascertained next day. Returning from firing at him I met Carey; his pluck had failed him, and he had dropped behind. On upbraiding him for not standing by me, he swore stoutly that he had stuck in the mud! as we had to cross a bog below the fountain in running for the shot. I thought this was good, and I said to myself, "I have got a name for you at last." But Carey was a good servant, and very attentive to me throughout my expedition.

The next morning I and Mutchuisho took up the spoor of my wounded elephant. He had gone off very slowly, with blood running from his trunk. After following the spoor some distance we lost it amongst others, and we then gave it up. I sent Carey to the waggons with the teeth, to act as guard, they being well worthy of an escort, and at night I watched the fountain along with three Bakalahari. We had not been long on the watch before three enormous old bull-elephants came; and, after much hesitation, and walking once or twice round the water, they came in and commenced drinking. I lay close to the edge of the fountain in a little hollow. The elephants came in to drink on the north side of a run which led away from the fountain, and I lay on the south side of it. Suddenly the finest bull of the three walked boldly through the run and came straight forward to where I lay. If I had remained still he would have walked upon me; but when he came within six or eight yards I gave a loud cough, upon which he tossed his head aloft and gave me a broadside, exposing his left side. I then gave him a shot from the big two-grooved rifle, and he dashed off with his two comrades in immense consternation, holding for the Limpopo.

CHAP. XXVIII.

Elephant Shooting by Moonlight

A FINE NIGHT'S SPORT. 285

The next day one of my steeds died of "tsetse." He had been bitten under the mountain range lying to the south of this fountain. The head and body of the poor animal swelled up in a most distressing manner before he died. His eyes were so swollen that he could not see, and in darkness he neighed for his comrades who stood feeding beside him.

CHAPTER XXVIII.

Paapaa Fountain—Watch by Moonlight from a Shooting-hole—Remarkable Sport with Elephants—Four bagged and eight mortally wounded in one night—Elephant-hunting with Horse and Dogs by Moonlight—A Troop of Lions—The Vultures with the shadowy Wings—Another Dog snapped up by a Crocodile—The Skeleton of an Elephant shot by me discovered—The Tusks being gone, strong measures are adopted for their recovery.

ON the 17th of September I resolved to leave the fountain of Seboono, as it was much disturbed, and to proceed with a few Bakalahari to a small yet famous water about six miles to the south-east. We accordingly saddled up and held thither. On reaching this fountain, which is called by the natives "Paapaa," I found the numerous footpaths leading to it covered, as I had anticipated, with fresh spoor of elephant and rhinoceros. I then at once proceeded to study the best spot on which to make our shooting-hole for the night. It would be impossible to prevent some of the game from getting our wind, for the footpaths led to it from every side. The prevailing wind was from the east, so I pitched upon the south-west corner of the fountain. The water was not more than twenty yards long and ten yards broad. The west side was bounded by tufous rock which rose abruptly from the water about five feet high. The top of this rock was level with the surrounding vley, and here all the elephants drank as if suspicious of treading on the muddy margin on the other three sides of the fountain.

I made our shooting-box within six or eight yards of the water, constructing it in a circular form, of bushes packed together so as to form a hedge about three feet high. On the top of the hedge I placed heavy dead old branches of trees, so as to form a fine clear rest for our rifles; these clean old branches were all lashed firmly together with strips of thorn bark. All being completed, I took the Bakalahari and our steeds to a shady tree, about a quarter of a mile to leeward of the fountain, where we formed a kraal and off-saddled. This day was particularly adapted to bring game to the water, the sun being extremely powerful, and a hot dry wind prevailing all the afternoon. I told Carey that we were certain of having a good night's sport, and I was right, for we undoubtedly had about the finest night's sport and the most wonderful that was ever enjoyed by man.

A little before the sun went down, leaving our kraal, we held to the fountain, having with us our heavy-metalled rifles, karosses, and two Bakalahari. We also had two small guns, my double-barrelled Westley Richards, and Carey's single-barrelled gun. As we approached the fountain a stately bull giraffe stood before us; the heat of the day had

18

brought him thither, but he feared to go in and drink; on observing us he walked slowly away. Two jackals were next detected. Guinea fowl, partridges, two or three sorts of pigeon and turtle-dove, and small birds in countless thousands, were pouring in to drink from every airt, as we walked up to our hiding-place and lay down. In a few minutes the sun was under; but the moon was strong and high (it being within three nights of the full), and the sky was clear, with scarcely a cloud.

Very soon a step was heard approaching from the east; it was a presuming black rhinoceros. He came up within ten yards of the hiding-hole, and, observing us with his sharp prying eye, he at once came slowly forward for a nearer inspection. I then shouted to him; but this he did not heed in the slightest. I then sprang up and waved my large kaross, shouting at the same time. This, however, only seemed to amuse Borèlé, for he stood within four yards of us, with his horn threatening our momentary destruction, nor would he wheel about until I threw a log of wood at him. Black rhinoceroses are very difficult to scare when they do not get the wind; the best way to do so is to hit them with a stone, —that is, in the event of the sportsman not wishing to fire off his gun.

Soon after Borèlé departed four old bull elephants drew near from the south. They were coming right on for the spot where we lay, and they seemed very likely to walk over the top of us. We therefore placed our two big rifles in position, and awaited their forward movement with intense interest. On they came with a slow and stately step, until within twenty yards of us, when the leading elephant took it into his head to pass to leeward. We let him come on until he got our wind; he was then within ten yards of the muzzles of our heavy-metalled rifles; on winding us he tossed his trunk aloft, and we instantly fired together. I caught him somewhere about the heart, and my big six-pound rifle burst in Carey's hands, very nearly killing us both. The elephant on being fired at wheeled about, and retreated to the forest at top speed. I now directed "Stick-in-the-mud" to make use of his single-barrelled twelve to the pound, in the event of more elephants coming up; and thanking my stars that the old Dutch rifle had not sent us both to the land of the leal, I sat down and watched the dark masses of trees that cut the sky on every side, in the hope of seeing a mass as high and wide come towering forward into the open space that surrounded the fountain.

Nor did I watch long in vain, for very soon three princely bull elephants appeared exactly where the first came on, and holding exactly the same course. They approached just as the first had done. When the leading elephant came within ten yards of us he got our wind, and tossed up his trunk, and was wheeling round to retreat, when we fired together and sent our bullets somewhere about his heart. He ran two hundred yards and then stood, being evidently dying. His comrades halted likewise, but one of them, the finest of the three, almost immediately turned his head once more to the fountain, and very slowly and warily came on. We now heard the wounded elephant utter the cry of death, and fall heavily on the earth. Carey, whose ears were damaged by the bursting of the big rifle, did not catch this sound, but swore that the elephant which now so stealthily approached the water was the one at which we had fired.

It was interesting to observe this grand old bull approach the fountain: he seemed to mistrust the very earth on which he stood, and smelt and examined with his trunk every yard of the ground before he trod on it, and sometimes stood five minutes on one spot without moving. At length, having gone round three sides of the fountain, and being apparently satisfied as to the correctness of everything, he stepped boldly forward on to the rock on the west, walking up within six or seven yards of the muzzles of our rifles, he turned his broadside, and, lowering his trunk into the water, drew up a volume of water, which he threw over his back to cool his person. This operation he repeated two or three times, after which he commenced drinking, by drawing the water into his trunk and then pouring it into his mouth. I determined to break his leg if possible, so, covering the limb about level with the lower line of his body, I fired, Carey firing for his heart. I made a lucky shot; and as the elephant turned and attempted to make away, his leg broke with a loud crack, and he stood upon his three sound ones. At once disabled and utterly incapable of escaping, he stood statue-like beside the fountain, within a few yards of where he had got the shot, and only occasionally made an attempt at locomotion.

The patch of my rifle fired at this elephant's comrade had ignited a large ball of dry old dung, about eight yards to leeward of our kraal, and fanned by the breeze, it was now burning away very brightly, the sparks flying in the wind. Presently, on looking about me, I beheld two bull elephants approaching by the selfsame footpath which the others had held. The first of these was a half-grown bull, the last was an out-and-out old fellow with enormous tusks. They came on as the first had done, but seemed inclined to pass to windward of us. The young bull however observed the fire; he at once walked up to it and smelling at it with his trunk he seemed extremely amused, and in a gambolling humour threw his trunk about, as if not knowing what to think of it. The larger bull now came up, and exposed a fine broadside; we took him behind the shoulder and fired together: on receiving the shots he wheeled about and held west with drooping ears, evidently mortally wounded.

Some time after this I detected an enormous old bull elephant approaching from the west. If we lay still where we were, he must in a few minutes get our wind, so we jumped up and ran forward out of his line of march. Here a borèlè opposed our farther progress, and we had to stone him out of our way. The elephant came on, and presently got the wind of where we had been lying. This at once seemed to awake his suspicions, for he stood still among the trees, stretching his trunk from side to side to catch the scent, and doubtful whether he should advance or retreat. We then ran towards him, and stalked in within forty yards of where he stood, and taking up a position behind a bush awaited his forward movement. The elephant came slowly forward, and I thought would pass to windward of us, when he suddenly altered his course, and walked boldly forward right for where we stood. He came on until within seven or eight yards, when I coughed loudly to turn him. He tossed up his trunk and turned quickly round to fly; as he turned, however, we fired together, when the elephant uttered a shrill cry of distress, and crashed away evidently hard hit. When this bull was standing before us, we both remarked that he was the finest we had seen that night: his tusks were extremely long, thick, and very unusually wide set.

We now returned to the fountain, and once more lay down to watch. Rhinoceroses, both black and white, were parading around us all night in every direction. We had lain but a short time when I detected a single old bull elephant approaching from the south by the same path which all the others had held. This elephant must have been very thirsty, for he came boldly on without any hesitation, and, keeping to windward, he walked past within about eight yards of us. We fired at the same moment; the elephant wheeled about, and after running a hundred yards reduced his pace to a slow walk. I clapped Carey on the shoulder, and said, "We have him." I had hardly uttered the words when he fell over on his side; he rose however again to his feet. At this moment the same presuming borèlé who had troubled us in the early part of the night came up to us again, and, declining as before to part by gentle hints, I thought it a fitting moment to put an end to his intrusion, and accordingly gave him a ball behind the shoulder. On receiving it he galloped off in tremendous consternation, and passed close under the dying elephant, who at the moment fell dead with a heavy crash, and broke one of his hind legs under him in the fall.

About an hour after two more elephants came touring on from the east. When they came up they stood for a long time motionless within forty yards of the water; and at length the finer of the two, which was a very first-rate old bull, and carrying immense tusks, walked boldly forward, and, passing round the north side of the fountain, commenced drinking on the rock just as the crippled bull had done. We both fired together, holding for his heart; the bullets must have gone nearly through him, for we had double charges of powder in our weapons. On receiving the shots he dropped a volume of water from his trunk, and, tossing it aloft, uttered a loud cry and made off, steering north; but before he was out of our sight he reduced his pace to a slow walk, and I could quite plainly hear, by the loud painful breathing through his trunk, that he was mortally wounded; but whether the natives were too lazy to seek him, or having found him would not tell me, I know not, but I never got him. We shot another bull elephant shortly after this; he too uttered a shrill cry, and went off holding the same course the last one did; that was, however, all that I ever saw of him.

It was now wearing on towards morning: the moon was low and the sky was cloudy; and feeling very sleepy, I set the two Bakalahari to watch whilst I lay down to rest. Carey was already enjoying a sound sleep, and snoring loudly. I had lain nearly an hour, and was neither waking nor sleeping, when the Bakalahari whispered "Clou toona, macoa," which signifies "Bull elephants, white man." I sat up on my kaross, and beheld three old bulls approaching from the west. At this moment there was a death-like calm in the atmosphere, and the sky looked very threatening all along the mountain range which bounds this favourite elephant district on the south-west. I greatly feared a thunderstorm. Suddenly a breeze came whistling from the mountains, and gave these three elephants our wind. We then left the fountain and held to our saddles, where we slept till the sun rose.

When the sun rose I proceeded with the Bakalahari to inspect the spoors of the wounded elephants. I was struck with astonishment when I thought over our night's sport: nine times had first-rate old bull elephants come up to drink, and we had fired at eight of these at distances of from six to ten yards, with cool steady rests. Two of them lay dead beside the fountain; another had a broken leg, and could not escape; and the only one which we imagined had escaped was the bull with the wide-set tusks, which we both felt certain was wounded too far back in the body.

The event, however, proved that our expectations were incorrect, for that afternoon we found this princely elephant lying dead very near our kraal. Both our shots were very far back, wounding him somewhere about the kidneys. We never saw anything of the four other elephants shot by us. The bull with the broken leg had gone nearly a mile from the fountain when we came up to him. At first he made vain attempts to escape, and then to charge; but finding he could neither escape nor catch any of us, he stood at bay beside a tree, and my after-riders began to assail him. It was curious to watch his movements as the boys at about twenty yards distance, pelted him with sticks, etc. Each thing as it was thrown he took up and hurled back at them. When, however, dry balls of elephants' dung were pitched at him, he contented himself with smelling at them with his trunk. At length, wishing to put an end to his existence, I gave him four shots behind the shoulder, when he at once exhibited signs of distress; water ran from his eyes, and he could barely keep them open; presently his gigantic form quivered, and, falling over, he expired. At night we again watched the fountain. Only one elephant appeared; late in the night he came up to leeward, and got our wind. I, however, shot two fine old muchocho, or white rhinoceroses, and wounded two or three borèlé, which were found by the natives.

On the 19th I proceeded with Carey and Piet, and a few Bakalahari, to a small fountain lying one mile to the south: here we made two shooting-boxes of boughs of trees. There were three pools at which the game drank, the largest not being more than twelve feet in breadth. I and Carey at night shot one fine bull elephant and four rhinoceroses, wounding two others, which escaped. On the night following we also wounded two elephants, which got away.

On the next night, on looking up the open vley to the south of the fountain, I beheld an unusually vast bull elephant coming freshly on to drink; but scared by a shot which I fired at other game, and hearing his courier crashing through the forest, he turned out of his course, and walked into the jungle. Presently, however, he again appeared a little to leeward of the dead elephant—this scared him a second time; again, a third time, he came on ; but on this occasion he got a puff of our wind, and a third time he retreated into the forest. It was now after midnight, the sky was clear and cloudless, and the moon was full.

I had long entertained an idea that elephants might be hunted in the saddle by moonlight with dogs, as in the day; but I thought it very probable that a man might get his eyes torn out by the wait-a-bits; I had also a notion that the elephants might prove more active, and perhaps more vicious. This night, however, I resolved to put the question to trial; I had horses and some of my best dogs in couples beside the fire, within two hundred yards of where we lay. When this mighty elephant retreated for the third time into the forest, the idea of hunting them in this manner again recurred to me, being very much annoyed at uselessly wounding and losing in the last week no less than ten first-rate old bull elephants. I communicated my idea to "Stick-in-the-mud," and we hastily proceeded to saddle my steed.

I led my dogs, eight in number, through the forest to leeward of where a bull who had come to the fountain to drink had gone in, and when I saw that they had got his wind I slipped them. They dashed forward, and next minute was heard the baying of the dogs and the crash and the trumpet of the elephant. He rushed away at first without halting, and held right for the mountains to the south-west. When, however, he found that his speed did not avail, and that he could not get away from his pursuers, he began to turn and dodge about in the thickest of the cover, occasionally making charges after the dogs. I followed on as best I could, shouting with all my might to encourage my good hounds. These, hearing their master's voice beside them, stuck well by the elephant, and fought better than in the day. I gave him my first two shots from the saddle; after which I rode close up to him, and, running in on foot, I gave him some deadly shots at distances of from fifteen to twenty yards.

The elephant very soon evinced signs of distress, and ceased to make away from us. Taking up positions in the densest parts of the cover, he caught up the red dust with his trunk, and throwing it over his head and back, endeavoured to conceal himself in a cloud. This was a fine opportunity to pour in my deadly shafts, and I took care to avail myself of it. When he had received about twelve shots he walked slowly forward in a dying state, the blood streaming from his trunk. I rode close up to him, and gave him a sharp right and left from the saddle: he turned and walked a few yards, then suddenly came down with tremendous violence on his vast stern, pitching his head and trunk aloft to a prodigious height, and, falling over on his side, he expired. This was an extremely large and handsome elephant, decidedly the finest bull I had shot this year. Afraid of taking cold or rheumatism, for I was in a most profuse perspiration, I hastened back to my fireside, having first secured all the dogs in their couples. Here I divested myself of my leather trousers, shooting-belt, and veltschoens, and, stretched on my kaross, I took tea, and wondered at the facility with which I had captured this mighty elephant.

Feeling fatigued, I intended to lie down and rest till morning. Just, however, as I was arranging my saddles for a pillow, I beheld another first-rate old bull elephant advancing up the vley from the south. I at once resolved that he, too, should run the gauntlet with the dogs. In immense haste, therefore, I once more pulled on my old leathers, and buckled on my shooting-belt; and ran down into the rank long grass beside the fountain to meet him, armed with the large two-grooved rifle, having directed Carey and Piet to come slowly up with the dogs and my horse and gun as soon as they were ready. The elephant came on, and stood drinking within thirty yards of me. When I saw Carey coming on with the dogs and steed I fired, but my rifle hung fire. The shot, however, gave the dogs good courage, and they fought well. The elephant took away at a rapid pace toward the other fountain where the Bechuanas lay, and at first led me through very bad wait-a-bit thorn cover, which once or twice nearly swept me out of the saddle. Presently he inclined to the west, and got into better country; I then rode close to him, and bowled him over with four shots. I also wounded a fine old black rhinoceros.

The next morning, my ammunition being expended, or very nearly so, I despatched Carey to camp for fresh supplies. When he was gone I walked through the forest around the fountain to seek for my wounded game. I first came upon the black rhinoceros of last night, and a little farther on I observed "Frachum" snuff up the wind and go ahead. I soon saw him returning, with two jackals trotting behind him, so I at once knew that there was some game lying dead in advance. When I had proceeded a little farther the dogs ran forward, and next moment a rush of many feet was heard charging towards where I stood. It was a troop of half-grown lions, with a lioness; which dashed past me, followed by the dogs. They had been feasting on a white rhinoceros, shot by me two nights previously, which I found lying a little in advance. Beside the carcase stood a fine fat calf—the poor thing, no doubt, fancying that its mother slept; heedless of lions, and all the other creatures that had trodden there, it had remained beside its dead mother for a day and two nights. Rhinoceroses' calves always stick to their mothers long after they are dead. The next night I was again successful in a night-hunt, and bagged a very fine bull elephant. This wound up my elephant night-shooting for that moon, for next day there was a most awful thunderstorm, which filled the forest with large pools of water.

While reviewing my extraordinary good fortune during the last week's hunting, I could not help deeply regretting that I had not earlier thought of pursuing the elephants at night with dogs and horses: if I had commenced with the dogs only a week sooner, I might have bagged eight or ten first-rate bulls, which I knew were mortally wounded, but were, nevertheless, not forthcoming. The ivory of these elephants would have brought me in upwards of £200; and it was vexing to think that many, if not all of them, were lying rotting in the surrounding forest. My only chance of finding them was by watching the vultures; but these birds, knowing that they cannot break the skin of the larger game, preferred remaining above and around the Bechuanas, where the butchering was going briskly forward. They perched in groups upon the old branches of the larger trees, or darkened the sky in hundreds with their broad and shadowy wings.

While, however, I mourned the loss of these wounded elephants, I reckoned that I had been favoured with immense good fortune in many instances during the past week. Ever intent upon embellishing and increasing my princely collection of African hunting-trophies, I placed great value upon any specimen I happened to shoot which I thought worth adorning it. Thus I neglected my real interest; and instead of devoting my attention to rendering my expedition profitable, I allowed this very necessary part of the business to remain quite a secondary consideration. Thus, when I shot an ordinary bull elephant, I was accustomed to say to myself, "Ah! a good bull; tusks at least fifty pounds each; 4s. 6d. a pound; bring me in £22 10s. Capital day's work; help to pay for the two horses that died last week, or the four that are bitten with 'tsetse,' and must die in a week or two." But if, on the other hand, I shot an elephant with a pair of tusks of unusual size, perfection, or beauty, I at once devoted them to my collection, and valued them at a tenfold price. This, then, was one thing in which I reckoned I had been extremely fortunate—I had secured the finest tusks in all that nest of patriarchial old bulls which I had so sadly cut up in one short week, and which perhaps the summers of a century had seen roaming through these boundless forests in peaceful security.

The night-shooting being at an end, on the 23rd I retraced my steps to the dead elephants, to assist Carey in superintending the cutting out of the ivory, and in escorting the same along with our supply of fat and flesh to the waggons. Early in the afternoon we had got all ready for a start. The Bechuana captains who were there, and had appropriated my elephants and rhinoceroses, and nearly all the fat, then brought up about fifty men, who shouldered my impedimenta, and we marched for camp. Carey went in front, I rode in the middle, and my after-riders brought up the rear. This long line of naked savages threading the mazes of the forest, and bearing home the spoils of a few days' hunting, formed a truly interesting and unusual picture. Every man that was there carried something of mine: some led the dogs, some carried the guns and extra ammunition, some cooking-vessels, axes, sickles, water-calibashes, provisions, rhinoceroses' horns, the elephants' teeth, and an immense supply of flesh and fat, etc., etc. We made the Limpopo as the sun went down, which we crossed all right, and brought everything safe to camp. I made other excursions from this encampment in quest of elephants, in which I was very successful; but as they did not differ in their details from the many already described, I shall not run the risk of wearying my reader with an account of them.

On the 30th one of those minor incidents occurred which the hunter in these parts must be prepared continually to encounter. As I awoke that morning I heard a scream which denoted that "Prince," a most worthless dog, was consumed by a crocodile. There were several of these terrible animals frequenting the still deep stream beside which we lay. They seemed ever to be on the look-out for prey, and I have not the slightest doubt they would have taken one of us if we had ventured in.

On the 2nd of October, in the morning, we packed the cap-tent waggon, and stowed carefully away in grass my favourite tusks, which I intended to keep as specimens.

The next afternoon, whilst making for the fountain called Setoque, accompanied by Kapain and a party from Bamangwato, I observed a number of crows and vultures, and came across the spoor of a party of Bakalahari. I at once felt convinced that one of my wounded elephants lay rotting near me, but, the sun being nearly under, I did not then wait, resolving to seek it at another time; Kapain promised to send two of his companions early next morning to see if I had not surmised correctly. These men next day arrived, bearing some putrid fat which they had got from the Bakalahari; and I at once said, "Oh, you have found my dead elephant?" They answered, "Yes, but the tusks are stolen." They also said that they had cut that fat out of the elephant. Kapain then promised me to do his best to recover the ivory for me; but I found out, very soon afterwards, that he was playing me false. Next day I shot an old bull elephant.

On the 5th I began to think of hunting no more across the Limpopo, as the season of rain was up; and any day I might come to the river, returning from hunting, and find myself cut off from camp by a mighty stream, which would probably remain impassable for months. I also wished to save, if possible, one or two of my horses from the "tsetse," as my stud was now reduced to five. I therefore resolved to return at once to camp, and cross the Limpopo no more. After an early breakfast I marched thither, with thirteen Bechuanas bearing the tusks, flesh, etc.

On my way I visited the remains of the elephant which Kapain's men had found; it was the carcase of an enormous old bull, no doubt the elephant which I had first shot on the night of the 16th of last month, for I had followed his spoor to within half a mile of the spot. His tusks were stolen as reported; they had not been cut out, but drawn. The skull remained perfect, and was finely cleaned by hyænas, vultures, and insects. On beholding the carcase, I at once knew that Kapain had lied in saying that his men had cut the fat I saw with them out of the elephant, for it was evident that all flesh and fat had been at an end many days previously: the tusks, however, had quite lately been drawn, perhaps on the preceding day. I felt quite certain that Kapain was deceiving me, so I at once charged him with falsehood, and resolved in my own mind to take some very strong measures for the recovery of the tusks. I suspected that a tribe of Bakalahari who lived not far from the elephant, upon the river, knew all about the tusks, for there were no other natives in that district; so I resolved to ride to the village early next morn, and threaten to shoot the chief if the teeth did not quickly appear.

Accordingly, on the morning of the 6th, before it was clear, four steeds were saddled; and having taken coffee, I crossed the Limpopo, accompanied by Carey, John, and Piet, bearing double-barrelled guns, and held down the river-side for the Bakalahari village, whith we made in about an hour. As soon as I observed the huts I dashed across their corn-lands at a racing pace, and was standing in the middle of the natives before they were aware of my approach.

The chief whom I wanted sat in the forum with most of his men, so, dismounting from my horse, I walked up to them, and sat down on the ground in native custom, and, taking snuff myself, I handed it round. While I was doing this, John and Carey, armed, occupied the two places of exit from the forum. I sat silent for a little, and then said, "My heart is very bitter with the chief of this village. You were hungry, and I killed much flesh and fat for you. I told you that many of my elephants were lying dead, and that I wanted their teeth. You promised me to watch the vultures, and bring me the teeth. I have traced your spoor home from one of these elephants. Why did the tusks not come to my waggons? I do not want to shed your blood, but I require the teeth to be laid immediately before me."

They all immediately exclaimed, "The teeth are forthcoming, they are forthcoming: wait a little, chief of the white men. We saw the vultures, and hid the teeth for you." I was delighted to hear this, but I pretended still to be very angry, and answered, "My heart is still very bitter, for you should have brought the teeth at once to me, and not caused me to come with guns to seek my teeth." The chief then at once despatched five or six active men to bring the teeth; and Bechuana beer and porridge were placed before me. In an hour the men returned, bearing the tusks of my lost elephant. I was right glad to see them; they were immense teeth, and very finely arched, and almost perfect. I then chose some skins of koodoo and blue wildebeests out of their kraals for packing my ivory in the waggons, for which I promised them beads; after which I returned to camp, the natives going before me, bearing the teeth and skins. These men had drawn the tusks, and concealed them somewhere close to the carcase of the elephant.

Here they would most probably have been concealed until I had left the country, when they would have forwarded them to their chief. Just as we reached the drift we met a string of natives returning from my last elephant, bearing flesh and fat. This was a fine opportunity for a seizure. I selected several large bundles of the flesh and some fat, and marched the same to camp on the shoulders of the Bakalahari, along with the ivory. When Kapain saw us arrive at camp, he was utterly confounded, and began to abuse the Bakalahari; thereupon I bundled him out of the kraal. In the afternoon we packed the ivory in the baggage-waggon; it had hitherto lain loose in the kraal. There were fifty-three tusks of bull, and seventeen tusks of cow elephants. Three pairs of these bulls' teeth I intended to keep in my collection; in the cap-tent were seven pairs of picked bulls' tusks, and two pairs of cow-elephants' tusks: all of which I likewise devoted to my collection.

CHAPTER XXIX.

We march up the Limpopo—The Guapa Mountains—Immense variety of Game—Stalk and shoot two Sable Antelopes—Several Hounds lost—Romantic Ravine in the Guapa Mountains—My Forest Home—Buck Koodoos—Stalking Sable Antelopes—Two of my Horses die from Tsetse—Continue our March—Countless Herds of Game.

ON the morning of the 8th of October we packed the waggons, and about midday inspanned, and left the Bakalahari village, where we had lain for nearly six weeks. The old chief of these Bakalahari looked extremely downhearted when he saw us preparing to depart; and could hardly refrain from crying. I had come there and found them starving; but ever since my arrival they had had more good flesh and fat than they could eat. I had also employed the women to stamp my barley and Bechuana corn, and had always rewarded them liberally with beads, which they made into native ornaments, and with which they adorned their persons. The old chief was distinguished by a snake-skin, which he wore round his head. I gave him some presents at parting, and we then trekked, holding up the river, but at a considerable distance from it, the Limpopo having at this part a very considerable bend. In the evening we came again upon the river, and halted at our old kraal, where I had been troubled with lions on the 5th of August. On the march I lost "Argyll," my best dog, of whom I have often made mention in former expeditions, he having weathered my two campaigns in the Bamangwato country. He was strangled on the trap of the waggon, where he was coupled along with the other dogs.

I now resolved to leave the Limpopo, and explore the country in a north-westerly direction. I was accompanied by a large body of Sicomy's men. These scoundrels would not give me any information either as to water or elephants, excepting in one direction which suited themselves, invariably answering my questions with "There is no water in that direction, there are no elephants there." Thus I was left entirely in the dark how to proceed, and was obliged to use my own discretion. About due north-west from where we lay, a bold mountain range rose blue above the forest. Thither in the morning I directed our course, and in the evening we halted at a small vley, which I found by following an elephant footpath; the rascally Bechuanas swearing that we should not find water till sundown next day. On the march we started an ostrich from her nest, in which we found sixteen large serviceable eggs. The country through which we passed was very soft and sandy, the forest often so dense as to compel us to halt and use our axes.

On the 13th we reached a strong succession of fountains, forming a running stream of pure water. Here the country became extremely beautiful; a very wide and finely wooded valley stretched away into the bosom of the mountains, ending in a bold ravine. This district I discovered to be the abode of a considerable tribe called "Moroking." Their cultivated corn-lands stretched away on every side of the fountain.

Here I outspanned, and presently the chief and all his people came to me, highly pleased that I had visited them. These men were dependents of Sicomy, and for some reason which I could not comprehend, had been instructed by the Bamangwato natives not to give me any information regarding the elephants or the waters in advance. At night we were visited by a terrible and long-protracted thunderstorm, and much rain fell, rendering the country very unfit for trekking.

The next morning I shot a large wild goose, a splendid bird, its general colour dark glossy green, with white patches on its sides and beneath its wings. While seeking for wild fowl along the edge of the stream I almost trod upon the tail of a fearful "cobra," which instantly reared its head on high and spread its neck out like the Indian cobra. Before it could strike, however, I sprang to one side and escaped its deadly fangs; Ruyter and I then slew him with sticks and stones. The chief of the Moroking, and all his people, both men and women, came again to see the white man, the waggons, and the oxen: they still persisted in saying that there were no elephants in advance. As the country was now quite unfit for trekking, and probably I might not find elephants until I had proceeded to a great distance, I resolved to turn back. Accordingly, after breakfast we trekked, and halted for the night at the fountain we had left on the preceding day. On the march I shot an extremely beautiful wood-pigeon; its back and tail were grass-green, its thighs bright orange, its bill and feet bright coral red.

On the 15th at sunrise we inspanned, and held on until late in the afternoon, steering for the mountain of Guapa, where I had seen sable antelope on the 16th of July. We halted for the night without water; during the night rain fell. On the march we saw spoor of eland; my troop of dogs took away after a herd of zebras, one of which broke Filbert's shoulder with a kick, so as I was obliged to shoot him. This was a sad loss to me; Filbert was the best dog I had left.

Next day at dawn we marched, holding for a vley close under the blue mountain in advance. Having proceeded some miles we fell in with springboks, zebras, blue gnoos; and, soon after, to my surprise, an old kookama or oryx, carrying a superb pair of horns, started away before the waggons. My dogs were fresh and hungry: they were instantly slipped, and dashed forward on the scent of the oryx. Unluckily, a wild dog sprang up right in their path, to which they at once gave chase, and thus I lost this most splendid antelope.

I walked ahead of the waggons with my rifle, and soon started two pairs of ostriches. I was going down wind, and kept starting the game. I next sent away a herd of zebras and brindled gnoos; next a sounder of wild boar; next a troop of giraffes; and, close to the vley where I intended to halt, I wounded a koodoo, which left a bloody spoor, that I did not choose to follow. The vley to which I had been trusting proved dry. We outspanned here for an hour, however, and then held round the western extremity of this fine mountain-range; and as the sun went down I halted my waggons on its south side, opposite the mouth of a bold and well-wooded ravine, which contained a strong fountain. On the march I rode ahead of my waggons on the spoor of two old buffaloes, which our waggon-whips had started; these had gone out of my course, so I did not follow far. Returning, I came to a black rhinoceros, which I wounded, but did not get. As I neared the ravine where I intended to halt, I stalked in close upon a second black rhinoceros, which on receiving two deadly shots charged madly forward and subsided in the dust. A few minutes after firing at Borèlé I was following a troop of pallahs close under the green rocky mountain, when, lo! a herd of the lovely sable antelope caught my attention. These were quietly browsing on a shoulder of the mountain among the green trees far, far above me. I instantly threw off my leathers, and proceeded to stalk in upon them. An old doe detected me, however, and, instantly sounding the alarm, the herd, which consisted of eight—three coal-black bucks and five does—dashed off, and took through a rocky ravine..

As it was too late in the day to follow them farther, I turned my face towards my horses, which I had left at the base of the mountain; and straining my eyes along the level forest beneath me to seek my waggons, which were now due, I detected them far out from the mountain, steering to go past the fountain. I then fired a signal shot, which brought them up. This unlucky shot started away two bull elephants which were feeding in the thorn cover close beneath me. I drew up my waggons in an open spot more than half a mile from the fountain, wait-a-bit thorns forbidding our nearer approach.

The 17th was a very cool and cloudy day; I took an early breakfast, and then held north-east, close in under the mountain-range, accompanied by Kapain and a party of Bakalahari, to seek elephants.

We fell in with immense herds of zebras and buffaloes numbering between three and five hundred in each herd, and towards evening with a numerous herd of elephants, when I killed one of the finest after an easy chase.

After several unsuccessful stalks for sable antelope I at length met with the success my perseverance deserved. Returning in the afternoon of the 20th homewards, I suddenly observed a herd of about ten of them in open cover on the mountain's ridge, upon which I commenced ascending the rugged acclivity as fast as I could, for the daylight would be gone in a very short time. When I got within two hundred yards of them, I found it impossible to get in any nearer, for I must cross a stony flat in sight of several of the ever wary does; it was, moreover, now so late that I could not well see the sights of my rifle. I had almost resolved not to disturb them, and to return to camp: on second thoughts, however, I resolved to give it a trial. I made a successful stalk, and crossed this dangerous rocky flat unobserved. There was no moss nor heather under my knees, but a mass of adamantine fragments of rock; yet this I did not heed, so I succeeded in my stalk.

Having crossed the flat, I soon stalked within shot, when, raising my rifle slowly, I fired at a lovely old doe which stood on my left. The ball passed right through her a little behind the shoulder; she bounded down hill, when I fired my second barrel at her, but, owing to the darkness, I missed. The potaquaines above me, seeing nothing and smelling nothing, stood bewildered until I had reloaded, lying on my side. I then shot another splendid doe with a perfect pair of wide-set horns, putting two bullets through her fore-quarters. She, however, took two more balls before she lay, when I put a fifth bullet into her to stop her kicking, as she was injuring her horns on the rocky ground. By this time the sun was under and the moon shone bright. Highly gratified at my success, I now cut off this magnificent antelope's head, and descended the mountain with a slow and careful step. The other potaquaine did not leave the ground, and I got her also next day.

I now reckoned my collection of African trophies as almost perfect. Last year I shot an old buck potaquaine in the Bamangwato country, which I had carefully preserved; and I had now shot two splendid does, which was what I most particularly required to complete my collection. I still wanted heads of the "bluebuck," or "kleenbok," "Vaal rheebok," "ourebi," and "reitbok ;" but these were abundant in the colony, and were not hard to get.

Next morning I ascended the mountain to secure the flesh of the dead potaquaine and to secure the wounded one. I found her still alive, and on seeing me she made off; I, however, followed her up, and, making a correct stalk barefooted, I shot her where she stood ; she proved a very old doe.

The 23rd was a very cool and cloudy morning, and looked likely for light rain. At an early hour I left my waggons with some provisions, and ascended the mountain to the north-east to seek sable antelope. Soon after gaining the upper heights of the mountain I had the satisfaction to detect a fine herd of these feeding among the trees on the table summit of a ridge of the mountain, which stretched away to the east. I determined to stalk them in true Highland fashion, and to use my very best endeavours to ensure success; accordingly, having surveyed the ground, I made a cast to leeward, and approached the herd upon my belly. When I got within two hundred yards of them I found it was impossible to approach nearer on that side, so I was obliged to creep away back again, and try to come upon them from another quarter. When next I crept in, the herd had vanished, and I could not find them for some time. At length, however, I came suddenly upon them, when the herd rushed in a semicircle round me. I ran forward as hard as I could, and, pulling suddenly up, fired at the big black buck as he dashed past me at top speed ; the ball told loudly, and the buck bent up his back to the shot.

They now charged for the southern ridge of the mountain, and disappeared over it at a tremendous pace. I quickly loaded, and proceeded to take up the spoor, and at once had the satisfaction to find great spouts of blood all along the spoor of the patriarchal old black buck. This gave me high hopes of success ; I waited a few minutes, and whistled for the Bechuanas, who immediately came up to me with "Bles" and "Affriar," two right good dogs. When the wounded buck had proceeded a short distance down the mountain's face, he left the herd and slanted away by himself. In a few minutes, however, I espied him : he stood about three hundred yards from me, under a low tree on the rocky mountain side, with drooping head and outstretched tail, which he kept constantly whisking from side to side, and he was evidently extremely sick. As he exhibited no intention of going farther, and as the waggons were near, I thought it would be a fine opportunity to give all the dogs blood; so I despatched Ruyter to camp to fetch them, and I remained stationary and watched the wounded potaquaine. After standing in one spot for some time, he made a few tottering steps, then lay heavily down in the grass as if dead, and nothing was visible but his side.

This was most satisfactory: there, on the side of his native rugged mountain, lay the ever-wary, the scarce, the lovely, long-sought sable antelope, and a most noble specimen—perhaps the finest buck in all the district. His ever-watchful eye was now sunk in the long grass; and as he was lying beside a little ravine, and a stiff breeze was blowing, I could, if I had chosen, have crept in within thirty yards of him, and shot him dead on the spot; but so far from doing this, I rather lamented that he was thus badly wounded, for I feared that he would not have life enough left to show a good fight when the dogs came up. It has been truly said that there is many a slip between the cup and the lip, and the truth of this old saying I was about most bitterly to experience. In half an hour the Bushman came on with three Bechuanas, leading all my best dogs. I went up to the potaquaine. He had arisen, and was looking at us as we came on; when I approached within a hundred and fifty yards of him he disappeared over the ridge. I did not, however, slip the trustless dogs until they should be on his scent or see him. When I gained the ridge I again beheld him standing within a hundred yards of me. I now slipped all my trustiest hounds; they ran forward towards the buck, and then took away up the hill, where, finding nothing, they presently came down again, and, after snuffing about for a little, followed up the scent of the buck.

All this time the potaquaine remained utterly motionless, regarding the dogs with a wicked eye. They, however, did not observe him until they were within about ten yards of him, when he stamped his foot, and turned as if to fight with them. The dogs opened a bay, and the next instant the potaquaine bounded through the middle of them, and, holding down the mountain side, was out of my sight in two seconds, the dogs all at his heels.

I pressed forward in the most perfect confidence of an immediate bay; but when I obtained a view of the open forest around the mountain's base, nor dog nor potaquaine could I see; neither could I hear a sound. I thought the chase must have led up wind, so I held on at my best pace along the rugged mountain's side.

I gained shoulder after shoulder, and opened fresh ground, but nothing living could I see, nor could I hear a sound. To make matters worse, it was blowing half a gale of wind. Most thoroughly confounded, I now in haste retraced my steps to the natives. These useless creatures I found sitting just where I had slipped the dogs. In vain I asked them whither they were gone; they only put me wrong, and lost me the day; for they declared that they had watched the ground below to leeward, and that no dog had gone in that course. They had, however, gone that way, and were at that moment baying a fresh buck very near me, but the unlucky wind prevented me from hearing them. I hastily retraced my steps once more up wind, and, after proceeding a little farther than I had been before, I saw "Alert," a very uncertain animal which I had long possessed, returning towards me.

The dogs have then gone up wind, I thought to myself, and they have the buck at bay in advance. Next moment, however, to my utter amazement, I beheld my wounded potaquaine standing in the forest below me, and not a single dog near him. I was now aware that my dogs had fallen in with some other bucks which I was not aware of, and were gone I knew not whither. After waiting an hour for them, I endeavoured to stalk in on the potaquaine; it was bad ground, and he saw me and made off. He went but a short distance, however, and stood again in a drooping attitude beneath a tree; the Bechuanas tried to drive him to a position which I took up, when he left the ground, and I never saw him again.

When I returned to my camp, my people told me that the dogs had bayed a buck for a long time under the mountain, within hearing of the waggons, and that the sounds had died away, as if they had pulled him down and killed him. On hearing this I at once saddled up two steeds, and rode in that direction to seek my dogs, but saw nothing of them, and, night setting in, I returned to camp. Next day three of the dogs returned; they were covered with the blood of the potaquaine they had killed, and one of them was wounded by his horns. I, however, never found the remains of either this buck or the one I had shot, nor did I see more of my three good dogs which were missing; no doubt they had all been found by the natives, and stolen by them.

I resolved on the 26th to make an expedition on foot across the mountain, and hunt in its northern limits for a few days. I accordingly started with Ruyter and four Bechuanas bearing my bedding, pots, water, and other impedimenta. Having ascended the upper heights of the mountain, I crossed to its western ridges, and held for its northern limits; and when the sun went down I halted beneath a green tree, where I slept.

I made my coffee by moonlight before the day dawned; and when it was clear I stalked along the upper ridges of the mountain. Presently, peeping over a rocky and well-wooded ridge, I saw a small troop of doe koodoos, one of which I shot for food. Immediately below where this koodoo fell was a lonely kraal of Bakalahari. These men had chosen for their place of residence a wild and most romantic ravine which here parted the mountain for a distance of about a mile, forming a deep and almost impassable gulf. At the upper end of this ravine was a most delicious fountain, forming a strong running stream, which wound along the shady depths of this wild and most secluded spot. When these Bakalahari heard the report of my rifle echoing through their valley, they left their pots upon their fires, and fled to a man. My Bechuanas, however, eventually got them to come back again, and they cut up for me my koodoo, and carried the flesh to a shady tree on the table summit of this tabular range, immediately above the strong fountain in the gulf beneath me.

SHOOTING SABLE ANTELOPE.

This spot I selected to be my forest home for a short time; and here I spent some merry days, and feasted like a prince on fat vension, marrow-bones, Bechuana corn, Bechuana beer, tea, coffee, biscuit, etc. I was also provided with a rich dessert consisting of a delicious African fruit called "moopooroo," which was now ripe and extremely abundant throughout this range. This fine fruit grows on a tree with a very dark green leaf; the fruit is the size and shape of a large olive, and when ripe is bright orange. In the afternoon I went out with Ruyter, and found four buck koodoos on the northern ridge of the mountain. I wounded one of these, and followed up his bloody spoor, and, coming on him in cover on the mountain side, I broke his fore-leg with a second shot; he, however, took away down to the level forest beneath, and there I lost him.

At earliest dawn next day I held down wind with Ruyter, and presently found fresh spoor of a herd of sable antelope which had got my wind, and they were off. I then inclined my steps in the direction in which their spoor led, and presently we observed them among the trees within three hundred yards of us, some lying and some standing. One of the old does soon observed us. We sat gently down in the grass, however, and I crept away back, and made a very fine stalk upon the herd in very difficult ground. I was obliged to do a hundred and fifty yards of it on my breast. A wary old doe kept sentry, and prevented my approaching within a hundred yards. I therefore took this doe, and shot her with a bullet in the shoulder. I then sent Ruyter for the natives and at once despatched the head to camp to be stuffed.

In the evening I fell in again with this same troop of potaquaines on the northern range of the mountain. They heard me coming on before I was aware of them, and held up wind over very rocky ground and through thick cover. I followed on in their wake like an old staghound, keeping close to them, and always halting when they halted; thus they did not observe me, and at last I got close in upon them. I could then have had a fine shot at several of the does, but I wanted the old black buck. I aimed for his heart, but an unlucky branch intervened, and, altering the line of my ball, lost me this most noble animal. I, however, fired a snap shot at him with my left barrel, and sent a bullet through his flank. The herd then dashed down the mountain side, making a tremendous rumpus among the loose masses of rock, the old buck leaving a bloody spoor. I did not disturb them further then, the sun being under, but returned to my home beneath the greenwood tree.

I followed the old buck up next day, but without success, and on the 31st I determined to return to my waggons. Accordingly, at dawn of day I rolled up my bedding, and, directing my Bechuanas to go and call Bakalahari to carry my flesh and impedimenta to camp, I held a south-westerly course across the mountains with Ruyter and a Bechuana boy. This morning richly repaid me for all my toil and exertions in following the sable antelope throughout these stony and rugged mountains. Having proceeded about a mile down wind, on looking over a height which commanded a fine view of well-wooded undulating table-land below me, I had the sincere pleasure to behold a beautiful herd of sable antelopes feeding quietly up wind a within a quarter of a mile of me. The herd consisted of seven does and one coal-black magnificent old buck. Even at the distance at which they then were, I could very plainly see that this buck was a most superb specimen; his horns seemed almost too large for him, and swept back over his shoulders with a determined and perfect curve.

I sat some time to watch their movements, and gazed upon them with intense delight. The ground on which they were feeding being very level, and observing that the does were extremely wary, I thought the best way to stalk them would be to cut in before them to windward, as they were proceeding in that direction, taking care of course to keep out of their way sufficiently far to ensure their not getting my wind. I then crept back from the ridge where I had observed them, and, describing a semicircle, crept in on my knees through the large rough stones. The does came freshly on, and inclined their course to the spot where I lay flat on my belly awaiting their forward movement. They continued to approach until one fine old doe was within range of my rifle. When, however, they had come thus far, they seemed all at once to change their minds, and after feeding about for a few minutes they took another track and altered their course from east to north. I then divested myself of my shoes and shooting-belt, and commenced following them up.

Presently, however, I observed a wary old doe, which had fed away among the trees apart from her comrades, standing looking at me. My position was a very awkward one; but I dared not alter it, as this would have lost me the day, so I remained motionless as the rocks over which I crept, and presently her patience was exhausted, and she ceased to suspect me, and held on to her comrades. I now made up my mind that it was impossible to do anything with them where they then were, and that it would be best to watch them from a distance until they should move into some more uneven ground, where a stalker would have some chance with them.

Having thus resolved, I beat a retreat, and returned to the ridge above, where I had at first made them out. Here I again sat, and with a longing heart watched the movements of these loveliest of Afric's lovely antelopes. I was struck with admiration at the magnificence of the noble old black buck, and I vowed in my heart to slay him, although I should follow him for a twelvemonth. The old fellow seemed very fidgety in his movements, and while the does fed steadily on he lagged far behind, occasionally taking a mouthful of grass, and then standing for a few minutes under the trees, rubbing his huge, knotted, scimitar-shaped horns upon their branches. At length the does had fed away a hundred and fifty yards from him, and he still lagged behind. This was the golden moment to make a rapid stalk in upon him, while his everwatchful sentinels were absent. I saw my chance, and stole rapidly down the rocky hill-side and gained the level on which the herd were pasturing. He was now obscured from my view by the bushy dwarfish trees which adorned the ground; the next move was to get my eye upon him before he should observe me: I stole stealthily forward and detected him. He was still feeding very slowly on after the does, and seemed quite unsuspicious. I then instantly cast off my shoes and shooting-belt, and, watching the lowering of his noble horns, my eye fixed tiger-like upon him, stalked rapidly in. My heart beat with anxiety as I advanced, and was almost within shot; twenty yards nearer and I would fire. Again he lowered his head to crop the young grass; I seized the moment, and the twenty yards were won.

Here was a young tree with a fork, from which I had resolved to fire. The potaquaine stood with his round stern right to me. I took a deadly aim and fired: the ball entered very near his tail, and passing through the length of his vitals rested in his breast. He staggered about for a second, and then, bounding forward about sixty yards, he halted, and looked to see from whence the deadly shaft had sped that had thus so unceremoniously disturbed his morning meal. The sights of my rifle were still fixed upon him, and just as he pulled up and exposed to me his full broadside a second bullet left the ringing steel, and crashed through the very centre of the old fellow's shoulder.

On receiving this second shot the sable antelope wheeled about and held after the does, and I knew from his movement, though his pace was good, that he had got the ball in his shoulder and could not go very far. I then walked leisurely back to seek my shoes and shooting-belt, and, having found them, I was loading my rifle, when the Bushman, who had been watching my stalk from the height above, joined me, and said that the buck had run but a short distance, and had lain down under a tree. I stole carefully forward and immediately observing him lying as if still alive, his noble head not laid on the ground, but in an upright posture. Fancying him still alive, and having too often been tricked with wounded antelopes, I then gave him a third bullet, but the dark form of this lovely habitant of the mountain quailed not to the shot; the spirit of the sable antelope had fled.

I was transported with delight when I came up and saw the surpassing beauty and magnificence of the invaluable trophy I had won. This potaquaine was very old, and his horns were enormous, fair set, perfect, and exquisitely beautiful. I cut off his head, and, leaving men to convey the flesh to camp, I held thither in advance, escorting my hard-won trophy. On my way to camp, coming down the footpath from the fountain, to my dejectment I found the untameable Mazeppa stretched to rise no more, and half consumed by hyænas and vultures; he had died of horse-sickness. The reduction of my stock by the fell hand of death during this week was, alas! not confined to Mazeppa only; the pony I bought of my cousin Colonel Campbell died of "tsetse," a valuable fore-ox died of some severe sickness, and "Fox," a very good dog, died of the African distemper; three of my very best dogs had also mysteriously disappeared the day they chased the potaquaine.

We remained in the neighbourhood frequented by the sable antelope for several days longer, but I did not succeed in killing another, although with other game of every kind I met with great success.

CHAPTER XXX.

Leave the Potaquaine Country—Absurd Ceremony—My Cattle fail me—Send to the Missionary Station for Aid—Encamp near the Limpopo—Indescribable Fish—A young Secretary—Nearly all my Oxen die—Assistance arrives from Mr. Livingstone—We reach the Residence of Sichely—A Hunter's Monument—We continue our March through a beautiful Country—An Adventure with two savage Lionesses—A violent Tempest—Mahura—Bakalahari driving Game towards their Pitfalls—We cross the Orange River and reach Colesberg.

On the 15th of November we inspanned, and left the mountains of Linguapa. Kapain and his Bechuanas held for Bamangwato; Seleka's Bechuanas held for their chief; and we held a south-westerly course for the Limpopo, which we reached in less than three hours.

Next day we trekked at dawn, and having marched a few miles we were joined by Bakalahari, who reported having seen elephants on the preceding day. A little after this I shot a waterbuck close to the river, when I outspanned.

During the day "Matsaca," chief of the Bamalette, visited me with a retinue: he brought a kaross for me, for which I was to cut him on the arm and shoulder and anoint him with medicine to make him shoot well with the gun which he had bought of me. In the evening I walked a short distance down the river's bank, and shot a lovely fawn of the serolomootlooque, and a buck pallah with a very handsome head.

On the 17th I went in quest of elephants, accompanied by the Bamalette men. We continued along the bank of the river for several miles, when we took up the spoor of three or four enormous old bulls. On our way I wounded a white rhinoceros, which I did not follow to secure. The elephants had fed very slowly away from the river, and before we had followed the spoor an hour we were close upon them. The Bechuanas chose to leave the spoor, and making a cast to windward they started the elephants. My dogs being much distressed with the sun, and I not being aware that the game were started, we at this very moment, unfortunately, sat down and rested for half an hour, which of course lost me the day. When I discovered that the elephants had moved off, I turned my face for camp, and before proceeding far I started an ostrich off her nest; the nest contained twenty eggs, which I directed the Bechuanas to bring to camp.

As we held up the side of the river I detected a very fine old black rhinoceros standing among some wait-a-bit thorn. Directing Piet, my dismounted after-rider (for my stud of fifteen was now reduced to one), to watch my movements, I commenced a stalk upon Borèlé, and, having got within about sixty yards of where he stood in dense cover, I signed to Piet to get on the other side and start him towards me; this plan succeeded, for he was charged out of the cover, and, holding for the bush behind which I was concealed, he passed within twelve yards. My first shot was a very deadly one. It set him charging round and round in a circle, when I gave him a second, and he made off mortally wounded. I then ran to my little mare, and, mounting her, I gave him chase, and presently dropped him with a shot behind the shoulder. Loud thunder was rumbling to windward of my camp, so I hastened to cut off Borèlé's horn, after which I rode home.

In course of the day I saw the fresh spoor of about twenty varieties of large game, and most of the animals themselves, viz., elephant, black, white, and long-horned rhinoceros, hippopotamus, camelopard, buffalo, blue wildebeest, zebra, waterbuck, sassayby, koodoo, pallah, springbok, serolomootlooque, wild boar, duiker, steinbok, lion, leopard. This district of Africa contains a larger variety of game than any other in the whole of this tract of the globe, and perhaps more than any other district throughout the world; for besides the game which I have just noted, the following are not uncommon, viz., keilton, or two-horned black rhinoceros, eland, oryx, roan antelope, sable antelope, hartebeest, klipspringer, and grys steinbuck: the reitbuck is also to be found, but not abundantly.

We inspanned on the 18th before it was day, and trekked up the Limpopo for about three hours. In the forenoon Matsaca arrived from the carcase of the borèlé: he brought with him a very fine leopard's skin kaross, and an elephant's tooth; these were for me, in return for which I was to cut him to make him shoot well. This I did in the following manner: opening a large book of natural history, containing prints of all the chief quadrupeds, I placed his forefinger successively on several of the prints of the commonest of the South African quadruped, and as I placed his finger on each I repeated some absurd sentence and anointed him with turpentine. When this was accomplished I made four cuts on his arm with a lancet, and then, anointing the bleeding wounds with gunpowder and turpentine, I told him that his gun had power over each of the animals which his finger had touched, provided he held it straight. Matsaca and his retinue seemed highly gratified, and presently took leave and departed: I afterwards trekked up the river till sundown.

On the succeeding day we marched with the dawn, and held up the river. In the afternoon Bechuanas from Seleka visited me, bearing a tooth of a bull-elephant, for which they wanted a gun; the tooth, however, being small, I would not give them one for it, although I might have done so at a fair profit. I found the game extremely abundant, counting no less than twenty-two rhinoceroses, nine of which were in one herd, feeding on the open plain. The wind was as foul as it could blow and kept continually starting the game. At length, late in the afternoon, I got within shot of four white rhinoceroses. The old bull stood next to me, so, resting my six-pound rifle on the trunk of a tree which an elephant had over-thrown, I took him on the shoulder and smashed his fore arm; he ran for thirty yards, and then rolled over on his back. He however regained his legs and ran a hundred yards farther, when his leg failed him, and coming up on his spoor I finished him in a few minutes. The waggons now came up, and I halted them on the river's bank, opposite to the rhinoceros.

On the 21st much rain fell throughout the day, rendering the country unfit for trekking. A birth and a death occurred among my cattle. In the afternoon a loud rushing noise was heard coming on like a hurricane:

this was a large troop of pallah pursued by a pack of about twenty wild dogs; they passed our camp in fine style within a hundred yards of us, and in two minutes the wild dogs had caught two of the pallahs, which my Bechuanas ran up and secured. A pallah in passing my camp cleared a distance of fifty feet in two successive bounds, and this on unfavourable ground, it being soft and slippery.

I left the sable antelopes' mountain mainly in consequence of a general falling off amongst my cattle. I did not then know to what cause to attribute this sad and to me all-important change in their condition, which only a few weeks before had been a source of admiration to us. Alas! it was now too evident that nearly all of them were dying, having been bitten by the fly "tsetse" at the mountain. The rains of the last three days had made this melancholy truth more strongly manifest; the cattle presented a most woful appearance. Listless and powerless, they cared not to feed, and, though the grass covered the country with the richest and most luxuriant pasturage, their sides remained hollow, and their whole bodies became daily more emaciated; the eyes also of many of them were closed and swollen.

The next morning being fair, I inspanned, although the country was very unfit for trekking; my heavily laden waggons sinking deep in the soft rich soil which lies along the banks of the Limpopo. My poor oxen, as expected, became knocked up on the march before they had proceeded three miles, and many of them lying down and refusing to proceed farther, or even to stand up. I was obliged in consequence to outspan one waggon and leave it behind, and to bring on the other waggon with the able oxen, and then send them back to assist their dying comrades in bringing up the second. I performed a short march, and halted on a fine sandy spot, where I made a strong thorn kraal for the cattle. Soon after we had outspanned the second waggon heavy rain set in, which continued at intervals throughout the night.

Light rains continued to fall throughout the 24th. I, however, performed a short march, and brought my waggons a few miles further up the Limpopo. I was obliged, as on the last march, to bring on one waggon at a time.

Heavy rains fell at intervals throughout the next day. "Ronoberg," a Natal ox, died during the night, and it was evident that many more would die in a few days; even now the half of them were utterly unfit to work. The heavy and continued rains which had lately set in made me feel my heavy misfortune with increased severity, for the country was hardly to be travelled with such loads as mine, even with oxen in good working condition. At length I found myself reduced to a stand, or the next thing to it. In this state of things I deemed it necessary to despatch natives to the nearest missionary station for assistance. I accordingly wrote a letter to Mr. Livingstone, the resident missionary at Sichely's, requesting the loan of two spans of oxen, and, having sealed up my epistle in a bottle, I sent it off with two natives, instructing them to use all possible speed. One of these men was a native in my service, named "Ramachumey;" the other was one of Sichely's subjects, having been on a visit to Seleka. They expected to reach Sichely in seven days.

For many succeeding days my difficulties with respect to bringing on the waggons continued to increase. The rain still poured down, rendering the country impossible to travel, and my oxen died daily of the tsetse-bite. In this condition my progress was slow and painful in the extreme, and I awaited anxiously the expected succour from Mr. Livingstone. At length I came fairly to a stand, not having sufficient oxen left to draw one waggon. I formed my camp in a shady bend of the river, and fortified it with a high hedge of thorny trees, and in a few days more all my cattle had died with the exception of two young oxen, which I inclined to think would survive the bite of the fatal "tsetse."

On the 7th of December I resolved to have some fishing; accordingly I routed out some old salmon-fishing tackle, and sallied forth with one of the waggon whip-sticks for a rod, and some string for a line. I baited my hook with a bit of blue wildebeest, and put on a cork for a bob. I cast in my bait in a quiet bend of the river, and anxiously watched the cork, which very soon began to bob. I then conjured up many forms in my mind, and wondered whether it would be a fair fish, such as I might expect in my own land's rivers, or something more like a young crocodile. I was not fated to live long upon conjecture however, for next moment under went the cork, and striking sharply I threw over my head a fine grey fish about a pound weight, and in appearance like a haddock, with a broad mouth and eight or ten feelers. My Bushman said the Boers about the Orange River knew this fish, and loved to catch and eat it. Presently my perseverance was rewarded by a second fish of the same kind as the first; and after this I hooked a very heavy fish, which I lost. I doubt not but most excellent sport might be obtained in the Limpopo.

In the evening Carey and I cut down a very dense thorn-tree to inspect the nest of a secretary. The summit of the tree was very wide, dense, and level, and from the terrible nature of the thorns it was utterly inaccessible without the aid of the hatchet. When the tree fell, out from its nest rolled a young secretary, and immediately disgorged its last meal, which consisted of "four lizards of different sorts (of which one was a cameleon), one locust, one quail, and a mouse."

A few days after this I sent out John and Carey into different airts to seek game, and each killed a pallah; but the sky threatening rain they did not wait to escort their venison, but left natives to bring it on. A considerable time having elapsed, and the Bakalahari not appearing, I despatched John and some of the natives in my service to look after them, and it was well I did so; for on reaching his pallah John found the Bakalahari whom he had left to convey it to camp, in the act of bolting with the half of it, having cunningly (as he thought) hacked the other half with a sharp stone, and dirtied the flesh with the entrails, thinking to persuade us that it had been done by a leopard or hyæna.

It was now twenty days since I despatched natives to the nearest missionary to inform him of my distress, and solicit assistance in oxen, and they might ere now have reached me, if all was well; this caused me many painful doubts and apprehensions. Day after day was passing away, and hourly I felt my situation more and more irksome and tedious. Moreover, my supplies were fast coming to an end. I certainly felt my fixed position most painful. At length, however, that aid which I so earnestly yet fearfully prayed for was at hand.

On the morning of the 16th, as I was preparing my breakfast, I suddenly beheld a civilized-looking native approach me; he wore a shirt, a pair of leather trousers, and a sailor's red nightcap, and carried a gun and shooting-belt. The instant I beheld him I said aloud, "Natives from Sichely—the oxen are at hand." It was even so: my messengers had found Mr. Livingstone at home, who, on hearing of my distress, had at once in the noblest manner despatched men with his whole stock of trek-oxen to my assistance. These I had now the inexpressible satisfaction to behold reach me in safety. We inspanned at once, and commenced our march, and continued to make good way for several days; and on the 26th we reached Kolubeng, the new residence of Sichely. In the morning that chief brought me two young oxen, which I all but purchased for an old saddle and two pounds of powder; but we split upon the cup of powder being level and not piled.

A day or two after I ascended the rocky hill above the town with Mr. Livingstone, to obtain a view of the surrounding country. I came upon a very high heap of well-bleached mouldering bones of many varieties of game, amassed and piled here by a mighty Nimrod, now no more, who had in days of yore chosen this hill for his habitation. Mr. Livingstone pointed out to me a range of tabular hills to the south-east, near the sources of the Kolubeng, throughout which he informed me the sable antelope was to be met with. In the evening Sichely came to trade with me, when I obtained several young oxen in barter from him.

On arriving at Sichely's I despatched natives to Bakatla, to fetch two spans of oxen which I had left on my way into the interior in charge of Mr. Edwards, and with these on the 3rd of the new year, we again inspanned and tried to make a start with twelve oxen in each waggon: they, however, finding the waggons extremely heavy, would not move them, nor could we prevail upon them to take to their wonted work, as they ought to do, until every ox had been most unmercifully flogged with both waggon-whips and jamboks. Our course for Bakatla was south-westerly, but owing to the position of the mountains we were obliged to make a very zigzag and circuitous march. We halted at sundown. The country here is the most pleasing I have seen in Africa—beautifully wooded, undulating plains, valleys, straths, and conical and tabular mountains of most fascinating appearance, invariably wooded to their summits, stretching away on every side.

We marched steadily for several days, and on the 7th reached Bakatla, which was looking extremely beautiful, being surrounded by very green fields of Bechuana corn. Here we remained a few days whilst I obtained fresh oxen, and then pushing on we gained the river Molopo. Early on the 4th I drew up my waggons on its northern bank, and in the forenoon I sallied forth to seek for reitbuck, which are here abundant. At this hour of the day, however, it was of little use to seek for them, as they were lying concealed in the endless dense reeds which enclose the Molopo, in some parts extending to a breadth of half a mile; their height averaging from twelve to twenty feet and upwards. I found plenty of spoor, including the fresh spoor of lions, which along the Molopo are always abundant. The day was excessively hot, and there was a most painful oppressive feeling in the atmosphere to an extent which I had rarely experienced. In the afternoon dark masses of clouds arose along the horizon on every side, and constant thunder bellowed in the distance: a little before the sun went down the sky above and all around looked extremely threatening, and I directed my people to prepare for a tempestuous night.

At this time I observed a reitbuck grazing beyond the dense reeds on the other side of the Molopo, and I at once held for him, with my little Moore rifle, accompanied by my Bushman. We had some difficulty in penetrating the dense reeds, and on gaining the other side a change in the direction of the wind started off the reitbuck; I then observed two other reitbuck, a buck and a doe, coming out to graze some distance to windward, and commenced a stalk in upon them. Having proceeded about half-way I suddenly observed two huge yellow lionesses, about a hundred and fifty yards to my left, walking along the edge of the reeds, holding a course parallel to my own. The reitbucks smelt the lions and lay down. I got very near them, but they started off, and bounded straight away from me: I fired and missed the buck.

Ruyter came towards me, and I ran forward to obtain a view beyond a slight rise in the ground to see whether the lionesses had gone. In so doing I came suddenly upon them, within about seventy yards; they were standing looking back at Ruyter. I then very rashly commenced making a rapid stalk in upon them, and fired at the nearest, having only one shot in my rifle. The ball told loudly, and the lioness at which I had fired wheeled right round, and came on lashing her tail, showing her teeth, and making that horrid murderous deep growl which an angry lion generally utters. At the same moment her comrade, who seemed better to know that she was in the presence of man, made a hasty retreat into the reeds. The instant the lioness came on I stood up to my full height, holding my rifle, and my arms extended, and high above my head. This checked her in her course, but on looking round and missing her comrade, and observing Ruyter slowly advancing, she was still more exasperated, and, fancying that she was being surrounded, she made another forward movement, growling terribly. This was a moment of great danger. I felt that my only chance of safety was extreme steadiness, so, standing motionless as a rock, with my eyes firmly fixed upon her, I called out in a clear commanding voice, "Holloa! old girl, what's the hurry? take it easy; holloa! holloa!" She instantly once more halted, and seemed perplexed, looking round for her comrade. I then thought it prudent to beat a retreat, which I very slowly did, talking to the lioness all the time. She seemed undecided as to her future movements, and was gazing after me and snuffing the ground when I last beheld her.

The sun was under, and terrific thunder which burst around proclaimed a coming tempest : I therefore deemed it safe to reach my camp with all possible speed, and, having loaded my rifle, we held thither at a sharp trot, holding for the old waggon-drift to avoid having to pass through the dense reeds. Before I reached the drift two reitbuck dashed past me, one of which I shot and bore to camp. On reaching camp the first move was to refresh the person. Before however I could accomplish this the tempest was upon us; it was one of the most violent I had experienced for years, the wind blowing a perfect hurricane, accompanied by rattling hailstones and rain, which fell in such torrents as in a few minutes to convert the dry ground into a befitting habitation for fish or water-fowl : the thunder and lightning were most appalling, and burst and flashed above and around us, threatening our momentary destruction.

The wind blew one side of my sail over the roof of the tent, the sail's fastenings having been insecure, leaving myself and my property exposed to the pelting rain, which in a few seconds had deluged bedding, blankets, pillows, rifles, sacks, leopard-skins, karosses, stuffed heads, etc., etc. I however quickly piped all hands to bend on another sail which I fortunately had in the waggon, and when this was accomplished my castle was once more waterproof. The violence of the wind had set my oxen at liberty, and when the tempest had passed away they were found to have passed away with it, which it may be supposed left me in no very placid temper, this being exactly the sort of night on which the stealthy prowling tyrant of the wilderness is ever found to be most active in his murderous pursuits; and, as if to add to my anxiety on the subject, lions immediately commenced roaring on every side, especially to leeward, being the course which cattle invariably take before a storm.

When day dawned men were despatched on the spoor of the oxen. I was busy all the forenoon drying my saturated property. The sun was high, and yet no tidings of my cattle. I began to be extremely anxious. About midday some of the Bakatla Bechuanas brought me one ox; it was "Youngman," the last of the Mohicans. On beholding him a pang of sorrow shot through my heart. He brought my melancholy losses all fresh as at a single glance before me; his appearance was worn and emaciated, and it was evident that soon the vulture and hyæna would leave his whitening bones to bleach upon the glowing plain.

Who then was "Youngman" that he could call up such melancholy associations ? "Youngman" was the only dying survivor of thirty selected trek-oxen which I had chosen to accompany me into the far interior, all of which I had seen pine away and die, and fail me in the hour of need. The men who brought me "Youngman" said that they had found him on the spoor of the other cattle, and about two hours afterwards I had the satisfaction to behold all the missing truants recovered. They had been seduced away by some young oxen I had obtained at Bakatla, which seemed to have resolved to return to their former masters, perhaps not relishing old Adonis's treatment of them in the yoke.

We now held on to the Meritsane (rendered famous among sportsmen by Harris's glowing description of its charms), and found it full of water. Before reaching this point, however, I left the old-established Kuruman waggon-road about three miles from the drift, my line of march being to visit Mahura, chief of the Batlapis, residing about the sources of the Hart River. This route is by many days shorter than by the old road, and has also the advantage of being through a firm grassy country. As we reached the Meritsane we started a cock and hen ostrich, with a large troop of extremely small young ones, which did not seem larger than guinea-fowls.

We held on for several days through a country abounding in game, and reached Mahura's town on the 25th. As we drew near to the town, Mahura was pointed out to me. He was walking in company with another old man, and carried a double-barrelled percussion rifle on his shoulder. He was dressed in a shirt, waistcoat, and baggy trousers, and wore a broad-rimmed hat à la Boer. Halting my waggons, I went up and shook hands with him, and asked his permission to outspan, which was graciously granted. Mahura and his aristocracy remained with us all the evening drinking my coffee, and fishing or pumping out all the news he could from me and my natives; and at a late hour this ill-expressioned cunning old tyrant took leave for the night, requesting that I would inspan in the morning, and bring up my waggons close to his dwelling-house, that he might enjoy as much of my society as possible during my stay at his town, and that we might trade with more facility.

Accordingly, in the morning I drove up my waggons, and very soon his highness made his appearance, and requested me to get ready some coffee. Presently about a dozen fine young oxen were brought up, which he said were to purchase powder, and after coffee we proceeded to trading. I selected one young ox, and offered him six pounds of powder for it. He then desired to see the powder, and on my measuring it out he said that I must add two more. From his manner it appeared to me that he did not intend to deal with me even if I gave him what he asked; so I said I would let him have one pound more, and if he did not like to take it we could not deal. He then, with the greatest nonchalence, said, "Lay by your powder," and commenced talking on some other subject. Being very anxious to obtain some good specimens of the large-horned oxen of the Kalihari, and Mahura being by report in possession of some, which he had lifted from the Bawangketse, I told him that if he would bring them up I would give him a good price for them. He said that he had cattle with large horns, and that he would send to one of his outposts for two oxen which would frighten me to look at.

In the evening the cattle came; these were two immensely tall, gaunt, hollow-sided, very remarkable-looking animals, and carried truly enormous horns. The head of one of them was very handsome; the horns were very wide and fair set, going out quite horizontally for some distance on leaving the head: their width, from point to point, might have been about eight feet. This ox was roan-coloured on his face and along the top of his back. The other was red; his horns were thicker than those of his comrade, and were of good length, with very good points, but their sweep was not graceful. They were neither of them so thick as the horns of my red Wangketse ox, Rob Roy, which I left with Fossey, nor by any means so handsome; yet, nevertheless, they were both very remarkable heads, and perhaps such another pair I might never again fall in with. I told Mahura that I possessed finer specimens, but I should be happy to have a deal with him. He then showed me two fine bull-elephant tusks, for which I offered him cash; but he said he had no understanding in cash, and that he would keep them until he saw something he stood in need of. His drift was to get one of my valuable double rifles out of me.

Next day Mahura brought me the two large-horned Kalihari oxen, and after coffee he asked me if I was going to buy. I asked him what he wanted for the oxen, when he said powder. I said that I would take them both, and give him eight pounds of powder for each. On hearing my offer he only laughed, and, turning round, ordered his herds to drive the cattle back to the post. I asked him what he wanted for them: this he would not state, but remarked, "You were wont to ride by the Motito road. They may well now say, 'Alas! we have lost that good trader; now may Mahura rejoice that that good man has gone to trade with him.'" The meaning of this speech was, that Mochuara, the chief at Motito, had presented me with an ox carrying very large horns, and that in return I had given him a gun. I now considered that I had already been too long with this ruffian, and I accordingly called for my oxen and marched for the Vaal River, distant a day and a half. We held on until sundown, having halted for an hour at mid-day.

We resumed our march at daybreak on the 28th, and held on through boundless open plains. As we advanced, game became more and more abundant. In about two hours we reached a fine fountain, beside which was a small cover of trees and bushes, which afforded an abundant supply of firewood. Here we outspanned for breakfast; it was a fine cool morning, with a pleasant breeze. The country was thickly covered with immense herds of game, consisting of zebra, wildebeest, blesbok, and springbok. There could not have been less than five or six thousand head of game in sight of me as I sat at breakfast. Presently the whole of this game began to take alarm. Herd joined herd, and took away up the wind; and in a few minutes other vast herds came pouring on up-wind, covering the whole breadth of the plain with a living mass of noble game.

Bakalahari now hove in sight, running at intervals across the plain, bearing parasols of black ostrich-feathers, which they brandished on high, to press on the panic-stricken herds. These fellows must have had good wind, for they held on at a steady trot, exactly like wild dogs (only that the wild dogs gallop and do not trot), and did not allow the game to get very far in advance. It was evident that they were driving it to a range of pitfalls in advance; but being without steeds, and in extreme pain from a swelled ankle, I was unable to follow them up and ascertain their success as I wished to have done. My ankle became daily worse. I applied leeches to it at Mahura's, which helped me a

CHAP. XXXI.

little, but the number was too small to be of a great benefit. I was now entirely unable to set my foot to the ground. Carey thought it was erysipelas, and I was very apprehensive that it would end in something extremely serious.

On the 29th we again set out, and in about three hours we reached the fair, long-wished for, yet much dreaded, Vaal River. I say much-dreaded, because, from the constant rains which had been continually falling this season, I had made up my mind that it was not improbable I might have to lie for many months upon the banks of this often impassable river. On this occasion, however, to my great satisfaction, and quite contrary to my expectations, I found the river low, and the drift, which I had never seen before, very good, and free from rocks or very large stones. The descent from our side was easy, but the ascent from the drift on the opposite side was steep and muddy; and some smart showers of rain, which had been falling during the last two hours, had rendered it so slippery that I deemed it best to outspan, and defer taking the drift until the ground should dry a little in the afternoon, when I got my waggons through in safety, taking one at a time with twenty steady oxen.

We now made the Vet River, which flows into the Vaal a little above the drift, and followed its course towards Colesberg. This we found to be an excellent road, but inclining too far to the east. Our march led us through vast herds of game, which I have before spoken of as frequenting the northern boundaries of the colony. On the 20th of February I crossed the Great Orange River at Alleman's Drift, and entered Colesberg next day. I found most of my old friends still here, and also my redoubtable friend old Murphy, as wild and as jolly as ever.

I hired the old barracks for my residence during my stay in Colesberg, and immediately set about sewing up my trophies in canvas, and stowing them away in cases. This was accomplished in about fourteen days. A fortnight more was spent in preparing for another hunting expedition. I purchased a new waggon from a Mr. Emslie for a hundred pounds, and a fresh stud of sixteen horses, a mule, and a span of oxen from various parties in town, and subsequently I increased my stud to twenty.

CHAPTER XXXI.

Start on my fifth and last Expedition into the Interior—Mr. Orpen accompanies me—Hurried March—Extraordinary Herd of Blesboks—The Hart River—Cattle attacked with Hoof Sickness—Three Lionesses fearfully mangle my pack of Dogs—Lion-hunts—Hyænas devour my Camp-stools—Meritsane—Six Buffaloes shot—Another Lion-hunt—Glorious Chase with Elands—Sichely's Kraal—We cross the Limpopo—A Lion attacks my Kraal and kills an Ox—A Field of Battle—Seboono—My hundredth Elephant!—We march down the Limpopo and hunt Hippopotami—Attacked by Rheumatic Fever—Mr. Orpen nearly killed by a Leopard.

ON the 19th of March, 1848, I left Colesberg with three waggons "well manned and stored," for my fifth and last cruise in the far interior. I was joined by a Mr. Orpen (a mighty Nimrod), who, notwithstanding my representing to him the dangers and hardships of an elephant-hunting expedition in their blackest colours, kindly agreed to favour me with his help and company on my lonely trip. My sojourn in Colesberg reduced me considerably, and I was glad once more to breathe the fresh air of the country. We got clear of Colesberg at about nine A.M., and commenced our march over the country I had so often marked with my wheel-tracks, and which my reader must now be fully acquainted with. On my way I completely recruited my oxen and stud, and prepared myself to take the field with an immense pack of stout serviceable dogs. I also engaged as after-rider a Bushman named Booi.

The game became plentiful in about ten days after we left Colesberg, but when we came to the Vet River I beheld with astonishment and delight decidedly one of the most wonderful displays which I had witnessed during my varied sporting career in Southern Africa. On my right and left the plain exhibited one purple mass of graceful blesboks, which extended without a break as far as my eyes could strain: the depth of their vast legions covered a breadth of about six hundred yards. On pressing upon them, they cantered along before me, not exhibiting much alarm, taking care, however, not to allow me to ride within at least four hundred yards of them. On, on I rode intensely excited with the wondrous scene before me, and hoped at length to get to windward of at least some portion of the endless living mass which darkened the plain, but in vain. Like squadrons of dragoons, the entire breadth of this countless herd held on their forward course as if aware of my intention, and resolved not to allow me to weather them.

At length I determined to play upon their ranks, and, pressing my horse to his utmost speed, I dashed forward, and, suddenly halting, sprang from the saddle, and, giving my rifle at least two feet of elevation, fired right and left into one of their darkest masses. A noble buck dropped to the right barrel, and the second shot told loudly; no buck, however, fell, and after lying half a minute the prostrate blesbok rose, and was quickly lost sight of among his retreating comrades. In half a minute I was again loaded, and after galloping a few hundred yards let drive into them, but still was unsuccessful. Excited, and annoyed at my want of luck, I resolved to follow them up, and blaze away while a shot remained in the locker, which I did; until, after riding about eight or nine miles, I found my ammunition expended, and not a single blesbok bagged, although at least a dozen must have been wounded. It was now high time to retrace my steps and seek my waggons. I accordingly took a point, and rode across the trackless country in the direction for which they were steering.

I very soon once more fell in with fresh herds of thousands of blesboks. As it was late in the day, and I being on the right side for the wind, the blesboks were very tame, and allowed me to ride along within rifle-shot of them, and those which ran charged resolutely past me up the wind in long-continued streams. I took a lucky course for the waggons, and came right upon them, after they had outspanned on the bank of the Vet River. I could willingly have devoted a month to blesbok-shooting in this hunter's elysium, but, having heard from a party of Bastards that the Vaal River was low, and being extremely anxious to push on, I inspanned, and continued my march by moonlight. Before proceeding far we discovered the deeply imprinted spoor of an enormous lion, which had walked along the waggon-track for several hundred yards. We continued our march till after midnight, vast herds of blesbok charging from us on every side. Lions were heard roaring for the first time during this night.

On the 22nd of April after some trouble we crossed the Vaal River, and on the 25th we reached Mahura's. I rode ahead of the waggons, and found the old ruffian busily engaged with some of his nobility in reducing with adzes a thornwood tree, which was to serve as a beam in a new dwelling-house he was about to erect. He was astonished to see me return so soon, and expressed much satisfaction thereat. I asked Mahura if he had still the two large-horned oxen which I had seen when last here; he replied they were still forthcoming. In half an hour the waggons arrived, and I drew them up outside the town. The chief shortly afterwards made his appearance, and had coffee with us.

For many days back our oxen had been looking very spare, and fallen off in condition, and one or two exhibited symptoms of the tongue sickness at the Vaal River. We now had the intense mortification to discover that nearly the whole of them were attacked with either tongue or hoof sickness. This discovery cast a sad gloom over our prospects. I was unacquainted with the nature of either of these maladies, and the Hottentots declared that an ox required months to recover from either of them, and that they often proved fatal. In this state of things I deemed it prudent to begin to purchase young oxen from Mahuara and his tribe, and I gave him to understand that I was willing to do so. The chief replied that his people would be unwilling to bring their oxen, because when I had last passed through his country they had brought oxen for barter, and I had purchased none of them; he however, promised to acquaint them with my wishes. In the afternoon, my waggons having outspanned at a great distance from the water, I inspanned, and trekked down to the Hart stream, which I crossed, and drew up on its opposite bank.

Next day the chief, instead of coming to trade as he had given me to understand he would, held a hunting party with a number of his people on the old Scottish principle of the ring, a common and successful mode of hunting among the South African tribes. On this occasion, however, the ring was mismanaged, and the game broke through. In the evening one large ox was brought for barter, but we did not agree about the price. Our oxen now presented a most woful appearance, the greater part of them being very lame, and nearly all more or less ailing. This was a most startling fact, and, as the Bechuanas did not seem disposed to bring oxen for barter, it threatened to oppose an insurmountable barrier to our progress either backwards or forwards.

Two hours having elapsed after breakfast the following morning, and the chief not having made his appearance according to promise, Mr. Orpen and I went up to the palace to ask him what were his intentions in respect to the trading. He replied that he could not force his people to bring me oxen, but that he had intimated my wishes to them. I then remarked that he would do me a friendship if he would set his people the example by first dealing with me himself, as I knew that I should then have no difficulty with them. The chief, after some demur, told me that oxen would be brought for barter, and requested me to go before him to the waggons, and get my coffee-kettle under weigh. In the evening I obtained one good-looking ox from one of his men for ammunition. When Mahura left I presented him with some sugar for his coffee and a whipstick.

The chief again made his appearance, accompanied by his interpreter and several of his people, early next day, bringing stout young cattle to barter for guns and ammunition. Having taken coffee, the chief called me aside, and, pointing out to me two good-looking young oxen, said they were his, and that he wanted powder for them. I asked him how much he would require, and he replied that he had brought a measure, and that if I would fill it with powder I could have the two oxen. When I beheld the wooden measure I thought the chief was going to drive a hard bargain with me. On filling it, however, with powder, I found that it held about eighteen pounds, and as this was not an exorbitant price for two good oxen, I was very glad to get them, and I told the chief I was satisfied with his measure. He and all his people seemed to think they had got a bargain, and, the example now being set, the trading went on rapidly, and by sundown I had purchased twenty-two oxen, twenty of which were quite fit for work. In the forenoon Mr. Orpen and I went to look at the cattle (which we allowed to remain night and day in the veld), and had the satisfaction to find a decided improvement in them.

The chief was in high spirits all day, and on leaving me in the forenoon he said he would give me a fat cow to kill for my people, and that he would bring me a large-horned ox to purchase. In the evening the fat cow was brought and slain, but the herds brought the wrong ox, so the chief sent it back again. A cousin of the chief, named Mokalliharri, anxious to cultivate my good graces, gave me a fat wether. We remained several days longer purchasing oxen, which, together with our horses, now amounted to one hundred and eleven, not counting our lame oxen, which we determined to leave with Mahura.

On the 3rd of May we again inspanned, and resumed our march for the far interior, steering our course across the boundless open plains which lie to the northward of the Hart River. On the 5th, having performed a considerable march, we halted about eleven A.M. beside a small fountain in a slightly elevated part of the country, where the grass was various, rank, and abundant. The country to the west was not frequented by the game, and here the grass was tall and rank; and covers of considerable size of thorn-trees and grey-leaved bushes were scattered over the landscape; it was a still and secluded spot. I observed several vultures soaring over one of these covers within a quarter of a mile of the waggons, and, thinking it very probable that they were attracted by some lion devouring his prey, I ordered a couple of horses to be saddled

Extraordinary Herd of Blesboks

CHAP. XXXI.

and rode towards the place, with one after-rider and about a dozen of my dogs. I was right in my conjecture; for, as I cantered along, I had the satisfaction to behold a majestic old black-maned lion walking parallel to me, and within a hundred yards. He had not yet observed me: he looked so dark, that at the first glance I mistook him in the long grass for a blue wildebeest; next moment, however, he turned his large, full, imposing face to me, and I knew that it was he. Shouting to the dogs with all my might, I at once dashed towards him, followed by my after-rider at a respectful distance carrying my rifle.

The lion, as I expected, was panic-stricken, and took to his heels, bounding through the long grass at top speed. The dogs went at him in gallant style, I following not far behind them, and yelling to encourage my pack. The lion, finding we had the speed of him, reduced his pace to a sulky trot, and the dogs came up and followed barking within a few yards on each side of him. In half a minute more I had passed ahead and halted my horse for a shot; but looking round for my after-rider, who carried my rifle, I beheld him slowly approaching, with pallid countenance, at least a hundred yards behind. The lion faced about, and, springing on Shepherd, one of my favourite dogs, he lay for several seconds upon him, and having bitten him so that he could not rise, he continued his course. A few moments after he knocked over another dog, called Vixen, which escaped with a slight scratch. The lion had now gained the edge of a small cover, and Booi, coming up at a very easy pace, handed me my rifle. In another minute the noble beast came to bay in a thick bush, and, facing round, lay down to await our attack. I then rode up to within twelve yards of him, and, halting my horse, I ended the grim lion's career with a single ball behind the shoulder, cutting the main arteries close to the heart. On receiving the ball his head dropped to the ground, and, gasping for a moment, he expired. I dismounted, and, plucking a lock of hair from his mane, I placed it in my bosom and returned to camp, having been absent barely ten minutes.

After breakfast a party went to inspect the lion, and bring home his trophies. On proceeding to seek for Shepherd, the dog which the lion had knocked over in the chase, I found him with his back broken and his bowels protruding from a gash in the stomach; I was, therefore, obliged to end his misery with a ball.

We marched again at sunrise, and at about ten A.M. I drew up my waggons beside the large pan where I had been storm-stayed for a week last season. On the march I shot a springbok; and observing vultures, Mr. Orpen and I rode towards them with a troop of the dogs, in the hope of falling in with a lion, but were disappointed. In the afternoon, directing the waggons to follow, I rode ahead with Booi; and on reaching the next large pan I drew the cover lying to the south of it, expecting to find a lion. When the waggons came up I formed my camp beside the thorn-grove, and, observing a herd of blue wildebeest making for my cattle, I proceeded to waylay them, and I fired two long shots. Next minute Booi came up to me, and said that on my firing he had observed a lion stick his head up in the long grass in the vley opposite to me. I felt inclined to doubt the veracity of his optics. I sent him back, however, with instructions to bring eight dogs, but Booi thought the whole pack would be better, and returned with thirty.

I then rode direct for the spot where the lion was supposed to be. Booi was correct; and on drawing near, two savage lionesses sat up in the grass and growled fiercely at us. An unlucky belt of reeds, about sixty yards long and twenty broad, intervened between me and the lionesses, and on perceiving their danger they at once dashed into this cover: then followed the most woful cutting up and destruction amongst my best and most valuable dogs. The lionesses had it all their own way. In vain I rode round and round the small cover endeavouring to obtain a peep of them, which would have enabled me to put a speedy conclusion to the murderous work within. The reeds were so tall and dense, that, although the lionesses were often at bay within eight or ten yards of me, it was impossible to see them. At length one came outside the cover on the opposite side, when I fired a shot from the saddle. My horse was unsteady, nevertheless I wounded her, and acknowledging the shot with angry growls, she re-entered the reeds.

A number of the dogs, which had gone off after a herd of blue wildebeests, now returned, and, coming down through the long grass, started a third lioness, which came growling down into the cover and joined her comrades. This was the signal for my united pack to make a bold sally into the centre of the lions' den, when they were savagely met by the three lionesses, who rushed furiously up and down, knocking the dogs about with just as much facility as three cats would have disposed of the same number of mice. For several minutes nothing was to be heard but the crashing of the reeds, the growling of the lions, and the barking and shrieking of the mangled pack: it was truly a most painful moment to my feelings. Carey, who had come up to assist, remarked to me that "there was an awful *massacree* going on among the dogs;" and he was right. Night now setting in put an end to this horrid work, and, with feelings of remorse and deep regret at my folly in not having at once called off my poor dogs, I wended my way to camp. On numbering the slain three of my best hounds were found to have forfeited their lives in the unequal contest, and seven or eight more were very badly wounded, exposing the most fearful gashes, from which several of them never recovered. Whilst I was occupied with the lions my followers were forming a kraal for the cattle.

Before the day began to break next morning lions were heard roaring to the west: accordingly, I rode in that direction with Booi and a detachment of dogs, still resolved to follow the king of beasts, notwithstanding the disasters of the former day. Having ridden about a mile, we reached the end of a long piece of cover, averaging a hundred yards in breadth, where I at once discovered the fresh spoor of a troop of lions. The dogs took it up and followed on at a wary pace, the hair bristling on their backs. On reaching the end of this cover a second one appeared several hundred yards to my right, whilst a little to my left was a small vley, and here I observed a jackal steal away, while a crow sounded his ominous voice in advance.

These signs bid fair for the promixity of lions, and I remarked to Booi that we must be upon them; it was so. Next moment I observed a yellow form on a barish spot two hundred yards ahead, which we knew must be the lion, and thither we rode at top speed. On observing us he raised his noble head, but quickly again laid it flat on the ground, intending to crouch in the hope that we should pass him by unnoticed. Within twenty yards of him lay a noble lioness with two half-grown young lions. On seeing that our course was direct for where they lay, they bounded up and charged for the cover to our right, the old lion displaying more cowardice than either his royal spouse or the young lions, and taking the lead at the best pace that he could muster. I did not wait for my rifle, but shouting to my dogs I pressed forward and tried to cut off his retreat. I was even with him and the lioness, and within twenty yards, when they reached the cover, which they sullenly entered. The dogs seemingly were apprehensive of following too near such dangerous game, probably warned by the fate of their comrades on the preceding day.

The noble game having thus retreated, I placed Booi at one end of the cover to keep watch, while I rode to the other end to beat up through the centre with the dogs. Twice I drew the cover unsuccessfully, but the third time the dogs found the lioness lying under a bushy tree. Then followed a bay, when I rode up and gave her both barrels behind the shoulder, which partially disabled her. My third shot entered beside her eye and blew away the entire half of her brain-pan. When riding up I had heard a dog shriek, and on looking round me I beheld poor Vitberg, a valuable dog, and one that was extremely attached to me, lying on the ground utterly disabled, with his hip so fearfully mangled that I was obliged to blow his brains out.

A fourth time we drew the cover for the old lion, but were still unsuccessful. Booi and I skinned the lioness, cut off her head, and returned to camp. Shortly after reaching the waggons I observed a blue wildebeest approaching my cattle, which I stalked and shot. The afternoon set in with a most terrific hailstorm, such as I never before witnessed; many of the stones were from two to three inches in diameter. The storm came on with a sound resembling the roaring of the sea: a dense intervening fall of rain obscuring our view, we were at a loss to think what it could be. The storm sent our cattle and horses flying before it for miles across the plain, and they were hardly recovered before the sun was under. It blew a gale of wind throughout the first half of the night; tremendous showers of hail and rain succeeding one another in quick succession, accompanied by appalling thunder and lightning.

As the day broke we heard lions moaning to the west, and I rode in quest of them, accompanied by Mr. Orpen and Carey, with a detachment of dogs. In drawing the cover beside which I had found the lions yesterday, I came upon two young lions, one of which, standing to give us battle, I finished with two shots: his comrade stole away, but after a sharp burst the dogs ran him to bay, when I rode up, and, dismounting, flogged the dogs off, and slew him with a single shot in the skull.

The next morning, which was the 9th, for several hours before the day dawned, a lion stood roaring terribly on a bushy eminence within two hundred yards of the waggons, and held west just as it became light, roaring occasionally as he went. We determined to give him battle if we could only find him, and before it was clear we were in our saddles pricking along the edge of the vley, accompanied by about a dozen of the dogs, who started the noble beast, but he got away unseen by any of us.

Our dogs kept up an incessant barking during the night, and we imagined that lions were prowling around our camp. In the morning, however, we discovered that we had been favoured with the presence of far less illustrious, yet more presuming visitors. A pack of audacious hyænas had visited our fireside, and, not content with cracking and swallowing the bones which they found there, they had eaten our table-cloth, which consisted of the skin of a sable antelope, and carried off the lid of our canteen and two large camp-stools, which I lately had made to order in Colesberg. One of these we had the good fortune to recover, minus the rheimpys; the other will probably be found in after years, and preserved as a Bechuana or Bushman relic.

On the 12th I drew up my waggons on the north bank of the famous Meritsane. Here I had the pleasure to find that, owing to a large tract of the country having been burnt by the Bakalahari some months previously, and favoured by the rainy season, a rich and verdant crop of young grass had sprung up, giving the uudulating plains a fresh and vernal appearance. I was delighted on beholding this, for I knew that it would have the effect of attracting the game hither from all the surrounding parts, and I confidently hoped to fall in with elands, as they are generally met with by the foremost hunters in the vicinity of the Meritsane.

Having breakfasted, I saddled up three of my fleetest steeds, and, accompanied by two after-riders, I rode forth in a northerly direction, and carefully sought for eland's spoor. Presently I crossed the old Kuruman road, and immediately discovered fresh spoor, similar to that of elands, but, in my opinion, a little too large. In a buffalo country I should have at once pronounced it to be the spoor of buffaloes, but these for many years had not frequented the Meritsane, and were not to be expected nearer the Molopo. Even in the days of Harris, twelve years ago, or upwards, buffaloes had forsaken the Meritsane. As I rode on, the spoor became more abundant, and very soon fresh dung disclosed to me that a very large herd of buffaloes had lately pastured there.

The spoor of zebras, blue wildebeests, hartebeests, and sassaybys was extremely abundant, and of all of these I fell in with very considerable herds. I had resolved, however, not to disturb the country, for fear of starting any elands which might be there, and rode past, leaving them unmolested. After proceeding for many miles, I had the mortification to ascertain that only a very few elands now frequented these parts, and after a fruitless search for these few I turned my face for camp, and resolved to fire into whatever game I might fall in with. I watched a large herd of blue wildebeest and a herd of hartebeests, and was very unfortunate, wounding several, but failing to secure one. This was to me most particularly annoying, our flesh in camp being completely exhausted, and my large pack of dogs famishing. I resolved therefore to march next morning for Lotlokane, and hunt in advance of the waggons.

The next day I rode forth with one after-rider, resolved to do my best to supply the deficiency in camp. I directed the waggons to follow, and outspan at the Flat Rocks, half-way to Lotlokane. I had proceeded but a short distance when I had the satisfaction to behold a magnificent herd of buffaloes quietly pasturing within half a mile of me on the opposite bank of the Meritsane. This was a first-rate look-out, and exactly what I stood in need of, considering the present low state of my commissariat. I returned to meet the waggons, where I saddled another steed, named Brown, which was steady under fire, and I once more rode forth, accompanied by Mr. Orpen, with two after-riders, and a large detachment of the dogs, resolved to deal death among the buffaloes. We rode to leeward of the herd to give the dogs their wind, and then galloped in upon them. At first bewildered, they stood gazing at us until we were within thirty yards of them, when, seeing their danger, a panic spread throughout the whole herd, and, wheeling about, they crashed along through the underwood in a dense mass, impeding one another's progress.

In two minutes I was alongside of the herd, and, dismounting, fired right and left into two old cows; one of these immediately dropped to the rear of the troop, and, staggering for a few seconds, fell over and expired. The herd now left the river and doubled back, passing through a belt of low cover. I halted a moment to load. Following on, I came right upon the other buffalo that I had wounded, standing with a comrade in a dense bush. I observed her before she could charge me, and three more shots laid her low. The reports of Mr. Orpen's gun now sounded ahead, and, galloping forward, I observed him to my right actively engaged with four old buffaloes, which stood at bay in a large bush in the open country; the herd had vanished. A single buffalo, however, was at this moment making off between me and Mr. O., to which I gave chase. My after-rider was up first, and headed it, when the buffalo charged him furiously, and next moment she charged me, but my trusty steed was too active for her, and I bowled her over with two good shots in the shoulder. I then rode up to assist Mr. O. Two of the four buffaloes were lying wounded in the bush. Riding up within forty yards of them, I fired into a fine old cow, when she and her comrade broke bay, and took down to the river. Some of my dogs now came up to my assistance, and brought the wounded buffalo to bay in the stream, and two more shots laid her low.

I then rode to meet my waggons, which were standing on the rising ground above; and as I was directing my men where to draw up, I observed two more buffaloes coming down the river's side, which, observing us, took shelter in a belt of lofty reeds. Most of my dogs having come up, I resolved to have another chase, and rode straight for the reeds where the buffaloes had disappeared. I came right upon a noble bull, within four yards of him. Fortunately for me he did not charge, but broke away up the river-side, followed by the dogs. He led me a sharp chase, and came to bay at last, when he fell with two shots within thirty yards of the second cow I had shot in the commencement of the chase. This made five old buffaloes I had bagged out of the herd; Mr. Orpen bagged his two, making in all seven.

After breakfast I despatched men with two spans of oxen, directing them to select four of the fattest buffaloes and drag them to the waggons. All hands were busy butchering and salting until sundown. In the evening I went out with my rifle in quest of a buffalo-calf, which had been left by the herd in the morning. On observing me, the savage young buffalo, to my utter astonishment, turned upon me, and charged down in the most determined manner. I stood his charge, with my rifle at my shoulder, and, covering his head until he was within four yards of me, I arrested him in full career, with a ball in the forehead.

Three of the buffaloes which we had shot having been left in the veld, I deemed it more than probable that a lion might be found on some one of them if sought for at early dawn; accordingly, having substituted a bowl of warm milk for coffee, I rode forth with an after-rider and a troop of my dogs to seek the king of beasts. On gaining the first buffalo, I found that my natives had left a flag of peace flying over him, which had guarded him from the attacks of the beasts of prey. Upon the second buffalo, however, a hundred vultures were feasting merrily, but, as I approached the third, the sudden rush of a flight of vultures over my head towards the buffalo told me that some occupant, which had hitherto kept them aloof, had that moment quitted the carcase; and on galloping forward and clearing an intervening rising ground, I had the satisfaction to behold a huge and shaggy lion trotting slowly off towards the cover along the banks of the river, within two hundred yards of me.

I instantly rode for him at top speed to get my dogs clear of the carrion, and, if possible, to bring the lion to bay before he should gain any bad cover. We came up with him just as he gained a small belt of reeds on the river's bank. The lion sprang into the river's bed and stood at bay. Riding up within fifteen yards, I disabled him with a shot in the shoulder, and then, springing from my horse, which was unsteady, I went up to within twelve yards on foot, and finished him with my second shot, which he got behind the shoulder. This was a fine old lion, with perfect tusks and a very beautiful coat of hair. Leaving Booi to protect him from the vultures, I rode to camp, and despatched men with instructions to flay him with the utmost care. In the afternoon I inspanned, intending to march, but continued showers of rain prevented me. Next day, however, we reached Lotlokane.

As morning dawned on the 16th a lion roared to the north within a quarter of a mile of us, and shortly after two other lions moaned to the east. I rode in quest of them with dogs and an after-rider. Hartebeests, zebras, and pallahs were standing about in all directions, and leading my dogs away I failed to find the lion. In the afternoon, anxious to obtain a gemsbok, I saddled up my three fleetest steeds, and rode in a northerly direction, with two after-riders, taking with me a light single-barrelled gun. I started several fine steinboks, which are here abundant. Having ridden a few miles, I entered upon a magnificent level park, adorned with groves of thorn-trees, on which were grazing large herds of blue wildebeests, zebras, hartebeests, and springboks. Knowing that eland and gemsbok are generally to be found in the vicinity of herds of other game, I resolved to ride in a semicircle to windward of these, and carefully examine the ground for the game I sought.

Having made a sweep for this purpose, we were slowly returning, when four superb elands charged up wind right in our faces. To these we instantly gave chase. Booi, coming up first, singled out the heaviest bull, which he broke from the troop, and drove towards camp. Coming up with the remaining three, I selected the best head, and, after a sharp chase, laid him low with a single shot in the shoulder. I then rode to assist Booi, who was about a quarter of a mile to windward on the plain below me: and coming up to him, we cannily drove on the noble eland, which we succeeded in bringing right up to the waggons, where I bowled him over with two shots in the shoulder. Not yet having a stuffed bull eland's head, and being a fair specimen, I directed it to be cut off for my collection.

We now held on for the Molopo, upon the banks of which I had some fine sport with roan antelope and reitbuck, and on the 29th of May reached Sichely's kraal on the Kouloubeng.

Within a mile of this chief's residence we were met by parties of the Baquaines: these men had been sent by Sichely to ascertain who we were, he having heard from some Bakalahari that three waggons were at hand. I saddled up and rode ahead of the waggons with Mr. Livingstone's letters.

On the 31st we again inspanned and held on for the Limpopo, reaching my old drift on that river on the 15th of June.

The greater part of the day was devoted to cutting down the opposite bank and getting the waggons through, which we accomplished by sundown, taking each waggon through with twenty oxen.

On the 18th, the moon being full, I crossed the river with Mr. Orpen, Carey, and attendants, and made for the fountain at Charebe, in the hope of enjoying some night-shooting with elephants. We had the ill luck to alarm the elephants frequenting the water and to drive them out of the district. On the 23rd, as I was returning to camp from the water at Guapa, we suddenly heard the cry of elephants about a quarter of a mile to windward. I took Ramachumie along with me and held forward for an inspection of the troop.

The cries of elephants were repeated in different directions, and I at once knew that there must be a very large herd of them. Having ascended a lofty thorn-tree, I obtained a view of the grey backs of some of the elephants appearing above the underwood of the forest. I sent Ramachumie back to bring up the dogs, and when they came I rode forward for a nearer inspection. It was a troop of upwards of a hundred elephants, but it consisted entirely of cows and young bulls. Having endeavoured for nearly half an hour to select a good elephant, I crept in within fifteen yards of a fairish bull, and gave him a shot behind the shoulder: my followers, however, failed to slip the dogs or to bring on my horse, and while I ran back for them the elephant got away in the herd. The dogs attacked another bull, which, after a long chase, I rolled over. The elephant had scarcely fallen, when old Mutchuisho, with a party of Bamangwato men, came up like a flight of vultures in quest of flesh. The next day I shot another elephant.

On the 29th I again inspanned, and in the afternoon crossed the Macoolwey and drew up on its opposite bank. On the march I hunted ahead of the waggons, and shot a waterbuck and doe, and started a troop of seven or eight lions, headed by a patriarchal-looking old fellow of unusual size.

One long march across country on the next day brought the waggons to the Basileka. I hunted ahead of the waggons, and shot two pallahs and a cow-camelopard. We formed the waggons at my old camp, but, observing tsetse on the horses, I at once resolved to leave Seleka's on the morrow.

About midnight a huge lion made a most daring attack on my cattle-kraal, charging recklessly through the thick thorn-hedge: he sent the panic-stricken cattle flying in dire confusion, and dashed to the ground a valuable ox, which lay groaning in his powerful grasp. I was awakened by the noise, and, instantly directing a troop of the dogs to be let loose, the cowardly lion was put to flight. The poor ox sprang to his feet and joined his companions, but I was obliged to shoot him next day, his fore and hind quarters having been fearfully lacerated.

About nine A.M. I left Seleka's, and at sundown halted on the Limpopo, opposite Guapa.

Here I remained for many days, making successful excursions with Mr. Orpen across the river in search of elephants. On these occasions, however, and likewise upon all subsequent encounters with the elephants, I had the mortification to remark that on coming up with the elephants my followers invariably yielded to a natural impulse, and thus throughout the entire expedition the whole brunt of the elephant-hunting lay upon my shoulders, not a single elephant being bagged or even wounded by any individual in my establishment except myself.

On our return from one of these expeditions we came upon a heart-sickening sight. The Bamalette tribe, through whose district we were now hunting, had been attacked and put to flight by Sicomy a few months before, when a large number of them were massacred, in consequence of which they had deserted their former town and ensconced themselves in an elevated ravine in the mountains. We visited their deserted town and the ground over which they had been pursued and slain. We were horrified to behold the bleaching bones and skulls of those who had fallen; the wolf and jackal had feasted on their remains, and laid the long grass flat round each skeleton. Hair and torn fragments of karosses lay scattered around, and the blood was still visible upon the stones.

On the 12th I had another hard day in the mountains after elephants, and at night I watched a fountain, and shot an old lioness. She came and drank within ten yards of me; the ball entered the centre of her breast, and rested in the skin in the middle of her back.

On the 13th I despatched men to camp with the skin of the lioness, and held south for Charebe, which I found still deserted by the elephants. In the evening the natives were all busy cooking the flesh of the lioness, which was excessively fat, and esteemed by them a particular delicacy. For my own part, although starving, and so weak from famine that I could scarcely walk, I could not persuade myself to partake of their repulsive repast. I had left my coffee-kettle, and other necessaries, for the use of Mr. Orpen, on the far side of the mountain, and had since that been unsuccessful in the chase. After a little rest I mustered strength to saunter to the fountain, where I had the good fortune to shoot a pallah.

On the 25th of July at sunrise we inspanned and held down the river, leaving three more of my stud behind me, two dead, and the other dying of tsetse. At sundown we halted about twenty miles down the river. Whilst on our march next morning we came across the fresh spoor of a troop of bull-elephants, when I immediately outspanned. I was proceeding to follow up the spoor of these elephants, when I was met by a party of Bakalahari, who informed me that other elephants had drunk on the opposite side, and some miles higher up the river, during the night. I accordingly resolved to go in quest of them. We crossed the Limpopo at a most rocky drift, where the horses were in danger of breaking their legs, and, holding up the river, we took up the spoor of three old bulls. Having followed it for five miles, we at length got into a country covered with locusts that the spoor was no longer visible. A large herd of elephants had, during several previous nights been there feasting upon these insects. After a little we made a cast in advance, and again discovered the spoor of the three bulls, and came up with them about an hour before sundown, in company with a noble troop of about fifteen other bull-elephants, and, the wind being favourable, they were not aware of our approach.

Whilst riding slowly round them on the lee side, endeavouring to select the best bull, a splendid old fellow broke across from my right, whose ivory far surpassed any other in the herd. To him I accordingly adhered, and laid him low after an easy battle, having only given him five shots. I received no assistance from my dogs, they, as is often the case, having packed upon the worst elephant in the troop. The tusks of this huge elephant being unusually perfect, I resolved to preserve the entire skill. I accordingly sent a messenger to camp to instruct my people to bring a waggon for the head, while I stood sentry over it. Three days passed before the waggon appeared, having had to cross the Limpopo at a ford many miles above my camp. I occupied myself in the mean time in preparing the feet of the elephant, which I preserved.

Returning to camp, I shot an unusually fine old bull giraffe, whose head I preserved. For several days following I hunted elephants in the forests east of the Limpopo with great success. On the 4th, having partaken of an eland which I shot on the preceding evening, I took up the spoor of elephants, which after following to a very great distance I found to have been started by a party of Bakalahari. At night I watched the fountain of Tetenie. Long after midnight, as the moon was waning, two giraffes drew near, which I mistook for an elephant, and unfortunately slipped the dogs. A troop of lions, on their way to the fountain, were prowling about to leeward of the cameleopards; a part of the dogs took after the cameleopards, but others, among which were my best, rashly gave chase to the lions. I galloped on in darkness vainly listening to hear the trumpet of the supposed elephant; a strong wind that was blowing rendered it difficult to hear any sound. Presently the loud moaning of a dog was heard to leeward, which I imagined was one of the dogs which had lost its way. On returning to the fountain we coupled up the dogs, and found all present except Spikbard, which I had obtained from my old friend Murphy in Colesberg; this was a large, handsome, rough, red dog, and by far the most sagacious and valuable in my pack.

Next day I was utterly at a loss to account for the rapid disappearance of the elephant of last night, and also of my favourite dog; but on proceeding to inspect the ground I found that no elephant had been there, and that I had been deluded by the lofty form of a couple of cameleopards. I then recollected the moaning of the preceding evening, and conjectured that Spikbard had been killed by a kick from one of them. In the afternoon, however, the sad fate of poor Spikbard was revealed by the vultures. Observing these fall in the forest in the direction in which I had heard moaning on the preceding evening, I rode thither, and, to my utter horror, I found poor Spikbard fearfully mangled by a troop of ruthless lions: the ground presented a fearful spectacle, being covered for yards by his blood and hair; the lions had chased others of the dogs, but had failed to capture them.

On the 7th we reached the village of Bakalahari where I had lain so long last year, where poor Hendrick had been dragged from the fire and killed by a lion. I found the village deserted, and the spoor and dung of elephants where last season the natives were wont to hold their parliament. We halted, and formed our camp a little below the deserted village, beside a widespreading green tree.

On the 8th I held for the fine fountain called Seboono to watch for elephants by moonlight. As we made the fountain a magnificent troop of twenty-two giraffes were drawn up by the edge of the forest on the opposite side, and a troop of seven or eight wild boars trotted away from the water with tails erect. In the evening the same troop of giraffes revisited the fountain, reinforced by another troop of bull giraffes: koodoos, zebras, and a princely old bull eland, also came to drink. I was surprised to see this eland come in and drink, having always been led to believe that elands never drink. About an hour after night set in, several parties of rhinoceros made their appearance, and presently a low rumbling noise announced the approach of an elephant; on he came, a mighty old bull, carrying only one tusk. When the dogs were slipped nearly all of them dashed off after a white rhinoceros, to which they most pertinaceously adhered for about two hours. I had extremely hard work with the elephant, the forest being dense and consisting

ELEPHANT AND HIPPOPOTAMI HUNT.

chiefly of thorn-trees, and the sky overcast with clouds: at length, however, I vanquished him, and he fell, having received about twenty-five balls. The dogs being still engaged with the rhinoceros, I rode thither and found a huge old muchocho standing at bay in a grove, which was either sulky or completely knocked up, for, on my coming up, he neither attempted to charge nor retreat, and allowed me to flog off the dogs unmolested, which I did and left him.

Next day I bent my steps for the fountain Pepe, where, in the preceding year, I had enjoyed such excellent night hunting. Here I hunted the elephants with dogs and horses, as before, and was particularly successful, as also with rhinoceros and cameleopard, etc. Some of these elephants were killed on very dark nights, when there was no moon, and the stars themselves were overcast by heavy banks of clouds. To illustrate this it may not be uninteresting to transcribe a few lines from my journal of the 15th :—

The moon rising late, at night I kept the first watch, and presently heard black and white rhinoceros blowing round the fountain ; it was much too dark to·see. Amid the noise of the rhinoceroses I fancied that I heard the sweeping step of an elephant in the water, and Carey and I accordingly went down and crept close in to the edge of the fountain. A huge dark mass was detected on the opposite side of the water, but so dark was the night that Carey pronounced it to be a black rhinoceros. He however presently turned his broadside, when I saw that it was an elephant, and directed Carey to fly and bring the dogs with all speed: both black and white rhinoceros of course stood right in the way of the dogs. I led these past the rhinoceroses, and in utter darkness I slipped one couple of dogs where I supposed the elephant to have been ; these took his scent, and presently my anxious ear was greeted by a bark, instantly followed by the shrill trumpet of a mighty bull elephant. I then slipped the remainder of the dogs; and after some difficult and dangerous work, owing to the pitchy darkness and the denseness of the wait-a-bits, I laid him low with about twenty bullets. While I was fighting with him the moon rose, and when the natives came up to catch the dogs her silvery horn was blinking through the trees.

By the 24th of August I had the satisfaction of making up my bag to a hundred and five select elephants killed in South Africa. We now found the district to be much deserted by the elephants, and accordingly on the 3rd of September we inspanned the waggons and marched down the Limpopo towards the district frequented by hippopotami.

On the 4th I rode up the river to shoot hippopotami. Of these I found three troops, and bagged one first-rate bull and wounded others. I saw several crocodiles of unusual vastness. Some of them must have been sixteen feet in length, with bodies as large as that of an ox. Returning to the waggons in the evening, I heard Mr. Orpen engaged with a huge invincible old bull-hippopotamus. On going to his assistance, and finding that he had expended his ammunition, I attacked the hippopotamus, which I barely finished with six or eight more shots.

On the 5th I rode down the river, accompanied by Mr. Orpen, to shoot hippopotami. We bagged seven very fine old specimens, two of which were bulls : one of these monsters of the river received sixteen bullets in the head before I could finish him. In the heat of the conflict a huge crocodile, attracted by the blood, suddenly made its appearance, and kept swimming round the hippopotamus in a state of great excitement, regardless of his struggles, which reminded me of a whale, and so agitated the broad river that considerable waves lashed the shores on either side. I slew the crocodile with a single ball, which crashed through the centre of his skull. On receiving the shot he turned over on his side, and remained motionless in that position for some minutes on the surface of the water, with one fore and one hind leg stretched and quivering in the air like a dying frog : after which, having emitted a smell of musk so powerful as to cause the little Bushman to run shrieking from the bank, he gently sank into his watery grave.

We rode down the river for several mornings hunting after hippopotami, a great number of which we killed. As the tusks of some of these were very fine, we chopped them out of the jaw-bones, a work of considerable difficulty. On the 17th I was attacked with acute rheumatic fever, which kept me to my bed, and gave me excruciating pain. Whilst I lay in this helpless state Mr. Orpen and Present, who had gone up the river to shoot sea-cows, fell in with an immense male leopard, which the latter wounded very badly. They then sent natives to camp to ask me for dogs, of which I sent them a pair. In about an hour the natives came running to camp and said that Orpen was killed by the leopard.

On further inquiry, however, I found that he was not really killed, but fearfully torn and bitten about the arms and head. They had rashly taken up the spoor on foot, the dogs following behind them, instead of going in advance. The consequence of this was, that they came right upon the leopard before they were aware of him, when Orpen fired and missed him. The leopard then sprang on his shoulders, and, dashing him to the ground, lay upon him growling and lacerating his hands, arms, and head most fearfully. In a few minutes the leopard's strength failed him, being faint from loss of blood, and, rolling over, he permitted Orpen to rise and come away. Where were the gallant Present and all the natives, that not a man of them moved to assist the unfortunate Orpen ? According to an established custom among all colonial servants, the instant the leopard sprang Present discharged his piece in the air, and then, dashing it to the ground, he rushed down the bank and jumped into the river, along which he swam some hundred yards before he would venture on terra firma. The natives, though numerous and armed, had likewise fled in another direction.

CHAPTER XXXII.

Mr. Orphen and myself in a helpless condition—We leave the low-lying Limpopo for the Mountains—Trading with Seleka—Ceremony to impart the power of successful Shooting—March to the Ngotwani and retrace our steps to the Limpopo—Enormous Herds of Buffaloes—An exciting Lion-hunt—Three of my

An Attack upon Four Patriarchal Lions

CHAP. XXXII.—1

LARGE HERDS OF BUFFALOES.

Dogs killed—The noble Beast takes the water, followed by a Dog and a Crocodile—A bold Mountain-range—Abundance of Game—A brilliant Lion-hunt—Two killed out of a troop of four—Rhinoceros-hunting—Leave the Mariqua River—Sublime Scenery—Another Lion-Hunt—A Buffalo rips up my After-rider's Horse—Camelopard-Chase—Sudden encounter with two huge Lions—Arrival at Sichely's Kraal.

BOTH Orpen and myself were now reduced to a state of utter helplessness—he from his wound, which were many and dangerous, and I from the fever, though I was slowly recovering. It was of no use therefore to remain longer in the low-lying district about the Limpopo, so I resolved to march on steadily to Sichely's country. We accordingly marched on the 27th of September, and on the 2nd of October I encamped on the bank of the Limpopo, a little above its junction with the Lepalala. Here Seleka's men requested me to halt for a day, as their chief wished to trade with me, which I agreed to do.

Next morning Seleka arrived with a considerable retinue, bringing some good specimens of Bechuana arms to barter for muskets and ammunition. He made me a present of some Bechuana beer, and a sort of fermented porridge; this, he said, he considered as a gift, but he expected that I, in return, would give him some gunpowder. This is usual style of *presents* in Southern Africa.

In the afternoon I exchanged a musket for nine very handsome assagais, a battle-axe, and two shields of buffalo-hide. I also exchanged some assagais for ammunition: and obtained other articles of native manufacture in payment for cutting the arms of two or three of the nobility, and rubbing medicine into the incisions, to enable them to shoot well. Whilst performing this absurd ceremony, in which the Bechuanas have unbounded faith, I held before the eyes of the inititated sportsman prints of each of the game quadrupeds of the country; at the same time anointing him with the medicine (which was common turpentine), and looking him most seriously in the face, I said, in his own language, "Slay the game well; let the course of thy bullet be through the hearts of the wild beasts, thine hand and heart be strong against the lion, against the great elephant, against the rhinoceros, against the buffalo," etc.

On the 5th we marched at sunrise, and, trekking steadily along, arrived on the 8th at the drift on the Limpopo where, on the former occasion, I had crossed the river. The game was very abundant in our course, but Carey and Present were rarely successful in killing and I was obliged, at length, weak as I was, to take the field, as we were sadly in want of flesh. On the 13th we made the banks of Ngotwani, up which we proceeded for several days; but finding that, owing to the long protracted droughts, its waters were dried up, and that it would be impossible to reached Sichely's country by this route, I determined to retrace my steps. We accordingly marched for the Limpopo, which I fell in with once more on the 23rd, having killed a noble old lion in my way.

We trekked up along the banks of the river for the Mariqua, and a little before sundown fell in with two enormous herds of buffaloes, one of which, consisting chiefly of bulls, stood under the shady trees on one side of the bank, whilst the other, composed chiefly of cows and calves, stood on the opposite side, a little higher up the river. In all there were at least three hundred. Thinking it probable that if I hunted them I might kill some old bull with a head perhaps worthy of my collection, I ordered my men to outspan, and, having saddled steeds, I gave chase to the herd of bulls, accompanied by Booi and my dogs. After a short burst they took through the river, whereby I lost sight of an old bull which carried the finest head in the herd. My dogs, however, brought a cow to bay as they crossed the river, which I shot standing in the water, but not before she had killed a particularly favourite bull-dog, named Pompey. I then continued the chase, and again came up with the herd, which was now considerably scattered; and after a sharp chase, part of which was through thick wait-a-bit thorn cover, I brought eight or nine fine bulls to bay in lofty reeds at the river's margin, exactly opposite to my camp: of these I singled out the two best heads, one of which I shot with five balls, and wounded the other badly, but he made off while I was engaged with his comrade.

In the morning I instructed four of my people to cross the river, and bring over a supply of buffalo beef. These men were very reluctant to go, fearing a lion might have taken possession of the carcase. On proceeding to reconnoitre from our side, they beheld the majestic beast they dreaded walk slowly up the opposite bank from the dead buffalo, and take up a position on the top of the bank under some shady thorn-trees. I resolved to give him battle, and rode forth with my double-barrelled Westley Richards rifle, followed by men leading the dogs. Present, who was one of the party, carried his *roer*, no doubt to perform wonders. The wind blew up the river; I accordingly held up to seek a drift, and crossed a short distance above where the buffalo lay. As we drew near the spot, I observed the lion sitting on the top of the bank, exactly where he had last been seen by my people. On my right, and within two hundred yards of me, was a very extensive troop of pallahs, which antelope invariably manages to be in the way when it is not at all wanted. On this occasion, however, I succeeded in preventing my dogs from observing them. When the lion saw us coming, he overhauled us for a moment, and then slunk down the bank for concealment; being well to leeward of him, I ordered the dogs to be slipped, and galloped forward.

On finding that he was attacked, the lion at first made a most determined bolt for it, followed by all the dogs at a racing pace; and when they came up with him he would not bay, but continued his course down the bank of the river, keeping close in beside the reeds, growling terribly at the dogs, which kept up an incessant angry barking. The bank of the river was intersected by deep watercourses, and, the ground being extremely slippery from the rain which had fallen during the night, I was unable to overtake him until he came to bay in a patch of lofty dense reeds which grew on the lower bank immediately adjacent to the river's margin. I had brought out eleven of my dogs, and before I could come up three of them were killed. On reaching the spot I found it impossible to obtain the smallest glimpse of the lion, although the ground favoured me, I having the upper bank to stand upon; so,

Hunting the White Rhinoceros.

CHAP. XXXII.—2

dismounting from my horse, I tried to guess, from his horrid growling, his exact position, and fired several shots on chance, but none of these hit him. I then commenced pelting him with lumps of earth and sticks, there being no stones at hand. This had the effect of making him shift his position, but he still kept in the densest part of the reeds, where I could do nothing with him.

Presently my followers came up, who, as a matter of course, at once established themselves safely in the tops of thorn-trees. After about ten minutes' bullying, the lion seemed to consider his quarters too hot for him, and suddenly made a rush to escape from his persecutors, continuing his course down along the edge of the river. The dogs, however, again gave him chase, and soon brought him to bay in another dense patch of reeds, just as bad as the last. Out of this in a few minutes I managed to start him, when he bolted up the river, and came to bay in a narrow strip of reeds. Here he lay so close that for a long time I could not ascertain his whereabouts; at length, however, he made a charge among the dogs, and, coming forward, took up a position near the outside of the reeds, where for the first time I was enabled to give him a shot. My ball entered his body a little behind the shoulder. On receiving it he charged growling after the dogs, but not farther than the edge of the reeds, out of which he was extremely reluctant to move. I gave him a second shot, firing for his head; my ball entered at the edge of his eye, and passed through the back of the roof of his mouth.

The lion then sprang up, and, facing about, dashed through the reeds, and plunged into the river, across which he swam, dyeing the waters with his blood; one black dog, named "Schwart," alone pursued him. A huge crocodile, attracted by the blood, followed in their wake, but fortunately did not take my dog, which I much feared he would do. Present fired at the lion as he swam, and missed him; both my barrels were empty. Before, however, the lion could make the opposite bank, I had one loaded without patch, and just as his feet gained the ground I made a fine shot at his neck, and turned him over dead on the spot. Present, Carollus, and Adonis then swam in and brought him through. We landed him by an old hippopotamus footpath, and, the day being damp and cold, we kindled a fire, beside which we skinned him. While this was going forward I had a painful duty to perform, viz. to load one barrel, and blow out Rascality's brains, whom the lion had utterly disabled in his after-quarters. Thus ended this protracted and all but unsuccessful hunt; for when I at length managed to shoot him, the dogs were quite tired of it, and, the reeds being green, I could not have set them on fire to force him out.

The lion proved to be a first-rate one; he was in the prime of life, and had an exquisitely beautiful coat of hair. His mane was not very rank; his awful teeth were quite perfect, a thing which in lions of his age is rather unusual; and he had the finest tuft of hair on the end of his tail that I had ever seen in a lion. In the chase my after-rider, who fortunately did not carry my rifle, got a tremendous capsize from bad riding, a common occurrence with most after-riders who have been employed in my service. The afternoon was spent in drying the wet mane of the lion, skinning out the feet, and preserving the skin with alum and arsenical soap.

On the 27th we reached the junction of the Mariqua with the Limpopo, when we once more bade farewell to the latter, and held up the northern bank of the Mariqua. This fine little river averages here about five or six yards in width, and meanders along in a very serpentine course through a very broad open vley, its banks being in many places destitute of cover, excepting reeds, and in others is densely clad with groves of thorn and willow trees, etc. Here I found reitbuck, which do not frequent the Limpopo in those parts which I have visited. The country looked fresh and green, and all the usual varieties of game were abundant. Elephants had been frequenting the district some months previously, but had now deserted it. About fifty miles to the south and east a very bold and rocky extensive blue mountain-chain towered in grand relief above the intervening level forest. The length of this mountain chain seemed to be about a hundred miles, its course about north-east, and it gradually became loftier and more rugged towards the north-eastern extremity. I believe the Limpopo rises somewhere to the east of this chain, and I felt a strong desire to follow it to its source, but under existing circumstances this measure was not advisable. On the march we passed a small village of Bakalahari, which was surrounded with heaps of bones and skulls of game.

Next day we marched about eight miles up the river, and outspanned in a wide open vley. On the march I shot one sassayby, and wounded two black rhinoceroses. In the afternoon I rode up the edge of the river with Ruyter, in quest of reitbuck, of which I saw several small troops, but did not kill any, not getting a chance of the old bucks, which I hunted for their heads. I however, shot one enormous crocodile, which we discovered fast asleep on the grassy bank of the river. He got two balls, one in the head, and the other behind the shoulder, yet nevertheless in the struggles of death he managed to roll into the water, and disappeared. I was extremely surprised to see so enormous a crocodile in so small a stream; his length was considerably greater than the width of the river at the spot where I shot him.

Marching again at sunrise, and I and Ruyter rode ahead to seek reitbuck. I detected one of these squatting beside the river to shun observation, and I shot him dead on the spot. He proved to be an old buck, but, both of his horns being broken in fighting, I did not keep the head. A little after this, two packs of wild dogs kept trotting and cantering slowly along before us, one on either side of the river; we had started them from two pallahs, which they had caught and were consuming. More reitbuck were seen, and presently an old buck, carrying unusually fine horns, started up before us in company with four does. By taking up a position in a hollow in the vley, and sending Ruyter to drive them towards me, I had the satisfaction to succeed in bowling over this fine old buck, which proved to be a princely specimen. I shot him running, and broke his back.

The waggons being opposite to us, we crossed the river, and deposited the head on my cardell; and having proceeded a short distance farther

Furious Charge of a Buffalo

CHAP. XXXII.—3

up, we discovered the fresh spoor of an immense herd of elephants, consisting mostly of old bulls. I drew up my waggons on a peninsular well-wooded spot, and proceeded to take up the spoor. These elephants had at first fed for many hours among thorns in the vicinity of the river, and then marched in a long string right away out of the country. After following the spoor for a great many miles I became annoyed, and gave it up.

On the 31st, as I was riding along the river's bank, about two miles below the spot where some days before I had fired at a large crocodile, I came upon a similar reptile lying asleep on the opposite side, which I shot dead on the spot, putting the ball through the spine close into the back of the head. On receiving the ball, he only made a slight convulsive movement, and then remained still and motionless as if asleep, not having in the slightest degree altered his position: a copious stream of blood issued from the wound, and coloured the shallow water in which he lay. Having crossed the river at a drift about a mile below, I rode up to inspect this hideous monster of the river, which, to my surprise, I found to be the same one at which, on the 28th, I had fired, and as I susppoosed killed. He bore the marks of both my bullets, one of which had fractured a part of his skull.

This crocodile was a very old fellow, and a fine specimen, its length being upwards of twelve feet. I resolved, therefore, to preserve the skin, and with this intention, in the forenoon, I marched down six men, who were occupied until sundown in the novel work of flaying the crocodile. When, however, they had accomplished their undertaking, I made up my mind that there was no room in the waggons for the entire skin, and determined only to keep the head, which we brought to camp. The night set in with a heavy storm of wind, accompanied with rain. Returning from skinning the crocodile to camp, I found the vley before me black with an immense herd of buffaloes, two of which I wounded, but did not follow till the ensuing day.

A few days after this, just as Swint had milked the cows, and was driving them from the wooded peninsula in which we lay, athwart the open ground, to graze with my other cattle in the forest beyond, he beheld four majestic lions walk slowly across the vley, a few hundred yards below my camp, and disappear over the river's bank, at a favourite drinking-place. These mighty monarchs of the waste had been holding a prolonged repast over the carcases of some zebras killed by Present, and had now come down to the river to slake their thirst. This being reported, I instantly saddled up two horses, and, directing my boys to lead after me as quickly as possible my small remaining pack of sore-footed dogs, I rode forth, accompanied by Carey carrying a spare gun, to give battle to the four grim lions. As I rode out of the peninsula, they showed themselves on the bank of the river, and, guessing that their first move would be a disgraceful retreat, I determined to ride so as to make them think that I had not observed them, until I should be able to cut off their retreat from the river, across the open vley, to the endless forest beyond. That point being gained, I knew that they, still doubtful of my having observed them, would hold their ground on the river's bank until my dogs came up, when I could more advantageously make the attack.

I cantered along, holding as if I meant to pass the lions at a distance of a quarter of a mile, until I was opposite to them, when I altered my course, and inclined a little nearer. The lions then showed symptoms of uneasiness; they rose to their feet, and, overhauling us for half a minute, disappeared over the bank. They reappeared, however, directly, a little farther down; and finding that their present position was bare, they walked majestically along the top of the bank to a spot a few hundred yards lower, where the bank was well wooded. Here they seemed half inclined to await my attack; two stretched out their massive arms, and lay down on the grass, and the other two sat up like dogs upon their haunches. Deeming it probable that when my dogs came up and I approached they would still retreat and make a bolt across the open vley, I directed Carey to canter forward and take up the ground in the centre of the vley about four hundred yards in advance; whereby the lions would be compelled either to give us battle or swim the river, which although narrow, I knew they would be very reluctant to do.

I now sat in my saddle, anxiously awaiting the arrival of the dogs; and whilst thus momentarily disengaged, I was much struck with the majestic and truly appalling appearance which these four noble lions exhibited. They were all full-grown immense males; and I felt, I must confess, a little nervous, and very uncertain as to what might be the issue of the attack. When the dogs came up I rode right in towards the lions. They sprang to their feet, and trotted slowly down along the bank of the river, once or twice halting and facing about for half a minute. Immediately below them there was a small determined bend in the stream, forming a sort of peninsula. Into this bend they disappeared, and next moment I was upon them with my dogs. They had taken shelter in a dense angle of the peninsula, well sheltered by high trees and reeds. Into this retreat the dogs at once boldly followed them, making a loud barking, which was instantly followed by the terrible voices of the lions, which turned about and charged to the edge of the cover. Next moment, however, I heard them plunge into the river, when I sprang from my horse, and, running to the top of the bank, I saw three of them ascending the opposite bank, the dogs following. One of them bounded away across the open plain at top speed, but the other two, finding themselves followed by the dogs, immediately turned to bay.

It was now my turn, so, taking them coolly right and left with my little rifle, I made the most glorious double shot that a sportsman's heart could desire, disabling them both in the shoulder before they were even aware of my position. Then snatching my other gun from Carey, who that moment had ridden up to my assistance, I finished the first lion with a shot about the heart, and brought the second to a standstill by disabling him in his hind quarters. He quickly crept into a dense, wide, dark green bush, in which for a long time it was impossible to obtain a glimpse of him. At length, a clod of earth falling near his hiding-place, he made a move which disclosed to me his position, when I finished him with three more shots, all along the middle of his back. Carey swam across the river to flog off the dogs; and when these came through to me, I beat up the peninsula in quest of the fourth lion, which had, however, made off. We then crossed the river a little higher up, and proceeded to inspect the noble prizes I had won. Both lions were well up in their years; I kept the skin and skull of the finest specimen, and only the nails and tail of the other, one of whose canine teeth was worn down to the socket with caries, which seemed to have affected his general condition.

On the 9th it rained unceasingly throughout the day, converting the rich soil on which we were encamped into one mass of soft sticky clay. In the forenoon, fearing the rain would continue so as to render the vley (through which we must pass to gain the firmer ground) impassable, I ordered my men to prepare to march, and leave the tent with its contents standing, the point which I wished to gain being distant only about five hundred yards. When the oxen were inspanned, however, and we attempted to move, we found my tackle, which was old, so rotten from the effects of the rain, that something gave way at every strain. Owing to this and to the softness of the vley, we laboured on till sundown, and only succeeded in bringing one waggon to its destination, the other two remaining fast in the mud in the middle of the vley. Next morning, luckily, the weather cleared up, when my men brought over the tent, and in the afternoon the other two waggons.

We followed up the banks of the river for several days with the usual allowance of sport. On the 16th we came suddenly upon an immense old bull muchocho rolling in mud. He sprang to his feet immediately he saw me, and, charging up the bank, so frightened our horses, that before I could get my rifle from my after-rider he was past us. I then gave him chase; and after a hard gallop of about a mile I sprang from my horse and gave him a good shot behind the shoulder. At this moment a cow rhinoceros of the same species, with her calf, charged out of some wait-a-bit thorn cover, and stood right in my path. Observing that she carried an unusually long horn, I turned my attention from the bull to her; and after a very long and severe chase I dropped her at the sixth shot. I carried one of my rifles, which gave me much trouble, that not being the tool required for this sort of work, where quick loading is indispensable.

After breakfast I sent men to cut off the head of this rhinoceros, and proceeded with Ruyter to take up the spoor of the bull wounded in the morning. We found that he was very severely hit, and having followed the spoor for about a mile through very dense thorn-cover, he suddenly rustled out of the bushes close ahead of us, accompanied by a whole host of rhinoceros birds. I mounted my horse and gave him chase, and in a few minutes he had received four severe shots. I managed to turn his course towards camp, when I ceased firing, as he seemed to be nearly done up, and Ruyter and I rode slowly behind him, occasionally shouting to guide his course. Presently, however, Chukuroo ceased taking any notice of us, and held leisurely on for the river, into a shallow part of which he walked, and after panting there and turning about for a quarter of an hour he fell over and expired. This was a remarkably fine old bull, and from his dentition it was not improbable that a hundred summers had seen him roaming a peaceful denizen of the forest and open glades along the fair banks of the secluded Mariqua.

During our march on the 19th we had to cross a range of very rocky hills, covered with large loose stones; and all hands were required to be actively employed for about an hour in clearing them out of the way to permit the waggons to pass. The work went on fast and furious, and the quantity of stones cleared was immense. We had now reached the spot where we were obliged to bid adieu to the Mariqua, and hold a westerly course across country for Sichely. At sundown we halted under a lofty mountain, the highest in the district, called "Lynché a Chény," or the Monkey's Mountain.

Next day at an early hour I rode out with Ruyter to hunt; my camp being entirely without flesh, and we having been rationed upon very tough old rhinoceros for several days past. It was a cloudy morning, and soon after starting it came on to rain heavily. I however held on, skirting a fine well-wooded range of mountains, and after riding several miles I shot a zebra. Having covered the carcase well over with branches to protect it from the vultures, I returned to camp, and, inspanning my waggons, took it up on the march. We continued trekking on until sundown, when we started an immense herd of buffaloes, into which I stalked and shot a huge old bull.

Our march this evening was through the most beautiful country I had ever seen in Africa. We skirted along an endless range of well-wooded stony mountains lying on our left, whilst to our right the country at first sloped gently off, and then stretched away into a level green forest (occasionally interspersed with open glades), boundless as the ocean. This green forest was, however, relieved in one direction by a chain of excessively bold, detached, well-wooded, rocky, pyramidal mountains, which stood forth in grand relief. In advance the picture was bounded by forest and mountain; one bold acclivity, in shape a dome, standing prominent among its fellows. It was a lovely evening: the sky, overcast and gloomy, threw an interesting, wild, mysterious colouring over the landscape. I gazed forth upon the romantic scene before me with intense delight, and felt melancholy and sorrowful at passing so fleetingly through it, and I could not help shouting out as I marched along, "Where is the coward who would not dare to die for such a land?"

In the morning we held for a fountain some miles ahead in a gorge in the mountains. As we approached the fountain, and were passing close in under a steep rocky hill side, well wooded to its summit, I unexpectedly beheld a lion stealing up the rocky face, and, halting behind a tree, he stood overhauling us for some minutes. I resolved to give him battle, and seizing my rifle marched against him, followed by Carey carrying a spare gun, and by three men leading my dogs, now reduced to eight. When we got close in to the base of the mountain, we found ourselves enveloped in dense jungle, which extended half way to its summit, and entirely obscured from our eyes objects which were quite apparent from the waggons. I slipped my dogs, however, which, after snuffing about, took right up the steep face on the spoor of the lions, for there was a troop of them—a lion and three lionesses.

The people at the waggons saw the chase in perfection. When the lions observed the dogs coming on, they took right up, and three of them crossed over the sky ridge. The dogs, however, turned one rattling old lioness, which came rumbling down the cover, close past me. I ran to meet her, and she came to bay in an open spot near the base of the mountain, whither I quickly followed; and coming up within thirty yards, bowled her over with my first shot, which broke her back. My second entered her shoulder; and fearing that she might hurt any of the dogs, as she still evinced signs of life, I finished her with a third in the breast. The bellies of all the four lions were much distended by some game they had been gorging, no doubt a buffalo, as a large herd started out of the jungle immediately under the spot where the noble beasts were first disturbed.

Showers of rain fell every hour throughout the 24th, and my men were employed in making feldtschoens, or in other words African brogues, for me. These shoes were worthy of a sportsman, being light, yet strong, and were entirely composed of the skins of game of my shooting. The soles were made of either buffalo or camelopard; the front part perhaps of koodoo, or hartebeest, or bushbuck; and the back of the shoe of lion, or hyæna, or sable antelope; while the rheimpy or thread with which the whole was sewn consisted of a thin strip of the skin of a steinbok.

On the forenoon of the 26th I rode forth to hunt, accompanied by Ruyter; we held west, skirting the wooded stony mountains. The natives had here many years before waged successful war with elephants, four of whose skulls I found. Presently I came across two sassaybys, one of which I knocked over; but while I was loading he regained his legs, and made off. We crossed a level stretch of forest, holding a northerly course for an opposite range of green well-wooded hills and valleys. I came upon a troop of six fine old bull buffaloes, into which I stalked, and wounded one princely fellow very severely behind the shoulder, bringing blood from his mouth; he, however, made off with his comrades, and, the ground being very rough, we failed to overtake him. After following the spoor for a couple of miles we dropped it, as it led right away from camp.

Returning from this chase, we had an adventure with another old bull buffalo, which shows the extreme danger of hunting buffaloes without dogs. We started him in a green hollow among the hills, and, his course inclining for camp, I gave him chase. He crossed the level broad strath and made for the opposite densely wooded range of mountains. Along the base of these, we followed him, sometimes in view, sometimes on the spoor, keeping the old fellow at a pace which made him pant. At length, finding himself much distressed, he had recourse to a singular stratagem. Doubling round some thick bushes which obscured him from our view, he found himself beside a small pool of rain-water, just deep enough to cover his body; into this he walked, and, facing about, lay gently down and awaited our on-coming, with nothing but his old grey face and massive horns above the water, and these concealed from view by rank overhanging herbage.

Our attention was entirely engrossed with the spoor, and thus we rode boldly on until within a few feet of him, when springing to his feet, he made a desperate charge after Ruyter, uttering a low stifled roar peculiar to buffaloes (somewhat similiar to the growl of a lion), and hurled horse and rider to the earth with fearful violence. His horn laid the poor horse's haunch open to the bone, making the most fearful rugged wound. In an instant Ruyter regained his feet, and ran for his life; which the buffalo observing, gave chase, but most fortunately came down with a tremendous somersault in the mud, his feet slipping from under him: thus the Bushman escaped certain destruction. The buffalo rose much discomfited, and, the wounded horse first catching his eye, he went a second time after him, but he got out of the way. At this moment I managed to send one of my patent pacificating pills into his shoulder, when he instantly quitted the field of action, and sought shelter in the dense cover on the mountain side, whither I deemed it imprudent to follow him. During my stay here I enjoyed excellent sport with buffaloes, koodoos, and other varieties of game.

On the 28th we marched at sunrise, when one of my waggon-drivers chose to turn his waggon too short, in opposition to my orders, whereby it was very nearly upset, for which I flogged him with a jambok, and then knocked him down. This man's name was Adonis: he was a determined old sinner on whom words had no effect. Our course lay through a wide, well-wooded strath, beautifully varied with open glades. As we proceeded, fresh spoor of buffalo and camelopard became abundant, and about breakfast-time, as we were crossing an elevated slope in the vicinity of the Ngotwani, I had the felicity to detect a magnificent herd of the latter browsing in the middle of the strath about half a mile to our left.

As I enjoyed very little sport with camelopard either in this or in last expedition, my time and attention having always been engrossed with elephants, I resolved to avail myself of this opportunity, and accordingly, having caught a couple of my mares, I rode for them, accompanied by Booi as after-rider. I had directed my men to outspan, and my intention was, if possible, to hunt one of the camelopards to my camp, but in this I failed. On disturbing the herd they separated into two divisions, one of which took right away down wind, being a tail-on-end chase from my camp; the finest bull went with this division, and him I followed. After a sharp burst of about a mile I headed and laid him low with two shots behind the shoulder. Having cut off his tail, we were returning to camp, and had proceeded about half way, when we came upon the other division of the herd. They were browsing quietly in company with a large herd of zebras; and observing amongst them another princely old bull, nothing short of the one I had already killed, I was tempted once more to give chase, and, directing

Booi to go home with the tail, I spurred my little mare, and dashed after the lofty giraffe.

In vain he sought the thickest depths of cover which the strath afforded, and put out the very utmost speed which he could muster. I followed close in his wake, and after a hard chase of about a mile over very rough ground, we gained a piece of hard level. Here I pressed my mare, and, getting close in under his stern, I fired at the gallop, and sent a bullet into him, and then passed ; in doing which I tried to fire a second shot, but my gun snapped. I had now headed the camelopard, so he altered his course and held away at a right angle across the level strath. A fresh cap was soon placed upon the nipple, when, pressing my mare, I once more rode past him. In passing I held my stock to my waist and fired : the ball entered behind the shoulder and ended the career of this gigantic and exquisitely beautiful habitant of the forest. Having run a few yards farther, his lofty frame tottered for a moment, when he came down with a crash which made the earth tremble.

On the 4th of December we inspanned at sunrise and marched to the Ngotwani, which we crossed after an hour of hard work in making a road ; having to remove some immense masses of rock, to cut down the banks with spades, and to throw some thorn-trees. In the afternoon I again marched, and halted at sundown within a few miles of my old spoor near the Poort or Pass of God. As the waggons were drawing up for the night a borèlé was detected, which Present and Carey stalked, and got within thirty yards, and then both fired and returned, stating that they had broken his shoulder.

Accordingly, on the following morning, I proceeded to take up the spoor of the wounded borèlé of the preceding evening, accompanied by Ruyter, and I very soon found that he was very little the worse for his wound. The spoor led me for several miles close along under the mountain-range to my right, and at length up into a long well-wooded basin in the mountains. Here I observed that two lions, having detected the blood, were spooring up the borèlé ; they had followed him up and driven him away from his lair, and had then lain down for the day.

When I came up I was within twenty yards of the lions before I was aware of their proximity. Observing me, they sprang to their feet, and, growling sulkily, trotted up the mountain-side. I only saw one of them at first, and ran forward for a shot. Having ascended the steep a short distance, the lion halted to have a look, giving me a fine broadside, when I shot him through the heart. On receiving the ball he bounded forward, and was instantly obscured by the trees. I advanced cautiously, and next moment the other lion sprang up with a growl, and marched with an air of most consummate independence up the mountain-side. I imagined that this lion was the one I had fired at, and I sent two more shots at him, both of which were too high ; after which he disappeared over a ridge immediately above.

On proceding to inspect the spot where the lion had been lying, I found that there were two beds, consequently that there must have been two lions, and I conjectured that I had killed one of them. In case, however, he should be only wounded, I deemed it prudent to ride down to the waggons which were then passing below me, to obtain some dogs to pioneer. Having procured these, I and Ruyter returned to the spot, and found the lion lying dead on the mountain-side. We then proceeded to skin him, and returned to the waggons with the spoils. The other lion had decamped; the dogs could not find him. Both of these were first-rate old lions, but the one that escaped was the larger of the two. In the afternoon I rode on to Sichely's kraal on the Kouloubeng, having directed my men to follow with the waggons.

On arriving at the station I found that Mr. Livingstone had left that morning to visit a tribe to the east of the Limpopo. I waited upon Mrs. Livingstone, who regaled me with tea and bread and butter, and gave me all the news. I remained a week in the station, and on the 12th I inspanned. At sundown we halted near the Pass of God, intending to hunt sable antelope, having seen a small troop of them in the month of May on a steep mountain-side, beneath which I formed my camp.

CHAPTER XXXIII.

The Pass of God—Hunt Sable and Roan Antelope—Sesetabie—My Cattle-losses in five Expeditions—My Cattle desperate for want of Water—Trading with Mahura—Inspanning young Oxen—We cross the Vaal River—The Country densely covered with Game—An Ostrich's Nest—Bloem Vonteyn—Multitudes of Antelope Skeletons cover the Plalns—The Great Orange River—We are detained by the Flood—Twenty-three Men drowned in attempting to cross—We have to take the Waggons to pieces—Arrival at Colesberg—Determine to revisit Old England and transport my collection of Trophies thither.

NEXT morning I rode through the Pass of God and held west, accompanied by two after-riders. I rode to within a couple of miles of .the Kouloubeng, and returned close in under the mountain-chain to the southward of the pass, having bagged a buffalo, a zebra, and a fine old cock ostrich. On the 14th, having breakfasted, I went forth on foot, accompanied by Ruyter, and ascended the mountain immediately above my camp to seek for sable antelope. I had the satisfaction to discover the spoor of three bucks on a piece of rocky table-ground on the highest summit of the range; and soon after I started a princely old buck from his lair. He was lying in long grass in a sandy spot behind a bush, within eighty yards of me. Starting from his mountain-bed, this gem of beauty rattled up a rocky slope beside which he had been lying, and, halting for a moment, looked back to see what had disturbed him, when I sent a bullet through his ribs, and as he disappeared over the ridge I lodged another in his vitals. Having loaded, I followed on the spoor, and soon I observed him within a hundred and fifty yards of me, standing in a green hollow far below, whisking his tail and evidently severely wounded.

A strong breeze which was then blowing was against me, as it shook a young tree of which I wished to avail myself for a rest. I nevertheless managed to make a fine shot, and sent a bullet through the centre of his shoulder, bringing him down on his face, and laming him. The potaquaine disappeared down the wooded mountain-side over a rocky ridge, but no rude fears agitated my breast; I had lamed him, and that was enough: if stalking should fail, there were dogs at my waggons that could very soon bring him to bay. I did not, however, wish to be put to the trouble of sending for the dogs, and continued to follow on his spoor with extreme caution. He had only gone a short distance down the hill when I found him without his seeing me, and, after a successful stalk, I finished him with three more shots, one of which was in his stern. This was a most splendid specimen of this very rare and most lovely antelope; his horns were enormous, very long, rough, and perfect. Having cut off the head for stuffing, and gralloched him, we covered him with many green boughs, and returned to camp, whence I despatched a party for the venison and the skin, which I preserved.

On the 15th I was occupied during the morning in stuffing the head of the sable antelope, after which I rode forth with two after-riders, and holding a northerly course I skirted the range of hills beneath which we were encamped. I soon reached a gorge in the hills, through which I rode, and at its upper extremity I discovered springs of water forming a little stream. In a basin in the hill-side opposite to this little stream, I observed a rattling old buck roan antelope, or bastard gemsbok, standing under the shade of some young trees, the sun being extremely powerful. I first endeavoured to stalk in upon him, but, finding that the ground would not admit of that, I laid a plot for him, and, guessing from the lay of the land what course he was most likely to take, I instructed Ruyter to give me about twenty minutes to steal forward, and then endeavour to move him towards me. Before, however, I could gain the point I wished, an eddy in the breeze apprised the roan antelope of my proximity, when he instantly started to pass a shoulder of the mountain opposite which I already was. As I was screened by some thorn-trees, I made a run to save the day. When the buck halted, I likewise halted; and when he ran, I also ran: thus, when he halted the second time, and looked down to see what had disturbed him, I had got within two hundred yards, and was standing in position, with my rifle steady on a branch of a thorn-tree. Giving it six inches of elevation, I fired, and the bullet caught him in the centre of the hollow behind the shoulder, and rested in the hide on his opposite side. Arching his back and bounding high, the rock-loving old roan antelope started forward, and was instantly concealed from my view by an abrupt rocky ridge. Having loaded, I inspected the spoor. Large blotches of his life-blood stained the rocks, and on clearing the ridge over which he had disappeared, I had the pleasure to find " Qualata " stretched to rise no more. This antelope carried the finest head I had ever seen; the horns were very long, fair set, immensely stout, and rough. I cut off the head for stuffing, and rode back to camp, where I found a trader named Jolly, with his waggons, who wished to travel along with me to the colony, being in fear of the rebel Bores.

Having heard from Mr. Livingstone that sable antelopes frequented the rocky mountains about the sources of the Kouloubeng, I resolved to march thither. Early on the 18th we inspanned, and in about four hours encamped on the Kouloubeng, at a spot where, three years before, Mr. Livingstone had made a garden to cultivate wheat, which, having sown, he left to the birds, having never returned to see how it had thriven.

In the morning I rode forth with the Bushman, and, holding a south-westerly course, examined the mountain-ranges and several fine straths in that direction. At length I started a small troop of zebras, and soon after I observed a fine old buck roan antelope, which got my wind. Returning from following this buck, I shot a steinbok; this shot at the steinbok started a troop of seven or eight old bull buffaloes, which Ruyter had found, from the summit of a rocky hillock. I followed, when the invariable rhinoceros birds started them, and I galloped on in their wake.

Presently they halted to look behind them, and I at the same instant sprang from my mare and lay down in the grass. My mare commenced eating the grass and whisking her tail, which the buffaloes observing, and fancying that she was some species of game, made up their minds that it was all right, and coming forward a few steps they took up a position under a wide shady tree, not evincing any further signs of fear. Thus I was enabled to take my time and select the finest head in the troop. After about twenty minutes spent in stuyding the set of the heads, I shot one princely old bull, when they all made off. Following on their spoor for a short distance, I found my bull lying dying beneath a thorn-tree, and his comrades standing near him. As the old bull died, he roared loudly, as buffaloes are wont to do. His comrades came forward and walked round him, smelling the blood, when I wounded two more, and a little after a third, which the natives discovered on the following day. On returning to camp I despatched men for the head of the buffalo and a supply of meat.

Next day, whilst exploring a fine mountainous tract of country to the south-west, I suddenly found myself in my old waggon-spoor of '45, within a short distance of the bold gorge in the mountains in which my oxen had been chased by lions. In this fine pass two streams of water meet: is is a first-rate district for game when the country has not been ransacked by Griqua hunters. I immediately found the spoor of a troop of buffaloes; it led me into a rich, green, and well-wooded glen in the hills, through which one of the afore-mentioned streams flowed. The wind was as foul as it could blow, and this troop got my wind. Returning from spooring them, however, I very soon fell in with another troop, reposing under dense shade in the same glen. I crept in within thirty yards of them, and there lay for upwards of an hour, endeavouring to select the finest head. The buffalo which I wanted was lying down, his body screened by stout thorn-branches. I might easily have shot any of the others through the heart, if I had wished to do so. One by one they rose, stretched themselves, rubbed their horns upon the trees, and again lay down. At length something, which I could not guess, alarmed them, when the buffalo I wanted sprang to his feet, affording me a certain shot, but my cap disappointed me. I then had a snap shot through the cover with my left barrel, and sent a bullet through his heart.

The herd took to the hills, and, by an extraordinary chance, I again fell in with them, while galloping along, half-way to my camp. Dismounting, I ran in after them, and, commanding their attention by a shrill whistle, the herd halted and faced half about, when I dropped a fine old cow with a single ball. On returning to camp I found a-party of Baquaines, among whom was a brother of Sichely's. These men informed me that the Boers had been making many inquiries concerning me: and that it was their intention to come in force on horseback, and take me prisoner. The Bechuanas, however, further stated that all the horses of the Boers were dead with the distemper. An attack from them being, however, by no means improbable, I deemed it prudent to hold myself in a certain degree prepared, and resolved, in the event of Mr. Edwards, the missionary of Bakatla, thinking the road by the Mamouri unsafe, to hold a more westerly course, and go out by the country of the Bawangketse. Another valuable black shooting-mare died of the fell distemper.

My losses in cattle this year were very considerable. Up to this time fourteen horses and fifteen head of cattle had died; making my losses in all four expeditions into the far interior amount to forty-five horses and seventy head of cattle, the value of these being at least £600. I also lost about seventy of my dogs.

We continued our march for several days through a country abounding in different kinds of game, affording good sport; and on the 1st of January, 1849, I rode into Bakatla, where I found Mr. Edwards and his family flourishing. The news was, that the Boers had met the Governor and the troops, etc., at a place called Boom Plaats, on the north side of the Orange River, and, after a bloody engagement of three hours, they had been defeated. Mr. Edwards stated that since this engagement the Boers had been flocking in about Mosega in great numbers, and that they were anxious to get possession of my waggons. He therefore advised me strongly not to proceed by my old line of march, but to get out of the country with all speed, taking the direct road across the mountain at the back of Bakatla. My prospects of doing this, however, were not heightened by an attack in the morning of fever brought on by over exertion and anxiety of mind.

On the 3rd we marched at dawn, and, after proceeding for many miles without finding water at the different spots where we were led to expect it, we had the pleasing prospect before us of not seeing any until the following day, when we might reach the Molopo. The sun's heat was most terrific, and my poor dogs were already on the verge of going mad; a number of my cattle were lame from hoof-sickness, and I myself was laid up with a rattling fever. In this state of things I halted my waggons, and despatched parties in different directions with spades to seek for water. Presently, to my great relief, Jolly rode up, and said that half a mile in advance there were several sheltered holes, containing sufficient rain-water for all the cattle; thither we accordingly moved with all speed. An attack from the Boers being not at all improbable, I ordered all my guns and rifles to be cleaned and loaded, and ammunition to be placed in readiness for action. I had also four good muskets cleaned and loaded, which in all gave me twenty shots at the first round; these, if well directed, in the open country, I calculated would keep off a whole host of Boers.

I pushed on the waggons as rapidly as I could, considering that the country was almost destitute of water, my cattle consequently being in a desperate condition; and in the afternoon of the 13th I reached the Hart River, where I outspanned within a quarter of a mile of the town or kraal of the Batlapis. The river was greatly swollen and quite impassable, the rain having been very heavy in certain parts of the country. Shortly after we arrived old Mahura with a party made his appearance and came down to greet me across the river, and beg for some coffee.

In the morning, by Mahura's request, I inspanned and crossed the Hart stream, and encamped on its southern bank. In the course of the day I obtained ten karosses in barter from the tribe, and one very good spotted cat as a present from the chief. I also obtained a large sack of Kaffir corn in barter for beads, and milk was pressed upon us to any amount. A few fine oxen were offered for barter, but I did not require them, preferring to purchase karosses. Mahura favoured me with a visit morning and evening, remaining at the waggons about three hours on each occasion, drinking coffee to an immense extent, and pestering me with requests for various articles of which he stood in need.

On the 16th I deemed it high time to be getting under way, being quite sick of the presence of Mahura and his retinue, who came down to my waggons and remained there for the greater part of the day, merely to eat and drink and pester me, not bringing articles of value for barter, and asking absurdly high prices. Accordingly at an early hour I ordered my men to count my cattle and inspan, and in about an hour we were on the move. Old Mahura was coming down to drink coffee, and met us as we were going past the town. He was evidently vexed at my sudden departure; I presented him with some coffee, sugar, and other articles equivalent in value to the kaross which he had given me, and took leave of him. In the afternoon we marched about six or seven miles nearer to the Vaal, and halted in the hollow where nearly ten months before I had coursed an old blue wildebeest with dogs.

Considerable delay was caused next day along the line of march by young oxen, which could not be persuaded to trek, notwithstanding an unusual application of both whip and jambok. About four hours after the sun rose we reached the fount beside a few acres of bush, where we outspanned. Our march was across boundless open country; we saw a good deal of game, blue and black wildebeest, blesbok, springbok, and a fine troop of about thirty hartebeests: in the afternoon I again marched, and at nightfall we encamped on the bank of the fair Vaal River. It was considerably swollen, heavy rains having lately fallen; but being upon the ebb, I deemed it well not to take the drift until the morrow; when, having arranged two trektows, we commenced crossing the Vaal, one waggon at a time, with twenty oxen, and in about two hours my three heavily-laden waggons were brought through in safety.

After two or three day's march we came in sight of several Boer encampments on both sides of the Vet River. Four Boers paid me a visit and drank coffee with me; I questioned them concerning the recent engagement between the rebels and the English. They said that nearly all the latter had fallen on that occasion and only six Boers, and told us many other equally extravagant tales. It was however very clear from their remarks that the Boers had received a lesson which they would not soon forget of the utter vanity of opposition to the English Government.

On the 24th our morning's march brought us into the district where in the commencement of last winter I had seen such overwhelming swarms of blesboks: Boers were encamped on the opposite side of the river. I outspanned beside some shady thorn-trees; lions' spoor was seen on the line of march. In the afternoon I lost my march, being obliged to halt soon after I inspanned to correct a bush of the iron-axletree waggon, which was loose.

The 25th was a cloudy morning, with a cool breeze. Our morning's march brought us to a forsaken Boer encampment, around which lay the remains of the different varieties of game frequenting the district. We halted for breakfast beside several acres of thorn-cover on the bank of the river.

As we were breakfasting on the 24th by the banks of the river, a trader from the Parl (a district near Cape Town), of French extraction, passed us with his two waggons laden with merchandise. He took a cup of tea with me and gave me the news of the colony. Observing the skull of an old bull buffalo fastened on one of my traps, he asked me if it was the head of an elephant. Another Boer had asked me a few days before if a crocodile's head, which was tied up at the back of Carollus's waggon, belonged to an elephant. In the afternoon, as we were inspanning, we were visited by a rebel Boer of very large proportions. This man told us plainly that the Boers did not consider themselves as conquered, and that they intended to try it on again.

We had now reached that point in our line of march where we were to take leave of the Vet River. I rode ahead of the waggons to hunt, and after proceeding about a mile, I found myself out of the country of sweet grass, and entering upon bare and boundless open plains, thinly clad with sour pasturage, the favourite haunt and continual residence of innumerable herds of black wildebeest, blesbok, and springbok. As I rode on, large troops of these excellent, sport-yielding antelopes gratified my eyes in every direction. I had been long away from them, far, far in the dense forest regions of the far interior, and now I gazed once more upon them with a lively feeling of pleasure and intense interest which no words can describe.

When the sun rose next morning I took coffee, and then rode west with two after-riders, in the hope of getting some blesbok-shooting. I found the boundless undulating plains thickly covered with game, thousands upon thousands chequering the landscape far as the eye could strain in every direction. The blesboks, which I was most desirous to obtain, were extremely wary, and kept pouring on, on, up the wind in long-continued streams of thousands, so swift and shy that it was impossible to get within six hundred yards of them, or even by any stratagem to waylay them, so boundless was the ground, and so cunningly did they avoid to cross our track.

I returned to camp, having bagged one springbok doe and one old bull wildebeest, which was in superb condition. Jolly and some of my people had been out, but without success.

On the 28th I rode in a north-westerly course, and gave chase to a noble herd of about two hundred black wildebeest. These being very wild, I yached them on the Boer principle, and, taking a double family shot at about three hundred yards, when the dust had blown past one fine bull was found to have bitten the dust: this was very near camp, so I despatched Ruyter for men and a pack-ox to bring the gnoo to camp. I held on in a westerly course, and found the game extremely shy, owing to the high wind.

In the afternoon I inspanned and marched, there being very little grass here for my cattle, and danger of the oxen taking a horrible and very fatal illness, called by the Boers "snot sickness," which cattle are very liable to from pasturing on ground frequented by black wildebeests. The sky to the north and west looked very threatening, and, before we had proceeded far, black masses of clouds came rolling up towards us, and vivid flashes of forked lightning, accompanied by appalling peals of thunder, proclaimed the approach of a storm. In a few minutes it was upon us, the rain falling in torrents. We held for a rocky coppice or hill, beside which we outspanned, and in about an hour the storm had passed away: vast herds of game surrounded us on every side.

Next day we marched, the country being very heavy for the bullocks, owing to the rain which had fallen. I held across country for a range of stony hills, dotted over with dwarfish trees and bushes, on which I expected to find sweet grass for my cattle. On my way thither the plains on every side of us presented the most lively display of game, and I was tempted by the endless streams of blesboks to halt my waggons for a minute to catch and saddle steeds and give them chase. They proved extremely shy, and in about four hours I rode to seek my waggons, having bagged a gnoo and a brace of blesboks.

While following the game one of my after-riders started an ostrich from her nest, which she had scooped in the sand; it was about seven feet in diameter, and contained thirty-four fine fresh eggs. I left Ruyter in charge of the nest, the eggs being in danger from jackals and vultures, and particularly from the ostrich herself, who would return in our absence and break every one of them. Having reached my camp, I despatched two men with leather sacks to fetch them.

Next morning I again rode forth to hunt on the plains below my camp, and took up positions, lying on my breast behind the anthills, while Booi and Ruyter moved up the game towards me. I had some exciting sport, the wildebeests several times coming charging madly down upon the very spot where I lay concealed. About midday I had bagged two old bulls, and found one of the wounded of the day before : he was still warm, and was in first-rate condition. Several thousand blesboks came pouring up wind between me and my camp as I was riding home : these had probably been hunted up by some Boer or Boers to leeward. In the evening I again rode out, and had the game moved toward me, when I shot a fourth old bull wildebeest, for which I despatched men with a pack-ox by moonlight, having left Booi in charge of the venison.

On the 1st of February we marched, and reached Bloem Vonteyn on the 3rd, where I was kindly received by the officers of the 45th and Cape Corps, stationed there. Here we remained a day or two, and then trekked on through a most desolate country, on which, together with vast herds of wildebeest, blesbok, and springbok, we found numbers of skeletons scattered over the plains on all sides. This great mortality had been caused either by famine or by a horrid mangy disease, called by the Dutch " brunt sickta," which often sweeps off whole hosts of the plain-frequenting game.

On the 17th we halted the waggons at Mr. Fossey's farm, within two miles of the Great Orange River. Mr. Fossey informed me that the river was full, and that he did not expect it would be fordable for several months. Norval's Punt had been smashed when the troops crossed over to fight the Boers at Boom Plaats some months before, and the new one constructed in the colony had not yet arrived. I was detained on the banks of this stream, much against my will, for several weeks; but at length, on the 8th of March, hearing that the Boers had constructed a float above Alleman's Drift, I inspanned and proceeded down the river to view it. The float was rather a dangerous affair—I mean for property—the stream being very rapid and deep. It was calculated to ferry over light waggons, but heavily-laden ones required to be off-loaded. At sundown I had taken over one waggon, and a span of twelve oxen, which I ferried across in two trips, taking six at a time.

Next morning when I awoke and looked to the river I found that it had grown greatly during the night, and was still increasing rapidly. Having off-loaded the greater part of the cargo of old Adonis's waggon, I managed to ferry it across the river, having narrowly escaped losing the whole in the middle of the stream. By this time the flood had increased so much that we deemed it dangerous to attempt to ferry over anything else, and we prudently resolved to await the ebbing of the river, which continued to grow rapidly the whole of the day. In the afternoon I was obliged to inspan the waggon which I had brought through on the preceding day, and remove it to a more elevated locality; and it was well that I did so, for before morning the river was running strong and deep on the ground which it had occupied. I entertained considerable apprehension for my waggons on the opposite side of the river, as they were now standing upon an island, and the flood had already nearly reached to their wheels.

The flood continued to increase steadily until the next afternoon, when it seemed to have reached its maximum, and about sundown it was evidently upon the ebb. During the whole of to-day and yesterday the flood presented an appearance of extreme grandeur; large blocks of wood and trunks of forest-trees were constantly sweeping past us, tossed on the troubled waters on their seaward course. In the course of the afternoon the stout new cable by which the float was worked, and which stretched across the river, each end being secured to a rock-rifted trunk of a tree, burst asunder, being unequal to resist the force of the swollen river.

On the 14th, with much difficulty, we got over the cable by which the raft was worked, and the Boers, by way of experiment, loaded her up with a party of Bechuana Caffres, and endeavoured to cross the river. There was a small boat attached to the float. When they had got about half-way across, the water rose partially over the float, when a panic came over both the Boers and Bechuanas, and a rush was made into the little boat. A capsize was the consequence; and at the same moment the rope which attached the boat to the float parted. The unfortunate men were then swept away down the rapid current; and of twenty-seven men who were on board of the punt, four only escaped. Two of those who were drowned were Boers. After this accident I directed my men, who were in an isolated position on the opposite side of the river, to inspan and remove down to Norval's boat, below Alleman's Drift, where I met them with the cap-tent waggon; and at sundown next day we had safely ferried over the other two waggons, and encamped once more on British territory.

The ferrying was a very laborious proceeding, each waggon having to be off-loaded, and then taken to pieces, and so brought over, bit by bit; the oxen and horses, etc., swam the river. My waggons were now all safely across, so, after loading them, we marched on the 18th about ten A.M. At sundown we entered the town of Colesberg, and drew up opposite to the old barracks, having been absent exactly twelve months.

As my waggons advanced into the town, the news of our arrival spread like wildfire, and multitudes both of men and good-looking young women rushed to see the old elephant-hunter, who had been mourned as dead. We were soon surrounded by nearly one-half of the population, who mobbed us until night setting in dispersed them to their homes.

My friend Mr. Orpen, being blessed by nature with an excellent constitution, had considerably recovered from the dreadful wounds which he received from the leopard on the banks of the Limpopo, but was still, I regret to say, obliged to carry his arms in slings. His father, the Rev. Dr. Orpen of Colesberg, informed me that he had great hope of restoring his arms to their former state, even at that late period, but of this I could not help being very doubtful.

During my stay in Colesberg I had much pleasure in meeting my friend, Mr. Oswell, of the Honourable East India Company's Service. He was then *en route* for the far interior, intending to penetrate the Kalihari in a north-westerly direction, and visit the lake of boats. This was an expedition which I myself had often thought of making, but a limited finance, and my fancy for collecting objects of natural history, led me to incline my course to the more verdant forests of the east, where I deemed I could more certainly first collect, and then export, the precious spoils of the elephant. Mr. Oswell being in want of draught oxen, I permitted him to select as many as he required from my extensive stock, with which he shortly set out, in company with Mr. Murray, on his interesting journey of discovery. I was occupied in Colesberg till the 12th of April, when I marched to "Cuil Vonteyn," a farm belonging to a Mrs. Van Blerk, which I reached in about three hours; the country all karroo, herds of springboks feeding in sight of the house. Here I found nine heavily-laden waggons drawn up, which I had hired and laden up to transport my collection of hunting trophies to the sea.

When I entered Colesberg I had almost made up my mind to make another shooting expedition into the interior; but a combination of circumstances induced me at length to leave Africa for a season, and re-visit my native land. I felt much sorrow and reluctance in coming to this resolution; for although I had now spent the greater part of five seasons in hunting in the far interior the various game of Southern Africa, I nevertheless did not feel in the slightest degree satiated with the sport which it afforded. On the contrary, the wild, free, healthy, roaming life of a hunter had grown upon me, and I loved it more and more. I could not help confessing to myself, however, that in the most laborious yet noble pursuit of elephant-hunting I was over-taxing my frame and too rapidly wearing down my constitution. Moreover, the time required to reach those extremely distant lands frequented by the elephant was so great that it consumed nearly one-half of the season in going and returning, and I ever found that my dogs and horses had lost much of their spirit by the time they reached those very remote districts. My nerves and constitution were considerably shaken by the power of a scorching African sun, and I considered that a voyage to England would greatly recruit my powers, and that on returning I should renew my pursuits with increased zest.

Having thus resolved to leave the colony, I directed my march towards Port Elizabeth, by way of Graff Reinett, crossing the bold mountain range of Snewberg. On the 10th of May I reached the shores of the ocean, which Ruyter and others of my followers, now beholding for the first time, gazed upon with wonder and with awe. On the 19th I took my passage for old England in the bark "Augusta." My valuable collection of trophies and my Cape waggon, weighing all together upwards of thirty tons, were then carefully shipped, and on the 7th of June I set sail (my little Bushman accompanying me) for my native land, after a sojourn of nearly five years in the wild hunting-grounds of Southern Africa.

THE END.

www.ingramcontent.com/pod-product-compliance
Lightning Source LLC
Chambersburg PA
CBHW030400230426
43664CB00007BB/675